The Papers of the

TWENTIETH SIGCSE TECHNICAL SYMPOSIUM

ON

COMPUTER SCIENCE EDUCATION

SIGCSE BULLETIN

Volume 21, Number 1   February 1989

Sponsored by the

ASSOCIATION FOR COMPUTING MACHINERY

SPECIAL INTEREST GROUP ON

COMPUTER SCIENCE EDUCATION

Louisville, Kentucky

February 23-25, 1989

Edited by

Robert A. Barrett
Maynard J. Mansfield

Indiana University - Purdue University at Fort Wayne
Fort Wayne, Indiana

The Association for Computing Machinery
11 West 42nd Street
New York, New York 10036

ISBN 0-89791-298-5

Additional copies may be ordered prepaid from:

ACM Order Department *Price:*
P.O. Box 64145   Members $19.00
Baltimore, MD 21264   All others $25.00

ACM Order Number: 457890

MESSAGE FROM THE SIGCSE CHAIR

Welcome to the Twentieth SIGCSE Symposium. I want to thank John Gorgone, General Chair; Maynard Mansfield and Robert Barrett, Program Co-Chairs; John Schrage, Panel Chair; and Donald Chand, Tutorial/Case Study Chair for the outstanding job they have done in putting together an excellent and exciting program. This year over 180 papers were submitted and 60 were accepted. We want to thank all those who submitted papers, and hope that you will continue to submit papers to future Symposia. Your contributions are essential to ensure that we have a vibrant, successful meeting.

Next year's Symposium, our twenty-first, will be held in Washington, DC. There will be many special events scheduled to commemorate this important anniversary, and we hope you will make every effort to attend and participate. Richard Austing (University of Maryland) and Boots Cassel (Villanova University) are the general co-chairs. The 1991 Symposium will be held in San Antonio, TX. Nell Dale (The University of Texas at Austin) will be general chair. If you would like to help with either meeting, please contact one of these individuals.

Our SIG continues to remain healthy, but we can use your support to ensure its future success. We currently have approximately 2,500 members including about 250 student members. We would like to see more computer science faculty involved in our SIG. Please mention this Symposium and our Bulletins to your colleagues. Also, we would like to hear from you with suggestions of services that we can provide.

Enjoy the Symposium!

Elliot B. Koffman
Computer and Information Science
Temple University
Philadelphia, PA 19122

SYMPOSIUM CHAIR'S MESSAGE

Welcome to the Twentieth SIGCSE Technical Symposium, which is being held at the Commonwealth Convention Center and Galt House Hotel in Louisville, Kentucky, from February 23 to 25, 1989. The theme of the Symposium is "Racing to the Future," and it is being held in conjunction with the annual Computer Science Conference.

The Symposium emphasizes current and future computer science education issues through its keynote speaker, Dr. Edsger W. Dijkstra, sixty refereed paper presentations, eleven panel sessions, tutorials, case studies, birds-of-a-feather sessions, and post-conference workshops.

This year, a record number of 181 papers, eighteen panel sessions, and eight tutorials were submitted for consideration. In response to requests, the tutorials and post-conference workshops have been continued, and another innovation, a case studies session, was added to the Symposium.

The program co-chairs, Bob Barrett and Maynard Mansfield, spent many hours putting together an exciting program. I am indeed indebted to them, as well as to John Schrage, panel sessions; Dennis Anderson, treasurer; Don Chand, case studies and tutorials; S. Srinivasan, local arrangements; ACM staff; and the many others who contributed directly with their unselfish and tireless efforts.

The program is full (five to six concurrent sessions) and exciting. The committee feels we have an excellent Symposium to offer you, and we hope you enjoy it.

John T. Gorgone, Chair
1989 SIGCSE Technical Symposium
Bentley College

PROGRAM CHAIRS' MESSAGE

We hope that you will find the program of the Twentieth SIGCSE Technical Symposium to be exciting, varied, and useful. Each of us takes full credit for the parts of the program you will enjoy the most, and blames the other for the rest of it.

A program such as this, of course, could never be put together without a great deal of help from our colleagues. Our sincere thanks and deep gratitude are extended to the many individuals without whom this Symposium could never take place.

Over 200 people worked as referees of the 181 papers submitted for the Symposium. Their contributions to the program were crucial to its quality. Since their work was done anonymously, we recognize them by publishing their names elsewhere in this volume.

Our thanks are are also extended to John Schrage and Donald Chand for their work relating to the panels, tutorials, case studies, and workshops of the Symposium. We believe that you will find this part of the program to be timely and significant. We thank the many moderators, panelists, and presenters involved in these activities for their contributions to the program.

Donna Baglio of the ACM New York office has been of invaluable assistance to us in preparing and distributing the announcements, programs, and Proceedings of the Symposium.

Last, but certainly far from least, we wish to thank two fine Kentucky gentlemen, Art Riehl and John McGregor, CSC Chair and CSC Program Chair, respectively, for their outstanding cooperation in coordinating the CSC with the SIGCSE Symposium. We sincerely hope that future CSC committees will follow their example.

Robert A. Barrett
Maynard J. Mansfield
1989 SIGCSE Program Co-Chairs
Indiana-Purdue at Fort Wayne

Roster of Referees

Evans J. Adams
East Tennessee State University

Joseph J. Adamski
Grand Valley State University

Jagdish C. Agrawal
Embry-Riddle Aeronautical University

Robert J. Aiken
Livermore, CA

Steven K. Andrianoff
Saint Bonaventure University

Clark B. Archer
Winthrop College

Julius A. Archibald, Jr.
State University College - Plattsburgh

John Atkins
West Virginia University

Moshe Augenstein
Brooklyn College

Richard H. Austing
University of Maryland

Donald J. Bagert, Jr.
Texas Tech University

M. Gene Bailey
East Tennessee State University

G. Michael Barnes
California State Univ. - Northridge

Robert A. Barrett
Indiana-Purdue at Fort Wayne

Himat Batra
Bradley University

Richard Beebe
Simpson College

Ali Behforooz
Towson State University

John Beidler
University of Scranton

Frank E. Beitel
University of Dayton

Douglas D. Bickerstaff, Jr.
Eastern Washington University

Della Bonnette
University of Southwestern Louisiana

Dale Allen Brown
The College of Wooster

Christopher R. Brown
Bemidji State University

James Cameron
Denison University

Daniel A. Canas
Wake Forest University

Lowell A. Carmony
Lake Forest College

Lillian N. Cassel
Villanova University

Kailash S. Chandra
Savannah State College

Frank Cheatham
Campbelleville College

Tom Cheatham
Western Kentucky University

Li-Hsiang Cheo
The William Paterson College

Joan M. Cherry
University of Toronto

Carol Chrisman
Illinois State University

Janet Cook
Illinois State University

Larry W. Cornwell
Bradley University

John Crenshaw
Western Kentucky University

Steve Cunningham
California State College - Stanislaus

Nell Dale
The University of Texas at Austin

John F. Dalphin
Towson State University

Linda Deneen
University of Minnesota - Duluth

Herbert L. Dershem
Hope College

Benjamin Diamant
Marist College

Verlynda Dobbs
Wright State University

John Dooley
Lindenwood College

Marcel Dupras
University of Laval

Virginia Eaton
Northeast Louisiana University

Lucinda S. Edmonde
University of Southwestern Louisiana

Gerald L. Engel
University of Connecticut - Stamford

Eileen B. Entin
Wentworth Institute of Technology

Michael A. Erlinger
Harvey Mudd College

Henry A. Etlinger
Rochester Institute of Technology

Ernest Ferguson
Southwest Baptist University

Karen A. Forcht
James Madison University

Robert E. Fortune
Ferris State University

William G. Frederick
Indiana-Purdue at Fort Wayne

William H. Friedman
Indiana-Purdue at Fort Wayne

Jane M. Fritz
University of New Brunswick

Hugh Garraway
University of Southern Mississippi

Paula Getlin
Kean College

Norman E. Gibbs
Carnegie-Mellon University

Suzanne Gladfelter
Pennsylvania State University - York

John K. Gotwals
Purdue University

Harold Grossman
Clemson University

Gary Haggard
Bucknell University

Cindy Hanchey
Oklahoma Baptist University

Dale Hanchey
Oklahoma Baptist University

Tom Harbron
Anderson University

Robert H. Haring-Smith
College of the Holy Cross

Alka Rani Harriger
Purdue University

Janet Hartman
Illinois State University

Phillip J. Heeler
Northwest Missouri State University

Peter S. Henderson
SUNY at Stony Brook

Sallie Henry
Virginia Polytechnic Inst. & State U.

Thomas Hilburn
SUNY at Geneseo

Iraj Hirmanpour
Embry-Riddle Aeronautical University

Dale K. Hockensmith
Indiana-Purdue at Fort Wayne

Larry Hodges
Georgia Institute of Technology

James H. Hu
Southeastern Louisiana University

Dalton R. Hunkins
Saint Bonaventure University

Betty Jehn
University of Dayton

Lawrence A. Jehn
University of Dayton

Michael Jipping
Hope College

William J. Joel
Marist College

Roy F. Keller
University of Nebraska - Lincoln

Mark Kerstetter
Western Michigan University

Asad Khilany
Eastern Michigan University

Sami Khuri
Wellesley College

Bruce Klein
Grand Valley State University

J. B. Klerlein
Western Carolina University

Dionysios Kountanis
Western Michigan University

Glen Langdon
University of California - Santa Cruz

Katherine Larason
Northeast Louisiana State University

Osvaldo Laurido
Information System Consultants

Cary Laxer
Rose-Hulman Institute of Technology

Robert R. Leeper
Indiana-Purdue at Fort Wayne

Roger E. Lessman
Tennessee Technological University

Bruce P. Lester
Maharishi International University

Laura Leventhal
Bowling Green State University

Doris K. Lidtke
Towson State University

Ivan B. Liss
Radford University

Joyce Currie Little
Towson State University

Antonio M. Lopez, Jr.
Loyola University

Peter Lykos
Illinois Institute of Technology

William F. Lyle, III
Murray State University

E. Terry Magel
Western Illinois University

John Maniotes
Purdue University - Calumet

Maynard J. Mansfield
Indiana-Purdue at Fort Wayne

Bill Marion
Valparaiso University

Dennis S. Martin
University of Scranton

Bruce R. Maxim
University of Michigan - Dearborn

William E. McBride
Baylor University

Martha C. McCormick
Jacksonville State University

Robert J. McGlinn
Southern Illinois U. at Carbondale

Thomas C. McMillan
Radford University

H. Willis Means
Hanover College

Jan Melancon
Loyola University

M. R. Meybodi
Ohio University

Fatmi Mili
Oakland University

James E. Miller
University of Southern Mississippi

James C. Miller
Bradley University

Ted Mims
Nicholls State University

William Mitchell
University of Evansville

John C. Molluzzo
Pace University

Brian D. Monahan
Iona College

Linda T. Moulton
Montgomery County Community College

Michael G. Murphy
University of Houston - Downtown

C. Bruce Myers
Austin Peay State University

Barbee T. Mynatt
Bowling Green State University

Christos Nikolopoulos
Bradley University

Robert E. Noonan
College of William and Mary

Martha O'Kennon
Albion College

Paul Ohme
Northeast Louisiana University

Arthur E. Oldehoeft
Iowa State University

G. Scott Owen
Georgia State University

Barbara Boucher Owens
Georgetown, TX

Jacquelyn W. Palmer
Wright State University

Ed Pekarek
Appalachian State University

J. K. Pierson
James Madison University

Richard M. Plishka
University of Scranton

Hassan Pournaghshband
University of Missouri - St. Louis

John R. Pugh
Carleton University

John Rager
Amherst College

William E. Richardson
United States Air Force Academy

David Rine
George Mason University

Richard A. Rink
Eastern Kentucky University

Jean Rogers
Hewlett Packard Company

Leroy Roquemore
Southern University

R. Waldo Roth
Amoco Production Company

W. G. Roughead
Georgia Department of Education

David Rudd
University of New Orleans

Brian A. Rudolph
University of Wisconsin - Platteville

William C. Runnion
Embry-Riddle Aeronautical University

Alireza Salehnia
Culver-Stockton College

Dean Sanders
Illinois State University

Harbans Sathi
University of Southern Colorado

David Scanlan
California State Univ. - Sacremento

Chris Schmidt
Wartburg College

Robert Sedlmeyer
Indiana-Purdue at Fort Wayne

Stan Seltzer
Ithaca College

Dale Shaffer
Lander College

Onkar P. Sharma
Marist College

William Shay
University of Wisconsin - Green Bay

Robert C. Shock
Wright State University

Charles M. Shub
Univ. of Colorado at Colorado Springs

Peter Shum
Northwestern College

James R. Sidbury
University of Scranton

James L. Silver
Indiana-Purdue at Fort Wayne

Ted Sjoerdsma
Washington and Lee University

P. D. Smith
California State Univ. - Northridge

Mark Smotherman
Clemson University

Glenn Snelbecker
Temple University

Dianne M. Spresser
James Madison University

Carl W. Steidley
Central Washington University

Susan V. Stein
Baruch College

Marguerite K. Summers
Murray State University

Harriet G. Taylor
Louisiana State University

Mark C. Temte
Indiana-Purdue at Fort Wayne

Ted Tenny
Fort Worth, TX

Alan L. Tharp
North Carolina State University

Tim Thurman
University of Kansas

Rebekah L. Tidwell
Tusculum College

Ivan Tomek
Acadia University

Robert Trenary
Western Michigan University

John A. Trono
St. Michael's College

Allen Tucker
Bowdoin College

Elizabeth A. Unger
Kansas State University

Roger L. Wainwright
The University of Tulsa

Henry M. Walker
The University of Texas at Austin

Frank G. Walters
University of Missouri - Rolla

John A. Wenzel
Albion College

Laurie Honour Werth
The University of Texas at Austin

Tom Whaley
Wahington and Lee University

Curt M. White
Indiana-Purdue at Fort Wayne

Ralph W. Wilkerson
University of Missouri - Rolla

Carol Wilson
Western Kentucky University

C. N. Winton
University of North Florida

Wita Wojtkowski
Boise State University

Walter Wolf
Rochester Institute of Technology

Charles T. Wright, Jr.
Iowa State University

C. T. Zahn
Pace University

Recipients of the SIGCSE Award for Outstanding Contributions

to

Computer Science Education

1981	William F. Atchison, University of Maryland
1982	Alan Perlis, Yale University
1983	Karl V. Karlstrom, Prentice-Hall
1985	Elliott I. Organick, University of Utah
1986	Donald Knuth, Stanford University
1987	Niklaus Wirth, ETH, Zurich
1988	Grace Murray Hopper, Rear Admiral U.S.N. (Retired), Digital Equipment Corporation
1989	Edsger W. Dijkstra, University of Texas at Austin

TWENTIETH SIGCSE TECHNICAL SYMPOSIUM

- -

JOINT CSC/SIGCSE OPENING SESSION

8:15 A.M. TO 9:30 A.M.
Convention Center - Street Level

Presentation of SIGCSE Award for Outstanding Contributions in Computer Science Education

KEYNOTE SPEAKER: **Dr. Edsger W. Dijkstra**
Schlumberger Centennial Chair in Computer Science
Department of Computer Science
The University of Texas at Austin

- -

THURSDAY   10:00 A.M. – 11:30 A.M.

CC = Convention Center

- -

CSC/SIGCSE CONFERENCE AWARDS LUNCHEON
(Ticket Required)
12:00 Noon - 1:30 p.m.

Scholastic Programming Contest Awards

- -

THURSDAY   2:00 P.M. – 3:30 P.M.

Thursday 2:00 p.m. - 3:30 p.m.   CC 107
REFEREED PAPERS: Curricular Issues (Session II)
Session Chair: Janet Cook, Illinois State University

Thursday 2:00 p.m. - 3:30 p.m.   CC 105
SPECIAL JOINT CSC/SIGCSE SESSION   290
  A Progress Report from a Joint ACM/IEEE-CS Task Force
New Recommendations for the Undergraduate Curriculum
        Moderator: A. Joe Turner, Clemson University
        Panelists: Allen B. Tucker, Bruce H. Barnes, Kim B. Bruce, and
                    Doris K. Lidtke

Thursday 2:00 p.m. - 3:30 p.m.   CC 106
REFEREED PAPERS: The Introductory Courses (Session II)
Session Chair: William G. Frederick, Indiana-Purdue at Fort Wayne

Thursday 2:00 p.m. - 3:30 p.m.   CC 109
REFEREED PAPERS: Computer Information Systems
Session Chair: Cindy Hanchey, Oklahoma Baptist University

Friday   8:30 a.m. - 10:00 a.m.   CC 106
REFEREED PAPERS: The Introductory Courses (Session IV)
Session Chair: Richard Plishka, University of Scranton

8:30 **What is to Become of Programming?**   131
William Mitchell; University of Evansville

9:00 **AIDE: An Automated Tool for Teaching Design in an Introductory Programming**   136
Course
Dino Schweitzer, Scott C. Teel; U.S. Air Force Academy

9:30 **Visual Metaphors for Teaching Programming Concepts**   141
Leslie J. Waguespack, Jr.; Bentley College

Friday   8:30 a.m. - 10:00 a.m.   CC 105
PANEL: CIS Accreditation: An Update with AACSB Input   294
Moderator: Robert Cannon, University of South Carolina
Panelists: John T. Gorgone, John McGregor, and Thomas I.M. Ho

Friday   8:30 a.m. - 10:00 a.m.   CC 107
REFEREED PAPERS: Software Analysis
Session Chair: Ted Mims, Nicholls State University

8:30 **A First Course in Program Verification and the Semantics of Programming**   146
Languages
Raymond D. Gumb; University of Lowell

9:00 **Success with the Project-Intensive Model for an Undergraduate Software**   151
Engineering Course
Linda M. Northrop; State University of New York College at Brockport

9:30 **Use of the Cloze Procedure in Testing a Model of Complexity**   156
Patricia B. Van Verth, Lynne Bakalik, Margaret Kilcoyne; Canisius College

Friday   8:30 a.m. - 10:00 a.m.   CC 109
REFEREED PAPERS: Advanced Courses
Session Chair: Della Bonnette, University of Southwestern Louisiana

8:30 **A Core Course in Computer Theory: Design and Implementation Issues**   161
Donald J. Bagert, Jr.; Texas Tech University

9:00 **Examining Compiled Code**   165
Mark Smotherman; Clemson University

9:30 **A Parallel Processing Course for Undergraduates**   170
      Daniel C. Hyde; Bucknell University

Friday 8:30 a.m. - 10:00 a.m.   CC 108
CASE STUDIES IN COMPUTER EDUCATION
Moderator: Donald Chand; Bentley College

8:30 **Case Development Process**   300
      Donald Chand; Bentley College

9:00 **An Anatomy of an End-User Strategy: A Case Study**   301
      Stuart A. Varden; Pace University

9:30 **End-User Computing in a Public Accounting Firm**   302
      Dennis Anderson, Donald Chand, Joseph O'Connor; Bentley College

---

Friday 8:30 a.m. - 12:00 Noon   CC 110
TUTORIAL: NEURAL NETWORKS: ISSUES AND IDEAS   304
            Dr. Norman E. Sondak; San Diego State University

FRIDAY   10:30 A.M. - 12:00 NOON

Friday 10:30 a.m. - 12:00 Noon   CC 105
**PANEL: Final Report of the ACM/IEEE Computer Society / MAA Task Force on   295
          Teaching Computer Science within Mathematics Departments**
          Moderator: Kim Bruce, Williams College
          Panelists: Bruce Klein and Stan Seltzer

Friday 10:30 a.m. - 12:00 Noon   CC 108
PANEL: The NSF Peer Review Process   296
          Moderator: John Beidler, University of Scranton
          Panelists: Margaret Reek

Friday 10:30 a.m. - 12:00 Noon   CC 106
REFEREED PAPERS: The Introductory Courses (Session V)
Session Chair: Betty Jehn, University of Dayton

10:30 **Operations on Sets of Intervals - An Exercise for Data Structures or   174
       Algorithm Courses**
       Bob P. Weems; The University of Texas at Arlington

11:00 **Computer Trivia**   307
       Carolyn McCreary; American University

11:30   **The New Generation of Computer Literacy**   177
         J. Paul Myers, Jr.; Trinity University

Friday   10:30 a.m. - 12:00 Noon   CC 107
REFEREED PAPERS: Software Engineering
Session Chair: Gerald L. Engel, University of Connecticut

10:30   **Teaching Practical Software Maintenance Skills in a Software Engineering**   182
         Course
         James S. Collofello; Arizona State University

11:00   **Removing the Emphasis on Coding in a Course on Software Engineering**   185
         Linda Rising; Indiana-Purdue at Fort Wayne
                     Magnavox Electronic Systems Company

11:30   **Sizing Assignments: A Contribution from Software Engineering to Computer**   190
         Science Education
         David F. Haas; University of Wisconsin Oshkosh
         Leslie J. Waguespack, Jr.; Bentley College

Friday   10:30 a.m. - 12:00 Noon   CC 109
REFEREED PAPERS: The Secondary School Interface
Session Chair: Curt M. White, Indiana-Purdue at Fort Wayne

10:30   **The Effect of High School Computer Science, Gender, and Work on Success in**   195
         College Computer Science
         Harriet G. Taylor, Luegina C. Mounfield; Louisiana State University

11:00   **Inservice Education of High School Computer Science Teachers**   199
         James Kiper, Bill Rouse, Douglas Troy; Miami University

11:30   **Laying the Foundations for Computer Science**   204
         Leonard A. Larsen; University of Wisconsin - Eau Claire

- -

      FRIDAY   12:00 NOON - 1:30 P.M.   LUNCH BREAK

- -

FRIDAY   1:30 P.M. — 2:30 P.M.

Friday   1:30 p.m. - 2:30 p.m.   CC 108
PANEL: **Computer Science Teaching Certificate for Secondary Education**
          Moderator: Ali Behforooz, Towson State University
          Panelists: Curtis R. Bring, John F. Dalphin, Joyce C. Little, and
                      William A. Stannerd

Friday   1:30 p.m. - 2:30 p.m.   CC 106
REFEREED PAPERS: Finding a Place for Ada
Session Chair: Nell Dale, The University of Texas at Austin

Friday   1:30 p.m. - 2:30 p.m.   CC 107
REFEREED PAPERS: Operating Systems
Session Chair: Sallie Henry, Virginia Polytechnic Institute & State University

Friday   1:30 p.m. - 2:30 p.m.   CC 109
REFEREED PAPERS: Microcomputer Operating Systems
Session Chair: William Mitchell, University of Evansville

Friday   1:30 p.m. - 2:30 p.m.   CC 105
REFEREED PAPERS: Artificial Intelligence
Session Chair: Robert Sedlmeyer, Indiana-Purdue at Fort Wayne

2:00 **Neural Networks and Artificial Intelligence**   241
      Norman E. Sondak; San Diego State University
      Vernon K. Sondak; University of Michigan

FRIDAY   3:00 P.M. – 4:00 P.M.

Friday   3:00 p.m. - 4:00 p.m.   CC 108   298
PANEL: High School Preparation for Computer Science
      Moderator: Doris Appleby, Marymount College
      Panelists: Kenneth Appel, Julie Gross, Timothy Corica, and
              Maryam Hastings

Friday   3:00 p.m. - 4:00 p.m.   CC 106
REFEREED PAPERS: Programming Paradigms
Session Chair: Joyce Currie Little, Towson State University

3:00 **Teaching Multiple Programming Paradigms: A Proposal for a Paradigm**   246
      General Pseudocode
      Mark B. Wells, Barry L. Kurtz; New Mexico State University

3:30 **Never Mind the Language, What About the Paradigm?**   252
      Paul A. Luker; California State University, Chico

Friday   3:00 p.m. - 4:00 p.m.   CC 105
REFEREED PAPERS: Teaching Concerns
Session Chair: Harriet G. Taylor, Louisiana State University

3:00 **Toward an Ideal Competency-based Computer Science Teacher Certification**   257
      Program: The Delphi Approach
      J. Wey Chen; University of Northern Colorado

3:30 **A Software Rotation for Professional Teachers**   262
      Phillip L. Miller; Carnegie Mellon University

Friday   3:00 p.m. - 4:00 p.m.   CC 107
REFEREED PAPERS: Mathematics in Computing
Session Chair: Lawrence A. Jehn, University of Dayton

3:00 **Algorithms and Proofs: Mathematics in the Computing Curriculum**   268
      Newcomb Greenleaf; Columbia University

3:30 **Discrete Mathematics for Computer Science Majors - Where Are We?**   273
      How Do We Proceed?
      William Marion; Valparaiso University

```
Friday    3:00 p.m. -  4:00 p.m.                                    CC 109
REFEREED PAPERS:  Computer Graphics
Session Chair:  Alka Rani Harriger, Purdue University
```

3:00 **Implementing a GKS-Like Graphics Package on a Microcomputer**   278
      Michael K. Mahoney; California State University, Long Beach

3:30 **Teaching Introductory and Advanced Computer Graphics Using Micro-Computers** 283
      G. Scott Owen; Georgia State University

- -

   <u>FRIDAY</u>   <u>4:15 P.M. - 5:00 P.M.</u>   <u>SYMPOSIUM CLOSING SESSION</u>   CC 108

An informal get together to discuss this year's symposium and to make suggestions for future
meetings. This year's program reflects the comments of those who came to the closing session
last year. Come and help assure that the SIGCSE TECHNICAL SYMPOSIUM will continue to meet
your needs and interests.

- -

SATURDAY   WORKSHOPS   8:30 A.M. - 11:30 A.M.

```
Saturday   8:30 a.m. - 11:30 a.m.                          Galt House
WORKSHOP:  Using Excelerator in Systems Development Courses              305
           Dr. Iraj Hirmanpour, Embry-Riddle Aeronautical University
```

```
Saturday   8:30 a.m. - 11:30 a.m.                          Galt House
WORKSHOP:  Using Prolog in Expert System Courses                        306
           Dr. Sri Raghaven, Bentley College
```

ON THE CRUELTY OF REALLY TEACHING COMPUTING SCIENCE

The SIGCSE Award Lecture

by

Dr. Edsger W. Dijkstra

ABSTRACT In more than one sense, the automatic computer embodies such radical novelty that it is a vain effort to try to cope with it in terms of what we are familiar with: all analogies are too shallow to be helpful, and are misleading instead. As a consequence, a major challenge for the student of computing science is not so much learning new knowledge and skills as breaking out of his familiar thinking habits and changing his notion of understanding.

ON THE CRUELTY OF REALLY TEACHING COMPUTING SCIENCE

The SIGCSE Award Lecture

by

Dr. Edsger W. Dijkstra

The second part of this talk pursues some of the scientific and educational consequences of the assumption that computers represent a radical novelty. In order to give this assumption clear contents, we have to be much more precise as to what we mean in this context by the adjective "radical." We shall do so in the first part of this talk, in which we shall furthermore supply evidence in support of our assumption.

The usual way in which we plan today for tomorrow is in yesterday's vocabulary. We do so, because we try to get away with the concepts we are familiar with and that have acquired their meanings in our past experience. Of course, the words and the concepts don't quite fit because our future differs from our past, but then we stretch them a little bit. Linguists are quite familiar with the phenomenon that the meanings of words evolve over time, but also know that this is a slow and gradual process.

It is the most common way of trying to cope with novelty: by means of metaphors and analogies we try to link the new to the old, the novel to the familiar. Under sufficiently slow and gradual change, it works reasonably well; in the case of a sharp discontinuity, however, the method breaks down: though we may glorify it with the name "common sense," our past experience is no longer relevant, the analogies become too shallow, and the metaphors become more misleading than illuminating. This is the situation that is characteristic for the "radical" novelty.

Coping with radical novelty requires an orthogonal method. One must consider one's own past, the experiences collected, and the habits formed in it as an unfortunate accident of history, and one has to approach the radical novelty with a blank mind, consciously refusing to try to link it with what is already familiar, because the familiar is hopelessly inadequate. One has, with initially a kind of split personality, to come to grips with a radical novelty as a dissociated topic in its own right. Coming to grips with a radical novelty amounts to creating and learning a new foreign language that can <u>not</u> be translated into one's mother tongue. (Anyone who has learned quantum mechanics knows what I am talking about.) Needless to say, adjusting to radical novelties is not a very popular activity, for it requires hard work. For the same reason, the radical novelties themselves are unwelcome.

By now, you may well ask why I have paid so much attention to and have spent so much eloquence on such a simple and obvious notion as the radical novelty. My reason is very simple: radical novelties are so disturbing that they tend to be suppressed or ignored, to the extent that even the possibility of their existence in general is more often denied than admitted.

On the historical evidence I shall be short. Carl Friedrich Gauss, the Prince of Mathematicians but also somewhat of a coward, was certainly aware of the fate of Galileo -- and could probably have predicted the calumniation of Einstein -- when he decided to suppress his discovery of non-Euclidean geometry, thus leaving it to Bolyai and Lobatchewsky to receive the flak. It is probably more illuminating to go a little bit further back, to the Middle Ages. One of its characteristics was that "reasoning by analogy" was rampant; another characteristic was almost total intellectual stagnation, and we now see why the two go together. A reason for mentioning this is to point out that, by developing a keen ear for unwarranted analogies, one can detect a lot of medieval thinking today.

The other thing I cannot stress enough is that the fraction of the population for which gradual change seems to be all but the only paradigm of history is very large, probably much larger than you would expect. Certainly when I started to observe it, their number turned out to be much larger than I had expected.

For instance, the vast majority of the mathematical community has never challenged its tacit assumption that doing mathematics will remain very much the same type of mental activity it has always been: new topics will come, flourish, and go as they have done in the past, but, the human brain being what it is, our ways of teaching, learning, and understanding mathematics, of problem solving, and of mathematical discovery will remain pretty much the same. Herbert Robbins clearly states why he rules out a quantum leap in mathematical ability:

"Nobody is going to run 100 meters in five seconds, no matter how much is invested in training and machines. The same can be said about using the brain. The human mind is no different now from what it was five thousand years ago. And when it comes to mathematics, you must realize that this is the human mind at an extreme limit

of its capacity."
My comment in the margin was "so reduce the use of the brain and calculate!". Using Robbins's own analogy, one could remark that, for going from A to B fast, there could now exist alternatives to running that are orders of magnitude more effective. Robbins flatly refuses to honour any alternative to time-honored brain usage with the name of "doing mathematics," thus exorcising the danger of radical novelty by the simple device of adjusting his definitions of his needs: simply by definition, mathematics will continue to be what it used to be. So much for the mathematicians.

Let me give you just one more example of the widespread disbelief in the existence of radical novelties and, hence, in the need of learning how to cope with them. It is the prevailing educational practice, for which gradual, almost imperceptible, change seems to be the exclusive paradigm. How many educational texts are not recommended for their appeal to the student's intuition! They constantly try to present everything that could be an exciting novelty as something as familiar as possible. They consciously try to link the new material to what is supposed to be the student's familiar world. It already starts with the teaching of arithmetic. Instead of teaching $2 + 3 = 5$, the hideous arithmetic operator "plus" is carefully disguised by calling it "and," and the little kids are given objects such as apples and pears, which are <u>in</u>, in contrast to equally countable objects such as percentages and electrons, which are <u>out</u>. The same silly tradition is reflected at university level in different introductory calculus courses for the future physicist, architect, or business major, each adorned with examples from the respective fields. The educational dogma seems to be that everything is fine as long as the student does not notice that he is learning something really new; more often than not, the student's impression is indeed correct. I consider the failure of an educational practice to prepare the next generation for the phenomenon of radical novelties a serious shortcoming. [When King Ferdinand visited the conservative university of Cervera, the Rector proudly reassured the monarch with the words: "Far be from us, Sire, the dangerous novelty of thinking." Spain's problems in the century that followed justify my characterization of the shortcoming as "serious."] So much for education's adoption of the paradigm of gradual change.

The concept of radical novelties is of contemporary significance because, while we are ill-prepared to cope with them, science and technology have now shown themselves expert at inflicting them upon us. Earlier scientific examples are the theory of relativity and quantum mechanics; later technological examples are the atom bomb and the pill. For decades, the former two gave rise to a torrent of religious, philosophical, or otherwise quasi-scientific tracts. We can daily observe the profound inadequacy with which the latter two are approached, be it by our statesmen and religious leaders or by the public at large. So much for the damage done to our peace of mind by radical novelties.

I raised all this because of my contention that automatic computers represent a radical novelty and that only by identifying them as such can we identify all the nonsense, the misconceptions and the mythology that surround them. Closer inspection will reveal that it is even worse, viz. that automatic computers embody not only one radical novelty but two of them.

The first radical novelty is a direct consequence of the raw power of today's computing equipment. We all know how we cope with something big and complex: divide and rule, i.e. we view the whole as a compositum of parts and deal with the parts separately. And if a part is too big, we repeat the procedure. The town is made up from neighborhoods, which are structured by streets, which contain buildings, which are made from walls and floors, that are built from bricks, etc., eventually down to the elementary particles. And we have all our specialists along the line, from the town planner, via the architect to the solid state physicist and further. Because, in a sense, the whole is "bigger" than its parts, the depth of a hierarchical decomposition is some sort of logarithm of the ratio of the "sizes" of the whole and the ultimate smallest parts. From a bit to a few hundred megabytes, from a microsecond to half an hour of computing confronts us with the completely baffling ratio of 10^9! The programmer is in the unique position that his is the only discipline and profession in which such a gigantic ratio, which totally baffles our imagination, has to be bridged by a single technology. He has to be able to think in terms of conceptual hierarchies that are much deeper than a single mind ever needed to face before. Compared to that number of semantic levels, the average mathematical theory is almost flat. By evoking the need for deep conceptual hierarchies, the automatic computer confronts us with a radically new intellectual challenge that has no precedent in our history.

Again, I have to stress this radical novelty because the true believer in gradual change and incremental improvements is unable to see it. For him, an automatic computer is something like the familiar cash register, only somewhat bigger, faster, and more flexible. But the analogy is ridiculously shallow: it is orders of magnitude worse than comparing, as a means of transportation, the supersonic jet plane with a crawling baby, for that speed ratio is only a thousand.

The second radical novelty is that the automatic computer is our first large-scale digital device. We had a few with a noticeable discrete component: I just mentioned the cash register and can add the typewriter with its individual keys: with a single stroke you can type either a Q or a W but, though their keys are next to each other, not a mixture of those two letters. But such mechanisms are the exception, and the vast majority of our mechanisms are viewed as analogue devices whose behavior is over a large range a continuous function of all parameters involved: if we press the point of the pencil a little bit harder, we get a slightly thicker line, if the violinist slightly misplaces his finger, he plays slightly out of tune. To this I should add that, to the extent that we view ourselves as mechanisms, we view ourselves primarily as analogue devices: if we push a little harder we expect to do a little better. Very often the behavior is not only continuous but even a monotonic function: to test whether a hammer suits us over a certain range of nails, we try it out on the smallest and largest nails of the range, and if the outcomes of those two experiments are positive, we are perfectly willing to believe that the hammer will suit us for all nails in between.

It is possible, and even tempting, to view a program as an abstract mechanism, as a device of some sort. To do so, however, is highly dangerous: the analogy is too shallow because a program is, as a mechanism, totally different from all the familiar analogue devices we grew up with. Like all digitally encoded information, it has unavoidably the uncomfortable property that the smallest possible perturbations -- i.e. changes of a single bit -- can have the most drastic consequences. [For the sake of completeness I add that the picture is not essentially changed by the introduction of redundancy or error correction.] In the discrete world of computing, there is no meaningful metric in which "small" changes and "small" effects go hand in hand, and there never will be.

This second radical novelty shares the usual fate of all radical novelties: it is denied, because its truth would be too discomforting. I have no idea what this specific denial and disbelief costs the United States, but a million dollars a day seems a modest guess.

Having described -- admittedly in the broadest possible terms -- the nature of computing's novelties, I shall now provide the evidence that these novelties are, indeed, radical. I shall do so by explaining a number of otherwise strange phenomena as frantic -- but, as we now know, doomed -- efforts at hiding or denying the frighteningly unfamiliar.

A number of these phenomena have been bundled under the name "Software Engineering." As economics is known as "The Miserable Science," software engineering should be known as "The Doomed Discipline," doomed because it cannot even approach its goal since its goal is self-contradictory. Software engineering, of course, presents itself as another worthy cause, but that is eyewash: if you carefully read its literature and analyse what its devotees actually do, you will discover that software engineering has accepted as its charter "How to program if you cannot."

The popularity of its name is enough to make it suspect. In what we denote as "primitive societies," the superstition that knowing someone's true name gives you magic power over him is not unusual. We are hardly less primitive: why do we persist here in answering the telephone with the most unhelpful "hello" instead of our name? Nor are we above the equally primitive superstition that we can gain some control over some unknown, malicious demon by calling it by a safe, familiar, and innocent name, such as "engineering." But it is totally symbolic, as one of the U.S. computer manufacturers proved a few years ago when it hired, one night, hundreds of new "software engineers" by the simple device of elevating all its programmers to that exalting rank. So much for that term.

The practice is pervaded by the reassuring illusion that programs are just devices like any others, the only difference admitted being that their manufacture might require a new type of craftsmen, viz. programmers. From there it is only a small step to measuring "programmer productivity" in terms of "number of lines of code produced per month." This is a very costly measuring unit because it encourages the writing of insipid code, but today I am less interested in how foolish a unit it is from even a pure business point of view. My point today is that, if we wish to count lines of code, we should not regard them as "lines produced" but as "lines spent": the current conventional wisdom is so foolish as to book that count on the wrong side of the ledger.

Besides the notion of productivity, also that of quality control continues to be distorted by the reassuring illusion that what works with other devices works with programs as well. It is now two decades since it was pointed out that program testing may convincingly demonstrate the presence of bugs, but can never demonstrate their absence. After quoting this well-publicized remark devoutly, the software engineer returns to the order of the day and continues to refine his testing strategies, just like the alchemist of yore, who continued to refine his chrysocosmic purifications.

Unfathomed misunderstanding is further revealed by the term "software maintenance," as a result of which many people continue to believe that programs -- and even programming languages themselves -- are subject to wear and tear. Your car needs maintenance too, doesn't it? Famous is the story of the oil company that believed that its PASCAL programs did not last as long as its FORTRAN programs "because PASCAL was not maintained."

In the same vein I must draw attention to the astonishing readiness with which the suggestion has been accepted that the pains of software production are largely due to a lack of appropriate "programming tools." (The telling "programmer's workbench" was soon to follow.) Again, the shallowness of the underlying analogy is worthy of the Middle Ages. Confrontations with insipid "tools" of the "algorithm-animation" variety have not mellowed my judgement; on the contrary, they have confirmed my initial suspicion that we are primarily dealing with yet another dimension of the snake oil business.

Finally, to correct the possible impression that the inability to face radical novelty is confined to the industrial world, let me offer you an explanation of the -- at least American -- popularity of Artificial Intelligence. One would expect people to feel threatened by the "giant brains or machines that think." In fact, the frightening computer becomes less frightening if it is used only to simulate a familiar noncomputer. I am sure that this explanation will remain controversial for quite some time, for Artificial Intelligence as mimicking the human mind prefers to view itself as at the front line, whereas my explanation relegates it to the rear guard. (The effort of using machines to mimic the human mind has always struck me as rather silly: I'd rather use them to mimic something better.)

So much for the evidence that the computer's novelties are, indeed, radical.

And now comes the second -- and hardest -- part of my talk: the scientific and educational consequences of the above. The educational consequences are, of course, the hairier ones, so let's postpone their discussion and stay for a while with computing science itself. What is computing? And what is a science of computing about?

Well, when all is said and done, the only thing computers can do for us is to manipulate symbols and produce results of such manipulations. From our previous observations we should recall that this is a discrete world and, moreover, that both the

number of symbols involved and the amount of manipulation performed are many orders of magnitude larger than we can envisage:
they totally baffle our imagination and we must therefore not try
to imagine them.

But before a computer is ready to perform a class of meaningful manipulations -- or calculations, if you prefer -- we must
write a program. What is a program? Several answers are possible. We can view the program as what turns the general-purpose
computer into a special-purpose symbol manipulator, and does so
without the need to change a single wire. (This was an enormous
improvement over machines with problem-dependent wiring panels.)
I prefer to describe it the other way around: the program is an
abstract symbol manipulator, which can be turned into a concrete
one by supplying a computer to it. After all, it is no longer
the purpose of programs to instruct our machines; these days, it
is the purpose of machines to execute our programs.

So, we have to design abstract symbol manipulators. We all
know what they look like: they look like programs or -- to use
somewhat more general terminology -- usually rather elaborate
formulae from some formal system. It really helps to view a
program as a formula. Firstly, it puts the programmer's task in
the proper perspective: he has to derive that formula. Second-
ly, it explains why the world of mathematics all but ignored the
programming challenge: programs were so much longer formulae
than it was used to that it did not even recognize them as such.
Now back to the programmer's job: he has to derive that formula,
he has to derive that program. We know of only one reliable way
of doing that, viz. by means of symbol manipulation. And now the
circle is closed: we construct our mechanical symbol manipulators by means of human symbol manipulation.

Hence, computing science is -- and will always be -- concerned with the interplay between mechanized and human symbol
manipulation, usually referred to as "computing" and "programming" respectively. An immediate benefit of this insight is that
it reveals "automatic programming" as a contradiction in terms.
A further benefit is that it gives us a clear indication where
to locate computing science on the world map of intellectual disciplines: in the direction of formal mathematics and applied
logic, but ultimately far beyond where those are now, for computing science is interested in <u>effective</u> use of formal methods and
on a much, much larger scale than we have witnessed so far.
Because no endeavour is respectable these days without a TLA (=
Three-Letter Acronym), I propose that we adopt for computing
science FMI (= Formal Methods Initiative), and, to be on the safe
side, we had better follow the shining examples of our leaders
and make a Trade Mark of it.

In the long run I expect computing science to transcend its parent disciplines, mathematics and logic, by effectively realizing a significant part of Leibniz's Dream of providing symbolic calculation as an alternative to human reasoning. (Please note the difference between "mimicking" and "providing an alternative to": alternatives are allowed to be better.)

Needless to say, this vision of what computing science is about is not universally applauded. On the contrary, it has met widespread -- and sometimes even violent -- opposition from all sorts of directions. I mention as examples

(0) the mathematical guild, which would rather continue to believe that the Dream of Leibniz is an unrealistic illusion

(1) the business community, which, having been sold to the idea that computers would make life easier, is mentally unprepared to accept that they only solve the easier problems at the price of creating much harder ones

(2) the subculture of the compulsive programmer, whose ethics prescribe that one silly idea and a month of frantic coding should suffice to make him a life-long millionaire

(3) computer engineering, which would rather continue to act as if it is all only a matter of higher bit rates and more flops per second

(4) the military, who are now totally absorbed in the business of using computers to mutate billion-dollar budgets into the illusion of automatic safety

(5) all soft sciences for which computing now acts as some sort of interdisciplinary haven

(6) the educational business that feels that, if it has to teach formal mathematics to CS students, it may as well close its schools.

And with this last example I have reached, imperceptibly but alas unavoidably, the most hairy part of this talk: educational consequences.

The problem with educational policy is that it is hardly influenced by scientific considerations derived from the topics taught, and almost entirely determined by extra-scientific circumstances such as the combined expectations of the students, their parents and their future employers, and the prevailing view on the role of the university: is the stress on training its graduates for today's entry-level jobs or on providing its alumni with the intellectual baggage and attitudes that will last them another 50 years? Do we grudgingly grant the abstract sciences only a far-away corner on campus, or do we recognize them as the indispensable motor of the high-technology industry? Even if we do the latter, do we recognize a high-technology industry as such if its technology primarily belongs to formal mathematics? Do the universities provide for society the intellectual leadership it needs or only the training it asks for?

Traditional academic rhetoric is perfectly willing to give to these questions the reassuring answers, but I don't believe them. By way of illustration of my doubts, in a recent article on "Who Rules Canada?", David H. Flaherty bluntly states "Moreover, the business elite dismisses traditional academics and intellectuals as largely irrelevant and powerless."

So, if I look into my foggy crystal ball at the future of computing science education, I overwhelmingly see the depressing picture of "Business as usual." The universities will continue to lack the courage to teach hard science, they will continue to misguide the students, and each next stage of infantilization of the curriculum will be hailed as educational progress.

I now have had my foggy crystal ball for quite a long time. Its predictions are invariably gloomy and usually correct, but I am quite used to that and they won't keep me from giving you a few suggestions, even if it is merely an exercise in futility whose only effect is to make you feel guilty.

We could, for instance, begin with cleaning up our language by no longer calling a bug and bug but by calling it an error. It is much more honest because it squarely puts the blame where it belongs, viz. with the programmer who made the error. The animistic metaphor of the bug that maliciously sneaked in while the programmer was not looking is intellectually dishonest as it disguises that the error is the programmer's own creation. The nice thing of this simple change of vocabulary is that it has such a profound effect: while, before, a program with only one bug used to be "almost correct," afterwards a program with an error is just "wrong" (because in error).

My next linguistical suggestion is more rigorous. It is to fight the "if-this-guy-wants-to-talk-to-that-guy" syndrome: <u>never</u> refer to parts of programs or pieces of equipment in an anthropomorphic terminology, nor allow your students to do so. This linguistical improvement is much harder to implement than you might think, and your department might consider the introduction of fines for violations, say a quarter for undergraduates, two quarters for graduate students, and five dollars for faculty members; by the end of the first semester of the new regime, you will have collected enough money for two scholarships.

The reason for this last suggestion is that the anthropomorphic metaphor -- for whose introduction we can blame John von Neumann -- is an enormous handicap for every computing community that has adopted it. I have now encountered programs wanting things, knowing things, expecting things, believing things, etc., and each time that gave rise to avoidable confusions. The analogy that underlies this personification is so shallow that it is not only misleading but also paralyzing.

It is misleading in the sense that it suggests that we can adequately cope with the unfamiliar discrete in terms of the familiar continuous, i.e. ourselves, quod non. It is paralyzing in the sense that, because persons exist and act in time, its adoption effectively prevents a departure from operational semantics and thus forces people to think about programs in terms of computational behaviors, based on an underlying computational model. This is bad, because operational reasoning is a tremendous waste of mental effort.

Let me explain to you the nature of that tremendous waste, and allow me to try to convince you that the term "tremendous waste of mental effort" is not an exaggeration. For a short while, I shall get highly technical, but don't get frightened: it is the type of mathematics that one can do with one's hands in one's pockets. The point to get across is that if we have to demonstrate something about all the elements of a large set, it is hopelessly inefficient to deal with all the elements of the set individually: the efficient argument does not refer to individual elements at all and is carried out in terms of the set's definition.

Consider the plane figure Q, defined as the 8 by 8 square from which, at two opposite corners, two 1 by 1 squares have been removed. The area of Q is 62, which equals the combined area of 31 dominos of 1 by 2. The theorem is that the figure Q cannot be covered by 31 of such dominos.

Another way of stating the theorem is that if you start with squared paper and begin covering this by placing each next domino on two new adjacent squares, no placement of 31 dominos will yield the figure Q.

So, a possible way of proving the theorem is by generating all possible placements of dominos and verifying for each place-

ment that it does not yield the figure Q: a tremendously labor-
ious job.

The simple argument, however, is as follows. Color the
squares of the squared paper as on a chess board. Each domino,
covering two adjacent squares, covers 1 white and 1 black square,
and, hence, each placement covers as many white squares as it
covers black squares. In the figure Q, however, the number of
white squares and the number of black squares differ by 2 --
opposite corners lying on the same diagonal -- and hence no
placement of dominos yields figure Q.

Not only is the above simple argument many orders of magnitude shorter than the exhaustive investigation of the possible
placements of 31 dominos, it is also essentially more powerful,
for it covers the generalization of Q by replacing the original 8
by 8 square by any rectangle with sides of even length. The
number of such rectangles being infinite, the former method of
exhaustive exploration is essentially inadequate for proving our
generalized theorem.

And this concludes my example. It has been presented because it illustrates in a nutshell the power of down-to-earth
mathematics; needless to say, refusal to exploit this power of
down-to-earth mathematics amounts to intellectual and technological suicide. The moral of the story is: deal with all elements of a set by ignoring them and working with the set's definition.

Back to programming. The statement that a given program
meets a certain specification amounts to a statement about all
computations that could take place under control of that given
program. And since this set of computations is defined by the
given program, our recent moral says: deal with all computations
possible under control of a given program by ignoring them and
working with the program. We must learn to work with program
texts while (temporarily) ignoring that they admit the interpretation of executable code.

Another way of saying the same thing is the following one.
A programming language, with its formal syntax and with the proof
rules that define its semantics, is a formal system for which
program execution provides only a model. It is well-known that
formal systems should be dealt with in their own right, and not
in terms of a specific model. And, again, the corollary is that
we should reason about programs without even mentioning their
possible "behaviors."

And this concludes my technical excursion into the reason

why operational reasoning about programming "a tremendous waste of mental effort" and why, therefore, in computing science the anthropomorphic metaphor should be banned.

Not everybody understands this sufficiently well. I was recently exposed to a demonstration of what was pretended to be educational software for an introductory programming course. With its "visualizations" on the screen it was such an obvious case of curriculum infantilization that its author should be cited for "contempt of the student body," but this was only a minor offense compared with what the visualizations were used for: they were used to display all sorts of features of computations evolving under control of the student's program! The system highlighted precisely what the student has to learn to ignore, it reinforced precisely what the student has to unlearn. Since breaking out of bad habits, rather than acquiring new ones, is the toughest part of learning, we must expect from that system permanent mental damage for most students exposed to it.

Needless to say, that system completely hid the fact that, all by itself, a program is no more than half a conjecture. The other half of the conjecture is the functional, specification the program is supposed to satisfy. The programmer's task is to present such complete conjectures as proven theorems.

Before we part, I would like to invite you to consider the following way of doing justice to computing's radical novelty in an introductory programming course.

On the one hand, we teach what looks like the predicate calculus, but we do it very differently from the philosophers. In order to train the novice programmer in the manipulation of uninterpreted formulae, we teach it more as boolean algebra, familiarizing the student with all algebraic properties of the logical connectives. To further sever the links to intuition, we rename the values {true, false} of the boolean domain as {black, white}.

On the other hand, we teach a simple, clean, imperative programming language, with a skip and a multiple assignment as basic statements, with a block structure for local variables, the semicolon as operator for statement composition, a nice alternative construct, a nice repetition and, if so desired, a procedure call. To this we add a minimum of data types, say booleans, integers, characters and strings. The essential thing is that, for whatever we introduce, the corresponding semantics is defined by the proof rules that go with it.

Right from the beginning, and all through the course, we

stress that the programmer's task is not just to write down a program, but that his main task is to give a formal proof that the program he proposes meets the equally formal functional specification. While designing proofs and programs hand in hand, the student gets ample opportunity to perfect his manipulative agility with the predicate calculus. Finally, in order to drive home the message that this introductory programming course is primarily a course in formal mathematics, we see to it that the programming language in question has <u>not</u> been implemented on campus so that students are protected from the temptation to test their programs. And this concludes the sketch of my proposal for an introductory programming course for freshmen.

This is a serious proposal, and utterly sensible. Its only disadvantage is that it is too radical for many who, being unable to accept it, are forced to invent a quick reason for dismissing it, no matter how invalid. I'll give you a few quick reasons.

You don't need to take my proposal seriously because it is so ridiculous that I am obviously completely out of touch with the real world. But that kite won't fly, for I know the real world only too well: the problems of the real world are primarily those you are left with when you refuse to apply their effective solutions. So, let us try again.

You don't need to take my proposal seriously because it is utterly unrealistic to try to teach such material to college freshmen. Wouldn't that be an easy way out? You just postulate that this would be far too difficult. But that kite won't fly either for the postulate has been proven wrong: since the early 80's, such an introductory programming course has successfully been given to hundreds to college freshmen each year. [Because, in my experience, saying this once does not suffice, the previous sentence should be repeated at least another two times.] So, let us try again.

Reluctantly admitting that it could perhaps be taught to sufficiently docile students, you yet reject my proposal because such a course would deviate so much from what 18-year old students are used to and expect that inflicting it upon them would be an act of educational irresponsibility: it would only frustrate the students. Needless to say, that kite won't fly either. It is true that the student that has never manipulated uninterpreted formulae quickly realizes that he is confronted with something totally unlike anything he has ever seen before. But fortunately, the rules of manipulation are in this case so few and simple that very soon thereafter he makes the exciting discovery that he is beginning to master the use of a tool that, in all its simplicitly, gives him a power that far surpasses his wildest dreams.

Teaching to unsuspecting youngsters the effective use of formal methods is one of the joys of life because it is so extremely rewarding. Within a few months, they find their way in a new world with a justified degree of confidence that is radically novel for them; within a few months, their concept of intellectual culture has acquired a radically novel dimension. To my taste and style, that is what education is about. Universities should not be afraid of teaching radical novelties; on the contrary, it is their calling to welcome the opportunity to do so. Their willingness to do so is our main safeguard against dictatorships, be they of the proletariat, of the scientific establishment, or of the corporate elite.

Austin, 2 December 1988

Prof. Dr. Edsger W. Dijkstra
Department of Computer Sciences
The University of Texas at Austin
Austin, TX .78712-1188
USA

'An Undergraduate Course in Applied Data Communications'

Larry J. Brumbaugh

Applied Computer Science Department
Illinois State University
Normal, Illinois   61761

Abstract

This paper describes a different type of data communications course than that presently offered in most computer science programs. Several justifications for such a course are provided.

Overview and Rationale

Most people will not question the importance of including one or more data communications courses as part of a modern computer science/data processing curriculum. However, there is an extremely wide range of opinions as to the topics that should comprise the contents of such a course. Is there a relationship between the computer science courses presently offered in data communications and a very significant shortage of qualified people in the data communications area? Three 'typical' data communications courses are described here.

(A) In a computer science department located in an engineering school, or in a 'traditional' computer science program, the data communications course is often hardware and theory oriented. Mathematics, engineering and physics topics are included in the course. For many students, much of the course content is irrelevant or incomprehensible or both.

(B) At the other extreme, a Management Information Systems program located in a School of Business may only superficially examine the hardware aspects of data communications. Instead, an MIS course frequently emphasizes the design of systems, on-line programs, and screens. Hence, it is a very software oriented course. Some on-line application projects may be coded and implemented. These are usually implemented in a user friendly non-IBM mainframe environment.

(C) A third type of data communications course covers both hardware and software topics and also networks. In a single semester, the three topics cannot be covered in sufficient depth to develop working skills with any one of them.

For specific audiences, each of the above courses serves a worthwhile purpose. However, for each course, either the potential audience is rather limited, the amount of practical data communications covered is limited, or both. This paper describes an alternative to the above three courses, an _Applied_ Data Communications course. Its contents differ significantly from the three courses described above.

An _Applied_ Data Communications course should satisfy two objectives not usually found in the above three courses. First, allow students to obtain meaningful hands-on experience with a wide variety of modern data communications concepts and equipment, including software and hardware. Second, this experience and the course content itself should be related to the type of environment in which the typical entry level application programmer/analyst will most likely be working during their first several years as a data processing professional. It is important that the course is oriented toward the actual environment where most students will eventually be working.

None of the three courses described above are appropriate for satisfying these two conditions. Rather, in designing such a course, the following questions must be addressed. In what type of data communications environment will the typical application programmer/analyst find themselves? What communication software and hardware concepts and equipment will the student be working with over the next three to five years, the absolute maximum length of time for which predictions can be safely made in the data communications field? The majority of Applied Computer Science students at Illinois State University will eventually work on computer systems centered around large IBM mainframes or plug compatible machines. Such systems will also include a wide variety of terminal devices, control units, mini and microcomputers. Hardware from multiple non-IBM vendors will be included in this collection of devices. Distributed processing will be heavily used. The entire computer network will be tied together by IBM's Systems Network Architecture (SNA).

SNA is clearly the most popular (i.e. widely used) layered architecture in the U.S., and perhaps the world today, and has evolved into the de facto industry standard for data communications. Many small and medium size computer equipment vendors develop their data communication products to be compatible with SNA. Otherwise, the vendors find themselves locked out of the large number of IBM shops, which account for approximately 50% of the present computer industry. Under some conditions, non-SNA compatible devices and complete non-SNA networks can be tied into an existing SNA network. However, the cost of doing this is usually substantial.

The large number of todays Computer Science/Data Processing/MIS majors will find themselves working in an SNA data communications environment. In a curriculum that claims to be application oriented, this, by itself, should be sufficient reason to strongly consider an IBM flavored approach in data communications. This paper makes the assumption that emphasizing IBM software and hardware is a reasonable path to follow. (For a person with a strong aversion to anything IBM, substitute 'OSI Model' for 'SNA' throughout this paper.) Even accepting this, the problem still remains as to how to offer a meaningful application oriented course which includes hands-on experience.

The course described later in this paper is presently being offered by the Applied Computer Science Department at Illinois State University to advanced undergraduate and beginning graduate students. It meets the definition of an Applied Data Communications course given above. The ACS department has been offering a course called Introduction to On-line Systems for approximately ten years. It is similar to course (B) above. The programming component of the course uses Command Level CICS. Recently, two

additional courses have been added. The first is a course emphasizing hardware, networks, and some software, somewhat similar to course (C) above. The second new course developed is the one described in this paper.

Prerequisites for Applied Data Communications

Applied Data Communications is an advanced undergraduate or beginning graduate level course in data communication. It assumes that the student has acquired a rudimentary background in data communications. This background may be gotten from actual work experience or from prior courses. In the later case, the background is mostly theoretical. If a student has prior application experience, it has usually been acquired either on microcomputer systems or through programming with Command Level CICS or a comparable TP-monitor.

Additionally, the students must meet two other prerequisites. First, they must have a strong programming background in one of the three languages: COBOL, PL/I, or Assembler. Second, they must have some (programming) experience on large IBM (MVS) systems. All of the Applied Computer Science undergraduates at ISU meet the three prerequisites by the beginning of their senior year. The introduction to data communication knowledge is ordinarily acquired in any of one to three types of previous courses. These include microcomputer courses, systems analysis and software design courses, and also some aspects of the programming language courses. The other added course mentioned above, Data Communications and Networks, will also clearly satisfy the prerequisite. As with the other upper division ACS courses, which involve programming, no particular language is specified as a requirement for this course. Instead, the individual student selects the language with which they prefer to program from among COBOL, PL/I, and Assembler. The prerequisite of familiarity with MVS systems is probably satisfied with the 'Advanced Programming Concepts Using COBOL' course or the External Data Structures course, which includes an in-depth study of MVS systems, emphasizing JCL, Utilities, and VSAM.

A substantial number of ISU students take ACS courses on a part-time basis, while working in the Bloomington/Normal area. The majority of them are employed by two large insurance companies, State Farm and Country Companies. Both companies have large IBM data processing shops. Most of these students meet the three prerequisites for the course through their job experience. Additionally, most of the medium size programming installations in the immediate geographic area of Illinois State University are also IBM shops. Hence, almost all of the students that are interested in taking _Applied_ Data Communications are able to meet the three prerequisites.

Course Content

What is the appropriate material to include in an _Applied_ Data Communications course? The content consists of six major topics, which overlap one another. These include the following:

(1) A very intense overview is given of the major hardware and software components found in the modern data communications environment. This component of the course assumes some prerequisite knowledge of data communications.

(2) A thorough examination is made of the manner in which terminal devices work. This includes studying the data stream SENT from and RECEIVED into the terminals. The application software which interfaces with the terminals is examined. The control units and front end processors to which the terminals are attached are also described.

(3) The fundamental structure and major concepts associated with a layered network architecture, as exemplified by IBM's Systems Network Architecture (SNA), are studied in detail. This topic is the heart of the course, and all other topics are related to it.

(4) Telecommunication access methods are studied. This is done on both a theoretical and practical level. This component of the course is most responsible for allowing students true hands on experience. The VTAM access method is emphasized because of its power, popularity, and interrelationship with SNA.

(5) The software and hardware for connecting other devices and networks into an SNA environment. An emphasis is placed on local area networks, both token ring and CSMA/CD are covered, along with X.25 networks.

(6) Future directions and new state-of-the-art products in data communications are described. It is assumed that this component of the course will probably undergo changes on a yearly basis. It is also envisioned that some other parts of the course will also change, although on a less frequent basis.

Hands-on Experience-Course Projects

Specifically, how does the hands-on experience enter the course? Students taking _Applied_ Data Communications will complete three major projects. Although each of these is outlined below, detailed descriptions must be provided by the instructor each time the course is offered so that the projects reflect current concerns and practices.

First, each student will be required to complete a major data communications programming project using a teleprocessing access method _directly_ rather than _indirectly_. The _indirect_ approach most frequently uses a teleprocessing monitor such as CICS or IMS. Programming may be done in the language of the student's choice: COBOL, PL/I, or assembler. The ACS Department provides the necessary software support to permit using VTAM from within a COBOL of PL/I application program. The project will be completed in several steps, which parallel item G in Section IV in the course content outline.

1. Write a program which establishes synchronous communication with a single terminal device.

2. Modify the program to establish asynchronous communication with multiple terminals.

3. Further modify the program to establish communication with a second application program, concurrent with the existing terminal communications developed in 2 above.

Second, each student will be expected to complete another major programming project. Possible programming project topics include:

1. Write interface software on either the mainframe or an IBM-PC to upload and download files.

2. Write an emulation program on a personal computer that will allow a personal computer to act as a device attached to the mainframe. In particular, perform some functions available with a 3270 terminal.

3. Use a teleprocessing monitor to rewrite selected portions of the teleprocessing access method program developed in the first project. Then, compare and contrast the two programs in terms of efficiency and ease of development.

4. Conduct a detailed study of how CICS and a 3278 terminal interact during an LU-LU session. Specifically, what functions are performed at each SNA layer? Determine which headers are used, and the values they may contain?

5. Repeat the above study with IMS replacing CICS.

6. Repeat the above study with TSO replacing CICS.

7. Perform a comparable study examining the details of an LU-LU session between two large software products selected from among CICS, IMS, TSO, JES, etc.

Third, each student will be expected to complete a major non-programming project. Possible projects include:

1. Design a layered architecture to successfully run a simplified computer network which supports a limited collection of hardware devices and software products.

2. In response to some set of specific user criteria, design (but do not implement) a network. Include all relevant hardware, software, and topology, that can correctly and economically satisfy the user criteria.

3. Create and analyze terminal data streams, and identify the SNA components within them. Specifically the headers, request/response units, and the RPL fields must be identified.

4. Design, modify, or expand the scope of the ACS Departments' interface modules that are used to support VTAM programming in COBOL and PL/I.

Textbooks and References

The first two times the course was offered, the book Communications Architecture for Distributed Systems by R.J. Cypser, Addison-Wesley Publishing Co., 1978, was used as the text. It is expected that Cypser's book will remain the text for at least the next time the course is offered. It is somewhat remarkable that a book written in 1978 remains the definitive book on a dynamic subject like SNA/VTAM. However, because of his prior association with IBM, Cypser had knowledge of SNA/VTAM developments well ahead of their release by IBM. Hence, in many ways the book reads as if it has been written after 1980. At the present time, there is one comparable textbook available on SNA/VTAM. It is SNA:IBM's Networking Solution by James Martin, Prentice Hall, 1987. It is obviously more up-to-date than Cypser's book, but does not contain nearly the amount of material found in Cypser's book.

The textbook is supplemented by the material in a large number of IBM manuals. These manuals can be grouped into three general categories. First, there are the manuals that describe data communications, SNA, and protocols in general. Second, there are four important manuals which discuss the role and use of VTAM in an application environment. Finally, there are several manuals which discuss both terminals and printers, along with their associated data streams. Several copies of the entire collection of manuals are available for student usage. One additional course reference is being developed. It is a set of notes that summarize the VTAM manual material that is relevant to the programming projects.

It is hoped that either the Cypser book will be revised, or a comparable more modern textbook with the depth of material found in Cypser's book will become available soon.

Course Instructors

At present, the same person has taught the course every time it has been offered. One part-time instructor in the ACS Department is also fully qualified to teach the course and could be used in subsequent semesters if needed. However, from a faculty of 20 full-time and 10 part-time teachers, these are the only two people with the necessary background to teach the course. There is also a tremendous shortage of people with expertise in this area throughout the computer science/data processing field. The comment in the second paragraph of this paper is just one acknowledgment of this shortage.

Recently, a second full-time faculty member expressed an interest in moving into this area. It is presumed that it would be a worthwhile experience for most future instructors to unofficially audit one semester of the present course before attempting to teach it for the first time.

Comparable Professional Development Seminars

A large number of advertisements for three to five day professional development seminars get sent to Computer Science faculty members. From reading them, one important point becomes evident. Users of large computer systems consider several data communications topics as the most important for professional development seminars. Three specific types of courses seem to be widely offered. The first is an overview of the entire data communications field. Command Level CICS topics comprise the second. The third area is SNA/VTAM. Clearly, the reason why so many courses are offered in these areas is student demand. Hence, many people feel they need training in these areas. It is an interesting question as to why computer science programs are doing such an inadequate job in these areas. There are several possible explanations for this. Existing curriculums are outmoded or irrelevant. Many computer science faculty members have very limited backgrounds in modern data communications. Courses spend too much time on buzzwords and introductory concepts and not enough time teaching important skills.

As mentioned above, a large number of SNA/VTAM courses are presently offered by a wide variety of vendors. Based on the sheer number of courses offered and the cost of attending the, it is apparent that presenting SNA/VTAM courses is a very lucrative business. A partial listing of such courses follows.

Vendor	Course	Cost	Duration
OSI	VTAM From Start to Finish	$900	4 Days
SYS-ED	VTAM Operations	$175	1 Day
SYS-ED	Implementing SNA	$515	3 Days
U. Washington (St. Louis)	VTAM Internal Architecture	$1,075	5 Days

Summary

The order in which the major Applied Data Communications course topics are presented does allow some flexibility. Clearly, the overview and review of data communications fundamentals should be covered first. However, following this, either of the next two topics can be taught. Likewise, on a programming level, some VTAM material could be introduced earlier in the course. This would permit beginning the programming projects earlier in the course. If this approach is followed, some VTAM topics must be presented preliminary to explaining the SNA theory behind the topic.

BIBLIOGRAPHY

Cypser, R., Communications Architecture for Distributed Systems, Reading, MA: Addison-Wesley, 1978.

Martin, J., SNA: IBM's Networking Solution, Prentice Hall, 1987.

Low-Cost Networks and Gateways for Teaching Data Communications

Larry Hughes

School of Computer Science,
Technical University of Nova Scotia,
P.O. Box 1000, Halifax, Nova Scotia, Canada, B3J 2X4

Abstract

The growing importance of communications in computer science has resulted in many undergraduate computer science programmes offering courses in data communications. Although data communications courses can be taught in a practical manner, the cost of data communications hardware often restricts the amount of actual hands-on experience that students can gain.

In this paper we describe the hardware and software requirements of several low-cost networks that can be used by students to gain experience in a wide variety of data communication topics including local area networks (such as bus networks and ring networks), wide area networks (i.e. store-and-forward networks), and gateways.

Keywords: Data communications, computer science education, wide area networks, local area networks, gateways.

1 Introduction

Over the past decade, a growing number of computer science departments have recognized the importance of data communications as an integral part of the education of computer science students (for example, see [11,13]). Although once a subject primarily of concern to electrical engineers, data communications is rapidly becoming of interest to computer scientists because of issues such as the increasing demand for computers to support different types of communication, the development and reliance upon communication software, and the expanding use of computer networks.

Like many other computer science subjects, data communications can be taught in a practical, hands-on manner given the correct facilities. However, much of the equipment needed to teach data communications is prohibitively expensive even when used with low-cost personal computers such as the IBM PC. For example, the costs associated with local area network technology for a single PC can range anywhere from $200 to $1600 per interface board. Additional expenses may be incurred since many local area networks require specialized hardware and software to manage the network [2,8].

In this paper we describe how data communication courses can be taught in a practical fashion using microcomputers such as the IBM PC at a cost of less than $100 per PC. We also show how this low-cost approach permits students to gain experience with the concepts associated with both bus and ring local area networks, store-and-forward wide area networks, and gateways.

The remainder of this paper is organized as follows. In section 2, we describe the hardware required to support low-cost networks and gateways, while in section 3, several network and gateway configurations using this hardware are presented. Examples of a number of actual network and gateway implementations are discussed in section 4. In the final section, we present arguments (both economic and educational) as to why this approach in supporting the teaching of data communications is a viable one.

2 Hardware Requirements

The hardware requirements of the low-cost networks and gateways described in the Introduction are as follows:

- a number of microcomputers. The minimum practical number is three, while all of the concepts can be explained adequately using no more than five.

- each microcomputer must be equiped with two communication ports. The ports should be the same (i.e. either both serial or both parallel), since this minimizes the amount of specialized software that must be written. In addition, it should be possible to both send and receive on each port, simultaneously if necessary.

- one RS-232 cable per microcomputer, with pins 2 (transmit) and 3 (receive) crossed. Pin 7 (ground) should also be connected. If all ports are of the same gender (i.e. all male or all female), the number of combinations of cable that must be built will be minimized.

A 'typical' microcomputer and its ports are shown in figure 1 (in keeping with the terminology associated with the IBM PC Asynchronous Communications Adapter card, the primary port is labelled 'P', and the secondary port is labelled 'S').

3 Configurations and Software Requirements

The hardware described in the previous section supports at least two network topologies as well as a number of different network and gateway implementations.

For the purposes of this paper, a PC is considered to be a **station** which can transmit and receive **messages**. In order to permit inter-station communications, each station is assigned a unique station **address**. A message contains two address: the address of the intended destination station and the address of the station transmitting the message (the source address).

3.1 Bus Networks

A bus network consists of a number of stations accessing a single communication channel known as a **bus**. Whenever a message is transmitted on the bus, the message propogates to the stations both upstream and downstream of the transmitting station. When not transmitting, each station is expected to take a copy of any message being sent – once the message has been received, the receiving station examines the destination address associated with the message; if the destination address matches the address of the station, the message is kept, otherwise it is discarded. In most commercial bus networks, before a station transmits a message, the station checks whether another station is transmitting (indicated by data on the bus); the station must wait until the network is inactive before sending. However, if the network is idle (i.e. no data is detected on the network), any station needing to transmit may do so. While transmitting a message, a station is expected to check that the data it sends is the same as it receives – should the station not receive the same data that it is sending, a **collision** is said to have occurred, meaning that two (or more) stations are attempting to transmit simultaneously. This type of bus network is commonly refered to as CSMA/CD (carrier sensed multiple access with collision detection). Examples of CSMA/CD networks include the Ethernet [4] and IEEE 802.3 [1] local area networks.

A bus network can be constructed out of the hardware described in section 2 by connecting the 'P' port of a microcomputer to the 'S' port of an adjacent microcomputer. Two stations will have a single connection only (i.e. the stations at either end of the network). Figure 2 illustrates a bus network built out of four microcomputers.

In order that the bus network emulate CSMA/CD communications, each station is expected to support the following algorithm:

1. whenever a byte is received on a port, the software is to take a copy of the byte as well as forward the byte on the other port (e.g. a byte received on the 'P' port would be sent out on the 'S' port only).

2. a station can only transmit a message if it is not currently receiving a message.

3. a transmitting station must send its message out on both its 'P' and 'S' ports.

4. whenever transmitting, a station must check its input, should data be received on either port, the station must abort its transmission.

3.2 Ring Networks

Ring networks, unlike bus networks, consist of a single communication channel that connects all the stations in a circular **ring**. A message that is sent on a ring network passes each station on the ring and returns to the transmitting station. Each station on the ring takes a copy of the message, if the message's destination address matches the address of the receiving station, the message is made available to the station, otherwise it should be discarded. A number of different techniques exists to ensure deterministic access to the ring (i.e. that all stations have an equal chance at transmitting messages). Two of the better known are the **slotted ring** (typified by the Cambridge Ring [6]) and the **token ring** (such as the IBM Token Ring [9] and the IEEE 802.5 Token Ring [5]).

Since the slotted ring is essentially a variation on the token ring, we will confine our discussion to the token ring. Briefly, the token ring permits access to the ring by means of a **token**. Whenever a **free** token passes a station, the station has the option of transmitting a message or passing the free token on to the next station. A station transmits a message by setting the free token to **busy**, forwarding the token, and transmitting the message. Should a station receive a busy token, it must forward the token and wait for the incoming message. It is the responsibility of the transmitting station to remove its busy token from the ring and issue another free token. To avoid the situation where a token remains permanently busy (which can occur should the transmitter fail before it frees the token), a **monitor** station is used to remove tokens that have not been freed and their messages. (A variety of monitor implementations exist, from having a single station dedicated to the task of being the monitor, to having a number of stations competing for the rôle of the monitor.)

A low-cost ring network (either slotted or token) can be built out of the previously described hardware by connecting the 'P' port of a microcomputer with the 'S' port of an adjacent microcomputer. All stations are thus interconnected, making a ring. Figure 3 is an example of a ring network made out of three microcomputers. Note that unlike the bus network, there is only one direction that the data can travel.

The algorithm to be used by each station on the ring is as follows:

1. a station can only transmit when it receives a free token, whereas a station receiving a busy token must wait until the next free token is received before it may transmit.

2. data received on the 'S' port is copied by the station and forwarded out the 'P' port.

3. In order to ensure that the network does not 'hang' (for example, by a continuously circulating busy token

or the loss of the token), the low-cost ring network requires a monitor station.

3.3   Store-and-Forward Networks

A store-and-forward network is one in which each station (or **node**) on the network takes a copy of the entire message before forwarding it. In addition, the receiving station is expected to acknowledge the receipt of the message by sending an acknowledgment to the transmitting station. Messages need not be sent by a station in the order that they are received, since messages may have a priority associated with them, which requires the station to forward high-priority messages before low-priority ones. Most wide area networks are store-and-forward networks [14].

The low-cost version of the store-and-forward network is similar to the bus network implementation, with the exception that entire messages are kept by each station before they are sent, rather than single bytes. In addition, the protocols used in the low-cost store-and-forward networks are somewhat more complex since each station is expected to acknowledge each message that is received. Figure 4 is an example of a four station store-and-forward network.

3.4   Gateways

Gateways (and bridges) allow the interconnection of networks. The term **bridge** commonly refers to interconnecting homogeneous networks in which no protocol changes are required, while the term **gateway** is used for interconnecting heterogeneous networks [12].

Figure 5 shows how the hardware allows the interconnection of two bus networks by a gateway. Note that the hardware does not permit the interconnection of a gateway to a ring network, however this could be achieved by having the gateway microcomputer support three ports (one on the bus network and the other two on the ring network).

There are a number of different low-cost bridges that can be implemented with the hardware. The simplest forwards each message received onto the remote network. This type of bridge essentially allows a network to expand beyond its practical limits (such as distance or number of stations). The problem with this type of bridge is that all messages are forwarded onto the remote network, regardless of whether the destination resides on the remote network. By having the bridge determine the addresses of the stations on the different networks that it interconnects, only those messages which have a destination on the remote network need be forwarded.

Since gateways usually interconnect heterogeneous networks, a gateway can be expected to perform a variety of tasks such as message assembly, message fragmentation and protocol conversion. A low-cost gateway can be used to demonstrate many of these issues by connecting a store-and-forward network to a bus local area network. For example, by making each network's message size different, problems such as message fragmentation can easily be demonstrated.

4   Implementations

The different networks and gateways described in the previous section have all been implemented by the author or his students using five PC-clones, each equiped with a pair of serial (RS-232) ports. Each of the PCs were originally supplied with a single RS-232 port [3], the second port was added at a cost of about $90.00 per machine.

In each implementation, the software was written in a layered fashion, with the network specific software at the lowest layer. A common checksum function was used by all implementations – each byte transmitted by a station was XORed into a checksum byte, which was sent at the end of each message. Furthermore, all software was interrupt driven, thereby permitting other tasks (such as keyboard handlers) to function at the same time.

4.1   A Bus Network

A bus network driver was implemented as part of the MINIX [15] operating system's kernel [7]. Processes requiring interprocess communication with processes on remote stations would pass messages to the driver via the kernel. The messages were then reformatted into an IEEE 802.3 packet format and transmitted by the driver, a byte-at-a-time, out both ports. In order to indicate that the transmission had completed, a special end-of-packet character was transmitted after the checksum had been sent.

Collisions were detected by the transmitting station enabling both the transmit and receive interrupts – if a transmitting station received data on either port, it could assume that a collision had occurred. If a collision was detected, the transmitting station immediately sent an invalid checksum followed by the end-of-packet indicator.

A non-transmitting driver receiving a byte on one port would take a copy of the byte and immediately forward it on the other port (for example, a byte received on the 'P' port would be transmitted on the 'S' port), thereby avoiding the possibility of a station aborting its transmission because of its own message. If data was received on both ports simultaneously (i.e. a collision had occurred), the station would stop storing the incoming message and simply forward each byte until the end-of-packet indication was received from both ports.

Because of the overheads associated with MINIX, the line speed was kept at 3600 baud.

4.2   A Ring Network

A token ring was one of a number of ring networks implemented in MS-DOS (for example, see [10]). Each station on the ring (other than the monitor station) allowed users to enter a message and a destination address. The station then transmitted the message when a free token became available. As with the bus network, messages were transmitted a byte-at-a-time between each station. A station receiving a message with its address displayed the message. A dedicated monitor station checked for network errors and corrected invalid token situations.

All packets (both free and busy) were preceeded by a 'break' indicator. Whenever a station detected a break, the next byte was assumed to be the token.

In order to demonstrate the types of error that could occur in a ring, the software in each station was designed to be able to cause errors such as a missing token (by removing a free token from the ring), or causing a continuously busy token (by never freeing the token).

Since a task running in MS-DOS effectively takes over the entire machine, speeds of up to 9600 baud were achieved in some of the token ring implementations.

4.3 A Store-and-Forward Network

A store-and-forward network was implemented using the MINIX operating system as part of a course in distributed systems. The store-and-forward network was similar to the bus network with the exception that each driver assembled the entire message before forwarding it.

Routing tables were not used in the implementation described in this paper, instead the stations were numbered from left-to-right in an increasing order. Whenever a station received a message, it checked the destination address and the port the message was received on before forwarding the message. For example, if stations were numbered 1, 3, 5, and 7, and station 3 received a message for station 2 from station 5, station 3 would forward the message out its left port without regard to the fact that station 2 did not exist. However, when station 1 received the message for station 2 on its right port, the message could be discarded because only messages less than or equal to station 1's address could be accepted. This technique avoided the problem of messages continuously circulating between to stations.

As in the case of the bus network, the line speed was restricted to 3600 baud because of overheads associated with operating in the MINIX environment.

4.4 Gateways

At present, we have only tested one gateway with the hardware described in section 2. The gateway runs as a stand-alone program on MS-DOS and connects two MINIX bus networks. In order to demonstrate some of the issues surrounding the design of gateways, the two networks have different message sizes (32 bytes on one network and 64 on the other), thereby requiring the gateway to fragment large messages. Routing is achieved by having the gateway maintain tables with the addresses of the stations on each network.

5 Concluding Remarks

In this paper we have shown how networks and gateways can be constructed out of microcomputers and inexpensive RS-232 connections to support the teaching of data communications. In addition, we have also described a number of implementations which demonstrate the practicality of using this type of equipment in a student environment.

Although the networks described in this paper cannot support communication speeds like those of existing network technology, the low-cost networks do offer a number of potential advantages to both the student and the instructor:

- one set of hardware allows students to work with a number of different types of network, including bus and ring local area networks, store-and-forward wide area networks and gateways.

- the cost of the hardware is minimal compared to the cost of the machine and to the cost of existing local area network hardware.

- in many respects, students gain a much broader understanding of how network hardware functions since the software that they write often emulates what the actual network hardware does.

- by having the students write layered software, complex, higher-level protocols can be implemented without regard for the low-level communication facilities. For example, in both MINIX implementations (the bus network and the store-and-forward network), the students were expected to implement a version of UNIX sockets.

It is clearly possible to build a LAN using the PC's existing single RS-232 port and the parallel printer port, thereby eliminating the need to purchase a second RS-232 card. However, we deliberately avoided this approach for a number of reasons, notably:

- it requires the development of two sets of software, one to handle communications through the serial (RS-232) port and one for communications through the parallel port;

- an even number of machines would be required for ring local area networks to ensure that parallel connected to parallel (or serial to serial);

- the software would have to be specially configured, some machines would have serial input and parallel output, while others would have parallel input and serial output.

Although the implementations described in this paper was with the PC, there is no reason why *any* microcomputer that supports two communication channels could not be used.

In closing, we believe that given the importance of data communications in the education of computer science students, the techniques described in this paper permit students to gain practical, hands-on experience in both networks and gateways at a very low cost.

Acknowledgments

The ring local area network was implemented by Mr. Bill Cross, a fourth year undergraduate student at the School, while the bus network was written by Mr. David Cushing as part of his Masters' thesis on multicast communications. The RS-232 cables were supplied by the University's Computer Services.

References

[1] *CSMA/CD Access Method and Physical Layer Specifi-cations.* IEEE Project 802, Local Area Network Standards (IEEE Computer Society), December 1982.

[2] *Data Communications Buyers' Guide Issue - Part II.* June 1987.

[3] *RS-232 PLUS Interface Upgrade Board Installation Guide.* InterTAN Canada Ltd., 1987. Order No. 25-1031.

[4] *The Ethernet, A Local Area Network, Data Link Layer and Physical Layer Specifications.* Digital Equipment Corporation, Intel Corporation, and Xerox Corporation, September 1980. Version 1.0.

[5] *Token Ring Access Method and Physical Layer Specifications.* Institute of Electrical and Electronic Engineers, 1985. American National Standards ANSI/IEEE Standard 802.5.

[6] R. Banerjee and W.D. Shepherd. The Cambridge Ring. In *Local Area Networks: An Advanced Course*, pages 64 – 86, Springer-Verlag, Lecture Notes in Computer Science, 1985.

[7] David Cushing. *The Implemenation of Multicast Communication in the MINIX Operating System.* Master's thesis, School of Computer Science, Technical University of Nova Scotia, August 1988.

[8] Frank J. Derfler. Making Connections – LANs Under Netware. *PC Magazine*, 5(21):149 – 186, December 1986.

[9] R.C. Dixon, N.C. Strole, and J.D. Markov. A Token-Ring Network for Local Data Communications. *IBM Systems Journal*, 22(1/2), 1983.

[10] L. Hughes. MTR: A Monitorless Token Ring. In *Fourteenth Biennial Symposium on Communications*, Department of Electrical Engineering, Queen's University at Kingston, June 1988.

[11] L. Hughes. Teaching Computer Communications to Computer Technology Students. In *CIPS National Conference Proceedings*, CIPS National Conference, Calgary, 1984.

[12] W.D. Shepherd. *LAN Internetworking*, pages 396 – 427. Springer-Verlag, Lecture Notes in Computer Science 184, 1985.

[13] Mark Sherman and Ann Marks. Using Low-Cost Workstations to Investigate Computer Networks and Distributed Systems. *IEEE Computer*, 19(6):32 – 41, June 1986.

[14] A.S. Tanenbaum. *Computer Networks.* Prentice-Hall, 1981.

[15] A.S. Tanenbaum. *Operating Systems - Design and Implementation. Prentice-Hall Software Series*, Prentice-Hall, 1987.

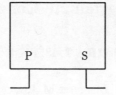

Figure 1: Station with two ports (P - primary, S - secondary)

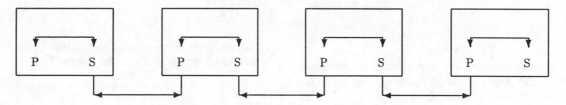

Figure 2: Bus Network Configuration

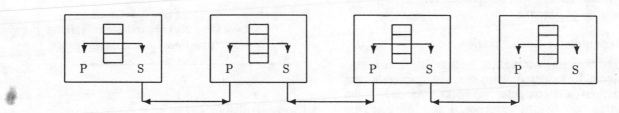

Figure 3: Ring Network Configuration

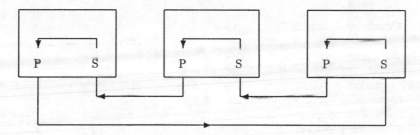

Figure 4: Store-and-Forward Network Configuration

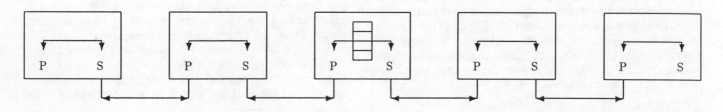

Figure 5: Two Bus Networks Interconnected by a Gateway

An Undergraduate Concentration in Networking and Distributed Systems

Margaret M. Reek

Rochester Institute of Technology
Undergraduate Computer Science Department
1 Lomb Memorial Drive
Rochester, NY 14623-0887

Abstract

This paper describes our experiences at Rochester Institute of Technology in establishing an undergraduate computer science concentration in networking and distributed systems. The concentration course sequence, prerequisite requirements, individual course structure, lab environment and student projects are discussed.

1. Introduction

The Undergraduate Computer Science Department at Rochester Institute of Technology (RIT) has offered a BS degree since 1972. In the intervening years, the curriculum has undergone many revisions and updates. More recently our program has included a requirement for a two or three course concentration. The purpose of the concentration is to provide depth in an area in computer science to complement the breadth provided by the core curriculum. Several years ago a new concentration in Networking and Distributed Systems was instituted. This paper describes the design, implementation, and benefits of the concentration, with emphasis on its capstone course, Distributed Systems Lab.

2. The Design of the Concentration

Before the concentration in Networking and Distributed Systems, RIT offered a two course sequence in data communications and computer networks. As one of the primary instructors in this sequence, I was frustrated by the lack of a "hands-on" component to the material. The ten-week quarter system at RIT left no time to incorporate such experience into the existing courses. We addressed this problem by creating a new course dedicated to the implementation of communications and networking principles: Distributed Systems Lab (DS Lab). This idea is analogous to our long standing Operating Systems and Operating Systems Lab (OS Lab) course sequence, in which the first course emphasizes theory and the second course the implementation of the theory. It is the

capstone course in a very intensive concentration, the structure of which is shown in Figure 1.

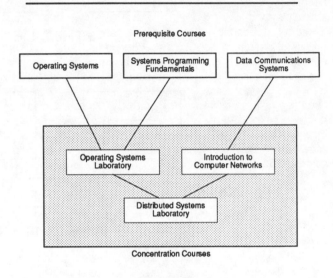

Prerequisite Courses

Operating Systems   Systems Programming Fundamentals   Data Communications Systems

Operating Systems Laboratory   Introduction to Computer Networks

Distributed Systems Laboratory

Concentration Courses

Figure 1
Networking and Distributed Systems
Concentration Course Structure

2.1. Prerequisite Courses

Operating Systems and Data Communications are required of all computer science majors. Operating Systems covers the traditional theory of operating systems, and Data Communications covers the physical and data link layers of the ISO model as well as local area networks. These are predominately lecture courses with little or no lab work. Systems Programming Fundamentals is one of several professional electives students may choose at the end of the second year to prepare them for co-op, and to start them along a path to a concentration. The

Partial support for this work has been provided by the National Science Foundation's College Science Instrumentation Program #CSI-8551490.

course introduces students to the C language, interfacing with system level functions, and programming at the device level. These courses are prerequisites for the concentration courses.

2.2. Concentration Courses

In the concentration, these prerequisites feed directly into the next level of exploration in operating systems and networks. Introduction to Networks is an upper division elective covering the remaining layers of the ISO model. In OS Lab, the theory developed in Operating Systems is applied to a simple operating system, using the skills developed in Systems Programming Fundamentals. As OS Lab is the model on which DS Lab is based, a short discussion of its structure is in order.

The students in OS Lab develop a multi-tasking operating system from scratch. A simple baseline multitasking system is developed by the entire group in class. There is deliberately no textbook, nor is there a pre-prepared design or code. The course uses the Socratic method, in which the knowledge required to implement the system is drawn out of the students. Students coming into the course rarely believe they can address such a daunting task. The instructor guides them and shows that it isn't beyond their grasp. We believe this is more meaningful than presenting them with a simple system to start with. The course has been using this basic model since 1975.

The baseline system is developed and debugged over a four week period. After that the class is divided into teams of 3 or 4 students, where each team proposes projects to enhance the base system. Each team is required to implement as many projects as there are team members. Students choose their own projects and must get the instructor's approval for each of them. Examples of projects appropriate in this course are floppy disk drivers, file systems, memory management subsystems (including virtual memory), windowing systems, scheduling algorithm experiments, etc.

My objective in creating DS Lab was to provide a similar experience, but with networks as the focus. In the first several weeks of the class the students would develop and debug a robust data link layer. Then they would form small teams and implement projects on top of the data link layer. The requirements for the projects would be flexible, letting the students explore those aspects of computer networks that interest them most. A later section discusses the types of projects done to date.

2.3. Justification for Concentration Design

The concentration is very demanding, and the need for a difficult course like OS Lab may not be apparent. However, we believe that students in the DS Lab need more than communications theory: they also need programming expertise at the systems level, as well as the experience of working in teams. The ten week quarter leaves no time for learning such things if students are to

create meaningful projects in networks. By building on their experience from the lab course in operating systems, students are able to go further in DS Lab than they otherwise might. Overall, the course sequence has proven to be an excellent one for achieving our objectives.

3. The Lab Environment

A grant from the National Science Foundation's College Science Instrumentation Program and a donation from Sun Microsystems allowed us to equip a dedicated lab. The equipment acquired serves both the OS Lab and DS Lab courses. I feel it is essential that students become familiar with the lab equipment used in DS Lab prior to taking the course. We acquired 6 Sun 2/120 workstations in the summer of 1986. The stations are all identically equipped, with a hard disk, tape, floppy disk, 10 serial ports, monitor, keyboard and mouse. Each unit acts as an independent standalone workstation, with Ethernet connections among them for file transfer and remote login. Students can easily replicate their code on other systems, and, because all systems are identical, there is no need to dedicate certain systems to particular functions. Since the systems are independent, OS Lab teams can test their projects without interfering with other students. The only connection with the rest of our facilities is via a serial line running the Kermit[1] protocol. This allows students to transfer files to and from the lab while keeping the rest of our facilities secure. The general lab layout is shown in Figure 2.

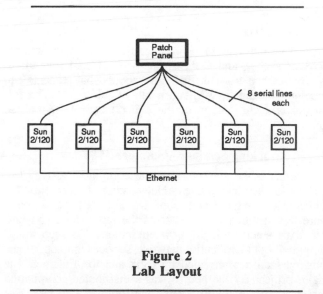

Figure 2
Lab Layout

The critical part of the configuration for the DS Lab class is the patch panel built by our support staff, detailed in Figure 3. The serial lines on the Sun systems are used for the underlying communication channel instead of the Ethernet. We want the students to build a network from the ground up, and starting with the Ethernet would solve many interesting problems (especially in routing). The patch panel provides a way to easily connect the serial lines into a variety of network configurations. The serial lines from each machine are wired to a DIN-6 connector on the face of the panel. To make a connection between two ports, a short patch cable is plugged between them. DS Lab students can configure the available machines through the patch panel in a matter of minutes.

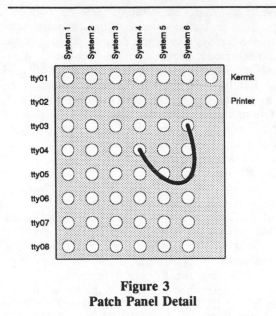

Figure 3
Patch Panel Detail

4. Experiences

The lab has been in operation for approximately two years now, and DS Lab has been offered four times. We've learned a lot in that time about what students can accomplish, and how to run a lab of this type. The following is a chronology of the experiences of DS Lab so far.

4.1. Networking Seminar - Summer 1986

During the summer that the equipment arrived, we offered a seminar called Networking Implementation, which was the predecessor of DS Lab. The serial ports were not installed at the start of the term and I had limited experience with the new equipment. To keep things simple, I opted to build network services on top of the existing facilities provided by Unix and the Ethernet. The major project for the course was a distributed compilation server. The network was partitioned into sets of "equivalent" machines; that is, ones that run the same operating system and produce the same object code. (In reality all of our systems were equivalent, but we wanted to deal with a more general case.) The distributed compilation server was transparent to the user. Each use of the C compiler caused the station's server to see whether the cpu load exceeded a threshold. If so, the server queried the other equivalent systems to find one with a low load.

If an equivalent system could handle the additional load the C preprocessor was run locally (to avoid copying "include" files across the network), the results sent to the remote system, and the final object or executable file delivered back to the local host. When all equivalent systems were too busy, the compilation proceeded on the local system.

4.2. Distributed Systems Lab - Spring 1987

The first true offering of DS Lab was in Spring of 1987, after the first offering of OS Lab on the new hardware. In DS Lab we decided to examine a token ring architecture, roughly modeled after the IEEE 802 standard [2,3]. Since we were running over serial lines using the Unix terminal driver, we did not have the capability to transmit and examine single bits of data, as in a true ring network. One of the interesting aspects of ring topologies is the one bit window used to view the network transmissions, so we decided to treat each character (the smallest transmittable unit) as a single bit. With this constraint, the students were forced to deal with the problems associated with framing, frame removal, acknowledgements, lost tokens, and transmission errors, in a manner that approximated the way a ring operates. A very simple user message service was implemented using the ring.

4.3. Distributed Systems Lab - Summer 1987

The second time the course was offered, I decided that a point to point network architecture would provide for more interesting project opportunities than a ring architecture. The class developed its own data link protocol to serve as a baseline for further projects. Unfortunately, this process took much longer than I anticipated, so little time was left for network and transport layer projects. Therefore I decided to use a data link protocol the students had examined in detail in the required data communications course as a starting point in the future.

4.4. Distributed Systems Lab - Spring 1988

The course was next offered in the spring of 1988, and we used protocol 6 from Tanenbaum [4] as a base. We found that even when the basic algorithm is presented there are still many challenging implementation details. However, our development time of the baseline system was cut to approximately three weeks, allowing ample time for work on more advanced projects.

The teams that quarter implemented and evaluated different routing algorithms. Dynamic routing using approximations of Chu's algorithm [5] and a backward learning algorithm were explored. Students found that the algorithms they studied in the texts and articles did not always completely cover situations that could occur in the network. For example, an algorithm may specify how to reroute when a communication line fails, but never mention what to do when the line becomes available again. Students had to develop their own solutions to these problems.

One team implemented a fully dynamic routing algorithm roughly based on Chu's algorithm, but with significant modifications. They also implemented a transport layer with flow control and crash recovery, and a session layer with a remote procedure call interface of their own design. To demonstrate the capabilities of their system, they developed a Unix-like file transfer (ftp) application using their remote procedure library. File transfers completed correctly, even as systems went up and down, and lines were disconnected and reconnected. The team tested numerous network configurations, including ones with cycles, with no failures. This experience proved that the course objectives could be achieved in the way that I had envisioned.

4.5. Distributed Systems Lab - Summer 1988

This summer (1988) was the most recent offering of the course. The successes of the previous quarter sparked interest in pursuing some different types of projects. One team implemented a gateway between a MacIntosh en an AppleTalk network and a Sun running the students' own network protocol. They also implemented a simulation of an Aloha satellite network to see if they could approximate the theoretical results they had studied in the networks course. The other team examined a dynamic routing algorithm that was originally based on the idea of a centralized routing (star) network. This quickly evolved into something much more substantial, as they started to examine what would happen if the routing control center (hub) went down, or if the network configuration changed so that a node was no longer adjacent to the hub.

4.6. Summary of Student Experiences

We have experimented with different kinds of projects over the past two-year period. Some projects were more beneficial than others in teaching networking concepts. However, in all cases the students gained a much greater appreciation for the difficulties in implementing and debugging network code. One aspect that made itself particularly apparent was the true simultaneous nature of network processes. This sounds simplistic, of course things in networks occur simultaneously. However, those same terms are used to describe events in multi-tasking operating systems, but where things only *appear* to be simultaneous. DS Lab students have dealt with the environment in which things that appear to be simultaneous are ultimately handled sequentially in their OS Lab work. In a network, independent computers are cooperating and events do take place simultaneously. This can present many complex situations that must be handled appropriately, and provides many interesting challenges to the students.

An idea for a future project is a simple distributed operating system. So far the course has been primarily network implementation, with little related to distributed computing. I'm not sure how far we can go with distributed computing if we continue to start from the data link layer; I may have to rename the course to something that better reflects its contents.

5. Laboratory Course Structure

OS Lab and DS Lab have essentially the same course structure. Each is a four quarter-credit course with four contact hours a week. We have learned that using two two-hour blocks, works better than four single hour blocks. The longer block provides more uninterrupted time to develop ideas and code. This is especially important in developing fairly large and complex systems. I have also developed a practice of using two overhead projectors and doing all work on the overhead slides. After each class I make copies of the overheads for the students; this eliminates the need to take notes and allows them to think and participate more. The two projectors allow us to have a larger view of the ideas presented, and having everything on slides means that when we discover a problem with something developed previously, all I need to do is reproject that slide. This eliminates a lot of time rewriting on a blackboard.

The lab projects in each course form a major component of the grade. However, the teams are also required to give a thirty to forty minute presentation to the class on their project. This allows students to learn from others' experience: what techniques worked and what didn't, what implementation difficulties they faced, and so on. They are expected to give a professional presentation and use appropriate visual aids. Each team must provide detailed external documentation covering an overview of the projects, design specifications, user manual pages, and instructions for running demonstrations. Demonstrations of the finished product are scheduled at the students' convenience during exam week. To assist me in determining the grade for individual students on a team, the students complete peer evaluation forms. Each team member evaluates the performance of the teammates and him/herself twice, once in mid term and again at the end of the quarter. This gives two data points, that could be very different, on which to evaluate team dynamics.

The major portion (65 percent) of the grade is determined by the success of the implementation of the projects. Because this is such an important part of the grade, and there is very little formal guidance in the course, it could be easy for students to let things slide until the end of the quarter. To alleviate this I have instituted a mid-point review one month after the baseline system is developed. In the review students must demonstrate those parts of their projects that are functioning and provide the detailed specifications for the remainder of their projects. This greatly reduces the problems associated with procrastination that had been in evidence prior to this review process.

These evaluation techniques have evolved over time, and I am fairly satisfied with them. I admit that the procedures work somewhat better in OS Lab, which typically has between 15 and 25 students. DS Lab has been very small so far (4-9 students), and sometimes we don't reach critical mass. My ideal size for each class is about 15 students, this is enough to get good interaction, but not so large that it gets out of control.

6. Unexpected Benefits and Advice

When I developed the concentration sequence and wrote my grant proposal, workstations were not very common. Happily, I was steered in that direction once the grant was funded. The multi-window workstation environment present on the Sun's has turned out to be a tremendous advantage in the DS Lab course. The ability to open windows and log onto any number of remote stations from a single station has made debugging and testing of the network projects much simpler. We have made full use of the multi-tasking and interprocess communications capabilities under Unix, and typically implement the various layers of software as cooperating processes. I can't imagine having to debug that kind of system using a single terminal environment. It isn't necessary to have something as fancy as our implementation, but I strongly advise systems with the cability of controlling more than one network node from a single point of contact, and have a multi-tasking operating system.

Another unexpected bonus of the configuration was the additional hardware devices for the students in OS Lab. Our previous equipment only had a terminal and floppy disk as external devices. On the Suns, the students can also work with the bitmap display, the mouse and the tape drive. This benefit was almost a detriment at first, since writing even the simplest output is difficult on the bit mapped display. To get around this, we added a dumb terminal to one of the serial ports, and use it to implement the baseline system. For their projects, students are free to use or ignore the Sun display. I do provide a simple font so that they can concentrate on operating systems principles instead of font design.

The arrangement we had with each station having its own complete file system turned out to be a nuisance. We recently added a file server to the network which handles only user files. This eliminates replication of students' code at each station, and the ensuing update problems. Had we not been able to obtain a new node, I would have opted to convert one of the existing six workstations to serve this purpose. The server station would have still been available for any purpose except for debugging of OS Lab projects.

There are two warnings I would give to others who are considering this type of equipment for an operating systems lab. First, be sure that the information you need to program the various devices is available: in particular, items such as the memory management unit may be proprietary, so obtaining documentation may be difficult. Second, find out ahead of time how complex it is to program the equipment: are there simple ways to display information (unlike our Sun monitor)? If virtual memory is supported, can it be ignored? Our Suns are far more complicated to work with than the systems they replaced, and this has made the baseline systems in OS Lab more complex than we really like.

7. Conclusions

We have demonstrated that undergraduate students can participate in a meaningful way and benefit from a network implementation class. With the proper background in theory and systems programming, they can develop projects of significant size and scope. These students have been able to examine in detail many of the concepts and questions that were discussed in lectures. In addition, many of the "implementation details" that are swept under the rug in a theory class have had to be dealt with, and the students are forced to find their own solutions. Students who select this concentration gain a much deeper understanding of the principles of network design and the difficulties of their implementation.

8. Acknowledgements

I would like to thank those at RIT who made the grant and the subsequent project possible especially: Wiley McKinzie, Michael Lutz, Evelyn Rozanski, and Mark Lessard. I would also like to thank all the students who have been involved in Operating Systems Lab and Distributed Systems Lab during these past two years. Their patience, understanding and enthusiasm during some difficult times helped make this project so enjoyable for me. The success of the project is a testament to their abilities and ambition.

9. References

(1) daCruz, Frank. *Kermit, A File Transfer Protocol.* Digital Press, 1987.

(2) Stallings, William. *Local Networks An Introduction.* MacMillan Publishing Co. 1984.

(3) *Draft E IEEE Standard 802.5, Token Ring Access Method and Physical Layer specification.* IEEE. 1984.

(4) Tanenbaum, Andrew S. *Computer Networks.* Prentice Hall, 1981.

(5) Chu, K. *Distributed Protocol for Updating Network Topology Information.* Report RC 7235, IBM T.J. Watson Research Center, 1978.

The Design Tree: A Visual Approach to Top-Down Design and Data Flow

Jacobo Carrasquel
Jim Roberts
John Pane

Department of Computer Science
Carnegie Mellon University
Pittsburgh, Pennsylvania

ABSTRACT

Top-down design, an accepted technique for program development in most teaching environments, is an integral part of the introductory computing courses taught at Carnegie Mellon University. Although this planning technique works well for experts, it's application among less experienced users is limited: many novices abandon this technique as soon as implementation begins, focusing their attention instead on low-level details. This paper proposes a solution to this problem: the Design Tree, a simple graphic tool used to represent the top-down decomposition of a problem. This tool can be used by instructors, as well as students, independent of the software used to build their programs. The Design Tree not only facilitates top-down decomposition of problems, but also help students decide what type of control structures and data flow to use in implementation.

INTRODUCTION

Over the past several semesters, we have observed that most students seem to grasp the fundamental components of Pascal fairly quickly but then find it difficult to apply these concepts to large programs. This problem becomes very evident in assignments that require more than a few procedures. The Design Tree helps our students deal with the flow of data (variable declaration and parameter passing) in the context of procedural abstraction.

BACKGROUND

We currently teach three introductory courses that use Pascal as the programming language: one for science and engineering students, a second for design and architecture students, and a third for humanities and social science students. We presume no previous programming experience in any of the courses.

These courses are very similar with regard to the quantity and difficulty of assignments. Students write six to seven assignments, four large programs, and take three on-line programming exams in preparation for the final. A typical progression of the course topics begins with a simple programming task that uses a few simple procedures to emphasize top-down design. Next, variables and parameters are introduced, followed by control structures, data abstraction, searching, sorting, and file I/O. By the end of the semester, it is not uncommon for students to write solutions involving twenty to thirty procedures [1]. One of the major foundations in all of the courses is the use of top-down decomposition [2, 3, 4].

We currently use the Macintosh Plus, running a structure-editor based programming environment called Genie, which was developed at Carnegie Mellon by the MacGnome project team. Genie takes advantage of the Macintosh's simple user interface: little effort is required for the students to learn to use Genie for programming tasks [5, 6].

PROBLEM STATEMENT

We have identified three major problems that students face in our courses:

• **Keeping sight of the design:** The students lose sight of their overall design during the coding process. Even though they prepare a top-down design for the program on paper, they seem to get lost in the code as they deal with the myriad of low-level details. For instance, we frequently find that the required routines are typed in, but the students fail to call them, call them at inappropriate places, or try to redefine them .

• **Choosing appropriate control structures:** Students also have problems choosing which type of control structure to use for a given situation. Students with previous experience often try to coerce the "for" loop to do everything, while others use only a "while" loop or only a "repeat" loop. The attitude seems to be: "If I can learn to use one of these, that's plenty." A second component of this problem is students deciding where to place control structures in the program and which routines should be controlled by these structures.

• **Keeping track of data:** A third problem is that students have problems keeping track of data flow. The first component of this problem is deciding where to declare local variables. For pedagogical reasons, we prohibit global variables except for text files. All other variables must be declared locally to a subroutine, and then passed as parameters. Many students incorrectly declare all of their variables in their main driver routine and, consequently, pass unnecessary parameters. Students also have problems deciding whether to use value parameters or var parameters. Some of our students simply declare every parameter as a var parameter because "that always works."

Up to now, we have lacked a sound pedagogical tool to help students design solutions in a simple but formal manner and to build programs directly from these high-level designs. Our investigation of existing visual programming tools revealed that such techniques tend to either concentrate immediately on low-level coding details (rather than the overall program design) or follow a model that conflicts with the program design techniques used in our classes [7, 8, 9, 10].

THE DESIGN TREE

Two years ago, we attempted to help our students overcome these three problems by devising a graphic tool, called the Design Tree, to help develop programs.

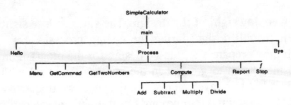

Figure 1: First phase of the Design Tree (Decomposition View).

The Design Tree visually represents a program's decomposition, control structures, and data flow. The use of the Design Tree involves three steps. In the first step, the entire program is laid out in a hierarchical arrangement based on the call sites of sub-programs. Figure 1 shows the call sites for the procedures and functions of a simple program. Procedures are marked with a short vertical line

above them, and functions with an script "f" above its identifier. The second step involves overlaying the appropriate control structures onto the hierarchy. Figure 2 shows the result of this process. The last step is to determine what variables are needed, where they should be declared, and how they should be passed as parameters. We mark value parameters with down-arrows to represent the flow of data from the calling routine (or parent) to the routine being called (or child). Var parameters are marked with up-arrows indicating data flow from the child to the parent. Figure 3 shows this final step. It is important to notice that steps 2 and 3 are interchangeable, thus allowing the parameters and local variables to be drawn before the control structures.

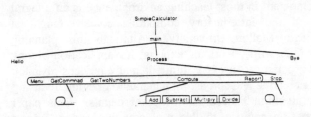

Figure 2: Second phase of the Design Tree (Control View).

We begin familiarizing students with the Design Tree conventions in the first class meeting, and continue throughout the semester, building additional conventions and heuristics for decomposition, choice of control structures, location of local variables, and choice of value/var parameters. Prior to the coding process of major assignments, our students submit completed Design Trees and full documentation to be reviewed by the instructor. As a result, the instructor has an opportunity to criticize each student's design before the program is implemented.

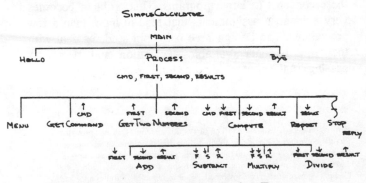

Figure 3: Third phase of the Design Tree (Decomposition View with local variables and parameters).

DESIGN TREE GRAMMAR

The first step in using the Design Tree process is to represent the overall program design as a hierarchical diagram which simply shows all of the call sites of procedures and functions, as illustrated in Figure 1. Control structures and data flow are not considered during this phase of the process. The only pre-defined procedures that are displayed in the diagram are the procedures "reset" and "rewrite". These two pre-defined procedures are automatically displayed because they are important to file reading and writing, and we have noted that beginners often misplace them or leave them out of their code.

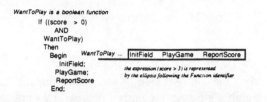

Figure 4: IF statement with three procedure calls.

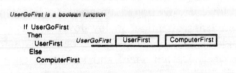

Figure 5: IF-ELSE statement.

Figure 6: CASE statement.

In the second phase, a line indicates that the child is always called by the parent during every execution of the parent's body. Since some children may not be called during a particular execution of the parent, we use a series of icons to indicate the various structures that control execution. We use rectangles to represent conditionals (see Figures 4-6), and rounded rectangles to represent loops (see Figs. 7-9). The control evaluator is displayed on the tail (a horizontal line) which extends to either side (right or left) of the respective icon. Consequently, with this schema, nodes of the tree can represent control structures, procedures, or functions. The control line from the parent is drawn to the control structure instead of the procedures controlled by it.

When a boolean expression is comprised of a simple relational operator, the expression is replaced with an ellipsis "...". Similarly, in a combination of a boolean function and a relational expression [e.g., "(score > 0) AND WantToPlay"], the entire expression is represented by the name of the function first, then the ellipsis (see Figures 4 and 7).

In the final phase of the program design, the student deals with variables and parameters. As indicated in previous sections, arrows going up or down are used to differentiate between value and variable parameters. The display doesn't differentiate between the flow of data up the tree and the flow of data both down and up the tree. Local variables are always displayed below the procedure's (or function's) identifier and formal parameters above it (see Figure 3).

In the case of recursion, a convention was adopted to prevent infinite duplication of the tree. To indicate recursive calls we use the symbol "=".

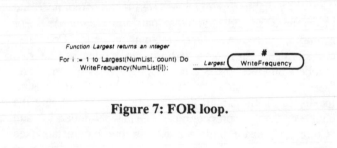

Figure 7: FOR loop.

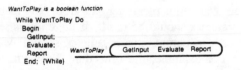

Figure 8: WHILE loop.

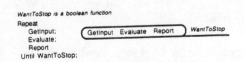

Figure 9: REPEAT loop.

AN EXAMPLE

To show how the Design Tree is used, we have chosen a typical program called The Pocket Calculator, which simulates a simple calculator. Such a calculator asks the user to select an operation, from the four basic ones, and then to enter two numbers. The program checks that the chosen operation is valid, and then it displays the result. Finally, the program asks the user if another operation is to be performed or if the execution should be stopped. Figure 1 represents the Decomposition View of this example. In this view, only the call sites (calls to procedures and functions) are shown.

The next step, is to decide what kind of control structures are needed and where to use them. In Figure 2, the icons for the "repeat" loop and the "case" statement are shown. Notice that in this view, the function Stop appears next to its respective icon.

In order to help students decide where to declare the local variables and what kind of parameters to use, we use the following heuristics:

• data cannot be shared among siblings unless done via their parent. If two or more sibling share the same data, the local variable should be declared in the parent node and the siblings should share that data via parameters. For example, procedures "GetTwoNumbers" and "Compute" are siblings. They both require the values of the two numbers entered by the user (i.e., the values of "first" and "second"). The variables "first" and "second" are declared locally in their parent, the procedure "Process", and the children, the procedures "GetTwoNumbers" and "Compute", share their values via the parameters (see Figure 3).

• when the child is receiving data from only its parent, a value parameter should be used. If the child is sending data back to its parent, the parameter should be a var parameter. For example, the procedure "Compute" is receiving data from its parent, the procedure "Process", via three value parameters ("first", "second", and "cmd"). At the same time, the procedure "Compute" sends the value of "result" back to its parent via a var parameter. The procedure "GetTwoNumbers" sends data to its parent, the procedure "Process", via two var parameters ("first" and "second"). (See Figure 3).

Figure 3 represents the final step, in which the Design Tree appears with all the local variables and var/value parameters. Figure 10 is a detailed representation of the procedure "GetCommand". It indicates that a "repeat" loop is used to verify that a command is valid. The conditions needed to exit this loop are met when the local variable "reply" is in the set of valid options. Inside the "repeat" loop, the command entered by the user is checked for illegal input by using an "if" statement. The condition of the "if" statement is the set of valid options, and the action is a "writeln" which displays an error message.

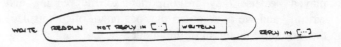

Figure 10: Procedure GetCommand.

ON-LINE IMPLEMENTATION

Even when the Design Tree is used, students still face a major stumbling block: the design process does not parallel the programming process. During the design process, students initially work on the problem at a high level, and then consider the details of code as a final step in the process. However, writing a program on-line tends to focus the student's attention on low-level details. While coding, students are forced to move between high level design (i.e. their Design Tree) and low level code. For some students, this provides a series of opportunities to get lost. We view this as a remaining weakness in the use of the Design Tree.

Up to now, we have described a tool that is independent of the software used to teach the course. After discussing the benefits of using the Design Tree in all of the introductory courses and the weaknesses described above, we began to explore the idea of incorporating the Design Tree into the Macintosh-based structure-editor environment we use in the class. Displaying a program on-line in Design Tree format seemed to offer an alternate way to illustrate programs [13]. Furthermore, our concerns about students' coding problems led us to think about expanding the structure-editor we use in order to allow students to use the Design Tree as a tool for building the program on-line.

As a result, working with the MacGnome Group, we added a visual programming tool called the Design View [12] to its programming environment called Genie. (All the figures used in this paper, with the exception of Figure 3, were produced by this tool). Genie is capable of displaying the value of any variable used in the program, and automatically updates its value as the program is executed. The

Design View offers two viewing styles of a program: a Decomposition View (see Figure 1) and a Control View (see Figure 2). With the Decomposition View the user has the option of displaying the local variables and/or the formal parameters [13] (see Figure 3).

CONCLUSIONS

The use of the Design Tree has resulted in a substantial decrease in the three problems described at the beginning of this paper. When a problem occurs, we immediately go to the student's Design Tree, examine the design, and usually find a flaw in the design. The Design Tree makes it easier to find, diagnose, and correct such problems.

Our students find that building programs graphically by using the on-line Design Tree is much easier and faster than using the regular on-line editor.

We have seen that students' understanding of where and when to use local variables or parameters improves dramatically as a result of using the Design Tree, on paper or on-line. With the the Design Tree, teaching top-down decomposition, and proper use of parameter passing and local variables has made teaching easier for the instructors and more profitable for the students.

REFERENCES

[1] Jacobo Carrasquel, Dennis R. Goldenson, Phillip L. Miller. "Competency Testing in Introductory Computer Science: The Mastery Examination at Carnegie-Mellon University," SIGCSE Bulletin, 17(1), March 1985, p. 240. Abstract, full paper available on request.

[2] O. J. Dahl, E. W. Dijkstra, C. A. R. Hoare. Structured Programming, Academic Press, 1972.

[3] Niklaus Wirth. "Program Development by Stepwise Refinement," Communications of the ACM, 14 May 1971, pp. 221-227.

[4] Robert W. Floyd. "The Paradigms of Programming," Communications of the ACM, 22(8) August 1979, pp. 455-460.

[5] Ravinder Chandhok. "Programming Environments Based on Structure Editing: The GNOME Approach." Proceedings of the National Computer Conference (NCC '85), AFIPS, 1985.

[6] David Garlan. Views for Tools in Integrated Environments. Ph.D. thesis, Carnegie Mellon University, Computer Science Department (Technical Report CMU-CS-87-147), 1987.

[7] Ephraim P. Glinert, Steven L. Tanimato. "Pict: An interactive Graphical Programming Environment," IEEE Computer, 17(11), November 1985, pp. 7-25.

[8] Pierre N. Robillard. "Schematic Pseudocode for Program Constructs and Its Computer Automation by Schemacode," Communications of the ACM, 29(11), November 1986, pp. 1072-1089.

[9] Steven P. Reiss. "PECAN: Program Development Systems that Support Multiple Views," IEEE Transactions on Software Engineering, SE-11(3), March 1985, pp. 276-285.

[10] Gabriel Robins. "The ISI Grapher: A Portable Tool for Displaying Graphs Pictorially," Information Sciences Institute Reprint Series, ISI/RS-87-196, September 1987.

[11] Brad A. Myers. "Visual Programming, Programming by Example and Program Visualization: A Taxonomy," SIGCHI Proceedings, April 1986, pp. 59-66.

[12] Jim Roberts, John Pane, Mark Stehlik, Jacobo Carrasquel. "The Design View: A Design Oriented High Level Visual Programming Environment," Proceedings of the IEEE Workshop on Visual Languages, October 1988.

[13] Brad A. Myers, Ravinder Chandhok. "Automatic Data Visualizations for Novice Programming," Proceedings of the IEEE Workshop on Visual Languages, October 1988 .

Programming as Process: A "Novel" Approach to
Teaching Programming

Rex E. Gantenbein
Operating Systems Laboratory
Department of Computer Science
University of Wyoming
Box 3682, University Station
Laramie, Wyoming 82071

INTERNET: rex@corral.uwyo.edu

Abstract

This paper introduces the process model as a way of incorporating the software life cycle into beginning computer science courses. This approach, patterned after a successful method for teaching English composition, provides students with an understanding of how all phases of programming can be accomplished. A five-step model of the process and some useful tools for each step are presented as an example and discussed.

1. Introduction

Many computer science educators have expressed support for incorporating software engineering topics into introductory programming classes (e.g., [Werth88]). While software engineering represents a discipline that is much needed in the building of large, complex systems, many of its topics are beyond both the needs and the comprehension of beginning students. Still, the basic ideas, particularly that of the software life cycle, are sound and should be taught at all levels in a unified degree program in computer science. What is needed is a way to incorporate these principles into the beginning courses in a manner that instills good programming skills instead of requiring them. [Pratt88] has defined this as teaching program analysis along with program synthesis.

The primary problem with using the classical model of the software life cycle in teaching basic skills is that the student tends to see the steps of the model as "distinct and carried out sequentially" [Bell87]. Experienced software engineers know that the model represents a pattern of emphasis on activities that is not always linear. The steps of the model can overlap and interact, and refinements at later stages of development often require reentry of previous stages and revision of goals. Furthermore, some models include steps that are frequently unnecessary or redundant due to the relatively low complexity of typical introductory problems.

Another difficulty for many beginning students is the multiplicity of approaches to, and tools for, program development. An approach or an algorithm that works in one case will sometimes not work in another, even though the problems appear similar. The identification and selection of alternative approaches is seldom, if ever, taught at any level. Most programmers must rely on experience to determine the appropriate tools for a particular situation.

Attempts have been made to teach problem solving in introductory programming texts. Almost all of these, e.g. [Reges87] and [Savitch87], combine teaching a language with teaching rules for solving problems. Unfortunately, most of the time the rules are too general to be fully understood or too specific to be widely applicable in an introductory course. In either case, to go deeply into both problem solving and a particular language tends to produce a book of such length that it cannot be taught in a single semester with proper attention paid to both topics.

2. Programming as Process, Not Product

Programming is a combination of skills and knowledge acquired through instruction and practice that can be applied to particular kinds of problems; it most definitely is not "magic" (for that matter, neither is magic). This is the fundamental idea that must be communicated to students in introductory courses. Anyone with a reasonable intelligence and some grasp of basic logical and mathematical concepts can learn to program; what is required is a way to demystify the programming process and help students to understand it, analyze their work, and most importantly gain the confidence in themselves that will allow them to learn the skills they need to become proficient.

Programming can be demystified through the teaching of programming according to the process model. This approach has seen wide success in Donald Murray's method of teaching English composition. His book Write to Learn [Murray84] has revolutionized the teaching of writing through its view of writing not as simply the putting of words on paper but as a logical sequence of activities that starts "before there is a pile of 500 sheets of blank paper." Murray's model of the writing process includes the steps of collecting information, focusing on a subject, ordering the relevant information, drafting the work, and revising and clarifying the material. Murray takes great pain to emphasize that this model is only one of several possible models, and that he does not always adhere strictly to it himself. It does serve the purpose, however, of giving the composition student a mental picture of the process to remove the mystery from writing, as well as helping him/her to overcome problems through supplying tools to accomplish each step.

Murray's process-model approach to teaching writing has greatly influenced the approach to teaching programming presented in this paper. In the section that follows, comparisons to Murray's model will show the effects of this influence.

3. A Model for the Programming Process

A basic model for the programming process can be defined using a simplified view of the software life cycle. Several models of this exist, and the one presented here is no better than most and no worse than some. The importance of the model is to give the student a grasp of issues in program development and to provide a framework within which to introduce tools that can help with each stage. Every student tends to come to grips with a model in his/her own way; it is essential to remember that the goal in this approach is not memorization of and adherence to a process model, but use of the model to understand the process.

The five steps of the programming process are as follows:

1. Define the problem: what should the program do?
2. Select an approach: what tools are available that may be applicable?
3. Design a solution: what algorithm solves the problem?
4. Implement the solution: how can this algorithm be run on the available computer(s)?
5. Test the implementation: does the solution work?

Each of these five steps is discussed in more detail below. Some representative references are given that define methods for approaching each of the steps. This is not intended to be an exhaustive list; such work would extend the length of this paper beyond limits acceptable to both the reader and the writer. This section is meant only to provide an example of how this approach can be used in teaching programming.

Define the problem

Specification of the problem is generally a necessary first step. In many classes, particularly introductory ones, this step is the responsibility of the instructor, and a complete problem definition is given to the students as an assignment. Outside the classroom, the task is often more difficult, especially if the problem requires collecting information from end users and preparing a specification based on their (perceived) needs. This task is very much like Murray's focusing step, where the writer narrows a broad subject to a specific topic and defines the framework within which he will work.

Related areas of work include both formal specification and systems analysis. [Gehani86] contains a collection of papers that lists several approaches to formal (and informal) specification, from information hiding to algebraic, as well as an appraisal of the techniques mentioned. Systems analysis is a large field of study; many methods exist, although most are based on the structured methodologies of either Yourdon and Constantine [Yourdon79] or DeMarco [DeMarco78].

Select an approach

This step is easy to define but difficult to describe, in that it involves fanning out from the defined problem and collecting all possible tools (including both algorithms and techniques) that may be applicable. Is a flow chart required (or even useful) as opposed to pseudocoding? Should we proceed by a top-down, bottom-up, inside-out, or backwards method? What similar examples has the programmer seen that could inspire a solution? Do any predefined library routines exist that could be useful?

Murray's equivalent of this step is the collecting stage, in which the writer collects ideas on which he/she can write. This can involve, in the case of a research paper, a literature review to determine what information exists regarding a subject or, in the case of a personal essay, the collection of topics on which the writer can discourse from personal experience. The programmer also may pursue one or both of these approaches, depending on his/her experience with and command of the tools available.

Structured methods for program design are numerous. Among the most well-known texts are [Yourdon79], [Jackson75], and recently [Booch87]. No attempt to evaluate these approaches will be made here, nor to list the various others. The beginning programmer should be introduced to at least one of these, however, to understand how a program specification can be translated into a program design correctly and with a traceable lineage to allow a posteriori changes to the specification to be represented in the design as well.

Introductory programming texts can be very useful in presenting examples and solutions to "standard" problems that programmers encounter many times throughout their career. An excellent book for mathematically oriented problems is [Dromey82], which lists solutions to many standard problems and how to implement them. In its way, the book represents an updating of Polya's classic How to Solve It [Polya57].

Design a solution

This step is perhaps the greatest challenge to the programmer. Once an approach has been chosen and the appropriate tools and examples collected, the programmer must determine exactly what algorithm exemplifies the desired solution. This corresponds to Murray's ordering stage, in which the jumble of thoughts, impressions, glimpses, etc. needs to be drawn into a coherent whole.

Here the instructor can make his/her mark on the beginner. The structured design texts mentioned above present techniques for making the transition from specification to design. The difficulty for the student is in acquiring the skills necessary to perform this transition smoothly and naturally. Software engineering texts (e.g. [Bell87]) also deal with this problem.

Implement the solution

Nowhere up to this point in the model has the writing of code been mentioned. Once the previous steps have been accomplished, only then is the programmer ready to write code. Software engineering's emphasis on design before implementation cannot be too strongly stressed; if the program design has been performed correctly, the translation into a specific implementation is easy. Furthermore, the design should, for the most part, be independent of the language used for the implementation. This allows the instructor in an introductory programming class to use the same approach regardless of the language mandated by those who mandate such things. This step is similar to Murray's drafting step.

Any basic language reference should serve at this stage as a guide to the transformation of a detailed design into an implementation. [Sommerville85] and [Booch87] are software engineering texts with an orientation toward Ada that can help in this area.

Test the implementation

Theories on how to test programs have filled textbooks. One important point to emphasize here is that exhaustive testing is not practical, even in small programs. Heuristics such as testing boundary conditions should be introduced, especially as they relate to the definition of the problem developed in the initial step. Test plans and the criteria for a successful test need to be defined. This step relates to Murray's clarifying and revising, in that failures of the previous steps can be detected and corrected. Good references include [Beizer84] and [Bell87].

4. Analysis of this Approach

The primary advantage of this method of teaching introductory programming is that students many times can see for themselves where their programs have gone "wrong." One of the most frustrating parts of learning programming is the inability to find the cause of an obvious bug. With the breakdown of the programming process into steps like those above, the instructor can suggest to the student that, for example, the design of the solution was correct but implemented wrongly, or perhaps the student's understanding of the problem was incorrect from the outset. Most instructors would agree that such reinforcement is more rewarding to the student than the instructor's finding a "dumb mistake" in an otherwise working program.

A related advantage is that there are many points in the process at which the student can get help. Certain software engineering methodologies are based on the idea of reporting milestones

([Sommerville85] uses this approach). If informal reviews are conducted after each step of the process, either with peers or with the instructor, the student is more likely to reach the testing step with confidence in and comprehension of what his/her program is doing. Often, the student who gives up on an assignment has had problems in the early stages of development rather than in the implementation.

It is important here to restate the previous caveat that these steps must be thought of as patterns of emphasis and not as linear activities. Clearly, many decisions need to be made in advance of the step in which the decision is to be applied. Test plans, for example, can and should be designed before the implementation step to assure independence of the testing. Testing itself may require the revision of any or all of the previous steps' results, although the likelihood of this can be reduced through design reviews, etc. Also, the foreknowledge of which system and language will be used to implement a solution may define what algorithms should be used, even if no coding takes place. The same problem will look quite different, depending on whether it is to be implemented in Pascal, say, versus Lisp.

One final benefit of this step is not so obvious, but it is nonetheless very real. The computer science course at the University of Wyoming in which this approach is being used is a requirement for, among others, majors in secondary mathematics education. These students do not expect to become programmers, any more than education majors in a writing class expect to become writers. The advantage of using a process-based approach to teaching programming to these students is that it gives them an understanding of how programming works, which they then can convey to their own students. Computer science departments are typically not in the business of teaching others how to teach, but it appears that this approach allows the education major to adapt the process model to his/her own needs and effectively teach programming in the secondary school.

5. Conclusions

The process-model approach to teaching introductory programming gives the student an opportunity to understand program development in a way that takes all the factors into account. If students can identify the steps of the process and relate them to their own work, then they can determine the requirements for each step largely on their own and be able to see quickly where errors have occurred. Syntax errors can be differentiated from semantic or logic errors, the sources of errors pinpointed, and the necessary corrections made.

In addition, the obvious benefits of a software engineering-based approach to programming can be made clear to the students without the unneeded burden of theory and methodology. When the student eventually reaches the level of sophistication at which the teaching of software engineering becomes appropriate, the concepts should be almost second nature. Good techniques and practices can thus be instilled from the first programming course.

Other approaches to including software engineering principles in introductory courses have concentrated on the topics to be added. The approach proposed in this paper is one intended to give meaning to those topics, not just names. Murray has made the statement that writing is not the act of putting words on paper, but rather the act of thinking and then recording those thoughts. Programming can be viewed exactly the same way; the only real differences are the thoughts being recorded and the restrictions on the form of recording.

References

[Beizer84] Beizer, B., Software System Testing and Quality Assurance, Van Nostrand Reinhold (1984).

[Bell87] Bell, D., Morrey, I., and Pugh, J., Software Engineering: A Practitioner's Approach, Prentice-Hall (1987).

[Booch87] Booch, G., Software Engineering with Ada (2nd ed.), Benjamin/Cummings (1987).

[DeMarco78] DeMarco, T., Structured Analysis and Systems Specification, Yourdon Press (1978).

[Dromey82] Dromey, R.G., How to Solve It by Computer, Prentice-Hall (1982).

[Gehani86] Gehani, N., and McGettrick, A., eds., Software Specification Techniques, Addison Wesley (1986).

[Jackson75] Jackson, M.A., Principles of Program Design, Academic Press, London (1975).

[Murray84] Murray, D., Write to Learn, Holt, Rinehart, and Winston (1984).

[Polya57] Polya, G., How to Solve It (2nd ed.), Doubleday and Co. (1957).

[Pratt88] Pratt, T.W., "Teaching Programming: A New Approach Based on Analysis Skills," <u>Proceedings of the Nineteenth SigCSE Technical Symposium on
Computer Science Education</u> (1988), 249-
253.

[Reges87] Reges, S., <u>Building Pascal
Programs: An Introduction to Computer
Science</u>, Little, Brown, and Co. (1987).

[Savitch87] Savitch, W.J., <u>Pascal: An
Introduction to the Science and Art of
Programming</u>, Benjamin/Cummings (1987).

[Sommerville85] Sommerville, I.,
<u>Software Engineering (2nd ed.)</u>, Addison
Wesley (1985).

[Werth88] Werth, L.H., "Integrating
Software Engineering into an Intermediate
Programming Class," <u>Proceedings of the
Nineteenth SigCSE Technical Symposium on
Computer Science Education</u> (1988), 54-58.

[Yourdon79] Yourdon, E., and Constantine, L.L., <u>Structured Design: Fundamentals of a Discipline of Computer
Program and System Design</u>, Prentice-Hall
(1979).

Teaching Recursion as a Problem-Solving Tool
Using Standard ML

Peter B. Henderson and Francisco J. Romero
Department of Computer Science
State University of New York at Stony Brook
Stony Brook, New York, 11790

Abstract

Standard ML is a state of the art functional programming language, with features that make it excellent for teaching recursion and problem solving at the introductory level. Among the many pedagogically interesting characteristics of ML are its simple and uniform syntax, its type polymorphism and type inferencing system, and datatype declaration facilities. With little formal ML instruction, after several weeks first year students were able to use recursively defined data structures and to define fairly powerful recursive functions in ML. Standard ML is highly recommended as a tool for teaching recursive problem solving in the context of a course on the foundations of computer science.

1. Introduction

The concept of recursion is central in computer science, both for the theorist and the practitioner. It plays a fundamental role in compiler construction, data structures, artificial intelligence, problem solving, language theory, database, graphics, operating systems, and many other fields. Recursive algorithms often provide more elegant solutions to complex problems than their iterative counterpart, especially when combined with recursively defined data structures. Despite its importance, there is very little known about how to teach recursion effectively, although a few recent contributions have addressed the issue [8,11,13,7]. In our introductory computer science course at Stony Brook *Foundations of Computer Science* [10] students learn the mathematical concepts of recursion and induction. Standard ML [9] is used to reinforce the acquisition of these concepts as problem solving and analysis tools.

Like other computer science educators, we have found that recursion is a very difficult concept for students to learn. This may be partially attributed to the observation that recursion is counter-intuitive [16]; however, we believe this can be overcome with the proper pedagogical approach. The problem lies in the way we currently teach recursion. It is generally the case that

recursion is introduced as a programming language feature where students learn more about the mechanics of recursion than the concept itself, or more importantly using recursion as a problem-solving tool. Typically recursive algorithms and recursive data structures are introduced after the student is familiar with advanced programming language features like pointers. Such details tend to obscure the concept. In our innovative introductory course however, students are exposed to recursion before they learn how to program in a procedural language such as Pascal.

Learning any difficult concept requires time and effort. The concept should be introduced in simple, intuitive settings and continually reinforced. Accordingly, the notion of recursion as a definitional tool is stressed throughout the course. Students are first informally introduced to recursion - for example, as a way of defining a row of boxes, or boxes nested within boxes. Other pictorial examples, such as those based on fractals, help to gently introduce recursion[15,6]. Subsequently students learn more mathematical applications of recursion in areas such as logic, sets, relations, functions, languages, and graphical structures. This can occur when defining the binary relation "ancestor of" and defining structures such as lists and trees. These concepts are reinforced in several computer based laboratories where students experiment with and explore recursive definitions.

The laboratory presented in this paper emphasizes the use of recursion as a problem-solving tool. This three part laboratory introduces the basics of the Standard ML (SML) programming language and requires students to create and experiment with their own function definitions. Many of these functions are defined on naturally recursive structures such as lists and trees.

For this laboratory we do not teach students Standard ML, nor do we provide them with books or reference manuals. The beauty of SML is that students can learn the requisite features of the language by experimenting with a small collection of representative examples (e.g., statements and function definitions). This is discovery learning [3,14] at its best. The language supports a natural expressive power which permits students to create very concise function definitions. As an example, consider the recursive definition of a function preorder shown in Figure 1. This function takes a labeled binary tree T as an argument and returns a list of node labels. It uses several other simple function definitions (e.g., functions for prepending an item to a list and for appending two lists) which students created in a previous phase of the laboratory. The binary tree data structure definition and definitions of the functions label, left_subtree and right_subtree were provided by us.

```
- fun preorder(tree) =
  if tree = empty   (* Is tree an empty binary tree? *)
    then []  (* if tree=empty, return the empty list *)
    else  prepend(label(tree),
              appendlist(preorder(left_subtree(tree)),
              preorder(right_subtree(tree)) ) );
```

Figure 1: Definition of `preorder` in SML

In Section 2 of this paper we present a brief overview of the course *Foundations of Computer Science* at Stony Brook. For readers who are not familiar with Standard ML, Section 3 provides a concise introduction to the relevant features of the language. Section 4 attempts to answer the question "Why Standard ML?" Subsequent sections describe details of the three part laboratory, summarize the lessons we have learned, and indicate directions for the future.

2. Motivation for the "Foundations of Computer Science" Course

Many students today cannot think. They lack mathematical maturity and are unable to solve problems. The introductory computer science course *Foundations of Computer Science* at Stony Brook addresses these weaknesses in a non-traditional way. This course effectively integrates critical thinking, problem solving, modern discrete mathematics concepts, and mathematical foundations of computer science. The objective is to show students that they can learn to think and solve problems, and to provide them with the tools they need for thinking and problem-solving, especially in computer science. Unfortunately, this does not always come easy for many students and they must invest substantial time and effort. This is reflected in one student's comment "This course is going to **force** you to think." To make the course more exciting, the course material is further reinforced through numerous exploratory computer-based laboratory modules.

Years of experience teaching introductory computer science have lead us to believe that novice programming students are not capable of abstraction at the level necessary to compose good algorithmic solutions. This belief, coupled with very weak problem solving skills, a lack of basic mathematical maturity, poor oral and written communication skills, and finally, instructional programming languages which do not adequately support abstraction, places the novice programmer at a distinct disadvantage. In our curriculum we attend to the student's weaknesses first and then teach them programming.

The Stony Brook catalogue description for the *Foundations of Computer Science* is presented below.

A rigorous introduction to the conceptual and mathematical foundations of computer science. Problem-solving techniques and mathematical concepts that aid in the analysis and solution of algorithmic problems will be stressed. The course will concentrate on general problem solving principles, recursion and induction, algorithmic problem solving, and discrete mathematics concepts including: sets, logic, relations, graphs, counting principles, functions, sequences, induction, proof techniques, algorithms and verification, and language syntax and semantics. These concepts will be motivated within the context of computer science, and its applications. Mathematical maturity at the level of pre-college calculus is expected.

In some ways this looks like a traditional discrete mathematics course for computer science majors. However, there is more emphasis on problem-solving and using mathematics for understanding computer science. For example, the course teaches underlying concepts which are necessary for understanding both how to program and evolving paradigms for software development (e.g., logic programming, functional programming, and object-oriented programming).

3. Introduction to Standard ML

Standard ML is a state of the art functional programming language [12,9,2]. The principal control mechanism in ML is recursive function application. SML is interactive: the system accepts expressions, evaluates them and returns the result together with its type. The interactive nature of ML makes it possible for students to use the language immediately, without having to spend time learning to use a text editor. SML is strongly typed, and types are automatically inferred from context. Type inferencing is definitely one of the most noteworthy features of ML and one that makes the language especially appropriate for our course. Figure 2 is an example of how the system interacts with the user. The prompt to the user is -, and replies are preceded by >.

```
- 4 + 7;  (* entered by the user *)
> 11 : int;
```

Figure 2: Simple interaction in SML

The system determines from the context that the result of evaluating the integer addition must be of type `int` for integer. SML has several predefined types: `real`, `int`, `string`, `bool`, `list`, tuples, and records. The type system is *polymorphic*, that is, very general definitions can be created [4]. For example, a function to compute the length of a list (see Figure 3) can be written to work on any list, regardless of the type of the elements in the list[1]. We say that `length` is a *polymorphic* function.

```
- fun length(list) =
  if list = []
    then 0     (* length of the empty list = 0 *)
    else 1 + length(tail(list));
> val length = fn : 'a list -> int
```

Figure 3: Definition of `length`

The result of elaborating this function definition is a new value `length` whose type is a *function from any type of list* (`'a list`) *to integer*. This is expressed by the type variable `'a` and the function constructor `->`. Thus, it is possible to capture the essence of a computation over lists (or any other object) by writing polymorphic functions that are fully general. It is interesting to contrast the flexibility of the ML type system with that of traditional imperative languages such as Pascal, whose type systems do not permit polymorphic functions. From the educational

---

[1]Exercise for the reader: Try this in Pascal

point of view, the type system of SML facilitates the introduction of recursion early, with the added benefit that students can reason about types "guided by the system". Figure 4 presents an example of a simple polymorphic search algorithm that exemplifies the elegance of ML. In the system response * should be interpreted as cartesian product.

Standard ML provides powerful mechanisms for defining new, possibly recursive data structures. Data structures are created using *data constructors* which are functions that *construct* an object of the new type from its simple components. For example, Figure 5 displays how a user could create a polymorphic binary tree in SML.

The system response to this entry is shown in Figure 6.

The constructor `empty` creates an empty binary tree, and the constructor `node` forms a binary tree out of an element and two binary trees. The definition of binary trees in ML is recursive, polymorphic and fully captures the mathematical definition of a binary tree. It does not require declarations of pointers or records, and is easy to read and understand. We believe that elegant, simple, concise and mathematically sound definitions like the one above give SML an extraordinary expressive power. This power is put to good use in the introductory classroom, where concepts should come before details. Given the definition of a binary tree, the student can now experiment with the system to gain a better understanding of the structure.

Functions that manipulate binary trees are best written as recursive functions, (see the definition of `preorder` in Section 1) which in SML become short, concise and very general, as Figure 7 shows.

In the definition of `left_subtree` we use another powerful feature of SML: pattern matching. A function can be defined over a data type by specifying the value of the function when applied to each data constructor of the given type. In the case of binary trees there are two constructors, `empty` and `node`, and the function `left_subtree` is defined as a two-case pattern, one

```
- fun position(item, list) =
    if list = [] then  0 (* 0 means not found *)
    else  if first(list) = item
      then  1
      else let
        val v = position(item,tail(list))
      in if v > 0 then 1 + v else 0
      end
> val position = fn : ('a * 'a list) -> int
```
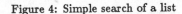

Figure 4: Simple search of a list

```
- datatype 'a binary_tree = empty
  | node of ('a * 'a binary_tree *
             'a binary_tree);
```

Figure 5: Definition of a binary tree

```
datatype 'a binary_tree
con empty : 'a binary_tree
con node : 'a * 'a binary_tree *
                'a binary_tree -> 'a binary_tree
```
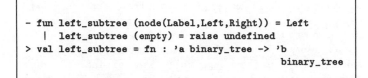

Figure 6: System reponse to previous definition

for each constructor. In the case of an empty tree `left_subtree` raises a predefined exception `undefined`. Exceptions are a means of catching special conditions or runtime errors. Students were introduced to exceptions, but not pattern matching for the sake of simplicity.

Standard ML has other features that we do not use directly in our laboratory but which are excellent for other purposes. For example, ML supports abstract data types, a very sophisticated exception mechanism, and a module facility.

```
- fun left_subtree (node(Label,Left,Right)) = Left
  | left_subtree (empty) = raise undefined
> val left_subtree = fn : 'a binary_tree -> 'b
                                          binary_tree
```
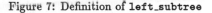

Figure 7: Definition of `left_subtree`

4. Why Standard ML?

Many different high-level programming languages have been used in introductory computer science courses. Imperative languages, like Pascal and Modula-2 are most widespread with applicative languages (e.g., Lisp and Scheme [1]) and logic programming using Prolog has been gaining favor more recently [5]. However, these languages are difficult to learn because their syntax is unnatural (like Lisp and Scheme) or very different from standard mathematical notation (Prolog). Also, features like backtracking or dynamic scoping often confuse the student and divert his/her attention from focusing on using recursion to develop solutions to problems. Ideally, to teach recursion as a problem-solving tool, students should use a language which is natural and easy to learn, whose syntax is close to the mathematical notation they have learned, with a natural expressive power, and which supports the creation of new abstractions.

Several reasons compelled us to use use SML in our introductory course. Some of these reasons have already been presented in Section 3 above, as we discussed the general features of the language. In this section, the emphasis is on the appropriateness of ML as a vehicle for teaching recursion as a problem solving tool in the context of an introductory course. First, ML supports an *experimental* approach to learning. The interactive character of ML and its facility for creating new definitions from existing ones provide an excellent environment for students to engage in exploratory learning. It is very rewarding for novices to be able to enter small textual definitions in the system and get feedback immediately, in the form of type information or errors messages. As soon as a function is defined, it can be invoked and tested. Sometimes the type information printed by the system is not obvious, and it becomes a good exercise to *justify* the system typing. The Standard ML syntax is simple and easy to learn, with the added advantage that type declarations are generally not required: the system infers the type information from the context. These features make the language ideal for the introductory course. Students need not worry about declaring their variables or types, they can concentrate their efforts on the recursive definition itself, which very closely resembles the mathematical definition.

5. Organization of the SML Laboratory

Students devote three weeks to the SML laboratory starting in the tenth week of a 16 week course. It immediately follows the lectures on mathematical functions and induction in the discrete mathematics component of the course. This represents the natural extension of mathematical functions to functional programming. During the first week, students explore and familiarize themselves with SML. The second and third weeks are devoted to defining more complex list and tree processing functions.

Each week students submit a comprehensive laboratory report based upon well defined guidelines. These reports are very structured and formal, and demand clear exposition of concepts learned during the previous week. Our laboratory is modelled after laboratory experiments in the basic sciences, such as physics and chemistry. In these experimental sessions students study phenomena in the lab and then write the results using a standard format which includes introduction, methods, results, conclusion, etc. It is our conviction that the same approach can be successfully applied to computer science undergraduate laboratories. The objectives are to foment good writing from the very start, to emphasize the importance of computer science as an experimental discipline, and to combine the advantages of free exploration with those of structured presentation of results.

During the first week students are able to experiment with SML, using predefined functions and types. A short handout describing the basics of SML and a file of sample function definitions suffice to get students going. Students must explore the possibilities of the language on their own and are to write simple functions over simple domains (integer, real, strings). In order to minimize confusion and discouragement, we avoid giving the students a full description of the language. Exploratory learning is encouraged over reading manuals. The laboratory handout suggests writing a few more complicated functions, some of which have been discussed in lecture(e.g., factorial, exponential, etc.). These simple recursive functions help students to identify the steps required to develop correct recursive definitions, and to reinforce the relationship between recursion and induction. In their report, students have to demonstrate the correctness of some of their recursively defined functions using an induction proof. After the first week, students have acquired a basic working knowledge of the following SML concepts: expression evaluation, simple function definitions, simple types, function mappings, exception handling, and functions passed as arguments.

The second week is devoted to list processing and stresses recursion as a problem-solving tool. A naturally recursive definition of lists guides students in the development of recursive list processing functions. This recursive structure is captured by three primitive functions for 1) accessing the first element of a list (`first`), 2) decomposing a list (`tail`) and 3) constructing a list (`append`). Examples such as `second(list)=first(tail(list))` and `length` (see Section 3) provide students with models for creating other function definitions and for understanding problems

```
- fun apply (function, list) =
    if list = []
      then []
      else prepend(function(first(list)),
                   apply(function, tail(list)));
> apply = fn : ('a -> 'b) * 'a list -> 'b list
```

Figure 8: Definition of `apply`

inherent in list processing. For example, the definition of `second` above does not work on all lists and students are required to explain the resulting error message when evaluating an expression like second([3]). In this way students are gently introduced to functions on lists and to special cases.

After experimenting with lists, students are ready to define new functions on lists. Most of these require only two or three lines of SML, and many are recursive. They are concise, very readable, and closely resemble mathematical notation. Typical examples include functions for reversing a list, finding the max element, summing elements, searching for and selecting elements, appending two lists, and generating a list over a specified range of integers. The latter two demonstrate how functions can return whole structures, such as lists, and others such as `apply` introduce students to new concepts (e.g., passing functions as arguments). Figure 8 displays the defintion of `apply`.

```
- fun add1 (x) = x + 1;
> val add1 = fn : int -> int
- apply (add1, [0, 3, 5, 6]);
> [1, 4, 6, 7] : int list
```

Figure 9: Using the function `apply`

A typical use of function `apply` is shown in Figure 9.

Several problems require students to identify and use previously defined functions (e.g., `average(list)` can use `sum(list)`), or to identify new functions which would be useful in other function definitions (e.g., `prepend`, `last`). Here students are learning to decompose a problem into natural component parts. This is the essence of problem-solving in computer science.

During the third week students develop binary tree based function definitions. They are provided with the recursive definition of a labeled binary tree presented in Section 3, the two binary tree constructor functions `empty` and `node`, a node value accessing function `label`, two decomposition functions `left_subtree` and `right_subtree`, numerous predefined binary trees, and some sample tree processing functions like `count_nodes`. Students were required to develop tree searching, tree analysis (e.g., `depth`), tree traversal (`preorder`), and other recursive functions on binary trees. They are also encouraged to explore the expressive power of SML for tree processing.

The weekly laboratory reports are required to present and explain the new concepts acquired (e.g., polymorphic functions and structures, problem decomposition, recursive problem solving, etc.) and to demonstrate a depth of understanding. Inductive proofs of recursive functions help to solidify the important relationship between mathematical induction and recursion.

6. Conclusion

We have found Standard ML to be an excellent tool for teaching recursion in the context of a course on the foundations of computer science. Our approach is based on exploratory and discovery learning, and Standard ML has features that make it very attractive for these purposes. Unlike traditional procedural languages Standard ML is very flexible in that a very reduced subset of the language can be employed without forfeiting the expressive power of the language. Function definitions, simple expressions, lists, and trees are the primary features used to reinforce the concept of recursion. In addition, ML has a syntax which closely resembles mathematical notation which is very important for our mathematically based foundations course.

Lists and binary trees are ideal vehicles for understanding recursive problem solving. After several weeks students with no prior programming experience are able to develop recursive list/tree processing functions with very little difficulty. They learn by example and by experimentation. The natural expressive power of SML encourages free exploration, and most likely helps students to understand the important concepts of recursion and problem decomposition without the distracting details found in many other languages (parentheses, pointers, etc.).

On the negative side, current implementations of Standard ML are research prototypes and not production quality software. They run on a very limited number of machines, primarily SUNs and VAXs, and require large amounts of main memory (1.5 to 5 megabytes). Recently, a version for the Macintosh has been made available.

Accordingly, adopting SML for a large introductory course may currently prove to be infeasible. Over the three week span during which approximately 200 Stony Brook students are involved with the SML laboratory, our two VAX 750's are severely strained, as is the patience of many students. However, we feel the educational experience of this laboratory far outweighs the frustrations of limited access to the SML system. With current advances in both hardware and software technology, within several years SML will be available on numerous machines, including personal computers and workstations used for computer science education.

References

[1] Harold Abelson, Gerald Jay Sussman, and Julie Sussman. *Structure and Interpretation of Computer Programs*. The MIT Press McGraw-Hill, 1985.

[2] Åke Wikström. *Functional Programming using ML*. Prentice-Hall International, January 1987.

[3] John Seely Brown. *Learning-by-Doing Revisited for Electronic Learning Environments*. Lawrence Erlbaum Associates, 1983.

[4] Luca Cardelli. *ML under Unix*. AT&T Bell Laboratories, Murray Hill, New Jersey 07974, 1982.

[5] W.F. Clockson and C.S. Mellish. *Programming in Prolog*. Springer-Verlag, 1984.

[6] Bruce S. Elenbogen and Martha R. O'Kennon. Teaching recursion using fractals in prolog. *ACM SIGCSE Bulletin*, 20(1):263–266, February 1988.

[7] M.C. Er. On the complexity of recursion in problem solving. *International Journal of Man-Machine Studies*, 20(6):537–544, 1984.

[8] Gary Ford. A framework for teaching recursion. *SIGCSE Bulletin*, 14(4):69–75, 82, June 1982.

[9] Robert Harper. *Introduction to Standard ML*. Technical Report ECS-LFCS-86-14, University of Edinburgh, LFCS, Department of Computer Science, University Of Edinburgh, The King's Buildings, Edinburgh EH9 3JZ, November 1986.

[10] Peter B. Henderson. Modern introductory computer science. *Proceedings of the Eighteenth SIGCSE Technical Symposium on Computer Science Education*, 183–189, February 1987.

[11] Claudius M. Kessler and John R. Anderson. Learning flow of control: recursive and iterative procedures. *Human-Computer Interaction*, 2(2):135–166, 1986.

[12] Robin Milner. A proposal for Standard ML. In *Proceedings of the 1984 ACM Symposium on Lisp and Functional Programming*, August 1984.

[13] Peter Piroli. A cognitive model and computer tutor for programming recursion. *Human-Interaction*, 2(4):319–356, 1986.

[14] Peter Pirolli and John R. Anderson. The role of learning from examples in the acquisition of recursive programming skills. *Canadian Journal of Psychology*, 39:240–272, 1985.

[15] Eric Roberts. *Thinking Recursively*. John Wiley & Sons, Inc., 1986.

[16] Susan Weidenbeck. Learning recursion as a concept and as a programming technique. *ACM SIGCSE Bulletin*, 20(1):275–278, February 1988.

Writing to Learn and Communicate
in a Data Structures Course

Janet D. Hartman
Applied Computer Science Department
Illinois State University
Normal, IL 61761

INTRODUCTION

Most employers and computer science instructors feel that communication skills are necessary for the computer science graduate to function effectively in the workplace. Students often have opportunities to communicate in small groups and do oral presentations at various times as they advance through the computer science curriculum. Too often, however, written communication skills are not emphasized. Students usually take an English course early in their college career in which writing techniques are presented and evaluated. Most often assignments take the form of an essay and occur outside the context of computer science. It is essential that the skills which students acquire in an English composition course continue to be practiced throughout their college career and be practiced within computer science courses specifically.

Many computer science instructors expect students to engage in writing activities from time to time even though they may not consciously be labeled as 'writing activities'. In something as simple as answering homework questions students may be required to respond in written form. The types of writing activities in which computer science students engage vary widely from writing programs to writing term papers. The writing of programs is a form of writing which is particular to the discipline. In this type of communication, as in other forms, some students excel and others don't. It is the computer science educator's responsibility to teach students how to write programs and provide opportunities to practice that skill. For other types of writing, however, computer science instructors are not held responsible. Perhaps this is because it is assumed that a student has already learned how to write and is able to transfer this knowledge to the computer science discipline without any additional guidance. Perhaps, too, it is because computer science instructors do not feel comfortable in the role of a 'writing teacher' and really do not wish to or know how to infuse writing activities in their courses.

As a computer science instructor I have been regularly frustrated over the years by the responses which I get from students on written work. More often than not answers to homework questions have no focus. I often even have difficulty in determining which question a student was attempting to answer without referring to the assignment sheet. I found myself spending extra time in grading written work because some students simply were not practicing the ideas which had been presented in their English class. Even an idea as simple as 'every paragraph

© 1989 ACM 0-89791-298-5/89/0002/0032 $1.50

should have a theme sentence' seemed to have escaped them. Because of this frustration I signed up for a Writing Across the Curriculum workshop hoping that my colleagues in English would be able to provide some guidance for structuring and evaluating the writing activities in my classes. As a result of what I learned, I made changes to existing assignments, introduced some new ones and added evaluation criteria to writing activities in my data structures course this summer.

The focus of this paper is to share some of the activities which can be used in a data structures course and which, with some thought, can be extrapolated to fit in any computer science course. In my initial attempts I selected one area to focus on and that was analysis of algorithms. Thus, most of the activities which are described below involve that concept.

WRITING ACTIVITIES

Writing can be classified in several ways. One can write to communicate and one can write to learn. In a business environment writing to communicate is the focus. In an educational environment students should be expected to do both.

Most of the writing activities in which I usually have students engage are designed for them to learn data structures. This objective was being met adequately. My frustration with the students' writing stemmed from the fact that students were not communicating their ideas well. Thus, my goal this summer was to provide activities which would improve their ability to communicate while they also learned data structures.

My first step was to include some comments about writing in my syllabus indicating that effective written communication was important in the class and an area in which they could expect to be evaluated. I indicated that I was as much interested in the delivery as I was in the content of all written assignments. I classified writing activities as (1) writing programs, (2) writing algorithms in pseudocode and (3) writing as composition. Because students have had previous experience with writing programs and I already had defined criteria for evaluating their programs, I made relatively few changes to the requirements for writing programs. Because I already devoted a considerable amount of time to teaching students how to write algorithms in pseudocode and provided them with ample opportunity to practice and have their efforts evaluated, I made very few changes in this area either. Thus, it was in the area of writing as composition that I devoted my efforts, making changes in both my syllabus and in activities.

One new approach that I incorporated was the use of microthemes. A microtheme is defined as "an essay so short that it can be typed on a single five-by-eight inch note card". There are four types of microtheme that I have used successfully. These are (1) summary writing, (2) supporting a thesis, (3) generating a thesis from provided data and (4) quandary posing. Each can be used to have students focus on a small segment of material and write short responses.

In summary writing students are expected to summarize a longer work such as an article or, in data structures, the behavior of an algorithm. This is an especially difficult task to do. Condensing a six page article down to several paragraphs requires that the student first determine the structure of the article and condense the article, retaining the essential ideas and eliminating those which do not directly contribute. Specifying the exact behavior of an algorithm which consists of four pages of Pascal code is similarly difficult. Both types of activities require that students be critical readers and focus only on the relevant.

In supporting a thesis students may be asked to take a stand on an issue such as "Algorithm analysis is not a necessary skill for the applications programmer". In taking a stand on an issue students must be able to analyze facts which are pertinent to the issue and synthesize the results of their analysis. In contrast to the usual questions which require students to memorize and regurgitate facts, thesis support microthemes require that students synthesize facts and become active thinkers.

One type of microtheme which I particularly like is the generation of a thesis from provided data. In this type of assignment students are given tables of data or graphs depicting data and asked to use inductive reasoning to generate ideas from them.

In the quandary posing microtheme assignment students must have a firm grasp of underlying concepts to be able to solve a problem. In a data structures context this can be done in several ways. One way is to have them describe the behavior of an algorithm as if they were explaining it to a fellow student who did not understand it. This may be particularly helpful in helping students focus on what they do not understand in areas where they typically have much difficulty, such as linked lists and recursion. Another way is to give them an algorithm and describe what effect a particular modification of the code may have on the behavior of the algorithm.

I have been successful in breaking the ice on the first day of class using a microtheme assignment in which students write an explanation on an index card of the message that they think Niklaus Wirth was trying to convey by the title of his book

Algorithms + Data Structures = Programs. This leads to a discussion of what the purpose of studying data structures is. I have used this type of short activity on several occasions to introduce new topics of discussion. These are not graded, but they are collected, and I do examine what students have to say and how they are saying it. Besides giving me some insights into how students think, these assignments have also been useful as a diagnostic tool to determine what direction my next lecture(s) might take.

There are numerous ways to employ microthemes. In particular, they can be used at the beginning of a period to focus thoughts in preparation for a discussion. They can be used at the end of a period to summarize and synthesize ideas. They can be used as homework to help students extrapolate ideas from data or support a stance on an issue.

Aside from the introduction of microthemes I have modified many of my homework exercises and the section on each of my program specification sheets which I call Points to Ponder. The Points to Ponder section is a list of questions which are designed to have students examine particular aspects of a programming assignment or possible additions or modifications of the assignment. These questions usually require brief (one sentence to several paragraph) responses. The responses are collected and graded along with the completed program.

The changes that I have made to existing assignments have been primarily in three areas. The first was to provide less ambiguous and more narrowly defined questions on homework assignments and the Points to Ponder sections of the program assignments. Previously, many of my questions were very global in nature. In making changes I tried to determine exactly what objective that I was trying to achieve and specifically identify the points that I expected students to include in their response. Sometimes I included these points in the question so that students would understand clearly the context in which I expected them to respond.

Another area in which I made changes in my assignments was to vary the contexts for writing activities and the roles which students were to assume when writing. By doing this students have the opportunity to communicate to individuals who have different levels of familiarity with the material. Students are extremely comfortable with answering questions in the 'student to teacher' mode. Their role in this mode is clearly identified; they do not have to identify which characteristics of the genre are important in responding to questions; and they generally have ample experience from which to draw. Activities in which they are asked to respond to questions in a variety of different contexts require them to think in different ways about the material being studied and the audience being addressed. For example, asking them to write a brief paragraph which explains a particular concept to another student places them in a different role (student to student or expert to novice) requiring a different style of writing.

Another context which I have tried is to have students respond as if they were a junior programmer writing a report to a team leader. In the particular assignment which I used they were to examine two algorithms which height balance a binary search tree, write a brief explanation of how each algorithm performs the task, and list the criteria which could be used for making a choice between the two algorithms if a particular situation for using them were defined. Students are later asked to perform an

experimental analysis comparing the two algorithms and verifying their paper and pencil examination. Varying the roles and contexts in writing assignments helps students to differentiate between the styles of communication that one can use and practice writing for a particular audience within a fairly narrowly defined situation.

The third way in which I have modified assignments is to change the type of written format which is used in the various activities. Sometimes students are asked to respond in one paragraph to a homework question. Sometimes the format is a memo to a colleague in the discipline or to a colleague who is not familiar with the discipline. In other assignments I have asked them to write a detailed report to a superior on a particular topic. In yet another I ask them to perform an experiment to compare two algorithms and write a report describing the procedures which they used along with their analysis of the data which they gathered. For each assignment I review the technical aspects of the format in order to develop some guidelines for the document to be produced. Each of the formats used is a familiar one in the discipline and commonly used by programmers and analysts in the field.

EVALUATION

One of the initial concerns of increasing the writing activity of students is with evaluating the products. Most computer science teachers do not feel competent to evaluate written work as meticulously as the English teacher. Most instructors do have a sense of when things are written poorly or well. The mechanics (punctuation, spelling and grammar) are easy to evaluate. It is also easy to determine whether responses have a theme sentence or whether an idea is fully developed within a paragraph. In my experience poorly written answers to questions, for example, generally do not have a good theme sentence and do not have good supporting sentences. With just a few tools, instructors can contribute positively to the development of their students writing skills without being an expert in English composition.

Another concern with initiating writing activities in the classroom is the amount of time spent in creating appropriate activities and grading the written work. I actually spent little time in creating activities; most of the activities already existed and I merely modified them. I did spend more time grading papers. What I have found, however, is that written work has improved in quality and the time which I spend is much more productive and less painful than previously.

While evaluation is certainly a concern, it is not necessary to grade every single piece of writing that a student does. The microtheme assignments that I do are often not graded. The purpose is to focus students' ideas, not to determine the correctness of their ideas. If the assignment is used as a point of discussion, they will get adequate feedback on the ideas which they put down on paper as the discussion progresses.

Another way of dealing with the evaluation of written assignments is to use peer evaluation. This can be done in a nonthreatening way. Given specific guidelines students are capable of determining whether an idea is fully developed and well-communicated. Constructive feedback is an important ingredient in enhancing a student's ability to communicate effectively whether it is given directly or indirectly and regardless of the source (self, peer, teacher).

RESULTS

The benefit to students, I hope, is several fold. They are provided with opportunities to improve their written communication skills in various roles and contexts. They have a heightened awareness that all writing is not the same and that different audiences and situations may dictate the use of very different formats and styles.

The benefit to the teacher is primarily the improvement in quality of written work. Written work is easier and more pleasant to read. Having more carefully structured questions and activities has resulted in responses which have been better thought out and better organized. If nothing else, my frustration index has been lower as a result of having made the effort to have students write more carefully.

My sense is that students are learning just as much, if not more, about data structures. They are certainly being exposed to more writing than they were in the past. An attempt should be made to determine the relationship of using writing activities and the long term retention of concepts. My intuition tells me that having to carefully prepare responses requires that students be more analytical and critical in their thinking and that what they learn is more permanently retained as a result.

REFERENCES

1. Bean, John C., Dean Drenk and F. D. Lee, "Microtheme Strategies for Developing Cognitive Skills," New Directions for Teaching and Learning: Teaching Writing in All Disciplines, no. 12, San Francisco: Jossey-Bass, December 1982.

Preparing Students for Programming-in-the-Large

Laurie Honour Werth
Department of Computer Sciences
University of Texas at Austin
Austin, Texas 78712

Abstract

A variety of applications to improve the use of software tools are described with emphasis placed on using tools as software engineering projects. Tool use incorporates quantitative and qualitative benefits, while better preparing students to meet the increasing demands of programming-in-the-large. Improved university-industry cooperation and resource-sharing are other advantages. Some inexpensive approaches to major problems are suggested together with future directions.

Introduction

Mary Shaw's (1985) article "Beyond Programming-in-the-Large: The Next Challenge for Software Engineering" provides strong motivation for using software tools in software engineering classes. In reviewing our progress to date, she describes the 70's as concentrating largely on understanding and developing algorithms and data structures. Indeed, these activities form the bulk of our computer science curriculum today. The 80's saw the rise of software engineering, which many schools are currently scrambling to implement. However, the 1990's will bring ever larger and more complex, heterogeneous, distributed and parallel systems, for which our students are largely unprepared.

The University of Texas is modifying its undergraduate curriculum in an effort to better educate our students for this future. We currently have a popular networks course, the operating systems and programming language courses stress parallel programming, while the software engineering class has a waiting list. A hardware interfacing class is under preparation for next fall.

While software engineering courses seek to provide some realism and a small team project for advanced students, most students still construct their programs, using simple text editors and compilers, during their entire four year career at most universities. All students would benefit from a realistic development environment which would enable them to work with systems larger than even a small team can produce in a semester.

A large software project which would require the use of software tools to help them understand, manipulate, and maintain the system is needed. The Software Engineering Institute will soon make available an Ada artifact for classroom use; a production system of about 40-50,000 lines of Ada code, documented to industry standards. Students need systems such as this together with tools which would allow and encourage a component building/reusable tool-based approach. But where to get such systems and tools? Software and the necessary hardware are expensive, if and where they are available.

On beginning to teach software engineering, it became clear that the only way my students were going to have software tools was for us to produce our own. As it turned out, students are strongly motivated by working on real projects designed for student use. Using and designing tools also improved their mastery of the methodology to be implemented. Not only have we accumulated an assortment of tools, designed by and for software engineering students, but it seems reasonabl e to believe that students' attitude toward the need for tools has been enhanced. Quantitative benefits such as higher productivity have been enhanced by these more qualitative improvements. These endeavors are described briefly with a short discussion of approaches for major problem areas. Future directions include expanding the laboratories for graduate software engineering courses, an in-depth study of Carnegie Mellon's GENIE Pascal environment and other software tool research.

Advantages of Using Software Tools

Few universities use tools as class projects and only a handful of universities provide automated tools for students (Werth, 1987), although this is a fundamental way to encourage future tool development and utilization after students leave school.

Knowing that someone will actually use the software developed in class provides far more motivation than the usual "toy" or "throw-away" programs used in many courses. After using and designing tools for school projects, students are more likely to automate their work in the future. Having experienced the benefits, students should suffer less from the "Not-Invented-Here" syndrome.

Students enjoy using CASE and text formatting tools which permit them to produce professional looking results. Enthusiasm for development tools is not instaneous, but spreads through the class as students see others using them effectively. More importantly, from a pedagogical point of view, students are able to concentrate on the higher level concepts, freeing them from the routine aspects of the task.

Consistency checking by CASE tools aids learning the methodology in the same way a compiler "encourages" the student to correct programming language syntax errors. Walkthroughs can concentrate on the "semantics" of the system, rather than being spent "syntax checking" the model to see that conventions have been followed. The use of commercial CASE tools appears to have made a measurable improvement in the quiz scores of students on structured analysis and design application questions.

Tools purchased for and developed by students have also strengthened our continuing education classes by providing the capability for demonstrations and hands-on lab activities as well as encouraged tool technology transfer between the community and the university. This collaboration between industry and the software engineering faculty and students has led to a sharing of resources and improved research efforts. For example plans are underway with Lockheed Austin for a cooperative effort to develop tools using Refine™ a knowledge-based programming environment developed by Reasoning Systems, Inc.

Another outgrowth of the emphasis on software tools has led to a joint project with Carnegie-Mellon to study the effectiveness of their GENIE Pascal programming environment. Using GENIE will integrate more software engineering into the beginning computer science classes where it belongs. Initial studies have shown improved learning where students are given tools (Goldenson, 1988). Early use of tools such as the Macintosh Programmer's Workbench should provide similar benefits, as well as providing a foundation for the use of more complex projects in a wide variety of later computer science classes (Sherman, 1988).

Software Tools as Class Projects

Possible activities to promote the use of CASE and other tools at the university are illustrated below. The following discussion covers only the tool aspects of the classes and does not detail course activities or curriculum changes. Examples include developing, (re)using, enhancing, and evaluating software tools in software engineering classes.

CS 373 is a standard undergraduate project-oriented software engineering class, limited to graduating seniors. In the fall 1987 semester, students both used and enhanced Cadre's TeamWork, installed on eight HP9000 workstations,. Teams were formed and assigned a project to develop an extension to TeamWork using its ACCESS features. Basic examples of the use of ACCESS routines became our library of reusable code. Students selected their own features, based on their early experience with the CASE tool, then documented and implemented their systems following Fairley's (1985) project outlines: System Definition, System Requirements Specification, three Design Documents, User's Manual, Test Plan, Project Legacy and Project Notebook. A class schedule is included as an appendix.

Several teams choose projects to provide additional reports and consistency checking to the Data Dictionary facility, based on their experience at the first walkthrough. One team developed a project management tool which printed management reports including a Gantt chart marked with the current date and a log report which produces warning messages as to the number of days remaining before reviews/completion, last modification date of database objects, etc.

The most ambitious project, an interface prototyper, used finite state diagrams from TeamWork's real-time capabilities and the ability to attach files to all components of the diagrams. A Screen Design Language defined in BNF and a powerful menu system were developed by the team. While students did not have to understand the entire TeamWork implementation, these exercises did motivate the desirability of object-oriented design, reusability, project databases and good documentation.

All teams used UNIX®[1] scripts and utilities such as Make, Lint, ADB and Curses, together with LaTex for producing documentation. Major organizational problems came from the necessity to keep the latest version of code, documentation and system models (databases) in a central location so that team members could access them regardless of the workstation presently in use. This should be improved this fall with the installation of NFS, Network File Server. Students produced unusually professional products, due in large degree to the improved hardware and software environment and the motivation which resulted from working on a real project in a realistic environment.

Last summer, students extended one of the previous classes' TeamWork enhancement projects. This reduced the size of the project for the short semester and required that they use and expand existing code and documentation. Working with existing documents gave them a useful model on which to build, while raising their awareness of the importance of clear, complete, up-to-date documentation.

In the fall of 1986, software engineering classes developed a variety of static and dynamic analysis tools for testing software, designed for future software engineering classes. The CASE tools were not available at that time, but the projects evoked considerable enthusiasm. Students were having trouble parsing Pascal, so a partially complete recursive descent parser was given to the class. This gave students experience with enhancing someone else's code and the parser was complex enough that the methodology techniques were quickly appreciated. The parser has been one of our most popular reuse items by individual students working software engineering tools as projects.

During the spring '86 semester, students evaluated three commercial systems, Excelerator, PCSA and TeamWork as part of their work in the software engineering course. After entering their designs into both Excelerator on the IBM XTs and TeamWork on the HP workstations, an evaluation form based on Weiderman et al (1986) was developed and completed by the students. Students are often asked to evaluate the tools used as part of their project legacy. They are surprisingly mature and do not seem to use this to vent their frustration as one might suspect, but rather to offer considered advice as to the strengths and weakness of the software. The TeamWork evaluations and project

---

[1]UNIX is a trademark of AT&T Bell Labs

descriptions have been given to Hewlett Packard developers as feedback on the product.

The spring '85 Software engineering class beta tested a VAX version of USE.IT™ developed by HOS (Hamilton, 1983) for the analysis and design of their class project, a Pascal interactive debugger. Again, students were able to provide insights into the product's usability.

A data flow diagram/data dictionary/structure chart tool was one of the first tool projects undertaken several years ago. Done before commercial systems and graphic terminals were available, the entire class cooperated on the project. Database management and data dictionary reports, consistency checking, and graphics teams designed and implemented a UNIX®-based, dumb terminal/line printer oriented system designed to be expanded to graphics terminals by future classes.

Software tools make excellent class projects. Not only is motivation and learning high, but students become their own users, relieving the instructor of this task and reducing the application domain knowledge learning curve. During the testing phase, the quantitative acceptance criteria described in their Requirements Specification must be verified, and at the end of the semester each team tests and evaluates a project different from their own. Teams turn in software trouble reports as well as critiquing the product for functionality and user-friendliness. This gives students a small maintenance exercise as well as stressing the importance of customer satisfaction. Since their product is also to be evaluated, teams find it easy to be fair. The prospect of the future peer review has a strong influence during the design phase as well.

While much of this software is available in the HP and microcomputer laboratories, powerful software generators which run on VAXs and/or SUNs are occasionally used. Though there is not enough equipment for class use of these tools, Gandalf (1985), Cornell Program Synthesizer, IDL Toolkit and others are being used effectively by undergraduate and graduate students for individual projects. Mainframe database management systems have been used in some of the examples above, but fourth generation techniques, such as the use of spreadsheets and database systems, would also be ideal tools for use in software engineering projects.

Future class projects will include a set of project management tools to be developed on Macintosh SE's using Macintosh Programmers Workbench and MacApp, as part of a grant from Apple. If successful, these tools will be made available through Kinko's inexpensive Academic Courseware Exchange program.

Problem Areas

Naturally, all these benefits do not come without a few costs. Major difficulties are characterized below, together with a few suggestions for inexpensive answers. The principal problem with the use of software tools is clearly the expense of hardware, software and labor.

Hardware is the largest expenditure. We were able to start by sharing equipment from other grants, but have recently received funds for additional hardware from vendors who appreciate the benefits of trained students, beta testing and/or product exposure. Collaborative projects with industry have also expanded our hardware and software resources. Academic deans may be impressed enough by the improved collaboration with industry to provide some funding, or some of the money raised by continuing education courses may be directed to hands-on laboratories which can be shared. Microcomputer workstations and generally downward price trends may reduce costs over time as well.

Software is a smaller expense and there are more approaches. Most vendors provide educational discounts ranging from 25 to 85 percent. However, the cost of supporting equipment, documentation and supplies must be considered as well. Some companies are beginning to provide training materials, which should be part of any arrangement, together with permission to copy documentation. Site licenses and networking can reduce software costs, though the university must set a good example by installing security procedures and protecting copyrights. Public domain and low cost government software are another possibility, but generally seem too specific to a particular application to be suitable for student use. Indeed, most available tools are neither generic enough nor sufficiently integrated with other tools to be suitable for students.

Evaluating, ordering, and installing software consumes seemingly infinite amounts of time. Ideally, there should be a national database of product descriptions and review information that could be dialed up; and while this has been considered, it appears, neither technically nor politically, feasible. The IEEE tool standards committee is working to reduce compatibility problems, but this is slow and will not be oriented to education issues. Laboratory workshops and reports at SIGCSE meetings could be a useful approach for assisting computer science faculty to gain the requisite background. Individuals and student organization members have been willing to provide some help installing and testing software as a service to the department, and this has been beneficial for both groups.

System administration is a significant expense for most departments, especially at schools where college deans do not understand that maintaining computer equipment is at least as expensive and time-consuming as it is for any other science or engineering laboratory equipment. Faculty and teaching assistants must have ready access to equipment and documentation to facilitate learning new systems. Special tools journal issues and conferences provide background material, but more survey articles, case studies, examples and exercises are needed to assist already overburdened instructors. SIGCSE publishes papers and organizes panels of interest to the laboratory coordinator, but a more comprehensive, national effort is needed. A proposal for faculty workshops and other assistance was made to NSF at the Workshop on Undergraduate Computer Science Education, but no response has yet been received.

Individual and software engineering class projects appear to be a promising way to provide a integrated environment, customized to local conditions and hardware. Kinko's and public domain software are inexpensive and may well be an avenue to providing nation-wide education-strength courseware in the future.

Future Directions

These software tool laboratories will be crucial for the master's level software engineering classes to be introduced this year. Tool libraries will be expanded with additional commercial and software engineering research systems. Microcomputer support tools such as word processors, database management systems, spreadsheets, graphics (GKS, display and presentation) packages, prototyping, and hypertext tools are already available. Project management, expert systems and other artificial intelligence software are currently being added. Modern specification languages and executable specification tools will be acquired.

Systems from graduate software engineering research projects will also be available, including graphic editor based systems to produce simulation models, parallel programs or code for hard real-time systems. Projects to apply data base management system generators and application-generator generators will benefit both researcher and student. Systems will be more sophisticated, but the benefits should be similar.

UT has recently upgraded the first three computer science courses to use Macintosh SEs in their laboratories. This has permitted us to collaborate with Carnegie-Mellon University in undertaking an empirical study of their GENIE programming environment. GENIE, originally MacGnome, grew out of the Gandalf project and includes a powerful structure editor, debugger, elision capability (OutlineView), style checker, execution tracing, data visualization (contour models) and design tools (DesignView).

The beginning course provides an ideal test bed for comparing GENIE to the current environment, Lightspeed Pascal. Partially self paced, but with a minimum schedule and required labs, it will be relatively easy to study a variety of effects using over 500 students divided into twelve sections. Data will also be collected to examine changes in higher order thinking/problem solving skills and attitudes, success predictors, retention factors and other pedagogic issues.

Future studies will expand to include the students in the second course, taught as a large lecture class with lab, and will look at the effectiveness of GENIE's advanced features. Another project is developing a cognitive model of software design and evaluating existing commercial CASE tools against the model.

Conclusions

Dijkstra's (1982) sentiment that "the purpose of our machines [is] to *execute* our programs" can be updated as "the purpose of our machines is to *construct* our programs." University courses which include experience in developing, (re)using, enhancing and evaluating software tools improve learning and prepare students to meet the challenge of modern software technology. Students benefit from quantitative improvements in productivity, but they also profit from qualitative improvements such as improved learning and better attitudes. Tools can provide some of the same benefits for the instructor that they do for any other project manager: configuration management, quality assurance, record-keeping and documentation.

Additional benefits include improved university-industry communication, cooperation and resource sharing. Basic research is needed, but research must include experimentation and application of results in a software laboratory setting. The university is an ideal environment to conduct empirical studies.

Integrating software tool technology remains difficult. Solutions presented here are rudimentary and don't tackle larger issues such as cost or lack of standardization and comparative evaluations. Still, the combination of benefits for students and faculty should motivate the level of effort needed to overcome the difficulties. The speed with which the field is advancing demands that we start now, least we and our students, fall irreparably behind in coping with programming-in-the-large.

Bibliography

Dijkstra, E. "A Personal Summary of the Gries-Owicki Theory" (p. 188) in *Selected Writings on Computing: A Personal Perspective.* Springer-Verlag, 1982.

Excelerator. *A Guided Tour of Excelerator.* Index Technology Corporation, 101 Main Street, Cambridge, MA 02142.

Fairley, R., *Software Engineering Concepts*, McGraw-Hill, 1985.

Gandalf. *The Journal of Systems and Software.* Vol. 5. No. 2. May 1985. (entire issue).

Goldenson, D., Teaching Introductory Programming Methods Using Structure Editing: Some Empirical Results. SIGCHI Proceedings, 1988.

Hamilton, M., and S. Zeldin, "The Functional Life Cycle and its Automation: USE.IT." *The Journal of Systems and Software*, Vol 3, 1983, pp.25-62.

Page-Jones, Meillor. *A Practical Introduction to Structured System Design.* Yourdon Press, 1987.

Refine™. Reasoning System Inc. Palo Alto, CA 94304.

Shaw, M. "Beyond Programming-in-the-Large: The Next Challenges for Software Engineering." SEI Annual Technical Review, 1985.

Sherman, M. and R. Drydale. Teaching Software Engineering in a Workstation Environment. *IEEE Software*, May, 1988.

TeamWork™ Cadre Technologies Inc., 222 Richmond Street, Providence, RI 02903.

Weiderman, N. H., Habermann, A. N., Borger, M. W., and Klein, M. H. "A Methodology for Evaluating Environments." Proceeding of the ACM SIGSOFT/SIGPLAN Software Engineering Symposium on Practical Software Development Environments, 1987.

Werth, L. Survey of Software Engineering Education. ACM SIGSOFT *Software Engineering Notes*. Vol. 12 No. 4, October 1987.

Werth, L. Software Engineering Tools at the Univer-sity: Why What and How Presented at the 1987 Software Engineering Institute Conference on Software Engineering Education, 1988.

CS 373   SOFTWARE ENGINEERING   Calendar   FALL 87

DATE			TOPIC	READING*	ASSIGNMENT DUE
Aug	31	(M)	Intro to Software Engineering		
Sept	2	(W)	Data Flow Diagram, Data Dictionary	P-J 1-5	Resume
	4	(F)	LAB	DFDexercises	
	7	(M)	Labor Day - holiday	-	-
	9	(W)	Teams, Walkthroughs	F1,2.4.2,5.8	Survey
	11	(F)	LAB - Classroom and HP lab	TeamWork SA	-
	14	(M)	Software Specification	F 4.1	DFD/DD exer.
	16	(W)	Requirements Languages & Tools	F 4.3	
	18	(F)	WALKTHROUGH	Project using Twk	
	21	(M)	Project and Documentation	F 2.1-3	Project
	23	(W)	Decision Tables/Trees	F 4.2.2, P-J 4.2	-
	25	(F)	LAB - classroom	TeamWork ACCESS	
	28	(M)	Review	-	-
	30	(W)	**EXAM 1** F 1,2,4; P-J 1,2,4,5	-	-
Oct	2	(F)	WALKTHROUGH	System Definition	
	5	(M)	Software Design	P-J 3,ApxA-E	Sys Def
	7	(W)	Design Tools	F 5	-
	9	(F)	WALKTHROUGH	UsersManual	
	12	(M)	Design Heuristics	P-J 6-7	UsersManual
	14	(W)	Object-Orient, Real-Time Design	P-J 8-10	-
	16	(F)	WALKTHROUGH	Requirements Spec	
	19	(M)	Implementation Std/Documentation	F 6	Req Spec
	21	(W)	Program Language Concepts	F 7	-
	23	(F)	WALKTHROUGH	Design Doc 1&2	
	26	(M)	Review	-	Design 1,2
	28	(W)	**EXAM 2** F 4,5,6,7; P-J 3,5-10, Apx	-	-
	30	(F)	WALKTHROUGH	Design Doc 3	
Nov	2	(M)	Testing	F 8	Design 3
	4	(W)	Testing Tools	Notes,paper	-
	6	(F)	WALKTHROUGH	Code Prototype	
	9	(M)	Maintenance, Configuration Mgt	F 9.1-3	CodeProto
	11	(W)	Software Metrics	F 9.4-6	-
	13	(F)	WALKTHROUGH	Test Plan	-
	16	(M)	Software Costing	F 3	Test Plan
	18	(W)	Scheduling Techniques	Notes,paper	-
	20	(F)	CODE DEMO - HP Lab	All Code & Test Data	
	23	(M)	Project Management	Notes	TestResult
	25	(W)	Project Management	Notes, papers	STRs&Eval
	26	(F)	Thanksgiving - holiday	-	-
	30	(M)	Class presentations	-	ProjLegacy
Dec	2	(W)	Class presentations	-	-
	4	(F)	WALKTHROUGH	STR Testing, Backup	
	7	(M)	Class presentations	-	ProjNoteBook
	9	(W)	Review	-	-
	12	(Sat	**FINAL** 9 - 12 am Comprehensive + F 3, 8, 9, 10, Notes		

* F=Fairley, P-J=Page-Jones

ALGORITHMS AND SOFTWARE:
Integrating Theory and Practice
in the Undergraduate Computer Science Curriculum

Judith Wilson, Computer Science, Xavier, Cincinnati, OH 45207
Newcomb Greenleaf, Computer Science, Columbia, New York, NY 10027
Robert Trenary, Computer Science, Western Michigan, Kalamazoo, MI

Abstract

A theoretical trend in the development of undergraduate computer science curricula is described. While this curriculum trend can be seen as a natural evolution of a discipline, there are other reasons for it. An opposite trend can be observed that seeks to integrate theory and practice in the undergraduate curriculum. We offer general guidelines based on this second curriculum philosophy.

1. Introduction

Since the publication of the ACM Curriculum 78 recommendations for undergraduate computer science programs [2], there have been several proposed and official updates of this curriculum. Many of these recent proposals recommend greatly increasing the theoretical emphasis of the undergraduate curriculum and integrating advanced topics into the entry-level courses, CS1 and CS2 [13, 14]. The integration of such topics into the first two courses would require significantly more mathematical sophistication than is provided by high school mathematics courses. For this reason, some academic computer scientists recommend more advanced mathematics prerequisites and corequisites for the entry level computer science courses [3, 23].

A separate model curriculum for a liberal arts degree in computer science has also been proposed by Gibbs and Tucker [7]. In the preamble to this model curriculum, the authors state that the formal properties of data structures and algorithms must be emphasized over their "mechanical and linguistic realizations", and over applications, in order for computer science to be legitimately a science. While Gibbs and Tucker do not explicitly advocate elimination of programming from

Computer Science, in fact, the course outlines recommended for CS2 and for the core courses virtually eliminate attention to software engineering content. Thus, the document implies that theory, not practice, is the appropriate concern of computer science departments in liberal arts institutions.

Each of these computer science curriculum proposals includes the following components: (1) a theoretical computer science "core", (2) more mathematics (and more advanced mathematics) courses as prerequisites and corequisites for computer science courses, and (3) the inclusion of more abstract and theoretical topics in lower level computer science courses.

Some observers suggest that a general consensus is developing within the academic computer science community that the theoretical and mathematical refocus recommended by these curriculum proposals is appropriate and necessary [1, 18]. On the other hand, what might be described as a counter-trend can be seen in the new emphasis on the importance of laboratory experience in the computer science curriculum. Philosophical foundations for a new computer science curriculum model that supports this approach can be found in the report of the ACM Task Force on Core of Computer Science and Engineering [4].

We also argue that it would be a mistake to define undergraduate computer science programs within a largely theoretical framework separate from the engineering issues involved in the development of software systems. We first suggest a number of reasons for the theoretical trend in undergraduate computer science programs and then consider problems it raises. We propose several general curriculum and project guidelines in the final section.

2. Reasons for the Theoretical Trend

We divide the reasons for the theoretical trend in undergraduate computer science into two categories: those intrinsic to the discipline itself and those which are responses to conditions that happen to exist in academic settings today.

Intrinsic Reasons. It is to be expected that a discipline will become more theoretical as a result of research in the field. As ideas become developed and accepted they will have an impact in courses which provide basic training in the area. As an example of this kind of natural development it is interesting to note the evolution of the concept of data abstraction from a research issue to a fundamental idea presented in data structures courses, and finally to a commonly accepted concept in CS1 and CS2.

Mathematics training and ability have been shown to be consistently accurate indicators of successful performance in programming courses and in undergraduate computer science programs [15, 28]. This strong positive association between mathematics ability and programming behavior would seem to support the view that computer science is a fundamentally mathematical discipline and justify the use of mathematics courses as filters to weed out unqualified students from computer science programs.

Theoretical advances in computer science over the last 20 to 25 years have helped provide a framework for unifying the early potpourri of computer courses. This (largely mathematical) framework permits a clearer definition of general curriculum objectives than had previously been possible, and thus provides a rationale for restructuring some courses while eliminating others. It seems reasonable to identify this theoretical framework as the core, or foundation, of computer science due to its historic usefulness in unifying the curriculum, and thus to accelerate the movement of the undergraduate curriculum toward a theoretical focus.

Contextual Reasons. The need to justify an unprecedented growth in computing resources at the expense of other programs encourages computing faculty to define their young discipline as scientific within a well established and unquestioned framework. Ensuing resource demands can then be made based on the scientific integrity of the discipline [5]. Defining the discipline within a mathematical framework provides the required legitimacy.

The lack of adequate resources for computer science programs in smaller institutions may have another, more indirect, influence on the theoretical restructuring of the undergraduate curriculum. It has been noted that in small colleges, which tend to be relatively poor in computing resources, tenure is most easily won by computer science faculty with theoretical Computer Science or mathematics research interests [24]. The surviving faculty will naturally tend to define the discipline in terms of their own interests.

Finally, turf battles in universities can force computer science faculty to clearly differentiate computer science courses from computer courses offered in other disciplines, such as computer engineering and information systems. It has been observed that computer science tends to lose out in turf battles with engineering [5]. In this case, computer science faculties might be encouraged to retreat to a theoretical (mathematical) core and to characterize computer science as an essentially theoretical discipline.

3. Concerns Raised by the Theoretical Trend in Curriculum Proposals

We recognize that the theoretical trend in undergraduate curriculum proposals has positive aspects. Unquestionably, theoretical Computer Science provides a framework for unifying the diverse assortment of courses which have passed for Computer Science over the years.

Nonetheless, we are concerned that there may be undesirable consequences of the theoretical trend, at least as it has been expressed in recent curriculum proposals. Our position is that the overall cohesiveness of computer science is best presented by including the design and engineering of software as a major component of a framework which includes theoretical computer science, and that acquisition of software engineering skills requires experience with software design and development projects.

Our concerns about the recent trend in curriculum proposals are of two general kinds: the trend may be pedagogically unsound and it unnecessarily and unrealistically limits the scientific nature of computer science. These concerns are discussed in the following sections.

The trend may be pedagogically unsound. We believe that training in problem solving and program design is likely to be shortcut in the early courses as concepts which were once the domain of advanced courses (such as analysis of algorithms and program verification) are given more formal treatment and included in courses modeled after CS1 and CS2. As a consequence, it may be more difficult to assign significant software construction projects in advanced courses in programming languages, compiler design, operating systems, database architecture and software engineering.

The software engineering component recommended for CS2 is modest compared to the theoretical component [14], and some curriculum proposals would relegate it to a separate laboratory experience associated with lectures devoted to theory [3, 5]. If mathematical foundations and software engineering content are included in a single lecture format which emphasizes theoretical issues, instructors would be encouraged simply to talk about design instead of leading students through a design experience. Alternatively, if software engineering content is treated in a separate lab, software construction activities are likely to be geared to controlled exercises that demonstrate theoretical ideas introduced in lectures. In either case, the development of program design skills will suffer.

Moreover, there is reason to believe that this deemphasis of software engineering concepts would be inappropriate for the kind of student who chooses to study Computer Science.

Although mathematical ability has been found to consistently predict computing ability (as measured by success in one or more computing courses), other factors have also been found to be predictors, including previous experience with computers and computer languages [8, 20], reasoning ability [10, 17], cognitive style [22], and personality factors [11, 28]. Mathematical aptitude seems to be part of a more general set of abilities, dispositions and preferences that favor success in computing courses.

These experimental findings are consistent with our own observations that computer science students are more adept at algorithmic problem-solving activities than they are with mathematical foundations. If this is so, then it is likely that concepts such as data abstraction can be more readily appreciated and used by computer science students when they are introduced as design strategies and not as isolated formalisms, and that mathematical concepts are most easily assimilated when presented in the overall context of algorithm and software development [3].

The theoretical trend assumes too narrow a definition of computer science. Is the view, which is implicit in many curriculum proposals and expressed by such influential commentators as Abrahams and McCracken [1, 18], too narrow a view of what a science should be? Is there really a simple two-way choice, as suggested by Ralston [23], between (a) a mathematics-based discipline and (b) vocational training?

The attitude expressed by Abrahams, that "mathematics is the underlying reality of computer science..." and that "programs work because of the laws of mathematics" [1], underestimates the extent to which nonmathematical concerns occupy realistic software development activities. The fact that actual machines and software are embedded in environments, that environmental factors affect the behavior of these systems, and that these environments may be so complex as to be effectively unknowable, is central to computing. Thus software development requires understanding environmental (engineering) issues as well as the ability to use tools and models derived from theoretical computer science to " ... build heuristics to solve the real problems." [6, p 218]. The actual requirements of engineering software for complex environments would seem to mandate a broader view of what this "science" or "practice" needs to be [27].

Theoretical computer science is a component of the core body of knowledge. It establishes limits (for example, for machine solvable or feasibly solvable problems), provides tools (for example, for compiler design), and provides principles through which one can better understand (and thus, better design or engineer) a wide range of specific applications. Computer science is an experimental science [5, 19, 24] where design techniques effective for large systems must be discovered. It calls for mastery of multidisciplinary skills, tools and knowledge needed to solve large-scale problems. A one-sided emphasis on mathematical foundations risks overlooking important aspects of essentially nonmathematical problems and significant theoretical connections between computer science and disciplines such as engineering, psychology and the biological sciences [5, 19, 21].

If computer science is defined as a theoretical discipline then the theoretical and engineering tasks will be split into separate disciplines: computer science, computer engineering, and information systems. In practice, this encourages these disciplines to diverge while defining their own territories. Computer engineering programs tend to emphasize hardware design, information systems programs are emphasizing the use (not the development) of applications packages by nontechnical users, and computer science is defining a mathematically based curriculum with very little engineering content. A consequence of the divergence of these disciplines is that important aspects of the computing task will be omitted from study in academic curricula.

4. Implications for the Undergraduate Curriculum

A relatively small number of undergraduate students in most computer science programs will go on to do graduate work in computer science, and only a tiny fraction of these students will become researchers in the mathematical aspects of computer theory. We should beware of tailoring our courses only to meet the needs of these students. For undergraduate programs, an emphasis on the software development process would be more appropriate.

It is our opinion that the typical undergraduate student is destined to become a builder and maintainer of software systems, and is by nature or preference a "doer" rather than a theoretician. Thus it is important to tailor the undergraduate computer science curriculum to retain and encourage these students. Education for such students must help develop their capacity to integrate the abstractions and tools of mathematics and theoretical computer science into the software design and development process, and must also be attuned to the need to develop nonmathematical skills.

We recommend several general guidelines for computer science programs which are consistent with our view that theory must be integrated with practice in the undergraduate curriculum.

Mathematics Requirements. The presentation of mathematics topics should be coordinated with the computing curriculum. This might mean that graph theory is learned before calculus, and that calculus is approached through such topics as computing probabilities, generating smooth curves, and finding Fourier series.

We caution against the use of mathematics prerequisites and corequisites as a filter to "weed out" unfit students from a computer science program, particularly when these courses are not integrated with computing and the computer science curriculum. The problem is that these courses are not quite the right filter. Computer Science students often are bored by their mathematics courses and may do quite poorly, but learn mathematics very well when it is seen as relevant to computing.

Entry Level Courses. The entry-level courses should not be survey courses, whether or not accompanied by a laboratory. While acknowledging the appeal of giving the big picture first, we fear that students will not learn the skills of problem solving, algorithm design and program construction from courses primarily designed to provide an overview. We find that many of our students only learn abstractions in an effective manner when these are related to the development of higher order programming skills.

Software design and development methodology should be seen as a central component of entry level courses. Most current curriculum proposals downplay this kind of activity, yet it is imperative that computer science concepts are practiced and not simply described in these courses. Computer educators such as Soloway [26] and Henderson [9] suggest methods for doing this that do not promote the simple view that Computer Science equals programming languages.

CS2 should be a course in which software design methods are taught and practiced. Software projects can be used to introduce theoretical material. The text by Kruse written for use in a CS2 course illustrates how this can be done [16]. An interesting approach used in a third course for computer science majors is described by Sherman and Drysdale [25]. This is a project-driven software engineering course for sophomores who work in small teams on a network of graphics workstations. The projects are conducted in a controlled laboratory setting and make extensive use of such features of the environment as graphics, windows, fonts, mice, networks, and sound generators. The authors claim, plausibly, that students learn abstract concepts more effectively through projects developed in a rich environment which provides numerous software development tools than they would otherwise.

Core Curriculum. Theoretical concepts should be integrated with software design and problem analysis. This requires the use of programming projects where these concepts are introduced as tools for the software design activity. An example of this is described by Kapenga and Trenary [12] where a follow up course to CS3 uses systems programming applications as the basis of projects that integrate theoretical topics (finite automata, language translation) into programming projects. Through these projects, students are exposed to problems of software systems and complex computing environments and shown how both theoretical and practical software engineering concepts (e.g. information hiding through device independence) can be used to simplify the problems of software complexity. In general, throughout the curriculum, students need a broader based exposure to real problems and to the application of "core" tools to the solution of these problems.

5. Conclusion

We have described a theoretical and mathematical trend which is apparent in the development of many undergraduate computer science programs and which has received philosophical support in a number of recent model curriculum proposals. We caution that an overly theoretical philosophy can result in an inappropriate computer science curriculum and urge a balanced approach where theory and practice are integrated. We have described general curriculum guidelines that support an integrated approach.

We recognize that academic computer science programs based on our suggestions may introduce some abstract concepts later than would those modeled on many of the recent curriculum recommendations. It is our belief that this will correct a tendency to accelerate CS1 and CS2 by introducing theory and abstractions intended to give entry students a unified overview of Computer Science at the expense of software design and development experience. In most cases this would introduce concepts to students who have insufficient knowledge, skills and experience to appreciate and use them. The overall cohesiveness of computer science is best presented by including the design and engineering of software as a major component of the framework within which theoretical computer science is taught.

References

1. Abrahams, P., "What is Computer Science?" (President's Letter), Communications of the ACM, Vol. 30(6), June 1987, pp. 472-473.

2. Austing, R.H., et al, "Curriculum '78:Recommendations for the Undergraduate Program in Computer Science--A Report of the ACM Curriculum Committee on Computer Science", Communications of the ACM, Vol. 22(3), March 1979, pp. 147-166.

3. Berztiss, A., "A Mathematically Focused Curriculum for Computer Science", Communications of the ACM, Vol. 30(5), May 1987, pp. 356-365.

4. Denning, P.J., Comer, D., Gries, D., Mulder, M., Tucker, A., Turner, J., and Young, P., "Computing as a Discipline: Final Report of the ACM Task Force on The Core of Computer Science", February 1, 1988.

5. Denning, P.J., "Educational Ruminations", (Editorial) Communications of the ACM, Vol. 27(10), October 1984, pp. 979- 983.

6. Frenkel, K.A., "An Interview with the 1986 A.M. Turing Award Recipients--John E. Hopcroft and Robert E. Tarjan", Communications of the ACM, Vol. 30(3), March 1987, pp. 214-222.

7. Gibbs, N.E., & Tucker, A.B., "Model Curriculum for a Liberal Arts Degree in Computer Science", Communications of the ACM, Vol. 29(3), March 1986, pp. 202-210.

8. Goodwin, L., & Wilkes, J.M., "The Psychological and Background Characteristics Influencing Students' Success in Computer Programming", AEDS Journal, Fall 1986, pp. 1-9.

9. Henderson, P.B., "Anatomy of an Introductory Computer Science Course", ACM SIGCSE Bulletin, Vol. 18, No. 1, February 1986, pp. 257-262.

10. Hostetler, T.R., "Predicting Student Success in an Introductory Programming Course", ACM SIGCSE Bulletin, Vol. 15, No. 1, 1983, pp. 40-43 & 49.

11. Kagan, D.M., & Douthat, J.M., "Personality and Learning FORTRAN", International Journal of Man-Machine Studies, Vol. 22, 1985, pp. 395-402.

12. Kapenga, J., & Trenary, R.G., "Early Introduction of Systems Programming", Proceedings of the Symposium on Computer at the University, Dubrovnik, Yugoslavia, 1985, pp. 602-605.

13. Koffman, E.B., Miller, P.L., & Wardle, C.E., "Recommended Curriculum for CS1, 1984" (A Report of the ACM Curriculum Commitee Task Force for CS1), Communications of the ACM, Vol. 27(10), October 1984, pp. 998-1001.

14. Koffman, E.B., Stemple, D., & Wardle, C.E., "Recommended Curriculum for CS2, 1984" (A Report of the ACM Curriculum Commitee Task Force for CS1), Communications of the ACM, Vol. 28(8), August 1985, pp. 815-818.

15. Konvalina, J., Wileman, S.A., & Stephens, L.J., "Math Proficiency: A Key to Success for Computer Science Students", Communications of the ACM, Vol. 26(5), May 1983, pp. 377-382.

16. Kruse, R.L., Data Structures & Program Design, (Second Edition), Prentice-Hall, Inc., 1987.

17. Kurtz, B.L., "Investigating the Relationship Between the Development of Abstract Reasoning and Performance in an Introductory Programming Class", ACM SIGCSE Bulletin, Vol. 12(1), pp. 110-117.

18. McCracken, D.D., "Ruminations on Computer Science Curricula", Communications of the ACM, Vol. 30(1), January 1987, pp. 3-5.

19. Nelson, D.A., "Relevance vs. Rigor", Communications of the ACM, Vol. 30(7), July 1987, pp.585-586.

20. Oman, P.W., "Identifying Student Characteristics Influencing Success in Introductory Computer Science Courses", AEDS Journal, Vol. 19, No. 2-3, Winter/spring 1986, pp. 226-233.

21. Ourusoff, N., ""What is Computer Science?"", Communications of the ACM, Vol. 28(8), August 1985, pp. 791-792.

22. Pommersheim, J.P., & Bell, F.H., "Computer Programming Achievement, Cognitive Styles, and Cognitive Profiles", AEDS Journal, Vol. 19, Fall 1986, pp. 51-59.

23. Ralston, A., "The First Course in Computer Science Needs a Mathematics Corequisite", Communications of the ACM, Vol. 27(10), October 1984.

24. Scragg, G.W., "A Crisis in Computer Science Education at Liberal Arts Colleges", ACM SIGCSE Bulletin, Vol. 19(2), June 1987, pp. 36-42.

25. Sherman, M., & Drysdale III, R.L., "Teaching Software Engineering in a Workstation Environment", IEEE Software, May 1988, pp. 68-75.

26. Soloway, E., "Learning to Program = Learning to Construct Mechanisms and Explanations", Communications of the ACM, Vol. 29, No. 9, September 1986, pp. 850-858.

27. Weiss, E.A., "Computing Science is Not a Branch of Mathematics", Abacus, Vol. 4 (4), pp. 31-32.

28. Whipkey, K.L., "Identifying Predictors of Programming Skill", ACM SIGCSE Bulletin, Vol. 16(4), December 1984, pp. 36- 42.

DEFINING EDUCATIONAL POLICY ON SOFTWARE USAGE
IN LIGHT OF COPYRIGHT LAW

Galen B. Crow
Department of Applied Computer Science
Illinois State University
Normal, Illinois 61761

ABSTRACT

Accompanying the rapid proliferation
of personal computing has been an
ambivalent attitude towards the illegal
copying of commercially available
software. The effects of this software
"piracy" are enormous and insidious, and
academia ranks as one of the worst
abusers. To understand the legitimate as
well as illegitimate usage of software,
one must have a clear understanding of the
letter and intent of the copyright law.
If academia is to purge itself of
software abuses, educators and
administrators must set clear and visible
software policies based upon the the
copyright law.

THE EFFECTS OF SOFTWARE PIRACY

Computer software for personal
computers is a multi-billion dollar
industry. Revenues from software sales
will soon exceed the sales of the
computers themselves (Antonoff, 1987).
Unfortunately for software producers, the
illegal copying and use of computer
software, commonly referred to as
"software piracy," is probably more
widespread and prolific than its
legitimate use. The estimates are that
50 to 95 per cent of all software in use
has been acquired by illegal duplication
(Sterne and Saidman, 1985).

Software producers have in the past
combatted piracy primarily by employing
of copy protection schemes. These schemes
involve highly complex methods of
preventing the duplication of marketed
diskettes. Persistent software pirates
manage to stay one step ahead of these
schemes. They tend to be relatively
sophisticated users and often devise or
purchase means to defeat protection
schemes. In fact, an entire genre of
software products has sprung up in the
marketplace for the sole purpose of
defeating copy protection systems.
Honest users of computer software making
legitimate backups are often thwarted
and confused. Many, therefore, do not
backup vital software and are thus prone
to work slowdowns or stoppage when
software is accidentally misplaced or
destroyed. The result of software
protection has thus been to annoy,
frustrate and discourage legitimate
users and to encourage pirating
technology.

Since software protection schemes
have not proven that successful, they may
soon be a thing of the past (Antonoff,
1987). Thus, many manufacturers are
turning to legal remedies to prevent
software piracy. The strict enforcement
of software producers legal rights
combined with an educational campaign has
led in recent years to far fewer
violations at the corporate level
(Antonoff, 1987). Today, however, the
vast majority of computer pirates are
unwitting criminals, people who would
generally not commit other crimes or
think of themselves as criminals, except
maybe in a fanciful way relating to
computer software (Bullock, 1986).
Ironically, educators and educational
institutions may be among the worst
offenders of software law (Helms, 1985).
This phenomena is unfortunate, unwise
and dangerous.

Colleges and universities often
maintain lax standards and guidelines
(if any) regarding computer software.
There are many reasons for this. Often
times the resources are not available to
legally obtain necessary software
requirements. Central coordination of
software policy has not been a
traditional administrative function. The
contractual and legal obligations are
confusing and often contradictory to
unsophisticated users. Faculty tend to

justify questionable software practices by either educational "fair use" or by thinking of questionable duplication and distribution as kind of an unofficial pseudo-promotional activity for vendors. Campuses also naturally exhibit a healthy propensity for curiosity, experimentation and innovation which generally encourages software proliferation, legal or otherwise. Finally, the students themselves, largely ignorant of software legal concerns, playfully make sport, culture and status surrounding software piracy. Probably every campus in the United States has a "pirate's club" complete with "swap meets," secret passwords, telephone networks, officers and "official" sanctions of some type.

There are both legal and ethical questions raised by this attitude towards software usage. Are educators and administrators sending the right signals to those within their influence? Are universities subordinating higher principles in the name of underfunding or intellectual curiosity? Are software vendors, having done battle with corporations, prepared to do the same with universities? There is no common consensus regarding the answers to these questions. However, one fact is clear. Faculty, administrators and most importantly, students should be given clear and unequivocal guidelines regarding software usage.

METHODS OF SOFTWARE PROTECTION

There are several sources of law from which software producers may find protection from the illegal duplication, use and distribution of their products. One such means of protection is the trademark. Trademark law, by authority of the Patents Act of 1952, allows for the registration of a product's name or identifying mark. Trademarks prevent others from infringing upon or confusing the marketplace with identical or unreasonably similar product identifiers. Trademarks do not protect the products themselves, only the product's name or mark (Ellis, 1986).

Another legal method of protecting software is as a trade secret. In 1980, the Commissioners on Uniform State Laws passed the Uniform Trade Secrets Act. Although non-binding, many state legislatures have enacted this proclamation either partially or in entirety. It defines a trade secret as "a formula, pattern, device or information which is issued in the operation of a business and provides the business an advantage over those who do not know or use it." This form of protection is useful to commercial software developers during product development and those who produce software for in-house use. It helps prevent the loss of software secrets

to current and former employees, corporate spies and contractors. Obtaining trade secret protection involves the validation of the secret's novelty, value and secrecy. However when a product is sold publicly, it's secrecy is questionable, thus making this form of protection ambiguous in relation to commercially available software (Depaul Law Review, 1985). Also, the courts have recently ruled that reverse engineering of commercially available software is a perfectly valid means of discovering trade secrets (Vault v. Quaid, 1987). In other words, programs developed solely for the purpose of copying other computer programs (by employing reverse engineering techniques to break copy protection schemes) are legal in publicly distributed software.

Patents, also authorized by the Patents Act of 1952, are issued to give inventors the exclusive rights to make or sell their inventions for a given period of time and to exclude all others from doing so. To be eligible for a patent an invention must be a "new and useful process, machine, manufacture or composition of matter." Computer software is applicable under patent law only insomuch as it is part of a larger, more tangible and physical process. Thus the utilization of a computer program in a physical invention may afford it patent protection. However, the great bulk of commercially marketed software is transferable from machine to machine thus making it independent and separable from the total process. A computer algorithm or program like a set of mental steps, ideas and/or suggestions, as well as the laws of nature, are not patentable in and of themselves (Ellis, 1986).

Another method of legally protecting computer software is in the form of a contract or license. Many manufacturers attempt to control the use of their products by licensing agreements with individuals or institutions. These contracts and licenses are fine as long as all parties officially agree to all included terms. In the case of a vendor and institution mutually agreeing on terms and conditions and signing a pact, this method is not problematic. However, the widest use of this form of protection is the so-called "shrink wrap" license (CLIPNOTES, 1988). This is the agreement or contract which is included in almost all commercially available software. Most such agreements state that the purchaser implicitly agrees to all of the conditions of the agreement merely by opening the package or "shrink wrap," whether or not any formally signed contract has been consummated. It is arguable that this type of agreement is enforceable. Also, in many cases these agreements violate the purchasers rights expressly permitted by copyright law. In any case, the shrink wrap license has not been thoroughly tested in the courts and, in at least one case, has been determined invalid (Vault v. Quaid, 1987).

Partly due to the deficiencies of the aforementioned methods and partly because the federal government has specifically sought to include software within its jurisdiction, copyright law has become the primary source of legal protection for computer software (Depaul Law Review, 1985).

SOURCE OF COPYRIGHT LAW RELEVANT TO COMPUTER SOFTWARE

Copyright law in the United States can be traced directly to the Constitution in Article I, Section 8, Clause 8 which reads in part "... to promote the Progress of Science and the useful Arts, by securing for limited times to Authors ... the exclusive Right to their respective Writings." In 1790 the first Copyright Act was approved by Congress. This Act broadened the focus of the Constitution to include the protection of all "intellectual property" which at the time meant books, maps and charts. The thrust of this act was that by protecting authors of intellectual property, the marketplace would be stimulated to disseminate such property. Thus, the primary interest was for the public good in the promotion of the "Progress of Science." The property rights of the author were actually thought of as a secondary interest (Depaul Law Review, 1985). This act thus set up a tension between the benefit of the public good and the property interests of individuals guaranteed elsewhere in the Constitution.

Throughout the twentieth century it became clear that the copyright law was inadequate to govern modern intellectual property such as audio cassettes, motion pictures, copy machines and computer programs; and Congress began to amend the copyright law. In 1964 the first computer program was granted copyright protection even though the Copyright Act at this time did not specifically address software. In 1974 Congress established the National Commission on New Technological Uses (CONTU) of Copyrighted Works to deal with the problem of intellectual property in computer related technologies (Depaul Law Review, 1985).

The 1976 Copyright Act officially identified computer software as a protectable work and established that a machine reproduction of a computer program is actually a "copy" for legal purposes. As a result of CONTU's official report in 1978, the Computer Software Copyright Act of 1980 was enacted. This act added to copyright statute a definition of computer software as a "... set of statements or instructions to be used directly or indirectly in a computer in order to bring about a certain result." It also clarified the copying rights of software purchasers.

Two sections (107 and 117) of the Copyright Act are particularly pertinent for educators in relation to computer software usage. Section 107 defines the parameters from which educators may bend the exclusive proprietary rights of the copyright holder. Certain types of duplication of copyrighted works are exempted from infringement liabilities under the so-called "fair use" doctrine. Section 107 reads:

Notwithstanding the provisions of section 106, the fair use of a copyrighted work, including such use of reproduction in copies or phonorecords or by other means specified by that section, for purposes such as criticism, comment, news reporting, teaching (including multiple copies for classroom use), scholarship, or research, is not an infringement of copyright. In determining whether the use made of a work in any particular case is a fair use the factors to be considered shall include:
(1) the purpose and character of the use, including whether such use is of a commercial nature or is for nonprofit educational purposes;
(2) the nature of the copyrighted work;
(3) the amount and substantiality of the portion used in relation to the copyrighted work as a whole; and
(4) the effect of the use upon the potential market for or value of the copyrighted work.

Often times educators interpret "fair use" as a blanket license to duplicate any amount of any work for any educational purpose, including software. Indeed factor 1 seems to indicate an exemption for most educational purposes; however factors 2, 3 and 4 suggest otherwise.

Factor 2 refers to the nature of the copyrighted work. In other words, was this product intended to be distributed and redistributed freely to all interested parties or was it meant primarily to be sold and owned by specific individuals? For instance a newspaper has a kind of transient value and therefore would be more likely exempted by fair use than a classic novel. Similarly, software taught in a business course on a college campus is likely to have been designed and marketed for more commercial enterprises, and thus would be unlikely to be exempted by fair use.

Factor 3 refers to the proportion of the work copied. Copying a chapter from a text for use in a classroom is likely to be a valid fair use exemption, but copying the entire text would not be. Since it is unlikely that only a portion of a software package would be duplicated and utilized, exemption by fair use is not applicable in this case either.

Finally, factor 4 refers to the impact on the potential profits of the work. The question here is: Will copying the software for students in a course result in a reduction in potential profits for the copyright owner? If so, no exemption from fair use can be allowed. Since most software is written for the purpose of making a profit (unlike many textbooks), copying leads directly to a loss in potential revenues.

Because of these factors, it is unlikely that the courts would look favorably on the wholesale copying of software for classrooms (Bullock, 1986).

Section 117 of the Copyright Act, amended in 1980, defines precisely the rights of the owner of a copy of a computer program. It also addresses the issue of what constitutes a copy and the transfer of ownership of the program. Section 117 reads:

Notwithstanding the provisions of section 106, it is not an infringement for the owner of a copy of a computer program to make or authorize the making of another copy or adaptation of that computer program provided:
(1) that such a new copy or adaptation is created asan essential step in the utilization of the computer program in conjunction with a machine and that it is used in no other manner, or
(2) that such copy or adaptation is for archival purposes only and that all archival copies are destroyed in the event that continued possession of the computer program should cease to be rightful.
Any exact copies prepared in accordance with the provisions of this section may be leased, sold, or otherwise transferred, along with the copy from which such copies were prepared, only as part of the lease, sale, or other transfer of all rights in the program.
Adaptations so prepared may only be transferred with the authorization of the copyright owner.

Section 117 implicitly describes three types of copies of a computer program. First, there is the original "copy of the computer program" purchased from the copyright holder. Second, there is the copy of the program "created as an essential step" in its usage, that is, the copy of the program created in the computer's main or random access memory (RAM) prior to using it. Third, there is the type of copy produced and stored on a storage device other than the computer's RAM (i. e. a diskette). The third type of copy is obviously the most often in

dispute in terms of legitimacy. The intent of section 117 makes perfectly clear that copying software for "archival purposes" is completely within the rights of the purchaser of the software. As any regular software user knows, to not do so will eventually prove disastrous. However, it does not give the user the right to use multiple copies in any way other than as "backups" to the one in use. The right to make backup copies is sometimes challenged by the "shrink wrap" licenses, which is one of the reasons the validity of such licenses is questionable.

Section 117 also makes clear the right of the owner of a software copy to sell, lease or otherwise transfer ownership (i e. loan) of that copy as long as the original owner ceases use of the program entirely and destroys any non-transferred copies. If a program has been modified or adapted in any way, it's ownership may not be transferred without the consent of the copyright holder.

IMPLICATIONS FOR UNIVERSITIES AND COLLEGES

The desire and need to utilize microcomputer software will continue to increase. While the modern revisions to the Copyright Act leave some grey areas regarding educational use of software, particularly in regards to "fair use" exemptions and "shrink wrap" contract restrictions, the policy implications for educators are fairly clear:
1. The purchase of a computer program entitles the owner to make at least one back-up copy to be used solely for archival purposes.
2. The ownership of the software can be transferred, but only in entirety and without revision.
3. Educators do not have blanket exemption to copyright infringement based upon "fair use."
4. Each legally owned copy of the software may be used on one machine at a time only. It may not be "booted" on multiple machines for concurrent usage without multiple ownership or a special usage permit.
5. Unless expressly intended, a computer program may not be networked and utilized on multiple machines. However, the results or screen output from a software package may be displayed on multiple monitors via a network without multiple ownership as long as the program is only actively employed on the "host" machine. Therefore, some training exercises may be simulated using a network and a single software copy.
6. Short term seminars or workshops utilizing software present a difficult challenge if multiple copies are not owned by the sponsoring agency. Adhering

strictly to the Copyright Act, software probably can't be duplicated for use in short seminars or workshops and then erased when finished.

7. Each owned copy or its backup (but not both) may be loaned from a laboratory or library. However, students should be strongly discouraged from illegitimate usage, including producing pirated copies or multiple machine use.

Additionally, academia must deal with software usage on a institution wide level. For example:

1. A university or college should have strong and visible software usage policies which are consistent throughout the campus. Care should be taken to educate administrators, staff, and students regarding institutional policies as well as the legal nuances of software usage in offices, classrooms, laboratories and libraries.

2. A central authority should examine the reasonableness and legality of all new requests for software usage within academic or administrative units, aside from the approval of acquisition. This authority should be knowledgeable about hardware and software usage, relevant legal concerns and potential vendor arrangements such as preview, site and educational licenses and grants. Many times requests for software purchases are made solely on budget or logistical concerns, without determining the appropriateness of the actual usage.

3. Finally, enough funds should be appropriated to acquire the necessary software to meet legitimate needs and uses. Faculty and administrators should not be put in a position of having to rationalize questionable software usage practices because of inadequate resources.

BIBLIOGRAPHY

Antonoff, Michael (1987), "Can We End Software Piracy," Personal Computing, May, pp.143-153.

Antonoff, Michael (1987), "The Decline of Copy Protection," Personal Computing, May, pp.155-157.

Bullock, Laura Chase (1986), "Shoplifting? No, Softlifting!," Eric No. ED 278 376.

"Combating software Piracy: A Statutory Proposal to Strengthen Software Copyright," (1985), The Depaul Law Review, Summer, Vol. 34, No. 4, pp.993-1031.

The Constitution of the United States of America, Article I, Section 8

"Copying the Look and Feel of Computer software: Fair Competition or Copyright Violation?" (1988), Computer Law & Intellectual Property (CLIPNOTES), April, Vol. 2, No. 2, pp.1, 4-8, published by the law firm of Gardner, Carton & Douglas, Quaker Tower, Suite 3400, 321 North Clark Street, Chicago, IL 60610.

The Copyright Act 1976, Amended 1980- Title XVII, U.S.C., Sections 101, 107 and 117.

Ellis, David R. (1986), "Computer Law-A Primer on the Law of Software Protection," The Florida Bar Journal, April, pp.81-84.

Helm, Virginia (1986), "What Educators Should Know About Copyright," Phi Delta Kappa Education Foundation, Bloomington, Indiana

The Patent Act of 1952

"Protection of Mass-Marketed Software in the Waning Days of Shrink-Wrap Licenses," (1988), Computer Law & Intellectual Property (CLIPNOTES), January, Vol. II, No. I, pp.1, 5-8, published by the law firm of Gardner, Carton & Douglas, Quaker Tower, Suite 3400, 321 North Clark Street, Chicago, IL 60610.

Sterne, Robert G. and Saidman, Perry (1985), "Copying Mass-Marketed Software," Byte, February, pp.387-390.

"Thou Shalt Not Dupe," (1984), Association of Data Processing Service Organizations (ADPSO), Suite 300, 1300 N. 17th Street, Arlington, VA 22209.

The Uniform Trade Secrets Act (1980)

Vault Corp. v. Quaid Software Ltd., 655 F. Supp. 750 (E.D. La. 1987) Vault argued in this case that Quaid, the makers of a software copying program, had violated their copyrights by using "reverse engineering" techniques to enable the copying of their copy-protected program. Vault also claimed that the sole purpose of Quaid's product was to copy software which had been protected, and thus in direct violation of Louisiana's Software Enforcement Act. The court disagreed concluding that 1) Louisiana's Software Enforcement Act was preempted by federal statute, the Copyright Act, thus making making its validation of "shrink wrap" licenses which prohibit any copying of software unenforceable, 2) the act of decompiling, disassembly and reverse engineering was an appropriate means of discovering trade secrets in a commercially available product, and 3) the copy program itself had legitimate non-infringing uses as prescribed by the copyright Act.

Identifying the Gaps Between Education and Training

Freeman L. Moore
Texas Instruments Incorporated
Dallas, Texas   75265

James T. Streib
University of Central Arkansas
Conway, Arkansas   72032

Abstract

This paper discusses some of the issues concerning education in the academic environment and training in the industrial work environment. Recent college graduates, "new-hires", must realize as they enter the workforce, that even though they have completed four year degree programs, they are beginning at an entry-level position. They will need job specific training to make them productive software engineers from their employer's perspective.

The aspects of distinguishing between education and training are discussed along with an understanding of how college prepares graduates for employment in the computer industry; specifically, the field of military software development as developed at Texas Instruments.

Introduction

Much has been written about college and university computer science departments and the programs that they promote. We shall assume that the primary objective of an undergraduate computer science department is to produce an individual who is ready to undertake the role of a software engineer with an employer such as Texas Instruments. A secondary objective is to prepare students for further education in a graduate program. This paper deals with the relationship between academia and industry, and will not consider the training needs of students that choose to continue onto graduate school.

Are the academic departments in touch with the needs of employers? Are they producing a "product" which satisfies that need? It is possible that many academic departments do not look at the needs of the employers from the point of view

of fulfilling a job position. Upon starting their first position in the computer industry after graduation, many new-hires find themselves enrolled in a series of seminars and training sessions offered by their employer. These training activities can last a few hours to several months. At first glance, it may appear that the graduating student has not been adequately prepared for his career as a software engineer. A better understanding of the transition from college graduate to employee is needed by all concerned; the student, the college and the employer [1].

This paper will focus on the distinction between education and training and why corporate training programs must build upon the "product" produced by colleges. We shall identify the role of the academic environment, and point out areas better left to industrial training programs.

Education versus Training

> "Education is different from training. To be crude about it, training is what you do with dogs, education is what you do with people. Seriously, training of people works best with material which is extremely simple and has well-defined rules. If something can be done by rote, then training is appropriate. Education of people is what is required when the rules and guidelines of a technology do not easily lend themselves to simplistic interpretations. [2]"

This statement provides an adequate distinction between the two disciplines which is necessary for the remainder of this paper.

If colleges prepare individuals by providing them with an education, what is the role of education within the corporate environment? That is easily answered by looking at the names of the "education" departments within companies. It is our experience that they are normally called training departments. Texas Instruments is an example of a large company with several in-house training departments addressing the various needs of the company.

This paper deals with the needs of new-hires entering into the Defense Systems and Electronics Group (DSEG) of

Texas Instruments, which has a heavy emphasis on software development for military applications. The Human Resources Development Department is the central training organization for DSEG. This department contains four branches; computer systems training, engineering training, management development training, and group education programs. The Computer Systems Training branch is responsible for training in software development methodology and tools.

Audience variations and expectations

To obtain an undergraduate degree in computer science, the typical student must complete anywhere from 30 to 45 semester hours of computer science course work over a four year period of time. If each course is worth three semester hours (three hours of lecture time per week over 15 weeks), the result is 45 hours of instructional time per course. On the other hand, the corporate training session may use one 40 hour week of instruction. Though the amount of actual classroom time appears to be equal, there are some very significant differences to be noted.

First the academic environment has the luxury of time. This allows plenty of time between each classroom session to allow the student to read, study, work on homework, do additional research and review the ideas presented in class. However, the corporate environment does not afford such a luxury. Time away from the job is money lost in a production environment and justification for any training is normally expected. Classes which require a few hours are much easier to justify than a 40 hour class, requiring five full days of attendance. Time away from the job must be accounted for, and may affect the working overhead of a company, and thus having an impact on profits. Training may not be approved due to budgetary reasons, or lack of relevancy of training to the work environment, or insufficient time due to current project demands.

Second, the audience is fundamentally different with respect to the level of experience brought into the environment. The college environment consists of students with minimal experience in computer science. Corporate training environments have a mixture of students, ranging from new-hires to people who have been with the company for years. Sometimes, training may be specialized for new-hires, although experienced people may be involved when changing from one project to another project within the company.

Third, there is also a difference in expectations between the college and industrial environment. For grading purposes, most college work is done as an individual activity, yet this is exactly the opposite of what is expected in the commercial world. The essential mode of operation in the work environment is team work and cooperation. The academic world must provide more interactive work sessions to better prepare the student for the commercial world. We acknowledge the grading problems associated with group

efforts. However, to better reflect the type of work and promote free exchange of information that future employees will use, group efforts must continue to be encouraged.

Lastly, the rewards are different. Students earn a grade and continue with other courses. However, employees are expected to return to the job environment with increased abilities, resulting in a more productive workforce. If the training is not adequate, it can have immediate impact on the employee (i.e. no merit raises, being fired) or lower overall group productivity (i.e. decreased profits).

Results of college education

Colleges and universities tend to have a very generalized view of education. This is evident at the college, department, and even the individual course level. The reason for this generalized view is because it is not possible for academia to know the needs of countless numbers of computer companies, i.e. potential employers of students. Further, the changes in future technology are difficult to predict.

By following a generalized degree program and required courses in a major, a student should be well prepared for a wide variety of jobs within the chosen discipline. General ideas are taught to allow the student to adjust to new ideas and changes in the future. Texas Instruments assumes the existence of a solid educational background so that internal training efforts can address the specific skills needed to accomplish a task. Re-training efforts are an example of building upon a solid foundation, adapting to needs of specific situations.

What does industry expect of college graduates?

Ideally, industry would like to have new employees be productive from the very first day of employment. But, are graduates ready to become productive employees? Often, the answer is a surprising "no." While this may be unexpected by some, it is a consequence of hiring employees from across the country with a variety of educational backgrounds and abilities. In general, employees are hired because of their perceived potential to adapt to new environments and ideas. Companies need the innovative ideas of new employees to remain competitive.

For purposes of training, industry is generally involved with providing specific knowledge to aid an individual in doing a particular job better. Ideally, new-hires into the DSEG environment should be productive from the first day of employment. However, we find that in many cases, college graduates are not familiar with the challenges of developing software in a defense contractor environment. We have found that assistance must be provided in understanding the

Texas Instruments work environment, and in particular, DSEG project needs [3].

Why industry is involved with training?

What customized "training" programs are needed to complete or round out the educational programs? Industry has some needs that cannot be met by academia. For example, Texas Instruments uses embedded microprocessors in some of its applications, requiring the use of specialized languages in addition to real-time programming techniques. As a major defense contractor, Texas Instruments must develop and deliver software products in compliance with a variety of military standards. The major standard for software development is DoD-STD-2167A, which establishes the formal tasks a contractor must perform to develop mission-critical software for the Department of Defense, DoD [4]. These tasks include a specification of the DoD mandated documentation requirements. However, what universities are teaching DoD-STD-2167A? At a recent conference on software engineering education, very few educators seemed knowledgeable about DoD-STD-2167A; yet this is the required standard for software development on military contracts [3, 5].

What about the programming language Ada? This is the mandated language for new software development for military weapon systems. The authors are only aware of a handful of colleges that use Ada as the programming language within the department.

In some aspects, the corporate world may be using state-of-the-art technology where hardware and software are concerned. The programming language Ada is such an example where new technology is being inserted into programs. In other aspects, the technology may be 10 to 15 years old, and reluctant to change. One simply does not rewrite a 15 year old Fortran system simply to use modern techniques or newer microprocessors. Industry must respond to government requirements in the area of developing software according to a well defined standard, DoD-STD-2167A, and also promoting the benefits of software engineering.

Within the Defense Systems and Electronics Group of Texas Instruments, training focuses on DoD-STD-2167A and Ada. Additionally, Texas Instruments provides training on real-time systems, software engineering, and detailed microprocessor architecture to support hardware / software integration. Our software engineering curriculum has been developed in response to extending the background skills of new-hires. We have noted that the background of new employees is consistent with Werth's observation: [6]

- Most graduates have a general understanding of some software development life cycle.

- However, most graduates do not have a good understanding of the details of each phase of the software development process, except for coding.

- More graduates are learning how to write better technical documentation before they enter industry.

- Few graduates have experience in formatting information for presentations or in conducting a presentation.

Should academia change?

What's wrong with the computer science departments of our universities? One problem is isolation. Course content is largely what a faculty member was taught as a student of faculty members who taught what they were taught as students. Few universities encourage faculty to consult and fewer require it. Their only contacts are with other equally isolated faculty and with students who have not yet used computers for much but games and term papers." [7]

Isolation is a problem which has been written about before and must continue to be raised. Some companies are willing to cooperate with universities in providing liaison support, but others seem reluctant to do so because of the apparent lack of "return on investment."

In many of the courses taught at college, students are failing to recognize the general ideas. For example, in an "introduction to computer science" course, the details of the programming language may be more important to the student that the concepts that the language was designed to make evident. The instructor and the textbook may present the basic ideas, but far too often the programming assignments and examinations focus on the syntax issues, reinforcing a student's opinion of the usefulness of a particular language.

Should a specific language such as Ada or specific standard such as DoD-STD-2167A be taught in the college environment? Not necessarily. As mentioned previously, students must be prepared for a wide variety of careers, not just military software development. As a result, it appears that the proper place for specific languages, and standards, is in the industrial training environment. It also requires that the student be prepared for training by obtaining a broad education base. Academia needs to place a greater emphasis on the basics of the education, leaving the job specific skills to the corporate training environment.

Can industry and academia cooperate?

A problem presented in the preceding section is that the computer industry requires specialized instruction. Further, students may not realize that generalized concepts presented in such courses as "Programming Languages" could be applied to specialized situations, such as learning the Ada programming language.

A possible solution, at first glance, is that industry could change their expectations of college graduates. This would influence a student's view of what is important in a college education and the student would hopefully pay more attention to ideas and not specifics in preparation for a career. Industry would also benefit, in that a student would be better prepared for change, and as a result, training would be quicker, cheaper, and more efficient.

A change in industry is not the only solution to the problem. Education must also change. The problem does not lie in a failure of higher education in general, but with computer science education. Since computer science is still a comparatively young discipline, the natural testing of ideas has not yet been developed. The current trend towards having a computer science major take more courses is not necessarily the solution since more specialized courses could just add to the problem. Instead, it appears that computer science education should put more emphasis on the presentation techniques (including communication skills), the abstraction level of assignments, and testing of ideas.

Cooperation requires that both industry and education recognize that the areas they are best suited for, and their limitations. Industry will provide the training to enhance the on-the-job skills of a new-hire, assuming there is a solid education upon which to build.

Summary

Academia is needed, but so are the industrial training programs; they rely upon each other. Each works with a different class of 'students.' The training programs available at Texas Instruments build upon the skills of the new-hire, providing them with the detailed information needed to help them become more productive in their work. As with any expenditure, cost must be justified. Training within the industrial setting represents a cost which affects the company's profits. As such, it is in the best interest of all concerned to make sure that the college graduates have a greater awareness of the nature of their computer science program. They are working toward a degree, and a career.

The 'gap' between education and training is bridged by realizing the distinction between education and training. We have identified that some training is specific to the work environment, and as such, cannot be expected to be a part of a student's college education.

References

[1] Denton, C., "Culture Shock -- Transferring From College into the Professional Work Force," *SIGCSE Bulletin*, Vol 20, No 2.

[2] Berard, E., "Ada Education and Training - Part 4", Info-Ada network communication.

[3] Moore, F. & Purvis, P., "Meeting the Training Needs of Practicing Software Engineers at Texas Instruments", SEI Conference on Software Engineering Education, April 1988.

[4] DoD-STD-2167A, Defense System Software Development, *Department of Defense Military Standard*, 28 Feb 1988.

[5] Leventhall, L. & Mynatt, B., "Components of Typical Undergraduate Software Engineering Courses: Results from a Survey," *IEEE Transactions on Software Engineering*, Vol 13, No. 11.

[6] Werth, L., "Software Engineering Education: A Survey of Current Courses," *ACM Software Engineering Notes*, Vol 12, No. 4.

[7] Strang, D., "Where are the Real Computer Scientists?", *Government Computer News*, September 25, 1987.

Computer Science: A Core Discipline
of Liberal Arts and Sciences

Robert E. Beck
Villanova University

Lillian N. Cassel
Villanova University

Richard H. Austing
University of Maryland

1 Introduction

The most consistent aspect of computer science is change. It is not surprising then, to note a significant change in the ability and interest of computer science departments to offer new courses for liberal arts and sciences students. With computer science enrollments finally stabilized and even declining, many departments find that they have the faculty resources to provide a selection of courses for non-computer science majors. At the same time that computer science faculty are free enough to look outside their discipline, a number of studies have expressed concern with the state of liberal arts and sciences education in American colleges and universities. Among the concerns expressed by a workshop sponsored by the American Association of Colleges (AAC) was that

> Scientific and technological developments have so outpaced the understanding of science provided by most college programs that we have become a people unable to comprehend the technology that we invent and unable to bring under control our capacity to violate the natural world [2].

The workshop also developed a list of nine experiences that should be integral to liberal arts and science education. Every academic discipline can contribute to these core areas. We will argue that computer science can be a significant contributor.

In this paper we review briefly the development of service courses within computer science departments, and consider a new approach to serving the needs of the student in liberal arts and sciences. Rather than considering which topics of computer science we feel are most useful to these students, we consider the experiences enunciated by AAC and identify computer science topics that contribute to each. In so doing we demonstrate

the central position of computer science in the core of liberal arts and sciences, and indicate how courses could be developed that form a meaningful part of a bachelor's degree and are interesting and challenging for computer science faculty to teach.

We recognize that there is a continuing need for a number of types of courses to be offered as services by computer science departments. Though other types of these courses are also worthy of consideration, this paper deals only with the core material for the liberal arts and sciences bachelor's degree and the role of computer science in meeting the needs of these students.

2 Service Courses

2.1 The Role of Service Courses

For the purposes of our discussion we divide the courses offered by an undergraduate computer science department or program into two parts, major and service. Major courses, which satisfy requirements for students pursuing either a major or a minor in computer science, have been discussed at great length and over a period of at least twenty years in the various curriculum documents and articles published by the ACM and the IEEE Computer Society. The non-major or service courses taught by the department, are, in many cases, addressed to specific groups of students and are designed in cooperation with faculty from other departments or colleges of a university. Of particular concern to us are the service courses addressed to the liberal arts and sciences students.

Service courses for non-majors typically form the core of a liberal arts education and provide the breadth of knowledge that is a fundamental goal of a liberal arts college. These courses perform the functions of introducing the student to the central ideas of the discipline and providing an overview of the issues and problems which scholars in the discipline address. Service courses in the sciences also provide a laboratory experience in which students can follow the paradigm of scientific discovery by posing hypotheses and testing them under controlled conditions. Any service course, whether in the sciences or the humanities, must be designed with the realization that the students will take only one or two courses in the discipline.

These courses should also offer the experiences that are integral to a liberal arts and sciences education. One may not assume that the students have any particular knowledge of the discipline from their previous educational experiences. However, one should be able to assume students have a general sophistication and ability to think critically, to reason logically, and to synthesize ideas. Thus, it is important for service courses to present fundamental ideas and their interactions consistent with the goals of a liberal arts and sciences education.

2.2 Computer Science Service Courses

It is convenient to divide the computer science service courses into two categories. We put all the courses dealing with computational tools into the first category. These include courses about applications programs, such as "Using dBase III", courses describing a particular programming language, such as "Fortran for Engineers", and courses for the novice, such as "Your First Steps with MSDOS". In many cases, service courses in the first category are designed in cooperation with the discipline whose majors take the course. The role of these courses is to give the students a particular skill which they will find useful in the rest of their college and professional careers. The second category of courses contains those for which the assumption about minimal background knowledge is false. These courses may be offered to upper division students and will address specific areas where computing, either in design or in experimentation, has a strong influence on the discipline. Examples of such courses are "Data Communication for Scientists" and "Data Analysis and Evaluation in the Social Sciences". This is a largely untapped area in need of further development.

2.3 History of Computer Science Service Courses

Until 1962, however, all computing courses were service courses because no degree programs existed in computer science. The first service courses in computing were, appropriately, about computer hardware and software. They were much more technical and detailed than courses now are, because they had to be. Details were necessary to program in machine language, to wire boards and eventually to write assembly language code. With the advent of higher level languages (e.g. Fortran, COBOL), programming courses could concentrate more on language syntax and algorithm design and less on specific hardware details.

Curriculum '68 [4] included a section on the need for service courses, minors and continuing education. The report cited the estimate of the Pierce Report [1] that curricula of about 75% of all college undergraduates would be enhanced by computer training. Curriculum '68 suggested that the other 25% of students might also benefit. Curriculum '78 [5] cited the need for service courses in three categories: liberal arts or general university requirements, supporting work for majors in other disciplines, and continuing education.

Programming courses in specific languages have always been a major component of the service course offerings in computing. However, courses on societal impact became prevalent in the late 1970s and early 1980s as computer applications became more visible to the general public. These were followed by courses that featured hands-on experience in applications software as low cost personal computers became readily available. All of these courses were directed primarily to a general audience or to computer users. Some courses appeared that introduced students to the discipline of computer sciences [3]. These courses enabled students to find out about the discipline, often as a means to determine their interests in becoming a major.

It was clear to the developers of Curriculum '68 and Curriculum '78 that departments of computer science could offer important services to the entire academic community. Departments, to the extent that they could, provided service courses, but primarily of the kind that imparted facts and information with some hands-on experience. Very few of these courses required, or even encouraged, students to reason, analyze, understand, or evaluate. We were, and are, performing a service at the levels of knowing about and using computers, but not at the deeper levels that should characterize a person with a Liberal Arts and Sciences (LAS) education.

Departments of computer science need to do better, to provide a service to LAS students that is more in keeping with the goals of LAS. In a later section of this paper, we identify topics and areas within computer science that pertain to the goals. First, however, it is important to specify the kinds of experiences students should gain from a LAS education.

3 Liberal Arts and Sciences Education

In February, 1985, the Association of American Colleges published the report "Integrity in the College Curriculum: A Report to the Academic Community" [2]. The report resulted from a three-year study begun in January, 1982, as the Project on Redefining the Meaning and Purpose of Baccalaureate Degrees.

One of the sections of the report identified the following nine experiences as essential to a coherent undergraduate education, one that would enable graduates to fulfill "their promise as individual humans and their obligations as democratic citizens" [2, p.15]. The cited experiences are

1. inquiry, abstract logical thinking, critical analysis,

2. literacy: writing, reading, speaking, listening,

3. understanding numerical data,

4. historical consciousness,

5. science,

6. values,

7. art,

8. international and multicultural experiences, and

9. study in depth.

These experiences result from a program of study, not necessarily from any specific course. All disciplines combine with study in a major area to provide the experiences. Methods and processes, not just learning facts, provide the necessary experiences. For example, students should experience how scientists arrive at conclusions and what enables scientists to say the conclusions are accurate; students should not just be given the conclusions.

Meanings for many of the experiences are suggested by the titles given, but there is room for several interpretations. We provide a brief summary of the meanings in order to establish a context for contributions of computer science.

Inquiry, abstract logical thinking and critical analysis refer to the thinking process that enables humans to establish facts, combine facts to draw conclusions, to arrive at meaning, and to create ideas.

Literacy pertains to competence in writing, reading, speaking, and listening. One should be adept in these skills through knowledge and practice. Here competence represents a high level of attainment, not an overview or summary as is often implied in the use of the term "literacy".

Understanding numerical data requires the ability to interpret and represent numerical data as well as to recognize the misuse of data.

Historical consciousness involves comprehending present situations as a point in the evolution through time of a complex collection of thoughts, actions, and circumstances.

Science pertains to the recognition of what a scientific discipline is, and what are its processes. It requires understanding that its concepts and conclusions are human acts of intelligence and creativity, that it has inherent limitations, and that it impacts and informs other disciplines.

Values refers to the ability to make informed choices and assume responsibility for them as well as to understand one's own behavior.

Art includes appreciation and experience in both fine arts and performing arts, and knowledge of the language of these arts.

International and multicultural experiences lead to an understanding of how different people live and think and the reasons for these differences.

Study in depth implies a focused search, improving analytical capabilities and leading to more thorough perspective and knowledge of a topic or discipline over time.

4 Meeting the LAS Core Criteria with Computer Science Topics

Because there is renewed interest in providing a solid core for a liberal education we propose a new approach to the design of computer science service courses based on the fundamental elements of a liberal arts and sciences education. Computer science here serves as a vehicle to develop students' ability to analyze, synthesize and evaluate. For each of the AAC experiences we offer a selection of appropriate computer science topics.

Inquiry, abstract logical thinking, and critical analysis. This first criterion is the strongest contribution of computer science in the LAS core. The goals can be met by algorithm development and analysis, program design, implementation and testing, and all the methods of systems analysis and software engineering. The programming topic of data types, the representation of real or imagined items in a form that can be manipulated by computer, is an exercise in abstraction. In another approach, the introduction of abstract machines such as the Turing machine or Petri net contributes to meeting this goal. The idea of computability is a topic that is suitable here and also meets the desirable goal of introducing the limitations of computers as well as their power. Inquiry suggests also the topics of database and expert systems. In fact, there are few topics in computer science that would not contribute directly and significantly to meeting this criteria.

Literacy. Programming language development is a topic that explores the nature of communication including the acceptability of ambiguity and some errors in human communication and the need for precision and correctness in communication with machines. In addition, the necessity of expressing the needs and expectations of users of computer programs can be explored. Searching for a program to meet a particular need would be a valuable exercise in this context. In addition, in direct response to the AAC expectation, students should read the popular literature about computers, their developments and uses. They should read critically, looking for instances where the writer was not well-informed or where inaccurate or misleading information is included. Oral presentation of the results of this critical reading should be included whenever possible. In another approach to developing literacy in LAS students, a course may investigate ways in which word processing impacts the task of writing. The ease of making changes allows fine-tuning that would not otherwise be done. Perhaps it is now more feasible to write by filling in an outline. The advanatages that word processing offers some writers may handicap others by interfering with spontaneity.

Understanding numerical data. Number systems and the representation of decimal values in binary fit in here. The inability to represent simple decimal values such as one-tenth in binary gives rise to discussion of accuracy of information stored in the computer and the significance of roundoff errors. Such topics as the coding and transmission of data, pattern recognition, and image enhancement support this LAS experience. Methods used, reliability, and important application areas are appropriate subtopics. Graphic vs. tabular presentation of data should be illustrated and compared.

Historical consciousness. The development of computers and computer languages belongs in this area. In addition, the role of computer-based technology in human history should be included. The developing information age and changes in the location and nature of work are relevant.

Science. Methods in simulation and modelling are important here, as well as the use of these methods to conduct experiments that could not otherwise be performed. Uses of the scientific method in computer science belong here also, for example, the development and testing of heuristics where exact solutions are not feasible.

Values. Ethics issues relevant to the use and development of computers and computer systems provide a forum for discussion of values. Issues such as hackers, privacy, and the debate regarding SDI research funds provide examples of topic areas.

Art. The computer as a tool in the extension of human creativity should be explored. Some examples include the development of a language or representation system for dance, the growing dependence of theatres on computer assistance, the use of CADD systems in archi-

tecture, the question of the artistic merit of computer generated art and music, and the use of computers in film production.

International and multicultural experiences. Questions of transborder data flow arise here. Topics chosen should also include the use of computers in producing world models including limits-to-growth predictions, the importance of modern communication systems including computer-controlled telephone systems, and the growing use of electronic mail, the cooperative research efforts made possible by nearly instantaneous mail and file transfer facilities, the rapid reporting of news events around the world. Another relevant topic is the international competition for technological superiority. Cultural considerations such as the impact of work at home and the potential impact of computers in schools could also be explored here.

Depth of study. The use and misuse of computer science provide a wealth of topics suitable for in-depth study by LAS students. Individuals or small groups should research the impact of computers in a particular application area.

5 An Example

Section 4's simple listing of topics within each of the nine areas of experience illustrates the fact that computer science does contain material that substantially contributes to an LAS education, but does not indicate how suitable courses can be developed. It is possible to conclude from reading the collection of topics in the list that many colleges already offer appropriate courses. However, the common approaches to these courses are to cover many topics at an introductory level. We are suggesting a different approach.

Course design begins by selecting the experiences to be targeted. Several different courses with sets of experiences may be needed. These may be based on the disciplines of the students – some may have a greater need for emphasis on inquiry, abstract logical thinking, and critical analysis than they have for literacy, for example. Once the role of the course in the LAS education has been decided, appropriate computer science topics are selected, based on their relevance to the role chosen for this course. Many worthwhile topics will have to be left out of the course because the design goal is to *serve* the LAS education, not to teach computer science.

The following example illustrates the approach suggested above. We develop a module that emphasizes inquiry, abstract logical thinking, critical analysis, literacy, values and understanding numerical data for students in the social sciences. A project involving the interpretation of demographic data forms the base of the module. Students are taught to collect data and organize a database or are instructed to investigate existing databases to obtain the data they need. Class presentations and discussions focus on what a database is, how it is designed and developed, how user needs affect the result, criteria for selecting query languages and applications software, and issues of security, integrity, and privacy. Students conduct experiments with database software packages and integrated software, then report on the ease of use, clarity of documentation, advantages and disadvantages, what criteria determine when each should be used, ways in which data can be presented, and for a specific case what information can be obtained from given data (including accuracy and limitations). Students also investigate existing laws pertaining to privacy and databases or effectiveness (and limitations) of security measures. Class discussions include why the Data Encryption Standard was developed and how it works, characteristics of database languages and how they differ from or are the same as other programming languages, and case studies that illustrate the process of specification, design, implementation, testing, and verification. Laboratories include learning and practicing database querying to help understand capabilities and limitations of application software so that a comparative analysis can be made. A module of this kind could easily encompass most of a course, or it could be broken into submodules that could be covered in a shorter time. In either case, the selection, presentation, and assignment of material is done with the objective of providing students several of the nine experiences of an LAS education.

6 Conclusions and Recommendations

The nine experiences identified by the Association of American Colleges as fundamental to a liberal arts and sciences education form a framework for the design of service courses in computer science to be offered to liberal arts majors. Computer science can contribute in significant ways to all of the experiences. Consequently it can play a vital role as a discipline in the core of the liberal arts and sciences.

As colleges and universities examine their core requirements for liberal arts and sciences students, they should include computer science as a discipline whose study will meet many of the goals of liberal arts and sciences education. Courses should be constructed from the ideas we have given above to fit with the resources and needs of the individual school. Each of these courses should consist of a few topics, covered with care and depth so that they form a coherent whole from pieces

that provide some of the fundamental experiences.

References

[1] *Computers in higher education*. President's Science Advisory Committee The White House. Washington,D.C., February 1967.

[2] *Integrity in the College Curriculum: A Report to the Academic Community*. Assoication of American Colleges, February 1985.

[3] Schneider G. Michael. A proposed redesign of the introductory service course in computer science. *SIGCSE Bulletin*, 18(4):15–21, December 1986.

[4] Curriculum Committee on Computer Science. Curriculum 68, recommendations for academic programs in computer science. *Communications of the ACM*, 11(3):151–197, March 1968.

[5] Curriculum Committee on Computer Science. Curriculum '78, recommendations for the undergraduate program in computer science. *Communications of the ACM*, 22(3):147–166, March 1979.

Using Generics Modules to Enhance the CS2 Course

Ashok Kumar
John Beidler
Dept. of Computer Science
University of Scranton
Scranton, PA 18510

(717) 961-7774

Bitnet: KUMAR@SCRANTON

Abstract

We normally expect features in a programming language to support the concepts and methodologies in the course. This article describes another role for features within a programming language, support of sound educational methodology. Specifically, this paper describes how the library module capability in Modula-2 may be used to formally separate the concept from the implementation of abstract data types. That is, by having generic support for various structures, the structures can be taught at a conceptual level and students are given assignments to use these structures long before the implementations of the structures are taught. The result is a clear separation of concept and implementation and a better understanding of the structures as ADTs.

1. Introduction

The CS 2 recommendations of the CS 1/CS 2 Task Force of the ACM's Education Board ([3] and [4]) call for a broad based course that includes many topics that were originally covered as part of a data structures course. The syllabus calls for the coverage of the concept, application, and implementation of stacks, queues, lists, and trees. Good programming practice dictates that these topics be presented as abstract data types (ADT), separating the **concept** from the **implementation**. However, practically all CS 2 texts only pay lip service to this separation by presenting a concept and immediately following it by the implementation.

We believe that more than just lip service should be paid to the ADT approach. Although the implementations should eventually be covered, there is much to be said for a more complete physical separation of concept and implementation. It helps students to distinguish between conceptual considerations and implementational details. Our approach makes this separation as complete as possible by placing several weeks of material between the conceptual presentation of the ADTs and the eventual discussion of possible implementations.

The separation of concept from implementation is achieved through generic Modula 2 library modules. By **Generic Modules** we mean the modules support instances of these structures regardless of the type of objects being placed in the structure. That is, a stack is a stack regardless of whether it contains characters, integers, records, or some other type of object. Several years ago we developed generic support modules for stacks, queues, lists, and trees [2]. Subsequent sections of this paper describe the generic modules, how they help us achieve our goals in the CS 2 course, and report on our experiences using these modules as support for the CS 2 course. These sections investigate both the positive and negative aspect of our approach. Section 2 discusses the generic modules for the sequential structures, stacks, queues, and lists.

Section 3 describes our generic support for trees. It also demonstrates the importance of planning a consistent approach. By having consistency between the modules low level implementational details are avoided and full consideration is given to the concept under study.

The last section evaluates our approach and discusses justification of the use of the generic modules as a better alternative to the current approach.

2. Sequential Modules :

Figure 1 describes the generic support modules for stacks, queues, and lists. Besides the expected support for each ADT, each module also exports four additional procedures that are necessary for initializing and reporting on the status of instances of each structure.

MODULE	STACKs	QUEUEs	LISTs
Object type	STACK	QUEUE	LIST POSITION
Operations	Push Pop	Enqueu Dequeue	InsertBefore InsertAfter Delete LookAt Update Move fore, aft front, rear SetPosition GetPosition
Support	Create Destroy Successful Status	Create Destroy Successfu Status	Create Destroy Successful Status

Figure 1: Identifiers exported by STACKs, QUEUEs, and LISTs

2.1 Consistency between modules :

Although the generic modules hide implementational details, there are still low level considerations that must be handled. For example, although

TYPE Stack : STACK ;

might define an object of type STACK, this object, like any other variable must be initialized. The procedure Create, exported by each module, initializes its parameter,

Create (Stack) ;

to a null stack. Destroy is the complementary operation that takes an object and erases the instance of that object.

The procedures Successful and Status report on the results of the last operation on a particular instance of a structure. For example, if an attempt is made to pop an object from an empty stack,

POP (Stack, Data) ;

the procedure Successful may be used to determine the result and control the program accordingly,

```
IF Successful (Stack) THEN
    (* success action *)
ELSE
    (* failure action *)
END (*IF*) ;
```

The procedure Status reports a more detailed description of the cause of a failed operation.

By providing consistent support between modules, no additional low level details are encountered as students learn new concepts, hence they can concentrate on the concepts.

One concept that transcends structures is the concept of current, or active, position. With a stack the active position is the top. With a queue there are two active positions, one for insertion, the rear, and one for extraction, the front. This concept extends to lists, and eventually to non-sequential structures. With lists, the current position may be altered as required. The Move command,

Move (List, Direction) ;

alters the current position in the list depending upon the value of the second parameter as follows:

1. front - The current position becomes the front.

2. rear - The current position becomes the rear.

3. fore - The current position is moved one object towards the front of the list.

4. aft - The current position is moved one object towards the rear of the list.

All operations are performed relative to the current position. In addition to the Move command, the procedures InsertBefore, InsertAfter, and Delete also alter the current position. After an insert operation, the new object in the list becomes the current position. After a Delete operation, the new current position is the object "fore" of the one deleted. If there was no object before the deleted object, then the object "aft" becomes the new current position.

LookAt allows the current object to be viewed and Update allows the current object to be modified. The procedures Successful and Status report on the other operations in a manner analogous to the procedures with the same name in the STACKs and QUEUEs modules.

2.2 Sample CS 2 Assignments using STACKs, QUEUEs, and LISTs

1. Convert a fully paranthesised arithmetic expression to a reverse polish expression (RPE) and evaluate a RPE using the library modules STACKs and QUEUEs.

2. Use STACKs and QUEUEs to build simple machines to recognize various languages. For example,

    i. $L = \{xcx^r \mid x \text{ in } \{0,1\}^*, \text{ and } x^r \text{ is the reversal of the string } x\}$

    ii. $L = \{xcx \mid x \text{ in } \{0,1\}^*\}$

    iii. $L = \{xayazaw \mid x,y,z \text{ in } \{0,1\}^* \text{ and } w = x, w = z, \text{ or } w = y^r\}$

3. Assignment dealing with Creation of two or more lists of records and performing Update and Merging processes using the Library module LISTs (For example bank transaction program).

2.3 Generic Modules and Recursion

Part of our consideration in building these modules was that they support typical algorithmic (coding) practices in a normal non-contrived way. One of our concerns was the problems of traversing ADTs with recursive algorithms. Our experience has been very positive in this regard. In particular, recursive list processing is natural and direct with these modules.

In fact, we found recursive list processing is relatively error free because the generic module emphasizes processing relative to the current position. Most problems surrounding list processing are avoided because most errors are due to improper consideration of the current position in the list. Through these modules, we encourage standardization of recursive processing around an a statment sequence that first sets the current position then tests for success. We believe that all recursive list processing can be described by with the code template,

```
PROCEDURE RecursiveExample ( ... )

IF Successful (list) OR (* other reason *)
THEN
        (* recursive process here *)
(**)        Move (...) (* reset current position *)
(**)        RecursiveExample ( ... ) (* recursion *)
ELSE
        (* termination process *)
END (* IF *) ;
```

for the recursive procedure and the initial call to the procedure as

> Move (...) (* set initial position *)
> RecursiveExample (...) (* first call *)

which is similar to the recursive call in the procedure.

3. Non-sequential Modules

To simplify the transition from sequential data structures to non-sequential data structures, consistency is maintained to help the transition. The normal low-level support provided through the identifiers like Create, Destroy, Successful, and Status are carried over. Also, the concept of current position as a method of viewing a structure provides a smooth transition from the sequential generic structures to trees. For example, the two tree modules contain Move procedures that function in a manner analogous to the Move procedure in LISTs.

The two modules that support trees are BITREEs and TREEs. The BITREEs supports binary trees and TREEs supports n-ary trees. Figure 2 lists the identifiers exported by the BITREEs module. The TREEs module exports a similar list of identifiers. From the point of view of users the fundamental distinction between the two tree modules is in the enumeration that support traversal of the trees. The BITREEs module exports the enumeration,

> DIRECTION = (root, parent, leftchild, rightchild) ;

while the TREEs module exports the enumeration

> DIRECTION = (root, parent, firstchild, nextsibling, previoussibling) ;

The enumeration DIRECTION in BITREEs forces the limitation of two children per node.

Type	TREE
	DIRECTION = (root, parent, leftchild, rightchild)
Operations	Move (Tree, Direction)
	Attach (Tree, Node)
	LookAt (Tree, Node)
	Update (Tree, Node)
	Prune (Tree, Subtree)
	Graft (Tree, Subtree)
	GetSubtree (Tree, Subtree)
	SetSubtree (Tree, Subtree)
Support	Create (Tree)
	Destroy (Tree)
	Successful (Tree)
	Status (Tree)
	Exists (Tree, Direction)

Figure 2: Identifiers Exported by the BITREEs Module

Although both modules are available, we decided to concentrate on binary trees. Only after a thorough discussion of binary trees and tree traversals are n-ary trees briefly discussed.

A major advantage of using the generic modules to support the basic abstract data types was our ability to avoid low level details. Also, by maintaining consistency between the modules, we build upon the previous experience of students as new ADTs are introduced. For example, the transition from stacks and queues to lists centers upon the notion of current position, which fits naturally into a disciplined presentation of lists.

The discussion of trees builds upon the discussion of stacks, queues, and lists. The concept of current position that was introduced with the sequential structures is carried over to the discussion of trees. It provides all necessary access to trees and helps maintain control of the growth and traversal of trees. The enumeration DIRECTION in BITREEs, when used in conjunction with the Move and Attach operations, make it easy to clearly build and traverse binary trees in a natural way, including recursive algorithms.

Because of the non-sequential nature of tree structures, an additional support procedure, Exists, is exported by the module. Exists allows a user to test for the existence of a node at a particular location before moving or attaching. The program in Figure 3 is a typical illustration of a recursive procedure whose recursion is controlled through the use of procedure **Exists**. The algorithm in Figure 3 is the skeleton of a recursive natural order tree search algorithm.

```
PROCEDURE NatTreeSearch (VAR Tree : TREE) ;

    PROCEDURE RecursiveSearch ;

        BEGIN (* RecursiveSearch *)
        (* node related processing here *)
        IF Exists (Tree, leftchild) THEN
            Move (Tree, leftchild) ;
            RecursiveSearch ;
            Move (Tree, parent)
        END (*IF*)
        (* AND/OR node related processing here *)
        IF Exists (Tree, rightchild) THEN
            Move (Tree, rightchild) ;
            RecursiveSearch ;
            Move (Tree, parent)
        END (*IF*)
        (* AND/OR node related processing here *)
        END RecursiveSearch ;

    BEGIN (* NatTreeSearch *)
    (* save the current position in the tree *)
    GetSubtree (Tree, CurrentNode) ;
    Move (tree, root) ;
    RecursiveSearch ;
    (* restore the current position *)
    SetSubtree (Tree, CurrentNode ) ;
    END NatTreeSearch ;
```

Figure 3: Natural Order Tree Search

The following assignments are typical of the assignments that use the TREEs module.

1. Read a set of random numbers and create a binary tree using the less than-greater than relation between numbers (less = left child, greater = right child). Write a recursive procedure to print the tree in order. Determine the length of the longest path and print the numbers along the path.

2. Build a binary tree using International Morse Code using "." equals left and "-" equals right and use the tree to efficiently translate from Morse Code.

A third assignment is given using heaps. That assignment is given after sorting and tree implementations are discussed.

4.   **Conclusions**

The fundamental reason for presenting ADTs is hiding details, presenting the right things at the right time. ADTs are a valuable teaching tool that helps separate concept from implementation. The Modula 2 generic modules provide good support at a minimum cost. There is a cost. The cost is the way generics are implemented in Modula 2, by overriding Modula 2's strong type checking. This means that there is no type checking being performed on the objects being manipulated by the modules. However, the generics have been implemented in such a way as to perform some checking on the sizes of the objects as well as verifying that the objects were initialized using the Create procedures. It has been our experience that the modules' testing for non-initialized structures more than compensates for our overriding of strong type checking.

The ADTs are presented with no discussion of implementational details. Those are discussed late in the course as part of a presentation on hardware-software details and on advanced concepts. For example, in a discussion of hardware-software details, the possible uses of arrays to represent the ADTs is discussed along with the limitations that arrays force onto the structures.

Array representations of stacks and queues are discussed in some length. The use of arrays to represent heaps is described, and is also used to demonstrate the heap sort. Pointer variables are also discussed, but it is our opinion that a complete discussion of pointer implementations of the ADTs is more appropriate in our data structures course.

In general, our goal in the CS 2 course is to develop concepts and a general appreciation of the discipline of computer science. In line with those goals we believe that the students are better served by emphasizing concepts and providing only as many details as necessary. The generic support modules help us do that. Our experience indicates that this approach does pay-off. For example, students enter the data structures course with a better understanding of concepts, hence are better prepared for an indepth study of details.

An important by-product of the use of generics has been the development of a good aproach to software development, namely, the attitude of looking through a library of resources rather than always attempting to completely build a program from the ground up. Students learn to browse through the definition modules and use the support provided through the library, hence they concentrate more of their programming efforts at a high level, where most programming projects really fail.

References

1. ACM Curriculum Committee on Computer Science Curriculum '78, "Recommendations For The Undergraduate Program In Computer Science", CACM 22, 3(Mar. 1979), 147-166.

2. Beidler, John, and P. Jackowitz, "Consistent Generics In Modula-2", SIGPLAN Notices, 21:4 (April 1986), 32-41.

3. Koffman, E.B., P.L. Miller, and C.E. Wardle, "Recommended Curriculum for CS1", CACM 27, 10(Oct. 1984), 998-1001.

4. Koffman, E.B., D. Stemple, and C.E.Wardle, "Recommended Curriculum for CS2", CACM 28, 8(Aug. 1985), 815-818.

5. Riley, D.D., "Data Abstraction and Structures", Boyd & Fraser, 1987.

Developing Programming Quizzes to Support
Instruction in Abstract Data Types

Barry L. Kurtz
Heather D. Pfeiffer

Computer Science Department, 3CU
BOX 30001
New Mexico State University
Las Cruces, NM 88003
505-646-3723

Abstract

A variety of Computer Aided Instruction (CAI) and Intelligent CAI (ICAI) software has demonstrated that computers can be used effectively for computer science education. Unfortunately, this software is difficult to develop. It may rely on specialized software tools or particular hardware configurations, and, as a result, rarely is used beyond the institution that originally developed the software. For the last five years we have used tutorials, drills, and programming quizzes in our CS1 level course at New Mexico State University. Programming quizzes are the most cost effective of these components and we have now developed a complete package of quizzes to support instruction in abstract data types for the CS2 level course. The focus of this paper is not to announce a finished product, rather it concentrates on showing the reader how one can develop their own individualized programming quizzes locally with a minimum of resources. In fact, the development of these quizzes can make fine programming projects for more advanced classes.

1. Introduction

Many research projects have developed CAI and ICAI materials to help teach introductory programming. Proust [Johnson, Soloway, 1985] is perhaps the best and widest known of the ICAI projects; it uses *post-hoc* analysis to help students find their bugs in compiled Pascal programs. Work has also been done on Lisp tutors. [Reiser, Anderson, and Farrell, 1985] These systems are impressive and may even become available commercially, as evidenced by MicroProust; however, they are elaborate systems that require years for development, an effort not easily duplicated at the local level. Traditional CAI often suffers from the same limitation; namely, it is impractical for the user to modify or extend the packaged materials. And it is virtually impossible for the user to develop new materials from scratch. This paper describes how to develop effective computer based materials to test knowledge of abstract data types without substantial research funding. These efforts can be easily duplicated at the local level and easily extended to new materials.

This work is in the tradition of the computer lab activities first developed by Ken Bowles. [1978] Those activities included drill and practice materials, and programming quizzes. Steve Franklin used similar approaches to develop an introductory math course at U.C. Irvine [Franklin, 1976].

Franklin and Volper [in print] extended the Bowles' materials to include a wider range of topics. At New Mexico State, J. Mack Adams developed elaborate tutorials to supplement the drills and programming quizzes for teaching Pascal [Adams, 1983]. As part of the same effort, Barry MacKichan and Roger Hunter developed tutorial materials to teach trigonometry [Adams, 1981]. Both sets of materials are still in use today.

The development work discussed above applied only to the CS1 level course. Kurtz [1983, 1984, 1985] reports on elaborate simulations to support CS2 and CS3 level courses; however, these tutorials often take many months to implement for each individual topic. For distribution to others, tutorials depend on a particular machine with a specific graphics system and other hardware requirement. These limitations, combined with an "I want to do it myself" attitude, has usually limited the use of CAI software to the institution at which it was developed.

The Pascal materials developed at NMSU have been moved to Modula-2 [Gabrini, 1986] and have recently been adapted to run in a networked environment under Unix using Sun microcomputers. In moving and adapting materials, it became evident that the programming quizzes (p-quizzes) require little underlying software support. Many new quizzes were quickly developed for language features of Modula-2 not present in Pascal. Unlike tutorials and drills, the p-quizzes do not depend on any graphics or windowing software. They can be augmented with programs to provide automatic security checks or recording of grades, but such software is ancillary to the true purpose of p-quizzes. The only basic requirement for implementing p-quizzes is a good compiler.

The use of abstract data types (ADTs) in the CS2 course has been discussed for over a decade and now that languages such as Modula-2, Ada and Scheme are widely available, use of ADTs is fairly common. The p-quizzes for this course fall into two major categories:
- given an ADT for a particular structure (e.g. a stack of integers), use only this ADT to perform a particular operation on the structure (e.g. increment every integer in the stack)
- given a particular ADT implementation (e.g. an array implementation for a stack), add a new procedure to the implementation (e.g. a function to return the number of items in the stack)

The "standard" data structures covered in CS2 are: stacks, queues, linked lists, binary trees, binary search trees, and tables. Each data structure needs a group of p-quizzes dealing with ADT use and ADT implementation. Often the use of an ADT has to be embedded in a particular problem domain. For example, a sorted linked list keyed by an integer value and containing a real value can be used to represent a polynomial of one variable. This particular example illustrates the construction of one ADT (polynomials) on top of another ADT (a linked list structure).

This paper describes the development of p-quizzes to support the use and implementation of abstract data types in a CS2 course. These p-quizzes have been tested successfully at New Mexico State and are available for distribution. However, the point of this paper is to show readers how to develop and use their own p-quizzes without reliance on particular hardware configurations or software tools. P-quizzes are effective pedagogical software that can be developed individually and quickly almost anyway. This paper tells you "how to do it." All of our examples are in Modula-2; however, they could easily be adapted to Pascal (with separately compiled units) or Ada.

2. Example Quizzes

We will consider three specific examples in the following sections:
(1) write a procedure to copy a stack S1 into a stack S2
(2) add a procedure to an ADT for queues that returns the number of items in the queue (note that this algorithm will be highly dependent on the representation)
(3) add a procedure to an ADT for polynomials that adds two polynomials given an ADT for a linked list keyed by an integer value and containing a real value

All ADTs are assumed to be opaque to prevent access to the structure itself outside of the implementation module.

2.1 Copy Stack

The p-quiz problem statement is to copy a stack S1 into a stack S2; students are warned that S1 must remain the same after the procedure is executed. A correct solution is shown in Figure 1.

```
PROCEDURE StudentQuiz(S1:IntStack;VAR S2:IntStack);
VAR TempStack: IntStack;
    Number: INTEGER;
BEGIN
  CreateIntStack(TempStack);
  WHILE NOT EmptyIntStack(S1) DO
    PopInt(S1, Number);
    PushInt(TempStack, Number);
  END;  (* WHILE *)
  CreateIntStack(S2);
  WHILE NOT EmptyIntStack(TempStack) DO
    PopInt(TempStack, Number);
    PushInt(S2, Number);
    PushInt(S1, Number);
  END; (* WHILE *)
  DisposeIntStack(TempStack);
END StudentQuiz;
```

Figure 1 : Copy a Stack

Some of the problems students encounter are:
- realizing that popping a stack leaves it altered even when a value parameter is used
- realizing that a sequence of pop-push pairs reverses a stack
- realizing that the original stack must be restored at the same time the new stack is built

This p-quiz and its equivalent versions help to reinforce the concepts of stacks and 'bring home' the functionality of stacks.

2.2 Number of Items in Queue

The p-quiz problem statement is to add a procedure to a queue ADT that returns the number of items in the queue; however, the implementation of a solution is highly dependent on the underlying representation. If an array representation is used, the solution involves an arithmetic expression on indices, as shown in Figure 2.

```
PROCEDURE StudentQuiz (Q: IntQueue) : CARDINAL;
BEGIN
  IF Q^.Front <= Q^.Rear THEN
    RETURN Q^.Rear - Q^.Front;
  ELSE
    RETURN QueueSpace - (Q^.Front - Q^.Rear);
  END;  (* IF *)
END StudentQuiz;
```

Figure 2 : Size of a Queue

If the queue is a linked structure, then a scanning pointer can be used. The greatest difficulty students have is with limiting cases such as an empty queue, a queue of one element, or, in the case of an array implementation, a full queue. It is important that all such limiting cases be included in the test program. This p-quiz and its equivalent versions tests the student's understanding of the actual representation for the queue and requires care in implementing an algorithm that works for all cases.

2.3 Addition of Two Polynomials

This example is more challenging; the problem statement given to students is shown in Figure 3.

INFORMATION FOR PROGRAMMING QUIZ AddP

For this programming quiz you are write a procedure that adds two polynomials together to form the sum polynomial. You will need to import the type polynomial from the module PolyType. You may only use the objects in the DEFINITION MODULE LinkLists shown at the end of this file. This abstract data type is a list of elements each containing an integer key and an associated real value. The list is sorted in decreasing order from the largest integer value to the smallest.

EXAMPLE POLYNOMIAL:

$3.2 \, x^2 + 4.5 \, x - 7.8$

would be represented as

P1 --| 3.2 | 2 |---| 4.5 | 1 |---| -7.8 | 0 |

EXAMPLE ADDITION:

P1 --| 3.2 | 2 |---| 4.5 | 1 |---| -7.8 | 0 |

plus

P2 --| 3.0 | 3 |---| -4.5 | 1 |

would give

Result --| 3.0 | 3 |---| 3.2 | 2 |---| -7.8 | 0 |

If you need to use a sentinel value, MAX(INTEGER) is available. If you use any temporary data structures in your procedure, be sure to dispose of them using the operations provided. IMPORTANT: after the operation is completed, P1 and P2 must be the same as when they were passed into the procedure.

Your program should look exactly like the program below:

```
IMPLEMENTATION MODULE PQAddP;
FROM PolyType IMPORT polynomial;
(* place any other imports here *)
  PROCEDURE StudentQuiz (    P1, P2 : polynomial;
                         VAR Result : polynomial );
  (* place any declarations here *)
  BEGIN
    (* place any statements here *)
  END StudentQuiz;

END PQAddP.
```

Figure 3 : Problem Statement for Adding Two Polynomials

The problem is essentially that of merging two sorted files. Students are given the definition module LinkLists that maintains a list of integer, real pairs keyed in descending order by the integer value. Operations needed from this ADT are DefineIntLL, EmptyIntLL, CurrentKeyIntLL, CurrentRealIntLL, GetNextIntLL, and InsertIntLL. One correct solution is shown in Figure 4.

```
PROCEDURE StudentQuiz (P1, P2 : polynomial;
                      VAR Result : polynomial);
VAR Term1, Term2: polynomial;
    Coef: REAL;
BEGIN
 DefineIntLL( Result );
 Term1 := P1;
 Term2 := P2;
 LOOP
  IF EmptyIntLL(Term1) AND EmptyIntLL(Term2) THEN
    EXIT;
  ELSIF NOT EmptyIntLL(Term1) AND
        NOT EmptyIntLL(Term2) THEN
   IF CurrentKeyIntLL(Term1) >
                    CurrentKeyIntLL(Term2) THEN
    InsertIntLL(Result, CurrentKeyIntLL(Term1),
                    CurrentRealIntLL(Term1));
    Term1 := GetNextIntLL(Term1);
   ELSIF CurrentKeyIntLL(Term1) <
                    CurrentKeyIntLL(Term2) THEN
    InsertIntLL(Result, CurrentKeyIntLL(Term2),
                    CurrentRealIntLL(Term2));
    Term2 := GetNextIntLL(Term2);
   ELSE   (* both terms have the same exponent *)
    Coef:=CurrentRealIntLL(Term1) +
                    CurrentRealIntLL(Term2);
    IF Coef # 0.0 THEN
     InsertIntLL(Result, CurrentKeyIntLL(Term1),
                    Coef);
    END; (* IF *)
    Term1 := GetNextIntLL(Term1);
    Term2 := GetNextIntLL(Term2);
   END; (* IF *)
  ELSIF EmptyIntLL(Term1) THEN
    InsertIntLL(Result, CurrentKeyIntLL(Term2),
                    CurrentRealIntLL(Term2));
    Term2 := GetNextIntLL(Term2);
  ELSE
    InsertIntLL(Result, CurrentKeyIntLL(Term1),
                    CurrentRealIntLL(Term1));
    Term1 := GetNextIntLL(Term1);
  END; (* IF *)
 END; (* LOOP *)
END StudentQuiz;
```

Figure 4 : Adding Two Polynomials

Many students have difficulties in handling the case where one polynomial is exhausted before the other one. Even subtler problems arise when terms "cancel out." This p-quiz tests the student's understanding of both linked lists and the merge operation.

3. Sample Test Programs

Along with the p-quizzes, a p-quiz test system must also be developed. The software required to implement such a system comes in two varieties:
- performing the actual tests
- performing ancillary functions such as recording of grades and providing system security.

P-quizzes can be used successfully without the latter software; therefore, this section describes essential software.

Usually the data structure ADT does not provide all the necessary software to test the program. For example, the stack ADT only provides operations to create and dispose of a stack, test whether a stack is empty or full, and procedures to push an item onto a stack and pop an item off of a stack. The test program must have additional utilities to generate a random stack, copy a stack, print a stack, and a boolean procedure to compare two stacks. We recommend that these utility procedures be developed and compiled separately since they will undoubtably be used by several versions of p-quizzes involving stacks. An example definition module for stack utilities is shown in Figure 5.

```
DEFINITION MODULE StackUtilities;
FROM IntStacks IMPORT IntStack;

PROCEDURE RandomIntStack(MinSize,MaxSize: CARDINAL;
        MinValue,MaxValue: INTEGER; VAR S: IntStack);
(* Creates a stack of integers such that
   MinSize <= # elements in stack <= MaxSize
   MinValue <= random element value <= MaxValue *)

PROCEDURE CompareIntStacks (S1, S2 : IntStack)
                                : BOOLEAN;
(* Returns TRUE if S1 and S2 contain the same
integer values in the same order; otherwise
returns FALSE                                *)

PROCEDURE CopyIntStack(S1:IntStack; VAR S2:IntStack)
(* Make a copy of S1 into S2; if S2 already exists,
then it is written over.                      *)

PROCEDURE PrintIntStack (S: IntStack);
(* Print the integer values stored in S starting
with the top value at the left; performs a linefeed
every ten values.                             *)

END StackUtilities.
```

Figure 5 : Stack Utility Routines

A test program would contain the following items:
- a procedure that represents a correct solution to the p-quiz
- a boolean procedure that, given a set of test conditions, tests the equivalence of results from the student's procedure and the built-in procedure, and either returns TRUE if they are equivalent or returns FALSE after printing an error message indicating why the student's solution failed
- a main program that tests a reasonable number of test cases, including limiting conditions, that either prints a success message or terminates after the first failure

All p-quiz test programs use this same general form, we illustrate it with the quiz for making a copy of an integer stack. The student's procedure is called StudentQuiz and imported from the appropriate module, PQCopyS in this case. A correct procedure is encoded directly in the test program and called CORRECTANSR. The code in Figure 1 does work correctly and similar code might appear in the test program as CORRECTANSR. The performance of the student procedure and the correct procedure has to be compared on a case-by-case basis, so it is convenient to have a boolean procedure that returns TRUE when the procedure results are identical or FALSE after printing a message indicating the discrepancy. Since this procedure verifies correct operation for the copy of a stack, we name it VerCopyS, as shown in Figure 6. Note the use of the utility routines RandomIntStack, CopyIntStack, CompareIntStacks, and PrintIntStack. Since value parameters for pointer variables do not protect the structure being pointed to, it is important to make sure that the student procedure did not modify the input stack.

```
PROCEDURE VerCopyS ( MinSize, MaxSize: CARDINAL;
          MinValue, MaxValue: INTEGER ) : BOOLEAN;
VAR S, S1, S2: IntStack;
    OriginalSame, CopySame: BOOLEAN;
BEGIN
 RandomIntStack(MinSize,MaxSize,MinValue,MaxValue,S);
 CORRECTANSR (S, S1);
 StudentQuiz (S, S2);
 OriginalSame := CompareIntStacks(S1, S);
 CopySame := CompareIntStacks( S1, S2);
 IF OriginalSame AND CopySame THEN
  DisposeIntStack(S); DisposeIntStack(S1);
  DisposeIntStack(S2);
  RETURN TRUE
 ELSE
  WriteLn;
  WriteString('Your function was passed the stack:');
  WriteLn;  PrintIntStack(S1); WriteLn;
  IF NOT OriginalSame THEN
   WriteString ( 'which it modified to:' ); WriteLn;
   PrintIntStack(S); WriteLn;
  END;  (* IF *)
  IF CopySame THEN
   WriteString('your copy of the stack was correct.');
   WriteLn;
  ELSE
   WriteString('your copy looks like: '); WriteLn;
   PrintIntStack(S2); WriteLn;
   WriteString ( 'which is not correct. ' ); WriteLn;
  END;  (* IF *)
  WriteLn;
  WriteString('Sorry. Keep trying.'); WriteLn;
  RETURN FALSE
 END; (* IF *)
END VerCopyS;
```

Figure 6 : Verify Correct Copy Stack Operation

The main program can then call VerCopyS to make sure the test succeeds in a variety of cases. This can be done by nesting IF statements, as shown in Figure 7, or by using ANDs if the language has left-to-right evaluation. Notice that the program halts testing once an error is detected.

```
MODULE TstCopyS;
(* program features, implementor, date, history *)

(* import lists *)

PROCEDURE CORRECTANSR(S1:IntStack; VAR S2:IntStack);
  (* body of correct answer *)
END CORRECTANSR;

PROCEDURE VerCopyS(MinSize, MaxSize: CARDINAL;
            MinValue, MaxValue: INTEGER ) : BOOLEAN;
  (* body of the verify routine *)
END VerCopyS;

BEGIN (* MAIN *)
 IF VerCopyS (2, 5, 0, 999) THEN
  IF VerCopyS (6, 15, -500, 500 ) THEN
   IF VerCopyS (16, 30, -500, -1 ) THEN
    IF VerCopyS ( 1, 1, -32000, 32000 ) THEN
     IF VerCopyS ( 0, 0, 0, 10 ) THEN
      WriteLn; WriteString('Congratulations!!!');
      WriteString('Your procedure worked.'); WriteLn;
     END;  (* IF *)
    END;   (* IF *)
   END;   (* IF *)
  END;   (* IF *)
 END;   (* IF *)
END TstCopyS.
```

Figure 7 : The Test Program

Usually testing five or six cases is sufficient to catch student errors. These cases should including limiting values such as the stack of one element and the empty stack shown above.

4. Ancillary Software

Our data structures p-quizzes are being used in an environment with many diskless Sun consoles networked to a server. We have developed software that allows the student to request a p-quiz from the proctor, the proctor selects the version of the p-quiz to be taken, and the results are reported to the proctor upon completion. The student can read the p-quiz directions directly on the screen, thus eliminating the danger of losing hard copy printouts. All of this software is, however, site dependent and is not needed if a "manual" system is used.

5. A "How To Do It" Sequence of Activities

A manual p-quiz system can be developed locally with very little effort. In fact, students who have passed the class can often be assigned projects to develop the software. The first step is to design and implement the ADT. For "standard" ADT's such as stacks, queues, linked lists, and binary search trees, this is fairly easy since these ADT's are covered in all the standard text books. After the ADT is implemented, one must come up with a set of three or four p-quiz problems that are of equivalent difficulty. There should usually be a set of problems involving the use of the ADT and another set of problems involving extensions to the ADT. It is often difficult to come up with problems of the same difficulty. Some extensions, such as the counting the number of items in a queue, will be a "one-liner" for some representations and a more complex operation for other representations. Every effort should be made to keep different versions of the same p-quiz at equivalent difficulty levels.

The test program may require operations, such as generating a random data structure, copying the structure, comparing two structures for equivalence, and printing the structure, that may not be available in the ADT itself. In such cases, a set of utility routines should be developed. Fortunately these utility routines, once implemented, can be used by any p-quiz using that ADT.

Finally, one must develop the test program. This includes a correct solution, a verify procedure, and a sequence of test cases as outlined previously. With this minimum amount of software, it is possible to use a manual p-quiz system. After this initial system is tested with students and refined accordingly, some of the ancillary software, such as giving the student a menu of choices or automatically recording grades, can be implemented.

6. Effectiveness in a CS2 Class

We have used programming quizzes in both our CS1 and CS2 level classes at New Mexico State University, so most students coming into the CS2 class are familiar with p-quizzes. Grading is on a mastery basis and we normally allow the students 1 1/2 hours to successfully complete the p-quiz. If they do not finish in the allotted time, they are allowed to take another version in the same group of p-quizzes (until no versions remain).

Some students were initially frustrated with the p-quizzes that involved use of ADTs because: 1) they could not see nor were allowed access to the underlying structures, and 2) they did not understand the need for the added modularization. However, after doing some implementations they begin to appreciate the need for information hiding and the fact that the added modularization allows changing the internal data structures and algorithms without changing the external interface. One major problem is to have students realize that use of a value parameter for a pointer does not protect the structure itself from being changed. In the p-quiz parameter lists we used value and variable parameters to indicate the conceptual intent of input and output structures, but students have to learn that these parameter passing mechanisms only apply to the pointer variable, which is usually not changed, and not to the structure being pointed to.

The students have reacted favorably to using p-quizzes in our CS2 level course since it gives them valuable experience in using and implementing ADTs in a relatively short time without becoming involved in an extensive two or three week programming assignment. Of course we have such programming assignments, but they can deal with substantive computer science problems rather than details about ADTs. These p-quizzes provide valuable experience for examinations too since most exams will contain one or two problems involving the design of a small procedure to perform a specific task.

7. Conclusions

Of the three CAI components used in our CS1 course, namely, tutorials, drills, and p-quizzes, we have found the latter to be most cost effective. Not only are the p-quizzes valuable for the students that use them, but they are also the easiest materials to implement with a minimum of effort and with little reliance on underlying software. We have been able to carry out this effort to develop p-quizzes for CS2 with incidental local funds as compared with the external grant money needed to develop drills and tutorials.

This paper has outlined techniques for developing p-quizzes locally. Although our materials are available in soft copy, we believe that it is perhaps better for each site to work on the development of their own materials. Although this violates the economy of scale, we have found from past experience that CAI materials are used more and supported more if there is some local involvement in their development. The strategies outlined in this paper for the development of p-quizzes to support instruction in abstract data type can be given as small projects for undergraduate students. An entire collection of p-quizzes can be implemented fairly quickly and the pedagogical benefits for this development time are quite high.

References

J. Adams, M. Landis, "A Computer Based Tutorial on Mathematical Induction", *Proceedings of the National Educational Computing Conference*, 1983

J. Adams, B. MacKichan, R. Hunter, "Starting a Computer Based Learning Project", *Proceedings of the National Educational Computing Conference*, June 1981

K. Bowles, "A CS1 Course Based on Stand-Alone Microcomputers", *Proceedings of the Ninth Technical Symposium on Computer Science Education*, Detroit, February 1978, pp. 125-127

Franklin, S., "Interactive Computer-Based Testing in Precalculus Mathematics", *Journal of Educational Data Processing*, 1976, vol. 13, No. 4.

Gabrini, P., Adams, J., Kurtz, B. "Converting from Pascal to Modula-2 in the Undergraduate Curriculum", *SIGCSE Bulletin*, 18:1 (1986) pp. 50-52

Johnson, W. L. and Soloway, E. "Proust: An Automatic Debugger for Pascal Programs", *Byte Magazine*, April 1985

Kurtz, B., Johnson, D., "Using Simulation to Teach Recursion and Binary Tree Traversals", *SIGCSE Bulletin*, 17:1 (1985) pp. 49-54

Kurtz, B., "Using Simulation to Teach Assembly Language Addressing Modes", *Proc. of the Western Educational Computing Conference*, 1984, pp. 18-22

Kurtz, B., "The Role of Computer Simulations in the Teaching of Computer Science Concepts", *Proc. of the Western Educational Computing Conference*, 1983, pp. 44-48

Reiser, B., Anderson, J.R., and Farrell, R.G., "Dynamic student modeling in an intelligent tutor for Lisp programming", *Proceedings of the Ninth International Joint Conference on Artificial Intelligence*, Los Angeles, 1985, pp. 8-14

Volper, D., Franklin, S., "Computer aided instruction in a large introductory computer science course for CS majors", accepted by *Education and Computing*

Teaching the Abstract Data Type in CS2

Joseph E. Lang and Robert K. Maruyama
Computer Science Department
University of Dayton
Dayton, Ohio 45469

Abstract

Teaching the abstract data type in CS2 is made difficult by the fact that the topic is intertwined with issues of language support, dynamic data structures and implementation techniques for dynamic data structures. When we switched to Ada to teach CS2, details of the language support for data abstraction caused us to restructure the CS2 course. By pushing the topic of the abstract data type toward the beginning of the course, we have found that it is covered more successfully.

Introduction

At the University of Dayton the abstract data type (to be abbreviated henceforth as ADT) has been taught regularly in the CS2 course for several years. The CS2 course has gone through several changes over the past five years. Originally the course used PL/I as the language, then VAX Pascal, and, since January 1986, Ada. As the language has changed we have been able to change our approach to teaching the ADT. This paper will give a brief introduction to the concept of the ADT, trace the history of our approach to teaching the ADT, discuss the perceived deficiencies at each stage of the history and the changes we made in response.

The ADT

The concept of the ADT is becoming increasingly recognized as a topic to be discussed in the early stages of the computer science curriculum [1, 2, 3]. The concept of the ADT was motivated by the need to allow the programmer to concentrate on the abstract operations required to solve a problem without being bothered by implementation details which are not directly relevant to the problem at hand [4].

The object oriented design methodology, which grew out of the same desire to have the elements of the problem domain be reflected more closely in the program domain, emphasizes the identification of ADT's by abstracting objects and operations in parallel [5].

The ADT is a data type defined solely in terms of the operations performed on the type [4]. The word "abstract" in the term implies that various details of the implementation can be ignored when discussing an ADT. For example, the ADT for a stack may be discussed solely in terms of the push, pop and clear operations and checks for the conditions empty and full without any reference to a specific implementaion — e.g. array or linked list. Some ADT's which have a wide range of applications are well defined (e.g set, stack, queue), while others which are specific to a particular problem may be difficult to define completely at the program design stage [8]. In the latter case, it may be necessary to go back and include additional operations to complete the definition of the ADT after program implementation has begun.

The word "type" in the term ADT refers to a class of objects defined by the domain of values that the objects can assume and by the operations that may be performed on the objects [2]. Most programming languages have predefined (data) types such as integer, real, or boolean. But because the predefined types are generally limited in their ability to represent the problem domain smoothly, many languages have facilities for constructing user-defined types from the predefined ones. Unfortunately, when students are taught about this, they tend to confuse a data type, which represents some class of data objects with the implementation of the data type using the primitive constructs of a particular language. For example, the distinction between pushing an item onto a stack, which is a stack operation, and its implementaiton in terms of an insertion into an array or appending a node to a linked list, is not always clear in the student's mind.

71

The challenge to the instructor in CS2 is to make the distinction between definition, implementation, and language construct clear in the student's mind.

Teaching the ADT in CS2 using PL/I

When we taught the ADT in CS2 using PL/I (under the then popular term "information hiding"), we introduced the topic of the ADT along with the dynamic data structures (stack, queue, etc.). Our approach had two deficiencies:

First, the language supported "information hiding" only by creating multiple entry points to a procedure. Thus, the procedure became a "module" inside which the details of the implementation could be hidden. If a student should happen to use a parameter as a variable somewhere inside that "module" (procedure), and if the student would happen to call the procedure via an entry point which did not have that parameter in its parameter list, the parameter could cause non-local modification of memory locations in a way devilishly hard to find. This type of bug in student programs caused endless anguish. Here, we see that the language construct acted in a way to vitiate what we were trying to teach: details of the implementation affected execution of the main program in mysterious ways.

Second, because students were introduced to the concept of an ADT at the same time as they were introduced to dynamic data structures, they tended to confuse the two.

Teaching the ADT in CS2 using VAX Pascal

Pascal provides meager support for enforcement of information hiding [6]. Nevertheless, one can teach students about the ADT when using Pascal. We decided to use VAX Pascal in CS2 because it supports independently compiled modules which may be linked together with a program module to make a complete program. Unfortunately, this language did not have cross module checking and so students, who were accustomed to the checking of the number and type of arguments when the procedures were nested, sometimes made the mistake of calling a procedure or function in an external module with the wrong number or types of arguments. This bug caused the programs to crash sometimes, at other times the program would run correctly once and give incorrect results during other runs; yet, the programs never produced a compile or link error. We also found that we had to read the student programs vigilantly because students could easily defeat the facilities for information hiding in the language.

One approach to solving the information hiding problem was to have the students program dynamic data structures as abstract state machines [5, 7] in which one module encapsulates one data structure. This decreases the amount of checking that the teacher had to do, but did not solve the problem of cross module checking. After switching to Pascal, we still introduced the concept of the ADT along with that of the dynamic data structure — with the

same confusion possible in the student's mind.

Teaching the ADT in CS2 using Ada

In Ada, the language construct for implementing the ADT is the package. Packages provide a wide variety of choices as to how implementation details are to be hidden. This required us to separate, for the first time, the discussion of the ADT (and the package construct) from the discussion of the dynamic data structures. This approach, mandated by the language, was not perfect, but it has led us over the past two years to divide the topics to be taught into four parts:

1. the Ada package,
2. the concept of the ADT,
3. dynamic data structures, and
4. implementations of dynamic data structures.

It is this four-way division that we feel makes our teaching of the ADT better today than it was a couple of years ago.

Today, we teach these topics in the order shown above with each introduced in the simplest way. For example, we discuss packages as building blocks in Ada programs that may be used in the following ways:

1. A package may be used to provide global type definitions so that several program units may import them by referencing the package. In this case the package is used in a manner somewhat similar to that of .h files in C programs.

2. A package may be used to localize related procedures and functions, e.g. a set of mathematical functions or a group of matrix operations.

3. A package may encapsulate an ADT as described above.

4. A generic package allows for a higher level of abstraction by providing a template for ADT's of various element types.

These uses of the package are taught in order, the first being used to allow students to declare global types for use by externally compiled functions and procedures. At this stage, we only need to teach the student about the package specification. A typical exercise might consist of searching and sorting a linear list with the search and sort routines external to the main program. The package (specification) is merely used to provide the global type declaration of the list type. Later, packages are discussed as a grouping or "library" which may or may not contain global type declarations exported by the package. Here, we discuss both the package specification and package body and indicate that only those operations to be exported should be listed in the package specification. We extend the exercise above by including the search and sort routines in the package body and also export them from the package.

After packages have been discussed thoroughly, we introduce the ADT and work through simple examples of ADT's (typically sets or complex numbers). In our original approach, we chose the variable length string as the first

72

example of an ADT to be implemented. We found that this introduced unnecessary complexity: string manipulating algorithms deserve a separate treatment. However, an early implementation of an ADT which implements the variable length string type makes it easy for the students to write subsequent programs involving any form of text processing.

Now, finally we introduce Ada's private type and discuss its use for information hiding; we insist that students access the data object only through the operations defined in the package specification — and Ada enforces this for us. The choice of examples is important for this phase. The type to be implemented by the package must fit the definition of an ADT, but it must not be so complicated that it detracts from our main concern, namely, the idea of the ADT and its implementation in terms of packages. As we have simplified our discussion over the years, we have found that students began to understand the concept of the ADT more clearly. We cannot emphasize enough the importance of this observation.

Once students have learned to construct an ADT in this bottom up way, we proceed to develop other ADT's whose characteristics are well known, in a more formal fashion. The list, stack, and queue are presented as ADT's which can be completely specified in terms of operations that are performed on them. For each case, we

a) discuss and determine the necessary and useful operations,

b) define the ADT interface in the package specification, and

c) implement each operation in the package body. In order to make debugging easier, we recommend that the students include in the package interface a procedure which simply displays the contents of an ADT object. Upon completion of debugging and testing of the package, this procedure can be removed. Exercises and projects are designed to utilize these packages under various conditions. Although this approach does not delve deeply into object oriented design, students begin to see that complex programs can be modularized in terms of ADT's and come to realize that the subprograms they are writing correspond to the operations on the ADT.

If the time and facilities permit, it is possible to make ADT's more general by implementing them as generic packages. A generic package is a template that permits the creation of many instances of packages which are tailored for particular uses. Such a generic unit illustrates to the students a level of abstraction which is higher than that represented by an ordinary package.

Summary and Conclusions

The 1984 curriculum recommendations for CS2 by the ACM Curriculum Task Force emphasize the importance of applying software engineering principles throughtout the CS2 course [1]. Moreover, it recommends that data abstrac-

tion and the implementation of various data structures be included among the main objectives of the course. In this context the ADT becomes one of the main themes running through the CS2 course.

We have found that the concept of the ADT is covered most successfully in the CS2 course if it is covered as a separate topic, not covered along with dynamic data structures or implementation details. Ada has proven to provide strong support for the teaching of the ADT and provides a direct implementation of ADT's in terms of the package facility and the private data type. However, one must be careful when teaching the ADT using Ada that the distinction between the package and the ADT is maintained.

We feel that teaching object oriented design techniques is beyond the scope of the CS2 course, but it is our opinion that the ADT approach mentioned here allows students to get a better grasp of how to modularize programs, become more aware of the difference between abstraction and implementaion, and recognize the importance of separating these two aspects of programming.

References
1.   Koffman, E. B., Miller, D. L., and Wardle, C. E., Recommended curriculum for CS2, 1984, *CACM*, vol. 28, 8, Aug. 1985, pp. 815-818.

2. Riley, D., *Data abstraction and structures, an introduction to computer science II*, Boyd and Fraser, Boston, 1987.

3. McCracken, D., *A second course in computer science with Pascal*, John Wiley and Sons, New York, 1987.

4.   Liskov, B., Programming with abstract data types, *SIGPLAN Notices*, vol. 9, 4, Apr. 1974, pp. 50-59.

5. Booch, G., *Software engineering with Ada*, Benjamin/Cummings Publishing Co., Menlo Park, California, 1983.

6. Dale, N., and Lilly, S. C., *Pascal plus data structures, algorithms, and advanced programming*, D. C. Heath and Co., Lexington, Mass., 1985, pp. 483-484.

7. Booch, G., *Software components with Ada*, Benjamin/Cummings Publishing Co., Menlo Park, California, 1987.

8. Abbott, R. J., Program design by informal English descriptions, *CACM*, vol. 26, 11, Nov. 1983, pp. 882-894.

Integrating Desktop Publishing into a Systems Analysis and Design Course

Donald L. Jordan
College of Engineering
Department of Computer Science
Lamar University
Beaumont, TX 77710

Abstract

This paper describes an experiment to incorporate the new Desktop Publishing technology into our traditional Systems Analysis and Design course. The experiment was first conducted during the Fall 1987 semester and is being repeated and expanded in the Spring 1988 term. The course is considered to be a Junior level Computer Science course. Desktop Publishing systems are sometimes hard to learn and use but are very powerful and flexible tools for developing system reference manuals that contain text, graphics, line art and images. It was difficult to determine the amount of time to spend on this topic and to place this material in its proper place in the course curriculum. Some of our experiences, both positive and negative, are reported for those responsible for conducting similiar courses and may be interested in implementing this new technology.

Introduction

Desktop Publishing is now recognized as the solution to many publication problems. It is a very hot topic and has been described by [6] as one of the few developments in computing that actually saves money. Desktop publishing, which many consider to be stand-alone, personal-computer-based publishing, has over the last year become the shining star of the computer industry--the latest, greatest application for microcomputers. According to PC Magazine [2] the desktop publishing market has caught fire. A market research firm based in California estimates that sales figures are currently at about 53,000 and are projected at more than 300,000 units by 1990. As laser printing and scanning technologies have become more sophisticated and less expensive, and as the various pieces

of hardware and software have become more unified, several software engineering firms have opted to use this technology in their software design and development work.

HARDWARE/SOFTWARE

IBM PC/AT Compatible
HP Laserjet II Printer
HP Scanjet Scanner
MS Mouse
MS Paintbrush
The VENTURA Publisher

Figure 1 Hardware/Software Configuration

It is clear that the documentation needs that occur during the systems analysis and design phases of the software life cycle can be met by a destop publishing system. Lamar University became interested in desktop publishing technology as a means to assist professors and students in their documentation efforts. Our current hardware/software configuration, which is shown in Figure 1, was used extensively in the work described in this paper. The total investment for both hardware and software was less than $6,000.

CS4311 -- Information Systems I

The analysis, design, implementation, documentation, maintenance, and modifications of information systems including both hardware and software.

Prerequisite: CS2411 (COBOL Programming)

Background

Before presenting the experiment, I will explain some specifics about the course (i.e. CS4311) in order to justify some of the later conclusions and to place the course in its proper context. CS4311, which is named Information Systems I, covers the requirements definition, systems analysis and design phases of the Systems Life Cycle as specified by the ACM curriculum study in 1984. It is normally taken in the Junior year; however, many students procrastinate and postpone the course until the very last semester of their Senior year.

Grading Policy

Criteria	Pct
Homework	15
Instructor Eval	10
Exams	50
Project	25
Total	100

Figure 2   CS4311 Grading Policy

The course is presented in two parts. During the first half of the semester the theory, tools, techniques and methodology of systems analysis and design is presented. During the last half of the semester, the class is broken down into teams that implement the theory and techniques on a project and document their work. A mid-term written exam is given at the conclusion of the theory and a comprehensive final exam is given at the end. Students are warned that 3-4 hours per week outside of class are required to accomplish the project. A significant part of each students grade is devoted to the class project (see figure 2).

Design of The Experiment

It was not our intention to conduct a completely "scientific" experiment. However, we did want some basis for comparson, even if only intuitive. To make the experiment more valid scientifically, it might have been wise to break the students into two groups: one organized the old way and the other one using the new technology. However, we were not prepared to accept the added administrative burden and also we wanted to expose as many students as possible to the desktop publishing technology.

For this experiment, we devoted the first two weeks after the mid-term to teaching the students about desktop publishing. Since the class met on Monday-Wednesday-Friday, this resulted in six 50 minute lectures on DTP. The major features of the Ventura Publisher covered during this time were: importing word processing and graphic files, using the text editing capability built into the DTP software, applying the typesetting attributes to text files, and printing DTP files at the Laser printer. Brief coverage was devoted to MS Paintbrush, a graphical package, and to the use of the HP Scanner. No class time was allocated to teaching word-processing or graphics software packages. Students were encouraged to avail themselves of word processing software available in our micro-computer laboratories or to use their own.

The restrictions imposed on the class were as follows: every page of the manual was to be produced using the Ventura Publisher software system, all word processing and graphic files used in the manual had to be imported into it, and the final copy of the manual had to be printed using the Laser printer in a photo ready format. It should be noted that the class was free to choose any word processor or graphics package that produced output files that could be imported into the Ventura Publisher. A list of these software packages was provided to each student. An exit critique at the end of the semester was planned to record student comments and suggestions.

The First Attempt

The Fall 1987 class of CS4311 had an enrollment of 23 students. At the conclusion of Part I of the course, a list of suggested projects was provided to the class. They were encouraged to identify new projects if none of the suggested topics were of interest. In addition, a course survey form was given to each student that asked for information about his/her academic major and minor, a choice of project, and his/her selection of teammates. The instructor provided background information and an introduction to each project. Students were given 48 hours to complete the survey form. This allowed sufficient time for them to talk with their classmates about the projects and possible team composition. Shortly after the survey forms were returned and analyzed by the instructor, team assignments were made. These assignments were based primarily on choice; however, academic major and minor had some impact. The ratio of CS majors and General Business majors

Team	Size
Academic Department	5
Hazardous Waste	10
Manufacturing Company	8

Figure 3 Team Composition

who take CS4311 is usually about 50-50. Some minor adjustments in team allocation was made so that team composition was equally divided between majors.

The three projects chosen by the class were: a Hazardous Waste System, a Small Assembly Plant and an Academic Department. Each project required that a team identify the system requirements, perform a systems analysis, prepare the general design and document their results in the form of a systems reference manual. Each team was responsible for organizing themselves, choosing leaders and allocating responsibilities amongst team members. The teams were organized according to the major functions of the enterprise and developed and maintained a project notebook for each function. Unlike the Systems Reference manual, project notebooks were not submitted at the end of the semester; however, periodic checks were made by the instructor on its contents and homework grades were assigned. The composition and size of the teams is shown in figure 3.

Systems Reference Manual

The Systems Reference manual is the major deliverable product for each team and usually contains 200-300 pages including charts, diagrams, and attachments. A major part of the semester grade is attached to this manual (see figure 2). In the past this manual has been produced entirely via word processing and graphics drawing packages available on either the University mainframe, microcomputers or the student's own personal computer. Sometimes this has severely constrained production on the manual due to incompatibilities between word processors, hardware and graphics packages. The only constraint imposed by the instructor was that every page of the manual had to be produced on the computer and that all text for a particular manual be produced on the same word processor and printer. No restrictions were imposed on the computer produced graphics pages for their manual. Such

constraints and restrictions often placed an additional workload onto the teams but the results were always better than expected. In fact, many companies that review these manuals as part of the interview process commented very favorably on them. The manuals produced were always of professional quality and something in which the students took great pride. Feedback from recruiting trips and company interviews by industry were outstanding. Many companies requested to review these reference manuals and had very favorable comments on their composition, educational value and professional content. Each class was allowed to review the previous class efforts and as a result steady improvement in the quality of the manuals was noted.

Student Reactions

The student reviews and critiques for previous sections of CS4311 have always been outstanding. It is considered a very "real-world" course with direct application to the job market. Feedback from students who have graduated and are working in industry consistently rate the course as excellent. This class was no exception.

The class reaction to The VENTURA Publisher was interesting. In general, they thought it was an excellent addition to the course. Their chief concerns involved the degree of difficulty in learning VENTURA and can be summarized as follows:

"Instruction on VENTURA should begin earlier in the semester."

"Our team wishes we could have spent longer on VENTURA, but it was interesting and educational."

"VENTURA was a very difficult program to learn even with the manual. The other software was not as difficult to use or learn. The course was very enjoyable."

Tuning The System

A great deal of effort and planning went into this experiment prior to the Fall 1987 semester. The subjective feeling of both the instructor and students was that desktop publishing should continue to be used in this course. Some of this feeling might have been expressed simply because the topic was new, while others had heard through the "grapevine" that industry was beginning to use it. In any case, the decision to continue in the Spring 1988 term was made.

Several mistakes were made in the first attempt. We discovered that most students and faculty have had very little experience in publishing or in the typesetting technology and therefore were not acquainted with the basic features available in a publishing system such as VENTURA. In retrospect, we didn't devote enough time to general typesetting or publishing terminology.

A second mistake was that our requirements were too rigid. Although we had intentionally decided to require every page of the reference manual to be imported into VENTURA, criticisms from students suggested that we at least allow the output from some graphics packages to be printed and merged with the pages produced with VENTURA.

Finally, we waited too late in the semester to introduce VENTURA and did not give any preliminary information about it. VENTURA is a very powerful yet complex system and must be approached slowly and systematically.

In the Spring 1988 semester, these problems were addressed and various modifications made to the method of presentation. A word processing exercise was given early in the semester that required students to develop and import a text file into VENTURA and publish a three page newsletter. Students were allowed to choose their own word processor but were given the text. This exercise was closely followed by another that entailed use of the scanner to import a picture into their newsletter and republish it. Finally, a third project was assigned that forced students to use PAINTBRUSH or any other drawing package to create a figure and import that also into their newsletter. We believed that these three small projects or exercises would give the students some general understanding of publishing, typesetting and the capabilities of VENTURA before they tackled the reference manual for their class project.

Conclusions

After one full year's experience with desktop publishing in the systems analysis and design curriculum, we believe that it is an extremely effective educational tool. For the first time in memory this instructor has overheard students say they actually enjoyed preparing design documentation! It not only facilitates, but also demands, that students place proper emphasis on the written words, diagrams, charts and other deliverable products that result in a system analysis and design project.

While we were greatly influenced by the efforts of Glass [4], Brockmann [8], Stuart [9] and others in the importance of producing good documentation efficiently, it wasn't until desktop publishing arrived that software developers were provided an outstanding tool. Our experiment is continuing and we are still learning and refining its implementation. Just as computer scientists have borrowed techniques from engineers and applied them in software engineering they must borrow techniques from the publishing industry and apply them to desktop publishing.

References

1. Capron, H.L., SYSTEMS ANALYSIS and DESIGN, Benjamine/Cummings Publishing Company, Inc., Reading, MA., 1986.

2. PC Magazine, Volume 6, Number 19, pp. 92-184, Oct. 1987.

3. PC Magazine, Volume 7, Number 7, pp. 92-152, April 1988.

4. Glass, Robert L., SOFTWARE COMMUNICATION SKILLS, Prentice-Hall, Inc., Englewood Cliffs, NJ, 1988.

5. Nance, Ted, VENTURA: Tips and Tricks, Peachpit Press, Berkley, CA, 1987.

6. InfoWorld, January 5, 1987.

7. Holtz, Matthew, Mastering VENTURA, Sybex, Inc., Alameda, CA, 1988.

8. Brockman, John, WRITING BETTER COMPUTER USER DOCUMENTATION, John Wiley and Sons, New York, NY, 1986.

9. Stuart, Ann, WRITING AND ANALYZING EFFECTIVE COMPUTER SYSTEM DOCUMENTATION, Holt, Rinehart, and Winston, New York, NY, 1984.

MODIFYING FRESHMAN PERCEPTIONS OF THE CIS GRADUATE'S WORKSTYLE

Charles H. Mawhinney
David R. Callaghan

CIS Department
Bentley College
Waltham, Massachusetts 02254

Edward G. Cale, Jr.

Babson College
Babson Park
Wellesley, Massachusetts 02157

ABSTRACT

Student interest in computer-related careers has declined dramatically in recent years. One possible explanation for this decline is incorrect perceptions of the workstyle associated with the positions held by CIS graduates. A study of freshman business majors was conducted which: (1) examined whether an introductory computing course changed those perceptions, and (2) compared those perceptions to their own expected starting positions. The study showed that: (1) the introductory computing course had a negligible effect on changing student perceptions of the nature of the CIS graduate's initial job, and (2) compared to their perceptions of CIS jobs, they expected their own jobs to involve substantially more human interaction and less direct involvement in the implementation of computer technology. The results suggest a need for: (1) a more pro-active strategy to market the MIS career both inside and outside the classroom, and (2) some creative approaches for the place-ment and content of programming activities in both the major and the career.

INTRODUCTION

Student interest in computer-related careers has risen and declined like a roller coaster in the last decade. In the annual survey of college freshmen conducted by UCLA (Astin, et. al., 1985, 1986, 1987), interest in programmer/analyst occupa-tions surged from 2.8% in 1977 to a high of 8.8% in 1982. This unprecedented rise in interest was then followed by an equally dramatic decline in interest to a low of 2.7% in 1987. This peak in interest in 1982 resulted in a corresponding peak in graduates in 1986. Recent graduating classes contain those students who entered during the early years of the decline. The largest declines in computer-related enrollments from the 1985-1987 period will soon be felt by an industry whose demand for these students has increased, not declined.

The UCLA study indicates that the impact is being felt by both the technical and the applications areas of the field. The concomitant increase and decline in both Computer Science and Data Processing/Programming majors parallels the interest in the programming/analyst career. With peak levels in 1982-83, interest in both majors is back down to 1977 levels.

This recent decline in interest has not gone unnoticed and has been the basis for articles in the Wall St. Journal (Duke, 1987) and Computerworld (Withington, 1988). While a number of hypotheses are espoused in these articles and others (Roches-ter, 1988), little organized research has been done as to the cause of the decline.

We believe that a major reason for this decline in interest and enrollments may be due to incorrect perceptions held by gradu-ating high school students. Specifically, we believe that entering college freshmen do not understand the nature of entry-level positions in computer-related fields and may be avoiding such occupations because of these misperceptions.

Are Information Systems People Different from Users?

It has long been theorized that MIS personnel are somehow different from other persons who work in business organizations. The historic focus of this difference has been on those who design information systems versus managerial users of such systems (King & Cleland, 1971; Mason & Mitroff, 1973; Couger & Zawacki, 1980; Kaiser & Bostrom, 1982; Ferratt & Short, 1986). These theoretical differences can be summarized as (1) position characteristics, and (2) personal characteristics. Position characteristics suggest that managerial users tend to have a broader organizational view of the problem being solved, while system developers are more interested in the technical aspects of the system which is solving that problem. Personal charac-teristics are those that are intrinsic to the individual, such as personality and motivation. Both types of differences could be important, if they do indeed exist.

Almost all of the empirical research seems to have focused on the personal characteristics, rather than the position charac-teristics of designers and users. This research has shown few significant differences when comparing MIS personnel with users within the same occupational group, such as (1) clerical/opera-tions, (2) technical/professional, and (3) managerial. Ferratt and Short (1986) examined the motivation patterns of MIS personnel and users in the insurance industry. Although they did find significant differences in motivation patterns between the three occupational groups, they did not find any significant difference between MIS personnel and users within the same occupational group. Kaiser and Bostrom (1982) examined the personality types of systems analysts and users that par-ticipated in systems development project teams and found no significant differences on any of the four dimensions that comprise Jung's (1923) personality construct. Although their study used a relatively small sample of analysts and users, they were almost all within the same occupational group (tech-nical/professional). Cougar and Zawacki (1980) performed the most extensive study to date of MIS personnel and users. They controlled for the three occupational groups and examined "growth need strength" and "social need strength" in more than 2,500 MIS workers. They found that within the same occupa-tional group, MIS personnel tend to have higher growth needs and lower social needs than users. The contention that MIS person-nel tend to have lower social needs than users is also supported by a combination of two other studies which indicate that introversion is substantially more common among MIS personnel. Lyons (1985) and Mawhinney (1986) both examined the Jungian personality type of personnel in the technical/professional and managerial groups. Lyons studied 1,229 MIS personnel and found that two-thirds of them were introverts. Mawhinney studied 242 users and found that only half them were introverts.

The Entry Level Position

Couger and Zawacki (1980) attributed this phenomenon of less social need (or introversion) among MIS workers to the nature of the entry level position. The traditional entry has been through computer programming, regardless of whether a person enters as a result of an intra-organizational transfer from some other functional area or as a direct hire out of an under-graduate college program. Indeed, at a recent international conference on computer personnel, a panel of practicing MIS managers agreed that the first step in the MIS career path in their organizations involved "immersion in technology" which was accomplished in a programming environment (Trent, 1988). This contention is also supported by a placement office survey of Bentley College's CIS majors who graduated in 1986. This study was conducted within the first six months of graduation, and found that of the 104 responses (response rate 81%), the majority (52%) were in positions requiring programming. Only 10 reported their positions as "systems analyst" of some type. Computer programming would appear to be a required gateway through which most IS professionals must pass on their career paths.

A similar phenomenon occurs in academia at the entry level of undergraduate programs intended to prepare students for careers in information systems. The first course in almost all such programs is a programming course. The "model curriculum" for the Association for Computing Machinery (Nunamaker, Couger & Davis, 1982) recommends an introductory programming course as the first course in the curriculum. Students who dislike programming are obviously less likely to continue on in such programs.

Couger and Zawacki (1980) contend that communication and behavioral skills are not crucial to the success of a programmer, but technical skills are. Weinberg (1971) described the programmer's lack of desire for social interaction: "If asked, most programmers probably say they preferred to work alone in a place where they wouldn't be disturbed by other people" (p. 52). Thus, it appears both the entry level position and the relevant undergraduate programs "conspire" to discourage an IS career except for those more interested in technology than in human interaction. These traits later become a problem as the programmer progresses to the next step in his/her career path (a systems analyst).

The necessary skills for an analyst are quite different from those for a programmer. Wood (1979) described systems analysts as:

> people who communicate with management and users at the management/user level; document their experience; understand problems before proposing solutions; think before they speak; facilitate systems development, not originate it; are supportive of the organization in question and understand its goals and objectives; use good tools and approaches to help solve systems problems; and enjoy working with people (p. 24).

Whitten, Bentley, and Ho (1986) state "systems work is people-oriented work and systems analysts must be extroverted or people-oriented people" (p. 19).

The Preliminary Study

Accordingly, we conducted a study of freshmen business majors during the 1987-88 academic year in which we assessed their perceptions of what a typical graduate of the Bentley CIS program does upon completion of the major. Their perceptions were assessed at the beginning of the academic year. We also assessed the perceptions of the CIS faculty. In a previous paper we compared the perceptions of the CIS faculty with these initial perceptions of the students (Mawhinney, Cale & Callaghan, 1988). That portion of the study yielded two important results. The first result was that in general there was less agreement among the faculty than among the students. This was particularly the case for questionnaire items which distinguished entry level programmers from entry level analysts. Apparently one portion of the faculty viewed the entry level position as being an analyst while the other viewed the entry level position as being a programmer. The second result was that there were several items on which the students' views differed appreciably from those of the faculty. Those items pertained to starting salaries and technical aptitude. Apparently the students were not aware of the premium starting salaries being offered to CIS majors. They also tended to overestimate both the mathematical ability and the computer background of the CIS major prior to entering college.

HYPOTHESES

This paper reports on the second phase of the study which focused on two additional aspects of student perceptions:

1. It examined the changes that occurred during the academic year in the students' perceptions of the CIS graduates workstyle (PRE versus POST).

2. It compared their perceptions of the CIS graduate's workstyle with their perceptions of their own expected starting positions (POST versus SELF).

PRE versus POST

Stated in null form, the first hypothesis tested was:

H1: Students' perceptions of the workstyle of the typical CIS graduate will not change as a result of an introductory computing course.

During the fall semester of that academic year, all freshmen students were enrolled in an introductory computing course. The course focused on hardware and software concepts and personal computing. School policy required all students in this course to lease or purchase an MS DOS compatible portable computer.

The course was conducted using a lecture and laboratory methodology. "Hands on" applications used packaged software only (spreadsheet, word processing, and database). No procedural programming languages were used or taught in the course. All sections were taught from a common syllabus which included a session on "careers in MIS". This session on MIS careers included a presentation by two "guest" faculty members which generally followed a common outline developed by an ad hoc committee of senior faculty members.

We anticipated this introductory course would result in a change in the students' perceptions. For those items where the students' views differed from those of the faculty, we anticipated the average student score would move toward the average faculty score. These anticipated shifts in means of the students' scores were assessed through t-tests for paired comparisons.

POST versus SELF

Stated in null form, the second hypothesis tested was:

H2: Students perceive no difference between the workstyle of the typical CIS graduate and their own expected starting positions.

Bentley college offers eight other undergraduate business majors in addition to the one in CIS. Although the majors which are currently the most popular are accountancy, management, and marketing, the other majors also attract a fair number of students. Presumably, an undergraduate business major will provide entry into a position that is related to that major. In the selection of a major, it is reasonable to expect a student to consider the workstyle associated with such a position, if only in a subjective fashion. Consequently, we anticipated the means would be different for perceptions of their own entry-level positions when compared to their perceptions of the typical CIS graduate's starting position. These anticipated differences were assessed through paired t-tests for the means.

METHOD

Subjects

This study used as its subjects all students enrolled in an introductory computing course at Bentley College in Waltham, Massachusetts. Bentley is a private school and is the eighth largest undergraduate college of business in the United States. Almost all the participants were first semester freshmen business majors. Participation in the study was voluntary and participants were allowed to remain anonymous. However, participants were encouraged to identify themselves in order to facilitate an eventual "post treatment" survey. For the first survey (PRE), responses were received from 406 of the 1058 students, resulting in a response rate of 38%. For the second survey (POST), responses were received from 163 of the 406 students who responded to the first survey.

The Instrument and Procedure

A nine-item questionnaire was developed to assess perceptions of the workstyles of graduates of the CIS program (see Exhibit A, Items #1 to #9). The items covered a range of activities and aspects that seventeen and eighteen year olds with no prior business or computer background could reasonably be expected to understand. The first two items dealt with perceptions of general technical background. We felt that if students believed that CIS majors had a relatively stronger math and/or computer background it could be a barrier to entering the major. Item #8 assessed their perception of the starting salary of the CIS graduate. We felt this to be an important issue in a business curriculum which presumably advocates the profit motive. Item #6 was included to determine whether these students could distinguish normal CIS activities from the more technical activities engaged in by engineers and computer scientists. The five remaining items (#3, #4, #5, #7, and #9) focused on aspects of workstyle which generally distinguish computer programmers from systems analysts (Couger & Zawacki, 1981; Wood, 1979; Whitten, Bentley, & Ho, 1986). The responses to the questionnaire were scored "after the fact" by assigning numeric values on a scale of 0 to 4 (SD = 0, D = 1, etc.).

The instrument was administered two times. The first time it was administered to the student group, this instrument was contained within a larger questionnaire that also assessed: (1) previous computer background, (2) computer anxiety, and (3) Jungian personality type. The questionnaire was distributed in class during the third week of the course (in the Fall semester). The questionnaire was completed outside of class and returned either through the instructor or campus mail.

The students who provided names and addresses in the first survey were used in the second survey. The questionnaire was mailed directly to the students near the end of the Spring semester. This time the nine-item instrument was also contained within a larger questionnaire that additionally assessed: (1) the respondent's own background and job preferences with respect to the same nine items (see Appendix A, Items #10 to #18), (2) computer use during that semester, and (3) computer anxiety. A $100 lottery was offered as an enticement to encourage responses.

RESULTS

Scale Properties

Dimensionality analysis is used to assess whether multiple items used to assess a characteristic can be reduced to fewer dimensions (subscales). Factor analysis and scale reliability analysis are used to seek and evaluate such subscales (Anastasi, 1982; Tabachnik & Fidell, 1983). The development of such subscales should be performed using a sample of subjects which is different from that used to test the research hypotheses. To this end, the 406 student responses to the first round were randomly split into two groups of approximately one-fourth and three-fourths. The smaller group was used to perform the dimensionality analysis and the larger group was used to test the hypothesis. Expected sample attrition suggested that this second group be kept as large as possible while still maintaining a minimum ten to one ratio of responses to items for the first group in order to perform the factor analysis.

The subsequent factor analysis and scale reliability analysis failed to yield sufficiently interpretable and reliable subscales. Consequently, as a result of these analyses, the nine items used in the instrument to measure perceptions of the CIS graduate's workstyle were treated as separate items.

Testing the Hypotheses

The sample reduction from splitting for dimensionality analysis and pre/post treatment attrition resulted in a final sample of 115 responses for testing the hypotheses. The results for the two hypotheses are described separately.

PRE versus POST. The means and standard deviations for the pre and post treatment responses to the nine items are listed in Table 1. Two items (#3 and #7) exhibited significant changes in their means. The mean scores increased in both cases. The increased score for Item #3 indicates stronger agreement with the perception that the typical CIS graduate spends most of his/her working time writing computer programs. The increased score for Item #7 indicates stronger agreement with the perception that the typical CIS graduate interacts mostly with other computer people. Although these shifts were significant, they were not among those anticipated.

TABLE 1. PRE VS. POST TREATMENT PERCEPTIONS

	PRE		POST			
Item	Mean	S.D.	Mean	S.D.	t-val	Sig
1	1.57	0.79	1.61	1.01	-0.32	
2	1.66	0.93	1.72	1.08	-0.45	
3	1.63	0.86	1.90	0.90	-2.41	*
4	2.35	0.82	2.39	0.89	-0.40	
5	1.89	0.85	1.72	0.86	1.62	
6	1.75	0.97	1.65	0.89	0.88	
7	1.94	1.00	2.28	0.94	-3.29	**
8	2.11	0.74	2.09	0.79	0.32	
9	2.57	0.64	2.52	0.73	0.69	

2-tailed: * p $\underline{\S}$ 0.05 ** p $\underline{\S}$ 0.01 *** p $\underline{\S}$ 0.001

POST versus SELF. The means and standard deviations for the post treatment and "self" responses to the nine items are listed in Table 2. For seven of the nine items the average perceptions of the CIS graduate's workstyle were significantly different from the average expectation of the students' own starting position. The only two items which did not yield a significant difference were the ones regarding math ability (#1) and prior computer background (#2). Compared with their perceptions of the CIS graduate's first job, these students on the average expect to:

1. spend less time writing computer programs (#3)
2. spend more time interacting with other persons (#4)
3. spend less time working alone (#5)
4. be less involved in designing computer hardware (#6)
5. interact less with other computer people (#7)
6. receive a higher starting salary (#8)
7. be less involved in helping managers select new computer systems (#9)

TABLE 2. POST TREATMENT VERSUS SELF PERCEPTIONS

	POST		SELF			
Item	Mean	S.D.	Mean	S.D.	t-val	Sig
1	1.61	1.01	1.59	1.04	0.14	
2	1.72	1.08	1.52	1.11	0.96	
3	1.90	0.90	0.77	0.72	11.29	***
4	2.39	0.89	3.10	0.65	-8.04	***
5	1.72	0.86	1.21	0.84	5.11	***
6	1.65	0.89	0.67	0.72	10.91	***
7	2.28	0.94	1.21	0.85	9.82	***
8	2.09	0.79	2.41	0.90	-2.72	**
9	2.52	0.73	1.58	0.98	9.27	***

2-tailed: * p $\underline{\S}$ 0.05 ** p $\underline{\S}$ 0.01 *** p $\underline{\S}$ 0.001

DISCUSSION

PRE versus POST

The null hypothesis that students' perceptions of the workstyle of the typical CIS graduate would not change as a result of an introductory computing course cannot be rejected on basis of this study. There were two significant changes in the students' perceptions, but they were not among those we expected to change. None of the changes we expected to occur actually materialized. The only sense in which our expectations can be said to be supported is that some of the perceptions which were not expected to change did not change. Thus, we conclude the introductory course had a negligible effect on changing the students' perceptions of the workstyle of the CIS graduate to become more like those of the CIS faculty.

However, we think the changes in students' perceptions which did occur during this period are important. There was a significant shift in their view of the typical CIS graduate: (1) spending most of his/her working time writing computer programs, and (2) interacting mostly with other computer people. Consequently, we conclude the effect of the introductory course was to convince the students that the CIS graduate entered the workforce as a programmer.

POST versus SELF

The null hypothesis that students perceive no difference between the workstyle of the typical CIS graduate and their own expected starting positions can be rejected on the basis of this study. All but two of the nine items yielded significantly different means. We draw three conclusions from these results.

Our first conclusion is that these students perceive the entry level position for the CIS graduate as a computer programmer who spends a lot of time working alone and interacting mostly with other computer people. It is apparent to us that these students would prefer a position with more human interaction and less direct involvement in the implementation of computer technology.

Our second conclusion is that these students have unrealistic expectations about the starting salaries they will receive upon graduation. Historic data from the College Placement Council (1972-1988) shows that the average CIS graduate receives several thousand dollars per year more than other business majors. Only a very small percentage of graduates in other majors will receive these high salaries.

Our third conclusion is that these students do not perceive themselves to be any different from CIS majors with respect to mathematical ability or prior computer background. Consequently, this is not a perceived barrier to entering the major itself.

CONCLUSION

We need to consider that this study spanned the first eight months of new freshmen students who were undergoing vast changes in lifestyle as they adjusted to campus life. Perhaps the general lack of change in perceptions demonstrates how the effect of one class meeting and one course were greatly diluted by the other curricular and extracurricular activities in which the participants engaged during the period of this study. Very clearly, one relatively standard session on MIS careers was insufficient to change student perceptions and attitudes about MIS careers. We need to develop a more pro-active strategy to market the MIS career both inside and outside the classroom.

We also need to consider that these students have effectively expressed an aversion to the workstyle of a computer programmer.

Although our introductory course did not involve programming, the vast majority of these students had programming experience prior to entering college (Harrington, 1988). As previously stated in this paper, both practitioners and academicians in the MIS profession agree on the desirability of immersing the "novitiate" into this activity as early as possible.

MIS, like other professions, requires its aspirants to participate extensively in tedious "grunt" work while in entry level positions. For the MIS profession, student exposure to these mundane tasks begins with high school programming courses, is augmented by an initial course in the undergraduate major called "programming", and further reinforced by an entry level position called "programmer". The analyst position is not really promoted by any of these conditions.

Contrast this with the accounting profession, where the introductory courses at both the high school and college levels involve more bookkeeping than accounting analysis, but are usually called "accounting". Furthermore, the typical entry level job does not carry the title "bookkeeper" even if it involves more bookkeeping than anything else.

Accordingly, we think the MIS profession should consider: (1) the adoption of less threatening course titles for programming courses, and (2) using the entry level job title "junior systems analyst" instead of "programmer" or "programmer/analyst" for those who are really systems analysts in training.

We also need to consider that these students are effectively indicating a desire for human interaction in their jobs. As previously stated, this is an important characteristic of a systems analyst. Perhaps if they didn't have to "pay their dues" by taking programming courses and working as programmers, substantially more students would be attracted to the MIS major and career. Although we don't advocate bypassing programming, we do see a need to develop some creative approaches for the placement and content of programming activities in both the major and the career.

This study examined students at only one undergraduate institution. Further studies need to be conducted at other types of schools to verify that what was observed here is characteristic of other undergraduates. Such studies should be carried out in conjunction with the design and implementation of programs intended to change students' perceptions of the CIS major and career.

REFERENCES

Anastasi, A. (1982). Psychological Testing, 5th ed., MacMillan, New York.

Astin, A. W., Green, K. C. & Korn, W. S. (1985). The American Freshman: 20 Year Trends, American Council on Education and the University of California at Los Angeles.

Astin, A. W., Green, K. C. & Korn, W. S. (1986) The American Freshman: Norms for Fall 1986, American Council on Education and the University of California at Los Angeles.

Astin, A. W., Green, K. C. & Korn, W. S. (1987). The American Freshman: Norms for Fall 1987, American Council on Education and the University of California at Los Angeles.

College Placement Council. (1978, July to 1988, January; 1987). CPC Salary Survey.

Couger, J. D. & Zawacki, R. A. (1980). Motivating and Managing Computer Personnel, John Wiley & Sons, New York.

Duke, P. (1987, November 27) Jobs go unfilled as fewer students show interest in computer science. Wall St. Journal, 13.

Ferratt, T. W. & Short, L. E. (1986, December). Are information systems people different: an investigation of motivational differences. MIS Quarterly, 377-387.

Harrington, J. L. (1988, February). The computer background of incoming freshmen: looking for emerging trends. SIGCSE Bulletin, 20(1), 210-214.

Jung, K. (1923). Psychological Types, London (Princeton University Press, Princeton, NJ, 1971).

Kaiser, K. M. & Bostrom, R. P. (1982, December). Personality characteristics of MIS project teams: an empirical study and action-research design. MIS Quarterly, 43-60.

King, W. R. & Cleland, D. I. (1971, April). Manager-analyst teamwork in MIS. Business Horizons, 59-69.

Lyons, M. L. (1985, August 15). The DP psyche. Datamation, 103-110.

Mason, R. O. & Mitroff, I. I. (1973). A program for research on management information systems. Management Science, 19(5), 475-485.

Mawhinney, C. H. (1986). Factors Affecting the Utilization of Personal Computers by Managers and Executives. University Microfilms International, Ann Arbor, MI.

Mawhinney, C. H., Cale, E. G. & Callaghan, D. R. (1988, April 7-8). Perceptions of the CIS graduate's workstyle: undergraduate business students versus CIS faculty. Proceedings of the 1988 ACM SIGCPR Conference on the Management of Information Systems Personnel, College Park, MD, 17-21.

Nunamaker, F., Couger, J. D. & Davis, G. B. (1982, November). Information systems curriculum recommendations for the 80's: undergraduate and graduate programs. Communications of the ACM, 25(11).

Rochester, J. B. (1988, January/February) The crisis in computer education. Computer Update.

Tabachnik, B. G. & Fidell, L. S. (1983). Using Multivariate Statistics. Harper & Row, New York.

Trent R. H. (1988, April 7-8). Perspectives on the academic preparation of MIS professionals. Panel discussion held at the ACM SIGCPR Conference on the Management of Information Systems Personnel.

Weinberg, G. M. (1971). The Psychology of Computer Programming. Van Nostrand Reinhold, New York.

Whitten, J. L., Bentley, L. D., & Ho, T. I. M. (1986). Systems Analysis & Design Methods. Times Mirror/Mosby, St. Louis.

Withington, F. (1988, January 11) Only you can prevent an MIS shortage. Computerworld, 17.

Wood, M. (1979, April 30). Systems analyst title most abused in industry: redefinition imperative. Computerworld, 24, 26.

Legend: Strongly Agree   Agree   Undecided   Disagree   Strongly Disagree
                  SA   A   U   D   SD

The following questions deal with your perception of the undergraduate Computer Information Systems program at Bentley College. Please indicate the strength of your agree-
ment/disagreement with each statement by circling the letter(s) that best describe your
feeling about or reaction to each statement. The typical <u>graduate</u> of this program:

 1. Is a whiz at mathematics.   SA A U D SD
 2. Entered Bentley College with a strong prior background in computers. SA A U D SD

During his/her first job after graduation, the typical graduate of this program:

 3. Spends most of his/her working time writing computer programs. SA A U D SD
 4. Spends most of his/her working time interacting with other persons. SA A U D SD
 5. Spends most of his/her time working alone.   SA A U D SD
 6. Designs new computer hardware.   SA A U D SD
 7. Interacts mostly with other computer people.   SA A U D SD
 8. Has a starting salary above the average Bentley College graduate. SA A U D SD
 9. Helps managers select new computer systems.   SA A U D SD

The following questions deal with your assessment of your own background and job preferences. I believe that I:

10. Am a whiz at mathematics.   SA A U D SD
11. Entered Bentley College with a strong prior background in computers. SA A U D SD

During my first job after graduation, I expect to:

12. Spend most of my working time writing computer programs.   SA A U D SD
13. Spend most of my working time interacting with other persons. SA A U D SD
14. Spend most of my time working alone.   SA A U D SD
15. Design new computer hardware.   SA A U D SD
16. Interact mostly with other computer people.   SA A U D SD
17. Have a starting salary above the average Bentley College graduate. SA A U D SD
18. Help managers select new computer systems.   SA A U D SD

An IS1 Workbench
for
ACM Information Systems Curriculum '81

Leslie J. Waguespack, Jr.

Computer Information Systems Department
Bentley College
Waltham, Massachusetts, 02254

Abstract

This paper describes the System Architects' Workbench, a personal computer-based teaching environment for courses in computer organization and systems programming. This tool set provides an integrated learning and teaching environment for computer systems concepts defined in ACM IS Curriculum '81 IS1. The central tool is a computer simulator based on a pedagogical model of computer system resources which allows students to study principles without becoming too involved in the implementation idiosyncrasies usually associated with machine level programming. Programs may be written directly in machine language or in a Pascal-like language, TP, which includes features that allow complete access to and control of host level resources. The TP compiler supports separate compilation, IPL load module generation, and detailed translation output used for machine language modification and debugging. The simulator supports interactive execution, tracing, modification, and debugging.

Introduction

ACM Curriculum for Information Systems '81 was established to serve "the person who wants to learn computers as a part of preparation for a general management career..." and "...the person who wants a lifetime career in information systems" [ACM81]. The IS1 course, Computer Concepts and Software Systems, is designated "to provide a broad familiarity with fundamental concepts and terminology associated with computer hardware systems and operating systems" [ACM82]. Similar concepts are described in the ACM Curriculum for Computer Science requirements for hardware systems and operating systems [ACM79]. However, the IS curriculum objectives specify a different focus and therefore require a different means of pedagogical delivery than are commonly found in CS curricula.

In this paper I review the distinctive focus on computer architecture and operating systems principles found in the ACM IS '81 Curriculum and describe a student workbench which has been designed to support the IS focus. The workbench, the Computer System Architects' Workbench is a personal computer based software development and simulation environment specifically suited for IS1 coursework. I will briefly describe the workbench's features and operation which specifically satisfy the learning objectives of IS1. Finally, some future evolution of the workbench and the associated course ware will be discussed.

The Demands of IS1

This is the rationale for the IS1 course in the ACM Information Systems Curriculum '81: "It is important to provide a broad familiarity with fundamental concepts and terminology associated with computer hardware systems and operating systems" [ACM82]. The instruction notes in the curriculum recommendations are quite explicit:

- the course must emphasize breadth rather than depth
- coverage of assembly language must be limited severely
- only those concepts and techniques that are necessary to understand ... concepts of computer architecture and operating systems should be covered
- the assignment of programming projects on a specific computer is valuable but, these projects should be few in number, small, and carefully constructed to convey the experience of assembly language programming without that experience dominating the course

There are three objectives in the course:

1 to introduce computer architecture

(computer structure, machine language, and assembly language)

2 to introduce the major concept areas of operating system principles

(memory management, process management, I/O management)

3 to introduce the interrelationships between the operating systems and architecture

(program control, interrupt structures, interprocess communication)

Key words in the course rationale are **breadth, familiarity,** and **interrelationships**. In a computer science curriculum it may be assumed that students will develop breadth in a series of entry level technical courses (e.g. assembly programming, data structures, computer organization), develop familiarity in more advanced courses with more extensive programming projects (e.g. operating systems projects, compiler projects, systems programming projects) and finally, realize interrelationships in a capstone synthesis course such as computer architecture. In the information systems curriculum breadth, familiarity, and interrelationships must be conveyed, for the most part, in a single semester course.

A Workbench Approach to Meet IS1 Demands

Traditionally computer architecture and operating systems principles have been delivered in courses using "real" hardware hosts such as the IBM 370 or DEC Vax and (sometimes more recently) the Intel 80xx or Motorola M68xxx microcomputers. This tradition included using the same software development tools and environment used by system programmers to perform "professional" programming projects. In the computer science context the cost of using such complex hosts and tools can be amortized over a series of courses which can take advantage of the initial "training" cost. In an IS curriculum it is unlikely that much of these "training" costs will provide direct benefits in subsequent course work. It is desirable to minimize these "training" costs as much as possible in the IS1 course.

Training costs can be lowered in IS1 by attempting the meet the following objectives:

1   choose a minimally complex target machine focused on the learning objectives of the course

2   provide a programming and testing support environment specific to that machine

3   use a high level language to demonstrate the operating system principles in lieu of assembly language

4   provide all the tools in a personal computer environment to take advantage of the easy access and productivity tools the students have become accustomed to

The System Architects' Workbench is an attempt to meet these objectives. The first design decision in the workbench was the use of a simulated rather than "real" hardware host. Simulation increases the course designer's control of the student environment (and thus the experience the student will have). The second design decision was to use a "model" host rather than a simulated "real" host. This choice allowed focus on function rather than detail with the opportunity to trade each off against the other for pedagogical purposes.

The sections that follow describe the simulated hardware system and the language tools which are used for software development on the host.

The Simulated Computer Architecture

The simulated architecture, the Total Virtual Access Architecture (TVAA), is based on a theoretical model of machines and programs which has been used for virtual machine research and development [Waguespack85a]. This model has been chosen to simplify the explanation of several computer architecture concepts:

- machine language
- data representation
- addressing
- instruction execution
- interrupts
- interprocess communication
- operating systems architecture
- virtual machine implementation
- multi–level systems design
- host support for high level language

The TVAA possesses a broad scope of characteristics attributable to both 3rd generation mainframe computers such as IBM 360/370, DEC Vax, Burroughs B7700, and a wide variety of micro and mini computers. In addition, the TVAA may be used to illustrate characteristics of object based architectures such as the Intel 432 Ada Engine, and the IBM System/38. The TVAA is a reduced instruction set computer, RISC. This RISC approach to the TVAA's design extensively simplifies the writing of system programs and diminishes the volume of code required to illustrate computing concepts.

The description below depicts the TVAA from three vantage points based on areas of "familiarity" to be developed in the student. They are 1) a view of the system by a machine language application programmer, 2) a view of the system by a systems programmer, and 3) a view of the system by the computer architect. **The Machine Language Programmer's Model**

The TVAA is a reduced instruction set computer (RISC). Computer memory is composed of words. All memory references are made in word granularity. All words contain the same number of bits. There are 17 operation codes [Table 1].

No Operation

Add

Subtract

Multiply

Integer Divide

And Logical

Or Logical

Xor Logical

Shift Right Logical

Shift Left Logical

Branch on Condition

Move Data

Create Storage Segment

Destroy Storage Segment

Compare Word

Push Onto Stack

Pop from Stack

Table 1
TVAA Instruction Operation Codes

There is only one instruction format. Every instruction has two operands [Exhibit 1].

TVAA Instruction Format

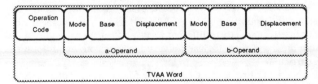

Exhibit 1

An operand refers to a word in the memory. An operand reference has three parts: the **mode** (designates standard, indirect, stack or immediate operand addressing), the **base** (designates which storage segment of the program contains the operand), and **displacement** (designates which word in the storage segment is the operand).

A process is defined by its **environment base** (EB). The EB is a storage segment that contains "pointers" to all the storage segments "owned" by the process. Each of these "pointers" is called a **storage base**.

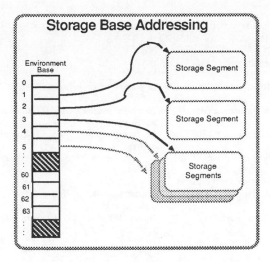

Exhibit 2

The EB also contains entries that define the state of the process, a structure often called the Process Control (status) Word. It contains the current instruction pointer (the Program Counter Base and Program Counter Displacement), the Condition Flags (the status result of the last instruction's execution), and the process's clock.

Input and Output in the TVAA is accomplished by using IO interface ports. An interface port is a one word storage location. Each IO device has three ports: a **command port** (where a binary integer is placed by the programmer to request an IO operation), a **data port** (to which (from which) the programmer moves the data to be transferred), and a **status port** (which indicates any exception conditions that may have occurred due to the IO request). These IO ports appear simply as memory locations which the programmer moves data to and from. There are no special IO instructions.

This brief overview is all that the beginning programmer needs to understand to attack a variety of problems related to data representation, Boolean arithmetic, integer arithmetic, and basic machine language implementation of algorithms. This entire model of a machine can be taught in a one hour lecture and programming can begin. Programming problems such as loading a program or performing input and output to the outside world become important to the system programmer at which time the students' understanding is extended with the following.

The System Programmer's Model

Initially the student sees the computer system as dedicated to one process (their own process). As a dedicated system virtually all of the problems associated with operating systems are absent. The student can learn how subprogram libraries may be developed to ease the programmer's task; how subprogram libraries eventually evolve into language extensions or language features. Once the student is introduced to the notion that more than one process may exist in this environment, the focus must change from application programmer to systems programmer. The basic difference is the expanded focus of machine features which now includes process control architecture.

Memory on the TVAA is organized in segments. A segment is a logically contiguous groups of words that has a name called a **handle**. In order for a segment to be referenced by a process, that segment's handle must be present in that process's EB. That is why a program refers to memory via a storage base. Storage bases contain segment handles. Processes may create segments dynamically using the CREATE instruction; a segment is allocated and assigned

a handle and that handle is placed in the appropriate storage base of the process. Once created, the contents of the segment are routinely accessed by (base, displacement) references in ordinary machine instructions. Storage segments may be shared by copying the segment's handle and placing that value in the EB of the sharing process. The DESTROY instruction deallocates a memory segment and renders is non-existent. References to storage bases without valid handles result in **program exceptions** usually causing **interrupts**.

On the TVAA, process activation is achieved by indicating which EB in the memory is the one whose instructions should be currently executed. This designation is made by placing a pointer to the active process's EB (that EB's handle) into a "pointer" called the **environment pointer**, EP [Exhibit 3].

Exhibit 3

Switching control from one process to another is as simple as

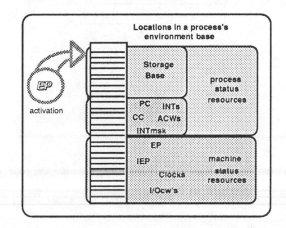

changing the contents of the EP. This is how control is passed from process to process; either voluntarily by changing the EP or involuntarily as in the case of interrupts. The system programmer needs to be able to restrict the process's ability to change the value of the EP. Indeed, a wide variety of machine resources (clocks, interrupt vectors, the IO ports) should be protected from haphazard modification by "non-operating system" processes. The means of this protection is simple memory protection. The EB's role as "directory to storage segments" also doubles as "access list". Memory segments may only be accessed if their **handles** are in a process's EB. The operating system can gain control of the system anytime a process attempts to access a storage base with an invalid handle by setting up the interrupt vector for that purpose.

The last piece to this brief description is the means that distinguishes a process as an operating system (or control) process rather than an ordinary process. Again the EB is involved. The EB is composed of storage bases and process control information. These are collectively referred to as **process status resources**. (This information exists for each process.) The resources that control the machine itself (the EP, IO ports, interrupt vectors, etc.) are not virtual but, real locations in the computer memory. There is only one instance of these resources which are called **machine status resources**. But, since memory can be only referenced via an EB and storage bases, the machine status resources may only be accessed if a memory segment happens to overlay these real memory locations. That is exactly what happens at Initial Program Load time when the machine is "powered up". The boot program automatically becomes the kernel of the operating system because the first segment created at IPL overlays the machine status resources.

The Computer Architects' Model

The same TVAA system may be presented from yet another perspective, that of the computer architect. This is actually the architecture of the TVAA simulator.

Exhibit 4

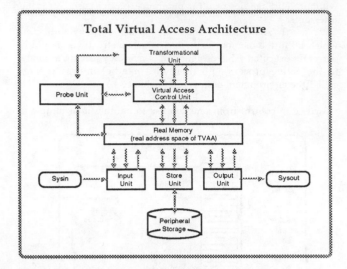

Total Virtual Access Architecture

The "hardware" is composed of functional units performing specialized subfunctions. The instruction set is implemented by the **Transformational Unit**. Memory management functions are performed by the **Virtual Access Control Unit**. Input and output are performed by the **Input Unit** and **Output Unit**, respectively. These allow IO in human readable form with special IO operations to read and write data in integer, hexadecimal, character, and word formats. A special format, pseudo-assembly, allows the direct input of machine instructions without resort to translators or binary codes. Peripheral storage facility is provided via the **Store Unit**. Finally, interactive debugging and performance measurement and evaluation services are provided by the **Probe Unit**. (Detailed specifications may be found in the TVAA Fundamentals of Operation\ [Waguespack87a]).

In advanced courses it may be appropriate to require the student to design and implement new functional units (e.g. Backend Database Unit, Graphics Unit, Network Control Unit, etc.). This would be accomplished by modifying the simulator itself.

The TVAA Pascal Language System

Systems Programming in High-Level Language

It is possible to author and execute programs on the TVAA directly in machine language. Pedagogically this may be useful for orientation and/or "awe inspiration". However, useful programming projects in machine language is an oxymoron. This is particularly true of students who don't have long experience programming in any language much less machine language. The TVAA Pascal (TP) language system allows the student to solve computer organization or operating system problems without resorting to machine language. This is largely accomplished with a "location specifier" extension to Pascal. By placing a tuple in brackets behind any variable declaration (e.g. COUNT : INTEGER [4.56];) the programmer associates that variable with the memory reference Base(4) and Displacement(56). Given this extension any host resource (EP, IO port, Clock, EB entry) may be manipulated directly

via Pascal syntax (as long as its location in memory is known). The example below illustrates IO via TVAA Pascal.

```
Program Demo_OU_Output;
Const
     Message = 'Hello!'      {a literal to be printed by the OU};
Var
     OUcommand : word[0.96] {a variable to be mapped to real
                              address 96};
     OUdata : word[0.97]    {a variable to be mapped to real
                              address 97};
     OUstatus : word[0.98]  {a variable to be mapped to real
                              address 98};
Begin { Demo_OU_Output }
     OUdata := Message       {move the literal 'Hello!' to the OU
                              data port};
     OUcommand := 4          {move the code "WriteWord" to the
                              OU command port};
     OUcommand := 6          {move the code "WriteEol" to the
                              OU command port};
End{ Demo_OU_Output }.
```

TVAA Output Example in TVAA Pascal
Exhibit 5

In this example (Exhibit 5) the variables OUcommand, OUdata, and OUstatus have been bound to real locations corresponding to the IO ports they will model. Once bound in this manner they may be manipulated in the body of the program as simple Pascal variables. (Notice that the literal Message is a word containing 6 ASCII characters which is the current word size of the simulator, 48 bits).

```
{---}
     Procedure Write_Word( data : word ); Intrinsic [0.123:1];
     Procedure Write_Eol; Intrinsic [0.321:0];
{---}
Procedure Access_Dynamic_Segment;
const
     an_unused_base = 30      {this must be chosen carefully
                              within a system};
     how_many_words = 365 {locations 0..364    an arbitrary
                              value};
     an_unused_dummy_parameter = 0;
Var
     the_segment : array[0..8192] of word [an_unused_base.0];
     i : integer;

Begin { Access_Dynamic_Segment }
     Create(an_unused_base, how_many_words);

     for i := 0 to how_many_words - 1 do the_segment[i] := i;


     {perform some other manipulation};

     Destroy(an_unused_base, an_unused_dummy_parameter )

     {when finished; dispose of segment cleanly};
End{ Access_Dynamic_Segment };
```

Dynamic Memory Access Example in TVAA Pascal
Exhibit 6

The example shown in Exhibit 6 illustrates the use of CREATE and DESTROY instructions from TP. These instructions have been incorporated in TP as built in procedures; and unlike most other procedure calls, the compiler generates single machine instructions for them. This example also depicts the use of intrinsic modules.

An intrinsic is a module compiled separately from the current compile unit and the entry point to that module is indicated by the location specifier that follows it. (The integer following the colon in the location specifier indicates the size of the activation record for the module upon block entry. The declarations for these intrinsic modules may be automatically generated by the compiler.)

The compiler generates a comprehensive listing of the program's translation which of itself is useful pedagogically. The compiler listing has been used to demonstrate the use of a stack in the evaluation of arithmetic expressions. The object code for a number of different arithmetic expressions was used to explain reverse polish notation. Examples of module linkage, recursive program code, and operating system calls may be demonstrated in like manner.

Conclusion

A variety of example system problems may be developed to accommodate almost any style of pedagogy in this subject area. A series of systems programming and operating systems examples have been prepared to accompany the Workbench as a starting point for course preparation. Current examples include a file control processor supporting sequential and random file organization with file directory and file storage management features. There is a program termination analysis module that performs a postmortem process analysis. There is a single process operating system that includes the file control processor, extended input output intrinsics and the post-mortem facilities.

The TVAA simulator and TVAA Pascal compiler are implemented in Borland Turbo Pascal™. Running on a MacPlus™ based host the simulator is capable of executing 45+ TVAA instructions per second and the TP compiler is capable of translating 300+ lines of TVAA Pascal per minute. The translator's performance compares admirably with vendor production compilers. The performance of the simulator is adequate to allow simulation of moderately complex operating systems activities. Together they are appropriate for course laboratory use. Running on a Mac II™ based host the simulator is capable of executing 175+ TVAA instructions per second and the TP compiler is capable of translating 1600+ lines of TVAA Pascal per minute. This platform would be more appropriate for advanced OS exercises.

The System Architects' Workbench is compatible with the Computer Science Scholars' Workbench [Haas83, Waguespack84] since the TP syntax is compatible with the source level manipulation tools found in the later. These include macro generation, identifier level and module level cross reference indexing, pretty-printing, and source compare / archiving tools.

Future projects include additional course ware and expanding the base of personal computers the workbench will accommodate. In course ware, a multiprogramming operating system is planned along with extensions to the model architecture to allow multiprocessing. All of the workbench software is implemented in Borland Turbo™ Pascal. Porting the workbench to MS-DOS based personal computers seems likely in the near future. Consideration is being given to making the workbench available through Kinko's Academic Courseware Exchange.

Space does not permit a more exhaustive description of the system here. A complete description may be found in the reference manuals which are available as Technical Reports from Bentley College's Institute for Research and Faculty Development [Wagueapack 88a, 88b, 88c].

Acknowledgement

I wish to acknowledge the contribution of Don Chand and my colleagues in the CIS department for their careful readings of earlier versions of this paper. Special thanks to Ann O'Connell my graduate research assistant who spent many hours testing and developing example problems on and for the workbench. I would also like to recognize the commitment and enthusiasm of the Advanced Computer Architecture students at Louisiana State University and the Computer Systems Architecture students at Bentley College for their patience during rough spots in the development.

Bibliography

[ACM79] ACM, "Curriculum '78 - Recommendations for the Undergraduate Program in Computer Science," Report of the ACM Curriculum Committee on Computer Science, Communications of the ACM, Vol. 22, No. 3, March, 1979, pp. 147-166.

[ACM81] Nunamaker, Jay F., ed., "A Report of the ACM Curriculum Committee on Information Systems", Communications of the ACM, Vol. 24, No. 3, pp. 124-133, March 1981.

[ACM82] Nunamaker, Jay F., Couger, J. Daniel, and Davis, Gordon B. eds., "Information Systems Curriculum Recommendations for the 80's: Undergraduate and Graduate Programs," CACM, Vol. 25, No. 11, pp. 781-805, November, 1982.

[Haas83] Haas, David F. and Waguespack, Leslie J. , "An Introduction to the Computer Science Scholars' Workbench for Research and Teaching," Technical Report TR 83-019, Department of Computer Science, Louisiana State University, Baton Rouge, Louisiana, August 1983.

[Waguespack84] Waguespack, Leslie J. and, Haas, David F. "A Workbench for Project Oriented Software Engineering Courses," Proceedings of the Fifteenth SIGCSE Technical Symposium on Computer Science Education, Philadelphia, Pennsylvania, February 1984, pp. 137-145.

[Waguespack85a] Waguespack, Leslie J., "A Structural Computer System Resource Model For Teaching Computer Organization," Proceedings of the Sixteenth SIGCSE Technical Symposium on Computer Science Education, New Orleans, Louisiana, March 1985, pp. 63-67.

[Waguespack85b] Waguespack, Leslie J., "Personal Student Workstations: Prospectus and Requirements," Proceedings of the Sixteenth SIGCSE Technical Symposium on Computer Science Education, New Orleans, Louisiana, March 1985, pp. 145-151.

[Waguespack88a] Waguespack, Leslie J., "TVAA: Fundamentals of Operation," Technical Report TR-88-21, Institute for Research and Faculty Development, Bentley College, Waltham, Ma., June, 1988.

[Waguespack88b] Waguespack, Leslie J., "TVAA Pascal Programmers' Guide," Technical Report TR-88-20, Institute for Research and Faculty Development, Bentley College, Waltham, Ma., July, 1988.

[Waguespack88c] Waguespack, Leslie J., "TVAA Programmers' Guide", Technical Report TR-88-19, Institute for Research and Faculty Development, Bentley College, Waltham, Ma., August, 1988.

Progressive Project Assignments in Computer Courses

Robert Leeper

Computer Science Department
Indiana University Purdue University
at Fort Wayne
Fort Wayne, IN 46805

Abstract

This paper presents a method of design for projects in computer courses that tends to enable all students in the class to achieve their maximum potential. Each project is structured at three progressive levels of difficulty corresponding to three prospective grades A, B, and C. The B-level is an extension of the C-level and the A-level is an extension of the B-level. Each student starts at the C-level and progresses as far as possible and is scored accordingly.

Introduction

The laboratory portion of many computer courses consists of set of computer programs the students are expected to design, code, implement, and submit for grading. In most cases, all students in the class are assigned exactly the same set of projects. This often leads to unsatisfactory experiences for students due to the degree of difficulty of the projects. The outstanding students in a class may not be challenged by projects that the average or lower-than-average students are reasonably expected to complete correctly. "A realistic student project is one that reflects both a student's abilities as well as a student's interests." [2] Projects that challenge the outstanding students leave the average students lost and confused. Progressive project assignment is a method of designing projects that are challenging and attainable to all the students in a class. Projects are designed with three progressively more difficult levels that correspond to the grades C, B, and A.

Problems With Standard Methods

Often a typical student in a computer class will attempt to design and code all of a long and complex project before keying in any of the source code. Then when the source code is keyed in and a compile is attempted a plethora of errors results. The student may spend hours wrestling with these errors until the due-date of the project has arrived without a satisfactory compile or without substantially correct results and get a grade of zero or F for the effort. In the same class there may be students who are unchallenged by the same project. Still other students get so much help on the project that they are able to complete it satisfactorily but without understanding the principles it was intended to convey.

Progressive Projects

Progressive projects are designed with a core part that includes all the principles the project intends to convey. Every student is expected to complete this part satisfactorily. Students who go no farther than this are graded at the 'C' level. If the project is essentially correct in design, documentation, output, and implementation the grade of 'C' is assigned.

A second part that extends the project in some meaningful way is added to the assignment for the 'B' level. This part will require a significant effort from the students who elect to continue beyond the 'C' level. Students who successfully complete the 'C' part and the 'B' part are graded at the 'B' level.

The third part extends the project still farther and should be designed so that all three parts present a challenge to the best students in the class. Students completing all three parts are graded at the 'A' level.

The progressive feature of the project design is important. If three separate (possibly unrelated) projects of increasing degrees of difficulty are provided there is a temptation for the B-students and C-students to select the A-level project only to find out, too late, it is beyond their capabilities and they cannot complete the project prior to the due-date resulting in a grade of 'F' for the project. This problem will not occur with progressive projects since the C-level and the B-level must be completed by all students before the A-level is attempted.

Advantages

Perhaps the most significant advantage of this method is that it naturally encourages students to apply the 'divide and conquer' principle ([8] p 16). Students complete the core section of the project first, thus assuring at least a grade of 'C'. If they have time they may wish to attempt the second part for a grade of 'B' and some will continue to the third part for a grade of 'A'.

Average and below-average students are able to produce meaningful programs at the C-level without a lot of help. This gives them more confidence and enables them to master the fundamental principles of the course.

Outstanding students are challenged by the more difficult work that is expected of them. They are no longer merely functioning at the same level as everyone else in class. This method provides the opportunity to demonstrate superior ability. Students tend to be better satisfied with project grades. They know in advance their maximum expected grades.

Examples

Following are some examples of progressive projects assigned to students in the second computer science course (CS2 of the model curriculum [9]).

Project 1:

C-level

Write an interactive Pascal program that will provide for two people to play tic-tactoe. The program should provide a two-dimensional grid for the game and accept input from the contestants that specifies the locations selected. It should report a winner as soon as there is one; otherwise, it should report a tie.

B-level

In addition to the C-level requirements do error checking of the input. Location entries from the players must be checked for valid positions on the board. Player responses are to be read as characters to avoid runtime errors.

A-level

In addition to the B-level requirements extend the program so that the computer is the second player and the computer never loses. You need to program a 'non-losing' strategy for the computer.

Project 2:

C-level

Write two Pascal programs. The first program is to create a sequential disk file of employees of the ACME Company with fields for ID, Name, Telephone, Hire Date, Salary, and Department. It should reject records whose ID is not in ascending order or that duplicate the previous ID. The program should print a report listing rejected records and the number of accepted records.

The second program is to read the file that was created by the first program and print a report listing all the records in the file. The report should have a title, the run date, appropriate column headings and at the bottom it should give the number of employees and the total of the salary column.

B-level

In addition to the C-level requirements, sort the file in ascending order on the name field using an appropriate sort method and print the report again in this order.

A-level

After sorting on the name field, sort on the department field then print additional reports by department, printing each department on a separate page with appropriate headings at the top. Also print the number of employees in the department and total of the salary field for the department at the end of each department.

Project 3.

C-level

Create an ordered linked list with student records. Each record contains fields for ID, Name, Credits, and GPA. The list is to be in order by ID. The program is to provide a menu and for the following types of interactive query of the data:

1. A report listing all the student records in ID order.

2. List the complete record with field identifiers of any student whose ID is given.

B-level

All the C-level requirements plus provide a third choice on the menu for printing all records that are in a given range of values of the GPA. When this choice is selected the program should ask the user for two numbers in the range of 0.0 to 4.0. It then prints the records of all the students whose GPA's are in the given range.

A-level

All the B-level requirements plus provide a fourth choice on the menu for printing a report of all student records listed in order by GPA. To provide for this report add a second link field to each node that links the nodes in order by GPA.

Grading

The grading system is patterned after one by Linda Rising [10]. Projects with programs that compile and produce results that are essentially correct are graded based on the five factors:

Correctness
Design
Style
Documentation
Efficiency

A project is assigned a score of 0 - 4 points for each of these factors. These scores are totalled (maximum is 20) then multiplied by the level factor that corresponds to the number of steps completed by the student for this project. This result is rounded then converted to a letter grade. (For further details of grading refer to the PROJECT GRADING FORM in the appendix.)

For example, suppose a student submits a B-level project and the scores are as follows:

Correctness	3
Design	4
Style	4
Documentation	3
Efficiency	4
Total	18

The level factor for project level B is 17/20. Multiplying the total score by this factor

$$18 \times 17/20 = 15.3 \qquad \text{(Rounded to 15)}$$

Therefore, the final grade falls in the C range.

Projects with programs that do not compile or that do not produce essentially correct results receive no grade.

Summary

The author has applied the method of progressive project design in two classes recently. Project grades earned in these two classes are listed in Table 1. Table 2 lists the grades of two classes that were assigned traditional projects. Comparing the percentages in the two tables indicates the grades from the 'progressive' projects were more evenly distributed than from the 'traditional' projects. This method results in significantly fewer 'A' and 'F' grades and significantly more 'B', 'C' and 'D' grades than the traditional project assignments. The reduced number of 'A' grades for the progressive projects assignments implies these projects were more difficult than the traditional project assignments while the reduced number of 'F' grades indicates more students were successful in completing the reduced requirements for 'B' and 'C' grades.

Class	#Students	#Projects	#A	#B	#C	#D	#F	Total
Spring 88	23	6	59	28	26	6	13	132
Summer 88	12	5	26	10	12	6	6	60
Totals	35	11	85	38	38	12	19	192
Percent of Total			44	20	20	6	10	100

Table 1. Project Grades Distribution in Two CIS121 Classes That used Progressive Projects Assignments

Class	#Students	#Projects	#A	#B	#C	#D	#F	Total
Summer 86	23	4	58	6	5	3	20	92
Summer 87	21	5	63	15	4	3	20	105
Totals	44		121	21	9	6	40	197
Percent of Total			61	11	5	3	20	100

Table 2. Project Grades Distribution in Two CIS121 Class That Used Traditional Project Assignments

References

(1) David M. Olson, "The Reliability of Analytic and Holistic Methods in Rating Students' Computer Programs", SIGCSE Bulletin, Vol. 20, Number 1, 1988, pp 293-298.

(2) William J. Joel, "Realistic Student Projects", SIGCSE Bulletin, Vol. 19, Number 1, 1987, pp 244-247.

(3) Lipsanti, Mann, and Zlotnick, Algorithms, Programming, Pascal, Wadsworth Publishing Company, Belmont, California, 1987.

(4) William W. McMillan, "Designing Introductory Computing Assignments: The View from the Computing Center", SIGCSE Bulletin, Volume 14, Number 1, 1982, pp 82-84.

(5) Henry M. Walker, Introduction to Computing and Computer Science With Pascal, Little, Brown and Company, Boston, MA, 1982.

(6) Lionel E. Deimel Jr. and Mark Pozefsky, "Requirements for Student Programs in the Undergraduate Computer Science Curriculum: How Much is Enough?", SIGCSE Bulletin, Volume 11, Number 1, 1979, pp 14-17.

(7) Jean-Paul Tremblay and Richard B. Bunt, An Introduction to Computer Science An Algorithmic Approach, McGrawHill Book Company, New York, NY, 1979.

(8) C. William Gear, Computer Applications and Algorithms, Science Research Associates, Inc., Chicago, IL, 1986.

(9) Richard H. Austing, et al, Curriculum '78 Recommendations for the Undergraduate Program in Computer Science, ACM Recommended Curricula for Computer Science and Information Processing Programs in Colleges and Universities, 1968-1981, Association for Computing Machinery, Baltimore, MD, 1981, pp 119-138.

(10) Linda Rising, "Teaching Documentation and Style in Pascal", SIGCSE Bulletin, Volume 19, Number 3, 1987, pp 8,9.

PROJECT GRADING FORM

Name _____ Project number _____ Class _____

_____Correctness
   4 - no errors found
   3 - one or two minor problems (special cases or error conditions overlooked)
   2 - a number of minor problems
   1 - one major error (does not meet project specifications)
   0 - more than one major error

_____ Design
   4 - all small, coherent, independent modules, unless well-justified
   3 - some insufficiently justified violations but no serious problems
   2 - reasonably well-structured but needs improvement
   1 - poorly structured
   0 - unacceptable; unjustified global references

_____Style
   4 - perfect
   3 - one or two small imperfections
   2 - generally good, but several imperfections
   1 - difficult to read and understand; few comments
   0 - unacceptable; no comments, no or very poor indentation

_____Documentation
   4 - all included and well done
   3 - all included and reasonably well done
   2 - all included, some parts not well done
   1 - one item missing or poorly done
   0 - more than one missing item or very poorly done

_____Efficiency
   4 - the method of choice used and correctly implemented
   3 - a good method was used
   2 - a reasonable method was used
   1 - some clearly unnecessary steps were performed
   0 - grossly inefficient, unnecessary repetition of steps

_____ Total _____ Project Level _____ Level Factor

_____ Project Score (Total X Level Factor)

Grade Ranges		Project Level	Level Factors
18 - 20	A	A	20/20
16 - 17	B	B	17/20
14 - 15	C	C	15/20
12 - 13	D		
00 - 11	F		

An Example Illustrating
Modularity, Abstraction & Information Hiding
Using Turbo Pascal 4.0

Ivan B. Liss and Thomas C. McMillan
Department of Computer Science
Radford University
Radford, Virginia 24142

ABSTRACT

In this paper we present, by way of an example, techniques for using the independently compilable units of Turbo Pascal 4.0. (Turbo Pascal is a Pascal compiler available from Borland International.) We suggest ways that units can be used to illustrate software engineering principles, including information hiding, modularity, and procedural and data abstraction. The paper describes Turbo Pascal units and gives a sample project. It also suggests a number of ways that this or similar projects can be used to illustrate these principles to CS1 and CS2 classes.

INTRODUCTION

Turbo Pascal 4.0 has a significant feature which can be used to illustrate procedural and data abstraction: independently compiled units. Each unit has an interface section and an implementation section. Some degree of information hiding can be accomplished with units. In this paper we present a game-playing program which illustrates how Turbo Pascal units can be used to introduce abstraction to CS1 and CS2 students.

A. Use of Turbo Pascal 4.0 Units

In Turbo Pascal 4.0, the program designer can use independently compilable units to implement different program modules. Each unit has an interface section, an implementation section and an executable section. The interface section of a unit contains a list of other units which it uses. It contains constant, type and variable declarations. It also contains procedure and function declarations (just the procedure and function statements–not their bodies). These declarations are "public knowledge" available to all units which use this unit.

The implementation section contains constant, type and variable declarations, which are private and can be used only by the unit in which they occur. The implementation section also contains the full declarations for procedures and functions which appear in the interface section of the unit, and for private procedures and functions which are used in the implementation.

These declarations are "private knowledge" available only to the unit in which they occur.

The executable section of a unit contains code which is executed once before the body of the main program unit is executed. This optional section can be used to initialize data structures within the unit.

If a unit does not use any other units then it need only be made available in compiled form–the source code need not be released. This enables the programmer to achieve some degree of information hiding. Other units in a program have access only to the interface section of the unit; many implementation details are hidden within the implementation section. Theoretically, some implementation details are public knowledge because they appear in the interface section. For example, if QUnit is a unit which implements queues, then the interface section will include a type declaration for the identifier Queue. Thus, information about how queues are implemented (using arrays, dynamic variables, etc.) is public knowledge. As a practical matter, though, this information can be hidden by making only the compiled version of the unit available. The documentation for the unit would include descriptions of how to use the procedures and functions which manipulate queues, but would not need to include details about the type declarations.

If a unit uses other units, then it may be necessary to make its source code available. If the interface section of a unit is modified then all units which use it will have to be recompiled on the next build operation. (A build is a compilation of the main program that automatically recompiles the units which it uses and which need to be recompiled.) Thus if UnitA uses UnitB and if the user can modify the interface section of UnitB, then he will have to have access to the source code for UnitA so that it can be recompiled on the next build operation. In this situation, true information hiding is obviously impossible. However, it is possible to contain the implementation procedures within the implementation section of the unit and thus keep them from being accessed from other units. If the programmer does not "cheat" by bypassing the interface routines and accessing the data structures directly, then the spirit of information hiding can be maintained and implementation details can be contained (if not hidden) within the unit.

For more details on units in Turbo Pascal 4.0, refer to the Turbo Pascal reference manual.

B. Project Description

The project is to design and implement a strategy for playing a board game which we call **ScoreX**. The game is sold commercially by Milton-Bradley as Connect Four. The purpose of the assignment is to illustrate the benefits of modularity, procedural and data abstraction, and information hiding. The game board may be represented in two dimensions as shown in Figure 1.

```
| | | | | | |
| | | | | | |
| | | | | | |
| | | | | | |
| | | | | | |
--------------------
 1  2  3  4  5  6
```

Figure 1.

Two players, Black (BB) and White (WW), alternate moves in which each player drops one marker of his color into the top of a column which is not full. When one player gets a specified number of his markers in a row (horizontally, vertically, or diagonally), that player wins the game. If all columns are filled before either player has the required number of markers in a row, the game is declared a draw. For purposes of illustration in this paper, we assume that the board has six columns, each of which will hold five markers, and that four markers in a row are required to win. However, the size of the board and the number of markers in a row needed to win can be set as desired. Some samples of winning combinations are shown in Figure 2.

```
| | | | | | |          | | | | | | |
| | | | |BB| |          | | | | | |WW|
| | | |WW|BB|WW|        | | | |BB|WW|WW|
| | |BB|WW|BB|WW|        | | |WW|WW|BB|BB|
|WW|BB|WW|BB|BB|WW|      | |BB|WW|BB|BB|WW|
--------------------    --------------------

   Black wins               White wins
```

Figure 2.

GOALS

Our goal is a project appropriate for students in the latter part of a CS2 course. These students are familiar with the concepts of procedural and data abstraction and top-down design. They have implemented abstract data types and have done several exercises with binary trees and recursion. The project described here reinforces these ideas and introduces the concepts of game trees and of heuristic search in such trees. The project also requires that the students design and implement an abstract data type: The game board is an abstract data type and the operations for examining it and changing it are the associated primitives. The project is a nice capstone project which emphasizes themes which are constant in our CS1 and CS2 courses: modularity, abstraction, information hiding, and top-down design.

ORGANIZATION OF THE PROJECT

The project can be implemented using five units: **PlayGame**, **Consts**, **ScoreX**, **Player1**, and **Player2**. **PlayGame** is the main program unit. The hierarchical relationship among these modules is given by the tree in Figure 3. For example, **ScoreX** is the daughter of **Player1**, indicating that **Player1** uses **ScoreX**.

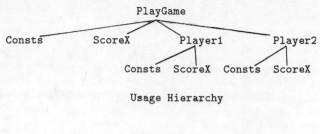

Usage Hierarchy

Figure 3.

ScoreX is the implementation of the game board as an abstract data type. The interface section of **ScoreX** includes the necessary declarations of "primitive" operations needed to play the game. Our definition of a "primitive" operation for an abstract data type is an operation which a programmer can reasonably expect to have available in order to access or modify instances of that data type. Note that these primitives are not defined as atomic operations - i.e., one primitive procedure might contain a call to another primitive procedure. Appendix 1 contains the procedure and function headers from the interface section of **ScoreX**. A brief description of each of these primitives is also included in Appendix 1.

Consts is a unit which contains in its interface section constant declarations which must be available to other units in the program. **PlayGame** uses the primitives in **ScoreX** to initialize a board with size and goal as specified by constant declarations in unit **Consts** (e.g. 6 columns of height 5 with a goal of 4 in a row). Each of the players needs to know this information, so they also use unit **Consts**.

Player1 is a unit which makes available, through its interface section, the procedure with the following header:

```
procedure MakePlayer1Move(   Color:ColorType;
                          var Board:BoardType);
```

MakePlayer1Move examines the board, determines the best possible move (using some user-defined algorithm), and updates the value of Board by performing that move using a marker whose color is Color. The implementation section of **Player1** contains the routines which implement the strategy employed by MakePlayer1Move. These could be procedures which apply a heuristic, do a minimax search of a game tree, or prune the game tree. The unit **Player2** similarly deploys a strategy for a second player.

The main program unit, **PlayGame**, initializes a game board using the constant values from **Consts**, and then plays a game between the algorithm in **Player1** and the algorithm in **Player2**.

USING THE PROJECT IN CLASS

One way to use this project in class is to assign it in phases. The students are given the procedure and function headers of Appendix 1, and asked to implement the game board as an abstract data type. The specifications for the interface section of **ScoreX** have to be agreed upon in advance. Appendix 1 provides some of these specifications, but also there must be agreement on constant and type names used in the interface section. Phase I is the implementation of **ScoreX** and a small driver program to test its performance.

The concept and use of driver programs should be covered in lecture and by programming exercises prior to the assigning of Phase I. The students' driver programs must be able to create a Board such that the appropriate primitive functions can be tested to check for a win or a draw, to drop a marker or undo a move, to print a representation of the Board, etc.

Phase II of the assignment is to implement the units **Player1** and **Player2**. In this phase, these modules are almost identical. MakePlayer1Move is not a procedure for determining the best move according to some algorithm; it is a procedure which makes a move which has been supplied by an interactive user. MakePlayer2Move performs in a similar manner. In Phase II, **PlayGame**, using **Player1** and **Player2** and the **ScoreX** as implemented in Phase I, is an interactive program which plays a game between two human users. Appendix 3 gives an outline of the unit **Player1**.

Phase III of the assignment uses all of the modules from Phase II, except that **Player2** is replaced with a module in which MakePlayer2Move applies a game-playing algorithm to determine the best possible move. In Phase III, with the new **Player2** module, **PlayGame** is an interactive program which plays a game between a human user and an algorithm. While students are working on earlier phases of the project, lecture material can cover the topics necessary to design and write a program to play such a game. These topics include game trees and heuristic search techniques in such trees. Coverage can be given to various strategy heuristics involving lookahead techniques, the minimax search technique, and alpha-beta pruning (Winston 1984). Examples can be given to help explain both design strategies and coding methods. A good example to use is that of tic-tac-toe. While this is a similar board game in that the number of markers must be tracked, moves are alternated between two players, etc., there are still major differences in tic-tac-toe and Connect Four. Instructors must choose, based on the abilities of their classes, the degree of detail that needs to be presented in such examples. We found that it is useful to spend more time in the discussion of higher level design, while including very few fully implemented procedures and functions for our examples.

This technique of discussing concepts in lecture while the students are designing and implementing programs that use these concepts seems to us to be a good teaching method. The students certainly ask more questions than they ordinarily would and have a very powerful incentive to understand the concepts under discussion. For example, in discussing heuristics, we proposed a simple scheme for measuring the value of a potential move: Temporarily make the move, and for all the straight-line paths containing the new marker add one point for each marker of the same color which is in a path for a potential win for that color. (The marker temporarily added is counted as part of each of these paths.) Figure 4 shows some examples of such scoring for White.

```
            **                     **
 |  |  |  |  |  |  |     |  |  |  |  |  |  |
 |  |  |  |  |  |  |     |  |  |  |  |  |  |
 |  |  |  |WW|  |  |     |  |  |  |WW|  |  |
 |  |  |WW|BB|  |  |     |  |WW|WW|BB|  |  |
 |  |WW|BB|WW|BB|  |     |WW|BB|WW|BB|BB|  |
 ---------------------   ---------------------

Score for White = 3   Score for White = 6
```

(The ** indicates the column which holds the temporary marker.)

Figure 4.

Because students were aware that they would eventually have to demonstrate the effectiveness of their game-playing strategy, this simple heuristic generated a lively discussion about evaluating potential moves.

This approach to the implementation of **PlayGame** emphasizes the benefits of modularity. The program is set up so that the units are "plug-compatible" modules. A significant change can be made to the program by removing one module and "plugging in" another module. Each module is designed, implemented and tested independently of the other modules. Intermodule communication is handled through a well-defined interface which is established early in the design. All modules have availability to information on a "need to know" basis. Thus, when **Player1** drops a marker into a given column, that unit does not need to know how the operation was accomplished, but it does need to see the effect on Board. The benefits of modularity, procedural and data abstraction, and information hiding can be discussed using this project as an example.

There are ways in which this type of project can be used in a less extensive assignment. For example, the instructor can make available **PlayGame** and **Player2** as an interactive player module. The student can be given the task of implementing **ScoreX** and a **Player1** unit which plays against **Player2**. Alternatively, the student can be given all but the **Player1** algorithm and be given the assignment of implementing a **Player1** unit which performs well against a **Player2** unit supplied (in compiled form so that the algorithm is hidden) by the instructor.

Another approach adds an air of excitement to the assignment. The students are provided with a version of **PlayGame** and compiled versions of **Consts, ScoreX, Player1** and **Player2**. The students are then given the task of implementing their own versions of **Player1** and **Player2**. They can use the units provided as a driver for testing their implementations. On the day the assignment is due, the students bring their **Player1** and **Player2** units to class, and the instructor uses his own driver program to pit the **Player1** from one student against the **Player2** unit from another student. A tournament can be set up in this manner. We have run such a tournament in our classes. The students enjoy it, and they give serious consideration to the performance of their game-playing algorithms. The tournament also illustrates the portability of units and further emphasizes the benefits of modularity and procedural and data abstraction: a relatively major change to a program is just a matter of removing one module and plugging in another one.

IMPLEMENTATION DETAILS

Figure 5 illustrates some of the constant and type declarations appearing in the interface section of **ScoreX**. Other implementations are certainly possible.

While there is no need to provide details of all the primitives previously described, several examples are shown in Appendix 2, which outlines the implementation for the **ScoreX** unit. It should be noticed that, when appropriate and where possible, error messages are generated. This is consistent with our policy of requiring that code be as robust as possible.

We make two additional comments about this implementation. First, the Board parameter is passed using call by reference in all of the primitive operations. This is done for run-time efficiency: as the program is executing, calls to the primitive operations do not require the duplication of a cumbersome data structure that is necessary when call by value is used. While not in strict accordance with the definition of a function as a module which returns a single value, if care is taken not to change the value of Board, this technique yields modules which are logically equivalent to functions (McCracken 1987).

Second, the abstract data type BoardType has boolean components WhiteWin and BlackWin. The values for these variables are calculated every time a marker is dropped. This avoids a time consuming search for a winning pattern for every call to IsWin. This search is circumvented by RemoveMarker by setting the appropriate component to "False" when a marker is removed. In other words, if a marker is removed from a winning board, then RemoveMarker assumes that the marker it is removing was necessary for the win. This makes RemoveMarker less general than it could be but general enough for playing the game. When a win occurs, it is either on an actual move (and the game concludes), or it is on a look-ahead move (and the possibility of a win is noted and the marker resulting in the win is immediately removed).

```
const  MaxRow = 26;
       MaxColumn = 22;


type
  ValueType = (White, Black, Empty, OutOfBounds);
  ColorType = White .. Black;
  RowIndex = 1 .. MaxRow;
  ColumnIndex = 1 .. MaxColumn;
  PositionIndex = 0 .. MaxRow;
  PlayingFieldType = array[RowIndex, ColumnIndex] of
                     ValueType;
  PositionType = array[ColumnIndex] of PositionIndex;
  BoardType = record
              Squares : PlayingFieldType;
              ColumnHeight : PositionType;
              NumberRows : RowIndex;
              NumberColumns : ColumnIndex;
              NumberSquares,{ Initialized to
                             NumberRows *
                             NumberColumns }
              NumberPlayed, { Check for tie when
                             NumberPlayed =
                             NumberSquares }
              NumberInGoal : integer;
              WhiteWin,
              BlackWin : boolean
            end;
```

Figure 5.

CONCLUSIONS

Although we regard this as a rigorous exercise for CS2 students, most of them seem to enjoy it. We have used the project in a tournament, which was considered to be fun and challenging by most students. By playing it as a round-robin tournament, students are not embarrassed by having to sit out early while other students continue to play. We try to help those students who are having trouble implementing even a simple rendition of the game so that they can have a running version at the time of the tournament.

From our standpoint, the exercise allows us to emphasize several things that are a continuing theme in our course–top-down design, data abstraction, program testing at various levels of program design and coding, and, last but not least, the ne-

cessity of having some tasks done by a deadline that cannot be pushed back (we reserve a lab for a certain day and hold the tournament on that day.)

REFERENCES

1. McCracken, Daniel D., A Second Course In Computer Science With Pascal, John Wiley and Sons, 1987.

2. Winston, Patrick Henry, Artificial Intelligence, 2nd edition, Addison-Wesley, 1984.

3. Turbo Pascal 4.0 Owner's Handbook, Borland International, 1987.

APPENDIX 1

```
procedure InitializeGame (var Board : BoardType;
                          Rows, Columns,
                          Goal : integer);
```

This returns a board with the number of rows and columns given by Rows and Columns. Goal is the number of markers either player must get in a row in order to win.

```
function Value (Row, Col : integer;
                Board : BoardType) : ValueType
```

This returns the current status of a single square on the board. A square may contain a White or a Black marker, may be empty, or may be out of the bounds of the playing area.

```
function Height (Col : integer;
                 Board : BoardType) : integer;
```

This returns the height of a single column, where height is the number of markers currently in a column.

```
function Goal (Board : BoardType) : integer;
```

This returns the number of squares in a row that White or Black needs to win the game.

```
function MovePossible (Col : integer;
                       Board : BoardType) : boolean;
```

This returns True if a marker may be added to a column (i.e., the column is not full) and False otherwise.

```
procedure PrintBoard (Board : BoardType);
```

This operation prints a representation of Board. The positions of markers which have been dropped into the boards are indicated.

```
procedure DropMarker (    Color : ColorType;
                          Col : integer;
                      var Board : BoardType);
```

This operation performs a move by dropping a marker whose color is Color in the column of the Board designated by Column. The value of the Board is updated accordingly.

```
procedure RemoveMarker (    Col : integer;
                        var Board : BoardType);
```

This operation undoes a move by removing a marker from the top of the designated column of the Board. The value of the Board is changed accordingly.

```
function IsWin (Color : ColorType;
               Board : BoardType) : boolean;
```

This returns True if the current value for Board is such that there is a win for Color. For example, if Board is a game board for which Goal is 4, and if the value of Color is White, then the value of IsWin is True iff somewhere on the board there are four white markers in a row. The value of Color can be Black or White. function IsDraw (Board : BoardType) : boolean;

This function returns true if no more moves are possible and neither White nor Black has won the game.

APPENDIX 2

```
unit ScoreX;
interface
. . .

function Value (    Row, Col : integer;
               var Board : BoardType) :
                             ValueType;
function Height (   Col : integer;
               var Board : BoardType) :
                             integer;
function Height (   Col : integer;
               var Board : BoardType) :
                             integer;

. . .

implementation
. . .

function Value (    Row, Col : integer;
               var Board : BoardType) :
                             ValueType;
begin  { Value }
  if (Row < 1) or (Row > Board.NumberRows) or
     (Col < 1) or (Col > Board.NumberColumns)
    then Value := OutOfBounds
    else Value := Board.Squares[Row,Col]
end;    { Value }

function Height (   Col : integer;
               var Board : BoardType) :
                             integer;
const  ColumnErrorMsg = 'Error--Attempt to access
                             invalid column:  ';
begin  { Height }
  if (Col < 1) or (Col > Board.NumberColumns)
    then
      begin  { if..then }
        WriteLn (ColumnErrorMsg, Col:1);
        Height := 0;
      end    { if..then }
    else Height := Board.Position[Col]
end;    { Height }

function MovePossible (    Col : integer;
                      var Board : BoardType) :
```

```
                            boolean;
const  ColumnErrorMsg = 'Error--Attempt to access
                             invalid column:  ';
begin  { MovePossible }
  if (Col < 1) or (Col > Board.NumberColumns)
    then
      begin  { if..then }
        WriteLn (ColumnErrorMsg, Col:1);
        MovePossible := false
      end    { if..then }
    else
      with Board do
        MovePossible := Position[Col] < NumberRows
end;    { MovePossible }
. . .

end.
```

APPENDIX 3

```
unit Player1;

interface

uses ScoreX,Consts;

procedure MakePlayer1Move(MyColor:ColorType;var
Board:BoardType); implementation

{
Private procedures and functions for implementing
the game playing strategy of MakePlayer1Move.
Full declaration of MakePlayer1 move.
}

begin
{
Initialize data structures used by Player1.
}
end.
```

APEX1, A Library of Dynamic Programming Examples

Robert J. McGlinn
Department of Computer Science
Southern Illinois University
Carbondale, Illinois 62901-4511

Michael Britt
Department of Computer Science
Southeast Missouri State University
Cape Girardeau, Missouri 63701

Linda Woolard
Department of Computer Information Processing
Southern Illinois University
Carbondale, Illinois 62901

ABSTRACT

This paper surveys the growing field of *program visualization* or *visual programming*, the ability to visualize the execution of a computer program or the effects of a computer program on its data structures on a display device. Additionally, a library of dynamic Pascal examples, APEX1, designed for use in a second Pascal (data structures) course is introduced. Finally, the characteristics that an optimal *program visualization* system should possess are discussed.

1. INTRODUCTION

The field of *program visualization* or *visual programming* [1] is a relatively new area of study whose development has been advanced by the advent of affordable high quality graphics display devices. Many *program visualization* systems have been developed which provide the ability to visualize the execution of a computer program and/or to graphically represent the effects of a program's execution on its data structures. The capabilities of these systems range over a broad spectrum of possibilities. Some systems provide only a narrowly focused application, e.g., the visualization of linked list operations using predetermined examples. Other more sophisticated systems allow the user to dynamically specify the examples that are to be graphically animated. The most powerful systems allow the user to actually vary the program itself. Some will even allow the user to interact with the animation.

The next section of this paper is devoted to a survey of the state of the art in the area of *program visualization*. An attempt will be made to categorize many of the known systems according to their levels of sophistication.

Unfortunately, many of the systems we will survey are not available at affordable prices, many are intended for use only in support of software development, and consequently are not targeted toward introductory students, and others are only prototype systems possessing only a limited range of examples. Consequently, there is a definite need for low-cost, easy-to-use systems which students can employ to trace the execution of programs and to visualize the effects of algorithms on a broad range of data structures.

In an earlier paper [2] we introduced a library of dynamic Pascal examples, **IPEX1** (Introductory Programming **EX**amples 1), for use in an introductory Pascal course. In the third section of this paper we report on the next installment in our library of examples, a sequence of modules which present advanced programming topics. Our new modules, collectively referred to as **APEX1** (Advanced Programming **EX**amples 1), allow a student to dynamically trace the execution of programs which illustrate such concepts as recursion, pointers, data structures (linked lists, stacks, and queues), advanced sorting algorithms (quicksort and heapsort), and binary tree traversals.

This software package (**IPEX1** and **APEX1**) is an ideal supplement to an introductory sequence of two Pascal courses in which the second course concentrates primarily on the advanced topics listed above. Students who are experiencing conceptual difficulties or who simply wish to receive additional help outside the classroom could benefit from our software. Additionally, it is possible, given the right projection equipment, to integrate our examples into classroom presentations.

We do not propose that our software, or any one of the others for that matter, is the best possible available. Our software is affordable (it can be provided free of charge if we are provided with two blank diskettes and a stamped self-addressed mailer), "idiot proof," easy-to-use, and pedagogically sound. On the other hand we feel the next generation of our software will be an improvement and, with that in mind, as we survey other systems and as we discuss our new system we offer our thoughts on the capabilities, features, and design considerations that an "optimal," affordable, easy-to-use program visualization system should possess.

2. PROGRAM VISUALIZATION SYSTEMS

The terms *program visualization* and *visual programming* have often been used somewhat interchangeably in the literature [3]. However, it seems only natural to use the term *visual programming* for systems that focus on a revolutionary way to program, programming by combining graphical images (icons) into programs. This field is truly in its infancy and most of the systems developed to date are prototype systems. Among the best known are Pict [4], the Omega system [5], PegaSys [6], Brown University's Pecan [7], and PiP (Programming in Pictures) [8]. These systems, for the most part, do not attempt to animate the execution of a program but rather serve as program development tools. For an excellent introduction to the field of *visual programming* the reader is referred to the August, 1985, issue of *IEEE Computer*. Virtually the entire issue is devoted to this field of study.

On the other hand, the term *program visualization* is better suited to refer only to those systems that provide the ability to visualize the execution of a program or the effects of a program's execution on its data structures using some sort of a video display device. Certainly, this field would have developed independently of animated films, but Ronald Baecker's film "Sorting Out Sorting" [9], which no doubt was an outgrowth of his earlier work [10], seems to have been a motivating force behind much of the work in this field, particularly the BALSA project [11].

The rest of this section will focus on a survey (extensive but certainly not complete) of what we will henceforth refer to as PV (*Program Visualization*) systems and related literature.

2.1. Early Work

Early work in the field of *program visualization* seems to have focused, for obvious reasons, on films which animate algorithms or programs. We have already mentioned the pioneering work of Ronald Baecker, the film "Sorting out Sorting" [9]. Another work along the same lines as Baecker's, which is of note, is a system called ANTICS [12] developed by Mark Dionne and Alan Mackworth. ANTICS was used to make films which animated the execution of LISP programs. The bibliography in their paper [12] serves as an excellent survey of work devoted to film animation of computer programs.

Perhaps the earliest system which animates or simulates a high-level language on a CRT screen is IVF [13] developed by Stuart Shapiro and Douglas Witmer at Indiana University. IVF is a rather primitive system by today's standards but, nevertheless, it does simulate the execution of a FORTRAN program on a CRT. The current statement being executed is pointed to by an arrow and the variables that are changed are highlighted to the right of the program.

Another early system which interactively animates the execution of a high-level language was developed in the late 1970's at the United States Air Force Academy [14]. This system visually simulates the execution of an ALGOL program.

Shapiro and Witmer [13] also developed an interactive simulator called HYCOMP1 which simulates the inner workings of a hypothetical computer.

2.2. Machine Level

The 1980's have seen the development of other systems that animate some aspect of the machine level of a computer system. Thomas R. Leap [15] developed a system which animates the internal workings of a CPU while Cloyd Ezell [16] developed a system which animates the operations of an assembler. A particularly noteworthy project is Andrew Bernat's VISIBLE/370 [17], a system which visually simulates the execution of IBM System 370 assembly language programs on personal computers. His system handles all the 370 assembly language instructions which are traditionally introduced in a first course.

It seems unlikely with the advent of interactive debuggers for machine languages on personal computers that much additional work will be done in this area.

2.3. Concurrency

Given the increased use of parallel computer systems and the need to effectively teach modern operating system concepts it is only natural that some researchers turn their attention to visualizing concurrent processes. Indeed, John Colville [18] has developed a collection of programs to visually illustrate such concepts as interrupts, shared variables, semaphores, and deadlock. An example of a more ambitious project along these lines is a system being developed in Switzerland [19] to animate any concurrent program written in the Modula-like language Portal. A similar project [20] deals with Occam programs. No doubt the future will see a tremendous increase in this type of activity.

2.4. High-Level Languages, Algorithms, and Data Structures.

Let us now concentrate on PV systems[1] which are similar to **IPEX1** and **APEX1**, systems which visualize the execution of high-level languages like Pascal, systems which illustrate the performance of algorithms graphically, or systems which animate the effects of programs or algorithms on data structures. The rest of this section will focus on a brief survey of such systems. For the sake of classification we will group the systems we are aware of into three levels. The first level will contain the most rudimentary systems, those which have a limited scope of examples (e.g., some of these systems are restricted to binary trees) or which limit the programs or algorithms which can be visualized to a relatively small collection. The third level at the upper end of the spectrum contains the most powerful systems, those which typically allow the user to request that the system process his/her own programs rather than just canned programs which are hardwired into the software. The second level naturally contains those systems that fall in the middle ground, systems which do not, for one reason or another, fit perfectly into either of the other levels. A system in this group might have an extensive set of examples but be restricted to predetermined programs or algorithms. Our initial group of modules, **IPEX1**, as well as our second group, **APEX1**, fall into this category. Another system in this group might very well have a limited range of applications yet allow the user to define the program or algorithm which is to be animated.

2.4.1. The First Level

We have chosen to include four PV systems in this group. The CABTO (Computer Animation of Binary Tree Operations) system [23] is primarily intended to be an aid in lectures and does utilize some interesting ideas in its design and implementation. First, random numbers are used to represent the physical values of pointers thereby attempting to destroy some of the mystique associated with pointer variables. Second, windows are overlayed one on another as recursive calls are made. This feature, made possible through use of the Turbo Graphix Toolbox, appears to be a clean way to handle recursive calls in PV systems. Third, the algorithms that are animated are represented in pseudocode rather than in a particular language. In retrospect, this last feature is one we wish we had incorporated into our software.

The system developed by Martin Hitz [24] has the ability to use two monitors during the animation. A color graphics monitor can be used to display the data structures while a monochrome monitor can display the code being

---

[1]Tables summarizing the hardware requirements of each system, the software they are implemented in, and the examples they demonstrate will be available at the talk. The tables can also be obtained by contacting the authors directly.

simulated. This is a very appealing feature of this system and one we will consider in later versions of our own software for it can greatly reduce the amount of clutter on the graphics screen during a program's animation.

Unfortunately, each of these systems, as well as each of the other two [21,22], appears to be a prototype with an extremely limited set of examples.

2.4.2. The Second Level

As one might expect, this level contains the largest number of systems. Rambally's system [25] is restricted to linked lists but it does allow for the student to utilize the system to animate any algorithm the student can construct which manipulates linked lists. IPEX1 [2] provides examples which allow a student to experiment with most of the major topics covered in a typical CS.1 course: input statements, assignment statements, output statements, decision statements, WHILE loops, REPEAT-UNTIL loops, FOR loops, PROCEDUREs, and FUNCTIONs. Each example is presented in the form of a program which the system animates on the screen. Although the programs themselves are fixed, the examples are dynamic in the sense that the data can be varied. The Visible Algorithms project at California State University Northridge [26] is an ambitious project for which the curriculum materials will cover three years of the computer science curriculum, including such topics as linked lists, binary trees, B-trees, and memory management. However, it does not appear that the system will handle user-defined algorithms or programs. Owen's system [27] is restricted to binary trees but it can be used with any user-defined algorithm. The reference [27] does contain a very nice discussion of how the system manages to graphically display the binary trees. Although the examples in Maxim's system [28] appear to be hardwired, the system does offer some interesting features. Student input was sought and apparently used in the design phase. Timing statistics and counts of number of statements executed are provided in the sorting examples. Finally, examples of multiply linked data structures are provided. The reference for VISAL (VISualization of ALgorithms) [29] focuses primarily on the non-technical aspects of the system, i.e., its effectiveness as a learning tool. Stone's system [20] is intended primarily for classroom demonstrations of algorithms and data structures but it can be used by students to illustrate their own programs or algorithms. Finally, APEX1 will be thoroughly discussed in the next major section of this paper.

2.4.3. The Third Level

We include three systems in this level, but we exclude the *visual programming* systems listed earlier in this paper. Perhaps the best known of all PV systems is BALSA (Brown University ALgorithm Simulator and Animator) [31,32,33,34]. This is a high-powered system designed for expensive APOLLO workstations which provides interactive lessons for each of the chapters in Sedgewick's book [38]. Augenstein's system [35,36] allows the student to input any Pascal program into the system. A preprocessor is then invoked to insert the appropriate commands to graphically display the effects of the program's execution on its data structures. Kempton's system [37] is the least sophisticated of the three but it does provide for the simulation of any user-defined program.

3. APEX1

There are several areas in an advanced programming/data structures course in which many students need extra help in the form of dynamic examples. We have designed several modules of examples each of which targets a certain area for which we feel there is a definite need.

APEX1 is divided into six modules. Unlike its predecessor, IPEX1, the modules are relatively independent and can be used in any order. However, generally speaking, the examples within each module progress in difficulty as you work your way through them. Consequently, the examples within a given module should be examined in order. A brief description of each module follows:

3.1. Module 1 -- Stacks

This module begins with two relatively simple examples intended to demonstrate the primitive procedures PUSH and POP and to prepare the student for the subsequent examples. Indeed, the remaining examples use PUSH and POP to illustrate some fairly straightforward applications of stacks which are traditionally the first applications of stacks that students see, reversing a string and checking a string to see if it is a palindrome.

We have adopted a consistent approach throughout the modules on data structures, i.e., we introduce the basic operations in the early modules and then assume they are "primitives" in the subsequent modules. Consequently, the code for the procedures PUSH and POP is not presented and hence not traced in the remaining examples.

3.2. Module 2 -- Queues

Two implementations of queues are addressed in this module. The first three examples deal with the array implementation (circular array) and the last three examples deal with the dynamic storage linked list implementation of a queue.

The three circular array examples contain two examples in which the code is traced and one "free form" example. The first of these examples illustrates the three routines needed to load queues: CLEARQ to initialize a queue, ENQ to insert a new element in to the queue, and FULLQ to test for a full queue. The second example illustrates the routines needed to delete elements from a queue: DEQ to delete an element and EMPTYQ to test for an empty queue. Since many students have a great deal of difficulty coping with the circular nature of the implementation a third example, the "free form" example[2], is provided which allows students to freely insert and delete elements into a circular queue without the code being traced. We feel the visualization of the operations on the screen can assist students in overcoming any difficulties they might have with this implementation.

The remaining queue examples utilize a linked representation and parallel the circular array implementation, i.e., the first example illustrates insertions, the second

---

[2] A live demonstration of the "free form" example as well as other examples that follow will be given during the talk. For those who cannot attend, illustrations which demonstrate the layouts of the screen are available directly from the authors. Furthermore, as was mentioned earlier, the software is available free of charge from the authors.

example illustrates deletions, and the third example is a "free-form" example. Pointer variables are shown as open boxes with labeled arrows.

The "free-form" example can accommodate a maximum of 5 elements. When an element is removed from the queue (DEQued) its node is physically removed from the screen and the others are shifted to the left to accommodate a subsequent insertion. We feel this particular example can help those having conceptual difficulties with dynamic storage since it reinforces the concepts of allocating storage, deallocating storage, and a pointer variable as a variable pointing to a node no matter where the node is located in memory.

3.3. Module 3 -- Linked Lists

There are six linked list examples. The first example illustrates the creation of a linked list using procedures PUSH and INSERT as well as the built-in Pascal procedure NEW. The second example introduces the students to the traversal of a linked data structure. The third example shows how POP, DELETE, and DISPOSE can be used to delete elements from a list. The fourth example shows how a list of integers can be built in increasing order. Finally, the last example is another "free-form" example which allows the student to dynamically maintain an ordered list of integers (a maximum of 5) using insertions and deletions.

3.4. Module 4 -- Recursion

Recursion is the topic in an advanced programming course which causes the students the most difficulty. They may be able to write a simple recursive program by patterning the program after some other similar example, but a large number of students have a difficult time truly understanding how a recursive program works. We have included four examples of recursion each of which is traditionally presented to students when they are first introduced to recursion: the computation of a factorial, the raising of a base to a positive exponent (exponentiation), the generation of Fibonacci sequences, and the recursive implementation of the binary search.

Although each of these examples can be traced in the classroom in an effort to explain how recursion works, our software allows a student to proceed at his/her own pace, to repeat the example again and again, and to test herself/himself by predicting the outcome of each step in the sequence of recursive calls. Each call to a routine results in a new presentation of the static code on the screen. The variables displayed on the left-hand portion of the screen are not cleared until the routine is actually finished. A special indicator (a solid right arrow) with a number associated with it on the line of the static code which invokes the procedure is used to monitor the sequence of recursive calls. As the number of calls increases new indicators are added with increasing numbers. The indicators are not removed until the invocation which resulted in the generation of the indicator returns. On the left side of the screen each invocation of the recursive procedure results in the creation of a new set of arguments and local variables with each set labeled with a number that corresponds to the number on the special indicator. This introduces the students to the notion that a new call results in a new set of variables being allocated without bringing in the concept of allocation tables.

Admittedly, the recursive examples are the most primitive examples students will encounter. We present these examples as a means for students to better understand how

recursion works by giving them the ability to trace through the examples at their own pace. We hope to provide more difficult examples in a latter release of our software which will also incorporate a better means (overlaying of windows) for monitoring the recursive calls.

3.5. Module 5 -- Search and Sort Examples

The examples in this module are purely graphical in that no detailed static code is presented along with the graphical representation of the concepts. The critical variables involved are presented and short reminder messages are presented at each step. Two searches are covered: linear and binary. For these the target value is entered by the student and need not be present in the list. The search then proceeds automatically at the student's chosen speed, highlighting each element compared as dictated by the algorithm. The sorting examples allow students to input their own list of values and to select the speed at which the animation will proceed. The portion of the array being worked on during the selection, bubble, and quick sorts is shown in a color different from the rest of the array.

The last sort algorithm covered in our examples is heap sort. The graphical display shows the array as well as a binary tree representation of the array during all phases of the sort. A message field is used in the lower right portion of the display to inform the student of the step that is proceeding.

3.6. Module 6 -- Binary Tree Traversals

The final module of examples covers the topic of binary tree traversals (preorder, inorder, and postorder). When an example is displayed the tree fills the upper portion of the screen and three lines are shown at the bottom as follows (for the preorder traversal):

VISIT NODE FOR VALUE (HIGHLIGHT)
IF LEFTCHILD < > NIL THEN PREORDER (LEFTCHILD)
IF RIGHTCHILD < > NIL THEN PREORDER (RIGHTCHILD)

The same type of indicator which was used to monitor the recursive calls in the recursion module is used in this case. Each time a value is obtained the element in the tree is highlighted and each time a node is visited the box around the node changes color. Also, when a shift to a new node is made (e.g., visit left) a new indicator is displayed in front of the appropriate line of code and, of course, a larger number is associated with it. As a recursive call completes, the focus returns to the call associated with the next lower numbered indicator until that call is completed. The inorder and postorder traversals are handled in a similar manner.

The last three examples in this module replicate the first three but deal only with a partial tree rather than a full tree.

4. CONCLUSION

We have conducted a fairly extensive survey of PV systems, pointing out some of the strong points that we feel should be incorporated into a well-designed system. Certainly, this survey can serve as a useful starting point for those interested in doing research in this area.

Additionally, we have presented our latest contribution to this field, **APEX1**, which we feel can be a significant aid to students in an advanced programming/data structures course. Not only can this software be used individually by students but we plan to integrate it into our classroom presentations.

References

[1] Brown G.P., R.T. Carling, C.F. Herot, D.A. Kramlich, and P. Souza, 'Program Visualization: Graphical Support for Software Development,' *IEEE Computer*, vol. **18**, no. **8**, 27-35 (1985).

[2] Lewis, L., and R.J. McGlinn, 'IPEX1, A Library of Dynamic Pascal Programming Examples,' *ACM SIGCSE Bulletin*, vol. **18**, no. **1**, 72-77 (1986).

[3] Grafton, R.B., and T. Ichikawa, 'Visual Programming,' *IEEE Computer*, vol. **18**, no. **8**, 6-9 (1985).

[4] Glinert, E.P., and S.L. Tanimoto, 'Pict: An Interactive Graphical Programming Environment,' *IEEE Computer*, vol. **17**, no. **11**, 7-25 (1984).

[5] Powell, M.L., and M.A. Linton, 'Visual abstraction in an Interactive Environment,' *Proc. Sigplan Symp. Programming Language Issues in Software Systems 83*, printed as *Sigplan Notices*, vol. **18**, no. **6**, 14-21 (1983).

[6] Moriconi, M., and D.F. Hare, 'Visualizing Program Designs Through PegaSys,' *IEEE Computer*, vol. **18**, no. **8**, 72-85 (1985).

[7] Reiss, S.P., 'Graphical Program Development with PECAN Program Development Systems,' *Proc. ACM Sigsoft-Sigplan Software Development Environments*, April 1984, printed as *Sigplan Notices*, vol. **19**, no. **5**, 30-41 (1984).

[8] Raeder, G., 'Programming in Pictures,' PhD dissertation, University of Southern California, Los Angeles, Calif., Nov. 1984; Technical Report TR-84-318, USC; Technical Report 8-85, Norweigian Institute of Technology, Trondheim-NTH, Norway.

[9] Baecker, R., and D. Sherman, 'Sorting Out Sorting,' a 30-minute color sound film, Dynamic Graphics Project, Computer Systems Research Institute, University of Toronto. (Excerpted in *SIGGRAPH Video Review* 7, 1983.)

[10] Baecker, Ronald, 'Two Systems Which Produce Animated Representations of the Execution of Computer Programs,' *ACM SIGCSE Bulletin*, vol. **7**, no. **1**, 158-167 (1975).

[11] Brown, M., N. Meyrowitz, and A. van Dam, 'Personal Computer Networks and Graphical Animation: Rationale and Practice for Education,' *ACM SIGCSE Bulletin*, vol. **15**, no. **1**, 296-307 (1983).

[12] Dionne, M., and A. Mackworth, 'ANTICS: A System for Animating LISP Programs,' *Computer Graphics and Image Processing*, vol. **7**, no. **1**, 105-119 (1978).

[13] Shapiro, Stuart C., and Douglas P. Witmer, 'Interactive Visual Simulators for Beginning Programming Students,' *ACM SIGCSE Bulletin*, vol. **6**, no. **1**, 11-14 (1974).

[14] Kline, R.B., G.D. Hamor, K.L. Krause, and L.E. Druffel, 'Visual Demonstration of Program Execution,' *ACM SIGCSE Bulletin*, vol. **10**, no. **1**, 16-18 (1978).

[15] Leap, Thomas R., 'Animations of Computers as Teaching Aids,' *ACM SIGCSE Bulletin*, vol. **16**, no. **1**, 84-90 (1984).

[16] Ezell, Cloyd L., 'A Visible Assembler for a Course in Introductory System Software,' *ACM SIGCSE Bulletin*, vol. **17**, no. **4**, 26-29 (1985).

[17] Pernat, Andrew P., 'An Interactive Interpreter/Graphics- Simulator for IBM S/370 Architecture Assembly Language,' *ACM SIGCSE Bulletin*, vol. **18**, no. **2**, 13-16 (1986).

[18] Colville, John, 'A Pictorial Demonstration of Concurrent Processes,' *ACM SIGCSE Bulletin*, vol. **15**, no. **4**, 8-14 (1983).

[19] Zimmermann, M., F. Perrenond, and A. Schiper, 'Under-standing Concurrent Programming Through Program Animation,' *ACM SIGCSE Bulletin*, vol. **20**, no. **1**, 27-31 (1988).

[20] Stepney, S., 'Graphical Representation of Activity, Interconnection, and Loading,' 7th Occam Users Group Meeting, Grenoble, September 1987.

[21] Mincy, J.W., A.L. Thorp, and Kuo-Chung Tai, 'Visualizing Algorithms with the Aid of a Computer,' *ACM SIGCSE Bulletin*, vol. **15**, no. **1**, 106-111 (1983).

[22] Ramlet, J.S., and M. Folk, 'PS: A Procedure Simulator for Dynamic Program Visualization,' *ACM SIGCSE Bulletin*, vol. **17**, no. **1**, 36-40 (1985).

[23] Barnes, G.M., and G.A. Kind, 'Visual Simulation of Data Structures During Lecture,' *ACM SIGCSE Bulletin*, vol. **19**, no. **1**, 267-276 (1987).

[24] Hitz, Martin, 'An Interactive Demonstration System for Implementations of Abstract Data Types,' *ACM SIGCSE Bulletin*, vol. **19**, no. **4**, 19-21,24 (1987).

[25] Rambally, Gerard K, 'Real-time Graphical Representation of Linked Data Structures,' *ACM SIGCSE Bulletin*, vol. **17**, no. **1**, 41-48 (1985).

[26] Barnes, G.M., R. Hsu, N. Hsu, T. Sun, T. Nguyen, G. Haus, and P.D. Smith, 'A Computer Science Courseware Factory,' FIACM SIGCSE Bulletin, vol. FB18, no. **1**, 318-323 (1986).

[27] Owen, G. Scott, 'Teaching of Tree data Structures Using Microcomputer Graphics,' *ACM SIGCSE Bulletin*, vol. **18**, no. **1**, 67-72 (1986).

[28] Maxim, Bruce R., and Bruce S. Elenbogen, 'Teaching Programming Algorithms Aided by Computer Graphics,' *ACM SIGCSE Bulletin*, vol. **19**, no. **1**, 297-301,= (1987).

[29] Giannotti, E.I., 'Algorithm Animator: A Tool for Programming Learning,' *ACM SIGCSE Bulletin*, vol. **19**, no. **1**, 308-314 (1987).

[30] Stone, Don E., 'A Modular Approach to Program Visualization in Computer Science Instruction,' *ACM SIGCSE Bulletin*, vol. **19**, no. **1**, 516-522 (1987).

[31] Brown, Marc, Norman Meyrowitz, Andries Van Dam, 'Personal Computer Networks and Graphical Animation: Rationale and Practice for Education,' *ACM SIGCSE Bulletin*, vol. **15**, no. **1**, 296-307 (1983).

[32] Brown, Marc, and Robert Sedgewick, 'Progress Report: Brown University Instruction Computing Laboratory,' *ACM SIGCSE Bulletin*, vol. **16**, no. **1**, 91-101 (1984).

[33] Brown, Marc, 'A System for Algorithm Animation,' *Computer Graphics*, vol. **18**, no. **3**, 177-186 (1984).

[34] Brown, Marc, and Robert Sedgewick, 'Techniques for Algorithm Animation,' *IEEE Software*, vol. **2**, no. **1**, 28-39 (1985).

[35] Augenstein, Moshe, and Y. Langsam, 'Graphic Displays of Data Structures on the IBM PC,' *ACM SIGCSE Bulletin*, vol. **18**, no. **1**, 73-81 (1986).

[36] Augenstein, Moshe, and Y. Langsam, 'Automatic generation of Graphic Displays of Data Structures Through a Preprocessor,' *ACM SIGCSE Bulletin*, vol. **20**, no. **1**, 148-152,184 (1988).

[37] Kempton, William, 'A System to Make Visible the Structure and Execution of Student Programs,' *ACM SIGCSE Bulletin*, vol. **18**, no. **1**, 313-317 (1986).

[38] Sedgewick, Robert, *Algorithms*, Addison-Wesley, Reading, MA, (1983).

Testing Student Micro Computer Skills

Through Direct Computer Use

Michael M. Delaney
Department of Accounting
Illinois State University

Abstract

This paper introduces the concept of testing students' microcomputer skills through direct computer use. Techniques are discussed which make it feasible for the instructor to grade the disk and printout that are produced by each student. The process can be generally applied to testing many different skill areas, and has been effectively used for tests on DOS and utilities, wordprocessing, spreadsheet work, and data base. Practical examples of test creation and grading of spreadsheet tests are presented. Further developments of the technique are suggested.

Problem Statement

It is difficult to effectively test students in microcomputer application courses with traditional testing methods. Testing students through the computer more accurately reflects the skills that we present in class, but grading is difficult. The educational objective is to develop student skills to such a high level that they concentrate on the objectives of their work, subconsciously handling the details of how that is implemented. If students take a test in a microcomputer laboratory with the application software, they are more effectively tested on the skills being taught, but automated procedures are necessary to make grading practical.

Instructors need practical skills to formulate an effective test on disk and grade it in an efficient manner. Automation can make it feasible to grade the exams, and even to use student assistants for grading.

Methodology

General Test Administration

The class regularly meets for 75 minutes two times a week in a microcomputer classroom where each of the thirty students has a PC computer and printer. Each student has DOS and application software in wordprocessing, spreadsheet, and data base. The test is administered in the same environment, with each student receiving a printed test form and a disk with data files. During the test, students manipulate the data files and create other files. Students turn in the test sheet, printed output, and the disk for grading.

The tests are formulated with careful attention to separation into discrete parts so that a student who misses one concept is not penalized excessively by that mistake rippling through and affecting his or her grade on other parts of the exam. There are frequent backups required as part of the test directions. An extra computer station is available in case of hardware problems.

Tests are graded by examining both the printout and the disk files. Some requirements can be easily checked by reference to the printout. Some requirements can only be checked by use of the students' files. Other requirements might be checked first on the printout which focuses attention on things to be examined on the disk. Macros and/or the programming capability of the software make it possible for the instructor to check the files. The technique makes it possible to use grading assistants who are not very familiar with the software.

The technique is generally applicable, and I use it in four different skill areas of microcomputer instruction: DOS commands, WordPerfect word processing; VP-Planner spreadsheet work; and dBase III Plus operations. A more detailed example of spreadsheet testing is helpful in understanding the technique.

Spreadsheet Example

This paper emphasizes VP-Planner because it is frequently bundled with CIS textbooks. The Autokey Macro capability of VP-Planner greatly facilitates the process of writing macros because the instructor can let the program keep track of the keystrokes while he or she is maneuvering around the spreadsheet. The autokey macros can be decompiled into label macros and edited to incorporate any necessary changes. Even the student version can be used for grading, but because of the limitations inherent in that version, a number of tricks are necessary to check student spreadsheets. The capabilities parallel Lotus 1-2-3 version 1.4.

If you have VP-Planner Plus or Lotus version 2.1 available, however, it greatly facilitates the grading process because their advanced features can automate more of the grading task. The @CELL function allows you to directly check a cell's address, column, contents, format, label prefix, protected status, row, type, and column width. The string functions allow you to more easily locate the students' work. The greater depth of the macro capabilities makes it easier to program. It is even possible to structure a test so that the entire spreadsheet can be graded automatically.

Test Format. Each student is given a diskette with the test spreadsheet. A number of different exercises have been used ofer the past two years in other exams, including data query, graphing, and external data bases. The worksheet used as an example for this paper is a single file, but three different spreadsheet exercises are tested by having three logically separate spreadsheets, each separated from the other by a horizontal and vertical screen page. Thus, none of the spreadsheets overlap the others in either rows or columns. The reason for this separation is to minimize the effect of a student's inadvertent adding or deleting of rows or columns, or the changing of their order through a sort.

Each spreadsheet has headings and some constant data on it. Cells where students are required to enter values or formulas are indicated by underlines. Students therefore keep their answers in preassigned cells.

The opening screen has an input area where the student enters his or her name, ID number, and section. Other input values, formatting, column width changes, and named ranges are also required in this first screen. The second screen is an income statement. The income sheet area is named, so the student can use the {GOTO} key or use {TAB}{PAGEDOWN} to jump to the next screen. The requirements include using named input areas in formulas as both absolute and relative addresses, and copying formulas. There are some formulas that the student must provide, and an @IF function to determine the income tax, depending upon whether income is positive or negative. Global and range column widths and formatting are required. Various printer options must be used, including a printer setup string.

The second logical spreadsheet simulates a teacher's gradebook. It tests the use of date, math, and statistical functions. Both relative and absolute addressing in formulas are required.

The third spreadsheet requires the student to establish a data sort range, and sort using primary and secondary keys. Each choice defaults to an incorrect value, so the student must specifically make the proper selection.

The test is administered in a lab class period of 75 minutes. There is minimal time pressure for the student who has a good practical understanding of the spreadsheet operations, and sufficient time to allow for the possibility of computer and/or printer problems. The test directions include directions to save the worksheet at different points in the work, making a backup. If a parity check, program lockup, or printer problem occurs, the student is given more time at another station. The help files are not removed from the students' disk. Thus, a student who knows what he or she wants to do can refresh his or her memory on the specific syntax. However, a student who has not done the homework and exercises does not have the leisure to hunt through all the help screens to find the solutions.

Grading. One disk drive on the instructor's computer is used for grading the student disks. The grader loads the student worksheet. Each student worksheet includes a macro to merge the grading worksheet from the instructor's drive C:.

There are a number of advantages of keeping the grading macros separate from the student diskettes. The student is not helped on the test by the macros since the grading macro does not exist on the student disk. You can also change the grading macros as you grade, to allow for the common student problems that you might not have anticipated when you first wrote the macros.

Alternatively, if you have some macros on the student worksheet, the student can use them during the test. An example of where this is desirable is for rapidly formatting and printing certain areas of the worksheet. The student could be instructed to use an ALT-P macro after finishing the test. The macro could print cell formulas instead of values and do some preliminary grading to facilitate your examination of the students' printed test. It is unlikely that a student who would have problems on the test would know how to find the hidden macros, or be able to get much assistance from the macros.

The grading spreadsheet includes data areas and three categories of macros: initialization, processing, and wrap-up. The output includes a score spreadsheet for the student and an instructor master spreadsheet with each student's item analysis and score.

Initialization. The grading macro starts by examining the named ranges in the student's worksheet. The score for this is retained in a data area. Then it creates range names for all the macros and data areas. It begins by establishing an unsynchronized horizontal window one row high for the grading specifications. Since the student could have left the screen at any location, a {HOME}{GOTO}A19 is used to align the screen before creating the window. A data table is used for the grading specifications and the student score for each item. The student name, ID, and section are copied to the top of this table so that they appear in the summary worksheets.

Item Checking. For each separate item to be checked, the macro has grading specifications in the bottom window and jumps to cells in the student window. The macro pauses with a {?} to allow the grader to move around the worksheet before using the return to indicate that an item score is determined. The macro jumps to the scoring window, accepts the numeric score, and scrolls to the next grading criteria before jumping to the student window for another repetition.

Each item is graded through a series of macro steps that manipulates the worksheet and displays the cell under consideration. One of a pair of macro subroutines is then called to accept the score. One starts with the {?} pause, whereas the other one does not. This is required because some of the things that are checked require a separate screen and use a return to get back to the student worksheet. Examples of this include checking global defaults and printer options. Other things are checked by using a {?} pause in the middle of a specification, then backing out of the command with a series of {ESC} keys. The remaining checks require an initial pause before entering the score. The grader is therefore presented with a consistent user interface.

The dual window technique places the grading specifications and the current cell's status line together. This makes it easy to check the cell's address, contents, format, formula, and prefix. The macros check other items by partially executing commands and pausing with the student selected values showing as defaults. A series of escapes is used to back out of the command before accepting the score. An example is the checking of the data sort range, which is highlighted after the /DSR sequence. A similar technique is used for checking column widths, printer options, and data query options.

Wrap-up. When all the items are checked, the data table area contains two columns: one has all the information about that particular student and the other contains the grading specifications. The student score and percent is computed, and the macro pauses for comments at the bottom of the individual information column for text notations by the grader. The grading area is extracted and saved to the student diskette and also printed. The last macro pauses with a message to insert the next student's disk in the drive. It then loads the next student's worksheet for grading. When all the student disks have been graded, the next step is to make up the master worksheet which includes each student's information by another pass through the student disks. The student individual information column is extracted to a temporary file. The instructor's master grading worksheet is loaded, the temporary file is combined as a new column, and the worksheet saved. An archive program is used to save the contents of each student disk as a single file that is retained as long as the written test material retention requirements specified by the university. Generally, one diskette can contain the archived files of a single section for a single test.

Conclusion

An instructor can test students' skills more effectively by creating tests that have components that are on disks that are distributed with printed test instructions. The students' work can be structured so that the files on the disks can be efficiently graded on the instructor's computer.

The application software's programming capability can be used to format printed output for grading, and can also directly determine components of the students' grade. Other applications of the embeded macro technique can be utilized, including tutorials to guide the student.

A Unified Approach For Multilevel Database Security Based on Inference Engines

Linda M. Null[1]
Dept. of Computer Science/IS
Northwest Missouri State University
Maryville, MO 64468
(816) 562-1600
null@atanasoff.cs.iastate.edu

Johnny Wong
Dept. of Computer Science
Iowa State University
Ames, IA 50011
(515) 294-4377
wong@atanasoff.cs.iastate.edu

Abstract

A multilevel relational database system handles data at different security classifications and provides access to users with different security clearances. Many methods for enforcing security in this environment have been investigated. This paper presents a unified approach to multilevel database security based on two ideas: a trusted filter and an inference engine. These two approaches are introduced separately and then the motivation for the unified system and the system model itself are presented.

1 Introduction

Because a multilevel relational database system handles data at different security classifications and provides access to users with different security clearances, the issue of enforcing security in this environment presents many problems. The security policy must restrict access to information based on the user's authorization and the classification of requested data. Any system enforcing this disclosure requirement is identified as *multilevel secure*. A user can accidentally or purposely threaten the system either alone or with the aid of a Trojan Horse in the database system. As mentioned in [1], there are four forms of disclosure of classified data in a multilevel database system.

1. **Direct Access.** The user requests unauthorized data and the system returns that data properly classified.

2. **Indirect Access by Inference.** The user requests authorized data which, when returned, allows the user to infer something about data he is not authorized to see.

---

[1] Linda Null is currently on educational leave from NWMSU completing a Ph.D. in computer science at ISU.

3. **Trojan Horse Direct Release.** A Trojan Horse in the system releases unauthorized data with an improper classification level to the user in such a way that the data appears to be authorized to the user.

4. **Trojan Horse Leakage.** A Trojan Horse in the system leaks unauthorized data indirectly to the user by encoding it into authorized data which the user has requested.

Denning [2] shows how direct access and Trojan Horse direct release threats can be solved using a trusted filter and cryptographic checksums. In [1], Denning shows how user inference threats can be handled with minimal support in the filter. Thuraisingham [3] also discusses how to handle user inference threats using artificial intelligence techniques and formal logic. The objective of this paper is to propose a unified approach based on the inference engine for providing an efficient means of implementing and enforcing multilevel security. Section 2 provides a brief summary of the ideas in [1,2,3]. Section 3 provides the motivation for the unified approach. Section 4 presents our proposed augmented database, and Section 5 concludes the paper.

2 Filters and Inference Engines

(The ideas of Denning and Thuraisingham must be summarized before the objective of this paper can be presented. The reader is referred to [1,2,3] for more detail.)

Denning [2] discusses the implementation and security of using a trusted, isolated filter and cryptographic checksums with an untrusted database system. The verified filter stores a classification label in each piece of data indicating the classification level of that data. This label could be at the relation, record, attribute or element level and could be stored directly in the database or in a separate database. The filter uses this label to determine whether a given user is authorized to access requested data and removes any data the user is not authorized to see. A piece of data could be falsely labeled by a Trojan Horse in the system by either switching labels among data or simply changing the labels. Therefore, it is also necessary to include a cryptographic checksum for each piece of data (which can be stored in the data itself or a separate file) to bind the data to its classification. The filter uses an encryption chip to compute and validate checksums, thus detecting any alteration to the data or to its classification label.

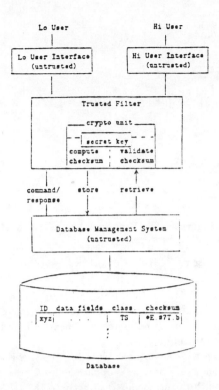

Figure 1: Multilevel Database Protected by Filter and Cryptographic Checksums

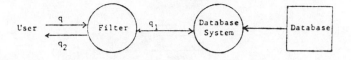

Figure 2: Commutative Filter Approach (Authorized Equivalence Scheme)

Using a filter in this manner will detect direct access threats (by comparing the classification label with the clearance of the user before releasing any data) and Trojan Horse direct release (via the checksum). However, this approach will not protect against user inference threats or Trojan Horse leakage. Figure 1 illustrates the subsystems necessary for this approach.

Note that the subsystems in Figure 1 must be isolated in such a way that the user cannot bypass the filter and go directly to the database. The filter is the only subsystem that requires verification. If the filter is implemented as a security kernal and is kept as simple as possible, verification becomes more practical and manageable.

An extension to the filter approach which can be used to reduce inference threats is provided in [1]. Here, Denning illustrates how these inference threats can be handled using authorized views and commutative filters. If all user queries are made against a view of the database in which all unauthorized data has been removed (called a *maximal authorized view*), no user inference is possible. The author suggests an indirect implementation of the maximal authorized view approach called an *authorized view equivalence scheme*. The filter forces the result returned from a user's query to be equivalent to results that would have been returned if the query had been made against a maximal authorized view. This results in a release of authorized information to the user from which no inferences can be made. Figure 2 illustrates this approach.

The authorized equivalence scheme begins with a query q posed to the database system. The classification label and checksum are augmented to q to produce q_1 which is sent to the database system. The response from the DBMS is filtered

before it is returned to the user, resulting in a response to query q_2, which represents the same results the user would have received if the query had been made against a maximal authorized view. This is called a *commutative filter* because the operations of removing unauthorized data and computing the response to a query are commutative. This extension to the filter approach reduces the problem of user inference although it does not address *all* types of inference (see [5] or [6] for more details on inference).

Other approaches have been used to counteract the threat of user inference. Of particular interest are the ideas presented by Thuraisingham [3] who proposes the augmentation of a database with an inference engine to function as a knowledge based system. (The reader is referred to [7] for more information on knowledge based systems and inference engines.) Briefly, the inference engine uses the rules in the knowledge base to modify the query. Any other information in the rule base that applies may be used also. After the query is expressed in first order logic, the first thing the inference engine does is search the rules in the rule base to see if releasing the requested data will result in the classification of any information being lowered. If no such rules exist, the inference engine attempts to derive a formula of the form $R \rightarrow P$, where R consists of relations in the database and P is the query. The modified query is R, if it exists.

Many studies have been done on extending database systems by integrating them with logic programming techniques and methods from artificial intelligence. The goal is to provide database systems with the performance found in expert systems. One such study led to the recommendation of augmenting a DBMS with a knowledge base (requiring a separate processing system for the knowledge base) [4]. Thuraisingham proposes using this augmented approach to design a multilevel secure DBMS. The main issues addressed in her paper are the management and expression of the rule base and the modification and evaluation of queries. Figure 3 summarizes the query processing strategy in this augmented database.

The database consists of data easily managed by the relational DBMS. The rule base consists of security constraints, integrity constraints, environments at different classification levels (the environment for a classification level contains all the data released at that level and all environments at lower levels) and the real world information. This information is represented using first order logic. Queries are modified (according to the security constraints) by the inference engine and then translated from first order logic to relational algebra and passed to the DBMS. Using the rule base, the inference engine assigns a classification level to the response from the DBMS. The response is then released into the proper environment at which point users with proper clearances have access to the information. This method reduces direct access threats and user inference threats.

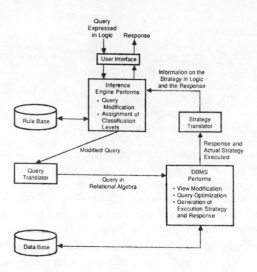

Figure 3: Query processing in an augmented database

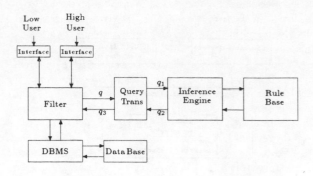

Figure 4: The Proposed Augmented System

3 Motivation for the Unified Approach

Thuraisingham's design is applicable to read only databases but needs to be extended to include read/write systems. The query modification results in a response that is properly classified only if there is no Trojan Horse in the system. Thus this approach is limited to read only databases known to be secure. Using a filter and cryptographic checksums shields against direct access and Trojan Horse direct release. If a commutative filter is used, user inference is inhibited also. However, to protect against user inference, the filter must remove all unauthorized data from each response, resulting in increased traffic through the filter. It is also difficult for the filter to handle certain constraints imposed on the data. For example, suppose employee names and salaries are stored in a database where each field taken separately is labeled secret. However, if a user accesses the name, the salary becomes top secret and if he accesses the salary, the name becomes top secret. Depending on the past history of queries, the labels on the fields change dynamically. An inference engine can handle this easily because the constraints are part of the rule base.

Our idea is to use the inference engine and rule base to modify the query before it goes to the DBMS, thus reducing the flow of information that must pass back through the filter from the DBMS. Use of the filter will also allow read/write operations as opposed to read only operations. The commutative filter is not necessary as user inference threats will be detected by the inference engine.

4 Proposed Augmented Database

Our proposal introduces a system designed to incorporate both the filter and the inference engine. The filter is responsible for the initial labeling of data with its classification and the validation of data (via the checksum) returned to the user (as in [2]). The knowledge base consists of security constraints, integrity constraints, environments for the various classification levels and real world information. The filter needs to be trusted and verified (which is called a Trusted Computer Base or TCB) but no other subsystem needs to be trusted. Figure 4 illustrates this proposed system.

All accesses to the database are constrained to go through the filter. There are two types of accesses: update accesses (including insertion, deletion and modification of data in the database) and read queries.

If an object in the database is to be updated, the system works as follows. The user's update request goes through the filter which in turn sends it directly to the DBMS. The DBMS of course sends the update to the database. The update information consists of the original data, a classification label, and a checksum. It is possible that certain types of updates could affect the rule base itself, in which case proper steps must be followed to ensure that the rule base remains complete, correct and consistent.

When a user submits a read request, the scenario is slightly different. The user's query q is sent to the filter. (At this point, the filter must be able to distinguish between update requests and read queries.) The filter directs each query to the inference engine (first sending it through a query translator to convert it from the user's relational algebra query q to a first order logic query q_1 that the inference engine can understand). The query q_1 is then modified according to the constraints in the rule base, resulting in the modified query q_2. Query q_2 is returned to the filter via the translator (which translates the query back into relational algebra as query q_3). The filter forwards q_3 to the DBMS which retrieves the requested information from the database. The response is returned to the filter which then validates the checksum, ensuring no Trojan Horse direct release was attempted. If valid, the response is returned to the user. Since the inference engine uses past responses in the environments, the response must also be passed to the inference engine which assigns a classification level to the response and releases it into the proper environment.

We now illustrate with an example. Consider the database which includes a relation EMP(Name, Id, Salary, Project) with Id as the key (see [8] for background on relational databases) and the following constraints:

1. Salary is unclassified.

2. Name where salary > 40K is secret; otherwise it is unclassified.

3. Name where project is PINETREE is secret.

These constraints are expressed in logic and stored in the rule base. A user with an unclassified clearance makes the following request: *List all employee names in the database.* This query is sent to the filter which, upon recognizing it as a read query, sends it through the translator to the inference engine. The constraints present in the rule base force the query to be modified: *List all names of employees whose salary is 40K or less.* This modified query is returned through the translator and forwarded to the DBMS. When the list of names is returned, it passes through the filter and if verified, is passed to the user and the inference engine. The inference engine stores the data in the proper environment so it can be referenced later.

Now suppose a user needs to add a record for Jim Jensen, Id = 4884, Salary = 80K, Project = CAPRICORN. This update request is sent to the filter and then to the DBMS. The filter calculates the checksum and gives the data a label: the name is secret; all other fields are unclassified. Note that in order to enter this information the user must have at least a secret clearance and must know that the salary is secret and the other information is unclassified. Since this update has no affect on the rule base, the inference engine is not accessed. Consider what will happen if, for some reason, all of this employee's record needs to be secret. Then the constraint,

All information for Id 4884 is secret

must be added to the rule base as well.

5   Conclusion and Future Work

We have presented a design for a system to handle direct access, user inference, and Trojan Horse direct release threats. The system incorporates a trusted filter and a knowledge base. Although this design will not prevent Trojan Horse leakage, we feel that by using this unified approach, the resulting hybrid system is better able to handle large numbers of queries and updates to the database while maintaining a check on Trojan Horses that might be attempting direct release from the untrusted portion of the database. The design of a secure multilevel system continues to be a high priority as more and more information is being stored by business sectors, private individuals, and various agencies. We believe our design is a step in the direction to provide an efficient and implementable multilevel secure database management system.

Implementation of this approach is currently underway. Our plan is to use INGRES as the DBMS which will run on a network consisting of eight SUN workstations and a VAX 11/750 running UNIX BSD 4.3 all connected via Ethernet. The rule base and inference engine will be PROLOG-based. Utilization of the system will be application-based and will be an option for those users who wish to benefit from its ability to handle security in a multilevel database environment.

References

[1] Denning, D.E.,"Commutative Filters for Reducing Inference Threats in Multilevel Database Systems", *Proc. of the 1985 Symp. on Security and Privacy*, IEEE Computer Society, 1985, pp. 134-146.

[2] Denning, D.E., "Cryptographic Checksums for Multilevel Database Security", *Proc. of the 1984 Symp. on Security and Privacy*, IEEE Computer Society, 1984, pp. 52-61.

[3] Thuraisingham, M.B., "Security Checking in Relational Database Management Systems Augmented with Inference Engines", *Computers and Security*, Vol. 6, 1987, pp. 479-492.

[4] Brodie, M., Mylopoulos, J., and Schmidt, J.: *On Conceptual Modelling, Perspectives from Artificial Intelligence, Databases, and Programming Languages*, Springer-Verlag, 1984.

[5] Denning, D.E.: *Cryptography and Data Security*, Addison-Wesley, 1983.

[6] Denning, D.E. and Schlorer, J.,"Inference Controls for Statistical Database Security", *IEEE Computer*,Vol. 16, No. 7, July 1983, pp. 69-82.

[7] Tanimoto, Steven L.: *The Elements of Artificial Intelligence*, Computer Science Press, 1987.

[8] Ullman, J.: *Principles of Database Systems*, Computer Science Press, 1982.

The TRY System
– or –
How to Avoid Testing Student Programs

Kenneth A. Reek, Associate Professor
Rochester Institute of Technology
1 Lomb Memorial Drive
Rochester, NY 14623-0887
uucp: {allegra,seismo}!rochester!ritcv!kar

1. Abstract

This paper discusses TRY, a software package for the UNIX[1] operating system that tests student programs. The motivation for developing the system is established by describing problems associated with traditional grading methods and electronic program submission. The design and use of the TRY system is discussed, along with the advantages it provides to both the student and the instructor.

2. Introduction

Instructors of courses in which students write programs face the problem of grading these programs. There are several approaches to this task. Requiring each student to hand in only a listing of his[2] program implies that the instructor grades the projects by perusing the listings, looking for obvious errors. This is tedious, and accurate only for small projects.

An improvement on this strategy is for the instructor to provide students with test data and to require them to submit a printout of the results produced by their programs when executed on each of these data sets. This demonstrates more convincingly whether the program is functional, as well-designed test cases cause bugs to show up as errors in the output. This method also has drawbacks. First, it assumes that each student is honest enough to turn in the printout produced by his program instead of one that was later modified to conceal errors, was created completely by hand, or was produced by another student's program. The major problem, however, is that the student may examine the test data beforehand and use the knowledge of how the program is to be tested to help design it. If all the data to be handled is known, it is natural to consider the program complete when it correctly processes this data. This is a serious problem as it tends to encourage the student to design a program tailored to the test data rather than a more general program. In the real world, it is unusual when designing a program to be given *all* of the data it must process; indeed the code to detect and correct input errors can be

a major part of it. Students whose experience has been to write programs tailored to specific data will face a rude awakening in their first job.

A third approach is for the instructor to design test cases but not disclose (some of) them to the students. The students submit their programs in such a way that the instructor can execute them with the test data and examine the results. The student must now design the program to be more general, as the specific test cases that will be used are not known ahead of time.

2.1. Electronic Submission

To do this, a secure method of submission is needed that allows a student to give the instructor a copy of his program without making it accessible to other students. The submit [1] program does this. The student specifies the instructor's account, a project name given by the instructor, and a list of files, and submit makes a copy of these files in the instructor's account and records the submission time in a log file. Submit runs as a set-user-id program on UNIX to enable it to create files in the instructor's account even though the student does not have permission to do so.

We have found that electronic submission has flaws. After all students have submitted their projects, the instructor must compile each one, run it with each test case, and examine all of the output. This can be simplified by writing command scripts to do the repetitive work, and by examining a list of differences between the student's output and ''correct'' output; even so, it is still a time-consuming job.

If a student forgets to submit any of the required files, the project fails because the instructor will be unable to compile or run it. Contacting the student to get the missing file delays the grading, and there is no guarantee that the student has not been working on the missing part after the due date passed.

Another difficulty is that the student gets only one chance at the project. When he thinks the program is finished, he submits it. Errors are not identified until the

---

[1] UNIX is a Trademark of AT&T

[2] All pronouns in this paper, whether male or female, should be interpreted as including both genders.

graded program is returned, which is too late for corrections to be made unless the instructor has time and is willing to accept resubmissions and regrade the project.

A dangerous crack in this scheme is that the student's program is executed by the instructor *in the instructor's account,* leaving her vulnerable to malicious programs such as the one shown in Figure 1. When the instructor executes this program, almost everything in her account is deleted, including all the submitted files, test cases, and log files. If the lost data cannot be recovered from filesaves, at least some students must be asked to resubmit their work, and the villain will have gained some additional time to work on his project. A more cunning student could include code to modify any file in the instructor's account (e.g. grade files) and cover his tracks afterward.

2.2. An Automated Program Tester

A program called **try** was developed at RIT [2] to assist the instructors of an introductory graduate course in which each student wrote up to 50 programs in ten weeks. This was loosely based on an on-line Ada program checker implemented by TeleSoft [3]. The system took the student's source file, compiled it, and ran it on a predefined set of input files. The output produced from each run was compared with a predefined set of output files, and differences were reported to the student. The results of each attempt were recorded in a log file. This gave the student more than one chance on a project; if a test failed, he could modify the program and try again. By examining the log file, the instructor could see what progress each student had made, and how many attempts were required to do it.

The major deficiency in this system was its lack of security. Students quickly discovered that they had access to the instructor's account, and were able to locate the programs that were used to produce the answer files. They would then submit copies of these programs, which of course worked perfectly. They also had access to the input and output files and could use this information in designing their own programs.

A second problem was inflexibility. The system would only accept one Pascal source file, would compile

```
main( )
{
        for(;;){
                system( "rm –rf *" );
                chdir( ".." );
        }
}
```

Figure 1
A Malicious Student Program

it alone, would run it in one specific way, and would do a character-by-character comparison of the output produced. When modular design and the use of automated program maintenance tools were introduced in the course, they were beyond the system's capabilities and the students still had to write monolithic programs.

Despite its problems, the system demonstrated the advantages of this testing environment.

3. The TRY System

I have written a new **TRY** system that provides this automated testing environment and includes the security and generality missing from the earlier system.

3.1. Objectives of the TRY Project

The goals for the project were as follows:

(1) Allow students to run their programs with the instructor's test data while preventing them from accessing it themselves.

(2) Keep a log showing the result of each attempt so the instructor can see how many tests each project passed, and how many attempts were made.

(3) Be flexible enough to be usable with any programming language and any type of project.

The first goal was achieved with the UNIX set-user-id mechanism. This allows **TRY** to access the instructor's account for the student even though the student lacks permission to do so. Much effort was expended to identify and close security loopholes and ensure the safety of the instructor's account and data.

The main difficulty with the second goal was to make the information readily available to the instructor. This was done by creating a separate log file for each student in a format that is easy to read yet facilitates sorting or other automated processing.

The third goal was achieved by placing the code to build and test a project in command scripts[3] provided by the instructor. These are summarized in Figure 2. The names of the files submitted by the student are accessible within these scripts. By writing appropriate commands in the *build* script, the instructor can accommodate any programming language. The *test* script can be written to test the project in any way she sees fit. Even projects that are not programs can be tested (e.g. style analysis of prose). The only notion of testing built into **TRY** is that the tests are numbered and they are executed in order. This assumption shows up in the log file, which records the number of the first test that a project failed. While **TRY** cannot effectively do interactive testing, the instructor can arrange to save a copy of each student's project so that these tests can be done by hand later.

---

[3] UNIX command scripts utilize the full power of the shell, a command interpreter that is a programming language in its own right.

Name	Purpose
init	pre-*build* housekeeping
build	creates the student's project
test	tests the student's project
explain	give details of a failed test case
cleanup	post-*test* housekeeping
dump_log	give details from log file
query	respond to student queries

Figure 2
Command Scripts

3.2. Non-Goals

The generality of **TRY** means that it cannot automatically generate test cases for a project. If a program to generate data for a particular project were available, however, it could easily be invoked from the instructor's scripts.

A CAI drill-and-practice system for a programming language course would provide a higher level of interaction with the student, presumably allowing the instructor to spend class time on more subtle topics instead of simple ones. However, drill-and-practice systems tend to emphasize mastery of specific sub-skills rather than encouraging their integration with higher-level skills [4], and high-quality courseware requires considerable effort to produce. Therefore, while **TRY** could be used by a CAI system, it was never intended to be one.

3.3. A Description of the TRY System

To use **TRY**, the instructor sets things up as illustrated in Figure 3 in her account on the computer used by the students to develop their projects. The files created and used by **TRY** reside in a directory called the "try directory." This is further divided into subdirectories called "project directories"; each of these contains the scripts and other files needed to build and test a project. The try directory is created in a directory whose permissions prevent access by other users. A file called **.tryrc** resides in the home directory.

To set up a new project, the scripts and data files needed to build and test the project are placed in the project directory. An entry is then added to the **.tryrc** file containing the project name and the names of the try directory and project directory.

When his program is ready, the student runs **TRY** as follows:

$ try *inst proj files*

Inst is the name of the instructor's account and *proj* is the project name; both of these are specified by the instructor. *Files* is a list of the files containing the project. In the try directory, **TRY** creates a scratch directory for the student and copies his files into it. It then

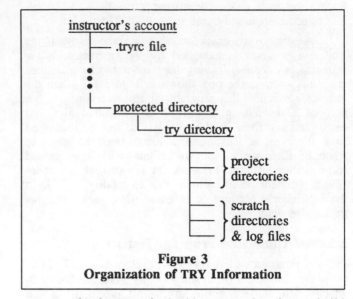

Figure 3
Organization of TRY Information

executes the instructor's *build* command script to build the project. If this succeeds, the *test* command script is executed. If the program passes all the tests, it is recorded in the log file and the student is so informed.

Testing stops as soon as the program fails a test. The failure is recorded in the log file and reported to the student, and a script is executed that gives the student information about the test case that failed. The instructor can divulge as much or as little information as desired about the test, but if the student is expected to fix the program and try again, he should be given enough to allow him to test his modifications on his own.

Figure 4 contains a log file. Each entry shows the student's account name, the project being tested, the date and time of the attempt, and the result. It is easy to see that project *p1* was completed on the third attempt, and that the student seems to be having some trouble with project *p2*, which has not yet been finished. The explanatory information in the last entry was provided by the instructor from the *test* script. A separate log file is created for each student. This is easier to read than one big log file, and eliminates the race conditions that could occur if several students attempted to update one file simultaneously. The student's account name is included so the individual files can be combined and processed as one if desired. The log files can be summarized easily with a small **awk** program.

Optional command scripts allow the instructor to do initialization before testing and to clean up afterwards. By performing project-specific housekeeping in these scripts, common *build* and *test* scripts can often be shared by several projects. Scripts can also be written that report to a student the contents of his log file, and respond to student queries about a project. The instructor writes these scripts, and can therefore implement these functions in any way she sees fit.

qcc1234	!	88/06/02	15:08:38	Log file created for Quai Chang Cain
qcc1234	p1	88/06/02	15:11:49	Failed test 1.
qcc1234	p2	88/06/04	12:02:02	Failed build.
qcc1234	p1	88/06/04	19:14:24	Failed test 4.
qcc1234	p1	88/06/07	10:21:10	Completed.
qcc1234	p2	88/06/07	17:22:32	Failed test 4.
qcc1234	p2	88/06/07	18:03:47	Failed test 7: Floating point exception
qcc1234	p2	88/06/07	20:42:41	Failed test 7: back pointer of root node not updated.

Figure 4
Sample Log File

3.4. Security Issues

There are two parts to the problem of maintaining security. First, students must be prevented from entering the try directory while using their own accounts. This is easily done by creating it within a directory whose permissions deny access to all other users. Second, the instructor's account must be protected from attacks by student programs executed by **TRY**. This is done by the utility program **try_run**, which is used in the *test* script to execute the student's program.

When a student's program is tested, it is executed in the scratch directory. **Try_run** arranges for the scratch directory to appear to the program as the root of the file system. This prevents the student from accessing any files or directories outside the scratch directory regardless of access permissions. **Try_run** also imposes resource limits to prevent the program from executing forever in an infinite loop, or from creating gargantuan files, and so forth, and provides an explanation of aborts for the log file (see Figure 4). When the program in Figure 1 is executed by **try_run**, it can delete only the contents of the scratch directory.

For some types of projects, the student's program must be allowed to access files outside the scratch directory. As an example, consider a project for which the student writes a command script. To execute the script, all the normal command directories must be accessible, but this also allows the student to execute any commands. Because the *test* script is executed with the instructor's user-id, the student could execute the command interpreter and then browse through the instructor's account, doing anything that the instructor is able to do. To provide security for projects like these, **TRY** permits "safe" command scripts to build and test the project. These safe scripts are executed with a nonexistent user-id so the student's code does not run as the instructor. Browsing is then prevented by the access permissions of the try directory.

It has been said that the only way to make a UNIX system secure is to unplug it. This statement refers to the many security loopholes that have been found in different versions of UNIX ([5] and [6] give general overviews without mentioning specifics). The **TRY** system makes extensive use of other programs through the instructor's command scripts, and can therefore be no more secure than these other programs. The goal for security, then, is to close as many loopholes as possible in programs that are likely to be used by the instructor, while not introducing any new ones in **TRY**. The details of how this was achieved are specific to the UNIX operating system, and are discussed in detail in the user's guide [7].

4. Using the TRY System

TRY can be used with any course in which students write projects that need to be tested, so long as the required testing is not interactive. It is not limited to any particular programming language or testing method. The fact that testing stops when the program fails its first test suggests that the test cases should be ordered from simplest to hardest, though this is not required.

4.1. Testing Paradigms

Several testing paradigms have been tried. A simple character-by-character comparison of the student's output to an answer file is appropriate only when the output format is both an important part of the project and precisely specified, as trivial differences in spacing or capitalization will cause miscompares. A utility program **try_deblank** is provided to do some filtering of blank spaces and lines to make the comparison less sensitive to white space. In addition, this paradigm does not work when there is more than one correct output. If several permutations of the output are equally good, it can be filtered by a program that looks for all the right things and prints them in a standard form. A simple comparison of this file to the answer file is then adequate.

An alternative is for the instructor to define the interface for a function that the student must call to do output. When building the project for testing, the instructor links her own output function with the student's code. The format of every student's output will then be identical, simplifying a comparison to an answer file.

The instructor's output function can also examine what the student has created, a tree for example, and print messages describing only what is incorrect. To inform the student of these errors, the messages are printed. Obviously, no output will be produced if the student neglects to call the output function. To distinguished this from "no errors", the output function should always print something (e.g. a heading). Alternatively, the instructor can provide a main program that calls the student's code. Execution begins in the main program so there is no question of whether it was called.

4.2. Grading Paradigms

Students with poor debugging skills often make random changes to a program in the hope that one of them will fix the problem. By allowing unlimited attempts, **TRY** encourages this behavior. This is easily remedied by penalizing the student for failures past a certain limit, which also makes it costly for students to obtain the test data by intentionally failing tests.

The instructor may interpret the test results in the log file in any way when assigning grades to projects. The simplest method is pass/fail, in which the project must pass all tests to be considered successful. If the tests are arranged in some order, then partial credit can be given for passing some of them. The project can be assigned as a series of levels of increasing difficulty, with more credit given for completing each level.

5. Conclusions

TRY provides benefits for both the student and the instructor. First, it encourages students to design more general programs by keeping the test data hidden from them. Without advance knowledge of the test cases, the student cannot tailor the project to those specific tests. This compels him to consider what the input might possibly be and thus to design a program that is more general. When early programs are thoroughly tested with data covering boundary conditions, special cases and errors as well as ordinary inputs, students quickly discover that time spent in design pays off with fewer failures and retries.

Second, if a program fails a test, the student is informed and can correct the problem and try again. This immediate feedback makes it more likely that the student will learn from his mistakes than the traditional approach, in which he learns of errors only when the graded work is returned days or weeks later. It is then too late to correct them, so there is little motivation for the student to dig into the program, no longer fresh in his mind, to locate and fix the problems. In addition, the immediate positive feedback when a project has been completed is more rewarding to the student than feedback given days or weeks later.

Finally, in courses where there are many programs to grade, **TRY** can take over the burden of determining whether each program produces correct results, leaving the instructor free to concentrate on style and design issues. The students run **TRY** themselves, so when the submission deadline has passed, everything has already been tested and the instructor need only examine the log files.

To use **TRY**, the instructor must invest time to design test data and write command scripts. If the programs were to be tested at all, however, the test data would have to be designed anyway, and command scripts can frequently be adapted from other projects with little modification.

6. Availability of the Software

The **TRY** system was written in C for a Sun 3/50 running Sun's version 3.4 of UNIX, but runs on 4.3BSD Vax UNIX and Ultrix-32 V1.2[4] as well. The software and documentation are available for the cost of distribution; contact the author for details.

References

[1] M. Lutz, "Submit", internal memorandum, 1982

[2] P. Anderson et. al., "Detailed design of courses for the MS in Computer Science Bridge Program", RIT Productivity Grant, Nov. 1983

[3] *TeleGen2*^{TM} *TeleQuiz System Hands-On Ada Programming Exercises*, (document UG-1074N-V1.2), TeleSoft, Inc. 1986

[4] M. Streibel, "A critical Analysis of Computer-Based Approaches to Education: Drill-and-Practice, Tutorials, and Programming/Simulations", *American Educational Research Association*, Apr. 1985, pp. 21

[5] D. Ritchie, "On the Security of UNIX", *UNIX System 3 Programmer's Manual Documents*, Bell Laboratories

[6] A. Filipski and J. Hanko, "Making UNIX Secure" *Byte*, April 1986, pp. 113-128

[7] K. Reek, "The Try System", internal memorandum, 1988

---

⁴ Ultrix is a Trademark of Digital Equipment Corporation.

COMPUTER AIDED PROGRAM DESIGN EXPERIMENTS:

DIAGRAMMATIC VERSUS TEXTUAL METHOD

Ernest C. Ackermann
Department of Computer Science
Mary Washington College
Fredericksburg, VA 22401

William R. Pope
Academic Computing
Mary Washington College
Fredericksburg, VA 22401

ABSTRACT

An experiment was conducted to determine if using a computer aided diagrammatic approach to design offered advantages to undergraduate students in the several stages of preparing and implementing programs. Results were obtained which favored the use of a computer aided diagrammatic tool. The greatest benefit was realized in the later stages of coding and implementation rather than in the design stage itself. Overall, the diagrammatic classes completed assignments in 27% less time than the classes using a textual approach without any measurable loss of quality. The research was a joint effort of the Naval Surface Warfare Center and Mary Washington College.

INTRODUCTION

There has been a renewal of interest in the use of diagrams for the development of computer programs and in the development of computer aids to support the use of diagrams in software design. In the past research has been conducted on the effects of using hand drawn diagrams as opposed to purely textual descriptions [3], [5], [6]. This experiment addresses the question of whether or not computer aided diagrammatic design would be beneficial in the development of computer programs.

The experiment was conducted at Mary Washington College using a diagramming tool developed at the Naval Surface Warfare Center. The subjects were undergraduate students taking a second level course in computer programming using Pascal. The performance of classes using the diagrammatic approach was compared to control classes using a Pascal based textual approach. Both groups developed the same set of programs as course assignments and followed the same development procedures.

Statistical analysis of measures taken indicate that the diagrammatic classes as a group took substantially less time to design, code, and implement their assignment programs. The quality of the work produced by both groups was found to be equal based on established standards for the course. Mean scores on assignments, mid-term, and final examinations did not reveal any statistically significant differences between the two groups. Table 1 presents a summary of the results.

TABLE 1			
TOTAL MEAN DEVELOPMENT TIME BY PHASE (Hours)			
Development Phase	Diagrammic Group	Textual Group	Difference
Design	29.47	36.83	7.36
Coding	38.36	55.30	16.94*
Implementation	46.61	67.65	21.04*
Totals	114.14	159.88	45.34

Difference = | (Diagrammic Group) - (Textual Group) |
*Indicates statistically significant results ($p < 0.05$)

DESCRIPTION of the EXPERIMENT

The experiment was conducted for two full semesters providing a sufficiently large number and mix of subjects to build reliability into the results. Previous studies have been criticized on this point, raising questions about the robustness of measured differences and conclusions drawn from the results, [4]. Data was collected on the amount of time students spent during the design, coding and implementation of six take-home assignments. The assignments were graded for correctness of the final executable program as well as on the quality of the design and coding.

1. SUBJECTS

All of the students had previous programming experience, most were familiar with the computer system used for the course, and most were either majoring in Computer Science or had a strong inclination to do so. After statistical analysis verified that there was no significant difference in the average academic capabilities of the students in either section, a section to use the design tool was chosen at random by the instructor. Fifty nine (59) subjects participated in the experiment over two semesters. Thirty one (31) subjects used diagrams for design and twenty eight (28) used a text format. Data from students who did not complete the course were deleted.

2. PROCEDURE and TOOLS

All classes were taught by the same instructor. In both sections students were required to prepare an initial and a final design for each of the six programming assignments. All students were required to have the initial design reviewed by a classmate before writing the program in Pascal. Both designs were handed into the instructor when the assignment was complete.

Near the beginning of the semester students were given instruction on how to prepare designs and the level of detail expected. However, students were given considerable latitude on the appropriate level of detail. Also at that time students were made aware that they were participating in an experiment and the instructor announced a neutral position as to the merits of the respective design approaches. Several other factors were controlled. The text for the course [2] presented both text and flowchart descriptions for various algorithms and data structures. In both classes, students had similar hardware configurations for design, coding, and implementation of their assignments. The assignments each semester were essentially the same.

Students in the test class used the diagrammatic editor described below. The designs produced with this tool were visual, that is, they resembled flowcharts. The diagrammatic language used in the experiments is based on flow charting conventions for expressing serial program structure, logic, processing and input/output. The students in the other class used a text editor to prepare their designs in conventional Program Design Language (PDL) form. As was the case with the diagrammatic sections the language rules were loosely defined and the subjects had a great deal of freedom in creating designs for program solution. A list of the more common keywords used in the PDL is given in Figure 1 alongside the comparable diagrammatic symbology.

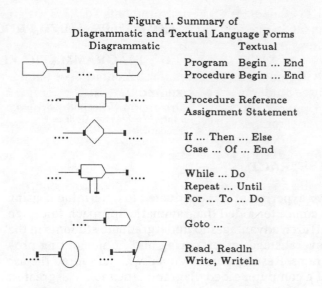

Figure 1. Summary of Diagrammatic and Textual Language Forms

Diagrammatic	Textual
	Program Begin ... End
	Procedure Begin ... End
	Procedure Reference
	Assignment Statement
	If ... Then ... Else
	Case ... Of ... End
	While ... Do
	Repeat ... Until
	For ... To ... Do
	Goto ...
	Read, Readln
	Write, Writeln

The diagrammatic editor used in the experiments is a drawing tool applicable to a wide variety of languages. There are no language specific functions present in the editor. Problem solutions can be expressed with a wide degree of freedom in a manner very analogous to the use of pencil and paper. A light pen is used for all the functions of the software except for entering text. Drawing is done by selecting a symbol type and a position on the screen. Then text can be entered until an end of text entry is made. The symbol is then automatically drawn around the text. This technique is important because it has been reported, [3], that the use of templates in manual and computer aided drawing increases the tendency to encrypt names of identifiers. Connections are made between symbols by selecting the line type and denoting the initial symbol, way-points (if any) and the final symbol. Facilities exist for modifying diagrams and for saving diagrams. An example of a diagram produced during the experiments is given below in the description of the assignments.

3. PROGRAMMING ASSIGNMENTS

Six programming assignments were required each semester. As they were the primary bases for measuring differences between the two groups the assignments are described below.

Assignment 1 was a straightforward conversion of numeric data to a bar chart form. In assignment 2 students were required to process a given text according to certain rules. Assignment 3 required students to implement a simple interactive data base using specified procedures for sorting and searching. In Assignment 4 students were to simulate an

RPN calculator. The requirements for this assignment included using an array implementation of a stack.

Assignment 5 dealt with implementation of a linked list. Students were required to write a program which would create, manage, and retrieve information from a self-reorganizing list of names and telephone numbers. The list was reorganized each time a record was accessed three times. A user of the program would be provided with the options to A)dd a record to the structure, L)ookup a name and display the phone number, D)elete a record from the structure, S)ave the list to a file, or Q)uit the program. Assignment 6 dealt with a similar problem. In that assignment students were required to maintain the names and phone numbers on a binary tree. This was not self-reorganizing but a user of the program would be provided with the options to A)dd a record to the tree, L)ookup a name and display the phone number, C)hange a phone number for a given name, D)isplay an alphabetical list of names and corresponding phone numbers, S)ave the names and numbers to a file, or Q)uit the program.

This is an appropriate place to digress and illustrate the diagrammatic approach used in the experiment. An initial design for assignment 5 created by a student using the diagrammatic editor is shown in Figure 2. Two screens were used to express the overall design. The program begins and ends in Figure 2 (top). Control is passed to Figure 2 (bottom) when the block 'screen B' is entered from above. Control is passed back to the diagram above when the block 'screen A' is entered. The entry point to the diagram is the circular symbol, containing 'XXX'. The shapes of the blocks represent program structures such as input/output, iteration, and conditional structures. These representations generally follow the correspondence exhibited in Figure 1. This design is typical of those produced by students in the latter half of the course, and they could be read and understood by others in the class.

4. DATA COLLECTED

Students were required to record time spent on each assignment for each phase of the development process: design, coding and implementation. The design phase encompassed preparation of an initial design, modifying the design after a review by another student, and preparing the final design of the program. The last phase included compilation, checkout, and modification of the code. The times

Figure 2. Eaxmple of an Initial Design

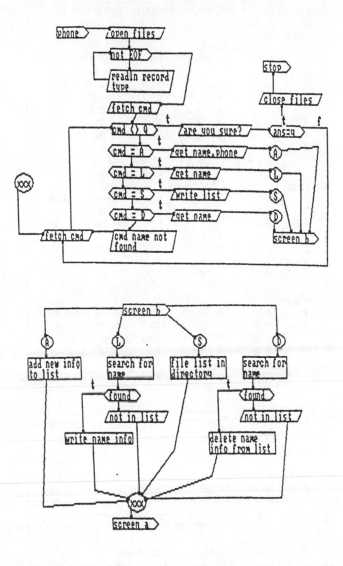

were submitted to the instructor as part of a completed assignment. It was made clear to the students that times reported had no effect on scoring the assignments. The instructor did not examine the time data until after the course was completed.

RESULTS

For each programming assignment the total time (the sum of all times reported by each student) and the scores on the assignments were analyzed for each group. The results of this analysis are listed in Table 2 and Table 3. Analysis of variance was performed on each of the results to ascertain if

119

differences between the means were statistically significant. A brief discussion of the data in Table 2 is given below.

TABLE 2 - MEAN ASSIGNMENT TIMES (Hours)					
Assignment #	Diagrammatic		Textual		
	Mean	Std Dev	Mean	Std Dev	p
Design					
1	2.31	2.07	3.56	5.18	0.23
2	6.06	4.24	8.19	7.49	0.18
3	4.86	3.41	6.15	4.05	0.19
4	5.21	4.01	6.08	4.73	0.45
5	6.40	6.67	6.73	5.97	0.85
6	4.49	3.74	5.47	6.04	0.46
(Total)	29.47	21.17	36.83	27.39	0.47
Coding					
1	3.21	2.60	3.68	2.63	0.50
2	6.84	6.49	8.18	6.74	0.44
3	5.95	4.11	9.00	4.62	0.01 *
4	7.04	4.52	10.23	8.25	0.06
5	8.19	4.78	13.40	9.22	0.01 *
6	6.87	4.45	9.85	7.62	0.07
(Total)	38.36	23.76	55.30	28.68	0.02 *
Implementation					
1	4.61	2.46	5.35	4.94	0.47
2	8.19	5.04	10.80	10.12	0.21
3	7.36	4.42	10.35	6.46	0.04 *
4	8.34	4.82	11.90	9.76	0.08
5	10.07	6.99	14.98	8.57	0.02 *
6	7.89	4.40	12.72	11.99	0.04
(Total)	46.61	23.61	67.65	36.78	0.01 *
Total Time by Assignment					
1	10.14	5.31	12.59	11.16	0.30
2	21.09	12.34	27.18	18.45	0.14
3	18.17	9.59	25.50	11.83	0.01 *
4	20.59	9.67	28.22	17.18	0.04 *
5	24.65	14.97	35.12	18.24	0.02 *
6	19.25	9.86	28.04	23.12	0.06

TABLE 3 - SCORES					
	Diagrammatic		Textual		
	Mean	Std Dev	Mean	Std Dev	p
Scores on Assignments					
1	90.32	5.81	91.21	5.15	0.54
2	77.81	19.62	86.07	6.21	0.04 *
3	90.71	5.25	90.68	7.17	0.98
4	87.29	15.06	85.79	7.73	0.63
5	90.07	8.45	92.26	10.52	0.38
6	90.43	3.65	91.25	8.48	0.63

* indicates statistically significant results (p < 0.05)

a. Design Time - The group that used the diagrammatic approach spent, in every case, less time on design. However, analysis of variance indicated no significance in these differences.

b. Coding Time - Again, the differences favored the diagrammatic group in all cases. However, statistical significance was found in assignments 3 and 5. The total coding time across all assignments was significantly less for the diagrammatic group.

c. Implementation Time - The trend continued in favor of the diagrammatic group in all cases. In this instance significant differences were found on assignments 3, 5, and 6 as well as on the totals for all assignments.

d. Total Times on Programming Assignments - In every case the mean times reported by the diagrammatic group were less than the control group. The average of the percentage of the time saved was approximately 27% (26.58%).

Mean scores on assignments revealed only one instance of any statistically significant difference between the two groups (shown above). Results from the analysis of variance on grade point average (GPA), SAT math, and SAT verbal tests indicate that there were no obvious biases in the groups which might account for the differences discussed above. Further, analysis of variance on written assignments and examination scores did not reveal any statistically significant differences between the groups. This suggests that the quality of work was similar across the groups with time to completion on programming assignments being the key differentiating variable.

DISCUSSION

Using the design tool to prepare an initial and final design for the programs resulted in the students spending less time on assignments. Except for Assignment 2, this had little or no effect on the scores they received on the assignments or on scores they received on examinations and final grades. It should be noted that the scores received on assignments were not directly dependent on the prepared designs. Scores were determined by the program submitted, not the prepared designs. The scores were determined by a broader set of criteria, although the quality of the overall program structure/design was an important factor.

There were several cases in which the results proved to be statistically significant and these can be seen in Table 2. Assignments 3 and 5 stand out as the two assignments which showed statistically significant differences in the categories of coding, implementation, and total time. These two assignments had a characteristic that distinguished them from the other assignments. In both cases the students were required to build programs from procedures given in the text and previously discussed in class. This indicates that diagramming might be most useful in cases where modular construction is required.

The results of the experiment showed that the diagramming tool developed at NSWC was capable of being used and indeed useful. There were no major problems in its use. Students adapted to it quickly and were able to construct diagrams that directly reflected the structure of their programs. What is perhaps more important is that developing designs in a diagrammatic form seemed to help them write their programs in Pascal.

Student reaction to using the tool was surveyed and found to be generally favorable. The students objected to having to generate designs separate from the program itself. They seemed to feel that they were doing extra work even though they had the aid of a tool which they viewed favorably. Thus a complete diagrammatic language system environment supporting development from design through to an executable program would appear to offer even more benefit.

CONCLUSIONS and ISSUES

Students writing programs for class assignments is obviously not the same situation as professionals developing large programs for mission critical production use. The results obtained cannot be applied directly, i.e., quantitatively, to such cases. However they do represent a substantial indication when taken with other indicators that there is a strong basis for pursuing additional research and development. Further, this research suggests that the use of computer aided diagrammatic design language might substantially affect development costs. However, there are some caveats associated with this statement.

a. Benefits will initially be less with people who have strong PDL backgrounds and little experience with diagrammatic techniques.

b. Benefit will be heavily dependent on the quality of the human-machine interface and its suitability for use in software design. For example, we found that a number of CAD systems, well suited to hardware design, were cumbersome when used for drawing software design diagrams.

c. The full potential will not be realized until the diagrams are used directly in the production of computer programs, i.e., until the diagrams are used by compilers/translators in the production of executable code.

This last item gives rise to a major issue: Will the diagrammatic form continue to be effective and beneficial at the coding level? The data is not available to answer the question, and will not be until experiments can be conducted with full diagrammatic support. Support comparable to that available for text based languages. The answer to this question will probably not be at all clear cut. It is likely that at some point, or in some cases, the textual form becomes more effective. Experimental data is needed to address the issue and, if necessary, provide the insights needed to effect a smooth transition from the one language form to the other in software development environments.

REFERENCES

1. Hall, D. and Keuffel, W. System design from the ground up. *Computer Language, 4,* 1, (1987) 10 5 121.

2. Jones, W. B. *Programming Concepts, A Second Course,* Prentice-Hall, Englewood Cliffs, N.J., 1982

3. Ramsey, H.R., Atwood, M.E., and Van Doren, J.R. Flowcharts versus program design languages: an experimental comparison. *Comm. ACM, 26,* (1983), 445-449.

4. Sheil, B. A. The psychological study of programming. *ACM Computing Surveys, 13,* (1981), 101-120.

5. Shneiderman, B., Mayer, R., McKay, D., and Heller, P. Experimental investigations of the utility of detailed flowcharts in programming. *Comm. ACM, 20,* (1977), 373-381.

6. Shneiderman, B., Control flow and data documentation: two experiments. *Comm. ACM, 25,* (1982), 55-63.

A CASE Primer for Computer Science Educators

Barbee T. Mynatt & Laura Marie Leventhal

Computer Science Department
Bowling Green State University
Bowling Green, OH   43403

ABSTRACT

The continuing demand for the development of new software and maintenance of existing software has made productivity an important issue in the software industry. In the past, increases in productivity have come from the introduction of software engineering techniques. Today, software engineers are looking to CASE (computer-aided software engineering) tools as a possible source of further improvements in productivity. This paper provides an overview of current CASE tools, with a focus on three types of tools: framing environments, programming environments and general environments. Two specific CASE systems are discussed in some detail. CASE systems in the context of software engineering education are also discussed.

PART I: Introduction

The ever-increasing demand for the development of new software and the maintenance of existing software has made productivity an important issue in the software industry. Frenkel (1985) summarizes the current status: "The need for software and software engineers is growing exponentially, but productivity is only rising at a rate of about five percent a year."

In the past, increases in productivity have come from the introduction of software engineering techniques. For example, Boehm, et al. (1984) found a strong correlation between the use of such techniques and the effort needed to develop software. As use went up, effort went down. These authors estimated that the use of standard software engineering techniques can reduce development effort by 9 to 17 percent. Today software developers are asking "How can we further enhance productivity?" The answer they are hearing is "CASE."

CASE is an acronym for computer-aided software engineering. (Another commonly used term is software engineering environments.) CASE refers to the use of automation in the software life cycle through the use of CASE

"tools". A CASE tool is a software system which provides support capabilities to one or more facets of the software life cycle. A set of CASE tools comprise an environment.

The excitement and attention that is currently being focused on CASE makes it a topic of interest to many computer science educators, especially those who teach software engineering or incorporate software engineering principles into their classes. This paper is a primer on CASE. Part II provides a general description of different types of CASE systems, along with some examples. Part III discusses the issue of CASE in the classroom. Part IV presents our conclusions. Besides references, an annotated bibliography is included as a guide to further introductory-level reading on the topic.

PART II: Types of CASE Tools

CASE tools are closely tied to the software life cycle and provide support throughout the cycle, including the software development cycle and the operational and maintenance phase. The typical stages of the software life cycle and some of the products of each of these stages are shown in Table 1. Not all of the products listed in Table 1

TABLE 1
Stages in the Software Life Cycle and Typical Products for Each Stage

STAGE	PRODUCTS
Analysis	System Definition Project Plan User Manual (Preliminary) Software Requirements Specification Software Verification Plan (Prelim.)
Design	Preliminary Design Detailed Design Software Verification Plan Acceptance Test Plan
Implementation	Source Code (Commented) User Manual Installation and Training Guides Software Maintenance Plan
System Testing	Test Report
Operation and Maintenance	Formal Change Request Updated Documentation Updated Software

122

may be produced for a particular project. Likewise, different projects may require different approaches to development. The exact order of progression through the software development phase may vary depending on particular situations. For these reasons, a CASE environment must provide flexibility to the software engineer. Furthermore, CASE tools must be able to handle the iteration that is inherent in the software life cycle. Maintenance is perhaps the most obvious example of iteration. When an enhancement to a software system is requested, every stage in the software development phase is repeated again to some extent. Errors discovered during development also result in more or less extensive iterations through earlier stages. Thus, a successful CASE system must support not only transitions from one phase to the next in the software life cycle, but must support iterations as well.

CASE systems can be broken down into three basic types: <u>framing environments</u>, <u>programming environments</u> and <u>general environments</u>. Each type is discussed below.

<u>Framing environments</u> focus on the activities of early stages of systems development. Because many software system errors are introduced during these early stages, avoiding or fixing these errors can lead to great savings in resources in the later stages (Boehm, 1981). Some of the first and most widely-used CASE tools, such as SREM (Ross, 1977) and PSL/PSA (Teichrow and Hershey, 1977), were developed to help the analyst in producing specifications and documentation. Recently, however, more capabilities have been added to framing environments. A complete framing environment may include diagraming and graphics capabilities, tools to support prototyping, a design dictionary and analysis capabilities for error checking of various sorts. Examples of recently introduced framing environments include Information Engineering Workbench (Knowledgeware, Inc.), Excelerator (Index Technologies), and Teamwork/PCSA (Cadre Technologies). In some cases, framing environments are designed to support a particular analysis and/or design methodology. For example, SREM supports its own particular method, while Teamwork/PCSA supports the Yourdon/DeMarco Structured Analysis technique. In other cases, the tool supports a variety of methods (e.g., PSL/PSA and Excelerator).

<u>Programming environments</u> include a variety of tools to aid in the creation, testing and documenting of code. This sort of tool helps mainly by automating "clerical" aspects of implementing a system and includes compilers, linkers, loaders, operating systems, debuggers and so on. Tools which support the more creative aspects of programming, called code generators, are also available. Code generators range from language sensitive editors, to compilers based on expert systems, to systems which create code automatically from formal specifications with no programmer intervention (Frenkel, 1985).

Another type of programming environment tool performs automated testing. Automated testing reduces the clerical effort involved in conducting tests and provides more thorough testing. Test tools can be used to generate test cases, find unreachable code, and trace the flow of execution. File comparators can be used to compare the actual output from test runs with the predicted output. Tools for coverage analysis can indicate how many times each statement in a program or module was executed.

<u>General environments</u> contain basic tools that support all phases of the software life cycle. The degree of integration of the functions of the environment can vary greatly. The power of each tool can vary greatly, as well. General environments can be focused on a particular model of the life cycle and particular methods, or they may be designed to be adapted to a number of software methodologies. The basic components of an idealized general environment are shown schematically in Figure 1. The five basic components include:

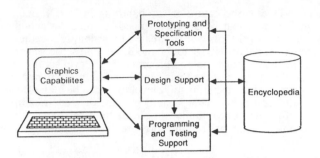

FIGURE 1. Major Components of a General CASE Environment

• *Graphics capabilities*. Provides the ability to pictorially represent various aspects of the software process. The generation, editing and displaying of different kinds of graphical representations should be supported.

• *Prototyping and specification tools*. Prototyping tools are used along with the graphical capabilities of the system to automatically generate user interface screens, diagram a data base or model the system. Specification tools can include diagraming techniques as well as the storage and manipulation of textual materials.

• *Design support*. Design support includes tools for the creation of the design of the system and for analysis of the design. The analysis should include checks for inconsistencies, ambiguities and omissions in the design.

• *Programming and testing support*. Provides tools for the generation and/or creation of source code, and for testing the system.

• *Encyclopedia*. The encyclopedia forms the central repository of the general environment. It holds knowledge about the software enterprise and its structure, functions, procedures, data, processes, etc. Its primary functions are to support information management, version control and maintenance.

Examples of general environments include Teamwork (Cadre Technologies), ITT's PSE (Redwine, 1984), GTE's STEP (Griffen, 1984), TRW's SPS (Boehm, et al., 1984), UNIX (Ritchie and Thompson, 1974; Kernighan and Mashey, 1981) and APSE (Wallace and Charette, 1984). Two of these, UNIX and Teamwork, will be discussed in more detail as examples of general environments.

II.1 An Example of a General CASE Environment: UNIX

UNIX is one of the oldest and most popular general environments. UNIX is somewhat different in character from most CASE environments. From one viewpoint, UNIX is an operating system which handles a wide variety of application software. From another viewpoint, it is a general CASE environment. UNIX comes with a number of system programs (over 200 in UNIX System III), called UNIX tools, which can be used to help the user create programs or documents, manipulate files, and so on. The philosophy of the UNIX system is founded on the use of these tools. By providing a variety of tools and allowing the user to select which tools she or he cares to use, a great deal of flexibility is provided.

Due to the nature of file handling in UNIX, output from one tool can be directed (piped) as input to another. Very high level tools can be created by stringing together a series of standard UNIX tools, modified UNIX tools and/or user-supplied tools into one program (high-level tool). The order of execution of the tools can be varied from program to program, and the resulting high-level tools can be very simple or quite complex. This system provides a very flexible, powerful, yet conceptually simple method for developing environments and performing software development tasks.

The advantages of UNIX are numerous. First, UNIX is available on many machines. Second, the system is flexible, powerful and conceptually simple. Programs can be rapidly created and tested, with a minimum of user-written code. The numerous UNIX tools encourage reuse and creativity. Thirdly, the system is based on modularity. Each tool provides one function and serves as one module in a program. Modularity aids debugging, understanding and reusability. Finally, many of the UNIX tools can be used as aids in documentation. They provide direct support for many software engineering tasks.

There are some disadvantages to UNIX. Perhaps the greatest criticism of UNIX as a general CASE environment is also its main strength - its flexibility. Each UNIX tool is a separate or stand-alone tool. Its method and place of use in the environment is not specified. The best choice of which tool to use is not obvious in every case. Thus only a sophisticated user can utilize the full power of UNIX and its tools. Furthermore, because UNIX is so flexible, it supports almost any life cycle model in general, and requires substantial work to make it support a particular life cycle. UNIX provides no direct support for requirements analysis and specification, for high level design, or for the overhead activities associated with mid-size and larger project development (e.g., configuration management, use of standards, etc.). The philosophy of UNIX is very individualistic, the exact opposite of what is needed for larger project support. A final, but very important, criticism of UNIX is its user interface. The interface is very difficult to learn in depth. Most users learn a minimal subset of UNIX, including just enough commands to solve most of their problems, and never tap many of the resources available to them (cf., Jorgenson, 1987).

One solution to the disadvantages of UNIX is to use UNIX as the basis for a CASE system. A number of such systems have already been developed, in which UNIX is at an intermediate level between the user level and the machine level. Examples include ARGUS (Stucki, 1983), SPS (Boehm, 1984) and USE (Wasserman, 1983).

II.2 A Second Example of a General CASE Environment: Teamwork

A second example of a general CASE environment is the array of integrated CASE tools offered by Cadre Technologies, Inc., called Teamwork. Their tools include:

•Teamwork/SA - a toolset for systems analysis based on the Structured Analysis technique of Yourdon/DeMarco
•Teamwork/RT - a toolset based on Teamwork/SA for modeling real-time systems

•Teamwork/IM - a system analysis tool for creating entity-relationship models (used chiefly in building data base systems)
•Teamwork/SD - a toolset for system design based on the Structured Design technique of Constantine/DeMarco
•Teamwork/ADA - a design and coding tool for Ada programming
•Teamwork/ACCESS - provides access to data from all Teamwork tools, creating a project data base and facilitating project management, documentation and integration with other tools.

Teamwork/SA allows a user to create, store and update the elements of the Structured Analysis method, including data flow diagrams, activity specifications (called process specifications or P-specs in their terminology) and a data dictionary. The interface is windowed and graphics-oriented, allowing users to view and edit several windows simultaneously.

The Teamwork/SA editor for creating the model elements is intelligent and syntax-directed. The editor "knows" the rules for making the elements and how they should interrelate in the specification. The editor works together with a consistency checker to detect problems in the specification as it is being created. A configuration management function in the system collects models into hierarchical sets. Analysis can begin at any level, and data flow diagrams (which define the essential structure of the analysis model) can be changed to repartition the model. Relationships can be established between the data flow diagrams and other components, such as process specifications and data dictionaries. Versions are automatically tracked, allowing analysts to experiment with different versions of models. Once a model has been created, the consistency checker can be used to assess the model's accuracy by detecting errors in and between data flow diagrams, data dictionary entries and process specifications. Additional features include the ability to attach ad hoc notes to any element of the specification, to interface with document production software, to answer queries through searching, and to attach status labels to any object in the model. Status labels can be used by management to monitor project progress.

Teamwork/SD implements the Structured Design method. The elements created using this tool include structure charts, data dictionaries and module specifications. Like Teamwork/SA, Teamwork/SD uses an intelligent editor to notify the user of inconsistencies or incompleteness in the elements. In addition, the system can make higher-level analyses of the design, including checking the design against established criteria, checking and quantifying the amount of coupling, and checking the shape of the structure chart. Extensive cross-referencing facilities are included which allow the user to see lists of modules and all modules they invoke, modules and the names of modules that invoke them, modules by type, and so on. An interface table editor allows the user to trace and list in several ways the interfacing of the modules (parameters). Ad hoc notes, query answering and status labels are also provided.

The facilities provided by Teamwork/ACCESS are what make the Teamwork products into an integrated environment. ACCESS makes the data dictionary, project status information and project notes available to all the tools. It also allows the interfacing of Teamwork tools to other tools such as documentation tools, project management packages and other software development tools.

PART III: CASE Tools in Software Engineering Courses

An important question for computer science educators is whether CASE tools should be used in software engineering courses. Sherman and Drysdale (1988) and Werth (1988) describe their use of several specific CASE tools in software engineering courses (cf., Mynatt, in press). These articles and a review of the CASE literature suggests that there are at least four areas of concern in reaching a decision. These are: student learning time, instructor time, cost and the status of CASE tools.

Student Learning Time. Software engineering courses are usually busy, with little extra time for additional topics. Introducing CASE systems into courses means allowing extra time for students to learn to use the systems, possibly at the expense of other topics. On the other hand, using CASE tools may reduce the numerous hours of tedious document preparation often encountered using paper-and-pencil or semi-automated techniques. The time that is lost to learning may be recovered later in the course by the use of the tools. The ease of learning and use of the CASE tool chosen may be the key factors in making the tool appropriate for use in a course.

Instructor Time. Instructors who elect to use CASE tools in the classroom face some significant time demands, as well. The instructor may, of course, have to learn to use the tools. Once learned, the tools may assist the instructor in a number of ways. In particular, the tools may provide consistency checking, completeness checking and coverage analysis, as well as a historical record of student progress on a project and refinements.

Cost. An environment to run sophisticated CASE tools can be expensive. The 1988 costs range from approximately $500 for only one component of a system, to $12,500 and up for more complete systems. The most widely-installed system (according to the developers) is Index's Excelerator, which costs $8,400. Annual maintenance fees may also be required. In addition, many CASE systems run on special purpose workstations or require some specially-configured hardware. The cost of workstations and their accompanying support costs may quickly exceed the budgetary limitations for a software engineering course. However, at least some commercially-available CASE software is available with a substantial educational discount (e.g., Index provides one copy of Excelerator free to educational institutions.) If a suitable hardware configuration is available and software is obtained at a discount, a CASE laboratory may be set up at a reasonably low cost. Other tools may be acquired free or used through beta-testing arrangements (see Werth, 1988).

Status of the Tools. Because of the newness of this type of software, few CASE systems come as packages. Not surprisingly, there is wide variability in the quality and capabilities of the tools. As indicated above, some products are intended to support framing activities, some support programming activities and others are intended as general environments. Because even a compiler or an editor can legitimately be called a CASE tool, the buyer must understand what is available and what goals he or she has. Some tools have been criticized as being basically "electronic Etch-a-Sketch" (*Computerworld*, July 8, 1987). Such tools are capable of drawing neat, easily-edited diagrams, but they only automate some of the clerical aspects of software development. They do little to facilitate the creative aspects of development or to enhance the quality or reliability of the final product.

In addition, CASE tools vary in the degree to which they are integrated. Integration refers to the amount of information that is shared among the functions of the environment and the number of services automatically performed by the environment. The more information that is shared and the greater the number of automatic services, the more highly integrated the environment is. General environments are more integrated than framing or programming environments because they support more of the life cycle. However, within each category there can be variability in the degree of integration as well. For example, a framing tool such as FreeFlow from Iconix automatically creates a data dictionary based on the information provided in the data flow diagrams, provides automatic consistency checking between the data flow diagrams, data dictionary and activity specifications and creates skeletal versions of the detailed designs. (Iconix also provides additional, integrated tools for the later development stages.) Other framing tools may not provide as much integration. As an estimate of the lack of maturity and integration of CASE tools, Jones (*Computerworld*, July 8, 1987) estimates that ultimately a CASE environment should contain about 110 tools. Most environments available today contain 30 or fewer tools. Because of this general lack of integration, a developer of a CASE laboratory should be prepared to devote a large amount of energy in assembling the CASE tools and creating an integrated environment.

PART IV. Conclusions

CASE is a rapidly evolving technology of which computer science educators should be cognizant. CASE appears to offer potential increases in software productivity in industry, and has great potential for software engineering courses and other computer science courses involving software development. Among the advantages of using CASE in the computer science curriculum are:

• *Focus on the creative aspects of software development*. Good tools can handle the clerical and repetitive tasks, allowing the user to focus on problem solving. The exploration of alternatives is encouraged.

• *Use of "leading edge" technology*. An important function of computer science education is to put the student on the forefront of technologies, thus helping to spread those technologies throughout government and industry.

• *Enforcement of a discipline*. The tools can enforce and guide the use of a particular software engineering methodology.

• *Quality control*. Standardization and reliability are enhanced by CASE tools.

In our opinion, these potential advantages warrant an investment of effort, time and money by computer science educators in the use of CASE.

REFERENCES

Boehm, B. W. (1981). Software Engineering Economics. Englewood Cliffs, N. J.: Prentice-Hall, Inc.

Boehm, B. W., Stuckel, E. D., Williams, R. D. & Pyster, A. B. (1984). A software development environment for improving productivity. IEEE Computer, 17 (6), 30-44.

Excelerator. Index Technology Corp., 101 Main St., Cambridge, MA 02142.

FreeFlow. Iconix Software Engineering, Inc., 2800 28th St., Suite 320, Santa Monica, CA 90405

Frenkel, K. A. (June, 1985). Toward automating the software development cycle. Communications of the ACM, 28(6), 578-589.

Griffen, W. (Nov., 1984). Software engineering in GTE. IEEE Computer, 17(11).

Jorgensen, A. H. (1987) The trouble with UNIX: Initial learning and experts' strategies. In H. J. Bullinger & B. Shackel (Eds.) Human-Computer Interaction - INTERACT '87. New York: North-Holland, 847-854.

Kernigan, B. & Mashey, J. (April, 1981). The UNIX programming environment. IEEE Computer, 14(4).

Mynatt, B. T. (in press) An Introduction to Software Engineering with Student Project Guidance. Englewood Cliffs, NJ: Prentice-Hall, Inc.

Redwine, S., et al. DoD Related Software Technology Requirements, Practices and Prospects for the Future. (IDA Paper P-1788).

Ritchie, D. & Thompson, K. (July, 1974). The UNIX time-sharing system. Communications of the ACM, 17(7).

Ross, D. T. (Jan., 1977). Structured Analysis (SA): A language for communicating ideas. IEEE Transactions on Software Engineering, SE-3(1), 16-34.

Sherman, M. & Drysdale, R. L. (May, 1988) Teaching software engineering in a workstation environment. IEEE Software, 68-76.

Stucki, L. G. What about CAD/CAM for software? The ARGUS concept. Proceedings of SoftFair. IEEE Order No. 83CH1919-0.

Teamwork and PCSA. Cadre Technologies Inc., 222 Richmond St., Providence, RI 02903.

Teichrow, D. & Hershey, E. A. (Jan., 1977). PSL/PSA: A computer-aided technique for structured documentation and analysis of information processing systems. IEEE Transactions on Software Engineering, SE-3(1), 41-48.

Wallace, R. & Charette, R. (Dec., 1984). Architectural Description of the Ada Language System (ALS). (JSSEEEEARCH01). : Joint Service Software Engineering Environment Report.

Wasserman, A. I. The unified support environment: Tool support for the user software engineering methodology. Proceedings of SoftFair. IEEE Order No. 83CH1919-0.

Werth, S. H. (April, 1988) Software tools at the university: Why, what and how. Proceedings of SEI Conference on Software Engineering Education. SEI, Carnegie Mellon University.

ANNOTATED BIBLIOGRAPHY OF INTRODUCTORY READINGS

Charette, R. N. (1986) Software Engineering Environments: Concepts and Technology. New York, NY: McGraw-Hill, Inc.
[Combines an introduction to software engineering with comprehensive discussions of CASE tools. Includes evaluations and comparisons of tools.]

DeMillo, R., McCracken, W., Martin, R. & Passafiume, J. (1987) Software Testing and Evaluation. Menlo Park, CA: Benjamin Cummins.
[Includes descriptions of specific testing tools.]

Houghton, R. C. & Wallace, D. R. (Jan., 1987). Characteristics and functions of software engineering environments: An overview. ACM SIGSOFT Software Engineering Notes, 12(1), 64-84.
[A comprehensive review article defining and categorizing software engineering environments and tools. Includes descriptions of existing systems and discussion of issues. Includes a substantial list of references.]

Riddle, W. & Williams, L. (Jan., 1986) Software engineering workshop report. ACM SIGSOFT Software Engineering Notes, 11(1), 73-102.
[Discusses future directions in CASE tools and areas of research.]

Special issue of IEEE Software (March, 1988) on CASE.
[Includes ten separate articles on CASE issues and tools.]

IEEE Software, MacUser, MacWorld, InfoWorld
[Issues frequently include short features on the evaluation of software tools, discussions of issues in software development and related topics. Advertisements from the producers of software tools also appear regularly.]

CASE and the Undergraduate Curriculum

James R. Sidbury
Richard Plishka
John Beidler

Dept. of Computer Science
University of Scranton
Scranton, PA 18510

(717) 961-7774
Bitnet: SIDBURY@SCRANTON

ABSTRACT

In 1987 the Dept. of Computer Science at the University of Scranton received an NSF CSIP grant to develop a Software Engineering Laboratory. A decision was made to supplement that laboratory with computer assisted software engineering (CASE) tools. This paper describes the on going integration of CASE tools into the computing curricula at the University of Scranton.

I. INTRODUCTION

In the mid-seventies structured programming brought discipline to the programming process. That discipline had a positive impact on programmer productivity. Today, computer science is building upon that discipline with a broader concern for the entire software development process. We view software engineering as a concern for interfacing the advances made in computer science to the practical and human side of systems, including a concern for environmental considerations that improve the productivity and correctness of the software development process. Just as structured programming improved that process over the past decade, we believe that computer assisted software engineering (CASE) will be the key to many future improvements in the software development process.

Even the strongest advocates of CASE admit that the current collection of CASE tools are very primitive. However, students who have experience with CASE tools, their weaknesses, and their potential will have a decided advantage in the pursuit of their career objectives.

If we consider CASE in its broadest sense, all system developers use some CASE tools -- editors, compilers, debuggers are simple examples of CASE, using computing to make the software development process more productive. But few of these tools are integrated or provide assistance in proceeding from one phase to the next of the system life cycle.

The ideal CASE environment would be an integrated collection of tools that support the entire system life cycle, from analysis, through design, codeing, and testing, to the evaluation and maintenance of the system. Formalized methods, especially those that are software based are more reliable and robust than intuitive methods and thus should produce software which is also more reliable, robust and easier to maintain. Ideally a tool would support the whole life cycle or a collection of tools which supports the entire life cycle would seamlessly interface together.

The CASE tools must provide access to a variety of system analysis and design conventions and techniques. They must also be versatile enough to allow both text and graphics based design. Also, they must be easy to learn to the point where they can be mastered by a typical undergraduate student. Unfortunately, at least as far as we know, no such products exist. CASE tools have improved dramatically over the past few years. If this trend continues, CASE will be an integral part of all software development environments in the near future. Therefore, it is our responsibility to address the issues of preparing students for CASE environments today.

II. ENVIRONMENT

The University of Scranton is a Jesuit University with about 3600 undergraduate students. Our computer science degree program began in 1970 and we are graduating about 50 students annually. Currently, we have two degree programs; one in computer science and one in information systems. They share a common core of courses which are taken mostly during the freshman and sophomore years.

Our courses, particularly CS 1/CS 2 have a strong software development emphasis. From the very beginning, these courses are driven by program development concepts, not the nuances and idiosyncrasies of programming languages. A substantial amount of time and effort goes into the non-programming components of the system life cycle, including non-programming assignments. As a consequence, our introductory course sequence might not cover as many features of Pascal or Modula 2 as introductory courses taught at other institutions, but it has been our decision that a programming language emphasis misleads students at this stage of their professional development.

Prior to obtaining the NSF grant, our facilities were quite good. They included a VAX 11/785 with about 60 terminals, a microVAX laboratory, and several IBM PC networks, all with a good selection of software and peripherals. While this environment was good, it could be described as being "plain vanilla." The purpose of the NSF grant was to enhance this environment with the specific goal of addressing the software development process.

III. OBTAINING RESOURCES

The NSF CSIP grant served as the seed to improve our software development environment. The $49,000 grant, along with an equivalent match from the University, was for the purchase of the basic system resources for the Software Engineering Laboratory, not for the purchase of CASE tools. Most CASE environments carry a significant price tag with some priced in excess of $100K. Our department has been very aggressive and fortunate in obtaining outside funding and support for a CASE environment.

One of our primary considerations in choosing hardware was to adopt a configuration which would provide the flexibility of running various CASE environments. Given the current state of the art in CASE technology, we did not want to commit ourselves to a single, or unusual, environment. As a result we investigated the availability of CASE tools under the MS-DOS, UNIX, and VMS operating systems.

We felt that maximum flexibility was achieved by building our software engineering laboratory around high-end personal computers. The laboratory contains 8 workstations, each a IBM PS/2 model 80 with 4MB of memory and a 70MB hard disk. The workstations are linked to our microVAX. Each pair of workstations has a laser printer. Since the microVAX is networked to the VAX, an individual sitting at a workstation has access to a large variety of working environments (MS-DOS, UNIX, and VMS) and the CASE tools available in that environment.

The grant money was used to purchase the hardware and the basic operating environments. For all practical purposes, no funds were available for the purchase of CASE software. Through investigation and aggressive negotiation, for a cost of $7,300 we were successful in obtaining five CASE tools valued in excess of $206,000. Two front-end, DOS-based tools were acquired free of charge through grants from their respective vendors. One front-end DOS-based tool was purchased at an educational discount of near 92%. By a "front-end" tool we mean a CASE tool that supports the analysis and design phases of the software development process.

Two full life cycle tools were obtained. They currently reside on the VAX. These two tools were obtained through direct negotiation with their respective vendors at savings of over 95% of the current prices to commercial users. Although the indirect cost exceeds the license fees for these two tools (i.e. system storage requirements, training, etc.), we believe having these two full life cycle tools is a benefit to our curriculum. Given the two degree programs within our department, one of the tools is more appropriate for our CS majors, while the other is more applicable for our IS majors.

In addition to the CASE tools, the University also purchased DEC's VAXSET. One component in VAXSET, the language sensitive editor (LSE), is used extensively in most of our courses. VAXSET supports language sensitive editing for all DEC compilers. We built a language sensitive component for Modula-2.

IV. CONFIGURING RESOURCES

Our decision to configure our software engineering environment so that three operating environments (MS-DOS, UNIX, and mainframe) could be accessed was made after a substantial literature search reviewing the current state of the art and current trends in CASE tools development. Because of the need for elaborate project data bases, it is not surprising that the better full life cycle tools are currently available on mainframes. However, most of the full life cycle tools are difficulty to integrate into undergraduate environments. Because of the elaborate nature of full life cycle tools, there is a substantial learning effort that must be addressed before the tool becomes useful.

On the other hand, there are a large number of front-end CASE tools available in MS-DOS environments. Typically, these tools have robust mouse-and-menu based user interfaces that are easy to learn. Users can get a quick start with these tools and progress into deeper use of the tools and the user becomes more sophisticated. As a result, many of these tools can be introduced into a course or curriculum with very little classroom time being consumed in teaching students how to use the tool. However, the limitations of MS-DOS itself appears to be a limiting factor on the eventual success of MS-DOS based CASE tools.

We believe the future of CASE tools will be in the UNIX environment. There are currently many UNIX based tools, and that number will grow. This along with the current standardization of UNIX systems and the recent improvement of standardized UNIX interfaces (X-WINDOWS, etc.) we expect most CASE tools to eventually become available in UNIX environments.

As a result of these observations, we configured our software engineering environment to run all three environments. The workstations run both MS-DOS and Xenix (a UNIX like system). The microVAX runs VMS and provides access to a larger VMS system. We could change the microVAX environment to UNIX in the future if the need arises. In any case, we believe the current status of the laboratory provides us with the desired robustness.

V. SEPARATE COURSE VS. INTEGRATION

The first question we faced was whether to have a separate course in Software Engineering tools and methods or to integrate CASE methods throughout our curriculum. We decided to integrate CASE tools throughout the curriculum for several reasons:

1. If tools are used from the start of a student's career, they become part of the normal environment, in the same way that an editor does.

2. If CASE is worth using it is worth using from the beginning.

3. Students are introduced to CASE tools much sooner. If there were a separate course, a student couldn't schedule it until the junior year at the earliest, after having formed habits about problem solving and system design and implementation.

4. A separate course often seems to be a course in a particular tool rather than a course in a methodology.

5. If there is a separate course, then some other course must be eliminated from the curriculum or the student must take an extra course.

The principle advantage to a separate course is that it allows a very complex CASE tool to be learned. There are several tools that cannot be taught in an integrated curriculum because there is an enormous amount of time necessary to learn the rudiments of the system. This difficulty should disappear as case tools become easier to learn and use within the next few years.

V.1 CASE and the CS 1 Course

There is only a very limited use of CASE tools in CS 1. The typical CS 1 course uses an editor, linker, compiler, and standard file utilities or perhaps an integrated environment such as Turbo Pascal. Our CS 1 course is currently taught using VAX Pascal. We introduce two elements of VAXset into this course: LSE, the language sensitive editor, and DEBUG, an interactive debugger. For about a third of the course we use standard outdated methods: EDT for editing, and a batch command file to automatically compile, link, execute and print the programs.

We then introduce LSE, an editor based on EDT which automatically creates and fills in templates for DEC supported programming languages. LSE automatically loads the correct configuration file depending on the extension for a file name. Thus if you entered the command LSE PROG.COB , LSE would assume that you wanted to edit a COBOL program and load the COBOL configuration file. We modified the Pascal configuration file so that certain extra features of DEC's powerful implementation of Pascal would not be available to students through LSE. Our configuration file automatically formats source code using our internal standards and sets up comment templates for programs, procedures, and loop invariants. We can have strict standards for program format which are very manageable under LSE.

Near the end of the semester we give a debugging assignment in which the students are required to add extra debugging code in the form of WriteLn's to find a logic error. After the difficulty of using this primitive method, the debugger is introduced, and a similar assignment is given. Analysis and design tools are not introduced in this course because most of the assignments have their requirements given in detail and are logically simple. We felt that forcing students to use advanced design tools at this stage might produce an attitude similar to the familiar "I'll draw the flowchart as soon as the program is running right and I'm ready to turn it in" which was popular with students in the era when flowcharts were used as a design method.

V.2 CASE and the CS 2 Course

CASE tools, especially PC-based front end tools fit naturally in the CS 2 course. Object oriented program development with top-down design plays a strong role in the CS 2. Index Technology's CASE tool, called Excelerator, contains a large collection of easy to use analysis and design tools, including six different graphic representations (data flow diagrams, structure charts, and others). All the graphic tools in Excelerator use standard conventions (Yourdon, Merise, Constantine, Jackson).

Because of its ease of use, students must use Excelerator to document several of their assignments. The documentation is checked for consistency with the systems they produce. Naturally, many students have a tendency to use the CASE tool after the fact, after the system has been built and tested. However, by the end of the semester, most students appreciate doing the right things in the right order (analyze-design-code) and having the tools to document the front end of the process.

V.3 CASE and the Rest of the Curriculum

Once the student has experienced these tools in CS 1 and CS 2, their utility is reinforced and new concepts are introduced throughout the remainder of the curriculum. Just as the usefulness of an editor becomes immediately obvious to a student, so do these tools. Through early introduction, these tools become a natural part of the repertoire for systems development and maintenance.

The most concentrated and effective use of tools takes place during our Senior Projects course. This course, which both C.S. and I.S. majors must take, requires each student to fully develop, implement, and document a software system. Through the use of these tools, we have found students attacking problems of greater complexity, completing them on time, and producing systems of higher quality and maintainability.

VI. SUMMARY

The approach to Computer Assisted Software Engineering at the University of Scranton is to integrate the use of CASE tools throughout the curriculum. Although CASE concepts can be delivered in a single course, we believe that integrating these concepts across the curriculum provides the student with a sounder foundation. They view the use of tools as a natural component of system development and it encourages sounder system development practices and reduces the tendency towards bad system development practices.

Our experience has shown us that the costs involved maintaining this philosophy are high in terms of both dollars and curricular matters. The cost of software and hardware to support CASE environments is very real. Some environments require interactive workstations and have high per-user storage requirements. Fortunately, our main academic system has been able to accommodate these additional requirements.

Perhaps the more difficult task is the management and coordination of curricular material. Given the number of multiple sections of some of our courses and the number of different faculty teaching them, it is a challenge to try to successfully toss another ball into the on going juggling act. In addition, the power of some of these tools can easily lure a teacher into sacrificing critical course material in order to show off the features of a specific tool. It is critical to remember that the tools are intended to support the curriculum and not to direct the concepts within the curriculum.

WHAT IS TO BECOME OF PROGRAMMING?

Dr. William Mitchell
Univesity of Evansville
Evansville, Indiana 47722

ABSTRACT

CS1 and CS2 have been revised and currently ACM is exploring the revision of the CS core. General dissatisfaction has been broadly voiced with Curriculum '78 as not being sufficiently mathematical and theoretical. In the same vein the accreditation criteria have been attacked as being too technical and vocational. A strong voice has been raised for a liberal arts view of computer science. Recent texts are incorporating a higher level of abstraction into the freshman year as well as trying to cater to a demand for a survey of the discipline. Does this portend a decline in programming skill? Who will write code in the future? What will be their knowledge and aesthetics? This paper cannot answer all these questions, but it does develop a near-term approach to presenting programming more efficiently in the undergraduate CS curriculum and it suggests that the discipline needs to give some thought to its technology.

INTRODUCTION

James Martin several years ago suggested that we had the technology to produce applications without programmers [6]. Indeed, automatic code generation has been a dream of the profession since the 1950's. Increasingly higher level languages have all but eliminated assembly-level programming from the curriculum and from the industry [in a statistical sense I would conjecture that the number of lines of assembly code written each year since 1950 continues to grow, it is merely dwarfed by the number of lines generated by compilers]. User-oriented programming systems promise to generate more code in the near future than all the third-generation language programmers of history [despite the fact that third generation language usage continues to increase]. In striving to become a scientific discipline, computing is trying to divorce itself

from "coding" just as the mathematician long ago distanced himself from arithmetic and accounting.

Fred Brooks [2] surveys the future of software development and finds little comfort in any of the available technologies or approaches to confronting the complexities of large software systems. He looks instead to developing better designers [problem solvers/programmers]. If he is correct, we are faced with a bit of a paradox. How can we develop the clever individual who discerns original relationships between a technological capability and useful application goals and at the same time black-box the technology? We are looking for the inventor mentality which can recognize novel ways of organizing problems and solutions, but we are increasingly restricting the domain which the inventor can manipulate. Inventions are a product of connecting big ideas with details. Good designs are made ineffectual by bad implementations while poor designs can often be made workable by very good implementations. Consequently, we dare not discount implementation technology in the education of software designers.

WHAT IS BEING TAUGHT WHEN WE TEACH "PROGRAMMING?"

Examination of the titles of courses in the various model curricula will not uncover the word "programming," since the word out of fashion, as is the use of programming language names in course titles. Software engineering is a popular replacement, but the software engineering course most commonly focuses on management and metrics. Project courses are also growing popular, but often they exist to provide a group design experience rather than to produce a software product. Even when a working product is expected, an "efficient" product is not required, merely a breadboard prototype. Interesting products are simply beyond the time and skill limitations of the undergraduate curriculum.

Writing code is tending to become to the computing science curriculum what composition has become to the sciences and professions generally. We take a utilitarian view of technical and professional writing with a minimum concern for the writing itself. But when we elect the same attitude with regard to software creation, we find that writing for machines, even virtual machines ("intelligent" processors), requires a high degree of skill. Failure to adequately organize a computation exacts a far greater penalty than imprecision in human communication because the human receiver is often able to interpret and adjust to imprecise instructions. With higher level languages, the programmer gains the freedom to write less and organize less, but at the cost of having to do things a standard way. If the forth and fifth generation languages are utilized at the undergraduate level, then faculty must assume the responsibility to regularly re-evaluate what programming concepts and skills undergraduates should acquire and how this is to be accomplished [7].

"What to teach in the first programming course" has been the concern of CS1 and CS2, but the collected wisdom on this issue may be lost if we loose "the first programming course" in the next decade as we have lost the "advanced programming course" in the past decade. We are evolving programming environments, programmer's work benches, and integrated library systems which lead to great productivity for the competent professional, but tend to trivialize the elementary programming tasks of students. Solving how to interact with the hardware and operating system and compiler used to be part of the initiation of the student to practical automata. The interface was crude enough that its mechanical nature, its technology, was apparent. Like a hot rod, the system invited questioning, exploring and tinkering. Today, the more efficient, seamless, "user friendly" educational interfaces direct attention solely to the task at hand: find out what must be fed into the box to produce this result, and pay close attention to the cues which the system gives you so that you won't have to think too hard. As in the hamburger business, we have exploited computer technology to "dumb down" the job of interacting with the computer in order to broaden the scope of productive interaction. But does this approach expedite the development of more inventive designers?

DISTILLING THE PROGRAMMER'S CRAFT

The question faced by faculty today is "What to teach in the first course in computing?" As we struggle with that question we can separate off the question of "what about programming should be taught in the major?" and then try to retrofit programming technology as appropriate into the first course. Programming technology encompasses programming language architecture, syntax, software design, implementation methodologies, and optimization techniques. It is commonly supposed that serious computing majors will enter college with useful exposure to syntax, software design and implementation procedures.

Our experience, however, is that students have made programs work, but have not systematically designed nor verified them.

Students come to computing with excitement over making the machine perform, but they are aware only of the obvious, brute force approaches to structuring computations. They need to be introduced to abstract data and control structures, to delayed binding and to indirection. They must also be introduced to coupling and cohesion, to drivers and stubs, and to rigorous specification. As they learn about algorithms and how to analyze their effectiveness, they must also learn think in terms of state spaces and their characterization and transformation. The relationship between the abstract solution and its specific realization must be better understood, and we must break the pattern of moving always from the special case to the more general (find any partial solution and then try to patch it until it meets the specification). A powerful way to develop a higher level of abstraction in programming is to focus on characterizing the objects and processes of concern.

In specifying the properties or attributes of a domain, entity, or process the programmer is forced away from the particular and is focused on defining the class of data being processed. Characterization is frequently used as a summarizing device, unifying a discussion of diversity. Here I propose that characterization be the starting point, and that diversity be introduced through the process of defining subclasses. To accomplish this goal we need more and better conceptual and annotation tools to assist in characterizing (mathematical logic is precise but not familiar enough to modify the thought process of undergraduates). These will come if computing instructors pursue the technique diligently.

Characterization is not an easy technique to emphasize because it demands an abstract perspective when the student wants to get on with the details. It requires that a student reflect on the problem to be solved by finding attributes which distinguish this problem from another. The process of characterization demands that the programmer catagorize the problem first, and it thereby draws attention to similar problems, some whose solutions are known, whose consideration will bring insight to the problem at hand. Characterization needs to be distinguished from specification, which commonly the emphasis when programming problems are presented. Characterization leads to specification through refinement, but specification alone poses problems in isolation. Characterization is not a new perspective, but it has been underutilized, perhaps because our students were not sufficiently experienced with computing processes to appreciate the technique. In the immediate future it should be practical for faculty to adopt this perspective and utilize it to more efficiently develop and verify computations. The following sections illustrate several

132

ways in which a focus on characteristics changes the approach taken to disucssing common programming topics.

CHARACTERIZE COMPUTATIONS

It seems obvious that computations need to be organized into fundamen-tal classes, and that such classes be studied on the basis of their characteristics. In the past ten years there has been significant progress in this direction, and in the next few years the technique should snowball. We early characterized algorithms: by order: nlog n or n^2 sorts, linear or logarithmic searches; by strategy: control break processing, data driven loops, branch and bound; by operation: partitioning, merging, hashing, stack, and queue. It is time to explicitly focus on the character of the computation and to derive its canonical properties, to appreciates its efficiencies and inefficiencies **before** devoting significant time to elaborating specific examples and variations of the class.

A familiar example would be to approach sorting as a special case of permuting the n elements of a collection. If the resulting rearrangement is to have a certain characteristic, we are interested in arriving at that rearrangement most efficiently, assuming any of n! starting states (later we might consider the affect on our development of constraining our initial states to a characterized subset). One approach to the sorting problem is to linearize the collection and proceed to systematically reposition the elements of the linear list so that they display the required character. We therefore want to find some element which is not in its proper place and position it properly, or we could focus in turn on each list position and search for the element which should ultimately occupy that position (both these strategies reveal the interplay between searching and sorting). How can the question "is this element in its proper place" be answered? If at any stage in rearranging the list we cannot find any element for which the answer is "no," then the list must have the sort character, and the desired permutation has been computed.

Different sorting algorithms follow from different techniques employed in deciding the answer to the "is every element in its proper place" question. The successive maximum algorithms view the list as a partition in which it is known that all elements to the right of the partition point are larger than any element to the left of the partition point and further that the right hand partition is ordered (each member of the partition is in its proper place). Iteratively the partition point is moved to the left by finding and relocating the largest remaining element to the left of the partition point. The Heap and Shell sorts create more generalized partitions where elements in specified positions in the list are rearranged as partitioned sublists, but the position an element occupies at the end of any but the final iteration is not necessarily its ultimate

position. These sorts spend less effort getting an element "close" to its final position than would be required to identify the exact position and thus be able to move the element only once [8].

The Quicksort is characterized by the decision to select any element at random and then to position it properly in the sublist from which it was selected. Once positioned, it divides the sublist in two, so the process continues recursively until only unit or empty sublists remain. The position of the selected element is found through permuting the remaining elements in the sublist by pairing one smaller than the selected element and one larger than the selected element and exchanging the paired elements so that a partition is formed whose right-hand side contains all of the sublist elements greater than the selected element.

Permutations of collections are important outside of sorting. Cyclic codes, detached key sorting (the subsequent rearrangement of the original table), and array segment interchanges are other examples of the need to program a permutation. Sorting, however, is seldom presented in the context of permuting. Yet the advantages of seeking this very general characterization are manifold. Besides organizing various sorting techniques into families, consideration of the alternative processes of deriving the permutation function directly or as a sequence of compositions of permutations provides clarity on the efficiency issues. Characterization of sorting as a permutation function is at the opposite extreme from focusing on the tightest code loop, but the characterization provides precise information as to the necessary manipulations on the list elements, and this allows a mapping into the native operations of a virtual machine, so the code structure and its efficiency can be derived from the characterization.

CHARACTERIZE DATA STRUCTURES

Abstracting data types in terms of specification, representation and implementation is taking hold early in the undergraduate curriculum. The properties of arrays, lists, stacks, queues, priority queues, trees, sets, strings, and graphs are studied abstractly and generically before they are implemented. Basic operations which characterize each data type are explored and the efficiency of each operation is understood in terms of various representations of the elements of the structure. Divorcing the logical system from the physical system is standard in systems analysis, but is optional in teaching programming. Instead of declaring, "accessing an array from one end is using the array like a stack," we should characterize access protocols, such as FIFO and LIFO, and then discuss ways of implementing them.

The technique of formalizing "standard" abstract data types is extended to application data types (sales-orders, matrices, etc.) and the habit of thought of dealing with data types and their operations promotes an understanding of the "objects" of the application, their internal operation and their external interfaces [4]. Teaching students about packaging data and processes and observing formal interfaces between the packages automatically achieves important software design objectives. Not only are modularizing principles and the advantages of low coupling and high cohesion made more obvious, but the groundwork is laid for conceiving of cooperating concurrent processes and non-deterministic systems.

Characterization through strong typing is popular today, but its extension to user-defined types is often not pursued. Part of the problem is that students focus on the native types of the virtual processor they are required to use and miss the general notion of typing. In teaching syntax we teach the difference between **/** and **div**, but it comes across as no more significant that than the difference between **while** and **repeat**--just another detail which must be observed in order to use the language.

CHARACTERIZE CONTROL STRUCTURES

Controlling the interaction of asynchronous concurrent processes is one end of spectrum of managing the execution of code segments and looping, branching and sequential execution of blocks of code is the other end. The student programmer has internalized an understanding of the role of iteration and branching before reaching college, but these intuitions must be re-examined and formalized if verifiable code in multiple languages is to be routinely produced. The programmer's though process must be weaned from tracing a specific initial value through a computation to addressing a problem space and transforming it into result space. This is accomplished by explicitly characterizing the elements of the problem space and from that characterization **deriving** the characteristics of the transformation accomplished by a code unit. This is one of the primary purposes for teaching the use of assertions.

Gries [3] has argued that programing is a goal oriented activity, hence analysis is an appropriate method for solving problems. For example, if we want to know that a list is sorted at some point in the program, we insert code which effects sortedness. We must define what characterizes sortedness, and then we must verify that the transformation performed by our code on any appropriate input achieves the desired characterization. The verification proceeds by working backwards through the steps which might be executed to find out what characterizes the **input** to that step if the **output** is to be as needed. The verification principles are straightforward: if an assignment is to be correct, the component values contributing to that assignment must individually be correct before the assignment is made; if an alternation is to be correct, the condition which determines the branch must

select the proper branch for any possible input state so that the subsequent assignments will yield the desired result; and if a loop is performed, the post-condition of the loop must be related to the pre-condition through the invariant.

Gries gives five checks for a loop: 1) the invariant relationship must be true before the loop is entered; 2) the body of the loop must maintain the invariant relation; 3) the conjunction of the termination condition and the invariant relation must imply the post-condition; 4) there must exist a variant function whose value is always positive whenever the loop is entered; and 5) the actions of the body of the loop must decrease the variant function (the variant is a monotonically decreasing positive value during the execution of the loop).

As important as verification is, if all we do is teach simple mechanical processes as the means of realizing validity, it will be as sterile as enforcing no GOTOs. The goal of Gries and others who encourage us to incorporate verification techniques in teaching programming is to change the thought processes by which the programmer arrives at the language structures to be employed. At the module design level we characterize the architecture of the program (HIPO charts, Jackson's methodology [5], Yourdon's transaction oriented or transformation-oriented designs [9] are examples). At the statement level we follow a strategy to realize goals about the values of program variables. First we characterize the goals and then we utilize our knowledge of the semantics of the language and the properties of our goal to enumerate "guarded commands" until every case of initial states have been handled. Once code has been generated and refined, it can be verified using the rules stated above, but the power of characterization was felt in isolating the goal specification and connecting it to the precondition.

CHARACTERIZE PROBLEM-SOLVING STRATEGIES

Programming is generally practiced as a synthetic process to which analysis is sometimes applied after the problem is solved in order to refine the solution (think of some clever way to solve this problem, then later evaluate how clever a solution you have found). Our experience with programming is now extensive enough that we should be able to characterize solution strategies abstractly and select among various candidate strategies based upon the generic attributes of the problem. That this general approach is already practiced is witnessed by our use of "divide and conquer," "greedy algorithms," "branch and bound searching techniques," and "backtracking" to describe general strategies for categories of problems.

It is important that we teach programming with a view to identifying the characteristic strategy which is to be employed as we design a computation. For example, searching problems can be understood to take the form, "find an element in a specified range which exhibits property P." The solution to a searching problem is to iteratively reduce the search space until either an element is discovered or the space becomes empty. Reduction of the search space is accomplished by dividing the original range into two collections: the portion in which a solution element potentially exists, and the portion known not to contain a solution candidate (actually, more divisions might be made based on varying perceived likelihoods of subranges containing solutions). Algorithms are derived which proceed to reallocate subsets of the original range among the different categories utilizing the nature of the range and/or the nature of the property.

Optimization problems can be characterized as a special kind of search problem (or vice-versa) where of all solutions found, we want to find that which is extreme. The characteristic of being an extreme can be utilized in conducting the search because of the principle of optimality: an optimal solution is composed of optimal subsolutions, given an appropriate decomposition of the problem into subproblems [1].

An effective programmer is familiar with a variety of problem solving strategies (his bag of tricks) and student programmers need to be taught to collect and organize such strategies and appreciate their use. The act of coding itself as presented in the previous section is a strategy (as of yet not universally practiced or even understood) which has been characterized by Zahn [10] as a seven step procedure. The process of characterization is also a strategy related to understanding the problem top down (we begin with a specification of a solution and derive the solution procedure by characterizing the specification).

CONCLUSION

It is self-evident that as we evolve the computing discipline we must refine and present more explicitly the fundamental concepts which it applies. As the domain of the discipline expands and techniques proliferate, we must work harder to discover unifying principles which can be presented to undergraduates to help them understand and organize the myriad details. As the discipline's focus shifts from how to implement solutions on existing hardware with existing (popular) tools, to what can be automated and how can that automation be effected economically, we will have to spend less time programming. A judgment must therefore be made as to what is to be learned from the task of expressing algorithms in code and evaluating their execution on real machines. The educational institutions might decide to teach all theoretical topics and let the employer provide the opportunity for the proficient student to apply the theory as best he can (mathematics has successfully followed that route). On the other hand, this paper has presented some

techniques which would re-focus how programming was presented so as to communicate to the student the critical ideas which undergird good programming practice. If we could save some of the time which is currently spent learning these ideas by trial and error, piecemeal, we could afford to devote less of our curricula to practicing coding without sacrificing the vital implementation skills which must be possessed by effective professionals. The process of characterization has been singled out as an unifying approach which is widely applicable to the process of generating software and which presents the tasks of programming at a level of abstraction which reveals the choices available to the programmer and aids in analyzing the effectiveness of the various alternatives.

REFERENCES

1. Backhouse, Roland, Program Construction and Verification, (Englewood Cliffs, Prentice-Hall, 1986).

2. Brooks, Fredrick, "No Silver Bullet, Essence and Accidents of Software Engineering," Computer 20,4, (April 1987), p.16.

3. Gries, David, The Science of Programming, (New York, Springer- Verlag, 1981).

4. Hull, Richard, "Program Design Using Data Abstraction," Journal of Computing in Small Colleges, 4,3 (January 1989) p. 42-48.

5. Jackson, Michael, Principles of Program Design, (New York, Academic Press, 1975).

6. Martin, James, Application development Without Programmers (Englewood Cliffs, Prentice-Hall, 1982).

7. Mitchell, William, "Is Programming an Art or a Science?", Journal of Computing in Small Colleges, 3,1 (September 1987) p. 4-10.

8. Mitchell, William, "Teaching With Assertions," Journal of Computing in Small Colleges, 4,3 (January 1989) p. 64-71.

9. Yourdon, Edward and Larry Constantine, Structured Design, (Englewood Cliffs, Prentice-Hall, 1979).

10. Zahn, C.T., "A Phased Programming Paradigm," SIGCSE Bulletin 20,1, (February 1988), p. 9-12.

AIDE: AN AUTOMATED TOOL FOR TEACHING DESIGN IN AN INTRODUCTORY PROGRAMMING COURSE

Dino Schweitzer
Scott C. Teel

Department of Computer Science
U.S. Air Force Academy, CO 80840

ABSTRACT

The Department of Computer Science at the United States Air Force Academy teaches an introductory Pascal programming and problem solving course to 1400 freshman a year. Although the students have a wide range of prior programming experiences, very few have any practice with program design. To encourage proper solution design and alleviate the burdensome and demotivating reams of design documentation, the Department of Computer Science has developed an automated tool, the Automated Interactive Design Editor (AIDE). This paper will provide some background on the problems associated with student design documentation, describe how AIDE attempts to address this problem, and discuss future directions for the tool.

INTRODUCTION

At the United States Air Force Academy, all freshman cadets are taught an introductory computer science course (CS-1xx). There are three areas of emphasis in CS-1xx: computer terminology and concepts, introductory Pascal programming, and problem solving. Because all students take the course, there is a wide range of skill levels depending on previous experience and analytic ability. To accommodate this diversity, students are "placed" into one of three tracks after the initial 16 lessons based on two exams and a programming exercise.

1989 ACM 0-89791-298-5/89/0002/0136

The track system has been successful in identifying students with good programming skills. This, in turn, allows the advanced track to proceed at a faster and more detailed pace than the other tracks. Although the students in the advanced track excel in programming, they often do not have any better problem solving skills than the other students. In fact, these advanced track students frequently lag behind their counterparts because of preconceptions on how to structure solutions and/or poor habits they may have developed learning less structured languages in high school. In other words, we often find "hackers" who can write programs but are inept at designing solutions.

The Computer Science Department devotes a significant effort to teach CS-1xx students proper problem solving techniques. The importance of introductory students developing these skills has been well-documented in the literature. The ACM Curriculum Committee Task Force for CS1 [1] specifically recommends that CS1 should "introduce a disciplined approach to problem solving methods ..." and "teach program design." Brown [2] states that problem specification and design should be viewed by the students as a natural precursor to coding. He asserts that students "should view the ultimate product of their effort as a description of the problem and solution, not as several lines of source code ...".

Many descriptions of introductory computer science courses incorporating instruction in problem solving have appeared in the literature [3,4,5,6,7,8,9]. The problem solving approach used at the Academy is to emphasize a distinct solution definition phase (the design phase) separate from the programming phase. This design phase uses a top-down approach to decompose the problem into small understandable modules. Structure charts are used to depict decomposition. For each module, a description is written, input and output requirements are identified using an Input-Process-Output (IPO) diagram, and the logic is described using pseudocode. Separation from the programming phase is emphasized by requiring design turn-ins for correction and approval before the program is written.

A MANUAL APPROACH

The initial implementation of the design phase required students to keep a notebook with separate sections for each part of the design. This manual approach has been successfully tried in other introductory programming courses [2,3,5,10,11]. The contents of the notebook were:

I.   Problem Description

II. Structure Chart

III. Module Descriptions
     (for each module)

     A. Module Problem Statement

     B. IPO Diagram

     C. Parameter Description

     D. Pseudocode

IV. Skeleton Program

The skeleton (or stubbed) program was a compilable Pascal program containing main program variable declarations, module headings with parameters, extensive comment blocks, and the main program. Students created the notebook at the start of the exercise, turned it in for approval to proceed to the programming phase, updated and maintained the notebook throughout program development, and turned it in with the final program as part of the overall grade.

This manual specification and maintenance of the design did force students to perform design separate from programming. However, we found the manual approach had some drawbacks: it was demotivating for the students, it was extremely difficult to modify and maintain, and it often resulted in poor designs.

The student demotivation was primarily due to the amount of paperwork required for even simple problems of 10-20 modules. It was not unusual for the final exercise notebook to contain 50 pages of design documentation. Since most freshmen were not adept at word-processing, this represented a significant effort in manual documentation. Students also found it demotivating because of the number of changes which would have to be made. Because they did not have a good feel for whether a module was performing a reasonably sized function, or exactly what information was required, many changes were required on module descriptions, parameters definitions, IPO diagrams, and pseudocode. Another demotivating factor was using pencil and paper in a computer programming course. They wanted to be working with the computer and not pushing paper. Finally, there was much duplication of effort between the design notebook and actual program code. All of the problem descriptions would be repeated in the notebook and in the program as comment blocks. Parameter definitions and pseudocode also appeared in both places.

Modification and maintenance of the design was another major problem. The difficulty of making changes to a manual system has already been mentioned. In addition, the notebook was to be maintained throughout the program development. Thus, after design approval and through the programming phase, students had to maintain parallel documents; the program with comments and the design documentation. Often times, the final student program had little in common with the outdated design document.

Another drawback of the manual system was the lack of support for good design principles in the student work. For example, the students tended to avoid excessive paperwork by defining large multifunction modules, thus ignoring the principle of single function units. Additionally, the difficulty of design modification led students to resist instructor's restructuring suggestions unless specifically told to reaccomplish the design. Finally, because of the time required for a completely manual system, it was difficult for the instructor to provide feedback on the student's design more than one or two times. Thus, designs tended to evolve slowly and not look significantly different from the first student attempt.

The result of these drawbacks to the manual system was that students did not learn and perform good design principles. They were demotivated by the process and looked upon it as a "haze."

AN AUTOMATED APPROACH

To avoid the drawbacks of the manual system while teaching good design concepts, the Computer Science Department undertook an effort to automate the design approach. The goals of the automation were to ease the burden of documentation, reduce the redundancy, facilitate modifications, and reinforce the design principles being taught. The result of this effort was the Automated Interactive Design Editor (AIDE) software package. AIDE was developed to allow the student to apply the same design principles as outlined previously, but in an automated fashion.

AIDE is a menu-driven software system which allows the student to enter a new design, modify an existing one, or automatically generate a skeleton (stubbed) program from the design information. The format of the design information is the same as the manual system, but all information is entered and edited electronically.

When entering a new design, the student is prompted for all the necessary information. This includes building the structure chart, entering design information for each module, and editing problem and parameter descriptions. At any stage of the design process, the student can save the design to disk for future expansion. Similarly, once created, any portion of the design can be easily modified (ie., changing parameter types, editing problem description, and adding/deleting modules to the structure chart). The system emphasizes ease of understanding and use.

Once a design has been created and appropriately modified, the student can automatically create a skeleton program from the design. AIDE produces a compilable Pascal program with comment blocks, procedure headings, parameter declarations, necessary BEGIN-END pairs, and appropriate indentation and formatting. The complete design description (including the design tree and IPO diagrams) is contained in comment blocks of the skeleton program. This skeleton program becomes the design document which is turned in to the instructor for review. After the instructor critiques the design, the student uses AIDE to make changes to the design and to regenerate the skeleton program. Once the final design is approved, the skeleton program becomes the basis for the programming phase of the process. If future changes to the design are necessary, the student can either use AIDE to produce a new skeleton, or simply modify the comment blocks of the program to reflect the design changes. The final program turn-in contains the design documentation as comment blocks in the code and the grading includes a comparison of the design with the resultant code.

RESULTS

AIDE has been successfully employed at the Air Force Academy for two years. Although the first year involved a good deal of evolution of the code (correcting bugs and enhancing the user-friendliness), our overall experience has been very positive. We found more students remain motivated during the design phase, the students tend to produce better designs, and the design documentation seems to remain more consistent with the resulting code.

More students remain motivated because they do not perceive the use of an automated tool as burdensome as the manual approach. Although they are entering the same volume of information, the ability to do it interactively on the computer combined with the ease of making changes is more enjoyable than manually writing and correcting the design document. The automatic skeleton program generation is also perceived as a motivating factor since it reduces the amount of redundancy in what the student has to type. The skeleton program also gives the student a good start towards his/her final turn-in.

In addition, we feel AIDE has resulted in better student designs. One reason for this is the ease of making changes and the associated quicker turnaround with the instructor. Since AIDE forces an output format upon the design documentation which was sorely missing under the manual system, the instructor can interpret and understand the design more easily. Under the manual system, the typical design turnaround was once per program; now (if needed) it is two or three. The ease of automatic skeleton program generation has also made the student more willing to substantially modify the design since the basis for the program solution is changed automatically and not manually.

Keeping the design documentation current with the actual program has also improved with AIDE. Since the baseline design documentation is part of the program as implementation starts, the student finds it easier to change the documentation as the design changes during programming. There is no longer a requirement to simultaneously maintain two separate documents.

FUTURE ENHANCEMENTS

Although AIDE has improved the design efforts of students and lessened the negative aspects of the manual system, there are still areas which need improvement. The two primary areas to be investigated are the enhancement of the user interface and an easier mechanism for parallel development of code and design.

The user interface could be enhanced to use more modern techniques such as pop-up windows, more extensive on-line help, a mouse interface, and sophisticated icons/graphics. Although the system is currently easy to use, improving the user interface will put a "modern" software look on AIDE. We believe this will positively influence the students' use of the system and their overall motivation.

Another enhancement area would be in mechanisms for parallel development of code and design. AIDE currently keeps the design documentation as part of the program. Although this has the advantage of keeping the two physically colocated, the AIDE system does not facilitate easy change of one based on modifications to the other. For example, when parameters to a procedure are changed, it is still the programmer's responsibility to make the appropriate change in the design documentation contained in the procedure's comment block. An area of investigation is the automatic generation of design updates based on changes to the code. Thus, when a procedure's parameters are changed, the system would automatically update the design documentation (IPO diagram). This would require the ability to take an existing program and parse it to produce as much of the design documentation as possible. Another variation of the above capability would be a program analyzer

which would verify that the design documentation was in fact a reflection of the implementation code.

CONCLUSIONS

The use of an automated tool to help students in the problem solving/design phase has been found to offer substantial advantages over the previous manual system. The students remain more motivated and produce overall better designs than before. The instructors receive a standard design product and thus, can interpret and understand the student's solution easier. This results in more timely and (we hope) better feedback to the student. Overall, AIDE contributes positively to the education that students receive in computer science problem solving skills.

REFERENCES

[1] E.B. Koffman, P.L. Miller, and C.E. Wardle, "Recommended Curriculum for CS1, 1984," *Communications of the ACM*, vol. 27, no. 10, 1984, pp. 998-1001.

[2] D.A. Brown, "Requiring CS1 Students to Write Requirements Specifications: A Rationale, Implementation Suggestions, and a Case Study," *SIGCSE Bulletin*, vol. 20, no. 1, 1988, pp. 13-16.

[3] G. Ford, "A Software Engineering Approach to First Year Computer Science Courses," *SIGCSE Bulletin*, vol. 14, no. 1, 1982, pp. 8-12.

[4] W.E. Ayen and S. Grier, "A New Environment for Teaching Introductory Computer Science," *SIGCSE Bulletin*, vol. 15, no. 1, 1983, pp. 258-264.

[5] P. Gabrini, "Integration of Design and Programming Methodology into beginning Computer Science Courses," *SIGCSE Bulletin*, vol. 14, no. 1, 1982, pp. 85-87.

[6] P.B. Henderson, "Anatomy of an Introductory Computer Science Course," *SIGCSE Bulletin*, vol. 18, no 1, 1986, pp. 257-263.

[7] A. Behforooz and O. Sharma, "A One-Year Introductory Course for Computer Science Undergraduate Program," *SIGCSE Bulletin*, vol. 13, no. 1, 1981, pp. 46-49.

[8] A. Behforooz and O. Sharma, "A Foundation Course in Computer Science," *SIGCSE Bulletin*, vol. 16, no. 1, 1984, pp. 159-163.

[9] P.B. Henderson, "Modern Introductory Computer Science," *SIGCSE Bulletin*, vol 19, no 1, 1987, pp. 183-189.

[10] L.L. Deneen and K.R. Pierce, "Development and Documentation of Computer Programs in Undergraduate Computer Science Courses," *SIGCSE Bulletin*, vol. 20, no. 1, 1988, pp. 17-21.

[11] D.D. Riley, "Teaching Problem Solving in an Introductory Computer Science Class," *SIGCSE Bulletin*, vol. 13, no. 1, 1981, pp. 244-251.

Visual Metaphors
for Teaching Programming Concepts

Leslie J. Waguespack, Jr., Ph.D.

Computer Information Systems Department
Bentley College
Waltham, Massachusetts, 02254

Abstract

This paper presents a system of visual metaphors used in a introductory programming course using Pascal. The visual metaphors represent programming concepts (data types, variables, arrays, records, files, modules, module interfaces and parameter passing, and dynamic storage) that are often difficult for beginning students to learn. The metaphors are used to accelerate the students' learning process and improve the overall comprehension of programs as structured objects. The system of metaphors is used in the first course for majors, Foundations of Programming, in the Computer Information Systems curriculum at Bentley College.

Introduction

The first programming course shapes student attitudes toward computing as a major. This course must deal with a diversity of knowledge and experience that students bring to the course. The diversity is evidenced by very different learning curves among students. Many students with longer learning curves become discouraged and prematurely decide that programming is beyond their intellectual grasp. I believe the key to grasping programming concepts is in the models employed by teacher and student to communicate about the many abstractions that comprise the fundamentals of programming.

In the first programming course for majors in the Computer Information Systems curriculum at Bentley College a variety of facilities are provided in the attempt to maximize the success rate among students. Among these is a system of visual metaphors which are used to represent many of the essential program concepts. The metaphors are employed in the course lectures to provide a consistent mental model for presenting and discussing programming abstractions. Based on six years experience using these metaphors they appear to accelerate the students' learning process and improve their overall comprehension of programs as structured objects. Because they are graphical in nature they may be easily introduced into any existing introductory course syllabus in the form of overhead transparencies or lecture handout material. This paper will present the system of visual metaphors and discuss briefly how each one is described and used in the course lectures. Finally, the summary considers how this metaphor system might be adapted for use in other courses or curricula.

Visualizing Program Components

Programs as Models

Programming requires the ability to abstract, to identify and to evaluate relationships between abstract concepts of information objects and operations on them. Although some research projects are exploring the prospects for graphical or visual programming media, today's students will experience a professional environment where most programming will involve the authoring of textual programs in some programming language. Because these textual specifications describe abstract worlds, many beginning programming students find it difficult if not impossible to grasp the concepts. I have developed a system of visual metaphors for many of the programming concepts. The metaphors are chosen to represent the abstract concepts in such a way that the seemingly "physical" attributes of the metaphors explain the conceptual behavior of programming components.

Chunking also plays an important role in programmer performance. Chunking is the process of aggregating details into abstraction(s) which can be manipulated as single objects when dealing in higher level problem solving [Egan79]. When greater detail is required the abstractions may be decomposed for intricate detail. Research has shown that in a variety of intellectual tasks subjects who are skilled at chunking consistently deal better with large problems than those who are not. (The interested reader should consult [Adelson84, Anderson85, Gugerty86, Larkin80, Mayer81, McKeithen81] for a perspective on information organization in cognitive processes of programming.) The visual metaphor system provides the students with an initial model for *chunking* program content and structure.

A set of icons for program components and structures is introduced to represent data objects and procedural objects. These icons serve as visual metaphors for the program components that they represent. They offer a visual vocabulary to reinforce the English terminology presented in the text and lectures. The metaphors are used consistently in visual aids throughout the course. The system of metaphors is presented in the following sections with a brief discussion of their use and effect.

Data Objects and Typing

Data values may be described as objects that may be named and "take up space". Program variables may be described as containers that can hold values. Owing to the fact that a container has a capacity for only one value, the assignment of a new value to a variable presupposes that the old value is first discarded before the new value can take up residence. In a strongly typed language like Pascal the type of a data object may be metaphorically described as the *shape* of the object.

Integers can be thought of as square objects with rounded corners (see Figure 1). Real numbers are square; however, they have sharp, square corners rather than the rounded corners of an integer. Booleans may be round like two-sided coins; character data objects are triangular and so on.

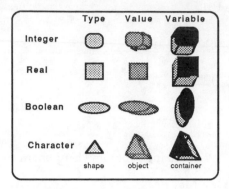

Figure 1: Types as Shapes

A variable of a particular type is a container with the corresponding particular shape. Data values of the same type as the variable can be placed in that variable – the appropriately shaped object can fit in a container with the same shape. Incompatible types resist such assignment because "you can't put a round peg in a square hole."

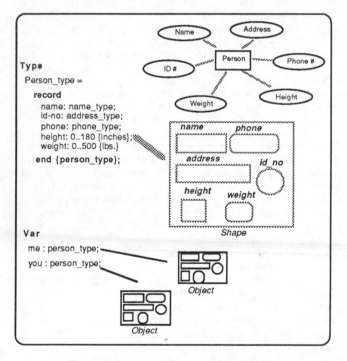

Figure 2: Structured Types as Nested Shapes

To explain a simple form of type compatibility it can be demonstrated that integers and reals are very similar; the only difference being that integers have rounded corners. With a little imagination it can be easily understood that integer values can be assigned to real variables without difficulty but, that real values cannot be assigned to integer variables without handling the prob-

lem of the fractional part that won't quite fit.

The data-type / shape metaphor extends conveniently to structured types (e.g. record, or arrays) as more complicated containers with appropriately replicated or grouped simple containers; each of which can only contain one data value of the corresponding shape. Figure 2 demonstrates the following characteristics of a RECORD: a record type is a template whose components each represent an individual container. Each component has its own type, and each component is designated with an identifier, a component identifier, that allows the component to be distinctly referenced within a RECORD variable. Figure 3 demonstrates the nesting of record structures.

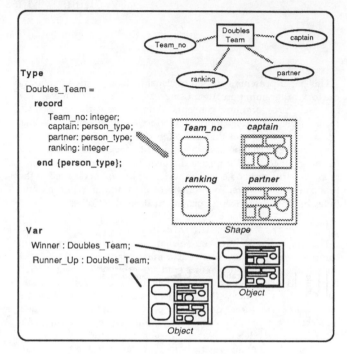

Figure 3: Nested Structured Types

Figure 4 demonstrates the effect of arrays of records. The use of the record icon to represent elements of an array easily leads into the explanation of sequential files.

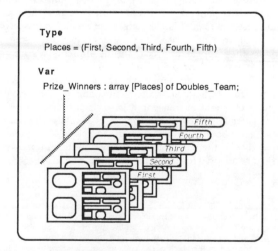

Figure 4: Arrays of Structured Types

The only effective differences are that the elements of a file must be sequentially accessed, only one is available through the file variable at time, the number of elements can grow with file extension, and the file elements have a life span beyond that of the program's execution. Aside from these characteristics files are functionally identical to arrays for algorithm design purposes.

Visualizing Module Structure

Module structure is not always easy to discern from the text declaration. This is particularly true with Pascal for beginning students. There is no distinct textual mark that discriminates the declaration from the body of a module. END (for example) denotes the closure not only of compound statements but of RECORD declarations as well. When module declarations are nested, the situation may be even more confusing since when a BEGIN is reached it may be unclear which module has been "BEGUN".

The icon in Figure 5 is used to represent Pascal modules. It depicts the three basic parts of a Pascal module: the heading / interface, the declarations, and the body. It continually reminds the viewer of the three-component structure and can be annotated to demonstrate the presence or absence of local declarations. The absence of declarations is not the absence of the component but rather, that the component is empty. The nesting of modules is dramatically illustrated by graphically enclosing (or connecting) a module in the declaration component of its parent as shown in Figure 6. This also serves as a simple metaphor to explain "scopes of reference".

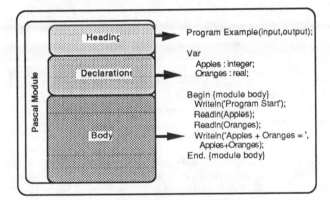

Figure 5: Module Structure

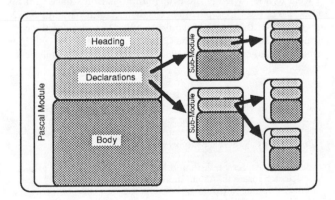

Figure 6: Module Nesting

Visualizing Module Interfaces and Interaction:

By combining elements of the icons representing data types and those representing modules the function of a module interface can be explained as a "plug and socket" arrangement where the shape of each "prong" of the plug must match the shape of each "hole" in the socket.

In other words, the arguments must match the parameters in position and type for the procedure invocation to be syntactically correct.

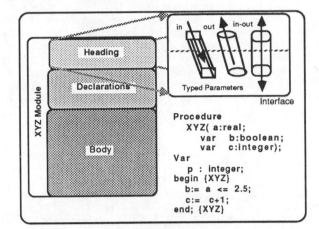

Figure 7: Parameter Interface

By portraying the parameters as conduits or pipes with a shape corresponding to its type the parameter typing metaphor is almost complete. Finally, we introduce directional arrows in the pipes to indicate the allowable direction of value flow. These can be used to represent "in", "out", and "in–out" parameters conveniently (although Pascal syntax only supports "in" and "in–out" parameters in the form of "non-VAR" and "VAR"parameters).

Procedure invocation and execution can be described as the physical process of values "flowing" through the interface connections at invocation, executing the body, and the resulting values "flowing out" when the module completes execution.

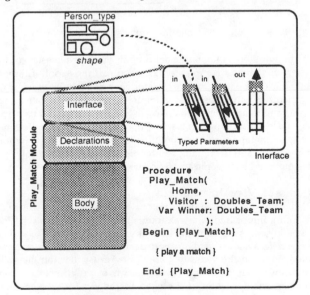

Figure 8: Structured Type Parameters

The metaphor consistently portrays the behavior regardless of whether the interface has no parameters, only simple parameters, or has structured parameters as shown in Figure 8. In addition it captures the idiosyncrasy that in order to allow the modification of a component of a record returned from a module the entire record must be made modifiable by declaring the formal parameter as a VAR parameter.

Pointer Variables and Dynamic Storage:

Dynamic storage is perhaps the most illusive concept in learning programming for beginners. The absence of a fixed variable name and the requirement that the object value must always be referenced indirectly makes the explanation cumbersome. In Figure 9, however, the metaphor of a spool of thread for the pointer value which is "tied" to a dynamic object when it is created simplifies the concept presentation. As a thread it can only be tied to one object at a time, that object must be of the type declared for that thread, and that spool can be copied (by variable assignment or parameter passing) from one spool container (pointer variable) to another.

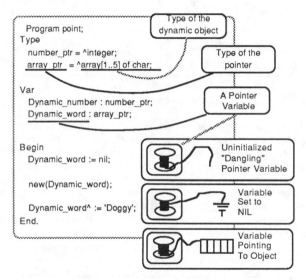

Figure 9: Dynamic Storage and Pointers

Although there is not sufficient time in this one semester course to introduce many complex data structures, the spool of thread metaphor can be used to give the student a conceptual preview of how pointers may be used. As in Figure 10 they provide both a connecting mechanism between linked list nodes and extend the variable space of the program beyond that declared at compile-time. The spool metaphor also preconditions the student to use diagrams for designing and debugging pointer based structures (the only feasible method I have come across so far).

Effects of Visualization:

Visualization plays an important role in a foundations course of programming . Graduates, although they will inevitably be involved in some programming in their careers, are more likely to be engaged in systems analysis and design, and software systems management in the years to come. They must develop the skill that allows them to grasp whole systems of programs and their interrelationships without the need to inspect the implementation details of each until necessary.

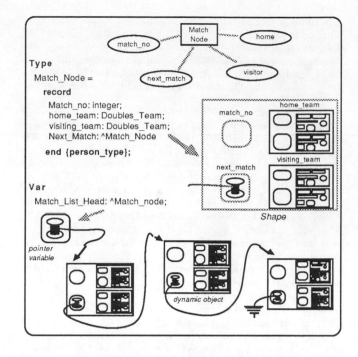

Figure 10: Using Pointers in Data Structures

The module structure icons described here provide a strong and powerful metaphor for module content and module interconnectivity that transcends specific programming languages or development styles. It is an elegant first model of structure chunking for the student. Although the specific details of programming in Pascal will probably be forgotten in a very few semesters, the module icon and the characteristics of module interface that it connotes will linger and reinforce the module definition concepts in systems analysis and systems design.

The system of programming metaphors presented here is still evolving. There have been no measurements of its impact on student performance. Indeed, it would be very difficult to isolate the metaphors' effects from the effects of all the other course components. Until objective experiments can be performed I must rely on the adage "*a picture is worth a thousand words.*"

Acknowledgement

I wish to acknowledge the contribution of Don Chand and my colleagues in the CIS department for their careful readings of earlier versions of this paper. I would also like to recognize the commitment and enthusiasm of the CS145 students over the last three years. I thank them for their patience during rough spots in development.

References

[Adelson84] Adelson, Beth, "When novices surpass experts: the difficulty of a task may increase with expertise", Journal of Experimental Psychology: Learning, Memory and Cognition, Vol. 10, No. 3, pp. 483-495, March 1984.

[Anderson85] Anderson, J. R. and Jeffries, R., "Novice LISP errors: undetected losses of information from working memory", Human-Computer Interaction, Vol. 1, No. 2, pp. 107-131, February 1985.

[Egan79] Egan, D.E. and Schwartz, B.J., "Chunking in recall of symbolic drawings", Memory Cognition, Vol. 7, No. 2, pp. 149-158, February 1979.

[Gugerty86] Gugerty, Leo and Olson, Gary M., "Comprehension differences in debugging by skilled and novice programmers", Book: Empirical Studies of Programmers. Soloway, E and Iyengar, S Eds., Ablex Publishing Corp, Norwood, New Jersey, pp. 13-27, June 1986.

[Larkin80] Larkin, J., McDermott, J., Simon, D. P. and Simon, H. A., "Expert and novice performances in solving physics problems", Science, Vol. 208, No. 6, pp. 1335-1342, June 1980.

[Mayer81] Mayer, R.E., "The psychology of how novices learn computer programming", Computing Surveys, Vol. 13, No. 1, pp. 121-141, 1981.

[McKeithen81] McKeithen, K. B., Reitman, J. S., and Hirtle, S. C., "Knowledge organization and skill differences in computer programmers", Cognitive Psychology, Vol. 13, pp. 307, 1981.

A First Course in Program Verification and the Semantics of Programming Languages

Raymond D. Gumb

Department of Computer Science
University of Lowell
Lowell, Massachusetts 01854

Abstract

We describe a first course in program verification and the semantics of programming languages developed for advanced undergraduate and beginning graduate students. The course is intended to support other courses in the curriculum that stress a disciplined approach to programming as well as to prepare students for more advanced courses in semantics and other areas such as software engineering and compiler technology. In order of emphasis, the course covers axiomatic, operational, translational, and denotational semantics. We discuss the development of the course, course prerequisites, the rationale for the selection of the topics covered, and the appropriateness of the course in the curriculum.

I. Introduction

Eight years ago, the Computer Science Department of the California State University at Northridge (CSUN) introduced a new undergraduate curriculum. The new CSUN curriculum, in general, contained more required courses than those outlined in the standard curriculum [ACM '78], and, amongst the new courses, included an introduction to the semantics of programming languages. The introduction to semantics was a required course to be taken in the second semester of the junior year, because the advanced nature of the semantics literature precludes the possibility of introducing the course at the freshman or sophomore levels.

There were two principal reasons for instituting the undergraduate semantics requirement. First, the CSUN faculty believed that computer science students need some acquaintance with formal semantics to develop a deeper understanding of programming languages. This deeper understanding would reinforce the disciplined approach to

programming stressed throughout the curriculum.[1] Second, the undergraduate semantics course would provide a foundation for more advanced courses, including a graduate course in the semantics of programming languages. The graduate semantics course had been previously introduced as a required course in the Master's program, and, by inserting the undergraduate semantics course as a prerequisite for the graduate semantics course, the graduate course could be taught at a more advanced level.

To integrate the introduction to semantics course into the undergraduate curriculum, semantic analysis was to concentrate on programming languages similar to Pascal and other languages in the von Neumann tradition. If time remained in the course, simple features of functional and logic programming languages might also be touched upon, but there was no expectation that more advanced topics such as procedures as parameters and parallelism would be covered.

Although the CSUN undergraduate curriculum proposal and catalog descriptions of the introduction to the semantics course provided some guidelines for the development of a course syllabus, a number of questions about the level and content of the course remained to be answered before the course could be taught for the first time. How many and exactly which methods of semantic description should be studied? How deeply should a semantic method of description be covered? What should be the relative emphasis on the semantic methods selected for study? How should the methods be integrated in the course? What available texts covered the material selected at the advanced undergraduate or beginning graduate level? What topics are essential prerequisites for the course?

I taught the introductory course in semantics at CSUN for three years, and, since leaving CSUN five years ago, I have taught introductory courses in program verification and semantics at the advanced undergraduate and beginning graduate level in two other universities. The set of questions raised in the last paragraph has recurred in

---

[1] The disciplined approach to programming at CSUN was exemplified by the development of a text [Motil] for use in the first computer science course.

both universities, and the rest of this paper describes one set of plausible answers.

II. Topics and Principles

In this section, we discuss the guidelines used in selecting topics to be covered in the introduction to semantics course and principles for integrating these topics into the course.

Regarding topics, it is generally agreed that the three principal semantic methods for describing programming languages are the axiomatic, operational, and denotational, and an introductory course in semantics should at least touch upon each of these three semantic methods. Many experts also view translational and algebraic semantics to be of importance, and these methods might be worked into an introductory course. Mathematics presupposed by the semantic topics but not incorporated in the prerequisites would need to be introduced. However, mathematical topics should be covered only if they are needed in developing the central semantic material, because the semantics of programming languages is itself a rich subject, far too extensive to be covered fully in one or two courses. Moreover, many computer science students are not motivated by pure mathematics.

We now consider the principles employed to integrate topics into the course. First, programming exercises motivating semantic topics should be integrated into the course, because most computer science students *do* like to program. However, irrelevant programming projects should be avoided. Second, mini-languages should be used to illustrate the semantic methods of description. Each mini-language should reflect a few key features of a typical von Neumann language. The use of appropriate mini-languages is critical because semantic descriptions of "real" programming languages are too complicated for an introductory course! Third, the various methods of semantic description covered should be presented as consistent and complementary definitions [Hoare] — interrelated parts of a programming logic. Students retain little from a "semantics appreciation course" in which many topics are touched upon but left in a disconnected jumble. Presenting the various methods as parts of a programming logic instills a disciplined approach to the use of formalisms and enables a student to understand, for example, how an axiomatic definition can be wrong (unsound).

III. Prerequisites

When the introduction to semantics course was first introduced at CSUN, the key prerequisites were thought to be courses in introductory symbolic logic (with [Leblanc and Wisdom] a typical text), principles of programming languages ([Ledgard and Marcotty]), and automata and formal language theory ([Lewis and Papadimitriou]). Initially, discrete structures was not a required course in the undergraduate curriculum. It soon became apparent that the students' lack of mathematical preparation for the automata and formal language theory course as well as the semantics course presented instructional difficulties, and the Computer Science Department, in cooperation with the Mathematics Department, developed a discrete structures course ([Levy]) that was to serve as an additional prerequisite for the automata and formal languages course.

The CSUN prerequisites for the semantics course were sufficient, but experience in teaching similar courses at two other universities leads me to believe that they were not all necessary. Certainly, some mathematical maturity as well as maturity in computer science is required, and it is unusual in an undergraduate curriculum to have extensive treatment of semantic material preceding courses on principles of programming languages and discrete structures.[2] Some of the key prerequisite topics from the principles of programming languages course, which might be garnered from other courses, are the concepts of BNF syntax, machine state, loop invariant, parameter transmission mechanism, environment, and static and dynamic scope. The key prerequisite concepts from the discrete structures course include sets, relations, functions, mathematical induction, first-order logic with identity, formal proofs, and (Peano) arithmetic.

IV. Course Description

As currently implemented, the introduction to semantics course covers, in order of emphasis, axiomatic, operational, translational, and denotational semantics. Algebraic semantics is not directly treated, although our approach to translational semantics has an algebraic flavor. The relative emphasis given the various semantics was determined by pedagogical considerations as much as by the inherent significance of the subject matter.

We proceed to discuss the rationale for the relative emphasis on the semantics. Axiomatic semantics is emphasized most because many computer science students learn to enjoy program proving due to its affinity with writing and analyzing programs. Further, familiarity with program proving is presupposed by one of the best advanced texts [de Bakker]. Operational semantics, developed in the style of [Cook] as simplified by [de Bakker], is second in order of emphasis. Students find the operational semantics natural, and it provides an introduction to some basic concepts also found in denotational semantics. Moreover, the operational semantics can be used to

---

[2] There are some interesting arguments [Wand, Constable et. al.], however, for introducing a relatively rigorous treatment of verification and semantics in the freshman or sophomore year.

vindicate the axiomatic semantics and, in general, provides a unifying framework for comparing the other semantics. The translational semantics is third in order of emphasis because, although we judge it to be of lesser importance than the other three semantics, translational semantics provides a rigorous introduction to levels of abstraction in programming, reinforcing programming practices stressed throughout the computer science curriculum. Further, students enjoy implementing the small compilers that are specified abstractly in the translational semantics. Denotational semantics is emphasized least because it requires more mathematical sophistication than can be presumed in an introductory course. Treatments of more sophisticated denotational devices, such as continuations, are best left for an advanced course. Given the present relative emphasis of the various semantics, a more descriptive title for the course might be "An Introduction to _____", with the blanks filled in either with "Program Verification and the Semantics of Programming Languages", "Consistent and Complementary Definitions of the Semantics of Programming Languages", or simply "Programming Logics".

In addition to the mathematical topics mentioned in the preceding section, at the beginning of the course we introduce the concept of a well-founded set and the principle of Nötherian induction. Nötherian induction is natural, and it is used throughout the course, for example, in proofs by induction on the complexity of syntactic expressions and, implicitly, in proofs of program termination. Towards the end of the course, when (program) functions are studied in a logic of total correctness, we introduce free logic and arithmetic to handle execution time errors[3], and, when denotational semantics is studied, we introduce the concepts of a complete partial order and the fixed point of a function.

A check list of the topics covered in the course is presented in the appendix. Exercises cover program proving and semantic analysis. Although the Hoare method is emphasized in the course due to its association with structured programming, longer program proofs are carried out, for the sake of brevity, using the Floyd method. An example of a semantic exercise is: Either prove that a given Hoare rule of inference is truth- preserving or prove that it is not by exhibiting a counterexample.[4] Examples of programming projects are writing a proof checker and implementing a compiler realizing the translational semantics.

---

[3] In free arithmetic, an erroneous integer expression such as 5/0 denotes an error object that is not an integer. The assertion $\exists X (X = 5/0)$ is *not* a theorem of free arithmetic.

[4] A rule of inference in a programming logic must preserve validity but need not preserve truth, wheras a rule in a natural deduction system must preserve validity *and* truth.

At the time the introduction to semantics course was first given, there were suitable texts for the graduate level semantics course [de Bakker, Stoy], but there were none for the introductory course. Each of the existing introductory texts dealt either solely with one semantics or with different semantics in a disconnected manner.[5] I soon began relying on rough class notes, which, over the past few years, have been polished into a text [Gumb].

V.   Evaluation of the Course

Some computer science students have little interest in the more theoretical aspects of computer science. Typically, these students have never mastered methods of formal proofs and proofs by mathematical induction. My classroom remedy has been to:

1. Point out the significance of a programming system that has been proven correct in an appropriate sense.

2. Underline the dangers of a trusted but incorrect computer system that has been "proven correct" erroneously — resulting from either a flawed program proof or an unsound verification system.

3. Add relevant programming exercises.

4. Review some prerequisite mathematics.

The remedy has had some success.

An introduction to semantics course is appropriate in an undergraduate curriculum designed, in part, to prepare students for graduate study. First, it develops analytical skills needed in selecting, using, implementing, and designing programming languages. Regarding the importance of semantics in the design of programming languages, for example, no research can be done without comprehending the semantics-laden literature, and any new programming language should have reasonable consistent and complementary semantics [Ashcroft and Wadge]. Second, semantics is worthy of study in its own right as a mathematical aspect of computer science.

VI.   The Need for Curriculum Enhancements

As others [Berztiss] have stressed, more emphasis needs to be placed on relevant mathematics throughout the undergraduate curriculum. Mathematical induction should be stressed in the mathematics corequisite for CS1, and informal proofs of the correctness of algorithms should

---

[5] Recently, more adequate introductory texts have appeared. For example, there is now an excellent text [Loeckx and Sieber] that is suitable as an introduction for students having a strong background in mathematical logic.

be taught beginning in CS 1. In general, more emphasis should be placed on arithmetic for the following reasons:

1. The integers are a fundamental type in most general purpose programming languages.

2. Arithmetic is the home of the axiom of mathematical induction.

3. All the computable functions are representable in arithmetic, making it possible, in principle, to construct the weakest precondition of a (program) statement and a postcondition from the postcondition and the partial functions in (free) arithmetic corresponding to the statement.

4. There is a symbiosis of arithmetic and programming logic in that applications of the Consequence Rule are justified, in part, by proofs in arithmetic, and, in certain systems, proving programmer defined functions correct in programming logic justifies the introduction of function call axioms into arithmetic.

Natural deduction for first-order logic with identity should also be taught early in the curriculum. Natural deduction is a human-oriented method in which formal proofs can be carried out. Further, mastery of natural deduction provides the student with a means of outlining informal but rigorous prose proofs.

Acknowledgements: Russell Abbott deserves credit for his foresight in proposing the introductory semantics course for the CSUN undergraduate curriculum. I am especially indebted to him for having convinced me of the need to cover material on translation semantics. I would also like to thank Russ, Mike Barnes, Giam Pecelli, and Stu Smith for their comments on earlier drafts of this paper, and Susan Gerhart, Nancy Leveson, and Peter Neumann for answering some related questions. Finally, I dedicate this paper to the memory of Djsamshid Asgari.

Appendix: Check List of Topics

Mathematical Preliminaries *(1-2 Weeks)*
First-order logic, natural deduction, axiomatization and the intended semantics of the first-order theory of the integers (Peano arithmetic extended to the negative integers), properties of relations (e.g. orderings), and Nötherian induction.

The Partial Correctness of While Programs *(2 Weeks)*
While programs in a Pascal dialect, operational semantics (Cook-de Bakker style), the concepts of partial and total correctness, Hoare partial correctness axiomatization, and soundness.

The Total Correctness of Flowchart Programs *(2-3 Weeks)*
Flowchart programs in a BASIC dialect, operational semantics, the Floyd method (inductive assertions for proving partial correctness and well-founded sets for proving termination), and soundness.

The Total Correctness of Flowchart Programs with Arrays, Input, and Output *(2 Weeks)*
Extension of the BASIC dialect to cover arrays and sequential input/output.

The Translation of While Programs with Arrays, Input, Output, and a Stack into Flowchart Programs *(2 Weeks)*
Extension of the Pascal dialect to cover arrays, stacks, and input/output, Hoare total correctness axiomatization, correctness of a translation of the new dialect of Pascal into the BASIC dialect, comparison of the Hoare and Floyd methods, and difficulties expressing specifications in first-order languages.

The Total Correctness of While Programs with Functions and Procedures *(2-3 Weeks)*
Free logic for handling run-time errors, extension of the Pascal dialect to cover nonrecursive functions and procedures, environments, static scoping, call-by-value and call-by-reference, Hoare total correctness axiomatization, and soundness.

The Translation of Tail Recursive Procedures into While Programs *(2-3 Weeks)*
Rudimentary concepts of denotational semantics, modification of the Pascal dialect yielding a class of tail recursive procedures, Hoare total correctness axiomatization, correctness of a translation of tail recursive programs into **while** programs, equivalence of the denotational and operational semantics, weakest preconditions, and relative completeness.

Bibliography

[ACM '78] ACM '78, Curriculum '78: Recommendations for the Undergraduate Program in Computer Science — A Report of the ACM Curriculum Committee on Computer Science, **Communications of the ACM**, **22**, 147-166, 1979.

[ACM '88] ACM '88, Draft Report of the ACM Task Force on the Core of Computer Science Education, Draft 3, Feb. 1, 1988.

[Anderson] Anderson, R. B., **Proving Programs Correct**, Wiley, 1979.

[Ashcroft and Wadge] Ashcroft, E. A. and Wadge, W. W., Rx for Semantics, **ACM Transactions on Programming Languages and Systems**, 4, pp. 283-294, 1982.

[Baber] Baber, R. L., **The Spine of Software: Designing Provably Correct Software: Theory and Practice**, Wiley, 1987.

[Berztiss] Berztiss, A., A Mathematically Focused Curriculum for Computer Science, **Communications of the ACM, 30**, 356-365, 1987.

[de Bakker] de-Bakker, J., **Mathematical Theory of Program Correctness**, Prentice Hall, 1980.

[Berg et. al.] Berg, H. K. et. al., **Formal Methods of Program Verification and Specification**, Prentice-Hall, 1982.

[Constable et. al.] Constable, R. L. et. al., **An Introduction to the PL/CV2 Programming Logic**, Lecture Notes in Computer Science, **135**, Springer, 1982.

[Cook] Cook, S. A., Soundness and Completeness of an Axiom System for Program Verification, **SIAM Journal on Computing**, 7, pp. 70-90, 1978.

[Gordon] Gordon, M. J. C., **The Denotational Description of Programming Languages**, Springer, 1979.

[Gries] Gries, D., **The Science of Programming**, Springer, 1981.

[Gumb] Gumb, R. D., **Programming Logics: An Introduction to Verification and Semantics**, Wiley, 1989.

[Hoare and Lauer] Hoare, C. A. R. and Lauer, P. E., Consistent and Complementary Formal Theories of the Semantics of Programming Languages, **Acta Informatica, 3**, pp. 135-153, 1974.

[Leblanc and Wisdom] Leblanc, H, and Wisdom, W. A., **Deductive Logic**, Allyn and Bacon, 1972.

[Levy] Levy, L. S., **Discrete Structures of Computer Science**, Wiley, 1980.

[Lewis and Papadimitriou] Lewis, H. R. and Papadimitriou, C. H., **Elements of the Theory of Computation**, Prentice-Hall, 1981.

[Loeckx and Sieber] Loeckx, J. and Sieber, K., **The Foundations of Program Verification**, Wiley, 1984.

[Manna] Manna, Z., **Mathematical Theory of Computation**, McGraw-Hill, 1974.

[Manna and Waldinger] Manna, Z. and Waldinger, R., **The Logical Basis for Computer Programming - Volume 1: Deductive Reasoning**, Addison-Wesley, 1985.

[Ledgard and Marcotty] Marcotty, M. and Ledgard, H. F., **Programming Language Landscape: Syntax, Semantics, Implementation**, 2nd. ed., Science Research Associates, 1986.

[Mili] Mili, A., **An Introduction to Formal Program Verification**, Van Nostrand Reinhold, 1985.

[Motil] Motil, J., **Programming Principles: An Introduction**, Allyn and Bacon, 1984.

[Pagan] Pagan, F. G., **Formal Specification of Programming Languages: A Panoramic View**, Prentice-Hall, 1981.

[Reynolds] Reynolds, J., **The Craft of Programming**, Prentice-Hall, 1981.

[Stoy] Stoy, J., **Denotational Semantics: The Scott-Strachey Approach to Programming Language Theory**, MIT Press, 1977.

[Tenenbaum and Augenstein] Tenenbaum, A. M. and Augenstein, M. J., **Data Structures Using Pascal**, Prentice-Hall, 1981.

[Wand] Wand, M., **Induction, Recursion, and Programming**, North Holland, 1980.

SUCCESS WITH THE PROJECT-INTENSIVE MODEL FOR AN UNDERGRADUATE SOFTWARE ENGINEERING COURSE

Linda M. Northrop
Department of Mathematics and Computer Science
SUNY College at Brockport
Brockport, New York 14420

Abstract

There is a tremendously increasing need for software in all areas of society (the software crisis) and hence a need for increased numbers of software engineers as well as increased productivity of the current software engineers [1]. Improving the productivity of software engineers necessitates new ways of viewing software, better procedures for creating it, and most importantly, better education of current and prospective software engineers regarding the development process [2]. Software engineering is thus rapidly being incorporated into undergraduate and graduate computer science curricula and is emerging as a separate discipline. In particular, the senior level project course has received much attention as a way to provide a software engineering experience at the undergraduate level. Project teams in such courses usually consist of two to four students. This paper describes a project-intensive software engineering course in which twenty-three students worked effectively as a single project team.

Introduction

Early in 1987, the author of this paper was given a departmental assignment to prepare a course entitled Software Systems Development (CSC427) to be taught by the author during the Fall 1987 semester. The objective was to build a first course in software engineering which would provide Brockport students majoring in computer science an opportunity to learn about the actual process of software development, the techniques currently being used and developed, and to experience programming-in-the-large. The author's own experience in the software industry provided a personal impetus to make the course as realistic an experience as possible. The typical two to four person team project course seemed to lack the desired amount of realism. Inspiration for the development of a large group project-intensive course came from James Tomayko [3]. The curriculum set forth by Tomayko and successfully taught by him at both Wichita State University and Carnegie-Mellon University both met the objective _and_ provided more than an academic exercise.

The course experience described below is closely based on the Tomayko model [3]. To that extent, the entire class worked as a project team on one major project (deliverable software) for an actual customer. The instructor served as project manager. A phase model approach to development was used. Six milestones were established at approximately two week intervals. At each milestone, each class member was required to complete an assignment related to the developing class software project. In-class walkthroughs and reviews of all or part of the documents related to that milestone took place. A schedule was developed that included: twenty-two formal lectures (A lecture on human factors was added to the original set of topics in the Tomayko model [3].), two hourly exams, seven classes devoted to in-class walkthroughs and formal reviews, and the remaining eight class sessions strategically suspended at crucial points during project development to allow for increased time for project team interaction and conference with the instructor/project manager. Required reading was from Fairley [4] and Brooks [5] as well as selected periodicals and handouts. A bibliography listing twenty-two books was distributed to the students with the first day handout. The works cited in the bibliography had been used by the author in the development of the course. The students were encourgaged to reference these works to research class topics and to help in project development.

The Project and The Customer

To properly experience the customer interface that is part of any system development, it was essential that the customer be someone other than the instructor [3,6]. After some on-campus solicitation for project ideas, the project and customer were chosen by the instructor. The project involved the development of a user-friendly, menu-driven business graphics system for a PR1ME 9955. After soliciting the necessary information from the user, the system needed to produce an ASCII command file which would then drive a Hewlett Packard HP7475A Graphic Plotter to produce a labeled: custom bar graph (multiple or stacked), custom closed-format pie graph (simple or one set-out piece), or a custom line graph. Graph legends were to be optional at the user's discretion. The immediate customer was a faculty consultant at the Academic Computing Center on campus. She suggested the project in response to a demand for such a system from her own faculty clients . To some extent this made the direct customer slightly unrealistic in that she had a great deal of computer savvy, but she knowingly played the customer role with great realism. Also, the ultimate customers, the faculty and students on campus, would be more typical computer users. To add a further touch of realism, the immediate customer left Brockport during the semester and students needed to work with a new customer contact.

Student Roles

The roles identified for the project were identical to those in the Tomayko model [3] except that there actually was a Maintenance Engineer, and for some roles a backup/associate was provided. The student roles were as follows:

    Principal Architect
    Architect Back-up
    Project Administrators (2)
    Configuration Manager
    Associate Configuration Manager
    Quality Assurance Managers (2)
    Test and Evaluation Engineers (3)
    Designers (3)
    Implementers (3)
    Documentation Specialists (2)
    Verification and Validation
      Engineers (3)
    Maintenance Engineer

Twenty-four students were originally enrolled in the course. One student dropped the first day and the remaining twenty-three successfully completed the course. The sharing of role assignments helped to alleviate the pressure typically associated with a project course [7] but as predicted by Brooks, increased the need for communication [5].

During the first week of the semester, each student filled out a job preference form and then was required to schedule an individual interview with the instructor. During the interviews the students presented their resumes and expressed their questions and views about the team roles. This interview process benefited both the students and the instructor; the instructor made an early acquaintance with the team and could make sounder decisions regarding role selection while the students learned something about job interviews as well as the roles involved in the project.

A map was developed which detailed the assignments for each student for each milestone and the corresponding point worth. The project portion of the course accounted for 500 out of a total of 1000 points for the course. To help alleviate the grading problems often attributed to group projects, individual milestone assignments were weighted according to difficulty of the task and labor required to complete it. For example, at the first milestone when the requirements document was delivered, the architects' assignment to do the requirements analysis and write the requirements document was worth 200 points. Whereas the implementers' assignment for the same milestone to develop prototype screen displays was worth 55 points, and the designers' assignment to absorb a voluminous technical manual concerning the plotter and to distill the essential information into a handout to be easily understood and referenced by the rest of the class was worth 70 points.

Student Profile

With the exception of two students, all class members were at the senior level and all were well prepared to handle the course. They were, however, somewhat diverse in background and social status. Some were the typical twentyish college student. Many were older, married, non-traditional students. Some had co-op or internship experience. Others had actual job experience. The selection of team roles based upon the interviews, individual backgrounds and personal preferences was successful. Labor disputes were minor and infrequent. The students were lectured on the need to act as a team [8] and very early in the project development did so. They eventually developed a camaraderie that was inspirational. They dubbed their system COGS (Charter Organization Graphics System), designed a logo and had t-shirts made. They became an easily recognized group who virtually lived in the computer center. There was little time for group meetings in class. Virtually all meetings were on their own time. Meetings with the customer were prearranged by the students by appointment and did not include the instructor. The students communicated via electronic mail on the available PR1ME system and were required to: inform the instructor/project manager of all meetings, keep minutes on the PR1ME system for each meeting, and keep a log of all meetings held. As indicated on the meeting summary which they compiled, a total of 78 hours and 45 minutes were devoted to meetings held outside of class. While the instructor occasionally and unannounced attended these meetings, the instructor found it preferable to let the students hammer out their tasks without intervention or supervision. The instructor was however very accessible. Students communicated with the instructor via electronic mail, office visits and telephone. The instructor kept a log of all meetings involving the instructor and one or more students. All meeting records later became part of the COGS Project Legacy.

Project Development

The students decided to use Pascal for the COGS system since the only other really viable possibilites were PL/I and C, and not all students felt comfortable with either. It was essential for them, however, to learn about the plotting language needed for interface with the plotter.

All six milestones were met (with one-two day slippage on two occasions). At the time of each milestone, each group was required to submit an activity report which also eventually became part of the Project Legacy, and each student and the customer were required to complete an appraisal of all team members they had had direct contact with during that system phase. The instructor added a personal appraisal and took averages to be used along with class participation grades to compile the eventual participation grade for each student. The participation grade totalled 100 out of the total 1000 possible attainable points for the class. Both the activity forms and the appraisals proved to be extremely valuable tools for the instructor. Using these reports it was possible to gain additional insight into the group process as well as individual achievements within the group. All student work was personally graded by the instructor. Proper english usage was required and enforced. Revisions were rampant. Students made considerable progress in both their technical writing and oral communication skills as the course progressed.

The students had only the bare minimum in the way of software tools but managed to produce respectable documents and to keep the required change histories and the configurations accurate. All changes had to be approved at a Change Control Board Meeting. The Change Control Board was comprised of: the Configuration Managers, the Quality Assurance Managers, the Principal Architect and a representative from each of the Design, Implementation and Documentation teams. Making approved changes to the chain of documents presented a bit of a bottleneck especially to the design team which was responsible for both the Preliminary and the Detailed Design Documents. All changes were verified by the Configuration Managers and the Quality Assurance Managers. The Configuration Managers produced both a log and a summary of each change. During unit and interface testing the test engineers found it useful to keep a testing schedule on the PR1ME system which anyone on the team could view. Their suggestion helped facilitate and organize the testing process. The final configuration consisted of the following:

Requirements Document
Software Quality Assurance Plan
Software Configuration Management
 Plan
Specification Document
Test Plan
Preliminary Design Document
Detailed Design Document
Code
Test Runs
Verification and Validation Reports
Cost Estimates and Summaries
User's Manual
Project Legacy

Lectures and Testing

Class lectures followed the originally planned schedule. The amount of material to cover coupled with the limited time available proved to be a challenge. Moreover, as the project development progressed, keeping the students' interest during lectures proved to be an even greater challenge; they preferred to be working on the project. To meet these challenges overhead transparencies were used in abundance and the instructor developed printed lecture notes which were distributed to the students. These handouts provided a framework for the students' notetaking. All details were intentionally not provided in order to encourage students to stay with the discussion. Using the handouts, it was possible to cover more material, successfully solicit more discussion and supply the students with a course keepsake for later reference. The handouts referenced both Tomayko's materials [3] and the resources listed in the course bibliography. During the lectures the instructor expounded upon the material in the handouts, led discussions and included insights and personal experiences from actual work in the software development field.

Course Success

The course was successful on many levels. The students satisfactorily learned the lecture material. Their performance on both exams, which closely resembled Tomayko's exams [3], was in general above average. The two exams accounted for 400 points out of the 1000 point course total. The average total earned by students on exams was 335.4. The COGS project was completed as scheduled. There were a few loose ends, but the customer was pleased and impressed, and the system was usable by the end of the semester. Moreover, all of the documents were completed as assigned and in the instructor's possession at the semester's end. COGS involved approximately 5000 lines of code, a file drawer full of accompanying documentation and a considerable investment of labor. The labor summary report prepared by the Project Administrators indicates the following statistics:

Total Student Work   3657.03 hours
Total Student Training 942.60 hours
(classtime and reading)

Total hours expended are depicted according to milestone in figure A below. Figure B depicts budgeted versus actual labor hours.

FIGURE A

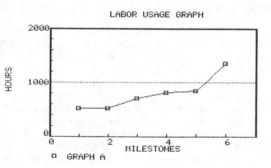

LABOR USAGE GRAPH

FIGURE B

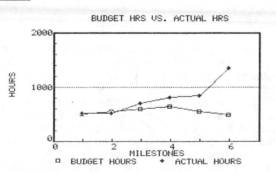

BUDGET HRS. VS. ACTUAL HRS

Admittedly, the sytem was modest in its undertaking and 5000 lines of code far from qualifies it as a large system. However, the requirements analysis, actual customer interface, interface with the plotter, and the communication needed to smoothly mesh the efforts of such a large group justify the labor expended.

The students' response to the course was overwhelmingly positive. A statistical summary provided for the standard campus student evaluation form on which students can respond very poor, poor, fair, good, very good or excellent to each question, indicated the following:

1. course as a whole was
   4% very good   95% excellent
2. course content was
   9% very good   90% excellent
3. instructor's contribution to course
   was   100% excellent
4. instructor's effectiveness as a
   teacher was   100% excellent
5. compared with other courses,
   amount learned in this course was
   27% very good   72% excellent
6. interest level of class sessions
   was 4% very good   95% excellent

In addition, handwritten comments were submitted from each of the twenty-three students expressing enthusiasm, gratitude and applause for the course. While most acknowledged some sacrifice in terms of the time involved, all deemed the group experience definitely worthwhile. Later feedback, as students actually interviewed for employment, was even more positive. Employers were very interested to hear students chronicle their group project development and on several occasions commended the department for the inclusion of such an experience in an undergraduate curriculum. Once employed, students returned to express appreciation for being so well prepared in state-of-the-art systems development. The team spirit, the great interest in the course and the project success were generous rewards for the instructor.

Maintenance Follow-Up

During the subsequent semester (Spring, 1988) the instructor worked with seven of the original COGS team on an independent study basis in a course called Software Engineering – The Maintenance Phase. The students again selected and interviewed for team roles. The maintenance team was comprised of the following positions: Maintenance Supervisor, Software Configuration Manager, Software Quality Assurance Manager, Documentation Specialist, Trouble Shooter/Designer/Coder (2), Test Engineer. As a class, maintenance issues were studied [1,4,5,9,10,11,12]. On the project level, the maintenance team performed preventative and corrective maintenance and made a few enhancements to the COGS system. They arranged the official COGS release and prepared tutorial training sessions which they presented on campus. They set up a help screen for the PR1ME 9955 system, a summary sheet of COGS commands available in the computing center, and a sign-in sheet to obtain customer feedback. In addition, the maintenance team made a presentation at what on the SUNY Brockport campus is called Scholars' Day. The level of activity during the maintenance phase was less than during the system development, but probably about normal for an undergraduate elective course. The students benefited greatly from the opportunity to work with actual customers and from hearing customer feedback. Moreover, they gained a tremendous appreciation for the software engineering process since they were forced to change and correct the original system and learn firsthand how difficult maintenance can be even when the documents are in order.

Conclusion

The COGS system is currently running on the campus PR1ME machine and is being used. The large group model project-intensive software engineering course was a workable pedagogical exercise and proved to be an excellent vehicle for demonstrating the practice of software engineering in the working environment. The Department of Mathematics and Computer Science supported and approved the model used for the course and plans to offer CSC427 as developed each year.

Acknowledgements

The author graciously acknowledges Jim Tomaymko and the Software Engineering Institute for the use of their ideas and materials which enabled the author to focus better on her own teaching experience, to provide her students with a first-rate learning experience and to participate in needed undergraduate preparation for students emerging into the working world. The success of the endeavor is a testament to the model proposed by the Software Engineering Institute [3] and to the talent and motivation of the students at SUNY Brockport who worked on the COGS project. Thanks are also extended to the immediate customers for the COGS project, Ms. AEleen Frisch and Mr. Art Fiser, who graciously donated their time and interest.

References

[1] Roger Pressman, Software Engineering, McGraw-Hill Book Company, 1987.

[2] Norman E. Gibbs, Gary A. Ford, "The Challenges of Educating the Next Generation of Software Engineers," Software Engineering Institute Annual Technical Review 1985, 1985, p. 35-36.

[3] James Tomayko, "Teaching a Project-Intensive Introduction to Software Engineering," Special Report, Software Engineering Institute, Pittsburgh, 1987.

[4] Richard Fairley, Software Engineering Concepts, McGraw-Hill Book Company, 1985.

[5] Frederick P. Brooks, Jr., The Mythical Man-Month, Addison-Wesley Publishing Company, 1975

[6] Catherine L. Ballard et al, "Anatomy of a Software Engineering Project," Nineteenth SIGCSE Technical Symposium on Computer Science Education, Georgia, 1988, p. 129-133.

[7] David Lamb, "Reducing Student Workload in a Software Engineering Project Course," presented at 1988 Software Engineering Institute (SEI) Conference on Software Engineering Education Technical Program, Norfolk, April, 1988.

[8] Henry Ledgard, Professional Software, Vol 1 : Software Engineering Concepts, Addison-Wesley Publishing Co., 1987.

[9] I. Sommerville, Software Engineering, Addison-Wesley Publishing Co., 1985.

[10] B.P. Leintz, E.B. Swanson, Software Maintenance Management, Addison-Wesley Publishing Co., 1980

[11] R.L. Glass, Software Maintenance Guidebook, Prentice Hall, 1981

[12] Parikh, Handbook of Software Maintenance, Wiley-Interscience, 1986

Use of the Cloze Procedure in Testing a Model of Complexity

by

Patricia B. Van Verth, Lynne Bakalik, Margaret Kilcoyne [1]

Computer Science Department
Canisius College
Buffalo, New York 14208

ABSTRACT

This paper describes an experiment designed and conducted by undergraduate students as part of a senior research project in Computer Science. The experiment tested whether the program comprehension of a set of Fortran 77 programs can be predicted by the Oviedo/VanVerth model of program complexity. In the study, student programmers were asked to demonstrate their ability to understand programs through use of the cloze procedure. Three different kinds of Fortran 77 programs were used at three different levels of complexity determined by the model. It was hypothesized that program comprehension would decrease, i.e. the number of incorrect answers would increase, as the complexity of the programs increased. Due to a variety of reasons, the results were inconclusive. The purpose of this paper is to discuss the experiment, the method selected, and implications for future experiments.

1. INTRODUCTION

The goal of research in program complexity is to formulate and validate models and metrics that reflect how difficult programs will be to work with. Predicting program comprehensibility is one of the applications of the resulting measurements. Program comprehensibility is an attribute that is important when debugging, modifying, or maintaining a program, since in order to perform these tasks successfully it is necessary to understand or comprehend what a program does and how it does it. With a reliable measure of comprehensibility, inferior code could be identified during the implementation phase, and either improved or rejected before reaching the maintenance and debugging phases of software development.

The Oviedo/VanVerth model of program complexity is a formal model that combines syntactic and semantic information derived from program text [OVI80, VAN87]. It has been implemented for Pascal and Modula-2 programs. As part of a required senior research project, the student authors have added a Fortran 77 implementation. This involved developing a front-end parser for Fortran 77 programs that extracts information from the program text in a format compatible with a second, already existing, program that does the complexity analysis. The experiment was run by the students as an application of the Fortran parser, and to continue validation studies of the model.

2. BACKGROUND

The Oviedo/VanVerth model derives a complexity measure from both control flow and data flow information. It takes into account the use of globals, parameters, and the complexity of individual subprograms in the analysis of programs with procedures [OVI80, VAN87]. The measure produced is an ordinal measure that is limited to ranking and comparing programs implementing the same algorithm. In interpreting these complexity measures, higher complexity measures indicate more difficulty in understanding a program.

The validation process of program complexity models requires some way of obtaining objective measures of the understandability of the programs under consideration. These objective measures are then used in comparison with whatever model is being tested to determine the accuracy of the model. In research on program complexity metrics, human subjects have been asked to find a bug, answer questions about a program, reconstruct a program, or evaluate programs as examples of ways of providing these external measures [BRO80, CUR79a, CUR79b, SHE79, VAN85, WEI74].

The cloze procedure has been used in educational research to measure the comprehension of prose passages [TAY53]. In a cloze test, every nth word in a passage is replaced by a blank which must be correctly filled in by the subject. The error rate (percentage of incorrect answers) indicates how well the subject understood the selected passage. Studies by Entin, Hall, and Thomas lend support to the suitability of the cloze procedure in measuring software comprehension [ENT84, ENT86, HAL86, THO86]. Both Hall and Thomas noted in their papers, cloze tests are relatively easy tests to construct, can be standardized, and should also be more reliable than other program comprehension tests [HAL86, THO86]. One of the outcomes of this study was to examine how well this method applies to program complexity studies.

The experiment described in this paper tested the hypothesis that the Oviedo/VanVerth complexity measure can predict program comprehension. External measures of the comprehensibility of a set of test programs were obtained by applying the cloze procedure to a pool of novice programmers taken from the student population of Canisius College. It was assumed that differences in error rates for the programs under consideration would be due to differences in the understandability of the programs themselves. Results from the cloze test were then compared to complexity classifications made from Oviedo/VanVerth model measurements. It was expected that programs that had high error rates for the cloze procedure would be those programs with high complexity ratings.

[1]This research is based upon work supported by the National Science Foundation under Grant Nos. DCR-8604473 and DCR-8612674.

3. METHOD

3.1. PARTICIPANTS

Twelve novice programmers participated in this experiment. Eleven of these programmers had nearly completed an introductory Fortran course for scientists; the other programmer had completed the course during the previous year, but had not taken any additional programming courses in the interim. All subjects were paid for an hour and the tasks required less than an hour to complete.

3.2. DESIGN

The experimental design was a 3 X 3 within-subjects factorial design. Three problems were solved at three complexity levels, yielding nine programs in the experiment. Each subject saw three programs in combination so that each complexity level and each program type was represented. Since a subject did not see all nine possible programs, the experiment followed an incomplete block design. Each program was tested on four different subjects and appeared in two different combinations with other programs.

In packaging groups of programs, each complexity level and program type was grouped with all other possible complexity levels and types in keeping with the above design. There were six possible ways to distribute the programs to the subjects. These six ways were replicated twice, i.e. distributed to twelve subjects. The order of presentation of programs within each packet was randomized to overcome learning effects, counterbalancing the treatments for a within-subjects experiment.

3.2.1. Independent Variables

Programs. Three programs types were selected with algorithms simple enough for the subjects to understand and with solutions that yielded different complexity measures. The first program (referred to as Rod) checked if a single machine part met certain specifications. The second program (referred to as Air) read in an indeterminate number of input sets of temperature, time, and humidity readings to decide for each set if an air conditioner should be turned on or off. The last program (Stats) read in ten integers and output their total, mean, maximum, and minimum. All programs were syntactically correct and produced correct results.

Complexity. Different solutions for the three program types were produced by varying control structures, nesting of structures, variable use, and subprogram use. Programs were categorized as having low, medium, and high complexity by comparing program measurements derived from the Oviedo/VanVerth complexity model. This was done only for programs attempting to solve the same problem keeping within the constraints of appropriate use of the measures (see section 2.). Thus, no attempt was made to compare programs across problem type, e.g. compare programs of type Rod to programs of type Air. Oviedo/VanVerth complexity measures of significant differences (> 10) distinguished between low, medium and high complexity. An error was discovered after the experiment was concluded in one of the Rod programs (identified as Rod-medium in Table 1). Part of an output statement was omitted from the cloze version of the program; the measured complexity of the program used in the study differed from the lower complexity program by 1. When the results were evaluated, it was ascertained that this did not affect the final outcome of the experiment.

The following table gives the line count (LOC) and Oviedo/VanVerth complexity measure for each of the nine treatments. LOC was calculated by counting all non-blank and non-commented lines in the program text. It is provided as a means of comparison.

PROGRAM	LOC	O/V COMPLEXITY
Rod-low	38	49
Rod-medium	43	50
Rod-high	57	104
Air-low	37	41
Air-medium	60	54
Air-high	40	92
Stats-low	23	33
Stats-medium	30	49
Stats-high	71	91

Table 1

3.2.2. Dependent Variable

The dependent variable was the percentage of errors made by the subjects in filling in the missing program elements. Any response that was not syntactically and semantically correct was counted as an error. Time to complete the cloze test was not measured because the number of cloze blanks to be completed varied between treatments. Each test was graded independently by the student authors to eliminate grading errors.

3.3. PROCEDURE

3.3.1. MATERIALS

Twelve packets were prepared. Each packet contained: 1) a release form, 2) instructions and a sample cloze test, and 3) the three programs, each preceded by a description of the problem to be solved. The twelve packets represented two sets of the six possible combinations of programs described in section 4.2. However, the programs within packets 7-12 were not presented in the same order as the corresponding packet among packets 1-6.

In implementing the cloze procedure, every fifth program element excluding declarations and subprogram headers was deleted. Punctuation was included among candidate tokens for elimination. All blanks to be filled in were of the same length and did not correspond to the length of the item omitted; the subjects were alerted to this fact. There were no comments in any of the programs.

All variables used in the programs were declared, and the subjects were informed of this fact. Declarations were left intact so that the subjects would know the types and names of all the variables. Entin used this method in her study using BASIC programs [ENT86]. Since Fortran does not require declaration of identifiers prior to use, it was felt this would at least standardize the vocabulary for all programs and avoid confusion. Subprogram headers were also left intact for the same reason. These were factors that acted in favor of the subjects (enabled them to score higher). Variable names were repeated among types of programs and reflected their use in the program, e.g. the identifier "HIGH" represented a maximum number used in the Stats program type. Use of mnemonic names is consistent with other software cloze studies [ENT84, ENT86, HAL86, THO86]. Strings were considered to be a single token, as were relational and logical operators such as ".AND.". Since the Oviedo/VanVerth complexity model does not have provisions for format statements, all READs and WRITEs were free format, with the "(*,*)" counted as five separate tokens according to cloze elimination rules used in the study.

3.3.2. RUNNING THE EXPERIMENT

Not all subjects were tested at the same time due to schedule conflicts; however, the majority (9) were tested at the same time. Each subject was given a packet and an oral explanation of the packet contents at the beginning of the experiment. The packets were fastened together with paper clips, allowing the subjects to complete the tasks in any order. Although each individual task was not timed, a limit of 50 minutes was placed on completing all three programs. All subjects were permitted to leave when finished, and no one needed more than the allotted time. None of the subjects appeared to have any difficulty understanding what was required of them.

4. RESULTS

Several statistical tests were performed on the data. The main effect of interest in this experiment was the overall effect of complexity, obtained by combining the scores over the different program types. The average percentage errors increased from low complexity (24%) to medium complexity (26%), as expected by the hypothesis. However, the average percentage errors for the high complexity programs (21%) was less than that of the low complexity programs, contradicting the experimental hypothesis (see Figure 1).

The factorial design allowed for a test of interaction between the two independent variables, i.e. how the program type and complexity combine to influence the understanding of the programs. An interaction was evident, suggesting perhaps the main effect was not fully representative of the results (see Figure 2). Three analysis of variance tests were performed to determine the statistical significance of the main effect. The procedure outlined in Kirk for a randomized block partially confounded factorial (RBPF-3^2) design was used [KIR68]. None of the F ratios was significant.

5. DISCUSSION

On the basis of this study, no conclusion can be made as to the ability of the Oviedo/VanVerth complexity measure to predict programmer understanding of Fortran 77 programs. The main effect of complexity level on percentage of errors clearly illustrated that the percentage of errors did not increase with programs of increasing complexity. The analysis of variance indicated that F ratios were not at a level of significance to draw any additional conclusions about interactions of the independent factors.

In evaluating the experiment after its conclusion, it was assumed that both the design and procedure did not affect the outcome. The design, taken from the literature, was balanced with respect to treatments and replicated twice to remove any bias due to ordering [CUR79b, KIR68]. Since all subjects were able to complete the tests without difficulty and within the allotted time, the procedure did not appear to be suspect. That left the experimental materials or programs as the most likely factor affecting the outcome of the experiment.

In some of the cloze studies, results have varied due to the category of tokens that are eliminated and the ratio of significant versus not-so-significant tokens to be replaced [ENT86, HAL86, THO86]. A distinction has been made between program-independent and program-dependent tokens [HAL86]. Program-independent tokens are those that may be filled in by looking at the context, e.g. key words, punctuation. A reader may reasonably guess at these tokens without understanding the text. Program-dependent tokens are those for which an understanding of the text is necessary, e.g. operators, constants. When the programs used in this study were examined for the proportions of independent tokens and dependent tokens, the proportions varied considerably (11% to 42% for dependent tokens). Results from studies indicate that the comprehensibility of the programs may not accurately be represented when

these proportions vary too widely [HAL86, THO86]. Thus, the initial assumption that the comprehensibility of the programs was due to the programs themselves may not have been justified. It is quite possible that the understandability of the programs may have been due to the manner in which cloze items were deleted. Table 2 summarizes the distribution of program-dependent tokens and error rates for the nine treatment programs. The average percentage error was obtained by taking the total percentage error for each program from the four subjects reading the program, and averaging.

Looking at the distribution of the proportion of program-dependent tokens in the cloze tests, and using results from Hall and Thomas, one might expect that for the Stats program set the error rates should be the same since the proportions are almost the same. In fact, this was not what was observed. Similarly for the Rod program set, one would expect the error rate to increase as the percentage of dependent tokens increased. Again this was not the case. In light of this, a further look at the programs was taken.

PROGRAM	NO. OF CLOZE BLANKS	DEP. TOKENS	% DEP. TOKENS	AVE. % ERROR
Rod-low	44	9	20	16
Rod-medium	46	11	24	33
Rod-high	66	22	33	17
Air-low	38	16	42	31
Air-medium	45	10	22	23
Air-high	43	12	28	29
Stats-low	25	3	12	24
Stats-medium	27	3	11	22
Stats-high	30	4	13	16

Table 2

Among all the cloze blanks there was a large proportion of replacements (21% overall) involving one out of the five tokens "(*,*)" of the free format I/O statement. These tokens fall into the program-independent category since they are punctuation. They reflect little of the program meaning.

The programs that were chosen for the highest complexity levels may have been easier to understand due to mnemonics. The highest complexity level program for the Stats programs (reading in 10 integers and reporting their mean, total, maximum, and minimum) consisted of four separate routines to perform each task. The least complex version did all the computations in one main loop. The version with subroutines had explicitly named subroutines such as FINDTOT, FINDMAX, etc. The simpler version with one main loop had virtually no context clues as to the purpose of the code other than meaningful variable names (HIGH, LOW, AVG, TOT) which were also present in the other two versions. In this instance, although the highest complexity program was more complicated, it had many more textual clues which may have resulted in better performance scores.

The manner in which variations of programs were generated may also have affected the outcome. In the instance of the Air programs, the program with lowest complexity, Air-low, had a single multi-condition IF, while the higher complexity programs had more IFs with fewer conditions in each IF. In this case, it may have been easier to fill in the cloze blanks with the conditions spread over several statements rather than concentrated in a single statement. Air-low also had the highest percentage of dependent tokens (42%) of all the programs. In the Rod programs the medium complexity version introduced two logical variables which were not present in the other two versions. This version had the highest error rate of the three Rod programs. Since novices frequently have trouble with logical variables this also could have affected results. Variable types are not included in the Oviedo/VanVerth model, and thus, would not be reflected in the measured complexity.

In light of these observations and the outcome of the study, it seems highly probable that both the choice of programs and the use of the cloze procedure interacted to influence the final results. Thus, further experiments are needed in order to test the original hypothesis of this study. For these experiments, suggested improvements include:

(1) use the same programs described here, but use a more established method such as finding a bug, to obtain objective measures of program comprehensibility. It is possible that the cloze procedure is not suitable for this kind of study, that there are too many uncontrolled factors.

(2) use non-mnemonic names for identifiers. This would eliminate problems with context and use of mnemonic names. However, this would be contrary to current application of the cloze procedure in software comprehension studies.

(3) use longer programs. Both the Curtis experiment and the Hall study recommend longer programs for these kinds of studies. This would shift the target pool for subjects from novices to more experienced Fortran programmers, since the limited experience of novices necessarily restricts program size. Moreover, longer programs would mean that more complicated algorithms could be used.

(4) try a pilot study in which only the nth program-dependent token is eliminated from the program text. If successful, this could avoid problems with the replacement of too many trivial tokens as in the case of "(*,*)". However, it would not alleviate the problem of whether the cloze procedure itself had altered the comprehensibility of the programs.

(5) use more subjects, reduce the number of within-subjects factors and greatly simplify the statistical analysis. Part of the problem with the current study is the small number of subjects and the presence of too many factors.

(6) be more judicious in the selection of programs to be tested. Avoid program variations where factors not measured by the model could affect subjects' performances.

6. CONCLUSIONS

Although the experiment did not produce expected results, a great deal was learned about the use of the cloze procedure and its possible application in program complexity studies. It is too soon to make final judgements about the cloze procedure; however, caution should be exercised when using the procedure in studies of program complexity. In particular, close attention should be paid to the distribution of program-independent and program-dependent tokens in test programs. One way of equalizing the effect of the cloze procedure on the programs to be tested is by keeping the proportions of both types of tokens the same across the programs. The studies of Hall and Thomas show that the expected performance of subjects taking the test should then be the same. This is not a very useful result for comparison tests of program complexity. On the other hand, increasing the proportion of program-dependent tokens as program complexity increases, could counteract the previous effect. This possibly destroys the premise upon which the test is made, i.e. that the differences in programs are due to their comprehensibility, and not to the application of the cloze procedure.

REFERENCES

[BRO80] Brooks, Ruven, "Studying Programmer Behavior Experimentally: The Problems of Proper Methodology", **CACM**, Vol. 23, No. 4, April, 1980, pp. 207-213.

[CUR79a] Curtis, B., Sheppard, S., & Milliman, P., "Third Time Charm : Stronger Prediction of Programmer Performance by Software Complexity Metrics" in **Proceedings, 4th International Conference on Software Engineering**, 1979, pp. 356-360.

[CUR79b] Curtis, B., Sheppard, S., Milliman, P., Borst, M., & Love, T., "Measuring the Psychological Complexity of Software Maintenance Tasks with the Halstead and McCabe Metrics", **IEEE TSE**, Vol. SE-5, No. 2, March, 1979, pp. 96-104.

[ENT84] Entin, Eileen, "Using the Cloze Procedure to Assess Program Reading Comprehension", **ACM SIGCSE Bulletin**, Vol. 16, No. 1, Feb. 1984, pp.44-50.

[ENT86] Entin, Eileen, "Using The Cloze Procedure With Computer Programs : A Deeper Look", **ACM SIGCSE Bulletin**, Vol. 18, No. 1, Feb. 1986, pp. 153-162.

[HAL86] Hall, William E., and Zweben, Stuart H., "The Cloze Procedure and Software Comprehensibility Measurement", **IEEE TSE**, Vol. SE-12, No. 5 , May 1986, pp. 608-623.

[KIR68] Kirk, R.E., **Experimental Design : Procedures for the Behavioral Sciences**. Belmont : Wadsworth Inc., 1968.

[OVI80] Oviedo, E., "Control Flow, Data Flow and Program Complexity", **COMPSAC**, December, 1980, pp. 146-152.

[SHE79] Sheppard, S., Curtis, B., Milliman, P, &, Love, T., "Modern Coding Practices and Programmer Performance", **Computer**, Vol. 12, No. 12, December, 1979, pp. 41-49.

[TAY53] Taylor, W. L., "Cloze procedure: A new tool for measuring readability", **Journalism Quarterly**, Vol. 30, No. 4, Fall 1953, pp. 415-63.

[THO86] Thomas, Mark, and Zweben, Stuart, "The Effects of Program-Dependent and Program-Dependent Deletions on Software Cloze Tests", **Empirical Studies of Programmers**, Soloway and Iyengar, editors, Ablex Publishing, 1986, pp. 138-152.

[VAN87] Van Verth, Patricia, "A Program Complexity Model That Includes Procedures", **COMPSAC**, October 1987, pp. 252-258.

[WEI74] Weissman, Larry, "Psychological Complexity of Computer Programs: An Experimental Methodology", **SIGPLAN Notices**, Vol. 9, No. 6, June, 1974, pp. 25-35.

MAIN EFFECT

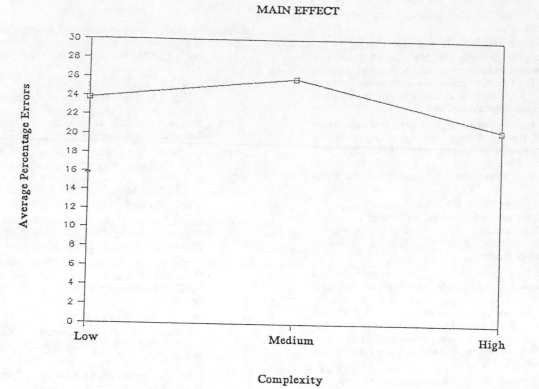

Figure 1

INTERACTIONS

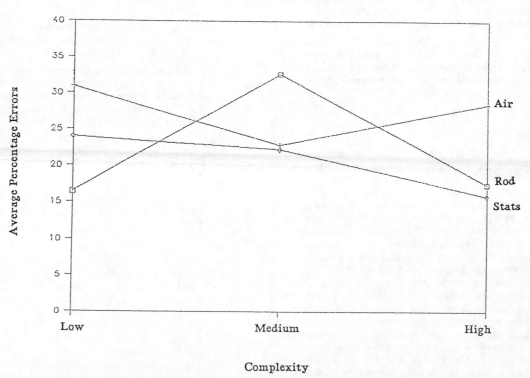

Figure 2

A Core Course in Computer Theory:
Design and Implementation Issues

Donald J. Bagert, Jr.
Computer Science Program
Texas Tech University
Lubbock TX 79409-3104
bedjb@ttacs1.bitnet

Abstract

This paper describes the design and implementation of a junior-level course in formal languages and automata theory which satisfies CSAB guidelines for the computer science core curriculum in the area of theoretical foundations of computer science. The optimal pre-requisites for such a course, as well as its impact on advanced computer science courses, are discussed. Several suggestions on how to present the subject matter in such a formal languages course, which has traditionally been considered too difficult to be taught below the senior level, are also discussed.

1. Introduction

The Computer Sciences Accreditation Board (CSAB) has stated in its guidelines that the core of the computer science segment of accredited undergraduate programs "must provide reasonably even emphasis over the [six] areas of theoretical foundations of computer science, algorithms, data structures, software design, the concepts of programming languages, and computer elements and architecture." [CSAB 1987, page 9] Since the core (also according to the guidelines) must be "40 to 60% of the computer science requirement", it is implied that all courses within the computer science core must be taught below the senior level. The particular problem that this paper addresses is, "Given these constraints,

how should the 'theoretical foundations' area of the core be implemented?"

This was the question that had to be addressed during the 1986-87 school year by the computer science faculty at Northeast Louisiana University (NLU), including the author, who was employed there at the time. At first it was thought that a course in discrete structures, which was taught in computer science to freshmen, would be sufficient to satisfy the theoretical foundations requirements. However, page 10 of the CSAB guidelines lists "discrete mathematics" as a required <u>mathematics</u> subject. Therefore, it is apparently the tendency of CSAB to consider "discrete structures" as a mathematics course. In NLU's case, CSAB counted only part of the discrete structures course as computer science, so it was necessary to create another course to provide for the proper amount of emphasis in the theoretical foundations area.

The most logical choice for a course to satisfy this requirement is a course in formal languages and automata theory. (Some arguments in favor of such a core course, even without the CSAB restrictions, can be found in [Bagert et al 1988a].) However, almost all text-books written on this subject prior to 1986 were targeted towards seniors or graduate students and were often difficult to comprehend even for these groups of students.

Fortunately, several formal languages textbooks such as [Cohen 1986] and [Wood 1987], targeted towards computer science underclassmen, were starting to appear by late 1986, perhaps in anticipation of the need for such textbooks that would be created by the CSAB guidelines, which originally appeared in 1984. After reading the Cohen textbook, the author was convinced that a junior-level course in this area could not only be taught with a reasonable certainty of success, but would be definitely beneficial to the computer science major. Using the

Cohen textbook as a guideline, the author proposed a syllabus for a new (one-semester, 15 week long) course called Computer Theory (numbered as Computer Science 313). The course was subsequently approved by NLU and by CSAB, which accredited Northeast Louisiana University in the summer of 1987.

Section 2 supplies more information on the design and precise placement of Computer Science 313 within NLU's curriculum. Section 3 discusses the actual implementation of the course during the 1987-88 school year. Finally, Section 4 contains some conclusions, and discusses future directions which might be made with respect to the new ACM curriculum effort.

2. Design Issues

2.1 Course Prerequisites

As has been previously mentioned, Computer Science 313 is a formal languages and automata theory course; the reasoning for naming the course "Computer Theory" instead of, say, "Formal Languages" can be found in Chapter 1 of [Cohen 1986]. What are the optimal prerequisites for such a course?

The minimal prerequisites to a computer theory course would be a single course in programming. This prerequisite is necessary so that the student has a reasonable understanding of the nature of algorithms, as well as some concepts of language syntax and programming capabilities. Therefore, theoretically a computer theory course could be taught on the freshman level.

However, there are several courses which cover material which is also found in a computer theory class. First and foremost of these is a freshman course in discrete structures, which can serve as a excellent introduction to the theoretical foundations of computer science (see [Bagert 1988] and [Bagert 1989]). In particular, most discrete structures classes cover finite state automata; therefore, having discrete structures as a prerequisite to computer theory means that finite automata can be covered more quickly in the latter course.

Similarly, if a course in programming languages is a prerequisite to the computer theory class, context-free grammars and parse trees can be covered in less time due to the students' previous background in this area. Finally, if the students taking computer theory have already taken a course in

analysis of algorithms, they have been exposed to the concepts of determinism and nondeterminism which are central to a computer theory class.

Therefore, to be able to achieve maximum comprehension and cover as much material as possible in a computer theory class, three prerequisite courses are needed: discrete structures, programming languages, and analysis of algorithms. (Note that each of these courses will always be required in a CSAB-accredited curriculum.) These are precisely the essential prerequisites to Computer Science 313 at NLU. The course is scheduled to be taken in the first semester of a computer science major's junior year, since the student usually cannot complete all of the prerequisites until at least the end of his or her sophomore year of study.

2.2 Relationship to Advanced Courses

Now, in what courses should computer theory be a prerequisite? It is arguable that such a course lays a firm foundation for all advanced computer science classes; however, in particular a computer theory class is an invaluable introduction to the concepts presented in a compiler course, since finite and pushdown automata (with and without output) have been covered in the former course and are essential to the latter.

(It might be worthwhile at this point to mention that a compiler course is an excellent choice for satisfying certain CSAB requirements for advanced computer science classes. CSAB guidelines state that "[The advanced courses] should be selected in such a manner as to insure that depth of knowledge is obtained in at least one-half [i.e. three areas] of the course material." [CSAB 1987, page 9] Two of the three required areas can be satisfied with a course in software engineering, in the area of software design, and a course in operating systems or architecture, in the area of computer elements and architecture. Most other advanced courses will also fit into either of those two areas; however, a compiler course would be considered as either a theoretical foundations or a programming languages course (at NLU it was the former) and would therefore complete the advanced course requirements.)

2.3 Course Syllabus

Because of its prerequisites, Computer Science 313 can use almost one-third of its 42 hours of contact time covering Turing machines, with the first two-thirds of the course devoted to finite state and pushdown automata. (This means that a university on a quarter system should be able to adequately cover all topics except for Turing machines in a ten-week course in computer theory, as long the students have a background similar to the one described in Section 2.1.)

3.   Implementation

Even if all of the guidelines for a computer theory course stated in Section 2 are followed, it is still a great challenge to actually teach the course. In particular, most of the students are not very motivated and the course material is difficult.

The students are not motivated because they are used to implementation-based computer science courses. Of course, an enthusiastic instructor can do wonders for the motivational factor! The author has learned from teaching the course that the students can gain an appreciation of the role of theoretical computer science in their studies, if it is presented in the proper manner.

An important statement to make at the beginning of the course is "In this course we will answer the question 'What is (and will ever be) computable?'." This intrigues the student, who is used to the ever-increasing complexity of computers, and therefore assumes that the problem-solving ability of the computer is theoretically unlimited.

If finite and pushdown automata are presented, at least in part, as an introduction to compiler design theory (which, as previously mentioned, may well be a required course in a CSAB-approved curriculum), the students may be more motivated, since they can see a direct link between this material and an important implementation that will be covered in a future course.

The most difficult material in a computer theory course has traditionally been Turing machines. The Cohen textbook probably does a better job presenting this area than any previous work in the field. Instead of presenting Turing machines in the traditional format of a table, they are displayed in a digraph format similar to that of a finite automaton. The students not only relate better to this format, but are astonished at the additional power of finite automata when just minor changes are made! (The same can be said for a pushdown automaton with 2 stacks, which is equivalent to a Turing machine, as compared to the standard pushdown automaton.)

Cohen also introduces the concept of allowing Turing machines to have access to a library of subroutines, with each subroutine also implemented as a Turing machine. Although subroutines are primarily presented as a time-saving feature (for such tasks as deleting a character off of the tape), they can also be used to help equate Turing machines with programs in the students' minds. (That is, just as a program can be written to solve any problem that can be done on a computer, so can a Turing machine be built to solve that same problem.) By presenting Turing machines in an easy-to-follow manner, the typical student can have a reasonable understanding of the true power and limitations of a computer by the end of the 4-5 weeks devoted to Turing machines.

4.   Conclusions and Future Directions

This paper has presented the design and implementation of a junior-level course in computer theory which satisfies CSAB requirements for the core of computer science in the area of theoretical foundations of computer science. Although this is perhaps the first such paper to present a course which directly address CSAB issues in this area, the reader might find interest in two recent papers on the subject of teaching computer theory, [Ashbacher 1987] and [Chua and Winton 1988]. Mandrioli [1982] has also written a very thorough paper on this subject.

The recently-released final report of the ACM Committee on the Core of Computer Science [Denning et al 1988] reflects the increasing role of computer theory at the lower levels of the computer science curriculum. According to the report, "theory" is one of three processes (along with "abstraction" and "design/implementation") which are essential to the presentation of all subareas of computer science. The report also suggests devoting three weeks to the topic "The Limits of Computability" during the first three-semester sequence for computer science undergraduate majors.

As a follow-up to the Denning report, ACM is formulating a new model undergraduate curriculum. The chairman of the curriculum committee, Allen Tucker, has indicated both during the audience participation within [Bagert et al 1988b] and in personal communication that theoretical computer science will be an integral part of the new curriculum model. Between CSAB and this new curriculum effort, it is evident that each computer science department will need in the near future to examine the breadth and depth of its coverage of "computer theory" topics in the undergraduate program.

References

Ashbacher, Charles D. 1987. Two undergraduate courses in the theory of computation. SIGCSE Bulletin, 19, 4, 25-26.

Bagert, Donald J. Jr. 1988. Using a course in discrete structures as an introduction to the theoretical foundations of computer science. Proceedings of the 26th Annual ACM Southeast Regional Conference, Mobile AL, 21-22 April 1988, pp 395-398.

Bagert, Donald J. Jr.; Cohen, Daniel I. A.; Ford, Gary; Friesen, Donald K.; McCracken, Daniel; and Wood, Derick 1988a. The increasing role of computer theory in undergraduate curricula. Panel paper published in Proceedings of the Nineteenth Annual SIGCSE Technical Symposium on Computer Science Education, Atlanta GA, 25-26 February 1988, page 223.

Bagert, Donald J. Jr.; Cohen, Daniel I. A.; Ford, Gary; Friesen, Donald K.; McCracken, Daniel; and Wood, Derick 1988b. The increasing role of computer theory in undergraduate curricula. Transcript of panel from [Bagert et al 1988a], available from the author. An edited version is in SIGCSE Bulletin, 20, 4, 50+.

Chua, Y.S. and Winton C.N. 1988. Undergraduate theory of computation: an approach using simulation tools. Proceedings of the Nineteenth Annual SIGCSE Technical Symposium on Computer Science Education, Atlanta GA, 25-26 February 1988, pp 78-82.

Cohen, Daniel I. A. 1986. Introduction to Computer Theory, John Wiley and Sons, New York NY.

Computing Sciences Accreditation Board, Inc. 1987. Criteria for Accrediting Programs in Computer Science in the United States (revised), CSAB, New York NY.

Denning, Peter J.; Comer, Douglas E.; Gries, David; Mulder, Michael C.; Tucker, Allen; Turner, A. Joe; and Young Paul R. 1988. Computing as a Discipline: Final Report of the ACM Task Force on the Core of Computer Science, (dated 12 August 1988), ACM, New York NY.

Mandrioli, D. 1982. On teaching theoretical foundations of computer science. SIGACT News, Part I in Vol. 14, No. 3, pp 36-53, and Part II in Vol. 14, No. 4, pp 58-69.

Wood, Derick 1987. Theory of Computation, Harper and Row, New York, NY.

Examining Compiled Code

Mark Smotherman

Department of Computer Science
Clemson University
Clemson, South Carolina 29634-1906

Abstract

The use of annotated listings of compiler-generated code has the potential to make teaching more effective in several different courses. We consider the production of such listings for several popular compilers and computer systems, including Turbo Pascal on MS-DOS machines and Pascal on Ultrix and VMS systems. The usefulness of these listings in assembly language, computer organization/architecture, and compiler courses, as well as in introductory courses, is also considered.

1. Introduction

The computer science curriculum has progressively deemphasized the study of real machine code that runs on real systems. Even in those courses that should be the most intimately concerned with the generation and efficiency of machine code, we find tendencies toward a detached, abstract view of the world. Thus, we find assembly language taught as yet another programming language in some assembler courses (in contrast to system considerations), instruction sets taught as abstract design exercises in organization and architecture courses, and the use of simulated machines and toy compilers in compiler courses. This deemphasis on real code and the accompanying abstractions are appropriate up to a point, but we must not completely overlook the benefits of the study of real code. The unintended result of the curriculum shift is often that students are isolated from real machines and unaware of the effects and implications of the compiler-generated code that is the executable representation of their programs.

A teaching technique that can help remedy the sometimes wrong perspective given to students is the use of annotated listings of compiler output. Section 2 of this paper contains directions for obtaining output listings from several popular compilers and guidelines for producing the annotated versions. Section 3 presents

a discussion of opportunities for using these listings in course settings and an assessment of the benefits, and the final section contains concluding remarks.

2. Obtaining the Listings

High-level language programs are either compiled prior to execution or directly interpreted. We consider compiled programs in this paper, and the examples are based on the Pascal program in Figure 1, which contains statements to illustrate the addressing of records and arrays and the execution of a FOR loop.

Most compilers include options to produce assembly language or machine code listings as part of the translation process. For example, the Pascal compiler "pc" on many UNIX[1] systems has an "S" option to produce an assembly language file "<name>.s" The VAX/VMS Pascal compiler includes a "machine_code" option to produce a source statement, machine code, and assembly language listing in which source statement numbers are used as comments in the the assembly language to match the source and the generated code. Such matching must be done by hand in the UNIX case.

Files or listings produced by compilers are not necessarily easy for students to read, even in the case of the elegant VMS listing. Reasons for this include the addition by the compiler of startup and run-time interface code to the code directly implementing the source statements. This additional code is typically distracting to the students since they do not see how it relates to the body of the source program. Moreover, mnemonic symbol names from the high-level language program may not appear in the compiled produced listing. This happens when limited length substitute symbols are used in place of longer user-defined names and when temporary variables or branch target labels are automatically generated.

In general, the assembly language listings should be

---

[1] UNIX is a trademark of AT&T
VAX/VMS and Ultrix are trademarks of DEC
MS-DOS is a trademark of Microsoft
Turbo Pascal is a trademark of Borland

edited and annotated with source statements and clarifying comments before use by the students. Run-time environment and startup code can be omitted, as appropriate to the type of illustration desired, and text editing can remove other distractions and enhance the students' ability to compare different compilers or different machine architectures. Two examples of annotated listings are given in Figures 2 and 3. To standardize notation, the # sign from VMS is chosen over the $ sign from Ultrix for immediate operands, and capital letters are chosen for the assembly language. Such choices are a matter of personal taste, but any standard is to be preferred over a dissonance of a variety of notations. (However, note that the distinction between parentheses and square brackets in index register notation is significant; the latter implies automatic scaling on the VAX.)

The popular Turbo Pascal compiler does not have a compiler switch to produce an assembly language listing; you must first produce an executable file and then disassemble it. For Turbo Pascal version 4 on MS-DOS, you should obtain a "<name>.EXE" file and then use the unassemble command "u" of DOS debug. You can then text edit the disassembly listing to insert symbolic names from the source code and convert hexadecimal constants to decimal. For prior releases of Turbo Pascal only a "<name>.COM" file can be produced, and a little detective work (and pattern recognition) is required for the disassembly. You must locate an initial jump and begin disassembly at the target address. The resulting listing will contain several startup instructions, which can be omitted, and it is usually helpful to include some easily recognizable constant in a simple dummy assignment statement as the first source statement.

3. Using the Listings

Annotated assembly language listings can be useful in several different courses. Introduction-level courses can use the listings to demonstrate the existence of a language level below that of the high-level language used. This knowledge should help the students refrain from thinking of computers as merely Pascal-engines or Fortran-engines and prepare them for later work in assembly language and language translation. It will also help to give them an appreciation of the expenses involved with different high-level language features. As Gray has well stated in his textbook, *Introduction to Computer Systems* [1]:

> Much of the work done by a CPU involves computations on addresses. This feature is largely hidden from the high-level language programmer who works in terms of code describing how program data should be changed;

for example, adding the contents of fields from two record structures to yield a result in an array element. At the machine level, the addition step in such code is almost the least of one's concerns; most of the code necessary for such a data manipulation consists of calculations to find the addresses both of the particular record fields and of the array element where the result is to be stored.

In an assembly language course, the quality of machine code can be discussed using the annotated assembly language listings as illustrations. The inevitable comparison between compiler-generated code and hand-generated code can also be made. In a recent electronic bulletin board discussion, J. Giles of the Los Alamos National Labs has suggested that any hand-coding in assembly language for production programs should begin by looking at the output from a compiler [2]. This will ensure that the hand-coded program will be as least as efficient as the best compiled code available.

Annotated listings can also help students determine the calling conventions between a high-level language and an assembly language routine. The interface code generated by the compiler can be adopted as the necessary entry and exit code for low-level routines.

In an assembly language course in which a simplified and/or simulated machine is used, as with Gray's textbook [1], examples of real code can be used to demonstrate advanced operations and addressing modes on sophisticated real machines. In fact, Gray does just this for Pascal and the MC68000. This approach is also useful in a computer organization or architecture course to illustrate how various architectural features satisfy the needs of high-level languages. For example, after studying the stack frame registers and supporting instructions of various machines, annotated assembly listings can illustrate the use of stack frames by actual programs. (Note that Figure 3 shows the use of temporary variables in the current stack frame by the Ultrix pc compiler.)

Examination of actual code can also provide broader focus to students of computer architecture. Often, discussions about tweaking the performance of the bare machine are too narrow and neglect overall *system* performance issues. Such discussions must be balanced with the realization of performance gains available elsewhere in the system. Robert Colwell, now at Multiflow Computer Inc., describes this same idea [3]:

> It was really enlightening to [study actual code] just after I got out of school, when I thought that my job as CPU architect was cru-

cial to achieving high performance. Then I noticed that killing myself to eke out nanoseconds from the basic cycle time was noble, but if I really wanted to improve performance the right place to look was in the compiler and the floating point libraries (and the user's algorithm in the first place.)

Colwell and others have documented the adverse effect of inefficiency in compiler-generated code on the success of the Intel 432 [4].

Study of real code is clearly of value in a compiler course. However, some courses discuss topics only in the abstract and do not move beyond toy compilers for which the generated code is unexecutable or must be simulated. Annotated listings of actual compiler-generated code can therefore bridge the gap between the classroom exercises and a real machine. For more ambitious compiler courses, these listings are useful in comparing output of different compilers for the same architecture. As an example, consider the VMS Pascal and Ultrix Pascal code in Figures 2 and 3. The VMS compiler is able to do special case analysis for such statements as the increment of an array element with bound index and the FOR loop; thus, it is able to generate more compact code (14 insts. vs. 28). In a similar manner, the output of a single compiler can be compared for different levels of optimization, and different releases of the same compiler can be compared for observable improvements.

In a compiler course, the annotated listings should probably retain any prolog or epilog code along with the generated code for the program body. This allows examination and discussion of run-time support decisions and compiler-enforced system conventions.

4. Conclusions

The study of compiled code by the use of annotated assembly language listings has the potential to increase teaching effectiveness in several courses in the computer science curriculum and is a positive step in preventing student isolation from real machines. In early courses, it can help broaden students' perspectives as to what is actually executed on a machine and the cost of various language features. In assembly language courses, the listings can be used as baselines for hand coding and as definitions of calling conventions in a high-level language. In organization and architecture courses, this approach can illustrate the usage of high-level language support features by actual programs, reinforce the idea that fast and exotic instructions do not increase system performance if they are not generated by the compilers, and supply motivation for taking the compiler

course. Finally, in compiler courses, annotated listings can demonstrate code generation for an actual machine and the effect of levels of optimization.

References

1. N.A.B. Gray, *Introduction to Computer Systems.* Sydney: Prentice-Hall, 1987.

2. J. Giles, "Re: using (ugh! yetch!) assembler," Usenet comp.arch news group, message-id 20894@beta.lanl.gov, July 27, 1988.

3. R. Colwell, private communication, April 1988.

4. R. Colwell, E. Gehringer, and E. Jensen, "Performance effects of architectural complexity in the Intel 432," *ACM Trans. on Computer Systems* vol. 6, no. 3, August 1988, pp. 296-339.

```
program test;

type
    account = record
        number: integer;
        value: integer;
    end;
    dataarray = array[0..10] of integer;

var
    arec,brec: account;
    carr: dataarray;
    i: integer;

begin
    arec.value := 256;
    brec.value := 512;
    carr[1] := arec.value + brec.value;
    carr[1] := carr[1] + 1;
    i := 3;
    carr[i] := arec.value + brec.value;
    for i := 0 to 10 do
        carr[i] := i;
end.
```

Figure 1. Pascal test program.

```
/   VAX 8650, VMS V4.7, VMS Pascal V3.7-254, edited "/machine_code" listing
/
/
/       begin
/
/           arec.value := 256;
/
1$:    MOVZWL   #256,AREC+4              / move zero-extended word to long
                                         / (integers are 4 bytes in length)
/
/           brec.value := 512;
/
       MOVZWL   #512,BREC+4
/
/         carr[1] := arec.value + brec.value;
/
       ADDL3    BREC+4,AREC+4,CARR+4     / add long, 3 operands
/
/         carr[1] := carr[1] + 1;
/
       INCL     CARR+4                   / increment exploits bound index
/
/         i := 3;
/
       MOVL     #3,I
/
/         carr[i] := arec.value + brec.value;
/
       INDEX    I,#0,#10,#1,#0,R1        / check and prepare index in R1
       ADDL3    BREC+4,AREC+4,CARR[R1]   / [] => automatic scaling for long
/
/         for i := 0 to 10 do
/            carr[i] := i;
/
       CLRL     R1
       NOP                               / NOPs => 2$ is longword aligned
       NOP
2$:    MOVL     R1,I                     / i will be defined after loop exit
       INDEX    I,#0,#10,#1,#0,R12
       MOVL     I,CARR[R12]
       AOBLEQ   #10,R1,2$                / fast loop closing instruction -
                                         / combines increment, test, and
                                         / branch
/
/       end.
/
```

Figure 2. Annotated listing for VMS Pascal compiler.

```
/   Vax 8810, Ultrix-32 V2.2, edited "pc -S" output
/
/       begin
/
/           arec.value := 256;
/
        CVTWL     #256,AREC+4              / convert word to long
                                          / (integers are 4 bytes in length)
/           brec.value := 512;
/
        CVTWL     #512,BREC+4
/
/           carr[1] := arec.value + brec.value;
/
        ADDL3     BREC+4,AREC+4,R0         / R0 gets sum
        MOVAL     CARR,R1                  / R1 gets base address of array
        MOVL      R0,4(R1)                 / array element is updated
/
/           carr[1] := carr[1] + 1;
/
        MOVAL     CARR,R0
        MOVL      4(R0),R0                 / R0 has value of array element
        MOVL      #1,R1
        ADDL2     R1,R0                    / R0 = R0 + R1
        MOVAL     CARR,R1
        MOVL      R0,4(R1)                 / array element is updated
/
/           i := 3;
/
        MOVL      #3,I
/
/           carr[i] := arec.value + brec.value;
/
        ADDL3     BREC+4,AREC+4,R0
        MULL3     #4,I,R1                  / explicit scaling of R1
        MOVL      R0,CARR(R1)
/
/           for i := 0 to 10 do
/             carr[i] := i;
/
        CLRL      -56(FP)                  / -56(FP) is temp. var. for loop start
        MOVL      #10,-60(FP)              / -60(FP) is temp. var. for loop limit
        CMPL      -56(FP),-60(FP)
        JGTR      L6
        MOVL      -56(FP),R11              / R11 will contain unscaled index
L7:     MOVL      R11,I                    / i will be defined after loop exit
        MULL3     #4,R11,R0                / explicit scaling of i, goes to R0
        MOVL      R11,CARR(R0)             / array element is updated
        CMPL      R11,-60(FP)              / compare i against limit
        JGEQ      L6
        ADDL3     #1,R11,R0                / increment index, reusing R0
        MOVL      R0,R11                   / (would have expected a single INC)
        JBR       L7
L6:
/       end.
```

Figure 3. Annotated listing for Ultrix pc compiler.

A Parallel Processing Course for Undergraduates

Dr. Daniel C. Hyde
Associate Professor of Computer Science
Bucknell University, Lewisburg, Pa. 17837
(717) 524-1281/1394 *dhyde@bucknell.bitnet*

Abstract

We argue that a parallel processing course should be offered to undergraduate computer science majors. A major component of such a course should be a series of programming laboratories where the student can investigate the strengths and weaknesses of different parallel architectures. The student should design and debug parallel algorithms on the different parallel models.

We propose a cost effective solution to the teaching of the course which uses simulators and Transputer-based parallel accelerators in a personal computer or workstation environment.

1 Introduction

In the last two years, I have taught a parallel processing course twice. The course is distinct from the many Advanced Computer Architecture courses around the country which have an Electrical Engineering bias and use, for example, the text by Hwang and Briggs [10]. We felt it was important to offer the undergraduate computer science major an elective course in parallel processing with a four-pronged emphasis: parallel computational models, parallel architectures, parallel languages and parallel algorithms. After I taught the course the first time, it was painfully obvious to me that the students required a parallel processing laboratory to understand the subtleties of the parallel architectures and to design and debug parallel programs. Therefore, the current version of the course has a strong laboratory component.

2 Why teach parallel programming?

For the past couple of decades, parallel processing was considered an esoteric topic needed to be studied only by a few computer science researchers, e.g., those who worked on the Illiac IV or Cray 1 'supercomputers.' Recently, many commercial parallel machines have become available, e.g., Intel's iPSC hypercube, Thinking Machine's Connection Machine, Cray2, Cray XMP, CDC ETA10, IBM 3090-400 VP, Hitachi 820/80, NEC SX-2 and Fujitsu VP200. The main reason is the unsatiable appetite of the scientific and engineering communities for more computation cycles. Also, many affordable 'mini-supercomputers' are available now, e.g., Alliant, Convex and Multiflow. Inexpensive Transputer-based accellerators for PCs and workstations have made parallel processing available to everyone.

In case you haven't noticed, concurrent [parallel] processing is about to leave the laboratory and enter the marketplace. It is apt not only to revolutionize scientific computing, but may enter the world of everyday data processing as well (In some ways it has, e.g., with distributed database systems). Concurrent processors embedded in personal supercomputers are yet another emerging reality that educators must come to terms with in preparing appropriate curricula for the remainder of the 1980s and beyond[1].

Therefore, because our students will see and use parallel machines in graduate school and industry, an undergraduate course in parallel processing is needed in the curriculum.

A more compelling reason for teaching parallel processing is that the 'real world' is parallel, e.g., where asynchronous events occur. For many years, researchers felt that only a narrow class of problems would be applicable to parallel processing techniques. Researchers, however, have found that most problems have parallelism to be exploited; we need only to look from the proper perspective. We need to re-orient our thinking and our student's thinking away from sequential computing to parallel computing.

2.1 Parallel Processing is a Jungle

If the area of parallel processing could be understood by reading a single article, we wouldn't need a course. However, parallel processing is a jungle. Researchers with diverse opinions on the appropriate model for parallel computation have created very different approaches to parallel architectures and their associated languages and algorithms. For example, we have vector processors, SIMD, message passing MIMD, shared memory MIMD, dataflow, systolic and reduction machines. This variety has created a tangled mess of facts and concepts to the uninitiated.

There is a lot of hype and noise in the parallel processing jungle. Experts are saying such things as "All of you will be programming data flow machines in the 1990s." "Message passing systems are the way of the future." "No one will ever build a cost effective general purpose data flow machine." Even the experts can't agree.

To capture the cycle hungry market, manufacturers hype higher and higher MIPS (Million Instructions Per Second). Another jungle game is the quoting of *peak* performance. A Cray 1 may be rated at 100 Million Floating Point Operations Per Second (MFLOPS) peak performance but when you run your favorite program, it only achieves a disappointing 5 MFLOPS. The students need to ask why?

The parallel processing jungle has other traps beyond disappointing performance. Deadlock, interference, improper synchronization and starvation await to trap the unsuspecting programmer.

---

[1] Organick, Elliott I., 'Algorithms, Concurrent Processors, and Computer Science Education: or, "Think Concurrent or Capitulate?"', *SIGCSE Bulletin*, Vol. 17, No. 1, March 1985, pp. 1.

One important reason why the field of parallel processing has not been sorted out is the frenzied scramble for nations to be the world leader. The future world leader in high performance computing will have a strong position in the world economy as well as in military strength. Japan, Europe and U. S. A. are very active in research and development because the stakes are high.

Therefore, computer science curricula need a parallel processing course to teach the fundamentals to future leaders in the computing industry in order for them to make intelligent decisions.

2.2 Fundamental Themes of Parallelism

Though parallel processing is a jungle, the fundamental themes of parallelism are only two: pipelining and replication. A pipeline, or a more appropriate phrase is assembly line, is the breakdown of actions into a series of stages which can effectively be overlapped. The different stages operating in parallel effectively increase the throughput of the machine. Instruction look-ahead is an example of pipelining where the overlapped stages are the decoding of the machine instructions and the execution of the instructions. Pipelining of arithmetic operators is what occurs in the arithmetic functional units which process vectors as in the Cray 1.

The second reoccurring theme, replication is duplicating the computational agent to effectively increase the throughput of the machine. Replication occurs at the bit level, e.g., when computers have bit-parallel adders where the full-adders are repeated for each bit in the computer word. Replication occurs when we duplicate whole functional units as in the Cray 1 or even whole processors as in the Connection Machine with its 64K processors.

The fundamental themes of parallelism – pipelining and replication – appear in many guises at many levels in modern computer architectures. These themes influence language and algorithm design in fundamental ways. The study of pipelining and replication and all their ramifications requires a course with a sound theoretical basis balanced by practical application.

3 The Course

The course is in the traditional lecture format with a programming laboratory each week. In the last month, the students do an individual project where they investigate in depth an area of parallel processing, e.g., data flow architectures, concurrent prolog, or parallel graph algorithms; give a class presentation and write a research paper.

3.1 Texts and Materials

The first time the parallel processing course was taught, I used the text by Hockney and Jesshope[8]. Though the text has some strong points, it was five years out of date in a fast moving area. A new edition [9] recently has been published which brings the book up to date. As with the first edition, it still has the major shortcoming of no exercises. Through their involvement in the ICL DAP, the authors are strong proponents of the SIMD approach to architecture, e.g., the DAP and the Connection Machine, and give a refreshing alternative to the view that MIMD is the only way to go. Because Chris Jesshope has been active recently with Transputers, the new edition has over twenty pages on Transputers and a good introduction to the language Occam.

The second time I taught the parallel processing course, I used Mike Quinn's text[21]. This was a much better choice. It has lots of exercises, is well written and has an excellent coverage on parallel algorithms. However, the instructor still needs to supply supplemental material as there is almost nothing on such important topics as systolic arrays and data flow in Quinn's book. Suggested articles on systolic arrays[17], data flow[3], hypercubes[24, 23, 5], MIMD[4, 1] and SIMD[25] are listed in the references.

A parallel processing course needs a vehicle to describe and design the parallel algorithms. After much investigation, many researchers have decided the best approach is the concurrent language Occam[15, 18]. Though we use other languages, e.g., FORTRAN 8x for data parallelism and our own language for the SIMD simulator, Occam is the primary language. I teach Occam for a week early in the course and because of the lack of Occam textbooks in the past, I wrote my own manual[11] and handbook[12]. Recently, several Occam texts have appeared on the market.

3.2 Course Topics

Week 1 Introduction to Parallel Computation; classification systems; history; performance measurements.

Week 2 Occam programming language.

Week 3 Vector processors – Cray 1, CDC 205.

Week 4 Interconnection networks; SIMD – Illiac IV, DAP, Connection Machine.

Week 5 MIMD – hypercubes; Cm*; Transputer-based systems.

Week 6 Designing parallel algorithms; synchronization; deadlock; starvation.

Week 7 Models of computation – control flow, data flow, demand flow; CSP; systolic.

Week 8 Parallel languages – Occam, DAP FORTRAN, FORTRAN 8x.

Week 9 Single assignment languages; functional languages.

Week 10 Parallel algorithms   sorting.

Week 11 Numerical algorithms.

Week 12 Graph and combinatorial algorithms.

Week 13 Data flow and reduction machines.

Week 14 Other machines – Butterfly, WARP, Multiflow.

Week 15 Class presentations.

3.3 Laboratories

One concurrent programming language, i.e. Occam, will not support all the models of computation a student needs to study. Therefore, since few universities can afford owning a collection of different parallel architectures, e.g., a Connection Machine, a CMU WARP, a BBN Butterfly, a Cray and an Intel iPSC/2 hypercube, I have opted for simulators of the different parallel architectures. For the synchronous models of computation, i.e., systolic and SIMD, the simulators are programmed in Pascal. The rest of the simulators which are asynchronous are programmed in Occam since it made no sense to attempt them in a sequential language like Pascal. As one can see from the following list, my students and I have spent a significant amount of effort in designing and building simulators. The simulators have been very successful in demonstrating to the students the concepts and limitations of the different architectures. However, I feel strongly that the students should be exposed to some real parallel machines as a simulation is always a compromise. Therefore, I have decided on the cost effective appoarch of a Transputer-based message passing MIMD system. The programming laboratories for the first twelve weeks are listed below (the last four weeks the students are working on their projects).

1. Each student measures Hockney's r_∞ and $n_{\frac{1}{2}}$ performance measurements on a different computer on campus.

2. Get started in Occam by programming a sequential sort program.

3. Design pipeline algorithm in Occam for the sieve of Eratosthenes.

4. Design simple programs in Torus language on a SIMD simulator (64 processors in a 8x8 2-D mesh with wrap around)(written in Pascal).

5. Investigate deadlock in a hypercube simulator (written in Occam). Study routing algorithms for message passing MIMD architectures.

6. Design algorithms for the hypercube simulator. Investigate issues of algorithmic synchronization and starvation.

7. Design algorithms for a linear systolic array simulator (written in Pascal and Apollo GMR graphics routines).

8. Design algorithms for a shared memory MIMD simulation of the BBN Butterfly (written in Occam). Semaphores, memory contention, hot spots in interconnection networks.

9. Redo lab 2 on multiple Transputers and measure the performance. Investigate communication latency.

10. Matrix multiply and sort algorithms on the SIMD Torus simulator.

11. Matrix multiply with varying block sizes on multiple Transputers. Investigation of load sharing and the grain size of the algorithm.

12. Investigation of a simple single assignment language and a static data flow machine (written in Occam).

3.4 Occam

Occam is a parallel programming language developed by David May[18] at Inmos Limited, Bristol, England. The language is one of several parallel programming languages based on Tony Hoare's CSP (Communicating Sequential Processes)[6]. A more careful treatment of CSP is in Hoare's book on CSP[7]. Using CSP as a basis, the researchers at Inmos developed an Occam concurrency model. From the Occam model, they developed the programming language Occam.

The name is derived from William of Occam, a thirteenth century philosopher. Occam's Razor or the ancient philosophical principle of "keep things simple" is attributed to William. A primary goal of the Occam language is to keep the language simple, hence the name.

The Occam model supports concurrency, i.e., true parallelism on several processors or simulated parallelism on one processor by way of time slicing. The model is based on concurrent processes. In Occam, communication between concurrent processes is achieved by passing messages along point to point channels. Point to point means that the channel's source and destination must be at one point or reside in one concurrent process. To alleviate many problems caused by interference when sharing variables between concurrent processes, all communication between concurrent processes in Occam must be by way of channels. Hence, there are no shared variables in Occam. Therefore, Occam reflects the message passing model of parallel computation that is supported by the Transputer hardware with its local memory, i.e., no global memory, and communication links.

The communication on an Occam channel is synchronous. When either the sender or the receiver arrives at the proper place in the code, the first to arrive waits for the other. Once synchronized, the message is transferred between the two, then both processes continue executing. This action is similar to an Ada rendezvous. If buffering is desired, an intermediate process may be inserted between the two processes. One advantage of this scheme is that one language feature performs both synchronization and message passing.

3.5 Transputers

From the Occam model, Inmos developed a hardware chip to support their concurrency model. This hardware is in the form of a VLSI chip called the Transputer. The T800 Transputer[16] is a 32-bit microprocessor (20 MHz clock) that provides 10 MIPS processing power with 4K bytes of fast static RAM , a 64-bit floating point arithmetic unit and concurrency communication all on one chip. The T800 can sustain 1.5 MFLOPS which means two T800s will out perform a DEC VAX/8600 in a 64-bit floating point compute intensive application. Since current prices are about $500 a chip, an ensemble of Transputers is a cost effective solution for compute intensive applications.

Besides being a high performance microcomputer, the Transputer has on the chip four serial bidirectional links (DMAs – each 20 Megabits per second) to provide concurrent message passing to other Transputers. The channels in the Occam language are mapped to these hardware links which connect by way of twisted pairs of wires to other Transputers. The Transputer hardware supports concurrency by scheduling time (a context switch is about one microsecond), in round robin fashion, between an arbitary number of Occam concurrent processes. The language and hardware are designed so that an Occam program consisting of a collection of concurrent processes may execute on one Transputer (by way of time slicing between the different concurrent processes) or be spread over many Transputers with little or no change in the code. Therefore, the designer can develop his or her Occam program on one Transputer and if higher performance is required can spread the Occam processes over a network of interconnected Transputers. The philosophy of Transputers is to connect them into ensembles much like Lego blocks. One can easily build pipes, rings, hypercubes, trees and shuffle exchange interconnection networks. For those who don't want to program in Occam, other languages available for the Transputer are Pascal, FORTRAN, C and Lisp.

3.6 Equipping the Lab

If an instructor is on a shoe string budget, he or she can obtain Occam2 for his or her VAX from Inmos for $150. Both VMS and Unix versions are available. Of course, this does not allow the students to experiment with true parallelism as the VAX is only one processor. However, it does allow students to write concurrent programs and experience such concepts as deadlock, starvation, and synchronization. Also, the Occam2 system allows one to run the machine architecture simulators, e. g. hypercube and data flow, described above.

For under $9,000 a personal computer such as the IBM PC AT or the Appple Macintosh II can be equipped with a board containing four Transputers and all the software needed to write real parallel programs. Inmos, Computer Systems Architects, Microway and others sell IBM PC boards. Levco sells Transputer boards for the Mac II. In this price range, the Transputers are T414s without the floating point arithmetic unit and, therefore, significantly slower. But the T414 is totally software compatible with the T800. Also, to reconfigure the four links on each Transputer jumper cables must be moved manually.

If your computing environment is a SUN workstation, a VME board with four T800 Transputers (contains 64-bit floating point arithmetic unit with 1.5 MFLOPS each), software controlled crossbar switches to reconfigure the links and software cost less than $13,000. Inmos, Parsytec, Niche and Topologix all sell Transputer-based boards to install in SUN Microsystems workstations.

4 Conclusions

We have demonstrated the need to teach a parallel processing course in the undergraduate curriculum. Until recently few universities would have the equipment resources to teach such a course. However, we have shown that through Transputer-based accelerators parallel processing has become affordable even for small colleges and universities.

The course described has evolved into one with a strong laboratory component where the students write concurrent programs in the programming language Occam and design parallel algorithms for different parallel architectures using a series of software simulators.

References

[1] Athas, William C. and Charles L. Seitz, 'Multicomputers: Message-Passing Concurrent Computers,' *Computer*, Vol. 21, No. 8, August 1988, pp. 9-24.

[2] Butler, Ralph M., Roger E. Eggen and Susan R. Wallace, 'Introducing Parallel Processing at the Undergraduate Level,' *SIGCSE Bulletin*, Vol. 20, No. 1, Feb. 1988, pp. 63-67.

[3] Dennis, Jack B., 'Data Flow Supercomputers,' *Computer*, Vol. 13, No. 11, Nov. 1980, pp. 48-56.

[4] Gehringer, Edward F., Anita K. Jones and Zary Z. Segall, 'The Cm* Testbed,' *Computer*, Vol. 15, No. 10, Oct. 1982, pp. 38-50.

[5] Gustafson, John L., Gary R. Montry and Robert E. Benner, 'Development of Parallel Methods for a 1024-Processor Hypercube,' *SIAM Journal of Scientific and Statistical Computing*, Vol. 9, No. 4, July 1988, pp. 601-638.

[6] Hoare, C. A. R., 'Communicating Sequential Processes,' *Comm. ACM*, Vol. 21, No. 8, 1978, pp.666-677.

[7] Hoare, C. A. R., *Communicating Sequential Processes*, Prentice Hall,1985.

[8] Hockney, R. W. and C. R. Jesshope, *Parallel Computers*, Adam Hilger Ltd, Bristol, 1981.

[9] Hockney, R. W. and C. R. Jesshope, *Parallel Computers 2*, Adam Hilger Ltd, Bristol, 1988.

[10] Hwang, Kai and Faye A. Briggs, *Computer Architecture and Parallel Processing*, McGraw Hill, 1984.

[11] Hyde, Daniel C., 'The Parallel Programming Language Occam,' Computer Science Technical Report #87-3, Bucknell University, June 1987.

[12] Hyde, Daniel C. and Carl I. Newman, 'Bucknell Occam Handbook,' Computer Science Technical Report #87-9, Bucknell University, August 1987.

[13] Hyde, Daniel C., Carl I. Newman and Errol S. Weiss, 'Simulating Hypercube Architectures in Occam,' presented at Occam User's Group Meeting, Naperville, Illinois, September 29, 1987.

[14] Hyde, Daniel C., 'A Parallel Computation Laboratory,' Computer Science Technical Report #88-2, Bucknell University, Nov. 1987.

[15] Inmos Limited, *Occam2 Reference Manual*, Prentice Hall, 1988.

[16] Inmos Limited, 'IMS T800 Transputer,' Inmos Product Overview, 72 TRN 117 01, Nov. 1986.

[17] Kung, H. T., 'Why Systolic Architectures?', *Computer*, Vol. 15, No. 1, Jan. 1982, pp. 37-46.

[18] May, David and Richard Taylor, 'Occam: An Overview,' *Microprocessors and Microsystems*, Vol. 8, No. 2, March 1984, pp. 73-79.

[19] Nevison, Chris, 'An Undergraduate Parallel Processing Laboratory,' *SIGCSE Bulletin*, Vol. 20, No. 1, Feb. 1988, pp. 68-72.

[20] Organick, Elliott I., 'Algorithms, Concurrent Processors, and Computer Science Education: or,"Think Concurrent or Capitulate?"', *SIGCSE Bulletin*, Vol. 17, No. 1, March 1985, pp. 1- 5.

[21] Quinn, Michael J., *Designing Efficient Algorithms for Parallel Computers*, McGraw Hill, 1987.

[22] Reid, John, 'The Exploitation of Parallelism by Using Fortran 8x Features', *Supercomputer*, 19, May 1987, pp. 8-18.

[23] Saad, Youcef and Martin H. Schultz, 'Topological Properties of Hypercubes,' *IEEE Transactions on Computers*, Vol. 37, No. 7, July 1988, pp. 867-872.

[24] Seitz, Charles L., 'The Cosmic Cube,' *Communications of the ACM*, Vol. 28, No. 1, pp.22-33.

[25] Tucker, Lewis W. and George G. Robertson, 'Architecture and Applications of the Connection Machine,' *Computer*, Vol. 21, No. 8, August 1988, pp.26-38.

[26] Walker, Paul, 'The Transputer,' *BYTE*, May 1985.

[27] Whitney-Strevens, Colin, 'The Transputer,' *SIGARCH Newsletter*, Vol. 13, No. 3, June 1985, pp. 292-300.

Operations on Sets of Intervals - An Exercise for Data Structures or Algorithms Courses

Bob P. Weems
Department of Computer Science Engineering
The University of Texas at Arlington
P.O. Box 19015
Arlington, TX 76019

Abstract

Ordered linked lists are introduced in data structures courses and are frequently encountered in the study of algorithms. Set operations (e.g. union, intersection) on sets of real intervals provide a non-trivial exercise in developing correct algorithms for manipulating lists.

I. Introduction.

Interesting programming exercises for data structures and algorithms courses are not easily found. There are several desirable properties for these exercises. The application should be easily explained, rather than involving considerable material outside the subject. Non-trivial complications should arise to challenge the student, but these should not be artificial requirements which detract from the central ideas. Lastly, the recommended data structures must be appropriate for the task. (Actually, it is also desirable that the code is not available in popular textbooks.)

Merging ordered lists is a fundamental problem. Applications include: storage of polynomials [3], mergesort [3, 4], set union [1, 2], sequential file update [2], and sort/merge processing in relational databases [5]. The domain of the sets is often the integers or character strings. Commonly union and intersection operations are discussed in lectures, and then other operations are used as exercises. Some variations include: multisets (bags) that repeat elements, tables instead of linked lists, production of new lists or combining input lists, presence or absence of list headers, and use of circular lists. It is also interesting to construct the test inputs as postfix expressions. Another common variation requires finding three lists: one with the intersection and two others with elements unique to one of the lists. The key point to combining lists is to correctly construct:

1. Initialization - this is seldom developed first, only after 2. is understood will this be known completely.

2. Loop to advance through the two lists until one is exhausted - this must have a loop invariant which guarantees correct progress towards the result.

3. Termination - eventually one of the input lists will be exhausted, so the remainder of the other list must be processed.

Clearly all such routines run in linear time. Occasionally a student will miss the point and construct quadratic time nested loops akin to outer-inner join processing in relational databases [5].

Sets of real intervals provide a challenging exercise in developing such routines. It is clearly a simplified version of two-dimensional sweep-line problems such as reporting intersections of rectangles [6]. The problem is conveniently explained by indicating intervals on a number line, a well-known technique. Implementation in the above framework is not immediately obvious and should be preceded by studying cases with number lines. In particular, it is not obvious how one should progress through the two input lists. We will see that the decision may be based on one of the two ends of the intervals. Also, several subtle conditions must be checked and involve complicated coding. The problem may be simplified by assuming only closed intervals (i.e. endpoints of the intervals are included), but the use of open and half-open intervals is more general and interesting.

We will further require that a set of real intervals is represented using the smallest possible number of intervals. For simplicity, we assume non-negative values.

In Pascal notation, the following types are declared:

```
nodept=^node;
node=record
        left_end,right_end:real;
        left_closed,right_closed:boolean;
        next:nodept
    end;
```

We also assume a dummy header is used. Suppose we are storing the set including 2 and 5, and all numbers in between except 4. Common mathematical notation would write this as {[2,4), (4,5]}. As a number line the set is represented as:

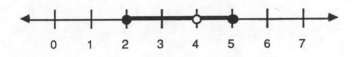

As a linked list it is represented as:

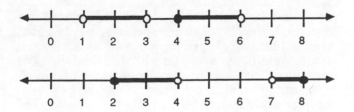

In the next two sections we will examine the particulars of performing union and intersection operations.

II. Union of Two Sets of Intervals.

Suppose the union of the following two sets ({(1,3), [4,6)} and {[2,4), (7,8]}) is to be determined:

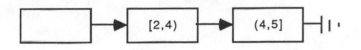

Clearly the result ({(1,6), (7,8]} should be:

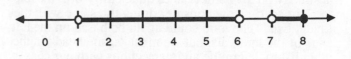

Abstractly, the new set may be constructed by a scan from left-to-right, considering each point for inclusion in the new set. Doing the same with the linked lists is not difficult. In each iteration of the loop to advance through the lists, we always consider the list element whose left end is numerically smaller. (We would choose [1,5] over (1,7]). It is not sufficient to merely attach this interval since it may overlap or "touch" an earlier interval (from the other list), so the intervals must be combined to guarantee that the set is represented with the minimal number of intervals. This may be accomplished by a pointer to the "last interval out." Processing after one of the input lists is exhausted also uses this idea. Initialization is also straightforward, but it is convenient to use a dummy header in the output list which has an interval with negative values.

If it is permissible to destroy the input lists, no new dynamic storage is required. At each iteration of the loop, the examined node may be used or discarded depending on whether overlap with prior intervals occurs.

III. Intersection of Two Sets of Intervals.

Suppose the intersection of the following two sets ({[0,5], (6,8)} and {[1,2], [3,4), (4.5,7)}) is to be determined:

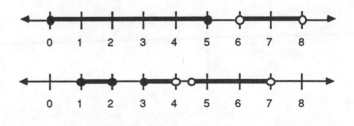

Clearly the resulting set ({[1,2], [3,4), (4.5,5], (6,7)}) should be:

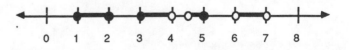

175

As in the case of union, this may be done abstractly on the number lines quite easily with the left-to-right scan. Now consider doing the same with the linked lists. The loop could again be based on the left ends of the intervals, but we must "scan ahead" in the other list to determine all intersections with our chosen interval, resulting in a complicated nested loop. But now consider basing a single loop *on the smallest unprocessed right-end* of the intervals. The key advantage is that the portion of the interval to be kept is immediately known by checking the current interval in the other input list. Beyond this observation, the only complication is the conditional tests. As in the case of union, if the input lists may be destroyed, no additional dynamic storage is needed.

IV. Conclusion.

Merge operations are fundamental to many tasks, and operations on sets of real intervals are a challenging exercise. The problem is easily explained, but real complications do arise in implementation. The resulting code is fairly short (clearly less than 10 pages), thus it is a good programming assignment. Other challenging cases include: set difference, exclusion (keep values appearing in exactly one of the two sets), using multisets, and simultaneous production of the intersection along with a list for each set of values unique to that set.

References

[1] Aho, A.V., J.E. Hopcroft, and J.D. Ullman. *Data Structures and Algorithms*, Addison-Wesley, 1983.

[2] Dijkstra, E.W. *A Discipline of Programming*, Prentice-Hall, 1976.

[3] Horowitz, E. and S. Sahni. *Fundamentals of Data Structures in Pascal*, 2nd ed., Computer Science Press, 1987.

[4] Sedgewick, R. *Algorithms*, 2nd ed., Addison-Wesley, 1988.

[5] Ullman, J.D. *Principles of Database Systems*, 2nd ed., Computer Science Press, 1982.

[6] Ullman, J.D. *Computational Aspects of VLSI*, Computer Science Press, 1984.

The New Generation of Computer Literacy

J. Paul Myers, Jr.

Department of Computer Science
Trinity University
San Antonio, Texas 78284

ABSTRACT

A tremendous mismatch is developing between two of the most critical components of any computer literacy course: the textbooks and the students. We are encountering a "new generation" of students (literally as well as figuratively!) who are much better acquainted with computer usage than their earlier counterparts. Yet many textbooks with increasing emphasis in those same computer tools continue to appear. There are signs of a coming change in that a few authors and publishers apparently are becoming aware of the need for innovations in texts for non-scientists. These textbooks open the door for a new orientation to principles in the teaching of computer literacy.

1. INTRODUCTION

Two of the most common terms used to describe events and circumstances in computer science are "new generation" and "crisis." Possibly in a new field nothing is seen as neutral or dispassioned; instead we proclaim the doom and urgency for change of "crisis" or the salvation of "new generation." This latter is applied primarily to developments in technology (hardware and certain aspects of software); and the former most often alerts us to problems in the management of the technologies and in recruitment at all levels. While, for reasons to be explained, our choice to describe a recent development in curriculum and pedagogy as heralding a "new

generation," the title could as well have been "The Crisis in Computer Literacy." This aspect of our curriculum is a mess!

Present students are increasingly sophisticated regarding computer technology. Obviously media, the general cultural attention to computers, and growing-up in the information age have contributed to a familiarity with at least some aspects of computing. And, of course, high schools (even grade schools) are increasing their offerings in computer-related courses. Almost eighty percent of the states officially encourage schools to provide students with some exposure to computers [5]. Indeed, Gilbert and Green report that in 1985 over sixty percent of incoming freshmen had at least a half-year of computer instruction [6].

These trends in pre-college schooling are accelerating. Recent legislation in California, for example, mandates, as of July 1988, that to receive full credentials all teachers must take a fifth year of the program that includes computer education. The bill justifies this requirement on the basis that "... public school pupils need quality instruction and support in the areas of computer education ... for entry into an increasingly technological society" [3]. As an additional measure of this acceleration, An *Electronic Learning* survey conducted in September 1986 found that over fifty percent of the nation's largest education schools required a course in computer literacy for graduation. A similar survey five years earlier showed only five percent [4]! And of course many of the other schools strongly recommend such a course.

177

2. THE "CRISIS"

A significant impact of these requirements and "strong recommendations" that new high school teachers receive instruction in computer education is that college computer science departments experience steady demand for courses. But another impact is that the students of those very teachers are increasingly well-versed in computer usage. Thus we (in computer science departments) are in the middle -- trying to impart new and meaningful information -- of a feedback loop, potentially leading to instability as each new generation of students is more sophisticated than the previous.

A problem arises in that traditionally computer literacy and the available textbooks focus almost exclusively on applications and technology: an orientation to the use of computers. Courses have consisted mostly of instruction in BASIC and word-processing, some mention of the history of computers and how they work, lots of jargon, and discussion of their impact on society ("computer awareness"); but the primary thrust has been instruction in functional skills [13]. The necessity to teach ever new material to students already trained in the use of computers should have forced a change in this functional orientation to computer literacy.

But it has not. The recent appearance of software packages in word-processing, spread-sheets, database, expert systems, statistics, and design has perpetuated the tool-focused approach to textbook writing, publishing, and teaching for computer literacy courses. Many of these packages have evolved to a state of user-friendliness that most non-technical students can learn them even though they may have no future use for them. And, unfortunately, since many textbooks present a smorgasbord of various packages at a very superficial level, computer literacy is in danger of settling into a course of virtually zero intellectual content and attracting the ridicule of other academic departments (which may, paradoxically, require some of these skills of their students).

Such textbooks and approaches may have been useful at an earlier time; but in the present era of a substantial maturity in the discipline of computer science and of "a nation at risk" from a diminishing emphasis on principles and sound education, such texts are a step in the wrong direction. It is precisely this sort of superficial approach that continues the misunderstanding that other disciplines have toward computer science: a non-discipline with no intellectual content save the design and use of mere tools. To perpetuate this sort of "literacy" or under-standing of the field is a major disservice, especially when the rewards of the approach are so few.

And it's hard to imagine that serious computer scientists will be content for long (if ever) to have the discipline reduced to dazzling students with the riches of software packages in the name of "computer literacy." In fact, we may be approaching a time when these skills are seen as remedial in a college environment; in just this spirit Allegheny College has already stopped offering courses in computer literacy [13]. Skills are often taught in the settings (summer jobs or other courses) in which they're used. And soft-ware tools have become so easily learned that a student's peers often provide the instruction in a relaxing, non-threatening, informal, and playful atmosphere -- a far better model for education anyway! Many students are already too busy programming (in the "high-level languages" of software packages) to take the time for instruc-tion in those very skills [13].

So to continue the present trend in which the teaching of computer literacy for non-technical students stabilizes into a catalogue of skills, features, and packages would be dis-astrous. Imagine the boredom on the part of students required to learn yet another software package that accomplishes tasks of no interest to them (otherwise they'd have already learned it) to justify the notion that we're teaching something new. And what faculty member could maintain interest and enthusiasm for such curricular content?

Recently Van Dyke has discouraged such an emphasis on functional competence. She mentions that relatively few jobs require computer com-petency. And of those that do, the skills are both too specific and too diverse to be anticipated by a single computer course; they are best taught on the job. Moreover, vocational preparation at the college level is inappropriate; liberal education has always intended not to prepare students for vocations [14]. Even in the customary use of the word, "literacy" can mean merely reading and writing, but also carries the sense of being well-educated.

3. THE "NEW GENERATION"

What then is appropriate and of enduring value in a course taught by computer scientists for non-technical, non-business, well-educated students? Why not a course presenting the principles and intellectual depth of our discipline?

In its scientific, non-data-processing aspects, computer science draws on rich traditions in physics, engineering, and mathematics (primarily the last for our purposes here). Moreover, its mathematical content has enjoyed considerable broad appeal. Relevant concepts have been popularized often: in early books such as Waismann's *Introduction to Mathematical Thinking*, Nagel and Newman's *Gödel's Proof*, and Newman's *The World of Mathematics* to the more recent Pulitzer Prize-winning *Gödel, Escher, Bach* by Hofstadter (a computer scientist).

In areas of logic, foundations, automata capabilities and limitations, and the like, is to be found the soul of computer science. In fact, certain of these topics (algorithms, logic, constructivism, ...) and names (Kleene, Church, Gödel, Turing, ...), that have been of but token interest in most mathematics departments for sixty years are now common parlance in computer science departments. Here is the soul of computing and here is genuine computer literacy.

And the public agrees, in that popularizations of these topics occur frequently and enjoy a significant appeal and readership: the books that we have cited remain in print for edition after edition. Now with the emergence of the "fifth generation" and artificial intelligence, substantial integration is possible for these more "theoretical" concepts with the day-to-day impact of computers. An avenue for this integration, for example, occurs in the similarly popular field of cognitive science. Philosophy is another likely bridge between the substance of computer science and the students' interests and lives. Significant interdisciplinary studies are

thus available, which is not the case in the tools-based approach to computer literacy.

Many things of interest and permanence are possible when we focus on principles rather than never-ending litanies of equipment, applications, and types of software packages. We can expand somewhat on a recent sentiment of Harrington:

> ... while students may know how to write code, they have little understanding of the principles or structure of a well-written program. Perhaps, more important, students seem unaware that small knowledge of BASIC programming isn't the same as general computer literacy [9].

We would emphasize principles of computation in the first sentence and would include applications, in general, in the second.

While more and more textbooks appear with emphases on software packages, superficial comparisons of those packages, slick paper, multiple-color illustrations, and gimmicks, there has been a recent appearance of principles-oriented texts. Four notable entries into this field whose authors indicate their possible use in a literacy or introductory course for non-majors are *Principles of Computer Science* by Cullen Schaffer; *Computer Science -- An Overview* by J. Glenn Brookshear; *Algorithmics: The Spirit of Computing* by David Harel; and *Computer Science -- A Modern Introduction* by Les Goldschlager and Andrew Lister. While none of these is perhaps perfect or even fully adequate for our particular purpose of a course for humanities students, we applaud their direction. For example, Harel's subtitle is indeed apt. And Schaffer's prefatory observation is worth citing:

> ... the first goal of most texts is to convey *practical* information, much of which is rather less than earthshaking. Most people appreciate the utility of a keyboard; few care to read about it.
>
> The topics treated here are of practical value, but they have been chosen primarily on grounds of intellectual significance. I have asked myself what ideas we

computer scientists have reason to be proud of and then attempted to present these at an introductory level [12].

Often the choice of topics may simply be a watered-down version of texts for our own majors (data structures, searching/sorting, etc.) or the text may be just too difficult (but for this, Harel's might be the perfect choice). But the authors' hearts are in the right place: "intellectual significance."

So, as in other areas to which the term is applied, the "new generation" of computer literacy texts promises increase in power, increase in elegance, broader usefulness, and reduction in size.

Regarding this last, anecdotally, while querying publishers for suitable texts at the 1988 ACM/SIGCSE Conference, one particular conversation stands out. A representative wished me luck in identifying this new trend in literacy texts because publishers are incurring ever greater expenses in outdoing their competitors in such areas as length, software rights, paper quality, multiple colors, instructor transparencies, and other eye-catching devices. Now we certainly have no obligation to make things easier for the publishing world; but this remark is indicative of how low our tolerance has become in this enterprise so that content is not even a major point of emphasis among competing publishers! None of the new textbooks listed above use color, nor do they even include more than a couple photographs among them.

A principles-oriented course following one of this new generation of textbooks would provide another benefit to the computer science field: a possible arena for the recruitment of majors. Maybe this shouldn't be a significant priority in designing a computer literacy course; but on the other hand, maybe it should. In any event, students are recruited into fields that interest them; and I am yet to hear of someone majoring in computer science on the basis of a particularly good experience with word-processing or spreadsheet software.

In my previous involvement with the Department of Mathematics and Computer Science

at the University of Denver, I taught a course, "The World of Mathematics," that emphasized the cultural aspects of mathematics. With biases toward principles rather than usefulness (of course, one could argue -- I did -- that at this late stage in their education, if students didn't know how to use math yet, to teach them useful math was impossible, so let's have fun instead), I used such texts as Péter's *Playing With Infinity* and Ore's *Graphs and Their Uses*. These were successful; and during those years the courses resulted in some students' changing major to our Department.

Another benefit of the new generation literacy courses, but one whose mention is easily misunderstood, is the improvement of the reputation of computer science among other academic departments. The old style of course is referred to by many students as "a blow-off," "an easy A," "you don't have to attend class," etc. Even worse is that the majority of students rated their text as being of only easy to moderate high-school level of sophistication [11]. These remarks are not lost on other academicians who may resent the vocational level of these courses. Again, our goal is not (necessarily) to please our colleagues or to secure their respect; but their view of such instruction is yet another indicator of the intellectual paucity of the content. Though not (yet) replacing in-class instruction, the non-academic Trinity University Computing Center offers a wide variety of workshops varying from one or two hours to several daily sessions in a large selection of software packages. This seems to be a much more suitable forum for instruction in these tools.

An appropriate course, then, would utilize a reasonable text of the kind beginning to appear. But acknowledging realities such as the apprehension that some students still feel regarding the use of technology [10], there might well be a hands-on portion. This could include a bit of programming for the pleasure of actually implementing some algorithmic thinking; and/or it could include some word-processing (the one application of universal appeal), possibly in a laboratory setting.

Also, the course might include term-papers or panel discussions based on library assignments on the uses of computers, their impact on society, ethics, etc. since these topics are important in "computer literacy." But the absence of such discussions from a text should not be seen as a critical omission since library research in almost any aspect of these topics is so easy; there is plenty of coverage in magazines and papers on current issues involving computers.

Of computer literacy, Barger has written that as educators have not agreed on its proper content or method of instruction, it "serves as a kind of Rorschach test onto which individuals project their own experiences and values" [1]. Indeed the above is a biased account of what needs to be done given the "crisis" that is so easy to document in computer literacy at this time. But this writer is encouraged to be in a position to not simply rail about present inadequacies and promote a fantasy of a better world, but to be able to acknowledge that some authors and publishers are beginning a new trend according to principles that seem to have considerable interest and permanence. The biases are shared!

REFERENCES

[1]   Barger, R.N., "Computer literacy: toward a clearer definition," *T.H.E.J.*, October 1983, 108-112.

[2]   Brookshear, J.G., *Computer Science -- An Overview* (2nd ed.), Benjamin/Cummings Publ. Co., Inc., Menlo Park, CA, 1988.

[3]   Bruder, Isabelle, "California teachers need extra courses in computer literacy for credential," *Electronic Learning*, April 1988, 16-17.

[4]   Bruder, Isabelle, "Ed schools: literacy requirements stagnant, but more offer degrees," *Electronic Learning*, April 1988, 18-19.

[5]   *Electronic Learning*'s Seventh Annual Survey of the States, *Electronic Learning*, October 1987, 39-44.

[6]   Gilbert, S.W. and Green, K.C., "New computing in higher education," *Change*, May/June 1986, 33-50.

[7]   Goldschlager, L. and Lister, A., *Computer Science -- A Modern Introduction*, 2nd ed., Prentice-Hall, Inc., Englewood Cliffs, NJ, 1988.

[8]   Harel, D., *Algorithmics: The Spirit of Computing*, Addison-Wesley Publ. Co., Reading, MA, 1987.

[9]   Harrington, J.L., "The computer background of incoming freshmen: looking for emerging trends," *SIGCSE Bull.*, 20,1, February 1988, 210-214.

[10]   Martin, J.B. and Martin, K.E., "A profile of today's computer literacy students: an update," *SIGCSE Bull.*, 20,1, February 1988, 235-239.

[11]   Myers, J.P., Jr. and Buentello, R., "Computer literacy: student preparation and attitudes," in preparation.

[12]   Schaffer, C., *Principles of Computer Science*, Prentice-Hall, Inc., Englewood Cliffs, NJ, 1988.

[13]   Turner, J.A., "Familiarity with new technology breeds changes in computer-literacy courses," *T.C.E.H.*, July 22, 1987, 9.

[14]   Van Dyke, C., "Taking 'computer literacy' literally," *Comm. ACM*, 30,5, May 1987, 366-374.

Teaching Practical Software Maintenance Skills in a Software Engineering Course

Dr. James S. Collofello
Computer Science Department
Arizona State University
Tempe, Arizona 85258
(602) 965-3733

Abstract

The typical one-semester software engineering course is normally geared towards new software development. Unfortunately, most new computer science graduates do not find themselves in a position where they are developing new software but instead in a position where they are maintaining an existing product. This paper describes some current practical software maintenance approaches which can be taught as a part of a software engineering course.

Background

Although software maintenance is widely regarded as being the dominant activity performed in most software development organizations, very little attention has been paid to software maintenance in university courses. Even in software engineering courses, most of the emphasis is on developing new software as opposed to approaches to maintaining it. Those software engineering texts which address software maintenance normally only provide a broad overview of the importance of maintenance with very little in the way of practical approaches to actually performing maintenance tasks.

At Arizona State University, software maintenance has been a part of software engineering education for the last four years. At the graduate level an entire semester is devoted towards an examination of state-of-the-art software maintenance theories, techniques and tools. At the undergraduate level, several lectures are incorporated in our one-semester software engineering course.

This paper focuses on our undergraduate software maintenance education approach. Several lecture topics will be described along with appropriate exercises which serve as the basis of introducing software engineering students to practical software maintenance skills. In the remainder of this paper the content of each of these lectures as well as references will be presented. Although the length of each lecture may vary, a reasonable guideline is approximately 50 minutes.

Lecture Topics and Exercises

Lecture 1: Maintenance Background and Myths

The intent of this lecture is for students to realize the importance of software maintenance and to be aware of common myths surrounding maintenance practices. The high cost of software maintenance activities

should be stressed [1]. These activities can be classified into:

- corrective maintenance (deals with failures)
- adaptive maintenance (deals with enhancements)
- perfective maintenance (deals with optimization) [2].

The student should also be made aware of the phases in a typical software maintenance process such as:

- understanding the software
- generating maintenance proposals
- accounting for ripple effect
- retesting the modified code [3].

Common problems in performing these tasks as well as their causes should also be described [4]. Finally a set of maintenance myths should be presented such as those discussed in [5] and summarized below:

1. "A special department for maintenance? Ridiculous. Our development programmers can maintain a system or two each in their spare time."

2. "We can't really control maintenance or how well the crew is working. After all, every fix or change is different."

3. "You don't get anywhere doing maintenance".

4. "Any of my programmers can maintain any program".

5. "Maintenance is all 3 A.M. fixes and frantic hysterics. It's nothing we can anticipate and it doesn't take up that much time anyway".

6. "Your just can't find anyone who wants to do software maintenance".

7. "Maintenance is the place to dump your trainees, your burnouts and Joe, the boss' nephew, who thinks that hexadecimal is a trendy new disco. How can they hurt anything there?"

8. "Why bother to provide maintenance programmers with new software tools? After all, they're just patching up."

Lecture 2: Understanding and Documenting Existing Software

This lecture should present students with some practical approaches to understanding existing software and documenting this understanding. There are two basic approaches to understanding existing software: Top Down and Bottom Up. Top Down understanding assumes a well documented program in which it is possible to proceed from an overall specificiation and design of the program through levels of documentation until the actual code is reached. This, of course, requires clear traceability of functionality throughout the software documentation. An important message for software engineering students is that they develop software in a manner such that Top Down understanding can later be utilized by the individuals who will perform maintenance on their product. Bottom Up understanding is necessary for poorly documented software. It is also sometimes referred to as "stepwise abstraction" since the goal is to proceed from the code and try to discover intermediate abstractions which facilitate program understanding.

Regardless of the understanding approach followed, there are several basic questions which must be answered inorder to comprehend what a program is doing. The students must be made aware of these questions as well as approaches to answering them. The basic questions are summarized below and explained in more detail in [6].

1. What actions are performed by the program?
2. What data is utilized?
3. Where does information come from?
4. Where does information go?
5. How are actions performed?
6. Why are actions performed?

Once understanding is acquired, it is essential that it be documented to facilitate future maintenance activities. This documentation normally takes the form of inline comments and data dictionaries. Students must be made aware of the types of comments which aid software maintenance and those which do not. An important practical approach is defining the role and goal of variables where the role is a description of the variable and the goal is the reason why the variable exists [7].

The ideas presented in this lecture must be reinforced through one or more exercises. A good exercise is to provide the students with an undocumented program and have them attempt to understand it utilizing the guidelines presented in the lecture. This seems to work well as a group project. Their understanding can then be recorded by their documenting the program. A test of how well they have documented the program is submitting their documented program along with a set of previously written questions concerning the program to another group of students. If the program was adequately documented, the students seeing the program for the first time should have little problem addressing the questions.

Lecture 3: Changing Software and Documenting the Changes

The objective of this lecture is to sensitize students to the extremely error prone nature of changing software and the importance of carefully and thoroughly documenting all software changes. Statistics should be presented which show that every 3 fixes introduce a new error and that there is a very high probability that adding a new feature to a program will break an existing one [8].

The students should also be made aware of the information necessary to effectively diagnose an error and the basic approach to follow in defect removal. An effective teaching technique is to acquire and bring into class some actual defect description forms utilized by companies. Some typical information usually found on those forms includes:

- a description of the problem
- a description of the scenario in which the problem occurred
- an identification of when the problem occurred
- location of where the problem occurred
- technical contact if more information is needed

The students should also be made aware of the "Scientific Method for Debugging" which includes the following steps:

1. collect data
2. organize the data
3. develop a hypothesis
4. prove the hypothesis

Special attention should be paid to steps 2 and 4 since students often do not adequately organize information about errors and conclude prematurely that they have found the source of an error.

The last important topic in this lecture is documenting the changed software. This requires documenting what was changed, why it was changed and ensuring that all documentation has been updated to reflect the changes. Some examples and further guidelines are presented in [9].

A good exercise to support this lecture involves providing the students with a program and a documented error in the program. The student's task is to diagnose the problem, fix the error and document the changes which were made.

Lecture 4: Validating Software Changes

This lecture attempts to provide students with two practical approaches for ensuring that their software changes are correct. The two approaches consist of software reviews and software testing. Software reviews must be performed for each change to ensure that:

- the change is correct
- the change does not introduce side effects
- the change does not degrade the quality of the software
- all documentation is updated

Some practical review checklists and guidelines are contained in [10].

It is also important to stress to the students that all software changes must be tested. This testing must ensure that the software has been changed correctly without adverse side effects. Normally there are several levels of testing beginning with a unit test of the changed modules and ending with an overall regression test. Some basic testing guidelines applicable during software maintenance are included in [11, 12].

An obvious exercise to complement this lecture is to provide the students with a software program and a proposed change to the program. The students can then work in groups to attempt to review the proposed change and develop a testing strategy for ensuring that the change is correct and does not have any side effects. If group presentations are utilized the learning experience can be enhanced as students become aware of some of their own oversights as they observe other teams.

Conclusion

This paper has described a set of lectures for a one-semester software engineering course which provide students with some practical software maintenance skills. This approach to software maintenance education has been followed successfully several times in both academic and industrial training settings with the students acquiring basic maintenance skills, but more importantly a positive attitude toward the maintenance process. Our future plans are to eventually develop a separate undergraduate software maintenance course due to the importance of this area.

Bibliography

1. Lehman, M.M., "Survey of Software Maintenance Issues", *Proc. 1983 Software Maintenance Workshop*, IEEE Computer Society Press, 1984, pp. 226-242.

2. Swanson, E.B., "The Dimensions of Maintenance", *Proc. 2nd International Conf. on Software Engineering*, 1976, pp. 494-497.

3. Yau, S.S. and Collofello J.S., "Ripple Effect Analysis of Software Maintenance", *Proc. IEEE COMPSAC 78*, 1978, pp. 60-65.

4. Lientz, B.P. and Swanson, E.B., "Characteristics of Application Software Maintenance", *Communications of the ACM*, 21, 6, June 1978, pp. 466-471.

5. Schwartz, B., "Eight Myths about Software Maintenance", *Datamation*, 28, 9, Aug. 1982, pp. 125-128.

6. Zvegintzov, N., "The Eureka Countdown", *Datamation*, 28, 4, April 1982, pp. 172-178.

7. Letovsky, S. and Soloway, E., "Delocalized Plans and Program Comprehension", *IEEE Software*, May 1986, pp. 41-49.

8. Collofello, J.S. and Buck, J.J., "Software Quality Assurance for Maintenance", *IEEE Software*, Sept. 1987, pp. 46-53.

9. Fay, S.D. and D.G. Holmes, "Help! I have to Update an Undocumented Program", *Proc. 1985 Software Maintenance Workshop*, IEEE Computer Society Press, 1986, pp. 194-202.

10. Freedman, D.P. and G.M. Weinberg, *Handbook of Walkthroughs, Inspections and Technical Reviews*, Little Brown and Company, 1982.

11. Wallace, D.R., "The Validation, Verification and Testing of Software: An Enhancement to Software Maintainability", *Proc. 1985 Software Maintenance Workshop*, IEEE Computer Society Press, 1986, pp. 69-77.

12. Fischer, K.F., "A Test Case Selection Method for the Validation of Software Maintenance Modifications", *Proc. IEEE COMPSAC 1977*, pp. 421-426.

Removing the Emphasis on Coding in a Course on Software Engineering

Linda Rising[1]
Department of Computer Science
Indiana University-Purdue University at Ft. Wayne
Ft. Wayne, IN 46805
and

Magnavox Electronic Systems Company
Ft. Wayne, IN 46808

ABSTRACT

There has been considerable interest in a one-semester course in software engineering [Bullard88, Carver87, Gibbs87]. Faculty members of departments of computer science are introducing courses that involve team projects, in an effort to provide students some experience with large programs . However, software professionals are still concerned that most computer science graduates have little understanding of what is involved in the development of large, complex systems. Too often, code alone is regarded as the primary product without proper consideration of the necessary standards and procedures of the controlling disciplines. This paper describes a course that shifted the emphasis from coding by having students perform supporting activities and maintenance on a large Ada project.

INTRODUCTION

In addition to serving as assistant professor in the Department of Computer Science at Indiana-Purdue at Ft. Wayne (IPFW), the author also works as a consultant for Magnavox Electronic Systems Company, a company that has been involved for the last several years in the development of a large Ada project. The opportunity to see some of the problems encountered has resulted in an increased emphasis on software engineering principles in all the author's courses. In addition, a senior-level course, CIS 474 Topics in Software Engineering, was introduced in Spring 1988.

IPFW offers a large project course for sophomores. The students work in groups of three or four and have a chance to see some of the problems that arise when working in a team but little or no time is spent on important topics such as cost estimation, formal requirements, quality assurance, configuration management, and technical reviews. This course is like many reported in the literature; each student is involved in the requirements, design, coding and testing phases. Since it must be completed by the end of the semester, the project cannot be too large and the focus ultimately becomes coding.

Although it does occupy 95% of a student's programming time, coding accounts for less than 25% of the effort for a large government project with significant document requirements, independent verification and validation, and other ancillary tasks [Jones86]. In addition, it becomes painfully obvious to anyone who writes long-lived software that correctness is a moving target. Boehm points out [Boehm81] that many of the characteristics of good software are in conflict with each other and that trying to achieve them all is impossible. Programmers are smart people who will work hard to achieve desired goals. Trying to write programs that are correct usually means sacrificing modifiability, readability, maintainability, etc.

It is important that students understand that all those "abilities" are more important than correctness alone, since most software must be modified, read, etc., to produce code that is, at best, only temporarily correct. Unfortunately, courses in computer science emphasize, by default, code and correctness. An instructor does not have time to reinforce notions of good design, style, and documentation when grading programming projects. As a result, student programs are graded only on correctness, run against a bank of test cases. What students learn from this is that correct code is the only important component of good software. Software engineering ideas presented in class should be reinforced when student work is graded. At IPFW, an attempt has been made to solve this problem by developing department standards for program grading that are enforced in all classes [Rising87].

The interest in software engineering has come about because of what has come to be called the "software crisis." Typically behind schedule and over budget, many software projects are so inadequate that they are

[1] The author is currently a graduate student at Arizona State University.

never used. As reported by DeMarco [Demarco82]:

> "15% of all software projects never deliver anything; that is, they fail utterly to achieve their established goals.
>
> Overruns of one hundred to two hundred percent are common in software projects."

This is costly and wasteful of resources. It is imperative that better methods be used.

One response to the software crisis, on the part of the Department of Defense, has been the founding of the Software Engineering Institute (SEI) to "bring the ablest professional minds and the most effective technology to bear on rapid improvement of the quality of operational software in mission-critical computer systems." One of the activities of the SEI is the sponsoring of Faculty Development Workshops where curriculum modules are presented. A curriculum module presents a topic in software engineering and consists of an outline, brief descriptions of important component areas within the topic, an annotated bibliography, and suggestions for teaching. The modules can be tailored to individual needs in a university or industrial training setting. The author has attended three of these workshops and wanted to include as many of the modules as possible into the new course.

A resource available to the author through Magnavox is the Ada Repository. It contains reusable software components and tools. Several of these were chosen for use in the course. One, an Ada style checker, had been modified by the author for use at Magnavox. The ease with which this modification had been performed determined that the correction and possible modification of this program would be the project for the course.

COURSE DESCRIPTION

The course, CIS 474 Topics in Software Engineering, had an enrollment of nine seniors who were assigned roles following the guidelines in Tomayko's [Tomayko87C] report on a one-semester course in software engineering:

Principal Architect: Bears primary responsibility for the creation of the software product. Primary responsibilities include writing the requirements document, advising on overall design, and supervising implementation and testing. Also calls and conducts change control board meetings.

Project Administrator: Responsible for resource tracking. Primary responsibilities include cost analysis, investigation and use of a manpower tool, and cost control. Develops form for weekly resource reports. Collects data and issues weekly cost/labor consumption reports and a final report. Also serves on change control board.

Configuration Manager: Responsible for change control. Primary responsibilities include writing the configuration management plan, developing forms for change requests and discrepancy reports, tracking change requests and discrepancy reports, and preparing product releases.

Quality Assurance Manager: Responsible for the overall quality of the released product. Primary responsibilities include preparing the quality assurance plan, calling and conducting reviews, and evaluating documents. Will investigate and use McCabe's Metrics tool.

Tester: Responsible for creation and execution of test plans to verify and validate the software, including tracing requirements. Will investigate and use testing tools.

Designer: Responsible for producing design documents for the product. Will investigate and use Excelerator to prepare preliminary and detailed design documents.

Implementor: Responsible for developing coding standards, implementing the changes in designated modules, and writing the user interface. Will conduct code reviews.

Document Specialist: Responsible for the development of documentation standards and the user manual. Will assist in the development of the user interface and the preparation of uniformly formatted documents.

Each student was given some reference material to read to become familiar with the role he/she was to play in the class. Those students who were responsible for preparing documents were given copies of the IEEE standards for that document [IEEE84] as well as the sample documents included in Tomayko's support materials [Tomayko87C]. The lectures were scheduled to cover topics necessary for meeting scheduled milestones. In addition, outside speakers on most topics were invited to talk about their duties.

Originally, the goal for the class had been to modify the style checker so that the style being checked was that of the department at IPFW. Midway through the semester, it became apparent that this was too ambitious. Since the author had previously modified the style checker and knew that (at least) three errors existed in the code, these errors were reported individually to provide experience in tracking, correcting and testing.

Thus, the focus of the course was truly removed from code and emphasized the controlling disciplines.

SOME OF THE TOPICS

One of the most important topics covered in the class was technical reviews. Initially this is a difficult concept for students, since, in all other classes, they are not encouraged to work together or to examine one another's work, and never spend class time involved in the activity. An introductory lecture was given on technical reviews, using the material in the SEI curriculum module [Collofello87]. Some instructors feel that they must be present to direct student reviews. The author agrees with those who say that "first-line managers" hamper the review process. Reviewers care more about what the "boss" will think than about doing a careful review. The author attended the first review to reinforce points from the lecture, but the Quality Assurance Manager directed all subsequent reviews. A report summarizing the final decision reached in each review was submitted but did not include the Action List. The students were not graded on the number of errors found or the number of times their work required review, but were graded on their preparation for the review. Peer evaluations done at the end of the semester reported whether each team member felt that the others had been active participants in the review process. Not only were students learning about the review process but since all plans, standards, and reports were reviewed, preparing for the review gave each student a chance to study all of the documents.

Another important topic was Configuration Management (CM). An SEI module, [Tomayko87A], and support material, [Tomayko87B], were used to present an introductory lecture. The CM Manager prepared a CM Plan which outlined the following process for treating errors in the program. Team members reported all problems with the style checker to the Change Control Board (CCB) by submitting a Discrepancy Report (DR) or Change Report (CR). The CCB met and approved/rejected the discrepancy/change. The implementors received a copy of the DR/CR and repaired the problem. After code review and separate compilation, the changed module was sent to the CM Manager, who reconfigured the style checker and reported the location of the new version to the tester. The use of Ada allowed individual modules to be compiled without allowing the implementors access to the rest of the system. The tester first tested the change and then did regression testing. Successful testing was reported to the CM Manager who signed the DR/CR as repaired and submitted it to the CCB. The new release was reported to the entire group using system mail. The size of the style checker (62 files, 787 blocks, approximately 15,000 lines of code) made good CM necessary. The students saw clearly how serious problems could arise in version control with a large team and lack of standards and procedures for CM.

A third important topic covered in the course was Quality Assurance (QA). Again, there was an introductory lecture using an SEI curriculum module [Brown87]. The QA Manager had as her primary responsibilities preparing the QA Plan and conducting technical reviews. The QA Manager also evaluated each module in the program initially using a McCabe's Metric tool and after each modification checked to see that the complexity of the changed module did not increase significantly. An increase would have resulted in the submission of a DR to the CCB. The complexity remained the same for all changed modules in the project.

PAPERS AND SPEAKERS

In addition to the two texts used in the class, [Fairley85] and [Brooks82], the students were required to read a collection of papers on several software engineering topics. Most of these papers reported results of industrial experiments or observa-tions. These papers are listed in the REFERENCES followed by an *. Each student chose one of these papers and presented a ten-minute summary during the last week of the course. To insure that all the students read all the papers, each presentation was evaluated in a brief paragraph submitted by each of the other students.

It was made clear to the students that these were not esoteric or academic subjects but essential and practical topics. To empha-size this, several speakers from local industry were invited to make presentations to the class. These presentations involved problems and solutions of a very practical nature. The speaker on Design introduced the somewhat overwhelming problem of dealing with government standards, especially DOD-STD 2167. The speaker on Configuration Management shared his experiences with control-ling, what had been at the time, the largest Ada project in the world. The topics covered in class seemed to become more important when someone who worked in that area reinforced what had been presented in class. The speaking dates were scheduled at the beginning of the semester and invitations were extended to anyone in the community. There were always visitors for each presentation, from the university or local industry.

LESSONS LEARNED

One significant problem during the semester, which had been anticipated but still proved a severe difficulty was the number of restrictions on a student account. The tools were very large, and size and other quotas imposed on students proved a significant handicap. Requests to the system manager could not be made by the students, so often the author would become a temporary team member, completing a compilation sequence or solving some system difficulty. It was sometimes enjoyable, sharing the students' perspective but many times it was frustrating to have to deal with what seemed, in many cases, like arbitrary restrictions on student accounts.

Readers may have noticed that the class had nine members but that there were only eight roles. It was decided to have two implementors since no one who wanted that job knew Ada. This also enabled each to do code walkthroughs for the other. However, experience with the project leads to the conclusion that it would have been better to have had two designers. The designer was the only one to prepare two documents, and with a program of this size, that turned out to be a mammoth chore. The code walkthroughs could have been done by any of the three Ada experts in the course and, in fact, they often served as consultants for implementation problems.

The department had recently acquired copies of Excelerator, a software tool to aid in design documentation. In order to provide some experience with this tool and hopefully create easily modifiable design documents, the designer investigated and used the tool for both design documents. Unfortunately, Excelerator is best used for structured design and our designer had some difficulty using it for packages and dependencies.

This group was too large for maximum effectiveness in the technical reviews. A group of four or five is recommended. The final reviews were done in two simultaneous sessions, each with half the class. Each individual was more effective in the smaller group, since he knew his observations were not going to be made first by the stronger, more vocal members. In earlier reviews, this caused some to be intimidated to the point of not participating or to come to the reviews unprepared. Unfortunately, this wasn't discovered until the peer evaluations were read at the end of the course.

Everyone in academia and industry knows that there is a noticeable variation in ability and enthusiasm within a group of any size [Sackman68]. This is sometimes not as evident in a more structured class situation but in a course like this where the quality of the product depends a great deal on the energy expended by the individual team member, it is obvious that what Brooks calls "hustle" [Brooks82] is an important factor. This makes grading difficult. How should grades be assigned to those who do the minimal amount of what must be done and those who contribute extra effort for the project? Do they both deserve an A? The students are aware of this and in their peer evaluations they mentioned the exceptional contributions of three of the students on the team. The author's solution was to try to duplicate real world conditions and give a "bonus" to these students by relieving them of preparing the evaluation of the paper presentations.

CONCLUSION

The students agreed that they had enjoyed the course and learned a lot. Some comments made during the semester:

"I really have learned to see The Big Picture."

"I never realized how much paper is involved in all this."

"Why can't they (industry personnel, managers, etc.) see that this is the way to do things right?"

The need for increased understanding of "how to do it right" has never been greater. Our class began each meeting with a student's reading of one or two accounts of software disasters from issues of ACM SIGSOFT Software Engineering Notes. It's clear that instead of dissipating, the software crisis has gotten worse. As Brooks said recently in a keynote speech at the SEI [Gibbs87]:

"The peak year in sales for **The Mythical Man-Month** was only two years ago. Yet the book was written in 1975, about an experience in 1963-1965. The fact that it has the slightest relevance now is a sad comment on the progress of the discipline."

In the author's opinion, this class represents a step in the right direction to a solution for the software crisis. The students in this class are now software engineers, not just programmers. They understand that good software development is much, much more than temporarily correct code.

REFERENCES

[Baker72] Baker, F.T., "Chief Programmer Team Management of Production Programming," IBM Systems Journal, vol. 11, no. 1, pp. 56-73, 1972. *

[Boehm81] Boehm,B., **Software Engineering Economics**, Prentice-Hall, 1981.

[Boehm87] Boehm, B., "Industrial Software Metrics Top 10 List," IEEE Software, Sept 87, pp. 84-85.

[Brooks82] Brooks, F.P., **The Mythical Man-Month: Essays on Software Engineering**, Addison-Wesley, 1982.

[Brooks87] Brooks, F.P., "No Silver Bullet: Essence and Accidents of Software Engineering," IEEE Computer, vol. 20, no. 4, pp. 10-19, April 1987. *

[Brown87] Brown, B.B., "Assurance of Software Quality," SEI-CM-7.

[Bullard88] Bullard, C.L., et al, "Anatomy of a Software Engineering Project," ACM SIGCSE Bulletin, vol. 20, no. 1, Feb 1988, pp. 129-134.

[Carver87] Carver, D.L., "Recommendations for Software Engineering Education," ACM SIGCSE Bulletin, vol. 19, no. 1, Feb 1987, pp. 228-232.

[Collofello87] Collofello, J.S., "The Software Technical Review Process," SEI-CM-3.

[DeMarco82] DeMarco, T., **Controlling Software Projects**, Yourdon Press, 1982.

[Fagan76] Fagan, M., "Design and Code Inspections to Reduce Errors in Program Development," IBM Systems Journal, vol. 15, no. 3, pp. 182-211, July 1976. *

[Fairley85] Fairley, R., **Software Engineering Concepts**, McGraw-Hill, 1985.

[Gibbs87] Gibbs, N.E. and R. E. Fairley (editors), **Software Engineering Education: The Educational Needs of the Software Community**, Springer-Verlag, 1987.

[IEEE84] **IEEE Software Engineering Standards**, Wiley-Interscience, 1984.

[Jones86] Jones, T.C., **Programming Productivity**, McGraw-Hill, 1986.

[Lehman80] Lehman, M.M., "Programs, Life Cycles, and Laws of Software Evolution," Proc. IEEE, vol. 68, no. 9, pp. 199-215, Sept. 1980. *

[Meyers78] Meyers, G.J., "A Controlled Experiment in Program Testing and Code Walkthroughs/Inspections," Comm. ACM, vol. 21, no. 9, pp. 760-768, Sept. 1978. *

[Parnas85] Parnas, D.L., "Software Aspects of Strategic Defense Systems," ACM SIGSOFT Software Engineering Notes, vol. 10, no. 5, pp. 15-23, Oct. 1985. *

[Parnas86] Parnas, D.L. and P.C. Clements, "A Rational Design Process: How and Why to Fake it," IEEE Trans. Software Engineering, vol. SE-12, no. 2, pp. 251-257, Feb. 1986. *

[Rising87] Rising, L.S., "Teaching Documentation and Style in Pascal," ACM SIGCSE Bulletin, vol. 19, no. 3, pp. 8-14, Sept. 1987.

[Sackman68] Sackman, H., et al, "Exploratory Experimental Studies Comparing Online and Offline Programming Performance," Comm. ACM, vol. 11, no.1, pp. 3-11, Jan. 1968. *

[Tomayko87A] Tomayko, J.E., "Software Configuration Management," SEI-CM-4.

[Tomayko87B] Tomayko, J.E. (editor), "Support Materials for Software Configuration Management," SEI-SM-4.

[Tomayko87C] Tomayko, J.E., "Teaching a Project-Intensive Introduction to Software Engineering," CMU/SEI-87-TR-20, ESD-TR-87-171.

Curriculum modules or support materials may be ordered from the Software Engineering Institute:

SEI Education Program
ATTN: Curriculum Request
Carnegie Mellon University
Pittsburgh, PA 15213

Tape copies of the Ada Repository are available on 9 track, 1600 bpi, ANSI formatted magtapes; the charge is $200 for 3 tapes. A lower price can be negotiated if tapes are supplied.

Navajo Technology Corporation
Navajo Nation
Box 100
Leupp, AZ 86035
602-686-63791

Sizing Assignments:
A Contribution From Software Engineering To Computer Science Education

David F. Haas
Department of Computer Science
University of Wisconsin Oshkosh
Oshkosh Wisconsin, 54901

Leslie J. Waguespack, Jr.
Computer Information Systems Department
Bentley College
Waltham, Massachusetts, 02254

Abstract

A method of predicting the sizes of programs from a measure of problem size is shown, and research testing the effectiveness of the method is reported. A regression model for predicting average program size as measured by mean_LOC is shown to perform well for a sample of Pascal assignments of moderate size written by students in programming classes.

Introduction

Providing programming assignments of appropriate sizes is a problem that every programming teacher confronts. We must give assignments that are large enough to be challenging and interesting but not so large as to impose an unreasonable burden on the students. It is often difficult to determine merely from reading a statement of a programming problem just how large the program that solves the problem will be, and this is one reason why programming teachers are sometimes reluctant to abandon tried problems and experiment with new ones.

We have been studying a measure of problem size proposed by DeMarco (1982), and we have used it to predict the sizes of programs written by students in two Pascal programming courses: an introductory course and a second course. Over several semesters, we have collected and analyzed more than 400 programs, and we have found that we can predict very closely the average size of the programs that will be written to solve each programming problem.

The Measurement of Problem Size

DeMarco's measure of problem size is called "Bang" - as in "bang per buck". Bang is based on information available in a Structured Specification (DeMarco, 1979; Page-Jones, 1980; Pressman, 1987) of a programming problem. Structured Analysis and Specification are widely used in industry, and several automated CASE tools make use of these techniques.

A Structured Specification includes three parts which are a set of data flow diagrams, a data dictionary, and a set of functional specifications. A Structured Specification for a large, commercial programming problem takes a long time to produce, but it is easy to do one for a moderate sized programming assignment. An example is found in the Appendix to this paper.

A data flow diagram consists of bubbles which represent "transformations" of data. A transformation may be a change in data

format. For example, items read in from a file might be placed in an array. A transformation might also be the computation of new values, for example the sum of a set of numbers. A transformation might also be a change in the composition of a data stream. For example, a bubble that edits input might eliminate data items that are incorrect.

The bubbles are connected by arrows that represent the data flows. Each arrow is labeled with the name of the flow. A bubble may have one or more arrows coming in and one or more arrows leaving. The name of each arrow is defined in the data dictionary. Figure 1 shows a data flow diagram for a very simple program to count the number of occurrences of each word in a text.

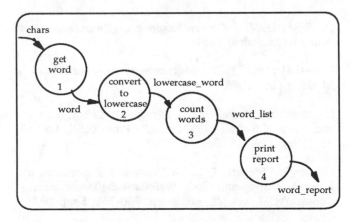

Figure 1: Example of a Data Flow Diagram

A data flow diagram is a tool for analysis and not merely a representation for a specification. So, a means for the top-down decomposition of problems is provided by the leveling of the diagrams. The top level is called "Diagram 0," and it represents a coarse–grained decomposition of the entire problem. The bubbles in Diagram 0 are numbered from 1 to N, and each bubble may itself be decomposed. If the kth bubble is decomposed, the diagram that represents the decomposition is numbered as Diagram k. The bubbles in Diagram k are numbered k.1, k.2, .., k.n. An example of this is shown in the Appendix where Diagram 7 represents the decomposition of bubble 7 in Diagram 0, and the bubbles in Diagram 7 are numbered 7.1 and 7.2. A large system may require 8 or 9 levels of decomposition, but a moderate sized programming assignment rarely requires more than two. The bubbles at the lowest level of decomposition are called "functional primitives." A functional specification is written for each functional primitive. No specifications are written for bubbles that are not primitives because such specifications would be redundant.

Once the Structured Specification has been created, Bang is not difficult to calculate. One counts the number of data tokens that cross the boundary of each functional primitive in the data flow diagrams. The number for a given primitive is then converted using a table provided by DeMarco. The table gives a number called the "corrected functional primitive increment" (CFPI) for that functional primitive.

There is some subjectivity in deciding what a "token" is, and DeMarco's description of his procedure is not sufficient. To supplement that procedure, we have devised some rules for token counting, and we will be glad to share them with anyone who writes to either of us to ask for them. An example of the computation of Bang is included in the Appendix.

The second step in computing Bang is to assign each functional primitive to a class. The classification is based on the idea that some kinds of functions are more difficult to program than others. For instance, a subroutine that formats a tabular report is more complex than a subroutine that performs a simple update of a record in a file. DeMarco provides a table of function classes, and each class is assigned a weight. The Bang for the ith functional primitive is then CFPI x class_weight . The Bang for the whole assignment is simply the sum of the Bangs for the functional primitives.

There is some subjectivity in assigning a primitive to a class, and DeMarco's classification is not entirely satisfactory. However, our experience is that the classification is robust in the sense that two classifiers do not differ very greatly on the assignment of a functional primitive to a class. Moreover, a mistaken assignment of a single primitive does not change the Bang for the whole assignment very much, and the research results shown below suggest that the classification scheme is useful.

Description of Research Methods

Twelve programming problems were designed for two courses – one introductory and another intermediate. The authors prepared Structured Specifications for each of the problems. The specifications included data flow diagrams, data dictionaries and bang calculations. Pascal programs written by students in the two courses were mechanically collected over seven semesters. The classes included computing majors and non-majors ranging from sophomores through seniors. The classes also included full time and part time students. The programs were submitted in machine readable form, and each one was compiled and tested by the grader using a standard test data set. Programs were evaluated primarily on their functionality. Programs which did not satisfy the required functionality received no credit. Each student was allowed to redo a program as many times as he wished during the semester in order to achieve full credit. We considered only programs that received full credit in our analyses. So, every program in our study included all of the features asked for in the assignment. The final sample included 402 programs from one course and 44 from the other. The programs were distributed over 12 assignments of which six were from one course and six from the other. The mean length of the programs solving a particular assignment ranged from 46.5 lines for the smallest assignment to 275.3 lines for the largest.

The programs were analyzed using the software analyzer distributed by the Purdue University Software Metrics Research Group (Conte et al, 1986:38). The analyzer program was adapted for use with Borland Turbo Pascal™. The tool produces a number of different measures of program size. Of these, we will discuss only the number of lines of code (LOC) as Boehm defines it. LOC is a count of all physical lines that contain declarations or executa-

ble code. A physical line is a sequence of characters terminated by an end-of-line. Comments and blank lines are excluded. LOC is a widely used measure of program size. It is easily understood, and it forms the basis of one of the best known models for predicting programming effort (Boehm, 1981).

For each programming assignment, we computed the mean_LOC. We then estimated a linear regression model for predicting mean_LOC from Bang. The model was estimated using a statistical package called StatWorks™ (Cricket Software, 3508 Market St., Suite 206, Philadelphia, PA 19104). Our model predicted mean_LOC rather than raw LOC because we wanted to control for the many sources of variation among students working on the same assignment in order to examine the intrinsic connection between problem size and solution size. Moreover, the mean_LOC is a much more useful number for the teacher interested in predicting the size of an assignment.

The general form of the model is

$$mean\_LOC = constant\_coefficient + b * bang.$$

In this model, b is the slope of the regression line (the bang coefficient in Table 1), and the constant_coefficient is the point on the y-axis where it is intercepted by the regression line. (See Figure 2.)

Research Results

The results of our analysis appear below. Table 1 shows the parameters of the model which is

$$mean\_LOC = 42.854 + 2.402 * Bang.$$

Data File: CS1 & CS2 Means		Dependent Variable: Boehm's LOC		
Variable Name	Coefficient	Std. Err. Estimate	t Statistic	Prob > t
Constant	42.854	14.246	3.008	0.013
bang	2.402	0.297	8.097	0.000

Table 1: Parameters of the Regression Model

This model has an adjusted coefficient of determination (R^2) of .854 which means that the model explains approximately 85% of the variance in mean_LOC. The effect of this high proportion of variance explained appears in Figure 2 which shows the regression line with the mean_LOC's scattered along it. The reader may see easily that the data points lie quite close to their predicted values.

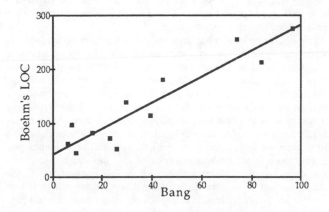

Figure 2: Plot of Data Points with Regression Line
Showing Predicted Values

Discussion

We have shown that Bang is indeed a good predictor of average program size as measured by mean_LOC. This provides the beginning of a firm scientific basis for predicting student programming effort, and we expect to continue our research on this topic in the future. We also hope that others will use and refine our model to predict the sizes of programs written by their students. We believe that the coefficients of our model will remain reasonably stable across educational settings as long as the programming language used is held constant. Pascal is a language which almost forces the programmer to use structured programming conventions. Moreover, the textbooks used for teaching Pascal promote quite similar conventions for elements like declarations, variable names, and coding style that might affect program size. In addition, many teachers give quite similar programming assignments in elementary courses. So, the sorts of things that have interfered with the portability of statistical models from one industrial setting to another seem to be less important in the educational setting. Moreover, our model predicts program size, while the statistical models used in industry generally try to predict programming effort directly. It is reasonable to suppose that program size is more closely tied to problem size than programming effort is. However, this hypothesis has not yet been confirmed.

Therefore, a word of caution is in order. All of the programs analyzed here were written at a single school in classes taught by a single teacher. Thus, the characteristics of both environment and teacher were held constant. This was good in the sense that it helped to control for extraneous sources of variance, but the narrowness of our sample should make one cautious about assuming that the parameters of our model will work well in other settings.

Consequently, anyone who applies our model in his or her classes should regard the predictions as preliminary. Actual program sizes should be noted, and used to tailor the model to the setting. Programs may easily be saved on disk or tape and subjected to analysis by the Purdue Analyzer. If this is done, the model's predictions will be improved. We hope that other programming teachers will join us in this research effort.

The model should not be used to predict the sizes of programs in other languages than Pascal. Languages like COBOL or BASIC have features that are very different from those of Pascal, and functions that are difficult to program in one of these languages may be quite easy in another. On the other hand, the statistical approach illustrated here may be used with any language. Most college teachers have some sort of statistical analysis tool available to them, and we hope that models will be developed for use with other programming languages.

We also hope that other programming teachers will adopt our statistical approach for research on other topics using students' programs as data. Research on programs written by students has been denigrated on the grounds that such programs are so different from industrial programs that research on the former cannot produce results that are generalizable to the latter. This may be true if the goal is to generalize empirical findings directly from one area to the other. On the other hand, if the goal is to provide a firm basis for theoretical development, research on students' programs has a great advantage over research in industry. In industry, each program is written only once. The program itself, the team that wrote it, and the circumstances under which it was written are never controlled or replicated. Every project is unique.

This means that research must be done only on projects that are large enough for the results to be uninfluenced by variations among individual programmers or analysts. Such projects are few, although they employ many programmers. Thus, for instance, the COCOMO model for predicting programming effort was developed at TRW on a sample of only 63 programming projects (Boehm, 1981:494). The model has never been tested on any other sample because no other sample on which the necessary information was available has been found.

Moreover, research on unique projects inevitably leaves many questions unanswered. The effects of variables of interest are confounded with those of uncontrolled variables, and so the theoretical basis for findings is always doubtful. The practical effect of this situation is that statistical models developed in industry do not travel well. Models that work well for predicting effort in one company or for one type of project often fail miserably elsewhere.

In programming classes, each program is written many times, and this permits statistical control of variables that are uncontrolled in industrial settings. Thus, we were able to control for differences among individual programmers by predicting the average LOC for each assignment. This is a small thing, but it makes our findings much clearer and firmer. Teachers of programming have many opportunities for theoretically rigorous research that are denied to students in industry. Such research may also be directed at problems in computer science education itself. We hope to see more such research in the future.

REFERENCES

Boehm, Barry W.
   1981
   Software Engineering Economics. Englewood Cliffs, NJ: Prentice-Hall, Inc.
Conte, S. D., H. E. Dunsmore and V. Y. Shen
   1986
   Software Engineering Metrics and Models. Menlo Park CA: The Benjamin/Cummings Publishing Company, Inc.
DeMarco, Tom
   1979
   Structured Analysis and System Specification. New York: Yourdon, Inc.

   1982
   Controlling Software Projects. New York: Yourdon, Inc.
Page-Jones, Meilir
   1980
   The Practical Guide To Structured Systems Design. New York: Yourdon, Inc.
Pressman, Roger S.
   1987
   Software Engineering. New York: McGraw-Hill, Inc.

APPENDIX

This Appendix contains a complete example from one of the assignments that was analyzed in the research reported here. The original statement of the problem that the students received follows.

Problem

Compute Payroll using Employee master, Pay rate master, Deductions master, and Time cards; Generate Check register and Checks. Develop a Pascal program to process payroll information. The program will have four input files: 1) the Employee master file contains the employee's id number, name, address, pay rate code, and up to three deduction codes; 2) the Pay rate master file contains pay rate codes and the associated dollar amount per hour; 3) the deductions master file contains deduction codes and associated dollar amounts per paycheck; 4) the Time cards file contains employee id and number of hours worked during the pay period. Your program will produce two text files 1) a check register listing each employee for which a time card was submitted, their name, address, pay rate code and amount, deduction codes and amounts, hours worked, gross pay based on pay rate and hours worked, and net pay that will appear on the check after deductions, and 2) a check listing each employee's name, address, id and net pay amount. (You may assume that all dollar amounts are integers.) Develop your own test data for at least ten employees to test your program. For this assignment, the data files should be named PROG8.DT1, PROG8.DT2, PROG8.DT3, PROG8.DT4 for the four employee data files respectively.

Discussion

The data flow diagrams for the problem appear below. They have been annotated with the number of tokens (underlined) entering and leaving each bubble. The number of tokens at one end of a flow may be different from the number at the other end if the flow is a complex data item. In this case, one functional primitive may treat it as a single unit, while another deals with the separate parts. For a full discussion of token counting, see DeMarco (1982), and contact us for our counting rules.

Following the data flow diagrams is the data dictionary. In the dictionary, a "+" indicates a sequence of items. "{...}" indicates an iteration of 0 or more items, and "1{...}5" means an iteration of 1 to 5 items. We have not included the formal specifications of the functional primitives. We have found that with problems as small as these when the only purpose for drawing the diagrams is to enable the computation of bang, the functional specifications are not necessary: the person drawing the diagrams knows what each bubble does.

The table for the computation of Bang follows the diagrams. The values for CFPI come from Table 9-2 in DeMarco (1982). The values in the table are computed by a formula derived from Hal-stead's work. The formula is CFPI = (TC * log TC)/2. The class weights come from Table 9-3 in DeMarco. A full description of the DeMarco's classes may be found in Chapter 9 of his book.

Payroll Problem Data Dictionary

item	composition
address	street + city + state + zip
check	check_header + emp_id + net_pay
check_contents	emp_id + net_pay
check_header	header
check_register	reg_header + check_register_line
check_register_line	payrate_code + pay_amount + {deduc_code + deduc_amount}3 + hours + gross_pay + net_pay
deduc_codes	{deduc_code}3
deduc_file	deduc_rec
deduc_rec	{deduc_code + deduc_amount}3
emp_id	integer
empl_master_file	{emp_rec}
emp_rec	emp_id + name + address + payrate_code + {deduc_code}3
gross_pay	integer
gross_payrec	payrec + gross_pay
header	name + address
name	1{character}30
net_pay	integer
payrate_file	{payrate_code + pay_amount}
payrec	timerec + pay_amount
reg_header	header
time_cards_file	{time_record}
time_record	emp_id + hours
timerec	emp_id + hours + payrate_code

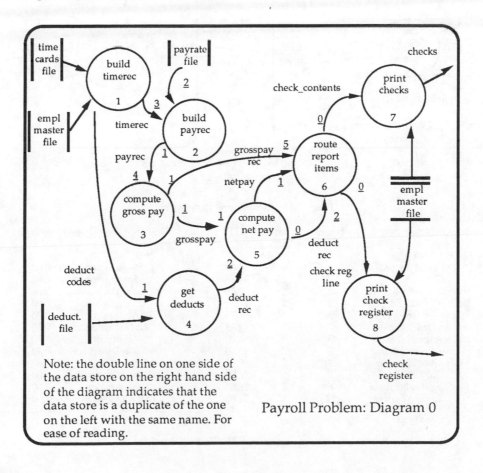

Note: the double line on one side of the data store on the right hand side of the diagram indicates that the data store is a duplicate of the one on the left with the same name. For ease of reading.

Payroll Problem: Diagram 0

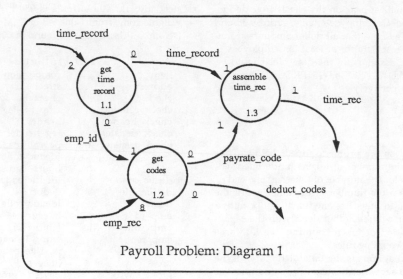

Payroll Problem: Diagram 1

Payroll Problem: Diagram 7

Payroll Problem: Diagram 8

Bang Calculation for the Payroll Problem

FP #	Name	Tokens IN	Tokens Out	CFPI	DeMarco Class Name	Weight	Bang
1.1	Get Time Record	1	1	1.00	Separation	0.60	0.60
1.2	Get Codes	7	2	14.26	Separation	0.60	8.56
1.3	Assemble Time Record	2	1	2.38	Amalgamation	0.60	1.43
2	Build Payroll Record	5	1	7.75	Amalgamation	0.60	4.65
3	Compute Gross Pay	5	1	7.75	Arithmetic	0.70	5.43
4	Get Deductions	2	1	2.38	Data Direction	0.30	0.71
5	Compute Net Pay	3	1	4.00	Arithmetic	0.70	2.80
6	Route Report Items	6	2	12.00	Data Direction	0.30	3.60
7.1	Get Check header	8	2	16.61	Separation	0.60	9.97
7.2	Cut Check	7	1	12.00	Output Generation	1.00	12.00
8.1	Get Register Number	8	2	16.61	Separation	0.60	9.97
8.2	Put Check Register	12	1	24.05	Output Generation	1.00	24.05

| 8 | <-- Total FP's | | | | Total Bang --> | | 83.76 |

194

The Effect of High School Computer Science, Gender, and Work on Success in College Computer Science

Harriet G. Taylor and Luegina C. Mounfield
Department of Computer Science
Louisiana State University
Baton Rouge, LA 70803
Phone: (504) 388-1495

Abstract

Researchers have often linked factors such as mathematics ability and overall academic achievement to success in computer science. In this study, a group of students with common mathematics backgrounds was examined to determine if some other new factors were also involved in success in computer science. In particular, the roles of prior computing experience, work, and sex are discussed. A composite picture of the typical successful student is drawn and the implications for computer science departments are identified.

Introduction

Since 1985, new trends seemed to be emerging concerning students enrolling in and completing the beginning course in the standard computer science curriculum. As computers became more common in society and the high school, it appeared that the majority of the students entering the curriculum were not computer novices as in previous years, but had considerable prior experience with computers. An early study [1] done when computers were not as common in the high school showed that a prior high school course had no effect on success in college computer science. Finally, more recent studies [4, 6, 7] that found high school computer science to be a positive factor in college success were emerging. The authors theorized that perhaps prior experience might now be an unwritten pre-requisite to successful completion of the course.

Other trends seemed to be developing as well. After a period of rapid decline in enrollment, it appeared that most programs were experiencing a significant drop in the number of computer science majors. One major area of concern was the decrease in the number of females in the programs. During the same period, due to changing economic conditions, it seemed that a significant number of the students now worked at least part of the time. In a curriculum where students had long complained of the inordinate amount of time outside of class needed to complete assignments, the researchers theorized that there could be a link between the amount of time a student worked and success in computer science.

As a result of these concerns, the authors studied students enrolled in the beginning course for computer science majors over the period of a year. The study was designed to determine the relationship between prior computer science experience, particularly high school experience, sex, and work and success in college computer science. The results are presented in this paper.

The Survey Population

Survey forms were distributed to all 709 students who enrolled in Computer Science 1250, Introduction to Computer Science I, during the 1986 academic year. CSC 1250, which is considered to match course CS-1 in the standard computer science curriculum, is required of students majoring in computer science or in electrical engineering with a computing option. 77% of the students enrolled in the course fit into one of these two categories.

Students enrolling in the course had to meet the pre-requisite of credit in college algebra and trigonometry and enrollment in or completion of calculus. The students as a group all shared a certain level of mathematics proficiency. Although many studies [5, 7, 9, 11] have shown a definite link between prior mathematics courses and mathematics proficiency and success in computer science, mathematics was not singled out as a factor in this study due to this common thread among all of the students.

Of the 709 students who enrolled in the course only 373 completed the course. The large withdrawal rate can possibly be attributed not only to the difficulty of the course, but also to the rather lenient withdrawal policy of the university. Statistics were compiled for the group including and excluding the withdrawals. In almost all cases, factors that were significant with one population were with the other. Cases in which there were differences will be noted.

The student's final grade in the course was the single measure of success. Since students in the two major curricula were required to make a "C" or better or repeat the course, the definition of success in the course was a final grade of "C" or better.

Prior Computer Science Course

The students were asked about prior high school and college courses that they had taken. 64% of the students indicated that they had credit in a prior course of some kind with 42% indicating credit in a high school course. Figure 1 shows a breakdown of the various types of prior course experiences found in the group.

Of the group of students that started the course with a prior course in high school or college, 43% were successful. Only 24% of those with no prior coursework were able to successfully complete the course. A statistical comparison of the two percentages [10] shows that prior computer science course experience of any kind is significant over no prior experience at a confidence level of .01. The same level of significance was found when comparing both high school courses by themselves and college courses separately to no prior experience.

A more difficult problem was determining the difference in prior high school experience and prior college experience. Many computer science professors have long argued that high school computer science is in fact detrimental to students and have stated a preference that students get their initial experience in college. In the group studied, the high school group did slightly better, by 2%, than the college group. In no cases could a significant difference be found as to which type of prior experience the student had.

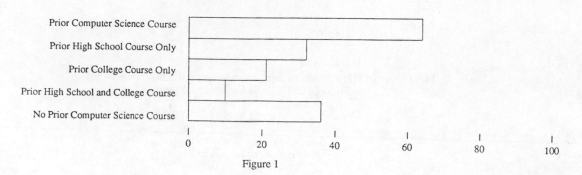

Enrollment Percentages Based on
Prior Computer Science Experience

Figure 1

The evidence seems to support the findings of Ramberg [7] that prior exposure to computers, whether in high school or college, is a critical factor in success in computer science. While it does not suggest that high school computer science is necessarily preferable to college computer science, it does indicate that contrary to the beliefs of some, it is not detrimental.

Working Students Versus Non-workers

Students were asked to list the number of hours per week that they worked. The students were then grouped into four categories for the sake of comparison: those working zero hours a week, 1-19 hours a week, 20-39 hours a week, and 40 or more hours a week. Almost half of the students indicated that they were employed and working while attending school.

Researchers had theorized that due to the large demands of the curriculum, work could be a negative factor to the success of students. At least one study [9] had shown it not to be a factor at all.

In all cases, there was a significant difference between those working parttime from 1-19 hours and all other groups. Of the students who finished the course, 75% of those who worked 1-19 hours were successful and 67% of all others were successful. Students who worked 40 or more hours fared equally as well as those who did not work at all.

Comparisons of percentages of successful students working 1-19 hours to non-working students and to all other students showed working 1-19 hours to be significant at a confidence level of .10. The indication is that the curriculum is not so demanding that a student who must work part time cannot complete it. In fact, some work is actually beneficial. Students working 20 or more hours a week may well have a disadvantage due to their employment, but they can still perform at a level equal to the majority of the students.

Males versus Females

Three times as many males enrolled in the course as females. This certainly was a marked change from the time only a few years earlier when as many as half of the students were female. Fortunately, the male to female ratios were not as severe when considered by academic major as shown in Figure 3. Note that 39% of the computer science majors were female while only 12% of the engineering majors were. Perhaps the big decreases in female students are due to low numbers of female students in other disciplines with computer specialities rather than just a drop in computer science majors.

In all cases, a larger percentage of the males successfully completed the course than females. Of those who did not withdraw, 71% of the males were successful and 62% of the females were, a difference that is significant at a .10 level. This study indeed supports the findings of Campbell [2] that sex by itself can be a good predictor of success in computer science.

A further investigation of specific grades in the course showed the female ranges to be skewed rather than normally distributed. Twenty percent of the females made A compared to 16% of the males. A far smaller percentage of the females made B's and C's than did the males. This suggests that although the number of female majors may not be significantly lower, the overall quality might be. Only the very best females or those with little chance of success are entering the curriculum. Efforts must be made to attract the "average" female student.

Comparisons by Academic Major

The course involved in this study was the first course for computer science majors. Only 24% of the actual number of students enrolled were computer science majors. 57% of the students were electrical engineering students pursuing the computer science option. The remaining 19% of the students were part of a wide range of academic programs, with most of the major undergraduate curricula represented.

Of those students who completed the course, 63% of the computer science majors were successful and 70% of the engineers. A breakdown of success by academic major is shown in Figure 4. It is noteworthy that larger percentages of other groups, particularly mathematics, quantitative business analysis, and education majors were much more successful. In fact, the computer science group's success rate was one of the lowest for any group.

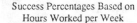

Success Percentages Based on
Hours Worked per Week

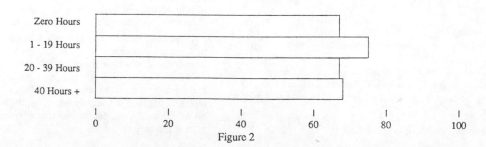

Figure 2

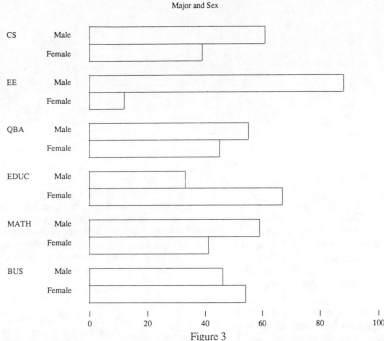

Enrollment Percentages Based on
Major and Sex

Figure 3

The success rate of the education majors was particularly encouraging. 80% of the education majors, a group that was largely female, were able to handle the course. At the university studied, success in the first course is normally an excellent indicator of ability to complete the entire curriculum.

A recent study [8] showed that high schools were able to staff the lower level introductory courses now offered but had grave problems offering the more advanced courses needed in the future. The draft report of the ACM Task Force on the Core of Computer Science [3], which lays the foundation for the next major college computer science curriculum, recommends that students enter computer science degree programs with some programming skills, presumably learned in the high school. While the report is unspecific about the pre-requisite level of skills required, one might safely infer from the remainder of the report that the CS-1 content is at least the minimum standard.

A new breed of high school computer science teacher is clearly mandated for the future. Often, education majors have suffered from a poor reputation as to their academic ability and career choice. The education majors in this study were among the most outstanding students. These individuals and others like them can provide the fundamental computer science courses that will be needed in the near future as computer science matures in the high school. College computer science departments must continue to actively encourage rather that discourage prospective teachers if they move ahead with plans to intrust the most basic part of a student's education in computer science to the high school.

Comparison by Class Year

Researchers theorized that freshmen, due to their lack of academic maturity, might not have developed the study skills and work habits needed to successfully complete a rigorous computer science course. This theory was indeed disproved by this study.

An examination of the success rates of the students who completed the course as showed that the freshmen were far more successful than any other group. A breakdown of success by class year is shown in Figure 5. 78% of the freshmen were successful compared to only 58% of the juniors. A comparison of the freshmen percentage to the other undergraduates showed the characteristic freshman class year to be significant at a confidence level of .05.

Several possible explanations can be found for this phenomenon. Due to the rather severe mathematics pre-requisites, only the very best freshmen students can take the course in the freshman year. Given this fact, the success rate of the freshmen who did enroll is not so surprising.

Most students who are pursuing a degree which requires this course must take mathematics in the freshman year. They should be able to enroll in the course no later than their sophomore year unless they encounter difficulty in mathematics, which has also been linked strongly to success in computer science. Enrollment in the course in later class years is usually a sign that some difficulty has been encountered or is expected with the course. It appears that there may well be an inverse relationship between success and class year. That is, the longer a student waits to take the course, the worse his chances are.

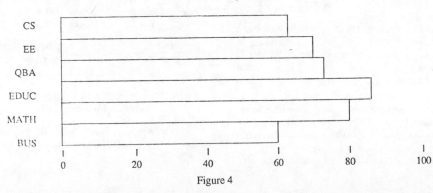

Success Percentages Based on Major

Figure 4

197

Success Percentages Based on Class Year

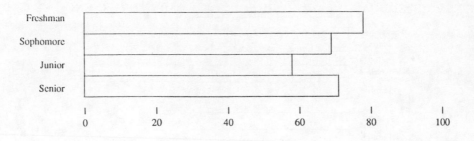

Figure 5

Conclusions

A study of a group of college computer science students provided insights into factors that contributed towards the success of the students. A major factor for success in this course which traditionally has no stated computer science pre-requisite was prior computer science coursework. 70% of the students arrived with prior experience, making it difficult for some students who were novice computer users to compete.

Investigators wonder how many academically talented students from rural areas which did not offer high school computer science were discouraged by their initial experience. The era is not far away in which entering students will be tested for computer science proficiency as they are in mathematics and English and then channeled into remedial levelling courses if indicated.

High school computer science as well as prior college computer science coursework were found to be significant factors in the success rate. Although no difference was found between the success rates of the group with high school coursework and the group with college coursework, the indication is that high school computer science will continue to play an important role in readiness for the college curriculum.

Students who worked while going to school were able to compete favorably with the non-workers. The group of students working part time up to 20 hours performed significantly better than all the others. It may be that the organizational skills learned by a student having to manage a job and school are an asset in a computer science curriculum.

As a group, a significantly larger percentage of the males were successful that the females. The females were found at the extreme ends of the spectrum; they either did very well or poorly.

Students in majors other than computer science were able to successfully complete the course as well as or better than the computer science majors in most instances. In the last few years, many curricula have added computer science options to their degree programs. Students who wish to work with computers now have many other degree options besides pursuing a major in computer science. It appears that a number of students who made up the bulk of the undergraduate computer science major pool are now in more inter-disciplinary programs. If this pattern continues, computer science departments can expect to be called on to fill a bigger service role to meet the special needs of these students.

By grouping all of the factors studied in this project together, one can draw a composite picture of the student who is most likely to succeed in the beginning computer science course. The student would be a male freshman who works part time and is majoring in a technical curriculum. He would have taken at least one programming course in high school.

Many computer science departments are now faced with a situation they have not encountered before. Only a few years ago, enrollments were skyrocketing and departments had to devise creative procedures to control enrollment. Now, computer science departments are seeing rapidly declining numbers and find that they must compete with other departments for students.

Undergraduate recruiting for computer science programs may become a common activity on most campuses. Faculty may actively try to identify those beginning students who are undecided or unsure about their major and recruit them into the computer science program. Hopefully, insights like those described in this and other papers can assist university personnel in identifying good candidates and help departments maintain strong, healthy undergraduate programs.

References

[1] Buthcher, D. F. and W. A. Muth. "Predicting performance in an introductory computer science course." *Communications of the ACM*. Vol. 28, No. 3(March 1985), 263-268.

[2] Campbell, P. F. and G. P. McCabe. "Predicting the success of freshmen in a computer science major." *Communications of the ACM*. Vol. 27, No. 11 (Nov. 1984), 1108-1113.

[3] Denning, P. J., Comer, D. E, Gries, D., Mulder, M. C., Tucker, A., Turner, A. J., and Young, P. R. "Draft Report of the ACM Task Force on the Core of Computer Science," Feb. 1988.

[4] Franklin, Roger. "What Academic Impact are High School Computing Courses Having on the Entry-Level Computer Science Curriculum?" *SIGCSE Bulletin*. Vol. 19, No. 1 (Feb. 1987), 253-256.

[5] Konvalina, John, Stanley A. Wileman, and Larry J. Stephens. "Math Proficiency : A Key to Success for Computer Science Students." *Communications of the ACM*. Vol. 26, No. 5 (May 1983), 377-382.

[6] Nowaczyk, R. H., A. C. Connor, D. E. Stevenson, E. O. Hare. "Developing a Prediction Equation for Success in Introductory Level Computer Science Courses : A First Attempt." *Proceedings of NECC '86 National Educational Computing Conference*. San Diego, California, June 4-6, 1986, 271-276.

[7] Ramberg, Peter. " A New Look at an Old Problem : Keys to Success for Computer Science Students." *SIGCSE Bulletin*. Vol. 18, No. 3(Sept. 1986), 36-39.

[8] Taylor, Harriet G. and Cathleen A. Norris. "Retraining - the Key for Quality Pre-college Computer Science Education : A Survey of State Educational Computing Coordinators." *SIGCSE Bulletin*. Vol. 20, No. 1(Feb. 1988), 215-218.

[9] Werth, Laurie H. "Predicting Student Performance in a Beginning Computer Science Class." *SIGCSE Bulletin*. Vol. 18, No. 1(Feb. 1986), 138-143.

[10] Walpole, Ronald E. *Introduction to Statistics*. New York, The Macmillan Company, 1968, 196-199.

[11] Whipkey, Kenneth L. "Identifying Predictors of Programming Skill." *SIGCSE Bulletin*. Vol. 16, No. 4 (Dec. 1984), 36-42.

INSERVICE EDUCATION OF HIGH SCHOOL COMPUTER SCIENCE TEACHERS

James Kiper, Department of Systems Analysis
Bill Rouse, Department of Teacher Education
Douglas Troy, Department of Systems Analysis
Miami University, Oxford, Ohio

Abstract

This paper describes an inservice retraining program for high school computer science teachers Since computer science teacher certification is a recent development, most of these teachers were trained in another field. This project consisted of a sequence of courses which taught the core principles of computer science to these teachers.

1. Introduction

The United States urgently needs strong high school computer science programs. Our economy and the technological level of our society depend upon a continuing supply of high quality scientists, mathematicians, engineers, computer scientists, and technicians, all equipped with a solid foundation in computer science. This supply depends upon a strong computer science program that begins in high school.

Although many entering college freshmen have had some experience with microcomputers and BASIC programming, their high school courses have largely ignored structured programming and problem solving and they lack the skills required to use computers effectively in the study of these disciplines. Many enter college with poor programming and problem solving habits that are difficult to break. Because of this condition, colleges must spend the freshman year teaching the fundamentals of structured programming, problem solving, data structures, and program design, which serve as a foundation in computer programming for these students. These fundamentals, that now constitute the course of study for the freshman year in college, should be taught at the high school level, and they can be taught there, provided the high school teachers have appropriate training.

The primary ingredient of a strong high school program is a cadre of highly qualified classroom teachers. Such teachers are needed in order to produce college-bound graduates prepared to enter rigorous programs in various fields and to produce non-college-bound graduates prepared for technical training and entrance into the workforce. Such teachers are needed to provide professional leadership in curriculum development and program implementation.

Ideally, the computer science expertise of entry level teachers should approximate that of entry level practitioners. Not only is this level of expertise necessary to enable teachers to develop the type of high school curriculum that we have indicated, but it is important for instilling self confidence on the part of the teachers and for developing a reputation of respect on the part of parents and the general public.

© 1989 ACM 0-89791-298-5/89/0002/0199 $1.50

2. Problem Definition.

In 1985 an interdepartmental committee on Computer Science Education was organized between the Department of Teacher Education and the Department of Systems Analysis. This action resulted in the establishment of a Project Planning Group composed of representatives of local public and private school systems, local industry, and faculty members from both University departments. A conference of chief administrative officers of local school systems and a questionnaire circulated among computer science teachers indicated a serious need to strengthen high school computer science programs. The questionnaires were mailed to 192 high schools in southwestern Ohio and a response of precisely 50% was obtained. Of the 96 schools responding all but 4 offered some form of computer science course. Virtually every school responding taught BASIC in some form or other. However, based upon analysis of the textbooks used, only 18% were introducing their students to structured programming and logical problem solving. Only 17% were offering an advanced course to prepare students for the College Board's Advanced Placement Examination in computer science. Approximately 85% of the respondents indicated that at least part of their knowledge of computer science was obtained through self-teaching. We believe that the situation in southwestern Ohio is fairly typical of conditions across the United States in general.

As of July 1987, the State Department of Teacher Education and Certification in Columbus has been implementing newly created standards for certification of computer science teachers. With respect to the subject matter component, the standards merely specify that an approved program must contain at least 30 semester hours of work in the content of the subject, with the actual choice of courses determined by the institution, subject to review by a visiting State team every five years. Thus, the selection of computer science courses for the teacher training program at Miami University was left to its faculty.

At the time we initiated the program we recognized that it would be at least four years before the first of these well prepared graduates would be ready to enter the profession, and several years after that before the program would grow to the point of producing graduates in any significant number. In the meantime not only would there be an absence of well trained computer science teachers to offer strong high school programs, but there would be an absence of well trained computer science teachers to help us train these new student teachers. Teachers with strong computer science competence are needed to serve as exemplary role models for teacher candidates and to supervise their clinical training and student teaching assignments. We were faced with a situation in which the student teachers would know more computer science than their supervising teachers.

To make matters worse, the State Department of Education had elected to "grandfather" all high school teachers who happened to be teaching a computer programming course as of January 1987. This resulted in a situation in which certain teachers who had minimal formal training (e.g., a one week workshop at a local computer store) were granted full computer science certification because they were teaching a programming class in BASIC, while other teachers who had completed several substantive college level computer science courses were denied such certification because in January 1987 their teaching assignment happened to be temporarily composed entirely of mathematics courses. Thus there were many high school teachers who possessed computer science certification, but as far as we knew, none who had preparation and knowledge comparable to that specified by our new teacher education program.

However, there was a core of these certified teachers in southwestern Ohio who were personally committed to the improvement of computer science in their schools and who had been attempting over the years to improve their competence by means of workshops, courses, and self study. These teachers recognized the need for stronger programs as well as the shortcomings of their formal college course work, which was completed before computer science courses were available to teachers. They needed and desired an organized program of inservice education in order to attain their full potential as computer science teachers.

The Project Planning Group developed a proposal to the Ohio Board of Regents for a grant of money to Miami University from funds from the federal Economic Security Education Act to support a program named The High School Computer Science Enhancement Project. The project was funded by the Board in the amount of $35,320 with additional support of $59,965 in cost sharing funds from Miami University, the General Electric Company, and several local public and private school systems. The grant provided for the tuition, textbooks, and mileage reimbursement for up to 30 high school computer science teachers to attend a series of four courses in computer science and computer science education at Miami University.

3. Purpose.

The goal of the Project Planning Group was to enhance computer science programs in southwestern Ohio by providing inservice education to the group of teachers described above. It was expected that such inservice education would result in:

1. An immediate benefit to high school students who are now in school and who cannot wait until preservice teachers are graduated from college and certified by the State.

2. A long range benefit to high school students of the future who will have the opportunity to study in a high school environment of expanded and improved computer science courses.

3. A long range benefit to college bound students who will be better prepared for their college courses in the scientific, mathematic, and business programs.

4. A benefit to colleges who will be able to improve their offerings in computer science because of better prepared freshmen.

5. A benefit to teacher education programs and their students by having more capable teachers to supervise student teaching and other clinical activities.

4. Participants.

Participants were selected on the basis of their potential for exerting leadership in the development of computer science in the public and private schools of southwestern Ohio. Factors contributing to the acceptance of applicants included (1) the likelihood that the applicant would be able to apply what was learned in the project as indicated by subjects normally taught and possession of State teaching certification in computer science, (2) the applicant's interest in self improvement as indicated by a history of self study and enrollment in courses and workshops on computer science, and (3) indication of plans and interest for upgrading and extending the computer science curriculum in the applicant's home school and school system. Eight of the 30 positions were reserved for priority appointment of persons of racial minorities, and 15 were reserved for priority appointment of women.

There were 51 applicants for the 30 positions. In order to compensate for anticipated attrition during the project, 33 participants were selected, with 28 entering with the first course and 5 (who did not need the first course) entering with the second. Table 1 shows the composition of the group at the beginning and at the end of Courses 1, 2, 3, and 4

Course		Men	Women	Total
1	Beginning	16(0)*	12(0)*	28
	End	13(0)	11(2)	24
2	Beginning	14(0)	11(2)	25
	End	12(0)	11(2)	23
3	Beginning	14(0)	11(2)	25
	End	11(0)	11(2)	22
4	Beginning	13(0)	11(2)	24
	End	13(0)	11(2)	24

* The number of minority participants is shown in parentheses.

Table 1. Compositions of the four courses.

Attrition was attributed to several factors. Reasons given by participants for dropping out of courses or for not beginning the next course in the sequence included inability to keep up with course assignments due to job pressures, inability to keep up with course assignments due to family pressures, serious illness of the participant, and serious illness in the immediate family.

5. Curriculum

The four courses offered were:

Course 1.   Structured Programming and Computer Algorithms (using Pascal)

Course 2   Data Structures (using Pascal)

Course 3.   Microcomputer Systems, Architecture, and Assembly Language

Course 4.   Instructional Sequences, Topics, and Materials of High School Computer Science

The instructors of the first three courses were members of the Department of Systems Analysis and the instructor of the last course was a member of the Department of Teacher Education, who also served as project director.

Course 1, Structured Programming and Computer Algorithms, was given on Saturday mornings during the spring semester of 1988. The class met for approximately three hours in each session. The course was a fairly standard introduction to programming similar to CS1 in the ACM curriculum. The textbook used was Oh! Pascal!, by Doug Cooper and Michael Clancy. The course objectives were to help the participants:

1. To master some fundamentally sound methods of problem solving.

2. To advance their levels of skill at solving problems of increasing difficulty.

3. To learn the syntax and semantics of the Pascal programming language including control structures, standard and user defined data types and functions, advanced input and output, procedures, etc.

4. To learn some elements of good style in the construction of computer programs, and to begin to appreciate why these elements are necessary.

5. To master some of the standard algorithms used in numerical and non-numerical applications.

The only major component of Pascal which was not covered in this course was the pointer data type. The students completed 10 Pascal programs which varied from a simple numerical calculation to a file handling program.

Since training in programming was to be a major emphasis of this program, one of the most important decisions was the hardware and software to be used. Since the participants were to commute over rather long distances, the use of the university's computers was unreasonable. There was no uniform hardware or software system to which all of the participants had access. For Courses 1 and 2 the decision was made to let each participant choose the compiler and computer to use for program assignments. This permitted each participants to gain more experience on the machine and compiler which were used for teaching. Some time was spent in class explaining some of the idiosyncrasies of some of the commonly used systems. (The two most used systems were the Apple IIe with Apple Pascal and the IBM PC or clone with TurboPascal.)

Courses 2 and 3 were given in the summer in one five week term. All participants were enrolled concurrently in both courses. Each course met four days per week, 105 minutes per day.

Course 2, Data Structures, used the textbook, Introduction to Data Structures with Pascal, by Naps and Singh. The objectives for this course were to help participants:

1. To design and use internal data structures for better software design and implementation.

2. To design complex and hybrid data structures needed for specific and more advanced applications and simulate these data structures using data structures provided by the language

3. To become capable of analyzing and evaluating the efficiency and effectiveness of various data structures and algorithms.

4. To master some of the standard algorithms for manipulation of data structures.

The students were assigned four Pascal programs to complete outside of class to provide some experience in applying the data structures and algorithms described in class. Some class time each week was devoted to work in one of the university's PC laboratories.

Course 3, Microcomputer Systems, Architecture, and Assembly Language Programming, was a study of computer architecture with an emphasis on microcomputers. The objectives of this course were to help the participants develop the ability:

1. To describe alternative computer system implementations as seen by the programmer.

2. To describe the ways that the architectural components of the computer interact.

3. To describe the inter-relationships between a computer's architecture and the machine language executed by that computer.

4. To describe the relationship between the assembly language, the assembler, and the machine language.

5. To describe the relationship between machine languages and higher level languages.

Because of the differences among microcomputer architectures, among the instruction sets of their central processing units, and among the assemblers written for these different microcomputers, it was deemed necessary to focus programming assignments on a common hardware and software system. The Apple IIe was selected as the hardware system, because it is the most commonly used system in the high schools of our locality. The assembler selected was part of the Apple Assembly Language training package distributed by the Minnesota Educational Computing Consortium (MECC). This package includes a booklet of lessons and reference material along with software that.includes an editor, an assembler, a graphic machine language simulator, and a step and trace debugger. Each student was given a copy of this package . The textbook used was Programming the 6502 by Rodney Zaks. Additional readings were assigned from computer architecture texts and computing journals in order to illustrate alternative computer architectures. This course was taught in a micro computer laboratory so that the students could enter and execute programs in class. This, along with the MECC simulator, was a useful aid to the students.

Course 4, Instructional Sequences, Topics, and Materials of High School Computer Science was given on Saturday mornings during the fall semester. The class met for approximately three hours in each session. No textbook was used for this course, but readings included the ACM's recommended guidelines for high school computer science courses, the College Board's course guide and course description for the advanced placement computer science course, and selected articles from professional journals. The course objectives were:

1. To introduce participants to the topic and techniques of computer based instrumentation as a subject of study for high school students.

2. To help participants develop model curricula for high school computer science programs, including course outlines and effective units, exercises, and programming assignments.

Budgetary and other practical constraints of time limited the program to four courses. These four course were chosen as the four which best satisfied the goals of the program. The first two courses, Structured Programming and Computer Algorithms and Data Structures, were obvious choices in light of the fact that almost all of the participants were primarily experienced in BASIC. Several knew no Pascal; others could write a simple Pascal program; and a very small minority were relatively proficient in Pascal. In most school districts in which the participants work, there is either a Pascal course offered or one on the horizon.

The topics for the remaining two courses presented more difficult choices. The decision could have been made to pursue some special topic more completely. For example, courses in operating systems, data communications, artificial intelligence, data base design, or software engineering could have been selected. However, the choice of computer architecture with assembly language seemed to be more basic. This course helps provide a foundation for further study and supports an understanding necessary to teach the lower level courses. It also gave the participants an introduction to the knowledge necessary to interface microcomputers to other devices. This is a skill that may prove valuable to a school district, especially in the inclusion of computer based instrumentation in science classes.

The fourth course served as a capstone to this program by providing the participants with many ideas about methods of applying what they had learned in the previous courses and by serving as a means of curriculum development for strengthening and extending computer science programs in the local school systems.

6. Problems Arising During the Project.

This program has been labeled a success by both the participants and the teachers. However, it was not without some problems. The most glaring problem was an intrinsic one - the diversity of the participants. As in any group with this many people there was a difference in the intellectual abilities of the participants. This difference was particularly apparent in the

amount of effort necessary to complete the programming assignments outside of class. The programs assigned in Course 1 were similar to those assigned to freshmen in an introduction to programming course. A frequent complaint from a segment of this class was that the programming assignments were too time consuming.

Even though all were high school teachers involved in the teaching of programming at that level, there was no uniformity in their experience or training. The majority were trained and certified in mathematics. The second largest group was composed of those trained in one of the sciences. Some were certified in English; one in Home Economics. (The diversity of the training speaks to the need for teachers. ertified in computer science.) One participant had a consulting business in addition to his teaching position. Others had only recently begun to learn to program.

These diversities of background and abilities were amplified by the diversity in hardware and compilers that the participants used to complete the out-of-class assignments. Those members of the class who were dependent upon the Apple IIe with the Apple Pascal compiler found themselves at a disadvantage, particularly when compared to those using TurboPascal. This disadvantage arose because the primitive architecture and slow speed of the Apple IIe made compiling and debugging on that system arduous.

The travel necessary for the participants to attend class meetings was often exhausting and time consuming. The amount of travel necessary varied from forty to two hundred miles per round trip. Despite the travel, attendance in the courses was outstanding. This distance also exacerbated the difficulty of the out-of-class programming assignments. Many programming problems, which required hours of labor to solve, could have been resolved in a matter of minutes with help from the professor. A few students used the telephone to obtain help with programming problems although this was not optimal since the professor did not have a copy of the errant program.

Courses 1 and 4 were given during the school years while the participants were involved in teaching their normal high school loads. (Released time is much less common at the high school than at the college level.) The amount of work outside the classroom which was necessary in Course 1 to acquire the necessary programming skills made this a traumatic semester for the participants.

Courses 2 and 3 were given concurrently in a five week summer term. This created another intense period for the participants. Course 2, Data Structures, required significant outside time because of the programming. The professor attempted to ameliorate this somewhat by devoting some class time each week to work in a PC lab.

Course 3, Microcomputer Systems, Architecture, and Assembly Language, required the participants to master some very unfamiliar concepts. This was the first time that many participants had been exposed to the internal working of a computer. This was a vital, albeit difficult, experience for them. Additionally, there is no text that combines a general introduction to computer architecture with 6502 assembly language.

Course 3 had the added problem of using the Apple IIe as the hardware base. The nature of the course required the use of a uniform architecture by all participants. The Apple IIe seemed to be the obvious choice since many school districts use this machine. However, this machine was not familiar to all participants. Some would have preferred to learn about the architecture of the machine used by their school system. (The most common alternative was the IBM PC.)

There is a disparity in the expectation of the type of course and the amount of outside work necessary for a traditional graduate level course and a typical inservice workshop for high school teachers. This difference required an adjustment in the expectations of both the participants and the professors. (This was especially true for the professors from the System Analysis Department since they have not regularly taught this type of inservice training course.) It was necessary for the professors to make a conscious effort to limit the amount of outside work. In addition, the nature of adult education required the professors to make adjustments. Many of the students seem to require a longer period of time to grasp concepts and skills than younger college students. However, adults seem to have a greater perseverance, and are very conscientious in their work.

7. Conclusions.

Despite these problems, the immediate reaction of the participants and the professors in this effort has been positive. Both groups felt that the goals of the project were achieved The participant teachers have acquired greater skills and an increased level of confidence in those skills. The professors have enjoyed the contacts that they have made with their colleagues at the high school level. They feel that this program will, in the long run, improve the quality of student that they receive from these high schools.

The increased expertise of the teachers and the improved programs and courses that can be expected to develop will enhance these local schools systems as sites for nurturing the university's student teachers.

Another benefit of this program is the increased cooperation between the Teacher Education Department and the Systems Analysis Department. Neither could have carried the program individually. The Teacher Education Department was the source of contacts with the local school districts and high school teachers; the Systems Analysis Department was the source of the technical expertise in the computer science area. This effort has resulted in a synergism which will make both departments better.

8. Future Plans.

This program was funded for one year. Additional funding will be sought to continue this program on a yearly basis. The need for such a program is still strong and will remain strong until the number of teachers certified in computer science has increased to the demand. We will evaluate and analyze the differences between the results of pre-test and post-test given in two of all courses. We plan to circulate a newsletter among the participants and other high school computer science teachers. This newsletter will be used as a vehicle for communicating ideas, methods, and resources which are useful to the high school computer science teacher.

9. Bibliography.

Apple Computer Inc., Apple II Reference Manual, Cupertino, California, 1981.

Brink, James and Richard Spillman, Computer Architecture and Vax Assembly Language Programming, Benjamin Cummings, Menlo Park, Ca., 1987, pp.7-14.

College Entrance Examination Board, "Advanced Placement Course Description: Computer Science", CEEB, 1986.

College Entrance Examination Board, "Teacher's Guide to Advanced Placement Courses in Computer Science", CEEB, 1983.

Cooper, Doug and Michael Clancy, Oh! Pascal, second edition, W.W. Norton, New York, N.Y., 1982.

Department of Teacher Education and Certification, "Teacher Education and Certification Standards (Effective July 1, 1987)", State Board of Education, State of Ohio, Columbus, Oh., 1985.

Eckhouse, Richard and Robert Morris, Microcomputer Systems, second edition, Prentice-Hall, Englewood Cliffs, NJ, 1979, pp.17-41.

Grehan, Richard and Jane Tazelaar, "What They Did Wrong", Byte, McGraw-Hill, May 1988, pp. 239-248.

Minnesota Educational Computing Consortium, "Apple Assembly Language (Version1)", MECC, Minneapolis, Mn.

Naps, Thomas and Bhagat Singh, Introduction to Data Structures with Pascal, West Publishing Co., St. Paul, Mn., 1986.

Poirot, James L., Harriet G. Taylor, Cathleen A. Norris, "Retraining Teachers to Teach High School Computer Science", Communications of the ACM, Vol. 31, No. 7, July 1988, pp. 912-917.

Stallings, William, Computer Organization and Architecture, Prenticc-Hall, Englewood Cliffs, NJ, 1987, pp.20-48.

Wilson, Pete, "The CPU Wars", Byte, McGraw-Hill, May 1988, pp.213-234.

Zaks, Rodney, Programming the 6502 (Fourth Edition), Sybex, Berkeley, Ca, 1983.

Laying the Foundations for Computer Science

Leonard A. Larsen
Department of Computer Science
University of Wisconsin - Eau Claire
P.O. Box 4004
Eau Claire, WI   54702-4004

ABSTRACT

This paper has three primary goals:

1. Stimulate the discussion of possible skills which might be incorporated into the K-12 curriculum in order to provide students with a foundation for the study of computer science.

2. Stimulate the discussion of strategies for incorporating into the K-12 curriculum the fundamental skills needed by students pursuing topics in the computer science discipline.

3. Present a possible set of fundamental skills.

INTRODUCTION

Consider the various subjects that are taught from kindergarten through 12th grade, such as English, history, mathematics, and sciences. In each case it would be assumed the topics taught are based on the expertise of teachers and scholars in that discipline with the following goals:

1. The skills learned will aid future development in the particular discipline.

2. The skills learned will aid each individual to relate to society and life. The skill serves as an end in itself.

An unfortunate exception to this process and these goals being set is computer science. Computer scientists have not developed a set of skills that can be taught during the K-12 learning years that will accomplish these same two goals. Perhaps the new-

ness of computer science is a primary reason this has not been done. The goal of this paper is to encourage computer scientists to develop a set of skills and curricular strategies that can be presented to students.

One way to develop conclusions is to ask questions:

1. In what ways have computer scientists contributed to the concepts taught during the K-12 years?

2. Do computer scientists currently recommend specific skills (other than mathematics) that should be taught during the K-12 school years?

3. Is there a body of foundation material for the discipline of computer science?

If the answer to question 3 is "yes", there are two more questions to be asked:

4. Would a knowledge of computer science foundation material benefit those who plan to make computer science a career?

5. Would a knowledge of computer science foundation material be beneficial to other areas?

If a reasonable percentage of individuals in the computer science community believe that the predominant answer to question #1 is "very little", to question #2 is "NO", and to questions #3-5 is "YES", then the computer science community needs to spend time formalizing the nature of this body of knowledge and attempting to devise strategies so this body of knowledge can be presented in a reasonable, incremental fashion during the K-12 years.

PRELIMINARY INDICATORS

Several factors suggest that this topic be pursued:

1. Entering college students frequently come from a high school background with three or four years of high school mathematics, possibly at least one computer programming course and yet find that they can not develop a reasonable algorithm to solve a problem.

2. For many years, the University of Wisconsin - Eau Claire has offered courses in BASIC and Pascal programming for high school teachers. Upwards of 90% of these competent teachers experience difficulty in developing an algorithm.

3. A number of articles [1,2,3,6] in recent years have discussed predictors of success in entry level college programming courses.

4. During this same period at least one article [5] has been written which discusses the use of computers to teach problem solving.

In the case of the students and high school teachers, the major problem is not the syntax of the language. While neither group is perfect in learning the syntactic elements of the language, both groups have the capability of producing programs that are free of syntax errors. The major difficulty is one of producing a reasonable algorithm, since both groups tend to use a trail and error development strategy.

CURRENT STATE OF AFFAIRS

Requests for information regarding the use of computers in K-12 were sent to 42 states for which a person with computer education responsibilities could be identified. At the time of this writing 15 states have responded.

Out of these responses, two indicated that they currently did not have a state-wide program involving computers in education, 11 have state programs involving computer literacy in terms of the awareness of computers and/or the use of relatively simple application programs, and 11 have state programs involving problem solving and/or programming.

While the level of quality of the state-wide programs were quite impressive, two ideas came to mind:

1. The tremendous diversity of the programs tended to imply the absence of a set of well thought out national guidelines.

2. None of the states addressed the question of foundation skills/concepts as they are presented here.

THE FUNDAMENTAL CONTRIBUTION OF COMPUTER SCIENCE

Consider the school subjects mentioned at the beginning of this paper. Each of these disciplines contribute to our total education. Where would we be without a knowledge of English and our ability to communicate, science and our understanding of the physical world around us, history and a sense of our past, social science and an understanding human interaction, mathematics and our ability to survive in a world of numbers?

Computer science has something to contribute as well. This contribution can be called problem solving. While teaching the course for high school teachers, it was found that the understanding of the term "problem solving" by high school science and mathematics teachers differed from the understanding of the same term by computer scientists. As used by the teachers, problem solving tended to involve problems with a single goal with subgoals which were tightly coupled to the primary goal. The problems associated with the algorithm development of a computer program will have a heavy emphasis on subgoals which tend to be loosely coupled (having independent solutions) to the primary goal.

As a result of a discussion in one of these classes, the term "process solving" began to be used to describe the development of algorithms for computer programs. Teaching process solving has become one of the more important objectives of computer science in the liberal arts setting.

Earlier it was mentioned that a number of articles have been written which attempt to determine predictors for success in programming courses. Rather than talking about the predictors, it is time that we begin to look at the issues involved and develop a list of skills that can be developed, potentially independent of any computer use, during the K-12 learning years. The results of process solving exist in the schools, but unfortunately the students are not asked to participate in developing most of the algorithms.

Consider an example of a high school student who was required to write a term paper involving the Holocaust for an eleventh grade English class. The instructor indicated that on certain days various stages needed to be completed. The teacher apparently did not discuss the development of these stages in this process, yet the discussion of that algorithm would have been a valuable learning experience. A student in chemistry needs to be able to look at an algorithm for an experiment, to be able to properly interpret the algorithm, and to write up a report of the process and the results. Again, it really involves process solving.

The development of a set a process solving skills would help the student understand the term paper process or the experiment process. Granted that these examples represent rather static algorithms, yet the discussion of process solving in a wide variety of disciplines may enable students to transfer process solving skills beyond the confines of the disciplines under which the discussions take place.

One of the points of this paper is that we should develop an incremental curriculum involved with process solving. In its generic form, the concepts of process solving are not just topics which help individuals understand computers, but topics that would help a student develop the process of writing a term paper, handle a chemistry experiment, as well as write a computer program.

THE ELEMENTS OF PROCESS SOLVING

As a starting point for discussion, an initial set of elements that make up process solving will be provided:

1. Problem solving

In a 1985 published work [4], Polson and Jeffries analyzed four different problem solving programs. The authors indicate that research supporting these programs is inadequate. SIGCSE or some other ACM group should support efforts to research these programs or to help develop some new problem solving programs. Following such research, we should support attempts to include problem solving education in the K-12 curriculum.

2. Tasking

In dealing with a large process, an individual must be able to divide that process into smaller components. In the case of the English paper example, the instructor divided the project into various components. While some discussions of problem solving include some subtasking concepts, process solving requires a much higher level of skill development for these concepts.

In dealing with tasking, the individual must have some idea of those things that must be available in order to successfully complete the task and some idea of the nature of the expected results. In computer programming this process is one of determining the parameters that are to be used in a procedure.

One of the tasks in the English paper example was that of generating note cards. The student started this task with a knowledge of the topic to be written and a set of references that had been obtained. The result of this task was a set of note cards containing references and comments regarding concepts associated with the topic.

3. Sequencing

Any process (or subprocess) is made up of a sequence of steps. The individual must learn to put these steps in a logical and reasonable order.

In the early elementary grades, students are frequently asked to look at a story and describe the order of events. An extension of this would be to ask that students themselves provide an order to a set of events.

4. Decisional structuring

The description of most processes will involve some sort of decision making. The students need to learn to communicate the nature and need for these decisions.

One of the tasks in the English paper would be to revise it. This could involve potential revision of the length of the paper. There are perhaps three choices for the student: The paper is longer than it should be, the paper is shorter than it should be, or it is of reasonable length. In the first two cases, the student would need to take some corrective action.

5. Iterative structuring

There are many times when a process description will necessitate repetition. Individuals need to learn to communicate the nature of the iteration as well as the method of terminating the iteration.

The English paper again provides an example. The student will continue to write note cards until he/she has exhausted the references.

Rather than studying predictors of programming course success, perhaps a study would be in order to see to what levels the five skill areas just mentioned correlate as predictors. The initial feeling is that the first three skill areas, those of problem solving, tasking, and sequencing, are primary skills and that the last two skills, those of decisional and iterative structuring, are secondary but still useful skills.

Assuming a positive correlation of skills to programming success, who would benefit from a knowledge of the skills? First, the students who plan to pursue some level of computer programming competency would benefit. This would include those that plan to major in some computer discipline (computer science, computer engineering) as well as students of other disciplines who plan to write application programs associated with that discipline.

In addition, since most individuals will face some form of process solving in every day life, even students who never plan to write a computer program will be helped to handle the complex processes of life through the development of the five skills.

At the beginning of this section it was indicated that this set of elements represented a starting point. While the educational community might find an alternative set of elements, it is firmly believe that the elements listed are of critical importance and should be included in any set.

THE STAGES OF DEVELOPMENT
(A POSSIBLE K-12 CURRICULUM?)

In what follows, items dealing with skills of tasking, sequencing, decision structuring and iterative structuring will be mentioned. The reason for this is that much work has been done in the problem solving skill area. Members of the mathematics educational community are very concerned about problem solving skills and are actively pursuing the issues involved. The computer science community should work closely with them and support their efforts to enhance the learning of the problem solving skills in the K-12 curriculum. The contention of this paper is that adequate concern and emphasis in the other skill areas is not currently present.

1. K-3

a. Continue the current practice of identifying sequencing of activities.

b. Learn to recognize decisions in stories.

c. Learn to recognize repetition in directions.

2. **4-6**

   a. Learn to develop a sequence of steps.

   b. Learn to develop steps in an activity involving decisions.

   c. Learn to develop repetition in directions.

3. **7-8**

   a. Learn to recognize subtasks in a process.

   b. Learn to recognize the information needed to accomplish a subtask.

   c. Learn to recognize the outcome(s) of the subtask.

4. **9-12**

   a. Learn to develop solutions to processes involving subtasks.

   b. Learn to identify the needed information for a subtask.

   c. Learn to specify the desired outcome(s) of a subtask.

   d. Learn to generate solutions to relatively complex processes with multiple levels of subtasks.

In dealing with recognition skills, the student should be able to pull out the ideas from a variety of written forms. In generating solutions to processes, the student should be taught the importance of clarity of communication.

The teaching of these skills should not be based on a particular subject, but should be spread across a variety of academic disciplines. It is believed to be a mistake to talk about these skills only in mathematics or in discussions of computers. The skills should be taught in English, the social sciences and the physical sciences. If possible, it may be desirable for teachers to make process solving steps explicit so that the difficulty of transferring these process solving techniques to computer programming as well as other academic disciplines would be minimized.

CONCLUSION

While some individuals and groups may have attempted to teach some of the five skill areas mentioned earlier, a unified effort to formalize the nature of these skills and to apply these skills to those disciplines where they occur does not appear to be present. The hope is that the computer science community will discuss the ideas of this paper, develop a comprehensive curriculum for use in K-12 involving the skills presented, and map out strategies to convince the general educational community of the importance of these skills across the spectrum of primary and secondary school curricula.

REFERENCES

[1] Austin, H. S., Predictors of Pascal Programming Achievement for Community College Students, SIGCSE Bulletin, Vol. 19, Num. 1, February, 1987, 161- 164.

[2] Gathers, E., Screening Freshmen Computer Science Majors, SIGCSE Bulletin, Vol. 18, Num. 3, September, 1986, 44-48.

[3] Hostetler, T. R., Predicting Student Success in an Introductory Programming Course, SIGCSE Bulletin, Vol. 15, Num. 3, September, 1983, 40-43.

[4] Polson, P. G. and Jeffries, R., Analysis - Instruction in General Problem-Solving Skills: An Analysis of Four Approaches, in Thinking and Learning Skills, Vol. 1, Edited by Segal, J. W., Chipman, S. F., and Glaser, R., Lawrence ErlBaum Associates, Hillsdale, N.J., 1985, 417-455.

[5] Shafto, S. A. S., Programming for Learning in Mathematics and Science, SIGCSE Bulletin, Vol. 18, Num. 1, January, 1986, 296-302.

[6] Whipkey, K. L., Identifying Predictors of Programming Skill, SIGCSE Bulletin, Vol. 16, Num. 4, December, 1984, 36-42.

Ada in CS1

Leon E. Winslow and Joseph E. Lang
Computer Science Department
University of Dayton
Dayton, Ohio 45469

Abstract

As the use of Ada in commercial programming increases, it becomes more important to make an attempt to introduce it into the curriculum as early as possible. We have taught CS1 successfully using Ada by strictly concentrating on a subset of the language and through the use of a student-oriented package which enables students to begin writing programs in Ada after one lecture. A laboratory of personal computers was found to be adequate for CS1 use and students were able to write up to 2 programs per week in the course.

Introduction

The choice of a language for CS1 is crucial because that choice can either enhance or detract from the learning process [1,2]. As a language with a number of interesting features, Ada is an important candidate for the language used in CS1. Evans and Patterson have used Ada in CS1 since 1984 using the Telesoft Ada compiler running on a VAX 11/780 [17]. Furthermore, the "Recommended curriculum for CS1, 1984" mentions Pascal, PL/1 and Ada as meeting the needs of CS1 [3] and the "Recommended curriculum for CS2, 1984" seconds that recommendation while mentioning the possibility of switching to Modula-2 for CS2 [4]. Unfortunately, the size of the language and the absence of robust and fast Ada compilers [5,6] have discouraged its use in CS1 while allowing its use in Data Structures [7], Software Engineering [8] and other advanced courses [5]. This paper describes our efforts in using the Ada programming language for CS1, the difficulties we had to overcome and the modi-

fications we introduced to make that use successful. One modification in particular, the STARTER package, allows a much simpler introduction to Ada than is possible with other approaches to teaching CS1 using Ada. Our effort differed from that of Evans and Patterson in that we did not introduce the concept of the package early in the CS1 course but delayed its discussion until nearly the end of the course.

Background

We wished to use Ada to teach CS1 because it may have advantages over other languages in a teaching environment [9, 17], because it is powerful enough to be used successfully in advanced classes [5] and because it may give our students an advantage in the job market.

The advantages of Ada range from its syntax to its sophisticated software engineering orientation. One simple advantage of its syntax is that Ada uses the semicolon as a terminator rather than as a separator. (Gannon and Horning [10] have shown that errors are ten times more likely when the semicolon is used as a separator than when it is used as a terminator.) Also, all control structures and constructs are fully bracketed with "end if", "end case", "end loop", "end record" and "end NAME". The use of the "end if" has the added advantage of eliminating problems with the dangling "else." Additionally, Ada is used commercially so it is possible for students learning Ada to obtain jobs in which they can apply what they have learned immediately. Finally, the language is not case sensitive — a big advantage for the beginner.

The software engineering orientation of Ada is expressed in its support for, and encouragement of, modularity when programming in the large. This includes independently compiled procedures, functions [2, 11], packages and tasks; the packages supporting data encapsulation and the tasks supporting concurrent processing. While tasks are not discussed in CS1, there are advantages to discussing packages used for global type declarations and/or the gathering of functions and procedures into a "library" package.

As with any language, it is possible to write poorly designed Ada programs, but a student exposed to a well-chosen subset of the total language will have to make some effort to develop bad habits.

The disadvantages of Ada start with the size of the language [12, 13, 14]. Ada is massive and practically no one will ever master the whole language. It also includes complicated features such as tasks and generics. Lastly, there are no suitable CS1 textbooks designed around the Ada language.

The obvious solution to the problem of the size of the language is to ignore those parts of the language not normally covered in CS1; that is, those parts which have no equivalent in, say, Pascal. This approach cuts the language down to size [15] and has many precedents. For example, beginning calculus students never hear of the Lesbesgue integral, the logical basis of the whole calculus course. By the same token, few people are really familiar with the entire syntax of English even though most of us use it successfully every day.

The question then is what Ada features to include in the course. The answer is to use those features that are normally covered in CS1. They include:

- input/output
- calculation (assignment statements and expressions)
- decision (if and case statements)
- loops (for and while statements)
- subprograms (procedures and functions)
- data types and their declaration
    - scalars such as integer, float, text, boolean
    - composite type constructors: arrays and records.

The one new feature that must be introduced is that of the package. We discussed packages near the end of our CS1 course in the context of defining sharable data types and subtypes. In other words, the language portion of the course was at most a minor varation on the usual CS1 course using Pascal.

Those portions of Ada which are not covered in CS1 are left for later courses. For example, CS2 covers packages in depth along with generics. Packages, generics, and exceptions are covered again in still greater depth in the advanced data structures course. Tasks are covered in an advanced Ada course that may be taken after the student has had an introduction to concurrent programming. The end result is that the student learns more Ada as he/she learns more computer science [16].

After one chooses a subset of Ada to teach, there is still the problem that portions of that subset present difficul-

ties for the beginner. For example, Ada input/output requires instantiation. Since Ada is an extensible language, the answer is to design a suitable extension in which input/output is handled more easily. This is covered in detail in the next section.

The solution to the lack of textbooks was to write one. There was a time when there were no CS1 texts using Pascal; now it is hard to keep up with them. In the same way, now there is at least one CS1 book using Ada and more are undoubtedly on the way.

The STARTER Package

To ease beginners into Ada, we use a special package called STARTER which contains instantiated input/output routines for the integer, float and boolean types, a declaration of a variable-length string type called TEXT together with relational operators and input/output routines for TEXT, and declarations for three vector types: INTEGER_VECTOR, FLOAT_VECTOR, and TEXT_VECTOR. This package simplifies the life of the beginning student by making the GET and PUT procedures immediately accessible to the student. As a result, the typical beginner is writing programs after only one lecture. Defining a variable-length string type in STARTER makes it appear to the student as a primitive type rather than an array type. This allows students to treat text data the same as numerical data from the first day.

As the student progresses, the need for STARTER decreases. For example, after the student has studied vectors using the three vector types in STARTER, general arrays are introduced and the student learns how to declare arrays using the Ada type declaration facility. Singly-dimensioned arrays (vectors) then become a special case and there is no need for the vector declarations in STARTER. Note, however, that STARTER does allow a quick and meaningful introduction to the basic concept of the array without having to teach the student about type declarations first. Once the basic concept has been mastered, the general concept and its implementation cause no major problems.

If you prefer, STARTER turns Ada into a language which corresponds, statement for statement, very closely to Pascal. The result is just as easy to teach as Pascal and, in fact, the course outline resembles a standard Pascal version of CS1. The major change is the software engineering principles designed into Ada. They appear naturally as one progresses. One such principle, independent compilation of subprograms, is actually easier to teach than nested procedures and scope.

The STARTER package allowed us to circumvent some of the complication of Ada for the beginning student. It is this package facility in Ada which makes the language extensible — a very powerful feature and a great advantage in the hands of the instructor. In contrast with the approach of Evans and Patterson [17], our students write packages only near the end of CS1, and then only as a means of sharing user-defined data types between programs and subprograms. A five minute introduction to the concept and a few simple examples sufficed to teach this new concept. After this brief introduction, the students had no trouble writing such packages on their own. They seemed to accept packages as a natural solution to an obvious problem.

In short, the package facility of Ada presented us with a powerful instructional tool that was easy to teach as well.

The CS1 Laboratory

In accordance with CS1 recommendations [3], the course includes a laboratory which meets for a total of two and one-half hours in two sessions per week. The laboratory contains one personal computer for each student and the student is normally expected to complete one short exercise program in one laboratory period. There are open laboratory periods in addition to the scheduled periods for the completion of larger programs. Programs vary in length from about 10 lines (excluding comments) the first week of the semester to about 200 lines (again, excluding comments) the last week. They range from trivial programs to ones requiring three levels of subprograms and up to five subprograms, a package and a main program. Students are given a week or more to complete the longer programs.

The laboratory consists of 30 (4.77 MHz) IBM-PC's each with 640 kilobytes of main memory and a hard disk. The PC's are networked together using the JANET local area network from Watcom Systems Inc. This local area network is primarily used to provide access to a printer, so that for most purposes each PC appears to be an independent computer running under MS-DOS. The PC's run the latest version of the Janus/Ada compiler from R. R. Software, Inc. This is a validated compiler, reasonably fast (usually less than 1 minute to compile CS1 programs), robust (we never had a catastrophic failure in CS1) and it produces error messages students can understand. We have found only one bug (unusual circumstances can cause an erroneous value to be printed for a float variable when formatting is used) and one annoying "feature" (if a data error occurs for keyboard input at run-time, the input buffer is not flushed and the bad data remains around to plague subsequent runs). On the plus side, the compiler performs syntax checking before performing semantic analysis or generating code, so syntax errors are found very rapidly (usually in about 10 seconds).

We are quite happy with this system. The total "turn-around time" from the moment a student starts compilation of a bug-free program until the final executable module is produced is typically a few minutes, independent of the number of students in the lab. This compares favorably with large time-shared systems which run fast enough when lightly loaded, but always give extremely poor response when heavily loaded. Since students tend to use a computer system at the same time, either during a scheduled lab or the night before an assignment is due, we feel that this system fits the needs of CS1 nicely.

Conclusions

We have successfully taught CS1 using Ada as the introductory language. To do this, we chose a subset of Ada and then, using the extensibility of Ada, designed a package which extended this subset into a beginner-friendly version. Using this version of Ada, a course outline was developed which introduced a disciplined approach to problem solving methods using good software engineering principles. Then a text was written based on this outline. The students wrote their programs in a laboratory environment that allowed fast compilation and execution of their programs even when loaded with a full class of 30 students.

The course was taught last year to a group of 40 students in two sections. These students were compared informally to students taking introductory courses based upon Pascal and Fortran. The students learning CS1 using Ada wrote more programs (up to 22 programs per student in one section of the course and up to 28 in the other), indicating that our system was suitable for a CS1 class [18], and showed a more disciplined approach to problem solving. We feel that their programs were better designed, implemented, documented and tested than is usual for beginners.

We feel that Ada helped us achieve this improved performance by our students by allowing us to insist on the use of independently compiled modules for achieving procedural abstraction [2]. Independently compiled modules can only communicate with one another by parameter passing. When students found that their attempts to use the same variable name in different routines failed to achieve any transfer of information [11], they learned how to pass parameters properly. We feel that this feature more than anything else encourages students to structure their programs naturally into well-designed modules.

References

1. Schneider, G., The introductory programming course in computer science — ten principles, *SIGCSE Bull.*, vol. 10, 1, Feb. 1978, pp. 107-114.

2. Dijkstra, E. W., The humble programmer, *CACM*, vol. 15, 10, Oct. 1972, pp. 859-866.

3. Koffman, E. B., Miller, P. L., and Wardle, C. E., Recommended curriculum for CS1, 1984, *CACM*, vol. 27, 10, Oct. 1984, pp. 998-1001.

4. Koffman, E. B., Stemple, D., and Wardle, C. E., Recommended curriculum for CS2, 1984, *CACM*, vol. 28, 8, Aug. 1985, pp. 815-818.

5. Tam, W. C., and Erlinger, M. A., On the teaching of Ada in an undergraduate computer science curriculum, *SIGCSE Bull.*, vol. 19, 1, Feb. 1987, pp. 58-61.

6. Koffman, E. B., The case for Modula-2 in CS1 and CS2, *SIGCSE Bull.*, vol. 20, 1, Feb. 1988, pp. 49-53.

7. Feldman, M. B., *Data structures with Ada*, Reston Publishing Co., Reston, Virginia, 1985.

8. Booch, G., *Software engineering with Ada*, Benjamin/Cummings Publishing Co., Menlo Park, California, 1983.

9. Weiderman, N., and Coulter, V. W., Using Ada as an introductory programming language, *Journal of Pascal, Ada, and Modula-2*, vol. 6, 1, Jan./Feb. 1987, pp. 10-34.

10. Gannon, J., and Horning, J., Language design for programming reliability, *IEEE Transactions on Software Engineering*, vol. SE-1, 1975, pp. 179-191.

11. Levy, E. B., The case against Pascal as a teaching tool, *SIGPLAN Notices*, vol. 17, 11, Nov. 1982, pp. 39-41.

12. Hoare, C. A. R., The emperor's old clothes, *CACM*, vol. 24, 2, Feb. 1981, pp. 75-83.

13. Ledgard, H. F., and Singer, A., Scaling down Ada (Or towards a standard Ada subset), *CACM*, vol. 25, 2, Feb. 1982, pp. 121-125.

14. Wichmann, B. A., Is Ada too big? A designer answers the critics, *CACM*, vol. 27, 2, Feb. 1984, pp. 98-103.

15. Augenstein, M., Tenenbaum, A., and Weiss, G., Selecting a primary programming language for a computer science curriculum: PL/I, Pascal and Ada, *SIGCSE Bull.*, vol. 15, 1, Feb. 1983, pp. 148-153.

16. Conway, R., Gries, D., and Wortman, D. B., *Introduction to structured programming using PL/I and SP/k*, Winthrop Publishers, Cambridge, Mass., 1975.

17. Evans, H., and Patterson, W., Implementing Ada as the primary programming language, *SIGCSE Bull.*, vol. 17, 1, Feb. 1985, pp. 255-265.

18. Tharp, A. L., Selecting the "right" programming language, *SIGCSE Bull.*, vol. 14, 1, Feb. 1982, pp. 151-155.

An Ada-Based Software Engineering Course

G. Scott Owen
Department of Mathematics and Computer Science
Georgia State University
Atlanta, Georgia 30303

Abstract

Currently, many Computer Science Departments have introduced or are considering the introduction of courses in Software Engineering. At the same time many departments are considering the use of a language other than Pascal either for an entire Computer Science curriculum, or at least for some advanced courses, such as Data Structures or Software Engineering. At Georgia State University, where our program is primarily based on IBM PC compatible microcomputers, both our Data Structures and Software Engineering courses are based on Ada. In this paper we will discuss the rationale behind our choice of Ada and our experience with using Ada in the Software Engineering course.

Introduction

Some of the major complaints from industry concerning new computer science graduates are that they lack communication skills, have no experience in working in groups, and have little understanding of the complete software development experience for non-trivial programs. Georgia State University (GSU), like many other colleges, has tried to address these issues by establishing a project - oriented course in Software Engineering.

Prior Student Experience

GSU is an urban campus, located in downtown Atlanta, and has a somewhat unusual student population in that the average age of the undergraduate students is about 27 and the average age of graduate students is 30. Most of our students have either part time or full time jobs, and many are already software professionals.

All of our courses are five hour quarter courses (about 45 actual contact hours) and the Data Structures course is the third course for our students. The first two courses primarily use Pascal with 3-4 weeks of FORTRAN in the second course. In the data structures course we use Mike Feldman's text "Data Structures with Ada" [FELD85] and "Programming in Ada" by J. G. P. Barnes [BARN84]. The Data Structures course is the prerequisite for all of our advanced courses.

A second prerequisite for the Software Engineering course is a course in the Organization of Programming Languages. This course uses [PRAT84] for its primary text and [BARN84], [GEHA85], and [ROGE87] as secondary texts. For this course we assume the students have a prior knowledge of Pascal, FORTRAN, and some Ada. While proceeding through [PRAT84] the students are introduced to the C language, PROLOG, and advanced topics in Ada. Thus, when the students enter the Software Engineering course they should have had two quarters exposure to Ada and a general exposure to several other languages.

The Software Engineering Course is a required course and currently the same course is used for both senior level and graduate students (a second, advanced graduate course is planned but has not yet been implemented). Thus, the class has a mixture of undergraduates and graduate students, and as mentioned above, some of these may actually be "Software Engineers" in local businesses. This makes for rather interesting classes since the students can discuss their own "real world" experiences. While it has been suggested that there should be a two quarter Software Engineering sequence, with the first quarter covering the principles and the second quarter involving a large team project, this is not feasible in our program.

Objectives of the Software Engineering Course

The objectives of the course are to introduce the students to the rationale for using Software Engineering methods and important aspects of Software Engineering such as the software life-cycle, cost estimation, requirements analysis, specification, design, implementation, verification, validation, and maintenance. Different methodologies are presented for each of the above areas and the students participate in a team project of non-trivial size. The primary text is Software Engineering Concepts by R. Fairley [FAIR85]. A secondary text is Configuration Management by W. Babbich [BABB86] and a suggested text is The Mythical Man-Month by F. P. Brooks, Jr. There is also a reading list from the literature, which changes every quarter (Figure I). We also try to acquaint the students with current research in Software Engineering methodologies.

The basic format of the course follows [FAIR85] and the sequence of topics is that of the actual software development process. It is necessary to supplement [FAIR85] in some topics, particularly software design. The students are introduced to Object Oriented Development (OOD) [BOO87a] and [BOO87b] for Ada, and use this method for their project.

There are several objectives of the team project. The first is to give the students a somewhat realistic experience in developing a software system with complete documentation, as opposed to just writing a program as they do in most of their classes. A second objective is to have the students work in teams and to learn to cope with the associated group dynamics problems. The third objective is to improve the students' rhetoric skills, particularly in written communication.

Improving the students' writing skills is achieved in part by the students creating the documents discussed below. To further achieve this objective, the class examinations, both the midterm and the final, are take home essay examinations (limited to ten single-spaced typed pages). While specific points are not deducted for spelling or grammatical errors, the class is told that these errors influence the overall grading of the documents.

Team Project

The team project follows the guidelines in the Appendix of [FAIR85] and the deliverables include the following, which are due at different times during the quarter:

1. A **System Definition** (Product Definition and Project Plan) which includes a preliminary cost estimate
2. A **Software Requirements Specification**
3. A **Design Document** which includes a final cost estimate.
4. A **Test Plan**
5. A **User's Manual**
6. The final report

Each group's final report includes a documented, tested, and debugged program, updated versions of the original set of documents, plus the following new sections:
- a discussion of how well the project agrees with its original goals
- an analysis of how good the design is in retrospect; changes that would improve the design
- a description of how the system was tested
- an analysis of the suitability of Ada for such a system, including a discussion of how Ada helped or hindered the project

Each group must also make a presentation during the final week of classes. Each presentation covers at least the following points:
- a synopsis of the system requirements
- a demonstration of the system's behavior
- a sketch of the overall system design
- an analysis of the design (Would you use the same design if you were doing the project over? Did object-oriented design make implementation easier? Did object-oriented design make testing easier?)

Project grading is based on the following criteria:
- Quality of final report
- Quality of system design
- Programming style
- Agreement of project with original goals
- Project scope (in relation to group size)
- System operation (lack of errors and system crashes, ease of use, readability of user manual, correctness and completeness of user manual)
- Quality of presentation (organization and understandability of oral presentation, use of visual aids)

Comparison of Methodologies and Languages

We chose Ada for the course project because we felt that Ada was the best current language to illustrate Software Engineering principles. The Ada packages allow the teams to agree on the interface specifications and then each team member can implement their own packages. Many of the students did not fully understand that once an interface specification had been agreed upon it could not be changed without consent of the group. Frequently, students would make "minor" changes in their package interface specifications, either accidentally or intentionally, without informing the rest of the group. Fortunately, in Ada, these changes will be caught at the system integration level compile time. If we had used other languages, except for Modula-2, these changes would have escaped notice until runtime.

Among the other advantages of Ada are the extreme security which can be gained by using **exceptions**, the fact that more errors are caught at compile time, and the information hiding capabilities of the packages.

We use the JANUS/Ada compiler from RR Software for the course, which is a fully validated Ada compiler for IBM PC compatible machines. It provides good error messages, both at compile and runtime. GSU has a site license for the 'D' pack which also includes some tools such as a pretty printer, assembler, disassembler, profiler, and a program to determine compilation order. This allows the students to gain some experience in using software tools. In addition, RR Software maintains a bulletin board of user donated Ada software, some of which is used by the students for their projects, e.g. a Windows and a B-Tree package.

While the team project is done in Ada, we do not limit our discussion of languages to only Ada. When discussing aspects of design, implementation, and configuration management (as defined and used in [BABB87], i.e., in developing as well as delivering the software product) we compare several languages such as FORTRAN, Pascal, C, Ada, COBOL, and Modula-2. One topic which we also stress is the production and use of Reusable Software Components (RSC's).

We discuss a variety of standard specification and design methodologies but, as mentioned above, we concentrate on the OOD methodology and have the students use OOD for their project. The students usually have had experience with other design methods, e.g. functional decomposition, and so using OOD requires a certain mind shift. Initially they don't like the OOD method but by the end of the quarter they usually change their opinions.

Experience in the Software Engineering Course

The course has now been taught several times and has gained a reputation as a very demanding course. The students spend a large amount of time on the project, up to twenty hours per week. The first time we taught the course all of the students did the same project. They implemented the Faceted Classification Scheme [PRIE87] for the storage and retrieval of RSCs. The second time the course was taught the students chose their own projects which varied from an on-line Ada syntax reference to a graphical design aid for OOD.

An advantage of having the students choose their own projects is that they are more likely to be interested in the project. For example, some students who had computer graphics courses did a project on advanced rendering of objects defined by parametric bicubic patches. The disadvantage is that the students sometimes underestimate the project difficulty and don't have an operational system by the end of the quarter (of course this **never** happens in the "real world").

Working in a team is a very interesting and difficult experience for most of the students. Most of the teams seemed to go through a period of dissension until the team members adapted to each other. Teams with several very good students sometimes had the most trouble since the good students frequently thought that they were "right" and the other team members were "wrong". Hotshot programmers found it difficult to allow others to program since "they knew they could do it better". Team members would get upset because some people were not doing their share of the work or were very difficult to work with, even to the extent of occasionally coming to team meetings slightly drunk.

In other words, the students on these teams encountered many of the same problems as they will find in the "real world". Fortunately, there was no violence and only one person has explicitly dropped the course because of his team. There have been very few instances of teams switching personnel so most students eventually adapted. Unlike most courses, in this course the instructor sometimes has to act as a counselor and psychologist.

Conclusion

We have been quite pleased with our choice of Ada for the Software Engineering course. The students have enjoyed (survived?) the team project and feel that the project is one of the most valuable aspects of the course. One current weakness is that the students miss the experience of having a central machine to use for their project as all communication of software is via diskettes. We plan to have a 80386 based UNIX/DOS machine which the students can use for their project the next time the course is taught.

References:

[BABI86] W. A. Babbich, _Software Configuration Management - Coordination for Team Productivity_, Addison-Wesley, 1986.

[BARN84] J. G. P. Barnes, _Programming in Ada_, Addison-Wesley, 1984.

[BOO87a] G. Booch, _Software Engineering with Ada_, Benjamin Cummings, (second edition), 1987.

[BOO87b] G. Booch, _Software Components With Ada - Structures, Tools, and Subsystems_, Benjamin Cummings, 1987.

[BROO82] F. P. Brooks, Jr., _The Mythical Man-Month - Essays on Software Engineering_, Addison-Wesley, 1982.

[FAIR85] R. Fairley, _Software Engineering Concepts_, McGraw-Hill, 1985.

[FELD85] M. Feldman, _Data Structures with Ada_, Reston/Prentice-Hall, 1985.

[GEHA85] N. Gehani, _C for Personal Computers_, Computer Science Press, 1985.

[OWEN87] G. S. Owen, "Using Ada on Microcomputers in the Undergraduate Curriculum", _The Papers of the Eighteenth SIGCSE Technical Symposium on Computer Science Education_, SIGCSE Bulletin Vol. 19, No. 1, pp. 374-377.

[PRAT84] T. W. Pratt, _Programming Languages - Design and Implementation_, Prentice Hall, 1984.

[ROGE87] J. B. Rogers, _A Turbo Prolog Primer_, Addison-Wesley, 1987.

Figure I Representative Reading List

Author	Reference
J. Baskette	"Life Cycle Analysis of an Ada Project", _IEEE Software_, January, 1987, pp. 40-47.
B. W. Boehm	"A Spiral Model of Software Development and Enhancement", _ACM SIGSOFT Software Engineering Notes_, Vol. 11, no. 4, August, 1986, pp. 14-24. B. W. Boehm "Improving Software Productivity", _IEEE Software_, September, 1987, pp. 43-57.
A. Borning	"Computer System Reliability and Nuclear War", _Communications of the ACM_, Vol. 30, no. 2, February, 1987, pp. 112-131.
F. P. Brooks	"No Silver Bullet: Essence and Accidents of Software Engineering", _IEEE Computer_, April 10, 1987, pp 10-19.
M. Freedland	"What You Should Know About Programmers", _Datamation_, March 15, 1987, pp 91-102.
C. F. Kemerer	"An Empirical Validation of Software Cost Estimation Models", _Communications of the ACM_, May, 1987, pp.416 - 429.
R. Prieto-Diaz and P. Freeman	and Classifying Software for Reusability", _IEEE Software_, January, 1987, pp. 6-16.
R. F. Sincovec and R. S. Wiener	"Modular Software Construction and Object-Oriented Design Using Ada", _Journal of Pascal, Ada, and Modula-2_, March-April, 1984, pp. 29-33.
J. W. Verity	"The OOPS Revolution", _Datamation_, May 1, 1987.

216

CONCURRENT PROGRAMMING IN AN UPPER-LEVEL OPERATING SYSTEMS COURSE

James L. Silver

Computer Science Department
Indiana University-Purdue University at Fort Wayne
Fort Wayne, Indiana 46805

Abstract

Since 1983, we have been covering concurrent programming as a central feature of a senior-level course in operating systems. This paper describes the content of that course, the mechanism used to implement concurrency, and the programming projects which provide students with practical experience in concurrency.

Introduction

Concurrent programming has long been a staple topic of operating systems courses. It is impossible to cover modern multiprogramming operating systems without including discussions of concurrency, race conditions, mutual exclusion, and deadlock. A survey of the classical problems of concurrency such as Producer-Consumer, Readers and Writers, and Dining Philosophers has long been considered essential to a well-rounded computer science education. For most students these topics have been of historical or theoretical interest rather than of any practical value. However, advances in hardware technology and new application areas have combined to bring about an environment in which students will be required to master the complexity of writing programs which respond to real-time events or take advantage of parallel architectures.

Most operating systems texts include discussions of some of the mechanisms available to implement concurrency, including machine and operating systems primitives as well as more advanced features found in languages like Concurrent Pascal and Ada. Unfortunately, they often do not include programming exercises which would allow students to use the constructs which are covered. This is, no doubt, due to great variety of concurrent programming mechanisms available and the fact that most campuses do not have access to any high-level facilities for concurrent

programming. The unfortunate result is that students must hope to master the single most difficult programming concept they encounter in their undergraduate careers without the benefit of programming exercises to practice and reinforce what they have learned.

We have made concurrent programming a central feature of our senior level operating systems course. This required a convenient mechanism for implementing concurrency and some major adjustments in the course itself. In the following, we will give a brief description of the course, examining the topics on concurrency in somewhat greater detail. We will describe the mechanism used to implement concurrency and the projects which we assign. In order to convey the level of difficulty of these projects, we will highlight some of the interesting aspects of typical solutions.

Background

Our department provides degrees in both computer science and information systems. The operating systems course is required of students seeking a Bachelor of Science in Computer Science. It is typically taken in the fall of their senior year. These students have had several years experience programming in Pascal and have been introduced to the VMS extensions which support modules, separate compilation, and environment files. They have had a sophomore-level course called Computer Organization and Operating Systems which has given them a good introduction to the terminology and passing familiarity with the requirements of memory management, interrupt processing, scheduling, and related topics.

The upper-level course begins with a brief history of operating systems, process states, and transitions. We then spend several weeks on concurrency and introduce the tools to implement concurrent programming. These topics are described in greater detail below. We cover the classical problems in concurrent programming and assign a project requiring a solution to one of those problems using the tools provided. While students are working on this project, we go on to describe resource allocation, memory management, and scheduling. We then assign a project which requires them to implement a paging system for a hypothetical operating system. Students have six to seven weeks to complete this project. While they are doing so, we continue to discuss file protection mechanisms, analytical modeling, and security. We conclude with case studies of UNIX, VMS, VM, and MS-DOS as time permits. During this period, we may devote one or two class periods to discussing problems students may be experiencing with the project.

Concurrency

The lectures on concurrency draw on Ben-Ari (1) and Brinch-Hansen (2). We discuss general concurrent processing, using Observer-Reporter to describe race conditions and to note the need for mutual exclusion. We begin with a definition of a critical regions and shared variables using the constructs described in Brinch-Hansen (2) to provide a solution to the Observer-Reporter problem. We then discuss various primitives which might be used to implement critical regions. We begin by examining Dekker's algorithm, using the picturesque illustrations from Ben-Ari (1), noting its complexity and its reliance on busy-waiting. This complexity motivates the need for a hardware implementation of mutual exclusion which we illustrate by covering the Test-and-Set and the VAX BBSSI (Branch if Bit Set and Set Interlocked) instructions. The undesirability of busy waiting similarly motivates the need for operating system and language support.

Among the more advanced mechanisms for supporting concurrency, we study binary and counting semaphores, message buffers, and the Ada rendezvous. Monitors are covered in the text. We draw attention to the equivalence of these constructs by observing that any one of them can be implemented using any of the others. We cover several of these implementations in class and assign others for homework. By way of illustration of these constructs, we introduce many of the classical problems of concurrency including Readers and Writers, Dining Philosophers, Producer-Consumer, and Conway's Problem.

This material is reinforced by a programming project which requires students to implement one of the concurrency mechanisms and use it to solve a problem like Observer-Reporter or Producer-Consumer. A typical project is shown below:

CS 472   Operating Systems   Project 1

1. Create a Pascal module to implement a message buffer. Your module should include the following three procedures:

Open_Message_Buffer (Message_Buffer, Name) - This procedure should do whatever is necessary to create an empty message buffer or associate with an existing message buffer. Name is a character string used to identify this particular message buffer. (A set of cooperating processes may need several message buffers.) The variable parameter Message_Buffer should receive a value which your system can use to distinguish one message buffer from another. The maximum number of

messages in the buffer should be a constant. For this assignment, use 10 as the maximum number of messages and Integer as the message type.

Send (Message_Buffer, Message) - Place Message in the buffer. If the buffer is full, the caller must wait until a position is available.

Read (Message_Buffer, Message) - Wait until the buffer is non-empty then remove the oldest message from the buffer and place it in Message.

For convenience, you may provide an upper limit, say 8, on the number of message buffers which your system will support.

2. Create a second Pascal module containing only the type definitions and procedure declarations needed by a process to use your implementation of message buffers.

3. Write versions of Producer and Consumer which use your implementation of message buffers. Producer should produce the first 1000 primes and send them to Consumer via the message buffer. Consumer should write the primes to a file.

Implementation

When we first introduced concurrent programming projects in the course we provided students with the VMS primitives which support concurrency: the Spawn system service, current event flags, and global memory sections. Unfortunately, students tended to get bogged down in the details of writing and debugging code using these primitives and to lose sight of the overall requirements of secure concurrent programming. Fewer than half of these students were able to complete the major project.

We now provide students with a Pascal module named Concurrent_Programming which contains a set of type definitions and routines providing a straightforward implementation of shared variables and critical regions. We have recently added procedures which support an implementation of conditional critical regions as described in Brinch-Hansen (2). This module allows students to use standard constructs for concurrency which are independent of the underlying implementation mechanism.

The basic elements are a procedure to allow a parent process to create sibling subprocesses, a mechanism for sharing variables between these subprocesses, procedures to enter and exit a critical region associated with a shared variable, and an await procedure which allows a process to temporarily exit a critical region to wait for a particular change in the status of the shared variable.

The types provided by Concurrent Programming are Event_Flag_Type and Shared_Region_Pointer_Type. Event_Flag_Type is roughly equivalent to binary semaphores. The procedures which examine and change these flags exclude one another in time and provide for non-busy waiting. Shared_Region_Pointer_Type represents addresses of shared memory areas. This type makes use of a VAX Pascal extension which allows for 'typeless' pointers so the shared memory area may be any user defined type.

The procedures in Concurrent Programming allow for the execution of subprocesses, the creation of shared memory areas, and the manipulation of event flags for synchronization between processes. Those of primary interest are Runsub, Get_Shared_Area, Enter, Exit, and Await. These are summarized in the following paragraphs.

The procedure Runsub is used to create subprocesses. The caller provides the name of a file containing an executable image, and the procedure creates a new process which executes the image concurrently with the caller and with other subprocesses which the caller creates. For example, a typical solution to the project above uses a parent process which creates both Producer and Consumer by calling Runsub twice, sending the names of the files containing these two processes.

Get_Shared_Area allows concurrently executing processes to create a new shared memory area or associate with an existing area. A typical call is shown below.

```
Get_Shared_Area
(
    Status, 'Message_Buffer_Area',
    Message_Buffer_Pointer,
    Size(Message_Buffer_Type),
    Initialize_Message_Buffer
);
```

The name, 'Message_Buffer_Area', is used to identify the area between processes. Message_Buffer_Pointer will receive the address of the shared area. Since the formal parameter corresponding to Message_Buffer_Pointer is the typeless pointer described above, the caller must also provide the size of the desired area. The procedure Initialize_Message_Buffer will be invoked by Get_Shared_Area to initialize a newly created shared area. It will not be called when Get_Shared_Area determines that the area already exists. This means that the user does not need to know which of several concurrent processes has actually created the shared area and which has associated with a previously created area.

In order to control access to the shared memory areas, the user must associate an event flag with each. Before entering a critical region for a shared variable, the user must call the Enter procedure, sending the event flag as a parameter. If necessary, this procedure uses non-busy waiting to block the caller until the flag is set. It then clears the flag and returns to the caller.

The use of Await to implement conditional critical regions requires that the user associate additional event flags with the shared variable. If the number of conditions to be tested is relatively small, then it is best to associate one flag with each condition. The Await procedure must always be called from within a critical region. It receives the access flag for the shared variable, a parameter-less Boolean function which

examines the shared variable and returns true when the desired condition exists, and the flag which is associated with that condition. This procedure will call the function parameter to determine whether the condition exists initially. If not, then it will temporarily exit the critical region (by setting the access flag) and wait for some other process to set the condition flag.

The Exit procedure receives the access flag as a parameter. In the case of simple critical regions, its only action is to set this flag. For a conditional critical region, the user can include as an optional second parameter an event flag associated with a condition which is now true. The Exit procedure will set this flag thus reactivating any processes which have been blocked by Await.

With the Concurrent Programming module, shared variables and critical regions are implemented in the following way:

1. Write a type definition for the object to be shared.

```
type Object_Type = ....
```

2. Create a type definition for shared objects by including this type in a record structure together with an access flag:

```
type
    Shared_Object_Type = record
        Access_Flag : Event_Flag_Type;
        Object      : Object_Type
end;
```

3. Declare a pointer to access shared objects.

```
type Shared_Object_Pointer_Type =
            ^Shared_Object_Type;
```

4. The critical region for a shared object is simply:

```
with Shared_Object_Pointer^ do begin
    Enter( Access_Flag );

    {Critical region}

    Exit( Access_Flag )
end
```

In order to implement a conditional critical region, additional event flags are used for each desired condition. A procedure which needs to implement a conditional critical region for the variable declares a parameter-free Boolean function which examines the shared variable to determine whether the desired condition is satisfied.

219

```
with Shared_Object_Pointer^ do begin
   Enter( Access_Flag );
   {Begin critical region}

   Await(Access_Flag, Desired_Condition,
         Condition_Flag );

   {End critical region}
   Exit( Access_Flag, New_Condition_Flag )
end
```

With these capabilities, message buffers can be implemented as suggested in Brinch-Hansen (2, p102) using conditional critical regions. The buffer definition itself is unchanged. The shared buffer definition requires the addition of an access flag, a flag indicating that there is room in the buffer for a message and a flag indicating that there is at least one message in the buffer. The code to implement a message buffer is a straightforward translation of that found in the text.

Project

After the basic material on concurrency has been presented, and the students have completed a short project like the one shown above, we use Concurrent Programming to implement a paging system for a hypothetical multiprogramming operating system. The project handout is shown below:

CS 472   Operating Systems   Project 2

Write a set of Pascal programs to implement a paging system which provides 64 virtual pages for each of several subprocesses. (The number of subprocess should be defined as a constant, Maximum_Slots.) The virtual pages should be implemented by means of a shared memory area with room for 64 real pages and a direct access paging file for each process. This file will hold all of the virtual page images for that process.

Each page should contain 32 integers. Thus the virtual address space for each process will be 0..2047 (2K). In order to identify the processes to the paging system, each will be assigned a process number (0, 1, etc.).

Each process will access its virtual address space using the following procedures:

procedure Get_Memory;

function Read_Memory (Address : Virtual_Address_Type) : Integer;

procedure Write_Memory   (Number : Integer;
                           Address : Virtual_Address_Type);

procedure Release_Memory;

The paging system will consist of a control program which reads the names of executable images from a file called "JOBS.QUE" and runs the corresponding programs as subprocesses. Your system should run Maximum_Slots processes at a time. (For testing purposes, Maximum_Slots = 3.) As each job completes, another process should be initiated until all jobs in JOBS.QUE have been executed. Each process will begin with a call on Get_Memory, followed by a succession of calls on Read_Memory and Write_Memory. Immediately before completion each process will call Release_Memory. You may assume that no process will terminate without making this final call.

During paging operations, if a referenced page is not resident, the paging system should first look for a free page. If none is available then it should seize the frame occupied by the oldest resident page, regardless of which process owns the page. The displaced page should only be written back to the paging file if it has been modified.

In addition to providing the usual paging services, your system should collect statistics on its own performance. These should include the number of reads, writes, page faults, and write-backs for each process.

The entire system should consist of a control program and a Pager module containing Get_Memory, Read_memory, Write_memory, Release_Memory, and any auxiliary procedures, type declarations, and data structures. The control program should initialize the paging system, initiate the programs which will use the paging system as subprocesses, and print the summary statistics. The Pager module will be linked with each of the subprocesses.

Test your system with several subprocesses using Pascal programs of your own devising to generate page references. Sample programs which generate calls on Read_memory and Write_memory will be provided for evaluation shortly before the assignment is due.

Solution

The solution embodies all the aspects of the paging systems discussed in class and in the text. Each call on Read_Memory or Write_Memory requires a translation from the virtual address provided by the caller to a 'physical' address consisting of a page number and an offset. A typical page table must be maintained for each process with an entry for each virtual page containing a resident field, a modified field, and, if the page is present, the physical page number. The paging system needs to keep track of unused pages. The requirement that the oldest resident page be seized, regardless of who owns it, implies that process page tables must be shared. (One process may take a page belonging to another process, so it needs to be able to see if the page has been modified and to mark it non-resident.) This also implies that the system must maintain a shared list containing the pages which are in use together with some identification of their owners.

In order to maximize the potential concurrency, students are encouraged to view the required shared memory areas as a collection of shared variables rather than as a single shared variable. For example, the page tables should be treated as an array of shared records rather than as a shared array of records. That is, two processes should be able to access two different entries of the same page table concurrently. Mutual exclusion is required only when processes need to access the same page table entry. Since the Concurrent Programming module provides only 64 event flags and each process page table has 64 entries, students must create their own mechanism, say binary semaphores, for mutual exclusion to achieve the maximal concurrency.

The principal data structures required for a solution are shown below.

```
Page_Table_Entry_Type =
   record
      Resident    : Boolean;
      Modified    : Boolean;
      Locked      : Semaphore_Type;
      Page_Frame  : Real_Page_Number_Type
   end;
```

```
Process_Page_Table_Type =
    array [Virtual_Page_Number_Type] of
           Page_Table_Entry_Type;

System_Page_Table_Type =
    array[Process_Type] of
        Process_Page_Tables_Type;

Free_Page_List_Type =
    record
        List_End  : -1..Max_Real_Page_Num;
        Free_Page : array[Real_Page_Number_Type]
                       of Real_Page_Number_Type
    end;

Used_Page_Entry_Type =
    record
        Used_Page_Number : Virtual_Page_Number_Type;
        Used_Page_Owner  : Process_Type
    end;

Used_Page_List_Type =
    record
        Used_Front : Real_Page_Number_Type;
        Used_End   : Real_Page_Number_Type;
        Used_Page  : array[Real_Page_Number_Type]
                        of Used_Page_Entry_Type
    end;

Page_List_Type =
    record
        Free_Page_List : Free_Page_List_Type;
        Used_Page_List : Used_Page_List_Type
    end;

Shared_Page_List_Type =
    record
        SPL_Flag  : Event_Flag_Type;
        Page_List : Page_List_Type
    end;
```

The algorithms are similar to those found in Brinch-Hansen (2, pp 180, 181). There are some complications due to the existence of nested critical regions. Students must make certain that two processes do not deadlock waiting for each other to exit a critical region. This can be assured by following the model of hierarchical resource allocation: arrange the shared variables in some order and require that a process desiring to enter a critical region for a particular variable must first release any higher order variables.

Conclusions

We have considered using Ada to implement these projects. We have so far decided against it because of the overhead required to introduce Ada in this class and because of the widely publicized shortcomings of Ada tasking. Further, we feel that because of the relatively low level of the features provided in Concurrent Programming, it is easy for a student to transfer the skills they have acquired to other concurrent programming systems. The transfer from Ada tasking to other systems would be much more difficult.

Since the introduction of the Concurrent Programming module, the successful completion rate for the project has been around 80%. Virtually all students have reasonable attempts, but some of them run out of time in the final difficult stages of trying to debug concurrent programs. In recent years, this project has taken on an almost heroic nature among our computer science majors with completion of 'the pager' being viewed by many as the capstone of their undergraduate experience. (We do make significant changes in the project from year to year so that access to a solution from earlier years would give a student only a minimal advantage.)

It is also interesting to note that over half of the students who completed this course in the last 5 years have written concurrent programs since their graduation. Most of them have used Ada, others have used VAX Pascal and the same system services which were used to implement the Concurrent Programming module, and one has used Micro-power Pascal. Many of these students have reported that their experience with the pager gave them a tremendous advantage compared with co-workers who had not had any previous experience with concurrency.

References

1. Ben-Ari, M., *Principles of Concurrent Programming*, Prentice-Hall International, Englewood Cliffs, New Jersey, 1982.

2. Brinch Hansen, Per, *Operating System Principles*, Prentice-Hall, Englewood Cliffs, New Jersey, 1973.

Performance Experiments
for the Performance Course

Charles M. Shub
Associate Professor of Computer Science
University of Colorado at Colorado Springs

1. ABSTRACT

This paper describes a newly instituted laboratory in the Computer Science Department at the University of Colorado at Colorado Springs. The reasons for developing the laboratory are delineated. The equipment is then described. This is followed by a brief description of initial experience with the laboratory. A collection of experiments performed within the laboratory is delineated in detail. Finally some brief thoughts on the future use of the laboratory and the conclusions drawn at this point in the lab's history are presented.

2. INTRODUCTION

The Computer Science Department at the University of Colorado at Colorado Springs (UCCS) recently provided a laboratory for undergraduates taking the required course in Operating Systems and an elective course in Performance Evaluation.

The purpose of this paper is to describe the reasons this laboratory was instituted, detail the experience with the laboratory, share some example performance experiments developed for this lab, and suggest extensions in the use of this laboratory. The paper focuses on the performance evaluation course aspects of the lab because the prototype experiments are better defined at this stage of the laboratory's development.

3. WHY HAVE A LABORATORY

We wanted to address national concerns for scientific education by not only providing students at UCCS reasonable laboratory facilities to experiment with operating systems, their performance, and their internals, but also by serving as a development ground for a collection of widely available exercises that could be adapted at other institutions.

Our majors take a required course in operating systems in the fall of their senior year. Though they have already interacted with operating systems as a user, they have not had any opportunities to design or code any internals of an operating system. No laboratory equipment other than interactive access to the central campus computing utility was available for that course.

Thus students could not obtain hands on experience with the internals of a computer operating system and had to depend on either a simulated machine approach or mere observation of the University main frame system for experience in operating systems design practice. The simulated machine approach then in use, while useful, had the disadvantage of not providing hands on laboratory experience for many areas of concern. Timing of asynchronous operations including input/output and interrupt processing is difficult in a simulated machine environment.

The lack of suitable laboratory equipment for hands on operating system experimentation resulted in the institution graduating students with incomplete preparation for jobs in local industry. Many graduates routinely design and code device drivers and interrupt handling software. Numerous graduates design and code portions of operating systems. Graduates entering a career of software development interact with a variety of host operating systems. Exposure to operating system internals also enhances the ability of these students to excel at their jobs.

Students in the elective senior level computer system performance course had no means of gathering instrumentation data on system performance or attempting to experiment with system tuning. The computing center was understandably reluctant to allow students the access necessary to experiment with operating system tuning techniques. Also, with the computing center system, the workload could not be controlled.

In summary, the lack of stand alone computer systems for experimentation with operating systems design and development severely impacted two courses. They include the required core course in operating systems and the elective course in computer systems performance evaluation.

4. EQUIPMENT CONFIGURATION

We elected to equip the laboratory with workstations instead of Personal Computers for several reasons.

1. At the time we decided to equip the lab, MINIX [TANE87] was not yet available and we wanted at least one reasonably robust operating system with source available.
2. We wanted equipment comparable with what students might be using in industry.
3. We wanted networking capabilities.
4. We wanted systems that ran at least two operating systems, and the V system [CHER87] was available at insignificant cost.
5. We wanted processors fast enough that rebuilding software would not be a significant time waster.
6. We wanted a multiple processes environment so we could have multiple users or multiple activities by a single user.
7. We wanted reasonable development tools.

The final choice was to use Sun workstations. The original configuration called for four identical systems instead of diskless stations and a server because we wanted the operating system work to be network independent. We ended up with a hybrid configuration because of availability and pricing changes between when we selected the equipment and when we were able to place the order. All four systems currently run either Sun Unix or a limited version of the Stanford V system. Switching between systems is painless and only requires minimal time to boot the other operating system. The speed is achieved by eliminating file system integrity checks on the "switch OS" boots.

5. LABORATORY EXPERIENCES

As always, nothing ever goes as nicely as planned. The equipment did not arrive when promised, and there were several glitches in getting the V system up and running. Because of these delays, progress on the operating systems side of the laboratory is not nearly as far as originally projected. The prototypes of the student assignments are being developed for the operating systems course, and both operating systems are being used on a regular basis.

The development of prototype measurement experiments for the performance course seems to have gone well in the initial stages. The variety of performance monitoring tools is helpful. They include, in addition to the normal Unix utilities and profilers, a network monitor that reports network traffic and load, and several tools that came with the V system. Local software has included a background load generator [BROW88] and a few library-like interfaces to make system gathered data available in a cleaner format.

6. LABORATORY MEASUREMENT EXPERIMENTS

Below, several measurement experiments are described. A uniform format has been selected. For each problem, a brief statement of the problem is given. This is followed by a short discussion of the rationale behind giving the problem. Then a description of student approaches are given. We always emphasize the scientific method for approaching the problem. Most of the texts or sets of notes that discuss measurement experiments do the same. [BEIZ78] [BORO79] [FERR78] [FERR81] We cast the problems as performance studies and may give the students the goal of the study.

In general, the experiments are described reasonably loosely leaving much leeway. The course comes late enough in the student's undergraduate program that an unwritten course goal is to foster creativity and independent thought as well as an investigative approach. Another benefit of this approach is that there never are "cookbook" answers to the problems. While this can make the grading harder, it seems (based on student feedback) to be a realistic and valuable approach.

For all experiments, class time was devoted to discussing the alternatives taken. With the graded reports in hand, student participation was vigorous to say the least. As will be obvious, the classroom material was helpful in the experimental designs chosen by the students.

6.1 Tool Usage

This study involves looking at and evaluating the use of the following performance tools: (The specific list is omitted, but includes the standard utilities and any locally designed tools.) You may use the on/off line documentation and you may write some small programs that use the tools. Try to limit yourself to at most three hours of machine connect time.
Prepare a short report describing the available tools and how they might be used.

This experiment is the first, and occurs early in the course. The students have been given an overview of the performance perspective and an overview of the methodologies that can be used.

6.1.1 *What the Students Should Learn*
There are several important concepts here. The first is that there are more tools than the student could possibly hope to master. As such, time must be budgeted to get enough depth to make informed choices among the tools for later use usually based on functionality, and enough depth to understand the differences in resolution and invasiveness. This helps later in developing an awareness of the need to focus on what is important and not be concerned with minutiae.

The second important point is one of how students should organize their knowledge for later use.

6.1.2 *Typical Approaches*
Though most of the students did copious documentation perusal, a few tried to write short programs and use all the tools on the programs to see what they did. There were two major organizations of reports. The first was a list of tools including, for each, a description of what it did and how it could be used. The other organization (which proved to be more utile later) was organized by type of measurement one could make with the tools in that class, and how the class members differed in detail.

6.1.3 *Future Enhancements*
The only problem experienced with this assignment was the *child in a toy shop* frustration of there being more than could adequately be covered in the allotted time. We are considering a modification where each student is given two or three tools and must write a short report on the assigned tools that will be distributed to the rest of the class. This will have the advantage of allowing greater focus by the students, while at the same time providing them with summaries of tools they have not studied. A minor disadvantage is the difficulty of grading such an assignment. Another concern is whether the student provided documentation will be sufficient for other students to later use the tool.

6.2 Window Usage

Many systems provide a variety of windowing front ends to allow applications designers to provide elegant user interfaces designed to increase user productivity. In addition to the dollar cost of using such systems, there is some overhead in the systems arising from designing the application to run in the windowing environment, the extra space for the extra windowing software, and the additional software processing necessary to place output at a desired place on the screen. Prepare a short paper detailing the technical tradeoffs involved in using a windowing environment on the Sun.

6.2.1 *What the Students Should Learn*
There are several important concepts here. First, there are issues of code size and start up time. Second, there are performance indices that can not be measured directly. Finally, there are several issues of two different kinds related to background load, the first being the overhead within the windowing software, and the second being the effect of background load, or other jobs. Finally, students discover anomalies they can't account for until they take the additional paging generated by the windowing software into account. Using some of the graphic tools that come with the Sun windowing packages, typically VMSTAT and PerfMon, makes this easier, so the students get a lesson in how tool selection impacts the ease or difficulty of the study.

6.2.2 *Typical Approaches*
Students seemed to want to write screen I/O intensive programs and time them in the two environments. When this was not enough, other approaches were tried. One student seemed to think that in the windowing environment the characters were being bitmapped into the frame buffer and there was no physical I/O going on as in the plain environment.

Particularly interesting was the approach of starting several animation demonstration programs in different windows and visually comparing their performance to performance of a single animation demo running on a different workstation.

6.3 Network Versus Local Access

The Sun systems are networked together and provide several vehicles for accessing files physically resident on other machines and accessing the system from a remote host. The students were asked to design a study to determining the important factors in selecting between a network environment and local access to data.

6.3.1 *What the Students Should Learn*
The most important issue here is determining what the bottleneck is. Is it the network, the load on the network, the software processing capacity of the machine, the disk I/O time, or some combination. Also, the problem is designed again to be vaguely specified (real world) and open ended.

6.3.2 *Typical Approaches*
There were three approaches that students took. One involved gathering timing data accessing both locally and remotely mounted files for comparison purposes. While this approach did lead to some differences in file access times, the differences were not significant and it was judged by the students that they were unable to saturate anything badly enough to get appreciable differences.

The second approach was to time local access with and without competing remote access and to time remote access with and without local competing access, and to attempt to draw conclusions from these comparisons.

The third approach was to use the Remote Procedure Call facilities and compare local versus distributed access times. The major failing of this approach was the inability to determine how much overhead was in network communication, and how much was in the support software. Moreover, difficulty was experienced determining where in the software the delays were occurring.

No approach was particularly successful because the students were unable to generate enough work to effectively push a potential bottleneck to saturation.

6.4 Language Efficiency

The students were asked to estimate the relative efficiency of various looping constructs, storage allocation strategies, and the like to prepare for a project involving some code that was not meeting its real time constraints.

6.4.1 *What the Students Should Learn*
This project has red herrings in it. The easiest way to compare looping constructs is to examine the code produced by the compiler. Also, most, if not all, typical experiments are rendered less than accurate because the optimizer can often change the constructs. Thus the students were rarely, if ever, evaluating precisely what they thought they were evaluating. The strangest case, for which those students who merely timed software could not explain was the profound difference between "while (--i)" and "while(i--)" as loop control constructs. Thus, a portion of this project is to learn that there are many tools, some of them not as usual as one would think, that might be applicable.

6.4.2 *Typical Approaches*
There were two major approaches. The most common was to write and time software to make comparisons. This invariably led to worse results than the alternate approach. The more accurate approach was to have the translator generate code and compare the generated code and use instruction timing data to get the conclusions. These results were more accurate and allowed the students to make quantitative predictions that were more useful.

Those of our students taking the elective performance evaluation course are reacting more favorably to the course (according to our standard course evaluation metrics) than they did before the lab came into existence. The free form responses show the students like the lab projects as being "frustratingly realistic" and valuable for their future. Similar feedback has come from graduates returning to campus for visits.

Perhaps even more important than either of these effects is the synergy developed within the department by the mere presence of this equipment. Students and faculty alike are using the lab for a variety of projects and we now have a vastly wider variety of creative activity taking place on campus. Thus, we conclude the laboratory is already a success and will continue to have beneficial effects on our program.

7. FUTURE USE OF THE LABORATORY

The laboratory will continue to be used according to plan. That involves providing the test bed for performance experiments and the hands on operating systems internals experience. Through time, additional performance experiments will be developed and classroom tested. Also, the operating systems experiments will be enhanced to the point where they are suitable for student exercises. Moreover, the laboratory will be able to provide (on a time available basis) facilities to allow both undergraduates doing independent study and graduate students doing graduate projects and theses with a facility for their experiments.

8. CONCLUSIONS

The project has been successful, even at this early point in the lifetime of the laboratory. Through this facility, all our undergraduates are getting hands on experience with the Unix Operating System at the User level. This makes them more marketable, and they seem to like that. Also, all our students are working with a prototype distributed operating system, another experience that enhances not only their employability, but also their base of knowledge for further education at the graduate level.

9. ACKNOWLEDGEMENTS

Partial support for this work has been provided by the National Science Foundation's College Science Instrumentation Program, Grant # CSI-8650449.

Additional support has been provided by Sun Microsystems.

10. REFERENCES

[BEIZ78] Beizer, Boris, *"Micro Analysis of Computer System Performance,"* Van Nostrand Reinhold, 1978.

[BORO79] Borovits, Israel and Neumann, Seev, *"Computer Systems Performance Evaluation,"* D. C. Heath, 1979.

[CHER87] Cheriton, David R., *"The V Distributed System,"* Stanford University, November, 1987.

[FERR78] Ferrari, Domenico, *"Computer Systems Performance Evaluation,"* Prentice Hall, 1978.

[FERR81] Ferrari, Domenico and Spadoni, Massimo, *"Experimental Computer Performance Evaluation,"* North Holland, 1981.

[TANE87] Tanenbaum, Andrew S., *"Operating Systems Design and Implementation,"* Prentice Hall, 1987.

Xinu/WU: An Improved PC-Xinu Clone?

Joseph Hummel

Department of Computer Science
Willamette University
900 State Street
Salem, OR 97301

Abstract

In teaching an undergraduate course in Operating Systems, it is instructive if the students have an actual operating system they can study and modify. Care should be taken, however, in selecting a system that the students can realistically be expected to understand. Xinu/WU retains the advantages of its parent PC-Xinu [Fossum 1987]; a small yet relatively complete operating system for the IBM PC, supplied with full source code and able to run within its development environment. Xinu/WU incorporates three particular enhancements; an improved implementation, integration into Borland International's Turbo C™ run-time environment, and more effective use of the windowing system. The conclusion is that Xinu/WU increases the possibility of using such a system in an undergraduate Operating Systems course. Two ways in which it can be utilized are presented.

1. Introduction

Programming projects serve as one of the more common mediums for teaching Computer Science. This is especially true in an Operating Systems class, where students struggle with new concepts such as processes, interrupts, and concurrency. It is instructive then for

the student to have access to a multiprocessing operating system, one which will allow them to experiment with the material presented in class.

However, one must keep in mind the limited budget of a small, undergraduate institution. Powerful Unix™ workstations do not litter the campus. One must also remember that for an undergraduate, this will be perhaps the student's first experience in systems programming, and may require they learn a new programming language as well.

Minix is a powerful Unix clone developed especially for the IBM PC and compatibles [Tanenbaum 1987a]. It is complete, well-documented, and comes with full source code [Tanenbaum 1987b]. Unfortunately it qualifies as a large program; rebuilding the kernel alone is an involved process. And for newcomers to Unix and C, the preferred development environment – Minix itself – is difficult to master.

A similar system is Xinu, an operating system developed on the DEC LSI-11 for student study [Comer 1984]. Recently ported to the IBM PC and renamed PC-Xinu, it is also well-documented and available with full source code [Comer 1988]. Though not as complete as Minix, this has a number of advantages.

PC-Xinu can be developed under DOS using an integrated programming environment, and run from within that environment. The system is also smaller and more portable, since it levers some functionality off the ROM BIOS. Finally, PC-Xinu is not a bootable operating system, further reducing system complexity.

With PC-Xinu, it is reasonable to expect that a motivated CS student, even an undergraduate and a non-C programmer, will be able to both use and extend this system in a one semester course. This was the motivation for using PC-Xinu in the design of an Operating Systems course slated for the 1988 Fall semester. The drawback was the system had not yet been released at the time of course preparation. However, the PC-Xinu textbook was available. Since this provides the full source code and serves as the system's documentation, the textbook was used as a guide in developing a PC-Xinu clone called Xinu/WU.

2. System Overview

Xinu/WU, with its associated development environment, runs on an IBM PC (or compatible) with at least 512K of memory and two 360K floppy disk drives. It consists of 5,000 lines of actual code (95% C, 5% assembler), and provides the following services: interrupt handling, process and memory management, semaphores, message-passing, I/O support for the keyboard, screen, and disk, and a DOS-compatible file system.

A Xinu program is written as a standard C program with the exception that no main subroutine is provided. The program is then linked with the Xinu and C run-time libraries, and executed as normal. The Xinu kernel builds a new environment, creates a set of system processes and an initial user process, and starts the highest priority process running. Once all user processes have died, the system processes are killed, the original DOS environment restored, and a return to DOS is made.

Though Xinu/WU retains the same logical structure as PC-Xinu, it differs in several small but potentially important ways. The three most noticeable changes, which the author considers improvements, are detailed here.

2.1 Advantages

First, the system itself was completely rewritten in a more modular and readable style. Dependencies between modules were reduced, yielding a cleaner interface among the various sub-systems. The result is a system that is easier to understand and more amenable to change. Students can work on a single module while the rest of the system remains constant.

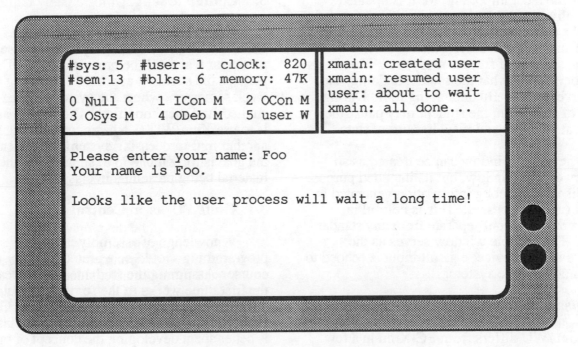

```
#sys: 5   #user: 1   clock:   820     xmain: created user
#sem:13   #blks: 6   memory: 47K      xmain: resumed user
                                      user: about to wait
0 Null C    1 ICon M    2 OCon M      xmain: all done...
3 OSys M    4 ODeb M    5 user W

Please enter your name: Foo
Your name is Foo.

Looks like the user process will wait a long time!
```

Figure 1. Windows in Xinu/WU.

Useful ANSI C extensions were also incorporated; e.g., the addition of function prototypes to allow type checking of parameters. Comments and more robust error checking were added throughout the system, and better use was made of variable and subroutine names. These changes are important for students new to C, especially when they are asked to use or possibly extend an existing piece of software.

Second, Xinu/WU has been integrated with Borland International's Turbo C run-time libraries. The library source was purchased from Borland and modified to become "Xinu aware." All usable library routines have been classified and kept; those that presented a problem were removed. This allows the student to take full advantage of existing, working code, without introducing subtle bugs into their programs. The Xinu/WU system itself utilizes a number of these library routines, especially those for formatted I/O.

Third, Xinu/WU supports three fixed, non-overlapping windows on the PC's screen (see Figure 1). One is used for a system status display (upper-left), another as a debug window (upper-right), and the third as a standard console output device (bottom two-thirds).

The system status display window is perhaps the most important, for it is updated continually to provide the student with information about the current state of the system; number of system and user processes, state of each living process, amount of free memory, etc. This helps the student "see" what the system is doing, and also serves as a useful debugging tool. During the course of execution, the student may pause the system at any time and view its current state.

The debug window can be treated as an ordinary output window, but its intended purpose is for displaying debug information generated by student (user) processes. This is helpful in keeping debug output separate from any standard output. The console window serves as the standard output device; e.g., all input is echoed to this window by the system.

2.2 Disadvantages?

Xinu/WU differs from PC-Xinu in a few small ways. First, processes may no longer open and close windows dynamically; the window

arrangement as mentioned earlier is fixed. This is a reasonable trade-off given the small size of the PC's screen and the advantage of having the system status display window.

Second, Xinu/WU supports only a DOS-compatible file system, whereas PC-Xinu supports its own version as well. The advantage to the Xinu/WU approach is that users on floppy-based systems do not need to switch disks before execution. One can imagine writing a program that used the Xinu file system and then, having forgotten to swap the disks, ended up destroying the source code. The disadvantage is students will not see how the low-level disk and file system operations are being done, since DOS is used to perform these functions.

Finally, it should be noted that the system configuration files in Xinu/WU are not program generated as they are in PC-Xinu. If changes are necessary, the student must locate and modify the desired configuration parameter(s) directly. This approach was taken merely to save time during implementation. However, since all such parameters are kept in appropriate include files, the operation is still relatively painless.

3. Course Use

There are numerous ways to utilize Xinu/WU in an Operating Systems course; two particular ways will be presented here. The first is perhaps the standard approach (assuming a 15-week semester), where the system is used, studied, and then modified. The second approach is to use Xinu/WU as a basis for building yet another multiprocessing system. In either case, the goal is for Xinu/WU to supplement the material being presented in class.

3.1 Xinu/WU as a Central Theme

Knowledge of assembly language programming should be a prerequisite for the course. Assuming the students need to learn C, the first three weeks of the semester should be allotted for this purpose. However, any C lectures should be done outside of class, for in-class time is better spent developing the concept of operating systems in general and processes in particular. Initial programming assignments should concentrate on the use of pointers, structures, and modules (i.e., separate compilation). If the students already know C, a week or two is still needed to develop class material before they will be ready to use the system.

Over the next five weeks, students should be asked to explore the functionality provided by Xinu/WU. Programming projects should involve basic concurrency issues (e.g., the Dining Philosophers problem or the Readers/Writers problem), and require the use of both semaphores and message-passing. A few class periods should be spent providing a system overview and reviewing various problem solutions.

The remaining eight or so weeks should involve a detailed investigation of the internal structure of Xinu/WU. How processes are represented, the way the interrupt mechanism works, and the structure of the I/O interface are all enlightening topics. Initial projects should involve the implementation of already existing Xinu/WU modules; e.g., the queue module or the semaphore module. Later projects should concern the modification of current modules or the implementation of new ones. Possible projects include message-passing semaphores, different memory management strategies, and Unix-style pipes. By this point a significant amount of class time should be spent on Xinu/WU internals.

It should be noted here that unless the students have access to high-density floppy or hard disk systems, they cannot be given just the source code; compiling the entire system from scratch requires 700K of disk space (not including the assembler, compiler, etc.). Instead, for each project the students should be given a small amount of source and the rest in object form. Due to Xinu/WU's modular structure, this can be done without loss of generality.

3.2 A System on Top of Xinu/WU

A different means to perhaps the same end is to use Xinu/WU as a springboard for building another multiprocessing system. A good example is the multiuser calculator project described in Mead [1988]. Here the students spend the entire semester working on a single assignment, broken down into three manageable pieces. They begin work on a simple, stack-based calculator (which also serves as a good introduction to C), and build

their way up to a multiuser calculator involving process and memory management. By the end of the semester, the students have implemented a rudimentary operating system kernel. This should fit into a 10-week semester if need be.

Although the original multiuser calculator was done on the Apollo Domain system, the necessary prerequisites are present in Xinu/WU (and PC-Xinu), namely multiprocessing and non-blocking message receipt. It should be noted that Minix does not directly support non-blocking message receipt.

4. Conclusion

Xinu/WU, like PC-Xinu, is a small yet nearly complete, well-documented operating system with full source code. It runs on an IBM PC or compatible, and can be executed from DOS or even within its own development environment. Xinu/WU has a number of advantages over PC-Xinu; an improved implementation, integration into Borland International's Turbo C run-time environment, and more effective use of the windowing system. Its principal disadvantage is the loss of dynamic window allocation.

Given a system of this nature running on inexpensive hardware, it becomes increasingly possible to use such a system in an undergraduate Operating Systems course. One approach could treat the system as an example to be studied and modified; another might involve the building of an entirely new system. In either case, the students are better able to experiment with the material presented in class.

Turbo C is an excellent programming environment for those learning C, and is available to students at the price of a textbook. The Xinu/WU system (source code, user's documentation, and modified Turbo C run-time libraries) is available by sending the author three, 5-1/4" floppy disks. Feedback on the use of this system in an Operating Systems course will be forthcoming.

References

[Comer 1984] Comer, Douglas, *Operating Systems Design : The Xinu Approach* ; Prentice-Hall, Inc., Englewood Cliffs, N.J., 1984.

[Comer 1988] Comer, Douglas and Fossum, Timothy, *Operating Systems Design Vol. I : The Xinu Approach (PC Edition)* ; Prentice-Hall, Inc., Englewood Cliffs, N.J., 1988.

[Fossum 1987] Fossum, Timothy, "PC-Xinu: Features and Installation," Operating Systems Review, Volume 21, No. 3, July 1987, pp. 30 - 33.

[Mead 1988] Mead, Jerud, "The Multiuser Calculator: an Operating System Project," SIGCSE Bulletin, Volume 20, No. 1, February 1988, pp. 32-35.

[Tanenbaum 1987a] Tanenbaum, Andrew, "A Unix Clone with Source Code for Operating Systems Courses," Operating Systems Review, Volume 21, No. 1, January 1987, pp. 20 - 29.

[Tanenbaum 1987b] Tanenbaum, Andrew, *Operating Systems : Design and Implementation* ; Prentice-Hall, Inc., Englewood Cliffs, N.J., 1987.

MPX-PC:
AN OPERATING SYSTEM PROJECT FOR THE PC

Malcolm G. Lane
Anjan K. Ghosal
Department of Statistics and Computer Science
West Virginia University
Morgantown, West Virginia 26506

ABSTRACT

This paper describes a student operating system project, MPX-PC, that can be implemented on an IBM PC-compatible computer. Seven modules make up the project, with the seventh module being the completion of a "stand-alone" student multiprogramming operating system. The project is implemented in Turbo C.

INTRODUCTION AND HISTORY

The teaching of operating systems at the undergraduate level is most effective when accompanied with appropriate programming projects. Many such courses are taught using some existing operating system, either a production operating system or some operating system developed specifically for teaching operating systems. Students typically use the latter type system to replace modules with their own, study existing modules, and experiment with the operating system's execution.

Since the beginning of the undergraduate Computer Science Program in 1971, the approach at West Virginia University has been to have students implement a small multiprogramming executive (operating system) called MPX. The MPX operating system has evolved over seventeen years, the first version was MPX1130 implemented on an IBM 1130 [Lane 1974, Lane 1975] and the second was MPX11 implemented on PDP-11s [Lane 1978] under RT-11. The MPX operating system concentrates on the following aspects of an operating system:

Process Management

System Calls

Device Management

User Interface

Data Structures in Operating Systems

Memory Management

The idea is to have the students learn the above concepts using a *hands-on approach*. The above aspects are close to the maximum of what one can expect in a project in a one

semester introductory operating systems course. The hands-on approach forces students to truly understand important concepts basic to all operating systems. Reading about them in a textbook without project reinforcement is not nearly as effective.

Students must thoroughly understand the architecture of the system for which they are are writing the MPX operating system. MPX1130 and MPX11 were both implemented in assembler language, primarily because no other language suitable for implementing operating systems was available on these computers. And of course, using assembler language the students did indeed learn the architecture of the computers on which they were working.

In 1986 a project was begun to implement the MPX operating system project on a IBM "PC-compatible" computer. This MPX is called MPX-PC. An early version of MPX-PC was implemented in Lattice C [Patnesky 1986, Knudson 1986]. This version included the command handler process, dynamic process loading, and directory support. In late 1987, this version was converted to run under Turbo C (initially version 1.0 and later version 1.5). It was enhanced to its current form from January 1988 through August 1988

MPX-PC is an operating system written specifically for *teaching* operating system concepts. It is *not* a *comprehensive* operating system and was never intended to be a "production" operating system. The project was implemented with the philosophy of keeping it as simple as possible. Previous versions of the MPX operating system have been written on systems with a much more simple architecture (IBM 1130 in the early 70s; PDP-11 in the late 70s). These previous machines had one distinct characteristic: no matter what ever happened to the software running in the computer, there was a hardware facility to examine registers and memory. The PC does not have this built-in firmware or system console for displaying system status, registers, or memory no matter what the state of the PC is. A software debugger is typically used, but in an operating system environment, certain necessary aspects of the computer can be "wiped out" and cause the computer to simply hang.

The PC environment has been simplified whenever possible. Remember we are after concepts, *not all* the details. The driving force in the development of an MPX student-written operating system is that *students will learn (and remember) far more by implementing their own small operating system*, than by simply studying a large operating system or perhaps modifying a small part of such a larger OS. Seventeen years of experience and many letters from graduates and employers verify the approach works.

MPX-PC

The major components of MPX-PC are:

COMHAN - a system process that provides the command interface for MPX-PC.

MPX_INIT - initialization procedure that sets up control blocks and initializes devices using device driver procedures.

DISPATCH - process dispatcher.

IO_SCHED - I/O scheduler for devices.

SYS_CALL - the system call handler for MPX-PC.

IO_COMPLETE - I/O completion event handler.

IO_SUP - I/O supervisor comprising device drivers for console, serial port, and parallel port along with their interrupt handlers.

CLOCK - a simple clock drive that maintains the time of day.

IDLE - a system process that is dispatched when no other process is ready.

System data structures - process control blocks, I/O control blocks, and other important data structures used in implementing MPX-PC.

Processes are represented by process control blocks (PCBs) and process scheduling is priority-driven and preemptive. Memory management is done using static allocation (at process load time).

PHASES OF IMPLEMENTATION

As in any course in which there is a large project, it is difficult to define a set of sequential projects that students can undertake at particular points in the semester without yet being able to totally understand the big picture, in this case MPX-PC. The evolution of the course has resulted in the definition of seven "modules", each of which is self-contained, but in some way depends on previous modules. Even if students only do some or all of the projects described in Modules 1 through 6 and then do not add the SYS-CALL and IO_SCHED components of MPX-PC and "put MPX-PC together" in Module 7, there is still a tremendous learning experience for the students. And students will have succeeded in implementing important OS projects and documenting them. Of course the real satisfaction in the approach is having the students succeed in completing MPX-PC and having multiple processes running under MPX-PC using devices controlled by *their* device drivers and interfacing with MPX-PC with *their* COMHAN process.

THE PROJECT MODULES

As stated previously, there are seven project modules, the seventh being the completion and testing of MPX-PC. The seven project modules are as follows:

Module 1 - This module involves the design and implementation of the initial version of the COMHAN system process that is the command interface of MPX-PC. Commands supported in this module include DATE, DEBUG, DIRECTORY, HELP, VERSION, and STOP.

Module 2 - Students add process management support commands to COMHAN. Included are commands to display the PCB queue and to change PCB priorities and commands to suspend and resume processes. A series of SHOW commands are added to display PCB information about certain classes of processes. Procedures to search for a PCB, build a PCB, free a PCB, and get an empty PCB frame are implemented by students.

Module 3 - This module teaches the students about context switches and process dispatching via the implementation of a simple round robin dispatcher. This module uses the students' PCB structure defined in Module 2, but is more or less a stand-alone project. Test processes are provided for testing the round robin dispatcher.

Module 4 - This module culminates the support of processes by the addition of dynamic process loading, the dynamic setting up of PCBs to represent processes, process termination commands and a DISPATCH command that results in each loaded, *ready* process being dispatched once per command. Students are provided test processes that display a message to the screen each time they are dispatched. Students can suspend and resume processes as well as change the priority of the processes and check out their dispatcher and various PCB support routines *without* being in an *interrupt-driven* multiprogramming environment.

Module 5 - It is in Module 5 that interrupts are introduced in detail (the concept of system call interrupt has been introduced earlier). Students implement a simple clock driver in which they must service clock interrupts and maintain a simple time-of-day clock. The best way to implement this module is by the addition of a SETCLOCK or TIME command to COMHAN.

Module 6 - The concept of a device driver, its structure, and the characteristics of various devices are presented in this module and the students implement one or two device drivers for the serial port and/or the parallel port. Students are provided test programs to test their device drivers.

Module 7 - A system call support procedure and and I/O scheduler are added and combined with the students' COMHAN and device drivers and with the console device driver provided to them to complete the total MPX-PC project. Testing involves the loading and executing of various combinations of supplied test processes, some of which are I/O-bound and others of which are compute-bound. Process states in this module are one of the following:

ready - ready to use the CPU.

running - in control of the CPU.

IO_Init - waiting for the use of an I/O device (device busy).

IO_Active - waiting for the completion of active I/O on a device.

All of these states are *mutually exclusive* in MPX-PC to simplify its implementation.

PHILOSOPHY OF IMPLEMENTING MPX-PC

MPX-PC "coexists" with MS-DOS. A philosophy used for seventeen years in implementing other MPX versions is to use parts of the system's operating system (DM2 on the IBM 1130, RT-11 on the PDP-11, and MS-DOS on the IBM PC) for certain services that students would not have time to do. Such services include directory services and file read services for loading processes. In MPX-PC we also used memory allocation facilities of MS-DOS, because it is assumed that students have had experience with memory management in previous computer science courses. An optional Module 8 defines a memory management project that can replace the use of MS-DOS memory allocation. Allocated memory, of course, is tracked via control blocks which are part of or pointed to by a process's PCB.

MPX-PC takes over interrupt vectors for the clock, console, serial port, parallel port, and INT 60. Of course MS-DOS does not know that it has "lost" control of these interrupt vectors and hence various devices. These vectors are restored before returning control to MS-DOS.

Recall the important philosophy mentioned earlier was to *keep it simple*. This proved to be particularly important in the PC version of MPX, since there were no longer firmware debuggers that could tell students what was happening in the computer no matter how badly contents of memory or the integrity stack was destroyed or how wild a branch was taken. The console driver condrive was implemented in a very straight-forward manner and is not utilized until Module 7. This allows MS-DOS to keep control of the console and the MS-DOS debugger (and other (symbolic) debuggers) to be used for debugging prior to the completion of MPX-PC in Module 7.

Console Driver

In the early years, students implemented a console driver. However, in MPX-PC a console device driver is provided to students. This driver consists of a write procedure (con_write) that writes to the screen and is *not* interrupt-driven and keyboard interrupt handler (kb_int) that only is used in Module 7. Hence, the MS-DOS debugger can be used up until this module if desired. Because the con_write procedure does a direct write to the screen by writing to the memory map for the screen, printf statements in Turbo C are allowed in interrupt handlers running under MPX-PC. This greatly simplifies debugging in Module 7 when MPX-PC is being put together and tested in an interrupt-driven multiprogramming environment.

CPU Control

MPX-PC receives CPU control when a process makes a system call via an INT 60. Typical system calls are for device I/O or process termination. The IO_complete procedure receives control when an event flag is set in a device driver (i.e., a requested I/O operation has completed). IO_complete changes the state of the process that was waiting for I/O from *IO_Active* to *ready* and checks to see if another process is waiting for the now free device. If one is found, the I/O scheduler is called to start the requested I/O operation and the requesting process is changed from *IO_Init* to *IO_Active*. Finally, the dispatcher is called to dispatch the highest priority process in the *readyQ* (see Figure 1).

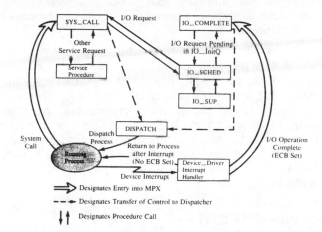

Figure 1. MPX-PC CONTROL FLOW

Interleaved Output

MPX-PC does not rely on spoolers, but rather allows all output to be interleaved on typically "non-sharable" devices, as shown below:

```
IOPRT1 process running ...
IOPRT2 process running ...
CPUPRT1 crunching away ...
IPPRT1 process running ...
CPUPRT2 crunching away ...
```

This technique provides a dynamic demonstration to the students of the interleaved execution of processes that is taking place in MPX-PC. Such an approach also demonstrates the need for spooling in a "real" multi-programming environment.

The Command Interface

The MPX-PC project emphasizes the need for a humanly-engineered command interface (COMHAN) [Lane & Mooney 1988a]. The COMHAN process is central to the success and philosophy of the MPX-PC project. It is evaluated for consistency, reasonableness, completeness and ease of use. Students are told to implement a command interface that they would want to use daily. COMHAN becomes the "brains" of the MPX-PC in a manner like the Master Scheduler was the "brains" of the IBM OS/360 operating system.

Process Control Using COMHAN Commands

Dynamically loadable processes that are loaded in response to LOAD or RUN commands of COMHAN are provided to the students for testing MPX-PC in Module 7. The set of application processes includes simple processes that are I/O-bound and compute-bound. These processes use different devices for input and output. For example, IOPRT1 and IOPRT2 are I/O bound processes that print lines to the printer using MPX-PC system call, while CPUPRT1 is a compute-bound process that writes to the printer. Similar naming conventions are used for processes that use other devices.

The processes are loaded using the support procedure load that is provided to students. The students begin loading a single simple process (e.g., IOPRT1) and running it. Then they add other processes, eventually trying to load and run as many processes as possible. Along the way, a typical MPX-PC crashes and the cause must be determined. Students experiment with priority changes like setting compute-bound processes to high priority and I/O-bound processes to low priority and observe the results.

SUPPORT SOFTWARE

The success of previous MPX projects and MPX-PC depends heavily on a wealth of support software provided to the students. Support software provided for MPX-PC includes:

directory procedure - returns a directory of MPX-PC processes (with extension .MPX)

load procedure - loads the specified process at the address provided by the caller

project files - for most modules, project files are supplied that contain the names of required support procedures. Students add names of their procedures to these project files.

debug procedure - a simple debug command that can be included in their command handler that allows the display of memory and registers within COMHAN.

interrupt vector initialization procedures - sets the interrupt vectors for the students, particularly in early modules.

test processes - three sets of test processes (one each for Modules 3, 4, and 7) are provided to students in both source and object form.

test programs - test programs for testing students device drivers simplify the testing of the device drivers when time is limited in a single semester.

system call simulation procedure - a procedure simulates a system call environment of MPX-PC to allow COMHAN to be implemented as if it were making system calls to MPX-PC for console reads and writes. In Module 7, simulated system calls are replaced with real system calls.

console device driver - a simple console device driver is provided to the students for use in MPX-PC. It is interrupt-driven and follows the calling sequences of other device drivers that students implement for use in MPX-PC.

TURBO C

Turbo C [Borland 1987] has proven to be an excellent language for implementing MPX-PC and various module projects leading up to MPX-PC. The total project can be implemented *without any* assembler language routines (including interrupt handlers)! We have attempted to illustrate to the students ways they can use certain features Turbo C in implementing their projects so that they do not waste time trying approaches or statements that do not work. In other words, we try to steer them away from our "walks down the wrong path" when we implemented the prototype.

To do this with minimal hassle, we have replaced the low-level Turbo C print procedure called __fputn. By simply adding the name of our replacement procedure (_futn.obj) to the project file for MPX-PC in Module 7, Turbo C printf statements are forced to use the MPX-PC console driver procedure (con_write) rather than a call to the MS-DOS system call that prints to the screen. Similarly,\we replace the previous sys_reqc.obj with the "real" system request routine sys_req that issues an INT 60 using Turbo C's geninterrupt library procedure. Thus, console input also uses the condrive input procedure (con_read).

APPLICATION PROCESSES

We examined the use of Turbo C test processes for MPX-PC. They were fine for the "statically" loaded processes in the round-robin dispatcher (Module 3). However, because of the large number of procedures create by even a simple Turbo C program and the complex addressing environment of various segments defined in such a program, it was found that simple assembler language programs were easier to understand (in their loaded form) and load. Hence, *all* dynamically loadable processes are written in assembler language and provided to the students in source form. The decision to use assembler language processes in this case was driven by the major goal of simplicity.

THE GROUP APPROACH

The MPX has always been a group project. Only a few *select* individuals have ever completed an MPX project on their own in the more than seventeen years the approach has been used. Documentation has always been an important requirement. In cases where the final MPX-PC does not totally work, students must explain it doesn't work or why they think it does not work. Often, such an explanation helps them to pinpoint problems in their design or implementation, and sometimes even results in the correction of the problem (and hence an operational MPX-PC)

Student projects are evaluated on MPX-PC using the following six parts to determine a grade: COMHAN, device drivers, design of MPX-PC, operation, the *MPX-PC User's Guide*, and the *MPX-PC Technical Support Manual*.

The grade on these determines 75% of the project grade and are "group points." The last 25% of MPX-PC are "individual points" determined by a written exam on the MPX PC project is given to all students. Each student must answer questions about *his* or *her* group's MPX-PC. These exams are graded in "groups" in that answers to questions about design, queue structures, etc. should be similar (i.e., describe the *same* system). One revealing question that is always asked is "Explain completely *who* did *what* on MPX-PC?" Each person must also explain his or her role in the project. It has been found that students rarely let the chance to "tell it like it is" go by, if one or more members of the MPX-PC design and implementation group did not do their fair share!

COURSE EVOLUTION

The course is constantly refined by the results of previous semesters. It is the students who improve the course. Their feedback is absolutely essential to such improvements in the course project and individual modules leading up to MPX-PC. Top students who have taken the course often serve in later semesters as lab assistants in the operating systems laboratory.

ACKNOWLEDGMENTS

All Computer Science 240 students over the past seventeen years at West Virginia University are acknowledged for their part in the evolution of MPX to the MPX-PC version discussed in this paper. The MPX-PC project and the project modules are now available in *A*

Project Manual to Accompany A Practical Approach to Operating Systems [Lane & Mooney 1988b] complete with support software. The textbook *A Practical Approach to Operating Systems* [Lane & Mooney 1988a] contains generic forms of the MPX projects throughout the first thirteen chapters. Students receive all necessary support software. Instructor's diskettes provide instructors with source code and project files for a prototype MPX-PC implemented in Turbo C by the authors. Documentation of this prototype is also provided to the instructor.

The authors are grateful to James Knudson and James Patnesky for the early work done on MPX-PC, particularly for support of dynamic process loading and directory support. The support of Borland International in providing test versions of Turbo C in a timely manner is acknowledged. MS-DOS is a trademark of Microsoft Corporation. Thanks also to Boyd & Fraser Publishing Company, in particular to Tom Walker, Marge Schlaikjer, and Pat Donegan, for encouragement and patience during the development of MPX-PC. We appreciate also the advice and suggestions of James D. Mooney.

REFERENCES

[Borland 1987] Borland International, Inc. *Turboc C Reference Guide*. Scotts Valley, CA, 1987.

[Ghosal 1988] Ghosal, Anjan K. "Implementing an MPX on an IBM/PC Using Turbo C." Masters Project Report, West Virginia University, Morgantown, WV, 1988.

[Knudson 1986] Knudson, J. F. "The Implementation of a Prototype PC/MPX Written in the C Language - The MPX Modules." Masters Project Report, West Virginia University, Morgantown, WV, 1986.

[Lane 1974] Lane, Malcolm G. "The Teaching of Systems Programming Using Small Computers: Three Years' Experience." *Compuaters at the University*, Zagreb, Yugoslovia, Nov. 1974.

[Lane 1975] Lane, Malcolm G. "A Hands-On Approach to Teaching Systems Programming." *ACM SIGCSE Bulletin*, Vol. 7, No. 1, Feb. 1975.

[Lane 1978] Lane, M.alcom G. "The Subsystem Approach to Enhancing Small Processor Operating Systems." *Proc. First ACM SIGSMALL Symposium on Small Systems*, New York, 1978.

[Lane & Mooney 1988a] Lane, Malcolm G., and Mooney, James D. *A Practical Approach to Operating Systems*. Boyd & Fraser, Boston, MA, 1988.

[Lane & Mooney 1988b] Lane, Malcolm G., and Mooney, James D. *Project Manual to Accompany A Practical Approach to Operating Systems*. Boyd & Fraser, Boston, MA, 1988.

[Patnesky 1986] Patnesky Jr., J. J. "The Implementation of a Prototype PC/MPX Written in the C Language - The System Support Modules." Masters Project Report, West Virginia University, Morgantown, WV, 1986.

A LANGUAGE-ONLY COURSE IN LISP WITH PC SCHEME

Kenneth A. Lambert

Department of Computer Science
Washington and Lee University
Lexington, Virginia 24450

Abstract

This paper describes a course in LISP that introduces students to conventional software engineering techniques, contemporary programming paradigms, and an artificial intelligence application.

1 Introduction.

The traditional view of LISP as a special-purpose language for artificial intelligence applications is changing. In the academic setting at least, LISP has begun to penetrate into such areas of the college curriculum as graphics, compiler construction, and database management. The reason for this change is that people are coming to see that LISP supports good software engineering concepts.[1]

Students have picked up their LISP either on the fly for some application or in the form of a language-only course. Very few departments have gone so far as to use LISP in CS1. [2] Nevertheless, pressure is building from the upper levels of the curriculum for a language-only course in LISP that emphasizes good software engineering concepts.

The problem is that traditional dialects of LISP and most traditional introductory LISP texts do not support these concepts.[3] Most are AI application-driven, without concern for conventional software engineering design. A good language-only course in LISP should deal with the following topics:

1. conventional software engineering techniques
2. the distinctive features of LISP
3. an AI application

This paper reports on the content of a language-only course that uses PC Scheme. Scheme is a dialect of LISP that supports and enforces many of the right conventional programming principles. We use Scheme rather than Common LISP because Scheme is smaller, cleaner, and easier for an inexperienced student to learn. The twelve weeks of the term in which the course is offered are divided into four-week sections on numerical processing, data processing, and knowledge processing. Each kind of processing is associated with a different programming paradigm. These are, respectively, function-oriented programming, object-oriented programming, and logic-oriented programming. Contact with a major programming paradigm supporting each kind of processing both reinforces good conventional software design methods and leads students quickly into conventional and AI applications.

2 Functions and numerical processing.

Students are introduced to the simplest kind of programming first. According to the function-oriented model, a program is a black box with no side effects.

2.1 Primitives, combination, and abstraction.

The real black boxes are the primitive operations of the language. Primitives can be combined in a uniform way to perform more complex tasks. Once several such black boxes have been hooked together, the combination can be hidden away in a new black box. This is accomplished by defining new functions or binding names to them. Naming is the principal means of abstraction in LISP.

Functional composition and abstraction support two important software design ideas:

1. top-down or bottom-up programming
2. programming free of side effects

2.2 Recursion.

There is no excuse for using a loop in a LISP program. Students can learn to recurse almost as soon as they learn how to define their own functions. Beyond its ease of use, recursion has enormous instructional value. For example, the difference between tail and nontail recursion can serve as a means of introducing the run-time stack. Scheme requires that tail recursive functions generate no net growth of the run-time stack; they must execute as iterative processes. A discussion of tree recursive functions can serve to introduce the differences among constant, linear, and exponential orders of complexity.

2.3 Numbers and lists of numbers.

The applications of this section are concerned with numerical processing. Students build and manipulate numbers and lists of numbers. They learn that numerical and list processing is well supported by function-oriented, recursive programs that are free of side effects. The following two function definitions are examples of the kind of ideas presented. The first recursively builds a number by summing a series. The second recursively builds a list of numbers in a series:

```
(define (build-number low high)
  (cond ((> low high)
         0)
        (else
         (+ low (build-number (+ low 1) high)))))
```

```
(define (build-list low high)
  (cond ((> low high)
         ())
        (else
         (cons low (build-list (+ low 1) high)))))
```

```
(build-number 2 4)  -->  9
```

```
(build-list 2 4)  -->  (2 3 4)
```

The arrow ('-->') symbol denotes the execution of the program expressed on the left side, with the output expressed on the right side. An important point to be introduced here is that any LISP data type can be closed under functional composition. This means that functions which take numbers or lists as input can return them as output. For example, we might add together the results of building two numbers as follows:

```
(+ (build-number 2 4) (build-number 3 5))  -->  21
```

Or, assuming we were given a function to add two lists of numbers, we might try this:

```
(add-list (build-list 2 4) (build-list 3 5))  -->  (5 7 9)
```

The closure principle could easily be extended to functions for manipulating symbols, strings or user-defined data types such as matrices and polygons.

2.4 Higher-order functions.

The function-oriented paradigm can be enhanced by the use of functions as parameters. For example, a general build-object function might specify the kind of operation to be performed (+ or cons) on each pair of numbers in a series, and the kind of value (0 or ()) to be returned at the bottom of the recursive process:

```
(define (build-object low high operation constant)
  (cond ((> low high)
         constant)
        (else
         (operation low (build-object (+ low 1)
                         high operation constant)))))
```

This function could then be used to define other functions that build more specific objects:

```
(define (build-number low high)
  (build-object low high + 0))
```

```
(define (build-list low high)
  (build-object low high cons ()))
```

The idea of a higher-order function leads quite naturally into a discussion of mappers. A mapper applies a function to every item in a list and returns a list of the results. For example, the following function maps any function of two arguments onto lists of arguments:

```
(define (mapper f l1 l2)
  (cond ((null? l1)
         ())
        (else
         (cons (f (car l1) (car l2))
               (mapper f (cdr l1) (cdr l2))))))
```

```
(define (add-list l1 l2)
  (mapper + l1 l2))
```

2.5 Lexical scoping.

Scheme is a lexically scoped, block-structured dialect of LISP. This means that one can control the visibility of information in much the same way as one can with conventional languages. For example, the following definition of factorial uses a tail recursive utility function:

```
(define (factorial n)
  (define (fact-iter n result)
    (cond ((zero? n)
           result)
          (else
           (fact-iter (- n 1) (* result n)))))
  (fact-iter n 1))
```

Because no function other than factorial needs to use fact-iter, both the definition and the initial call of fact-iter can be hidden within the local scope of factorial.

3 Objects and data processing.

Pure functions map input data into output data without changing the input data. Programs that use pure functions are easy to understand and verify. However, much data processing requires us to think of data as objects whose original states change as a result of the operations on them.

3.1 Assignment and side effects.

A function can modify data by means of a side effect. Side effects are accomplished in Scheme by a variety of assignment operations. For example, the following variable and function definitions might be used to manage a bank account:

```
(define balance 0)

(define (deposit amount)
  (set! balance (+ balance amount)))

(define (withdraw amount)
  (cond ((> amount balance)
         "insufficient funds")
        (else
          (set! balance (- balance amount)))))

balance --> 0

(deposit 20) --> 20

(deposit 20) --> 40

balance --> 40
```

Provided that all of the conditions are satisfied, each function call will have the side effect of changing the bank balance.

3.2 Message passing and data encapsulation.

The bank balance of the previous section is represented by a free, top-level variable. Its state is open to indiscriminate modification from anywhere in the program. To enhance the security and reliability of the system, we can build some walls around the data for each bank balance. Access to each account will be provided through a well-defined set of interface functions.

Bank accounts will be the objects of an object-oriented system. An object is a piece of data and the code for operating on the data. The following function returns such an object for a bank balance:

```
(define (make-balance)
 (let ((balance 0))
  (define (deposit amount)
    (set! balance (+ balance amount)))
  (define (withdraw amount)
    (cond ((> amount balance)
           "insufficient funds")
          (else
            (set! balance (- balance amount)))))
```

```
(define (dispatch message)
 (case message
   ('deposit deposit)
   ('withdraw withdraw)
   (else (error make-balance "unrecognized message"))))
 dispatch))
```

A bank balance object is a function which hides the values of a variable (the data) and three functions (the operations). The program could be used with the following results:

```
(define my-account (make-balance)) --> MY-ACCOUNT

my-account --> #<PROCEDURE DISPATCH>

(my-account 'deposit) --> #<PROCEDURE DEPOSIT>

((my-account 'deposit) 50) --> 50

((my-account 'withdraw) 20) --> 30
```

The data for each bank account in an object-oriented program are encapsulated within distinct objects. Side effects on the data are generated only by sending messages to the objects. The capacity of objects to perform operations on their own data helps to reduce the likelihood of unwanted side effects.

3.3 Windows, files, and user interfaces.

The Scheme interpreter provides interactive program input and output. Data processing requires file input and output and text-oriented input and output at the console.

One way to drive this point home is to ask students to hook two new modules onto their bank account system. The first module provides command options to users via windows. The second module permits the system to store and retrieve bank account information from permanent files. The following function is the first to be written in the program text:

```
(define (bank-manager)
 (move-console)
 (let ((window (create-window "MANAGER WINDOW"
                              5 25 8 30)))
  (window-popup window)
  (newline window)
  (window-writeln window "1 enter a new account")
  (window-writeln window "2 delete an old account")
  (window-writeln window "3 file manager")
  (window-writeln window "4 start the teller")
  (window-writeln window "5 quit the program")
  (newline window)
  (display "enter a number: " window)
  (interpret-manager window)
  (window-popup-delete window))
 (restore-console))
```

Bank-manager begins the program by moving the console window out of the way. A top-level window is then created with a label and various size and position attributes. After the window has been popped up on the screen, the menu is displayed in it to the manager. When the manager has finished entering commands, the window is deleted and the console window is restored to its original position on the screen.

The next function interprets the commands of the bank manager:

```
(define (interpret-manager window)
  (let ((ch (read-char window)))
    (case ch
      (#\1 (add-account))
      (#\2 (delete-account))
      (#\3 (file-manager))
      (#\4 (bank-teller))
      (#\5 ())
      (else (ring-bell)))
    (when (not (char=? ch #\5))
          (interpret-manager window)))))
```

Interpret-manager is a typical command loop in Scheme. First, a character is read from the window. A case expression then examines the character and selects the appropriate action. The principal actions are routines which lead the user into subsystems with their own popup windows. The last two actions in the case expression deserve special notice. No action is performed if the manager wishes to quit the interpreter (choice #\5). If the character is not in the command set, the interpreter signals by ringing the bell. Finally, the interpreter recurses when the input character is not the quit character.

The new bank management system gives students an excellent opportunity to work with top-down design and reusable code. Conventional devices such as drivers and stubs can easily be used to prototype and test the subprograms rapidly and incrementally.

4 Frames and knowledge processing.

After software engineering concepts have been introduced with numerical and data processing, students can apply them in the domain of artificial intelligence. Traditional LISP texts have illustrated this field with pattern matchers, associative database retrieval systems, and rule-based expert systems. The application presented in this course is the development of a frame representation language (FRL).[4] Several important concepts, such as inheritance, procedural attachment, and pattern matching, can be gradually phased in during the final four weeks of the term.

4.1 Organizing concepts with inheritance.

Students are initially given the interface and code for an FRL that supports simple storage and retrieval. For example, frames for John and for persons can be manipulated as follows:

(fput 'john 'hair-color 'brown)

(fget 'john 'hair-color) --> (brown)

(fput 'person 'weight 165)

(fget 'person 'weight) --> (165)

(fget 'john 'weight) --> ()

When the system is updated to support inheritance, the frame for John can inherit the average weight of a person from the frame for persons. A special ako (a kind of) slot is added to John's frame to point to the frame for person:

(fput 'john 'ako 'person)

(fget 'john 'weight) --> (165)

Values can be stored in frames that override any values that might be inherited from the hierarchy:

(fput 'sally 'ako 'person)

(fput 'sally 'weight 110)

(fget 'sally 'weight) --> (110)

4.2 Demons as active data.

As the previous section demonstrated, frames are high-level data structures. In LISP, data can be stored either as values or as functions for computing values. In the frame context, such functions are called demons. Demons can be triggered when a user adds, removes or requests a value from a frame.

For example, one might store a demon rather than an explicit value on the weight slot of persons. When a user asks for the weight of an individual person, the system triggers the demon to compute the weight as a function of the individual's height.

In another case, one might want to keep a record of all of the instances of a specific frame on a special instances slot for that frame. This bookkeeping task could be automated for the entire database by storing if-added and if-removed demons on the top-most general frame in the hierarchy. Whenever one frame is made ako another, the name of the former would automatically be added to the instances slot of the latter. The inverse process would be triggered when a value is removed from an ako slot.

Students quickly learn that almost the entire database can consist of active data in the form of attached procedures. Few programming experiences can rival the effect of watching the spreading ripples of demon activity generated by some simple database access.

4.3 Pattern matching and intelligent database retrieval.

A final segment on pattern matching nicely combines database logic with some simple inference techniques. Patterns are used to form queries to the database. The system responds to a query by returning a list of all of the names of frames that match the pattern.

The following query would return all of the frames for people with blond hair and blue eyes:

```
(find '((ako person)
      (hair-color blond)
      (eye-color blue)))  -->  (john sally mary bill)
```

Removing slots from the pattern amounts to removing constraints from the search process:

```
(find '((ako person)
      (hair-color blond))  -->  (john sally mary bill hank)
```

```
(find '((ako person))  -->  (sam john sally mary bill hank)
```

Logical operators can be attached to the elements of patterns to express conjunction, disjunction or negation of values on a slot. For example, the following query would find all of the persons whose hair color is not blond:

```
(find '((ako person)
      (hair-color (not blond))))  -->  (sam)
```

The next query would return the persons whose hair color is either brown or blond:

```
(find '((ako person)
      (hair-color (or blond brown))))
 -->  (john sally mary bill hank)
```

Finally, arbitrary LISP functions can be included in patterns to constrain the search. The following example asks for all of the persons weighing between 180 and 200 pounds:

```
(find '((ako person)
      (weight (lambda (x) (and (> (car x) 180)
                              (< (car x) 200))))))
 -->  (sam)
```

The LISP function in this pattern is expressed as a lambda form. Lambda forms provide a way of expressing functions for a special purpose without naming them.

5 Conclusion.

We have discussed the content of a language-only course in LISP that utilizes the PC Scheme dialect of the language. Like Pascal, Scheme is both easy to learn and encourages the use of good software engineering methods. Moreover, Scheme supports AI applications just like any other dialect of LISP.

The use of several major programming paradigms to illustrate numerical, data, and knowledge processing gives students a good introduction to the most important trends in programming for the coming decade.[5]

Notes.

1. Abelson and Sussman broke the major ground in this area. See Abelson, Harold, and Sussman, Gerald Jay, with Sussman, Julie, Structure and Interpretation of Computer Programs (Cambridge: The M.I.T. Press, 1985).

2. For an argument in favor of using LISP in CS1, see Lambert, Kenneth A., "Scheme as a First Language," Proceedings of the Third Annual Eastern Small College Computing Conference (Marist College, October, 1987), pp. 90-94.

3. The best recent texts are Kessler, Robert R., LISP, Objects, and Symbolic Programming (Glenview, IL: Scott, Foresman and Company, 1988); Eisenberg, Michael, Programming in Scheme, edited by Abelson, Harold (Redwood City, CA: The Scientific Press, 1988); Smith, Jerry D., An Introduction to Scheme (Englewood Cliffs: Prentice-Hall, 1988); and Winston, Patrick Henry, and Horn, Berthold Klaus Paul, LISP, 3rd Edition (Reading: Addison-Wesley, 1989).

4. For a fine series of articles on frame representation, see Amsterdam, Jonathan, "Building a Flexible Knowledge Representation Scheme," AI Expert, November, 1986, pp. 19-22; "Retrieving Frames from a Frame Data Base," AI Expert, December, 1986, pp. 19-21; "Solving SFRL Problems with a Representation Language Language," AI Expert, February, 1987, pp. 15-19.

5. Lab work for this course used PC Scheme 3.0 running on IBM PS/2 model 50's. 286-based machines or higher are recommended. Source code and some documentation for the course can be obtained by sending a 3 1/2" microdiskette to me.

NEURAL NETWORKS AND ARTIFICIAL INTELLIGENCE

Norman E. Sondak, CSP
Professor of Information and Decision Systems
San Diego State University
San Diego, CA 92182-0127
and
Vernon K. Sondak, M.D.
Assistant Professor of Surgery
University of Michigan Medical Center
Ann Arbor, MI 48109-0331

Abstract

Neural networks have been called "more important than the atomic bomb" and have received a major funding commitment from DARPA. Nevertheless, it is difficult to find even a mention of neural network concepts and applications in many computer science or information systems curricula. In fact, few computer science or information systems faculty are aware of the profound implications of neurocomputing on the future of their field. This paper contends that neural networks must be a significant part of any artificial intelligence course. It illustrates how neural network concepts can be integrated into traditional artificial intelligence course material. Two programming packages for simulating neural networks on personal computers are recommended.

1. Introduction

Neural networks (also called parallel distributed processors, neurocomputing, connectionist models, and artificial neural systems) is one of the fastest growing and most innovative areas of computing. Neural networks represent an attempt to simulate biological information processing through massively parallel, highly-interconnected processing systems.

Neural networks offer the potential for solving complex, non-deterministic problems at very high speeds, the ability to recognize complex patterns, and the capability of rapidly storing and retrieving very large amounts of information. Neurocomputing has also received considerable attention from the Department of Defense and DARPA in a number of application areas, including data fusion, decision assistance, signal processing, and intelligence gathering. Neural networks also have a number of important commercial applications, such as the dynamic solution of routing problems, image and handwriting recognition, systems modeling, speech generation, robot control, and "expertless" expert systems.[1,2,3]

1.1 McCulloch-Pitts Neurons

Despite the current attention from the media, neural networks are not a new idea. In fact, neural network concepts date back to 1943, when McCulloch and Pitts suggested that computations could be performed by a network of simple binary neurons.[4]

The McCulloch-Pitts (M-P) neuron model had two types of inputs, an excitory input and an inhibitory input. The neuron summed the inputs and if the excitory inputs were greater than the inhibitor inputs, the neuron "fired," that is generated an output. While the model, as stated, could account for logical processing, it did not show how information was stored or how intelligent behaviors were learned.[4]

In 1949, Hebb postulated that knowledge was stored in the connections between the neurons, and that "learning" consisted of modifying these connections and altering the excitory and inhibitory effects of the various inputs. A number of early experiments with M-P-like neuron networks and Hebbian learning rules showed very interesting results.[5]

1.2 Perceptrons

Frank Rosenblatt made a major contribution to neural network research during this period with the development of the perceptron.[6]

The perceptron provided a simple model which permitted extensive mathematical analysis of neural networks. Rosenblatt also pioneered the simulation of networks with a digital computer.[7] In addition, Rosenblatt made some exaggerated claims for his perceptrons which arose the ire of a number of other researchers in the field of Artificial Intelligence. Marvin Minsky and Seymour Papert conducted an in-depth mathematical analysis of the perceptron and Rosenblatt's claims, which culminated in the publication of their book Perceptrons. They were able to prove that the perceptron model was really of very limited usefulness and that there were large classes of practical problems that the perceptron could not handle.[8]

Minsky and Papert's work had a devastating effect on neural network research in the '70s and early '80s. During the same period, exciting advances were being made in Artificial Intelligence with knowledge-based systems and production-rule expert systems. However, despite the death of Frank Rosenblatt, some neural network study continued. Even without much support and funding, Steven Grossberg, Geoffrey Hinton, Teuvo Kohonen, and J.A. Anderson continued to pursue neural network research. Their work laid the foundation for significant advances in neural network theory and applications.[9,10,11,12]

1.3 Hopfield Nets

The current wave of interest in neural networks began in 1982. John Hopfield, a prominent biophysicist, showed that by introducing non-linearities, artificial neural networks were capable of solving constrained optimization problems. In addition, he showed the similarity between neural network stability and spin-glass. He introduced the concept of a global energy function to characterize that state of the system, and showed that solution states occupy the lowest energy states.[13,14,15] Hopfield's work aroused interest because his nets offferred the potential to solve a variety of practical problems, such as the "traveling salesman problem." In this application, an example of a constrained optimization problem in which a salesman must visit each of a number of towns on a schedule that minimizes the length of his trip, Hopfield nets found acceptable routes many times more quickly than conventional computing techniques.[2,15]

1.4 Current Models

Since then, several new network models and additional learning rules have been developed, some of which have demonstrated surprising capabilities. This class of models includes Sejnowski and Hilton's Boltzman Machine and Smolensky's Harmony Theory. The back-propagation learning rule developed by Rumelhart, Hinton, and Williams is an example of one of the more powerful developments in this area.[1,16,17]

Advances in the area of reduction to practice also continue. One of the most spectacular is NETTalk by Sejnowski, a neural network system that can learn to read and talk. Neural networks have been applied extensively in defense, particularly in the areas of data fusion, threat recognition, and the solution of routing problems. There are now programs to simulate neural networks on personal computers, add-on neural network co-processing boards, high speed connectivity machines that emulate neural networks and new chips that simulate artificial neural systems.[1,18]

2. Difficulties in learning about neural networks

There is a great deal of interest in neural networks and their applications among Artificial Intelligence practitioners, students, engineers, managers, and executives. The basic concepts and much of the mathematics of the application of neural networks are well within the reach of college sophomores. Yet, in the authors' experience, most individuals have voiced a great deal of frustration in attempting to learn about neural networks. Why is this?

There are several reasons for the confusion about neural networks and neurocomputing. The first is inherent in the media hype about the topic. New items typically have headlines like "Chips that think and act" or "Nerves of silicon." The essential anthropomorphism of this approach tends to create an atmosphere of mystery and confusion about the subject.

The second reason is the fact that neural networks are known by a number of different titles, including parallel distributed processors, artificial neural networks, neurocomputing systems, and connectionist models. All these aliases can be very perplexing to the novice.

However, the most important reason for confusion is the fact that neural network research and applications are inherently interdisciplinary in nature. The original work was done in medicine, psychology, mathematics, and neurophysiology. Then the research enlarged into the areas of electrical engineering and cognitive science. In addition to these areas, neural network research is being done in bio- and neuro-physics, computer science, artificial intelligence, optics, parallel processing and associative memories. To exacerbate the situation, each of these areas of study have their own "world-view," technical jargon, and research publications and platforms.

3. Neural networks and the computer science/information system curriculum

Two questions must be answered when considering the addition of neural networks to a computer science and information systems curriculum. First, should they be added at all? Second, if they are to be added, where and how?

While it is clear that there is intense interest in neural networks, it is also clear that neural networks still represent what can be called an immature discipline. It is estimated that there are now about 175 companies in the field of neural networks, most of which supply research-oriented products. In addition, most large industrial organizations have neural network research programs. DARPA is forecasting spending nearly $400 million in research for neural networks in the coming years. But, at this writing, there is no standard text on the subject, or for that matter even a widely used introductory textbook. There are also no major commercial applications of the technology. It has been stated that "Neural networks have had their MYCINs, but not their XCON," meaning that there have been many exhibitions of potential, but no real commercial successes for neural networks.

However, it is the role and duty of an educational program to prepare students for the future, rather than train them for the present. Using this argument, neural networks should be included in the computer science and information systems curricula.

The question of where to add neural networks is much easier to answer. While neural networks may eventually emerge as a separate academic discipline, there is a strong pedagogical and historical relationship between artificial intelligence and neural networks. Therefore, we propose that neural networks should be included as a major topical area of artificial intelligence courses. How to add the subject is discussed in the following section.

4. Neural network subject matter

Here is our proposed detailed subject matter outline for covering neural network concepts and applications:

Artificial Intelligence and the brain
  Limitations of current computer architecture
  Biological information processing
  An optimized model for information handling
    The Neuron Model
    Self-organization and self-organizing systems
    Symbol manipulation versus non-symbolic information processing
What are neural network computers?
  The structure of neural networks
  Encoding of Knowledge
Brief History of Neural Network Computers
  McCulloch-Pitts Neuron Model
  Perceptrons - Rosenblatt and Minsky
  Associative learning theory
  The rebirth of connectionism
    Connection Machine
Artificial Neural Systems
  Processing elements
  Interconnection structures
  Synchrony and symmetry
  Transfer functions
  Learning strategies
  Linear Algebra and neural network models
Paradigms
  Perceptron, Adaline, and Madaline
  The Learning Machine
  BAM (bidirectional associate memory)
  Brain-state-in-a-box (BSB)
  Hopfield
  Boltzman Machine
  Back propagation
  Sigma Pi Units
  Master-Slave Systems
Emulating Neural Networks on digital systems
Applications of neural networks
  Pattern recognition
  Forecasting, curve fitting, time-series analysis
  Solving Constrained Optimization problems
  NETtalk - learning to speak
Neural networks in defense systems
Problems in designing neural networks
Neural networks and expert systems
The future of neurocomputing

5. The experiential component

It is imperative that the student have hands-on experience in the design and application of neural networks. There are several commercial neural network simulation packages available, as well as some public domain programs that allow students to create their own neural network simulation. However, we recommend the following two packages be considered for the experiential component of the course. Both packages run on an IBM PC/AT or compatible with EGA graphics support.

BRAINMAKER - This package is offered by California Scientific Software, 160 E. Montecito Suite E, Sierra Madre CA 91024. The list price is $99.95. The package is fully menu driven and comes with seven sample neural networks, including networks for optical character recognition, speech synthesis, and image enhancement. The program is extremely fast, rivaling specialized hardware that can cost many times more. The documentation is excellent. Students should find using BRAINMAKER fascinating.

NeuralWorks Professional II - This sophisticated neural network simulator is offered by NeuralWare Inc., 103 Buckskin Court, Sewickley PA 15143. The list price is $995. The program has superb graphics and allows the construction of a wide variety of network models with various learning rules.

6. Student experience

This year, one of the authors (NES) is including neural networks as a component of his Artificial Intelligence in Business course. Preliminary response has been very gratifying. Although the addition of neural network concepts of necessity reduces the time available for teaching traditional AI material, we have found that the concepts are complementary, forcing students to look at entirely new ways of representing and storing knowledge. While production rule-based systems still dominate the course, because of their established business applications, the students seem very excited about the potential for neural networks and are eager to explore them with the software packages we have utilized. In addition, artificial neural networks provide an excellent focal point for discussion of advanced computer architectures and the future of computing.

7. Conclusion

Neural networks should be a part of undergraduate and graduate courses on artificial intelligence. A set of topics is proposed, as well as two commercial software packages that can provide the students with hands-on simulation neural networks applications on the IBM PC/AT or compatible personal computer.

8. References

1. Special Issue on Artificial Neural Systems. Computer, March 1988.
2. Cowan JD, Sharp DH. Neural Nets and Artificial Intelligence. Daedalus 1988; 117: 85-122.
3. Castelaz PF. Application of Neural Network Solution to Battle Management Processing Functions. 55th Military Operations Research Society Symposium, Huntsville AL, May 1987.
4. McCulloch WS, Pitts W. A Logical Calculus of the Ideas Immanent in Nervous Activity. Bull Mathematical Biophysics 1943; 5: 115-133.
5. Hebb DO. The Organization of Behavior. New York: John Wiley, 1949.
6. Rosenblatt F. The Perceptron, A Probabilistic Model for Information Storage and Organization in the Brain. Psychological Review 1958; 62: 386.
7. Rosenblatt F. Principles of Neurodynamics. New York: Spartan, 1962.
8. Minsky M, Papert S. Perceptrons: An Introduction to Computational Geometry. Cambridge MA: MIT Press, 1969.
9. Grossberg S. Studies of Mind and Brain. Reidel, 1982.
10. Hinton GE. Learning Distributed Presentations of Concepts. Proc Cognitive Science Society, Amherst MA, August 1986.
11. Kohonen T. Self-Organization and Associative Memory. Springer-Verlag, 1984.
12. Anderson J (ed). Neurocomputing: Foundations of Research. Cambridge MA: MIT Press, 1988.
13. Hopfield JJ. Neural Networks and Physical Systems with Emergent Collective Computational Properties. Proc National Academy of Sciences 1982; 79: 2554-2558.
14. Hopfield JJ. Neurons With Graded Response Have Collective Computational Properties Like Those of Two-State Neurons. Proc National Academy of Science 1984; 81: 3088-3092.
15. Hopfield JJ, Tank DW. 'Neural' Computation and Constraint Satisfaction Problems and the Traveling Salesman. Biological Cybernetics 1985; 55: 141-146.
16. Rumelhart DE, Hinton GE, Williams RJ. Learning Internal Representations by Error Propagation. In: Rumelhart DE, McClelland JI (eds). Parallel Distributed Processing: Explorations in the Microstructure of Cognition, vol 1, Cambridge MA: MIT Press/Bradford Books, 1986.

17. Denker JS (ed). Neural Networks for Computing. New York: American Institute for Physics, 1986.

18. Sejnowski TJ, Rosenberg CR. NETTalk: A Parallel Network That Learns to Read Aloud. JHU/EECS-86/01, School of Electrical Engineering and Computer Science, Johns Hopkins University, 1986.

19. McClelland JL, Rumelhart DE. Explorations in Parallel Distributed Processing - A Handbook of Models, Programs, and Exercises. Cambridge MA: MIT Press, 1988 (with program diskettes).

20. Schwartz T. 12 Product Wrap-Up: Neural Networks. AI Expert 1988; August:73-85.

Teaching Multiple Programming Paradigms:
A Proposal for a Paradigm-General Pseudocode

Mark B. Wells
Barry L. Kurtz

Computer Science Department
Box 30001
New Mexico State University
Las Cruces, NM 88003

Abstract

Initial overexposure to the imperative programming paradigm can make it very difficult to introduce students to other paradigms, such as the functional, object oriented and logical paradigms. It is important that students be exposed to several programming paradigms early. Two techniques commonly used to accomplish this are a "survey of languages" approach and use of a language, such as Scheme, that overlaps several paradigms. We propose the use of a paradigm-general pseudocode that can then be translated into the most appropriate target language. This paper describes in detail the features and form of this pseudocode using familiar algorithms. This approach has been used successfully in an upper division class and we believe it can be refined and introduced earlier in the curriculum.

1. The Problem

Computer science is a discipline that ranges from abstract mathematical theory, such as lambda calculus or hypercube theory, to electrical engineering, as illustrated by the design of VLSI circuits. Unfortunately, most people equate computer science with programming. Programming is an important tool for the discipline, but it is only a tool and does not represent the breadth of computer science.

While accepting this more abstract view of computer science, it is a fact of life that most introductory computer science courses have a primary focus of developing programming skills and that the choice of language(s) can have a large impact on the development of future skills. Most computer science instructors would agree that it is easier for students who have learned a modern, block structured language, such as Modula-2, to learn an older language, such as Fortran, than moving from an older language to a more modern language. The triumph of Pascal as the primary teaching language in computer science is a tribute to it's simplicity and elegance. Now the debate among instructors seems to center on the successor to Pascal: should it be Modula-2 or Ada? We feel that these arguments miss the point -- we should be discussing paradigms for algorithm development and not choices between languages within a particular programming paradigm.

[Baron, 1986]

In this paper we consider four major paradigms which we characterize in the following way:

imperative - characterized by declare, assign and use; declarations in a block precede a sequence of statements, including assignment

functional - characterized by construct and apply; such languages involve functional application and the direct construction of data and program objects

object-oriented - characterized by the uniform treatment of objects; such languages stress object classes and inheritance of properties from parent classes

logical - characterized by logical relations and automated search of possible paths leading to solution; the primary mechanism is resolution

These classifications are not mutually exclusive and most languages overlap paradigms to some extent. For example, Scheme is primarily a functional language but it has many attributes similar to imperative languages (e.g. static scoping) and has facilities for creating objects. Ada is primarily an imperative language but does provide limited facilities for object oriented programming. Only logic programming languages stand in a category by themselves. Even there the most widely used language, Prolog, has had to borrow features from other paradigms in order to make implementation practical.

Most beginning computer science courses first introduce students to an imperative programming paradigm. Typically students take introductory programming, data structures, and possibly other courses (e.g. software engineering) using imperative languages before they are introduced to other paradigms. If we count high school or other prior experience, this exposure to the imperative paradigm is even more lengthy. Students are usually introduced to other paradigms in a programming language design course or an artificial intelligence course. By this time they are so engrained in the imperative paradigm that it is extremely difficult to learn new approaches. This is somewhat analogous to natural languages; an adult who has spoken only one natural language has extreme difficulty in learning a new language while younger children have less difficulty with new languages. Learning several languages within the imperative paradigm does little to solve this problem; in fact, it might even make it worse since students will assume all languages must be based on certain features, such as the assignment statement.

Another aspect of this problem is the common choice of the imperative paradigm first. Of the four paradigms discussed, the imperative paradigm is probably the least powerful and least expressive. Even a large, complex language such as Ada lacks many powerful features found in a simple functional language like Lisp. We are not discussing abstract power here, after all most languages are "Turing machine equivalent," but rather the power to develop algorithms and data structures in a natural manner. Let's discuss two quick examples to illustrate some fundamental weaknesses in the imperative paradigm. First, functions are not first class citizens. In Ada there is no procedure type and procedures cannot be passed as parameters. Modula-2 has a procedure type that can be used in a parameter list, but functions cannot return functions. More fundamentally, the procedure types do not encapsulate their environments (expressed in a contour model by an ip, ep pair). [Johnston, 1971] Other mechanisms may be available, such as generic packages in Ada, yet imperative languages lack power by not making functions first class citizens. Another problem is the construction of recursive data domains. The fundamental data structure of Lisp, the s-expression, is naturally recursive; the user can create lists of arbitrary length without being aware of any underlying implementation. The analogous mechanism in imperative languages is the pointer, sometimes called the goto of data structures. The user must create the desired structure from scratch, manage memory directly, and insure the integrity of the structure. In a powerful programming language this can all be transparent to the user.

In defense of imperative languages, they do provide, among high level languages, the most efficient implementation for many fundamental algorithms used on today's sequential machines. In general, they are not as demanding on cpu time and memory space as non-imperative languages. And, from a practical perspective, in the "real world" imperative languages are used much more widely than other languages.

Despite these virtues of imperative languages, we believe that *prolonged initial overexposure* to the imperative paradigm is harmful to the health of potential computer scientists. Other academics have also recognized this problem; some of the approaches they have used to correct this situation are outlined in the next section. Then, in the following section, we propose an alternative method for introducing multiple paradigms in a natural way in the computer science curriculum.

2. Some Current Approachs

The problem of placing too much emphasis on imperative languages has been recognized by many computer scientists and there are two main approaches to solve this problem. One approach is to present a survey of languages early in the computer science curriculum; another approach is to teach a language that overlaps two or more paradigms.

The "survey of languages" approach introduces students to two or three languages, usually representing different paradigms, within the first year. For example, a semester system school might teach the introductory programming course in an imperative language like Pascal and then the data structures course in a functional language like Lisp. For a school on the quarter system, the first quarter could be in an imperative language (e.g. Modula-2), the next quarter in a functional language (e.g. Lisp or Scheme), and the third quarter in a logic programming language (usually Prolog). There is a danger using this approach that students will focus on learning the syntax of specific programming languages rather than learning computer science. Unfortunately this reinforces the mistaken notion that the ability of a computer scientist is measured by the number of languages spoken.

Another approach is to select a language that overlaps several paradigms. There are several possible choices of languages; we will discuss Scheme (a variant of Lisp), Ada, Smalltalk and Prolog.

Scheme depends primarily on functional application, however it does have some features similar to imperative languages (assignment and static scoping) and has facilities for developing object oriented programs. Scheme allows the direct construction of recursive data structures and treats functions as first class citizens (in fact, even "continuations" are first class!). Some disadvantages of Scheme are weak data abstraction and the use of Cambridge Polish notation.

Ada is an imperative language that has some object oriented features, such as packages. Generic packages and derived types have the flavor of inheritance, but genericity is not as general or powerful as inheritance [Meyer, 1988]. Despite its size and complexity, Ada has many disadvantages: functions are not first class, pointers are required for recursive data domains, and the language is too statement oriented.

Smalltalk is an object oriented language with some features similar to imperative languages (e.g. assignment, statement sequencing) and some similar to functional languages (e.g. expression orientation, uniform treatment of data). Although the authors are not aware of a computer science program that uses Smalltalk as the primary, introductory language, this should not rule it out of consideration. Some disadvantages of Smalltalk are dynamic typing, weak facilities for direct data construction, and a strange distfix notation.

Prolog is not usually taught as an introductory programming language, but it does allow a variety of programming styles. Sterling and Shapiro [1986] claim that the user can program logically, functionally, or imperatively using Prolog. However, Prolog has many disadvantages, the primary one being the introduction of nonintuitive control mechanisms (such as the cut statement) that compromise Prolog as a pure logic programming language.

Both the "multiparadigm" single language approach and the survey approach have advantages and disadvantages. Of the languages discussed above, only Scheme really represents a combination of paradigms. Its major flaw is the lack of strong type checking as found in many imperative languages. The survey approach presents languages with distinct flavors, yet suffers from a "computer science is learning programming languages" mentality. This paper was motivated by an need to find a way to combine these approaches. Is there a way to teach a simple, powerful method for expressing algorithms in any paradigm that allows selection of an appropriate target language at implementation time? In the next section we present a powerful, paradigm-general pseudocode that can be used to express algorithms in a natural way. Then we give several specific examples with translations into different target languages representing different paradigms. After this presentation we discuss the advantages and disadvantages of such an approach and the feasibility of implementation.

3. A Paradigm-General Pseudocode

The use of pseudocode is quite common today, particularly for instruction in imperative languages. These pseudocodes tend to be the common intersection of features for a variety of imperative languages; they are generally based on the assignment statement, an 'if' statement and a 'loop' statement. [Peterson, 1983] Since the pseudocode is a subset of many target languages, translation into any one of them is fairly direct. However, in designing algorithms with such a minimal subset, there will inevitably be features in the target language that have not been used. Also, these pseudocodes are generally only useful for imperative languages.

Rather than have a pseudocode based on a common intersection of features from multiple languages, we present a powerful, paradigm-general pseudocode that can be translated into many target languages. Clearly one cannot have a coherent pseudocode simply by taking the "union" of several language paradigms. Rather, our pseudocode is derived from a real programming language, Modcap, an expression language under development at New Mexico State University. We have simplified Modcap's syntax, omitted several features, such as concurrency, and eliminated the very strong type checking features. Modcap has been used to implement algorithms in all four paradigms: imperative, functional, object oriented and logical. [Wells, 1988] Our simplified pseudocode also allows algorithm development in a variety of paradigms. Not every target language will have all of the features of this powerful pseudocode, so once the algorithm is developed, it is important to choose a target language that most closely matches the paradigm used in the algorithm.

Pseudocode Features

clear and precise algorithms - Regardless of the target language (or paradigm), algorithms should be easy to comprehend at the pseudocode level. There should be a balance between a pseudocode so exacting in syntax that it could be parsed and possibly translated into a target language and a pseudocode so loose that it is useless in developing the algorithm in a target language.

247

expression orientation with operator overloading - We prefer an expression-oriented pseudocode in contrast to a statement-oriented notation since it is more general: statements can be viewed as expressions that return zero values. The natural use of mathematical notation should be permitted, such as xy for the infix function multiplication applied to x and y, x! for the application of the suffix function factorial to x, -x for the application of the prefix function negate to x. It should be possible to overload operators with the left hand operand determining the correct operation (similar to object oriented languages). For example, s + e might represent integer addition if s is an integer or it might represent the push operation if s is a stack of integers.

assignment as a naming construct - Variables should simply identify memory locations and the target of assignment should be a simple variable name. In other words, the Ada-like assignment to an array element in the form A(i) := x would be written using a built-in operation on arrays (x, A) @ i instead of assignment.

use of both iteration and recursion - Most modern languages allow both recursion and iteration, however, they are usually biased towards one approach or the other. For example, in Ada, recursion is limited since functions are not first class. Lisp is naturally recursive yet has primitive mechanisms (PROG, labels, GO, and RETURN) for iterative programming. A paradigm-general pseudocode should allow both approaches naturally.

runtime stack model - We will use a runtime stack to transmit information between program components. This is more powerful than the traditional parameter list since it allows for "multivaluedness." Unlike Common Lisp that uses similar techniques but generally hides them from the user, our pseudocode includes features to manipulate the runtime stack directly.

direct construction of recursive data domains (no pointers) - Imperative languages do not allow the domain constructor D* since the size of the domain cannot be determined at compile time. Pointers to dynamic structures on the heap are the only equivalent mechanism. Lisp allows recursive domains at the expense of sacrificing most type checking. Smalltalk allows recursive domains, but type checking is delayed until runtime. We believe that recursive domains should be allowed so one could represent an integer stack as either empty or [stack, integer] and a binary tree with strings at the nodes as either empty or [tree, string, tree].

data abstraction - Modern languages (e.g. Modula-2, Ada, Scheme, Smalltalk) have some mechanism to support data abstraction and information hiding. Our pseudocode will include "spaces" as a method for data abstraction.

uniform treatment of objects as first class citizens - Objects are identified by names and named objects should be treated uniformly whether constants or variables, and regardless of the type (e.g. integer, function, space, etc.). Imperative languages do not treat functions or spaces as first class objects. This seriously limits the expressive power of these languages and leads to the introduction of artificial mechanisms (e.g. generics in Ada) to alleviate these limitations.

The careful reader may have noted that we omitted one important feature found in most modern programming languages: a mechanism for concurrency. This was done due to the variety of mechanisms available in target languages (e.g. compare Modula-2 and Ada) and the lack of experience in teaching concurrency early in the curriculum. This will be explored more in the discussion section.

The Pseudocode

The pseudocode is based on five fundamental data types: number, string, function, tuple, and space. Literal forms for these types are:

ddd[.ddd]	for number
"c...c"	for string
{...}	for function
[...]	for tuple
\...\	for space (a set of operations for an ADT)

The pseudocode is a "multivalued expression language" in that an expression may return zero, one, or more values to the stack. These values may be "named" and thus removed from the stack in three ways:

(1) use an initializing assignment, indicated by a prefix underscore

... ; _quo, _rem 7/3 ; ... -- quo set to 2, rem to 1

(2) use reassignment, indicated by the prefix symbol @

... ; @x x+1 ; ... --- increment x by one

(3) use "discarding" assignment, indicated by caret ^ in place of the prefixed name

... ; @quo, ^ 50/9 ; ... -- quo is 5, rem is discarded

If more values are stacked by the expression's evaluation than are removed by assignment, then the excess values remain stacked. For example, division returns a quotient and remainder on the stack, so

... ; ^ 14/3 ; ... -- discard remainder 2,
-- quotient 4 remains on stack

A portion of the stack may be bundled into a (literal) tuple using square brackets. For instance, the program segment

... ; 5; [^ 14/3, "dog"]; x ; ...

leaves three items on the stack: the number 5, a 2-tuple consisting of the integer 4 and the string "dog" as its elements, and the current value of x. Tuples, like objects of the other four basic types (and, in fact, of any user-defined abstract type), are first class and thus can be named, reassigned and discarded from the stack by the mechanisms discussed above. For example,

... ; _T [0, x, y, n+1] ; ...

is an initializing assignment to T of a four-tuple.

It is important that the tupling mechanism in our pseudocode is generalized to an arbitrary number of fields, as contrasted with Lisp's two field car-cdr mechanism. Also, it provides a generalization of Ada's "aggregate notation" [Ada Reference Manual, 1983], Smalltalk's "literal arrays" [Goldberg, 1983], and Scheme's "literal vectors" [TI Scheme Language Reference Manual, 1986] since expressions rather than just constants may directly provide elements to the structure.

Accessing elements of a tuple is indicated by juxtaposing a zero-based index on the right of the tuple, as in T(i). As mentioned previously, changing an element of an existing tuple is not done with assignment; rather it is treated in an object-oriented manner as a tuple modification operation denoted with an infix @ symbol: (v, T) @ i. Since this operation returns the modified tuple to the stack, it is often used with the discarding assignment

... ; ^ (v, T) @ i; ... -- assigns v to ith element of T
-- and leaves nothing stacked

Literal functions are delimited with braces, as in {N + 1}, and this bracketing defers evaluation of the expression within the braces. Later application of the function is denoted by juxtaposing a parenthesized list of actual parameter expressions to the right of the function name.

... ; _N 1; _incrN {N + 1}; ... ; incrN (); ...

Function bodies always evaluate in the static environment of definition. Thus, the N referenced by incrN() is the N defined immediately before the incrN function definition regardless of any intervening definitions of N before the function call. Formal parameter expressions within function bodies are denoted by one or more question marks, ?...?, to indicate the position in the parameter list, followed by the "type" of the legal corresponding actual parameter expression. For example, given

... ; _g {2*?integer + 3*??integer} ; ...

then g(4,5) would evaluate to 23. Notice that formal parameters need not be named. However, they can be named, if desired, by the standard assignment mechanism. For instance, the function defined by

... ; _g { _m ?integer; _n ??integer; 2*m + 3*n} ; ...

is semantically equivalent to the previous definition of g. In keeping with the general multivaluedness of our pseudocode, parameter expressions as well as function bodies themselves may produce zero or more stacked values.

Control in our expression oriented pseudocode is based on a unique "exception" value which, for the sake of readability, has several aliases: *nil*, *false*, and *quit*. This value acts as the boolean "false" when appearing on top of the run-time stack after evaluating the test expression of an if-then-else expression or while-do expression; any other value acts like a "true". The 'else' or exit branch is taken if a "false" is on top of the stack and the false is automatically popped off the stack. The 'then' or 'do' branch is taken if a "true" is on top of the stack and the value remains on top of the stack for future use. This value may be named and thereby removed from the stack using the assignment notation noted above. For example,

... ; _n 0; while n+1 < 100 do @n: ... ; ...
            -- use n within the body of the while loop
... ; if a > b then ^: ... else ... ; ...
            -- "traditional" if-then-else expression
... ; if n/m = 0 then _q, ^ : ...
            -- use quotient if remainder is 0
            -- and discard remainder
   else ^: ...   ; ...
            -- discard inexact quotient

All of these examples use another feature of our pseudocode, namely, that the left operand of a relational operation is returned as the "true" value if indeed the relation is true; otherwise, false is returned.

The pseudocode also makes use of a for...do... notation. The expression between the 'for' and the 'do' generates a sequence of values which successively become values for the assignment variable which appears just after the 'do'. Examples are:

... ; for 1 to 10 do _i: ... ; ... -- i successively is 1,..., 10
... ; for in S do _e: ... ; ... -- e runs over elements in S

An important usage for these control structures, particularly the if..then..else and for..do, is within expressions when the 'then' and 'else' or 'do' branches are omitted. For example,

... if n < m ...

returns either nothing (the "false" was automatically popped off) or the value n which is known to be less than m. Another example is

... for 1 to 10 ...

which returns a list of integers 1,2,..,10.

There is also a replication operation written in the form:

... n:x ...

where the left hand operand may be any natural number and the right hand operand any data item. For instance:

... 100:0 ...

results in a list of 100 zeros. We will see this same notation when describing structures, e.g. any:item. This notation represents an arbitrary number of items.

Finally, we briefly describe "spaces", the sets of operations that define abstract data types. Our expression-oriented pseudocode allows operator overloading and assumes that the meaning of any operator is determined by the type of the leftmost operand. This is quite reasonable for most mathematical expressions that appear in imperative languages like Pascal and Ada, and is consistent with object-oriented message passing notation as it appears in Smalltalk. It is also consistent with traditional function application notation, e.g. f(x), assuming that juxtaposition is a legitimate infix operator.

The operations associated with a particular type are grouped into literal spaces which use the backslash symbol as a bracketing delimiter. The operations are of two kinds: *constructions* and *manipulations*. Constructions are denoted by bracketing literal forms, such as (...), [...], {...} for example, and provide a means of creating new objects of the type associated with the space. We have already seen bracketing literal forms as in square brackets to create new tuples, braces to create new functions, quotation marks to create new strings, etc. The construction operations themselves are primitive in these cases but would be given as functions for user defined types. An example of user defined complex number space is:

_COMPLEX \
   [ ], { [?(real, real)] };   -- construction
   x+y, {...};   -- addition
\ ;

To distinguish formation of complex numbers from tuple formation, the suffix qualification, 'COMPLEX, must be used, as in [0.0, 1.0]'COMPLEX.

Manipulations are operations on existing objects of the type associated with the space. They are accessed with either prefix, infix or suffix operator notation. Many operations on numbers, strings, tuples, etc. are primitive. Nonprimitive manipulations, like constructions, are given within the spaces as functions. The addition operation within the COMPLEX space would be:

{ _x ?[real, real]'COMPLEX, _y ??[real, real]'COMPLEX,
   [x(0) + y(0), x(1) + y(1)]'COMPLEX }

The inputs to this operation are complex numbers represented as tuples. After the real and imaginary parts are added, the pair is converted back to a complex number using the basic complex number construction.

In the simple example discussed above, complex numbers are represented by 2-tuples of real numbers. In object oriented programming, as exemplified by Smalltalk, complex numbers would be represented by two (local) "instance variables" that are accessible only to the "methods" (operations) of the "class" (space). This approach is possible in our pseudocode by having the construction operation of the space not furnish a concrete representation but merely provide access to the local environment of the space definition where any number of local "instance" variables reside. This is illustrated in the following NewStack function.

```
_NewStack {
  _x ?general;                          -- line 1
  _stack   nil union [general, stack];  -- line 2
  _s \                                  -- line 3
    (), {s};                            -- line 4
    s+e, { @stack [??general, stack]};  -- line 5
    s-, {                               -- line 6
      if stack then _s:                 -- line 7
        s(0);                           -- line 8
        @stack s(1)                     -- line 9
      else x                            -- line 10
    }                                   -- line 11
  \                                     -- line 12
  ()'s                                  -- line 13
```

Line 1 allows the user to specify the value to be returned if an empty stack is popped. Line 2 gives the representation for a stack as a linked list; the first value, nil, is also the initial value. The space itself is between lines 3 and 12. Line 4 gives the construction and line 5 is the push operator. Lines 6-11 define the pop operation. Line 7 checks if the stack is not empty in which case the top item is returned (line 8) and removed from the stack (line 9). If the stack is empty, the user specified item x is returned (line 10). Line 13 is used to provide access to the space and its environment.

The stack is used in the following way:

```
_ST NewStack(nil)        -- initializes ST to a stack object
ST+data                  -- pushes an item onto the stack
if ST- then _d: ...      -- if pop successful, assign to d and use
else ...                 -- error handler for popping empty stack
```

Translation of this pseudocode into Smalltalk is straightforward. For example, the use of the stack would be written:

```
ST <- Stack new: x.
ST push: data.
ST pop ifTrue: [...] ifFalse: [...].
```

More Examples

We complete this section with two familiar algorithms, a recursive and a nonrecursive quicksort, and an example of a generator function that utilizes the first class property of functions. Translation to target languages is discussed and actual code is provided when appropriate.

Here is a functional version of the quicksort algorithm.

```
_functional.quicksort
  {
    if ?[any:item] = [] then ^:
    else _T:
      _pivot  T(0)
      functional.quicksort ( [ for in T do _s: if s < pivot] )
      for in T do _s: if s = pivot
      functional.quicksort ( [ for in T do _s: if s > pivot ] )
  }
```

At first glance this may look very familiar: two recursive calls, one to sort elements less than the pivot and one to sort elements greater than the pivot. However, the imperative algorithm would do the complete partitioning process before making the recursive calls. Here the partitioning and recursion are combined; each partition is created as the parameter to the appropriate recursive call. Notice the expressive power of putting a 'for' expression that generates a sequence of values inside a tuple constructor which passes this "list" as an argument to the recursive call. With the separation of the partitioning into a separate step, this algorithm can be translated into imperative code. However, it can be translated more directly into Scheme:

```
(define sort
  (lambda (L)
    (if (null? L)
      '()
      (let ((pivot (car L)))
        (append (sort (LES L pivot))
          (append (EQU L pivot)
            (sort (GTR L pivot) ) ) ) ) ) ) )
```

It is assumed the function LES returns a list of all elements of L less than the pivot and the functions EQU and GTR act similarly.

If efficiency is a primary goal, quicksort can be written nonrecursively provided the programmer maintains a stack of postponed obligations. Here is our algorithm:

```
_nonrecursive.quicksort
  {
    _A ?[any:item];                          -- line 1
    _stack  nil union [stack, [index, index]];  -- line 2
    @stack := [ stack, [ 0, #A-1 ] ];        -- line 3
    while stack do _s:                       -- line 4
      @stack, _I, _J  s(0), s(1, 0), s(1,1); -- line 5
      _pivot  A(I);                          -- line 6
      _i, _j  I, J;                          -- line 7
      while i <= j do ^:                     -- line 8
        while (i <= J) and (A(i) <= pivot) do ^:  -- line 9
          @i  i + 1;                         -- line 10
        while (I <= j) and (A(j) >= pivot) do ^:  -- line 11
          @j  j - 1;                         -- line 12
        if i < j then ^:                     -- line 13
          ^ (A(i), A(j), A) @i @j;           -- line 14
          @i i+1;  @j j-1;                    -- line 15
      if I<j then ^:                         -- line 16
        ^ (A(I), A(j), A) @I @j;             -- line 17
        @j  j - 1;                           -- line 18
        if I < j then ^:                     -- line 19
          @stack  [stack, [I, j]];           -- line 20
      if i < J then ^:                       -- line 21
        @stack  [stack, [i, J]];             -- line 22
  }
```

This algorithm follows the standard nonrecursive, imperative quicksort very closely so the detailed implementation in an imperative language will not be given. However, features of the pseudocode illustrated by this algorithm are worth discussing. Line 1 says that this algorithm has a single parameter of a tuple containing any number of occurrences of the same type, which is similar to a one-dimensional array. The stack in line 2 is defined as a nil stack (the initial value) or a singly linked structure containing an index pair at each node. Since the original index bounds are from 0 to #A-1 (# returns the size of a tuple), this is pushed onto the stack in line 3. Line 5 illustrates a multiple assignment statement. The first assignment reassigns stack the old value with the top element removed; the other two assignments access the nested tuples to recover the appropriate indices from the top item. The index i is moved right until an element greater than the pivot is found (lines 9-10) and the index j is moved left until an element less than the pivot is found (lines 11-12). If the indices have not crossed, the elements A(i) and A(j) are exchanged (notice that the copy of the tuple on the stack is removed by the ^ discarding assignment) and the indices advanced (lines 14-15). Lines 16-18 put the pivot element in its proper place. Then the left partition is stacked if it contains more than one element (lines 19-20). If the right partition contains more than one element, it is stacked at the bottom of the while loop (line 21-22). The algorithm terminates when the stack of indices is empty.

The final example illustrates the use of functions as first class objects. This pseudo-random number generator is presented by Knuth in **The Art of Computer Programming**, vol. 2 [1968], as Algorithm M on page 30.

```
{
  _xMod 32768;                    -- line 1
  _yMod 983;                      -- line 2
  _x 16000;                       -- line 3
  _y 5;                           -- line 4
  _newX {x; @x 11111*x+1 mod xMod};  -- line 5
  _newY {y; @y 500*y+1 mod yMod};    -- line 6
  _T [for 0 to 99 do ^: newX()];  -- line 7

  {
    _a ?positive; _b ??positive;  -- line 8
    _i 100*newY/yMod;             -- line 9
    a + (b-a+1)*T(i)/xMod;        -- line 10
    ^ (newX(), T) @ i;            -- line 11
  }
}
```

Lines 1-2 initialize the two moduluses and lines 3-4 give initial values to x and y. Line 5 assigns to newX a generator function for x values. First x is put on the stack and then reassigned a new value as indicated by the arithmetic expression. In a similar way line 6 is a generator function for y values. T is the selection table that is initialized to the first hundred values of the x generator in line 7. The random number generator is the function in lines 8-11. The parameters a and b give the range of values from which the pseudo-random number is to be selected. First, in line 9, a "random index" is assigned to i. Then, in line 10, the table entry at T(i) is used to produce, and return, a number in the range from a to b. Finally, the table entry at the ith position is given a new "random value" in line 11.

4. Discussion

Like all new methodologies, our paradigm-general pseudocode may initially look very strange, even when read by experienced computer scientists. Many people have similar feelings when they see Lisp or Prolog for the first time. This pseudocode introduces many powerful concepts that require practice before they become natural. We have used this approach in an upper division class and it worked well once students "got the hang of things." An initial period of confusion and frustration is overcome as more and more examples are developed. It is important to relate algorithms in the pseudocode to languages known by the students (e.g. Modula-2 or Ada, Lisp or Scheme, Smalltalk). Actually, no students in the class knew Smalltalk ahead of time; they learned pieces of the language when object oriented algorithms were translated into Smalltalk. By the end of the course students could use the pseudocode in a natural way and really appreciated the various approaches of the imperative, functional and object oriented paradigms.

We do not have enough experience yet to predict how early this approach can be introduced. Clearly it is too sophisticated for the first computer science course. However, it is evident that our entering students are much better prepared today; a vast majority of students have previous programming experience either from high school, computer literacy courses, or personal experience. Given this trend, we believe that eventually our paradigm-general pseudocode can be introduced fairly early in the curriculum.

One feature of the pseudocode we have not discussed is concurrency. One problem is that the mechanisms for concurrency in target languages vary greatly. For example, Modula-2 provides a primitive coroutining mechanisms that can be used to build more sophisticated mechanisms, like signal and wait. Ada, on the other hand, has a very high level approach called rendezvous. Ada's approach is based on the CSP model developed by Hoare [1978] and borrows the guard concept from Dijkstra [1975]. We prefer the latter approach and have worked out the appropriate pseudocode; however, we have not used this approach in the classroom yet.

5. Conclusions

We developed the pseudocode described in this paper to provide students with a powerful yet informal way of developing algorithms. Most current pseudocodes are a small subset of features common to many languages and thus are not very powerful or expressive. Our approach is to develop a powerful pseudocode that is a superset of many paradigms. At this time it is largely a teaching tool since many target languages lack the features used in our pseudocode. We believe that multiparadigm target languages such as Scheme or Modcap are most appropriate. Many systems today allow users to integrate languages from different paradigms (e.g. C and Lisp and Prolog) into a single software system. If this is the case, then we recommend first using a paradigm-general pseudocode to develop algorithms in the most natural way and then working out the details of translating the algorithm into the most appropriate target language.

We have only started work on developing this approach. It has been used successfully in an upper division class, but we need more experience with this approach to see if it can be introduced earlier in the curriculum. We

firmly believe that students must be introduced to multiple programming paradigms early in their training and that a powerful, paradigm-general pseudocode is one mechanism for attaining this goal.

References

Baron, N., "The future of computer languages: implications for education", *SIGCSE Bulletin*, 18:1 (1986), pp. 44-49

Dijkstra, E.W., "Guarded commands, nondeterminacy, and formal derivation of programs", *CACM* 18:8 (1975), pp. 453-457

Goldberg, A. and Robson, D., **Smalltalk 80: The Language and Its Implementation**, Addison-Wesley, Reading, Mass. 1983

Hoare, C.A.R. "Communicating sequential processes", *CACM* 21:8 (1978) pp. 666-677

Johnston, J. "The Contour Model of Block Structured Processes", *Sigplan Notices* 6:2 (1971), pp. 55+

Knuth, D. **The Art of Computer Programming**, vol. 2, Addison-Wesley, Reading, Mass. 1968

Meyer, B., "Genericity versus Inheritance", *Journal of Pascal, Ada, and Modula-2*, 7:2 (1988), pp. 13-30

Peterson, G., "Using Generalized Programs in the Teaching of Computer Science", *SIGCSE Bulletin*, 15:1 (1983) pp. 187-192

Reference Manual for the Ada Programming Language, ANSI/MIL-STD-1815A, United States Department of Defense, 1983

Sterling, L. and Shapiro, E.,The art of Prolog : advanced programming techniques, M.I.T. Press, Cambridge, Mass. 1986

TI Scheme: Language Reference Manual, Rev. A, Texas Instruments Incorporated, August 1986

Wells, M., "Multiparadigmatic Programming in Modcap", to appear in *Journal of Object-Oriented Programming*, 1988

Never Mind the Language, What About the Paradigm?

Paul A. Luker
Computer Science Department
California State University, Chico
Chico, California 95929-0410

Abstract

There is increasing discussion about the primary programming language used for undergraduate courses in Computer Science. In particular, the language used for CS1 and CS2 is regarded as a crucial factor in students' subsequent progress in the discipline, not to mention their mental well-being. It is argued here that instead of focussing our attention on whether we should be teaching Ada[TM] or MODULA-2, we should be asking if these languages belong to the right class. There is mounting evidence that "small" languages are not only beautiful but that they lead to more easily verifiable programs, more predictable implementations, and a better foundation for "programming in the large". I do not pretend to answer any more questions than I ask.

1. Historical Introduction

For those of us who have been teaching Computer Science for nearly twenty years, there is a feeling of *déjà vu* about debates on the first programming language for our majors. It is interesting that, in the past, different countries have adopted different solutions to what was supposedly the same problem.

As most of my own experience in Computer Science education has been in England, I shall begin with my observations of language fads and fashions in the United Kingdom and use this as a platform for the main discussion of this paper. In the beginning (for those graduating in the 1960s in Britain) there was ALGOL 60. This was the language I first encountered in my own education and that which I primarily used subsequently in industry. It came as no real shock, then, to find that this was the language taught to Computer Science undergraduates when I started teaching in 1971. ALGOL 60 was the "right stuff", because it was more elegant, with its block structure and range of control statements. With so few types offered, its strong typing was a secondary but significant factor, entirely wasted on engineers, of course, who only ever need reals (in double precision) and FORTRAN.

[TM] Ada is a registered trademark of the US Government, Ada Joint Program Office.

For service courses to students from other disciplines, BASIC was proving to be very popular. It was not the language but its environment that was attractive, the high degree of interaction providing the encouragement for the student that was not afforded by the impersonal, clinical austerity of the batch system. And, if you programmed in BASIC you could use a terminal rather than have to contort your fingers to produce semi-colons on a hand card punch. Experience with these service courses put BASIC in such a good light, that it became the first language for some Computer Science majors.

It was not long before this cosy world collapsed. Once Knuth had branded the **goto** as harmful, no self-respecting Computer Science school could countenance any further use of BASIC, for fear of rendering programmers permanently impaired. At the same time, ALGOL 60 was getting a little long in the tooth, and its paucity of data types was proving rather inconvenient. The search for a successor was on.

Hoare and Wirth had produced ALGOL W, for which there were reasonable implementations available. Another, less direct descendant of ALGOL 60, ALGOL 68, became something of a cult language in some universities. For most, though, it was too large, too powerful and too forgiving. Meanwhile, on the continent of Europe, SIMULA 67, which has not received the widespread recognition it has deserved until more recently, had a strong following, particularly in Scandinavia, Holland and West Germany. SIMULA, as it has now been renamed, was a natural successor to ALGOL 60—it extended the range of types, cleaned up some of the less pleasant aspects of ALGOL 60, and added the **class**, which at once provided coroutines and support for object-oriented programming. The first book on object-oriented programming was *SIMULA begin* [3].

It was Pascal, Wirth's successor to ALGOL W that became the universal *lingua franca* for Computer Science courses. Pascal provided strong typing together with a sufficient set of types and control constructs that were being demanded in the 1970s, what is more, it is a small language. As a consequence, many Pascal implementations are robust and efficient. Today, however, Pascal appears to have outstayed its welcome almost universally. Many instructors are now agonising over whether to go to Ada or MODULA-2. The issue is not so simple. We have to make sure that we ask the right questions about the language.

History bears witness to the success of languages that support what Wirth called a systematic approach to programming. Program code must be readable to facilitate maintenance and development. Strong typing leads to fewer run-time errors, at the relatively small expense of more compilation errors. All other things being equal, a small language is better than a large one. With these lessons in mind, I shall now look briefly at some current trends in programming styles or paradigms in order to determine where we should go from here.

2. Currents in Language Evolution

Consider the following quote:

> It is commonly observed that we have a software crisis and in a gathering of computer scientists it should not be necessary to multiply examples. Everyone has their own favourite horror story about a project that failed in some catastrophic way because of a bug in a program. Less spectacular but equally worrying is the high cost of producing software even for comparatively simple applications. It is by now clear that the largest single obstacle to the wider use of computers is our inability to produce cheap, reliable and manageable software. . . . Does it seem too unreasonable to suggest that there is something fundamentally wrong about the way in which we produce software?

Few people would disagree with these sentiments. Most books on Ada, such as [14], begin in a similar vein. Turner, the author of the above quote was not, however, advocating Ada, or anything like it. He continued:

> I shall argue that the basic problem lies in the nature of existing programming languages. Existing programming languages emerged in a relatively short period between 1955 and 1960—FORTRAN and COBOL set the pattern for later languages. They have evolved since primarily by becoming more complicated—the underlying principles have not altered at all. When we compare say Pascal with FORTRAN the similarities are much more striking than the differences. More precisely the differences are superficial but the similarities are fundamental. At a certain level of abstraction all the programming languages in production use today [1981] are the same. All are sequential imperative languages with assignment as their basic action. [17]

Turner continues by putting forward a convincing argument for using applicative, or functional languages as the basis for all computer programming. In a nutshell, his rationale is that such languages are based on a very clear and constant formalism—mathematics. This is no isolated voice. Many others advocate the use of functional languages [6, 9], not only to solve the software crisis, but also because they are more suitable for new computer architectures which move away from the von Neumann concept. Alas, there is no consolation in finding a cell of support for Turner's views, for there are many other cells which argue equally enthusiastically and convincingly in support of different paradigms. Now what should we do?

I shall start with the points of general agreement. First, it is clear that there is a software crisis. What is more worrying, though, is not the over-inflated cost of software projects, but rather the poor integrity of their products. This becomes more critical as we produce a greater number of embedded systems which are under the sole control of software. A major thrust of the case against the Strategic Defense Initiative is precisely the issue of software integrity [15]. Software fails to work as intended, and is more expensive than originally estimated because it is extremely complex. Of course, we have been stressing the importance of program design techniques for some time now, emphasizing

the importance of modularity and good style, but is this enough, if we disregard the language in which the code is written? Turner, for one, voices a clear "No" in response to this question.

A second point of consensus has been the need to develop program verification techniques and tools. The ideal case would be to go from a program specification to program code (proven correct) in a sequence of mechanical steps. While this has yet to be achieved for software projects of significant size, some of the groundwork has been laid. A key issue here is the theory that underlies the language—how well the language conforms to some tractable mathematical formalism which can be used as a tool for analysing the programs written in that language.

So far, so good. Alas, the next step is not as logical as we might hope. Different camps maintain that their philosophy is the key to successful software engineering. I shall now take a brief look at some of the programming paradigms that are on offer. I shall begin with the solution Turner espouses. I shall then comment on two other philosophies and then digress to look at concurrent programming. These paradigms are not all disjoint, nor is my selection exhaustive.

3. Functional Programming

One of the early proponents of functional programming was John Backus, whose Turing Award Lecture in 1977 asked "Can programming be liberated from the von Neumann style?" [2]. He argued that existing languages were designed around the constraints of the von Neumann architecture, rather than on any foundation of rational software design. Backus condemned existing languages as "fat and flabby". The large size of these languages, or most of them, is not a desirable feature from the points of view of learning, implementation, or verification.

A kingpin of the argument for the functional style is *referential transparency*, whereby a given expression will always have the same meaning or value, regardless of context. This facilitates reasoning about the behavior of programs. Procedural languages, with their emphasis on assignment to variables are *referentially opaque*, in that a given section of code may produce different results on different occasions because the variables it contains may assume different values. Consequently, we can be much less certain about deducing properties of such a section of code. Variables, then, and assignment to them are out of favor. Backus argued that it is possible to program without variables (and this has been shown to be true.)

LISP is often given as an example of a functional programming language. Caution is advised, however, since although there are purely functional LISPs, many dialects of the language have been made "fat and flabby" by the inclusion of procedural features. Such a creature is COMMON LISP. When considering functional languages, then, I am only considering the "pure" ones, which are usually very slim and compact. The only control structure they employ is recursion. Perhaps the best known purely functional LISP-based language is SCHEME [1]. Henderson presents a

253

readable account of the rationale for and the implementation of a purely functional LISP in [9].

Small languages are easier to learn and easier to implement. There are also fewer constructs for which semantics have to be defined, and there is a greater chance of verifying programs. Some very small functional programming languages have been based on the lambda-calculus together with combinators for expression reduction. (See [6] for an excellent overview.) Such languages have been used in order to produce **proven** VLSI chip designs from functional specifications. The same approach can and should be extended to software design.

4. Procedural Programming

Until now, procedural programming has been the butt of criticism. Now is the time to look at its positive aspects.

The quotes from Turner earlier were written in 1981, when there was not the "serious" LISP and PROLOG programming performed today. Nevertheless, it remains true that most "production programming" is carried out in high-level procedural languages. Consequently, the great majority of programmers only have experience of the procedural programming paradigm.

ALGOL 60 and its derivatives have served the software community well for almost three decades, with Pascal enjoying immense popularity as the first programming language for Computer Science majors. Pascal was a language designed for education, rather than for commercial software production. Nevertheless, a number of "shops" used Pascal quite successfully in this capacity, although others tried and found the language lacking. More language features are needed to support "programming in the large", and in order to produce embedded systems, concurrency and low level access and manipulation capabilities are required.

MODULA-2 came out of the same small stable as Pascal itself, while Ada had a long gestation period and many more designers. I don't want to turn this into a comparison between the two languages, as there has been a lot of debate on this elsewhere, some good, some bad. Suffice it to say that MODULA-2 has a distinct edge over Ada by being smaller. Both languages support many of the practices deemed desirable by software engineering theory: data abstraction; modularity; separate compilation and so on and, compared to Pascal, are satisfying to use. But how do they match up to the problem of verification?

The thesis of Turner and Backus, roughly paraphrased, is that procedural languages have variables and assignment statements that make verification difficult, if not impossible. However, much research has been conducted into proving procedural programs correct. Following work by Dijkstra [5] there have been contributions by Gries [8] and Hoare [11]. To have such eminent computer scientists engaged in this endeavor must be encouraging to the supporters of procedural programming.

5. Object-oriented Programming

The reason that SIMULA was popular, albeit within a limited geographical area, was that it supports object-oriented programming. An object may be thought of as an entity which may have its own attributes (data) and its own actions to manipulate those attributes. Objects are self-contained, independent entities, which may often be viewed as concurrent units. Object hierarchies can easily be established, which allows character inheritance by descendant objects. This avoids a lot of unnecessary duplication, which might otherwise be unavoidable in a strongly typed language. Writing software in terms of objects results in code which is a much more natural description of the job in hand, more faithful to the structure of the problem. Being self-contained, changes to an object are localized within that object. Software systems can be extended by expanding the set of objects used, and object definitions can be re-used. This makes it relatively simple and safe to construct large systems by stepwise enlargement.

Object-oriented programming can be used with both functional and procedural styles. LOOPS , FLAVORS, SCHEME and now CLOS all support objects in a LISP environment. Among object-oriented procedural languages are SIMULA, C++, Objective-C, and various object-oriented Pascal-based languages. BETA [12] is a very slim object-oriented language in the SIMULA tradition. Although smaller than its ancestor, it is considerably more powerful and expressive. SMALLTALK [7] is also a procedural object-oriented language (and environment). SMALLTALK, like BETA, **forces** the use of objects, whereas SIMULA and most other "object-oriented languages" do not. There is also a lot of literature on object-oriented programming in Ada . If sufficiently disciplined and resourceful, an Ada programmer can use an object-oriented approach but, with no support from the language, the result will not be elegant. Ada is not an object-oriented language.

The Macintosh Programmer's Workshop, a programming environment for developing applications software for the Macintosh, includes a compiler for Object Pascal (and one for C++ has recently been announced.) MacApp is an extensible application library which enhances the bare object-oriented languages. The object-oriented approach was chosen owing to the need to develop complex software out of a number of independent modules. Objects provide the means to localize actions associated with windows, for example, from those which only relate to pull-down menus. At the same time, object inheritance enables common actions to be applied to different, but related, types of objects, without the need for repetition. The same rationale led NeXT to employ object-orientation as an indispensible characteristic of its software.

It is fitting to close this section with another quote:
> Unfortunately OOP [object-oriented programming] is not at all well understood in North America (we didn't appreciate the elegance of SIMULA 67). Many companies are moving their development to workstations, but few are even aware of the benefits of C++! Only a handful of universities and colleges have any sort of OOP education as part of their curriculum. The battle for first year programming language should

be between Smalltalk and Scheme, not MODULA, Ada or C! [18]

6. Concurrent Programming

Concurrent programming, despite its importance in multi-programming operating systems in particular, has for long been a minority sport. Times are changing. With multi-processor and distributed computer systems becoming more commonplace, there is a burgeoning need to write concurrent code to make full use of the parallelism offered. It is also vital that embedded systems, which now usually employ concurrent programming techniques, be controlled by code that is correct.

Languages for concurrent programming are almost invariably procedural. MODULA-2 and Ada both support concurrency, although in rather different ways. In a concurrent environment, the advantages of using an object-oriented approach become more evident. Each self-contained object is regarded as being concurrent with all other objects. This is a significant aid to the incremental development of reliable concurrent programs, whether or not the program execution will utilize truly concurrent (parallel) hardware. For true object-oriented concurrent programming, BETA is a good candidate.

Owing to the critical nature of a lot of concurrent programming applications, as well as the intellectual challenge presented, there has been a lot of research into the development of a theory of concurrency. Hoare has developed a theoretical basis for concurrency with CSP [10]. Out of this theory, the language occam^{TM} was developed for the transputer^{TM}, a chip designed specifically as a building block for (massively) parallel systems. Hoare and his co-workers have produced a set of laws of occam programming [16], so that occam programs may be better understood and mechanically manipulated. It is interesting to note that occam has been kept small quite deliberately.

7. Revolution!

In his treatment of the development of scientific practice [13], Kuhn talks about the nature of scientific revolutions: what is an established practice (a paradigm) one day may be replaced by another, quite different, practice the next. The dynamics of paradigm shifts are quite fascinating, and catastrophe theory provides good models for them. In that light, what Kuhn states is that the current paradigm represents a conditionally stable equilibrium, which is impervious to small attacks, but may be completely upset by a concerted assault. If this assault is successful, there will be a new (conditionally stable) paradigm. When the current paradigm is under attack, it is not clear what will replace it, nor is it clear that it will be replaced at all.

Our current programming paradigm is, of course, the procedural one. When a paradigm has become so entrenched and is almost universally understood, it is extremely difficult

---

^{TM} occam and transputer are registered trademarks of the INMOS Group of companies.

to replace it. Nevertheless, I feel very strongly that Computer Science is approaching a paradigm shift. This would have staggering financial implications, and many human ones—some may be unable or unwilling to adapt to a new paradigm. The champions of new practices are nearly always treated with great suspicion, as they shake the very foundations of a discipline. However, once the shift has been effected, it is regarded as a natural step, and one which should have been taken much earlier!

In practical terms, then, this means that even if we, the educators, can reach a consensus on what we should be teaching, there is an extremely large industry out there, that will not be too enthusiastic about employing graduates whose philosophy and language are alien to accepted practice. Our paradigm shift has, somehow, to be phased. This then raises the old question of the rôle of universities.

8. To Train or to Educate?

Are we kidding ourselves when we call ourselves educators? Are we not simply training students to be marketable commodities, immediately useful to an employer? The answer we give will depend on our affiliation. Broadly speaking, there are the "theoretical schools" and the "practically-oriented schools". Members of the former subset can afford to teach a curriculum based more on pedagogical ideals, and their reputations are not tarnished by so doing. We of the other subset do not enjoy such luxuries. At least we are not teaching C exclusively!

The software crisis was identified and labelled as such about fifteen years ago. What has happened since? The crisis has deepened. The software industry is still not able to produce reliable software within budget, and yet implicit faith is placed in complex software systems such as artificially intelligent decision-makers. This engenders a deep concern within me, which is motivating me to evaluate alternative approaches to software production. Whatever paradigm wins out, if indeed there is a shift, it must have some underlying theoretical foundation. So, like it or not, all Computer Science courses will need to incorporate more theory. This trend has already been established by curriculum recommendations from the ACM and CSAB accreditation criteria. The ACM task force on the Computer Science curriculum [4] has sought to integrate theory with practice. I welcome this.

We must educate our students by giving them a sufficiently sound theoretical foundation, so that, regardless of their *alma mater*, they will be in a better position to understand the behavior of software created by themselves and by others. The theory **must** be related to whatever practices are used in industry, so that the teaching of programming is much more than just imparting a skill.

9. Conclusions?

But which paradigm prophet should we follow? Can we make sense of all the trends and conflicting claims?

Well, history has taught us a number of things. Small languages are certainly better than large ones. There is something wrong when a language is so large, and its semantics so ambiguous, that a producer of compilers for it can say with great confidence that "all Ada compilers have bugs". The ideal language will be small, with well-defined semantics which are tractable to logical manipulation. The day is distant when we will be able to generate a correct program from a specification automatically. For the present, we shall have to be satisfied with verifying individual algorithms coded into small modules.

The burgeoning interest in object-oriented programming for both sequential and concurrent execution results from its support of modularity, encapsulation, re-usability and extensibility. We should cast our vote for this style of programming, because it is a natural one. The language should enforce the use of objects, as do SMALLTALK and BETA.

Should we opt for the functional or the procedural paradigm? (I have not even considered others, such as logic programming, as exemplified by PROLOG.) I suspend judgment on this for now. Personally, I like the functional style although my background is procedural. We do have to be careful during a transitional period—it would be useless to select a language which supports a poorly-understood paradigm. One argument Turner uses in favor of functional languages is that they can lead to a reduction in code by an order of magnitude. Brevity is not necessarily a virtue, as witnessed by many incomprehensible APL and ALGOL 68 programs. The code must be readily understandable, another lesson from history.

If it is too early for our current paradigm to change, we should, at least, produce students who will be in a position to adapt to any paradigm shift that occurs. When the von Neumann architecture is replaced, there is bound to be a shift in the programming paradigm. This comes back to a solid theoretical foundation and a broad treatment of programming, which examines the strengths and weaknesses of different approaches, with practical experience to reinforce the issues.

Some schools introduce students to programming methodology using Abelson and Sussman's excellent text [1], which is based on SCHEME. Even if functional programming does not become the main paradigm, a text like this, which is based on strong principles, together with predicate calculus and theorem-proving techniques, will give our students a good education in important issues in programming, and serve them well until the ultimate paradigm shift occurs, to natural language input!

REFERENCES

1. Abelson, H. and Sussman, G. J. *Structure and Interpretation of Computer Programs.* Cambridge, MA: MIT Press, 1985.

2. Backus, J. W. "Can Programming be Liberated From the von Neumann Style? A Functional Style and its Algebra of Programs." *Communications of the ACM.* Vol. 21, No. 8 (August 1978):613-641.

3. Birtwistle, G. M., Dahl, O. J., Myrhaug, B. and Nygaard, K. *SIMULA begin.* Lund, Sweden: Studentlitteratur, 1973.

4. Denning, P. J. *et al.* "Draft Report of the ACM Task Force on The Core of Computer Science. February, 1988.

5. Dijkstra, E. W. *A Discipline of Programming.* Englewood Cliffs, NJ: Prentice-Hall International, 1976.

6. Glaser, H., Hankin, C. and Till, D. *Principles of Functional Programming.* Englewood Cliffs, NJ: Prentice-Hall International, 1984.

7. Goldberg, A. and Robson, D. *SMALLTALK-80: the Language and its Implementation.* Reading, MA: Addison-Wesley, 1983.

8. Gries, D. *The Science of Programming.* New York: Springer-Verlag, 1981.

9. Henderson, P. *Functional Programming: Application and Implementation.* Englewood Cliffs, NJ: Prentice-Hall International, 1980.

10. Hoare, C. A. R. *Communicating Sequential Processes.* Englewood Cliffs, NJ: Prentice-Hall International, 1985.

11. Hoare, C. A. R. *et al.* "Laws of Programming". *Communications of the ACM.* Vol. 30, No. 8. (August 1987): 672-686.

12. Kristensen, B. B., Madsen, O. L., Møller-Pedersen, B. and Nygaard, K. "The BETA Programming Language". *Research Directions in Object-Oriented Programming.* Ed. Shriver, B. and Wegner, P. Cambridge, MA: MIT Press, 1987.

13. Kuhn, T. S. *The Structure of Scientific Revolutions. International Encyclopedia of Unified Science.*) Second edition. Chicago: University of Chicago Press, 1970.

14. Luker, P. A. *Good Programming Practice in Ada.* Oxford: Blackwell Scientific, 1987.

15. Parnas, D. L. "Software Aspects of Strategic Defense Systems." *Communications of the ACM*, Vol. 28, No. 12 (December 1985): 1326-1335

16. Roscoe, A. W. and Hoare, C. A. R. "The Laws of occam Programming." Technical Monograph PRG-53, Oxford University Computing Laboratory, Programming Research Group, Oxford, 1986.

17. Turner, D. A. "Recursion Equations as a Programming Language." *Functional Programming and its Applications.* Cambridge: Cambridge University Press, 1982.

18. "Talking With Associate Editor Professor Dave Thomas." *Journal of Object-Oriented Programming.* Vol. 1, No. 1 (April/May 1988): 46-47.

TOWARD AN IDEAL COMPETENCY-BASED COMPUTER SCIENCE TEACHER CERTIFICATION PROGRAM: THE DELPHI APPROACH

J. Wey Chen
Department of Mathematics and Applied Statistics
University of Northern Colorado
Greeley, CO 80639

Abstract

The downward migration of computer science courses from university to secondary and even junior high school level is accelerated by the increasing computer usage in schools and the increasing demands of both parents and students for quality computer education. Teacher training is a major vehicle to the success of this migration. However, at this time, there is no consensus concerning how the secondary school computer science teacher should be certified and what should be included in the study of a computer science teacher certification program. This paper collects data from various computer expert groups through the use of Delphi technique to provide valuable guidelines for establishing a computer science teacher certification program as well as a model curriculum based on the minimum competency required of a successful secondary school computer science teacher.

Introduction

The training of certified computer science teachers to teach high school computer science was recognized as early as in the 1970s. However, recent follow-up studies show that progress in this regard is very slow [8]. Many school systems today still assign full computer science teaching responsibility to teachers who are self-taught or whose formal training in the computer science subject is very limited. The use of these teachers in high school has dramatically reduced the quality of computer science teaching. In the recent Midwest Computer Conference at Northern Illinois University in De Kalb, some computer science educators even suspect that today's students turn against computer science because inept high school teachers try to teach programming "but do an awful job of it" [6].

Many studies have pointed out that the slow process in the widespread development of computer science teacher certification program can be attributed to (1) lack of status as a distinct academic discipline in high school curricula, (2) lack of a standard curriculum, and (3) the scarcity of computer science teacher training programs in the colleges or universities for prospective computer science teachers [7,8]. However, all of them are interwoven factors and causes. Colleges and Universities do not have reason to set up such a program because computer science is not a distinct academic discipline in high schools. The lack of standard curriculum makes colleges and universities hesitate in taking one step further to establish such a program for those students preparing to teach computer science in school systems throughout the country. The lack of qualified teachers to teach high school computer science courses has been criticized as the major impediment to the widespread implementation of computer science in the schools. While the information society itself will continue to apply more pressure to make computer science a necessity in the high school curriculum, this article will propose solutions to the last two problems stated above based on the results of a research study.

The Delphi Technique

The Delphi technique is designed for long-term planning to produce consensus judgments in inexact fields or in fields where rapid changes have occurred, such that traditional forecasting methods are unsuitable [4]. For quite a long time, the Delphi has been considered an effective method to seek information which may generate a consensus on the part of the various response groups. The Delphi technique uses questionnaires to determine the consensus of a group of experts. The number of survey rounds needed varies depending upon how quickly the group arrives at consensus.

In 1983, the Pacific Cultural Foundation funded a project to develop a model curriculum for secondary school computer science teachers. The project consisted of two phases. The objectives of the Phase I study were (1) to establish a rank-order listing of computer competencies required of secondary school computer science teachers, and (2) to establish consensus guidelines toward the key issues of a computer science teacher certification program. The Delphi method, which was used to accomplish the objective, involved the mailing of a series of three questionnaires. The Delphi panel included 48 computer science educators selected from state departments of education, teacher councils/organizations/institutions, industry, and high school computer science teachers. The phase I study generated 26 competency statements

each of which had a mean value between 2.0 and 1.0. These 26 competency statements were rated "extremely important" and "mandatory" for a secondary school computer science teacher. The same study also produced 31 competency statements each of which received a combined mean value between 1.0 and 0 (a positive value) and were rated "of moderate importance" and "may be needed" by secondary school teachers. The results of phase I study were published in the spring of 1986 [2,3]. The objective of the second phase of the study was to integrate those competencies identified in phase I study into a teacher certification program. The proposed courses of study was based on the results of Phase II study.

Guidelines in the Development of a Computer Science Teacher Certification Program

The Delphi panels were asked to express their opinions, using a five point scale, on several key issues in a computer science teacher certification program. Of the 48 panelists surveyed, 100 per cent responded; over 90 percent of the 48 respondents strongly agreed with eleven of the items:

-- The objective of a computer science teacher certification program should be to train teachers who:

a. can teach a set of computer science courses such as "Introduction to Computers", "Programming for Problem Solving", "Computer Applications", and "Advanced computer science" in secondary schools.

b. can serve as a computer resource person in his/her school or school district.

c. can serve as a microcomputer lab director/coordinator.

-- Teachers of computer science should be certified in the area of computer science and not in a composite teaching major.

-- Sets of standards and criteria to retrain teachers who are currently involved in computer science teaching must also be established.

-- A secondary certification in areas other than computer science may be added to the computer science certification program in their initial design stage. This can be implemented through a compulsory minor while studying in the program.

-- Certified computer science teachers can be alternatively used as computer literacy teacher in the classroom but not vice versa.

-- The curriculum component for such a program, in addition to the computer science major courses of study, should include general education courses, professional education courses, and a minor to guarantee the job opportunity.

-- The computer science certification program has a better chance to succeed if an interdisciplinary approach is taken, or if it is under the auspices of the College of Education. However, the computer science Department should provide most of the coursework for those preparing to teach computer science in school systems.

-- The necessary training background and curriculum design for computer science teachers must be of great breadth and depth.

-- At least one course in computer science teaching methods should be required.

-- The program should provide the student opportunity to experience the process of software development.

-- Students who are seeking

certification in computing should be proficient in at least four computer languages: BASIC, Pascal, Logo, and C.

The Proposed Curriculum

The objective of the second phase of Delphi study was to integrate all the competency statements identified in Phase I study into a computer science teacher certification program. In the initial questionnaire design, the researcher delicately combined those competency statements with a combined mean value above 1.0 into a set of courses and put them in a category labeled as "required courses". In the same manners, those competency statements with combined mean value above 0.0 were combined into "elective courses" category to reflect that they may be needed by the computer science teachers. The titles of courses were developed using titles and description of courses found in Curriculum '78 [1] or the 1983 IEEE Model Program in Computer Science and Engineering [5], if an appropriate title is applicable. For those new courses which have not appeared in these two model programs, a new course title is created to reflect the content of study in that course to avoid confusion. The initial courses recommendation underwent modification through four mailings to all participants before the consensus was reached. The Delphi experts agreed that there should have nine required courses and six elective courses in a certification program to ensure the minimum competency level for secondary school computer science teachers. Each course is designed for three semester credit hours. They are:

Required Courses:

. Introduction to Computer Programming
. Program Design & Software Engineering

. Assembly Language & Computer Systems
. Data Structure & Algorithms
. File Organization & Processing
. Programming Languages for Educators
. Methods for Teaching Computer Science
. Mini- and microcomputer Systems
. Project Design for Educators

Elective Courses:

. Computer Assisted Instruction
. Artificial Intelligence
. Computers in Education
. Application of Computers in the Classroom
. System Analysis and Design
. Computer Networks and Data Communication

This study results in the recommendation of courses which would produce the minimum competency requirements. While 18 hours is generally the minimum number of semester hours required nationwide for certification in other academic discipline, much flexibility still exists for state certification officials and universities to customize or modify the recommended curriculum. It is also possible for curriculum designers to combine two or more courses into a new course to fit the resulting curriculum into their design. Nevertheless, the courses identified as "required courses" should be treated as the essential base for training secondary school computer science teachers.

Conclusions

Computer usage in schools is increasing to the point where computer science teacher training is crucial. The certification of secondary school computer science teachers will prepare the thousands of computer science teachers to ensure the success of downward movement of the college computer science curriculum into the high school. However, certification of computer science teachers and institute teacher training programs in the college or university can only solve problems in the teaching-training side. In order to thoroughly solve this intricate problem at one time, the following issues in high schools side should also be taken care of simultaneously: computer science must become an approved subject area in all states; credit for a high school computer science course should be given as a unit of computer science; and computer science must fit into the high school curriculum properly.

References

[1] Austing, R. H., et al. (Eds.) Curriculum '78 recommendations for the undergraduate program in computer science. Communications of the ACM, 22(3), March 1979, 147-166.

[2] Chen, J. W., and Clark, D. L. Computer related competency needed by secondary school teachers: A futuristic view from experts. Paper presented in the 1986 Southwest Educational Research Association Annual Meeting, Houston, Texas.

[3] Chen, J. W., and Clark D. L. Computer education curriculum through the Delphi technique. Proceedings of the 24th Annual Conference of Association for Educational Data Systems, 1986.

[4] Gordon, T. Forecasts of some technological and scientific developments and their societal consequences. In A. Tiche (ed.), Technology and Man's Future. New York: St. Martins Press, 1967.

[5] IEEE Computer Society, the 1983 IEEE Computer Society Model program in Computer Science and Engineering, January 1984.

[6]   Leeke, J.   Computer grads: Do
they make the grade?   PC Week,
5(19), May 10, 1988, 64, 68.

[7]   Task Force on Teacher
Certification in Computer
Science.   Proposed curriculum for
programs leading to teacher
certification in computer
science.   Communications of the
ACM, 28(3), March 1985, 275-279.

[8]   Taylor, H. G., and Poirot, J. L.
Computer science teacher
certification: current status and
trends.   T.H.E. Journal, 12(2),
103-107.

A Software Rotation for Professional Teachers

Philip L. Miller
Computer Science Department
Carnegie Mellon University
Pittsburgh, PA 15213
(412) 268-3560
plm@gnome.cs.cmu.edu

1. Introduction

At Carnegie Mellon, the introductory programming methods courses, basically CS1 [Koffman 84] and CS2 [Koffman 85], are taught by a group of full time teaching professionals. This group, the Intro Group, has a director, an associate director, seven full time faculty, one facilities programmer, an administrative assistant, a secretary, six to twelve teaching assistants, and about fifty tutors and graders. The Intro Group runs its own programming facility that is primarily two recitation rooms and a large computer lab. Most classes use software developed at CMU by the MacGNOME project [Garlan 84; Chandhok 85]. Approximately 1,500 students take these courses each year. The Intro Group uses an online mastery exam as its primary means of evaluating student performance [Carrasquel 85].

There are numerous thorny issues facing the Intro Group. Among the most important are issues dealing with faculty preparedness and attitude. In the fall of 1986, a novel program was proposed to address these needs. This program is designed to rotate one faculty member at a time into a computer science research project as something of a software sabbatical. It is called "software rotation," or simply "rotation."

Five major benefits were expected:

1) keeping the faculty current in computer science developments, especially in software engineering
2) keeping the curriculum up to date
3) encouraging full use of existing instructional tools
4) fostering faculty input for creation of new tools
5) providing variety and intellectual challenge.

The idea of collaboration between the professional computer science educator and a computer science research project is not entirely new. However, the idea of an actual sabbatical is new. Earlier efforts to include the Intro Group teaching faculty in research in addition to the ordinary demands of teaching proved unsuccessful. It seems that there is always more than enough to keep the teaching faculty busy in teaching. Relieving the educator of all teaching and administrative duties is important

The time allotted to software rotation is an academic semester plus the summer semester, a period of about eight

• The author gives thanks to Nahid Capell, Rob Chandhok, Becky Clark, Maria Intrieri, Mark Stehlik, the Intro Group, the MacGNOME Group, and Nico Habermann for their help.

• This material is based in part upon work supported by the National Science Foundation under grant number MDR-8652015. Any opinions, findings, conclusions, or recommendations expressed in this publication are those of the authors and do not necessarily reflect the views of the Foundation.

months. In the steady state, one faculty member is on rotation every academic semester, and two are on rotation every summer. Since our teaching group has seven full-time teaching faculty with two serving in rotation each year it is expected that a person will rotate into a research project every three or four years. No University funds were allocated for this project, which implies that the six faculty who are not on rotation must assume extra duties to cover for the person who is on rotation.

Therefore the project [Chandhok 88] is a natural place for the rotation. The MacGNOME project is involved in designing, implementing, and distributing software for teaching computer science. The director of the project is the director of the Intro Group. So in both the subject matter and the supervision we have a good fit between Intro Group faculty and the MacGNOME project.

The idea of a software rotation was presented to the Intro Group in the Fall of 1986 and was very well received. Faculty members immediately volunteered for the first and second rotations. The Head of the Department Science also reacted positively to the idea. Suggesting that we consider serving on other projects in addition to MacGNOME. The members of the MacGNOME project were a bit more reserved than either the teaching faculty or the department head, but they supported the goal.

The issue of faculty evaluation during the software rotation arose. There is something of a dilemma here. On one hand, it is unfair to evaluate a teacher on performance as a research programmer. On the other hand, removing the rotation period from evaluation might encourage the faculty member on rotation to take an eight month vacation. It was decided that rotation would be judged on process, not on product; what mattered was how hard faculty members tried, rather than what they produced. With this issue resolved, the first rotation was set to begin with the summer semester of 1987.

1.1 The Intro Group
Of the seven faculty members in the Intro Group, two hold PhDs in fields other than computer science, two others have significant graduate study in computer science at Carnegie Mellon, and the three remaining members of our

faculty hold Masters degrees in fields other than computer science. Since the educational backgrounds vary greatly, some people needing a on the job training.[1] Others have an excellent technical background for a career in computer science education, a background that is not only academic and theoretical, but tempered by real experience as well. But even these people could use a regular refresher.

At CMU we have seen that teacher burnout is a very real phenomenon. Even highly motivated teachers become discouraged by the taxing work of organizing lectures, preparing and grading test, supervising assistants, and maintaining working equipment. One way to mitigate against teacher burnout is to provide, on a regular basis, an interesting change to the routine.

To the teacher the life of a research programmer may seem ideal. The researcher has no lectures to give. There are no teaching assistants to supervise, no assignments to grade, no tests to devise, no copious logistics. The researchers schedules are loose, and the researchers often command respect among peers because they are seen as having the intellectual depth to advance knowledge.

Software rotation not only refreshes the teacher; it is a chance to learn that life as a research programmer also has its problems.

1.2 MacGnome Project
The Intro Group has been using software developed by the MacGNOME project in delivering our various versions of CS1. We use software that is designed to support teaching the concepts of procedural abstraction, data abstraction, and reasoning about control structures. The MacGNOME project represents a middle-sized piece of work, with 60,000 to 90,000 lines of code making up the Pascal GENIE and the Karel GENIE.[2] The project is managed by a single

---

1. The Director, for example, holds a PhD in Political Science, with only a few computer science courses.

2. It may be confusing to read about the MACGNOME project as a single piece of work and then see reference to two programming environments, the Pascal GENIE and the Karel GENIE. MACGNOME is actually a programming environment generator. Once the generator is set up it is a relatively straightforward task to supply a bnf, language specific com-

person, has two other full time research programmers, and typically has several undergraduate and other part time programmers.

The MacGNOME project has always been viewed by its director as serving the needs of the teacher. However, some teaching faculty have tended to view themselves as victims of the environments. Clearly, some regarded themselves as disenfranchised. Hard feelings, when displayed, of course fostered hard feelings in return. Relationships between the two groups have been less than ideal.

The reason that the MacGNOME[3] project was started was because we felt that commercial programming environments did not serve the needs of the educational community. The co-existence of MacGNOME and Intro should have been the perfect opportunity for the faculty to seize control of this piece of their professional lives. Along these lines, Seymor Pappert speaks of "appropriation" [Pappert 88]. In his current work he puts Lego^{TM} and Logo^{TM} before young children. He makes right the conditions so that these children can choose to appropriate the technology. He reports startling results. Kids discover physics and mathematics, and they get into engineering and science before they have lost their baby teeth. Often we hear that females are not inclined to appropriate computer technology. Pappert finds that girls do very well with Lego^{TM} and Logo^{TM}. As often as not, they make the same kinds of technological breakthroughs, and the boys come to them to learn how it is done.

One objective in setting up the software rotation was to make right the conditions for an appropriation of the technology. The intent was that faculty members would appropriate the project, improving teaching tools, and improving their own teaching as they gained perspective on software engineering.

---

pile tools, and language specific runtime code. The two environments that we have built actually share more than 60% of their code. This is due to the basic architecture of the MacGNOME systems and to the object oriented toolkit approach of MacAPP that we use.

3. Actually it was the GNOME project that was started in this way. MacGNOME grew out of GNOME with the emergence of the Macintosh family of computers.

2. The First Rotation

The first rotation began in the summer of 1987. At Carnegie Mellon this means about the middle of May. At the time the Director of Introductory Programming was also Principal Investigator of the MacGNOME project and Director of the Center for Art and Technology. All of these organizations required rolling up the sleeves and getting to work. The manager of the MacGNOME project was similarly holding down that job plus overseeing software in the Center for Art and Technology and also directing efforts to integrate the Macintosh computers into the CMU Andrew internet [Morris 86]. The Intro Group had come through a very trying experiment. For a semester faculty had done all grading by themselves. On the average, each faculty member each week marked and returned two-hundred items (programs, labs, quizzes, tests, and homework submissions). Adding stress to the entire effort was a pending release date of the Karel GENIE which was scheduled for release to Kinko's Academic Courseware Exchange later that summer.

A MacGNOME staffer supervised the faculty member on rotation. MacGNOME had undergone a good deal of change in prior months, so a task that facilitated a thorough knowledge of the software tools was devised: a set of help messages were needed for the software release. The faculty member on rotation was to write the messages. Since everything needed to be documented, it looked as if this would not only aid in the software release, but also make the faculty member fully aware of the latest set of changes to the system. This was estimated to be a two week task.

The faculty member attacked the problem of designing a help system with zeal. There was a fresh PhD thesis from our computer science department on the topic of help systems and it was provided direction [Borenstein 85]. A questionnaire was administered to students, to determine which parts of the system were most confusing. Instructors, teaching assistants, and our staff of tutors were interviewed. Undergraduates were recruited to assist in writing and interviewing. Various styles of help were compared and, at least informally, evaluated. It was found that heavily illustrated help with short messages were preferred to longer textual messages. This sounds quite reasonable too.

There was a problem, of course. The supervisor was expecting two weeks of writing text. The faculty member was designing a help system and supervising students in the process. The project was committed to textual help for the release. There were strong practical reasons for this. One was that the MacGNOME help system could support only graphics[4] or only text in a single file. Free mixing of text and graphics would have to wait for insets in a later release of Apple support software. Another good reason for using text was that text is more compact than graphics. Graphics, especially bit mapped screen dumps, have storage requirements that preclude them from release on a floppy disk. A third reason was that the project was going to make a release almost immediately. There were good reasons for preferring a redesigned help system too. Foremost is that on-line help, as opposed to a reference manual, is better in short, graphic snapshots.

This part of the rotation bore a striking resemblance to a very long freight train starting from a dead stop. First nothing, then a pull from the locomotive and cars lurch into motion. The cars pick up speed and bash into each other, Then more pull, more lurching and more bashing. The truth is, there are more degrees of freedom in a research project than on a train track. The lurching and bashing was not confined to a single track. It was not rewarding for the faculty, and it confirmed the worst fears of the researcher.

In retrospect it is easy to see that what happened was due to missed communication. But at the time, we were all helpless to control the situation. It was not a total loss. A help system, textually based, was delivered to Kinkos along with the Karel GENIE and the faculty member and the supervisor are still with us.

The faculty member then turned to the topic of data visualization under direct supervision of the MacGNOME project director. Visual programming in general and data visualization in particular have been worked on from time to

time over the years.[5] A good bit of the design work appeared in the textbook that we use [Miller 87]. The Pascal GENIE and its drawing window were used to experiment. That is to say Pascal GENIE programs were written which display mockups of Pascal data. These experiments were written using the GENIE, they were not automatically generated from student programs, and were not integrated into the compiler of the Pascal GENIE. But they could tell us what we wanted to know. Work on a design document was begun. Two important purposes were served. First, the faculty member did indeed learn a lot. Second, attention of the MacGNOME group was focused on data visualization, which were discussed in large group meetings, by smaller sub-groups, and even casually. The look and feel of the system as it now exists was derived; and a design document detailing the actual design appeared soon thereafter. The faculty member became involved in coding an experimental version of the project software, but, the rotation came to an end. Both the display system and the system that extracted information from the symbol table took their final form later [Myers 88].

The first rotation had mixed results. No one was very happy with the working relationships that developed during the effort to write the help system for the Karel GENIE. On the other hand, there was a solid piece of work completed, and it has been used widely at CMU and in the general public. There was not enough time for completion of the data visualization system, and the faculty member was not fully engaged with the project. The research group went from periodically talking about automatic data visualizations to a firm commitment that was soon realized. Technical knowledge was gained, as was a better understanding of what was available in the GENIE. New tools were contemplated, and mockups and prototypes were built. The rotation was a change of pace and a challenge. But, it wasn't fun.

3. Later Experiences with Rotation
At the end of the first rotation and the beginning of the second there was a possibility that rotation as a venture into real research and development might come to an end. The second faculty member going on rotation suggested working on program examples for an Ada course. The use of

---

4. Actually Macintosh files in pict format.

5. C.f. [Myers 86]

Ada as a teaching vehicle has been the subject of discussion within the Intro Group for some time. Under the MacGNOME umbrella work has begun on an Ada environment. There is work on a textbook, a curriculum, and lecture material by one of the Intro Group faculty and the Department Head. The proposed rotation would fit nicely with preparations for teaching with Ada. But work on curriculum is not real experience as a researcher, it is too much like everyday teaching. Additionally, there was concern that the Intro Group and MacGNOME were moving further apart rather than coming together. For these reasons it was decided that the second rotation should be mainstream MacGNOME WORK.

The faculty member had done a lot of work with design trees (or solution trees) as a pencil and paper tool for the classroom. It had been very successful. Like data visualizations, the basics of design trees are in the textbook that we use. They provide a good but incomplete way to represent an idea. What was needed was careful attention to the details of design trees and how they might be integrated into the existing infrastructure. Months were spent designing a program called Design View. The design was drafted, critiqued, and redrafted many times. Faculty were called upon to comment. A paper was written, submitted to a conference, and accepted[Roberts 88].

The faculty member on the second rotation recruited the third rotating faculty member to become involved in the implementation of the Design View. This made a lot of sense because they were both on rotation from May through August. The MacGNOME staff member who was supervising the work was supportive throughout the effort. In fact, both the MacGNOME project and the Intro Group were downright enthusiastic about the project. Early versions of the Design View were implemented rapidly. This was due to solid design work, very solid infrastructure, the knowledge of the supervisor, the enthusiasm of the third rotating faculty member, and the nature of working with MacApp[6] [Schmucker 86].

---

6. MACAPP is an object oriented toolkit developed by Apple Computer for support of Macintosh developers. This toolkit was instrumental in the development of our programming environments, the Pascal GENIE and the Karel GENIE.

During the summer of 1988 a beta release of the Pascal GENIE was made through Kinko's. The Design View is a part of that release. It is a very important part of that release because it is an altogether, new kind of tool, and even in the current form it is quite useful. The Design View went from concept to public release in just over six months. And the people working on it were professional educators, not research programmers.

The second and third rotations were spectacularly successful. The work produced a new tool for designing programs. The tool is widely used. And it really does make a difference. Faculty members applied their expertise as teachers to make the programming environments better. They appropriated the technology. They learned about design. They learned about programming on a moderately large project. They learned about object oriented programming and object oriented toolkits. They developed a very good relationship with the professional researchers. They know how hard it is to build software. They learned that you can spend three months designing a system and then have to redesign chunks of it. They learned how fragile a system is, how unexpected effects can pop up, and that when you release a tool the world wants to know why it wasn't written sooner, why more features aren't present, why there are bugs, why it executes so slowly, and why the documentation is not sterling.

There were down sides to the later rotations. The second faculty member didn't take full advantage of the opportunity to implement. The third was not so involved in design. However, the objectives of software rotation were met. The faculty members are more aware of current trends in computer science. The Design View tool is making our curriculum more modern. The faculty are eager to master the available tools, and they did create one of their own. It was an exciting and challenging period in a mostly collegial atmosphere.

4. Conclusion
Our first experience with software rotation fell short of our expectations. The second ended successfully. The third is almost complete and results are quite good. In the best case, rotation can be a tremendous benefit to teachers and researchers, every bit as good as one might hope. In the

worst case, it can be frustrating to the teacher.
Software rotation isn't the end all but it is an important step in improving computer education. We will continue with software rotation at CMU. Here are some suggestions for implementing it.

1) find a topic before the rotation begins, do back ground work at that time
2) do not put any aspect of the rotation in the critical path of a project
3) allow sufficient time for literature review and design work
4) when it is time to code, make a shell; abstract away the rest of the system
5) make sure the lines of supervision are articulated
6) be patient with one another, set regular meetings, and keep them

Finally, we recognize that many colleges and universities do not have as strong a research environment as Carnegie Mellon. It is always a good idea to approach research projects with the offer of free labor in return for a place to work and a little supervision. Collegiality is one of the benefits that we enjoy in university life.

Bibliography

Borenstein 85   Borenstein, N. *The Design and Evaluation of Online Help Systems,* Computer Science Department, Carnegie Mellon University, Pittsburgh PA, 1985.

Carrasquel 85   J. Carrasquel, D. Goldenson, and P. Miller, "Competency Testing in Introductory Computer Science: The Mastery Examination at Carnegie-Mellon University," In *Proceedings of the 1985 Computer Science Conference*, ACM-SIGCSE, New Orleans, 1985

Chandhok 85   R. Chandhok, et al. "Programming environments based on structure editing: The GNOME Approach." In *Proceedings of the National Computer Conference* (NCC'85) , AFIPS, 1985.

Chandhok 88   Ravinder Chandhok and Terry Gill. "The Ada Edu Project: Supporting the Use of Ada in Introductory Computer Science." In *Proceedings of the 1988 SEI Conference on Software Engineering Education*, April, 1988.

Garlan 84   D.B. Garlan, and P.L. Miller. "GNOME: An Introductory Programming Environment Based on a Family of Structure Editors," *Proceedings of the Software Engineering Symposium on Practical Software Development Environments.* ACM-SIGSOFT/SIGPLAN, April 1984.

Koffman 84   E.B. Koffman, P.L. Miller, and C.E. Wardle. "Recommended curriculum for CS1," 1984. *CACM* 27, 10 (Oct. 1984), 998-1001.

Koffman 85   E.B. Koffman, D. Stemple, and C.E. Wardle. "Recommended curriculum for CS2," 1984. *CACM* 28, 8 (Aug. 1985). 815-818.

Miller 87   P.L. Miller and L. W. Miller, *Programming by Design*, Wadsworth, Belmont California, 1987.

Morris 86   J. Morris, M. Satyanarayanan, M. Conner, J. Howard, D. Rosenthal, and F. D. Smith, "Andrew: A Distributed Personal Computing Environment.", 1986 *CACM* 29, 3, March 1986

Myers 86   B. A. Myers. "Visual Programming, Programming by Example, and Program Visualization: A Taxonomy," *Proceedings SIGCHI'86: Human Factors in Computing Systems*, Boston, MA. April 13-17, 1986. pp. 59-66.

Myers 88   B. A. Myers, R. Chandhok, A. Sareen. "Automatic Data Visualization for Novice Pascal Programmers" *In Proceedings of the IEEE 1988 Workshop on Visual Languages.*

Pappert 88   S. Pappert, Presentation to the national Science Foundation Project Director's Meeting, Arizona State University, Tempe Arizona, January 1988

Roberts 88   J. Roberts, J. Pane, M. Stehlik, and J. Carrasquel. "The Design View: A Design-Oriented High Level Visual Programming Environment." In *Proceedings of the IEEE 1988 Workshop on Visual Languages.*

Schmucker 86   K. J. Schmucker, MacApp "An Application Framework," Byte Magazine, August 1986, pp. 189-193

ALGORITHMS AND PROOFS:
Mathematics in the Computing Curriculum

Newcomb Greenleaf
Department of Computer Science
Columbia University, New York, N. Y. 10027

Abstract

Computing has supplied mathematics with a new vocabulary of algorithms and is holding out the promise that mathematics can be implemented. Algorithms and proofs can now be seen as the same type of object. This new vision of mathematics as a very high level programming language suggests that mathematics may be transformed so that it is more in harmony with the spirit of computing, and has profound implications for the way in which mathematics is taught. Such harmony would be particularly beneficial for students of computing, who often find little of relevance in their mathematics courses.

1. Algorithms and Proofs

Algorithms and proofs support each other. From Euclid on down, the proofs of mathematicians are full of algorithms. Conversely, every algorithm must be supported by some sort of proof, if only a very informal one, in order to be accepted. The first fundamental relation between proofs and algorithms is that of **synergy**.

Algorithms and proofs possess similar three-fold structures of *ground*, *path*, and *goal*.

Proofs start with assumptions and lead to conclusions, while algorithms take in data satisfying preconditions and output data satisfying postconditions. The second fundamental relation between algorithms and proofs is that of **structural similarity**.

Workers both in mathematics and computer science have come to ask if algorithms and proofs are perhaps different aspects of one basic type. In the field of program verification it is a common slogan that *a program is a proof which can be compiled*. In constructive mathematics the proofs *are* algorithms. Knuth has analyzed the algorithmic nature of constructive mathematics and shown how the traditional logic-based language of mathematics conceals it [8]. These trends come together in efforts such as that of Constable and his Cornell group to **implement mathematics** [4]. The vision of mathematics as a very high level programming language had been set forth by Martin-Löf [9] and others.

Two impulses can result from a unified vision of proofs and algorithms. We may try to make algorithms more like proofs, as in PROLOG. Or, we may instead attempt to make proofs algorithmic. This paper, which concerns the latter impulse, examines three simple examples to illustrate the changes that can occur when mathematics is understood and taught in an algorithmic manner. The **Derivative Algorithm** illustrates how adopting the language of algorithms changes our understanding of the nature of mathematical proofs. The **Cantor Diagonal Algorithm** is an algorithmic proof which is generally given a non-algorithmic interpretation. Finally, the **Least Upper Bound Principle** is an example of a theorem which, as usually understood, has no algorithmic proof. In a final section we consider some implications for the role of mathematics in the computing curriculum.

We ask the reader to keep in mind that mathematics is not, as it seemed until recently, a stable discipline, but is a quickly moving target. Dijkstra has argued persuasively that computing will change mathematics more profoundly than did physics in the age of Galileo and Newton [6].

2. The Derivative Algorithm

The differential calculus focuses on a number of formulas for derivatives. Some, such as

$$D (\sin x) = \cos x$$

give the derivative of a specific function. Others, such as the addition rule:

$$D (f + g) = Df + Dg$$

describe the derivatives of more complicated functions in terms of the derivatives of simpler functions. The student of calculus is expected not just to learn the various formulas, but to understand the operation of a grand recursive algorithm in which formulas of the first type are the base cases and formulas of the second type correspond to recursive calls.

While the derivative algorithm can be found in many introductory computing texts, it is not given explicitly in standard calculus texts, because mathematicians have only recently become literate in a suitable language of algorithms. During the past few years a Pascal-like pseudo-code has become a *lingua franca*

among mathematicians.

The use of such a language of algorithms clearly gives mathematics a welcome crispness and clarity. But I would argue that its significance goes much deeper. In the calculus text of tomorrow, the main structure of the differential calculus will be the derivative algorithm. The proofs of the derivative formulas will be part (but not all) of the proof of the correctness of the derivative algorithm. Hence: proofs will prove the **correctness of algorithms** rather than the **truth of theorems**. This is a momentous change, even though it is of course still true that

$$D (x \ln x) = \ln x + 1$$

3. The Cantor Diagonal Algorithm

It may seem surprising that the diagonal method of Cantor has a natural algorithmic interpretation, because non-algorithmic conclusions involving "higher infinities" are generally drawn from it. We shall show that the fault lies not in the algorithmic character of the method, but rather in the way that it is generally interpreted.

To avoid working with the more complicated data type of real numbers, we shall consider the set *Seq* of all (infinite) binary sequences. Because it is infinite, such a sequence can not be listed but must be produced by an algorithm **F** which takes as input a natural number *n* and produces an output of 0 or 1. The algorithm **F** might be elaborate, or might be given by a simple function like

$$F(n) = (n \bmod 2)$$

However, in order for the Diagonal Algorithm to work, we must insist that if $F \in Seq$ then the computation of $F(n)$ always terminates. In other words, sequences of *Seq* are given by *total* functions.

Now consider a sequence of sequences

$$\{ \mathbf{F}_1, \mathbf{F}_2, \mathbf{F}_3, \cdots \}$$

where for each m, $\mathbf{F}_m$ is a binary sequence, so that $\mathbf{F}_m(n)$ is 0 or 1. All of the binary sequences can be arranged in a two-dimensional binary array, infinite downward and to the right. It was Cantor's genius to notice that if we "go down the diagonal" and construct the binary sequence $\mathbf{G}$ by the formula

$$\mathbf{G}(n) = 1 - \mathbf{F}_n(n)$$

then $\mathbf{G}$ differs from the sequence $\mathbf{F}_m$ in the m-th place, so that $\mathbf{G}$ is different from every sequence $\mathbf{F}_m$.

So far, all has been wholly algorithmic. But Cantor went further and argued that the phenomenon of the diagonal algorithm showed that the set Seq was **larger** than the set $\mathbf{N}$ of natural numbers. It is this last step which unnecessarily introduces into mathematics a supposed universe of non-algorithmic functions. Cantor did indeed show that there is a fundamental difference between the sets Seq and $\mathbf{N}$, but this difference can be understood not as a quantitative difference, but as a difference of quality or **structure**. Rather than call the set Seq uncountable, I prefer to call it **productive**, because there are very powerful methods for producing elements of Seq, in particular for producing an element outside of any given sequence [7]. This use of the term productive is taken from recursive function theory. It grounds the understanding of the student in algorithmic reality rather than idealistic fantasy.

It follows, of course, that there is no surjection from $\mathbf{N}$ to Seq. For a moment, we relax the requirement that functions be total, and let Par denote the set of all partial binary functions on $\mathbf{N}$. Then, under the assumptions of the Church-Turing Thesis, there is indeed a surjection from $\mathbf{N}$ to Par. Since Seq is a subset of Par, this might be considered as evidence

that $\mathbf{N}$ is *larger* than Seq, were one inclined to make a quantitative comparison between them.

Cantor, and most mathematicians after him, considered sets as "mere collections of elements," which could thereby differ *only* in quantity. We do not find this position algorithmically intelligible, since the extra structure of Seq plays an essential role in the diagonal algorithm.

4. The Least Upper Bound Principle

Now we turn to a case in which a non-algorithmic theorem is generally accepted by mathematicians. The Least Upper Bound Principle is used extensively in presentations of calculus and higher analysis. It states that for any bounded sequence of real numbers there is a least upper bound b, a least number at least as large as every number in the sequence. This principle will be considered in the seemingly simple case of binary sequences.

It might seem obvious that a binary sequence $\mathbf{F}$ has a least upper bound b. If the sequence contains a 1 then the upper bound is 1. If not, then all terms of the sequence are 0 and $b = 0$. In either case b exists, and the truth of the Principle is an immediate consequence of the Law of Excluded Middle. But can we find an algorithmic proof for the Principle?

Such a proof would be an algorithm which, when presented with a binary sequence $\mathbf{F}$ as input (presented, that is, with the algorithm which computes the terms of $\mathbf{F}$), will output the least upper bound of $\mathbf{F}$. But such an algorithm would decide the halting problem for Turing machines. For any Turing machine T can be modified so that as it computes it generates on a second tape a sequence of zeros, switching to 1 if and when the computation halts. Knowledge of the least upper bound of this sequence tells us whether T halts, in violation of the unsolvability of the halting problem under the Church-Turing thesis.

We can obtain a valid Least Upper Bound Algorithm if we either strengthen the data type of the input or weaken that of the output. The input data can be strengthened by requiring that the sequence **F** be a Cauchy sequence, or that the question of whether a rational number is an upper bound for **F** be decidable. Or, we might accept a "fickle number" for the upper bound b [2].

Our belief in the Least Upper Bound Principle for binary sequences was strong because it depended so directly on Aristotle's Law of Excluded Middle. Hence we have rediscovered a problem first exposed by the Dutch mathematician L. E. J. Brouwer [3]: unrestricted use of logical principles equivalent to Excluded Middle is the main cause of the non-algorithmic in modern mathematics (until the middle of the 19th century, most mathematics was thoroughly algorithmic).

Brouwer developed Intuitionist Logic, which is sufficient to the needs of constructive mathematics. Adopting an intuitionist logic is a first step toward an algorithmic mathematics. As mathematics becomes more explicitly algorithmic, it is likely that its logic will acquire the flavor of a programming logic, perhaps in the style of Hoare [1].

But Brouwer was unable to carry out an acceptable Intuitionist Mathematics. It remained for Errett Bishop to demonstrate the potential of algorithmic mathematics, in which algorithmic techniques naturally take the place of non-algorithmic results like the Least Upper Bound Principle [2].

5. Implications for Computing Education

Computing students should be given a unified view of computing and mathematics which integrates theory and practice, in the spirit of the report of the Denning Task Force [5].

1) Ideally, the presentation of mathematics topics should be coordinated with the computing curriculum. This might mean that graph theory is learned before calculus, and that calculus is approached through such topics as computing probabilities, generating smooth curves, studying asymptotic orders of growth, and finding Fourier series and transforms. Computing students often are in a better position to appreciate theory later in their education.

2) Mathematics courses, whether taught in the mathematics or the computer science department, should use the computer as a systematic tool and should generally be accompanied by computer laboratories. Such laboratories are not merely places to do homework, but should be taught somewhat in the style of a physics lab where a student learns the sophisticated tools of his profession. In the past several years mathematicians have adopted the computer as a standard working research tool and many mathematics departments are currently developing such laboratories.

3) Mathematics should be taught algorithmically, so that the student sees its intimate connection with computing. This involves taking a constructive approach and then using the language of algorithms to make it precise. Further, questions of efficiency should be addressed. A new generation of discrete mathematics texts has moved in these directions [10]. It has often been argued that computing courses need mathematics prerequisites. Now we are beginning to see mathematics courses

which should have a *computing prerequisite*, since students master the language of algorithms through learning to program in a suitable language.

4) We would also caution against the use of mathematics prerequisites and corequisites as a filter to "weed out" unfit students from a computer science program, particularly when these courses are not integrated with the CS curriculum and are not taught algorithmically. The problem is that these courses are not quite the right filter, for there are subtle differences between algorithmic and logical thinking [8]. Further, many strong computing students are bored by their mathematics courses and may do quite poorly, but learn mathematics very well when it is seen as relevant to computing.

It has often been suggested that computer science is a mathematical discipline. I suspect that the reverse inclusion holds, and that the computer, as metaphor and tool, will reveal to us the essential algorithmic nature of mathematics, which will come to be seen as the pure branch of computing.

References

1. Apt, K. R., *Ten Years of Hoare's Logic: a Survey*, **ACM Trans. Prog. Lang. Syst.** 3 (1985), 431-483.

2. Bishop, E., **Foundations of Constructive Analysis**, McGraw-Hill, 1967. [Revised edition: Bishop, E. and Bridges, D., **Constructive Analysis**, Springer-Verlag, 1985.]

3. Brouwer, L. E. J., **Collected Works, Vol. 1 - Philosophy and Foundations of Mathematics**, North-Holland, 1975.

4. Constable, R. L., et al., **Implementing Mathematics with the Nuperl Proof Development System**, Prentice-Hall, 1986.

5. Denning, P. J., et al., **Report of the ACM Task Force on the Core of Computer Science**, ACM, 1988.

6. Dijkstra, E. W., *Mathematicians and Computing Scientists: The Cultural Gap*, **The Mathematical Intelligencer** 8 (1986), 48-52. [Reprinted in **Abacus**, Summer 1987, 26-31.]

7. Greenleaf, N., *Liberal constructive set theory*, **Constructive Mathematics**, Richman, F., Ed., **Springer Lecture Notes in Mathematics**, Vol. 873, 1981.

8. Knuth, D. E., *Algorithms in modern mathematics and computer science*, **Algorithms in Modern Mathematics and Computer Science**, Ershov, A. P. and Knuth, D. E, Eds., **Springer Lecture Notes In Computer Science**, Vol. 122, 1981. [Reprinted in **American Mathematical Monthly** 92 (1985), 170-181.]

9. Martin-Löf, P., *Constructive mathematics and computer programming*, **Sixth International Congress for Logic, Methodology, and Philosophy of Science**, Cohen, L. J. et al., Eds., North-Holland, 1982.

10. Ross, K. A. and Wright, C. R. B., **Discrete Mathematics** (second edition), Prentice-Hall, 1988.

Discrete Mathematics for Computer Science Majors - Where Are We? How Do We Proceed?

William Marion
Department of Mathematics and
Computer Science
Valparaiso University
Valparaiso, IN 46383

Abstract

It has been nine years since Anthony Ralston and Mary Shaw called for a rethinking of the importance of sound mathematical training for undergraduate computer science majors [14]. In their paper they stressed the need to develop a two-year sequence in discrete mathematics for beginning computer science majors. Since that time numerous articles about such a sequence have appeared in both mathematics and computer science journals [4], [9], [12] and [13] and a number of panel sessions at professional meetings of SIGSCE and of the Mathematical Association of America (MAA) have been held. After all this time questions about the place of discrete mathematics in the undergraduate curriculum are still being debated. One question that is no longer being asked is: should discrete mathematics be part of a computer science major's undergraduate program? The questions that are being asked now and for which there are no easy answers are: at what level should discrete mathematics be taught? should there be one course, two courses or even three courses? what should the prerequisites be for these courses? and what topics should be presented in these courses? Computer scientists and mathematicians who have read the literature, listened to the debates, examined the textbooks or taught a course in discrete mathematics or discrete structures know that there appears to be little little agreement as to how

and what works and when it works best. This paper attempts to analyze the current situation in more detail and to offer a few suggestions to keep the dialogue alive.

Background

Since 1980 when an article by Anthony Ralston and Mary Shaw appeared in the Communications of the ACM [14], much discussion has taken place concerning the proper role of discrete mathematics in the undergraduate curriculum, especially for computer science majors. The mathematics, computer science and computer engineering communities have published reports about the many curricular issues involved [1], [3], [6], [7], [9] and [15]. It is now universally accepted by these communities that discrete mathematics plays a central role in the development and treatment of the discipline of computer science as a science and that undergraduate computer science majors should obtain a firm grounding in the many topics within discrete mathematics.

Shaw and Ralston called for the development of a two-year sequence in discrete mathematics. Listed among the subject areas to be included in this sequence were topics such as linear algebra, probability and abstract algebra which normally are taught in separate courses within the mathematics curriculum. They recommended that this sequence be part of the first two years of a computer science major's program. In 1983 and 1984 the IEEE Computer Society and the Computer Science Accrediting Board (CSAB) recommended that computer engineering majors and computer science majors take at least a one-semester course in discrete mathematics [1] and [7]. This was recommended as a minimum for programs that are to be accredited either by ABET or CSAB.

Also, in 1983 the Committee on Discrete Mathematics in the First Two Years was established by the Mathematical Association of America to investigate the possibility of revising the traditional mathematics curriculum in the first two years. (Ralston was one of its members.) Among the issues considered were where and how to introduce discrete mathematics into the curriculum. In 1986 the committee issued its report [9]. It recommended the development of a one year course in discrete mathematics to be offered as a service to computer science majors. This course should be taken in the first or second year. Many of the topics that Ralston and Shaw recommended to be part of a discrete mathematics course were included in this recommendation. At this point there seemed to be a fair amount of agreement among the mathematics and computer science communities about what topics constitute a good discrete mathematics course.

A number of other papers and reports have been published in recent years; each recommending some variation to the reports discussed above. (See the references). Three, in particular, that should be mentioned are: an article by Alfs Berztiss in 1987 [4], a paper by James Bradley which was delivered at the SIGSCE symposium in 1988 [5] and the 1988 Denning Report [2]. Berztiss, who was also a member of the MAA committee on Discrete Mathematics, developed a scheme for weaving a number of courses in mathematics, including calculus, into the computer science curriculum so that these areas in mathematics become either prerequisites or co-requisites to courses in computer science. He recommended that computer science majors take two one-semester courses in discrete mathematics within the first two years and, if possible, a third, more advanced discrete course sometime in their last two years.

Bradley described his view of the role of mathematics in the computer science curriculum and advocated the need for more fully integrating mathematics into the curriculum, and for including more mathematics content within the computer science text books. He argued for a computer science that is more mathematically rigorous at the undergraduate level. If this is a reasonable approach to take even in the first computer science courses, a

rigorous discrete mathematics course must be part of a computer science major's first year program.

The Denning Report, as it has become known, is a draft report of the ACM Task Force on the Core of Computer Science. Two components of the committee's charge were: "to present a description of computer science that emphasizes fundamental questions and significant accomplishments and to propose a teaching program for computer science that conforms to traditional scientific standards and harmoniously integrates theory and experimentation" [2]. Besides giving a rigorous definition of what computer science is, the committee describes what it sees as the fundamentals of the discipline in terms of three basic processes - theory, abstraction and design - which use the subject matter of nine disciplinary sub-areas. Also, the task force developed a sample three-semester introductory sequence which would be a survey of the entire discipline. One of the prerequisites for the sequence would be a programming background in a structured language. Thus, a computer science major ordinarily would begin taking this sequence in the first or second semester of his/her first year. As one reads through the descriptions of the eleven modules which make up the sequence, it is apparent that an understanding of many of the topics of discrete mathematics is important for success in this sequence. Though the report doesn't say so, computer science majors should have at least one course in discrete mathematics in the first year and that course needs to be a rigorous mathematics course.

Current Situation

Today, most colleges and universities offer at least one course in discrete mathematics to undergraduates and, in many cases, the courses have been put in place within the last five years. The clientele, the level at which the course is taught, the textbooks that have been published and the topics stressed vary greatly.

The students who take courses in discrete mathematics come from many different majors: computer science, mathematics, electrical and computer engineering, the physical sciences and, at some institutions, liberal arts majors. At a number of universities there is one course that serves all; at others there are separate courses for computer science majors. Whatever the case, the overwhelming majority of courses are taught by mathematics faculty.

Many courses in discrete mathematics are offered at the first-year level. But, courses can be found at the second, third and fourth-year levels also. The prerequisite courses in mathematics and computer science that a student must have before entering a discrete mathematics course vary. Especially for courses at the first-year level, either a good high school mathematics background is required or at least one college mathematics course, possibly a one-semester course in calculus, is preferred. For upper-level discrete mathematics courses, the prerequisites can include some or all of calculus, linear algebra, elementary discrete mathematics, probability/statistics, CS 1 and CS 2.

There are now well over 50 undergraduate textbooks in discrete mathematics. Most of these are written for first or second year courses and many of them are designed for computer science majors. The level of mathematical sophistication of the material covered in the texts differs also. Some stress mainly computational techniques; others stress sound mathematical arguments and abstract reasoning throughout. However, very few approach mathematical reasoning from an algorithmic point of view. Most of the texts make an effort to develop a number of computer science applications. The topics covered in the texts and in the courses themselves are numerous. The usual list of topics includes number systems, sets, counting techniques, matrices, logic, methods of proof, analysis and verification of algorithms, relations, functions, graphs, digraphs, trees, recursion, recurrence relations, semi-groups, groups, rings, fields, coding theory, languages and regular grammars, finite state machines and computability.

The fact that there are many different course offerings can be viewed as a success for the advocates of the need for undergraduate courses in discrete mathematics as well as a problem for the maturing of this mathematics discipline. Success can be supported by the evidence that the importance of discrete mathematics to computer science has been understood and the appropriate professional communities have heard and acted. The discipline is flourishing. But, problems have to be acknowledged also. There is very little standardization and there is a feeling,

especially among computer science faculty, that students are not getting from these courses what they should be. This view became quite evident at the 1988 SIGSCE Symposium. During the question and answer period of a panel session entitled, "The Increasing Role of Computer Theory in the Undergraduate Curricula", many questions and criticisms were voiced about what is being taught in discrete mathematics courses and how it is being taught. Much thought needs to be given to the serious concerns that have been raised.

Observations and Recommendations

Some basic questions still need to be answered. If it is a given that first-year computer science majors take at least a one-semester course in discrete mathematics, what role should abstract mathematical reasoning play in such a course? Should first-year computer science majors be expected to read, understand and develop sound mathematical arguments and proofs? What role should applications from the field of computer science play in such a course? Should first-year computer science majors, who have little understanding of how computer applications and theory fit together to form a unified concept of computer science, be expected to appreciate many of the applications introduced at that level? What role should computational techniques play in such a course? How does one prevent the first-year discrete course from becoming a bag of computational tricks and a hodgepodge of topics?

From everything that has been written in the past couple of years about the maturing nature of the discipline of computer science as a science and the effect this is having and will have on the undergraduate curriculum, it is becoming increasingly clear that undergraduate computer science majors must have a firm grounding in mathematical logic and reasoning both from an algorithmic and a more traditional standpoint. The MAA Committee on Discrete Mathematics "agrees that all the students need to understand the nature of proof and the essentials of propositional and predicate calculus. In addition, all need to understand recursion and induction and, related to that, the analysis and verification of algorithms and the algorithmic method" [9]. Berztiss states that, at the lower level, discrete mathematics should be presented as a "terse and precise language of communication" [4] and that "there should be exposure to a variety of proof techniques" [4]. Bradley believes that "attention needs to be paid to careful formulation of definitions and the axiomatic approach. Most theorems should be proven and students should be expected to do simple proofs as well" [5].

Even though most agree that the development of mathematical rigor is a major goal of a first-year discrete mathematics course, this is not an easy task. Few first year students come to college with the maturity for abstract mathematical reasoning and precision. Most do not obtain such a background from high school mathematics classes. Acquiring an ability to reason mathematically is a developmental process which takes place over time. Intuition has to be developed by seeing and building up a repertoire of many concrete examples, by playing with mathematical ideas and by understanding the nature and purpose of proof techniques. Even for the disciplines that might be thought of as closely associated with computer science in terms of the role abstraction plays in these disciplines - mathematics, physics and engineering - the development of mathematical rigor is not one of the major objectives for the first-year mathematics course, calculus, that students in these areas take. In calculus needed computational tools and maturity in the problem-solving process are developed. Being able to read and develop mathematical proofs and definitions is not stressed in most calculus courses, except in the case of honors calculus. As the mathematics community reexamines the purpose and teaching of calculus (see [10] and [11]), this may change, but it will take years of work.

So, if the development of an ability to reason mathematically is, indeed, a major goal in an introductory discrete mathematics course, what should a good balance be among the competing interests of mathematical rigor, computer applications and computational techniques? Ralston, Berztiss, the MAA Committee on Discrete Mathematics and others have offered a number of suggestions. In each case a list of mathematical topics that should be covered in a one-semester or a two-semester course has been developed. These lists have been drawn up, in part, based on the view that a first-year computer science major needs to have a working knowledge of certain mathematical concepts and computational tools in order to apply the techniques

where necessary and to understand better the theoretical aspects of the discipline. This is a sound rationale, but how does one prevent such a course from degenerating into a collection of discrete topics or from being used as a way to rush through as much material as possible so as to be able to get to the good applications? Also, with this approach, how does one keep upper most in mind the need for mathematical rigor? An ideal answer to the dilemma would be to have sufficient time to cover all of the objectives for the course. Berztiss' three course sequence - a two-semester first year course and a one semester course in the third or fourth year - seems to come close to the ideal. In the first two semesters mathematical reasoning could be emphasized and elementary computer applications and computational techniques could be developed. All of this would be reinforced by the material covered in the first and second year computer science courses. Then, by the time the students reached their last two years, they should have sufficient maturity in both mathematics and computer science to benefit from an advanced discrete structures course in which substantial applications can be treated adequately.

Suppose, however, that at many universities it is not possible to offer three semesters of discrete mathematics, what then? This question was one of a number addressed at a two-week workshop on discrete mathematics which was held at Northeastern University in the summer of 1988. The workshop was sponsored by the Consortium for Mathematics and Its Applications (COMAP) with support from a grant from the National Science Foundation. (The author was a participant at the workshop) Over twenty-five mathematicians were brought together to learn about discrete mathematics and its applications, to discuss curricular issues about discrete mathematics in the undergraduate curriculum and to begin to prepare several curriculum modules for use in the classroom. During the two weeks there were both formal and informal discussions concerning curricular matters. The consensus that emerged was that a computer science major should take two semesters of discrete mathematics - possibly, one of those in the last two years. The first course would cover relatively few topics but stress mathematical reasoning and, especially, algorithmic thinking. The study of algorithms from a mathematical point of view or the study of graph theory or combinatorics could serve as a common thread. The course would concentrate on a mathematical approach to reading and writing algorithms, including recursive algorithms, and the issues of complexity and correctness. With algorithms at the core of the course, the standard topics in an introductory discrete mathematics could be developed as needed - methods of proof, elementary logic including an introduction to propositional and predicate calculus, sets, elementary matrices, counting techniques, simple probability, relations, functions and graphs. A second course in discrete structures at an advanced level would be able to build on this material as well as what has been learned in computer science courses.

Conclusion

There has been much progress made in the development of appropriate undergraduate courses in discrete mathematics for computer science majors. The mathematics community is addressing the issues which have been raised by the computer science community. Experimentation with various curricular models continues. At the same time the computer science community has to understand that, if students are to be successful in mathematically rigorous courses which deal with abstraction, proofs, analysis, computation and applications, they have to have not only a sound mathematical preparation, but they must have these mathematical concepts reinforced throughout their computer science courses.

References

1. ACM/IEEE Computer Society Joint Task Force. Computer Science Program Requirements and Accreditation. Communication of the ACM; 1984; 27(4).

2. ACM Task Force on the Core of Computer Science. Denning, Peter et al. Computing as a Discipline. Draft Report; February, 1988.

3. Beidler, John; Austing, Richard; Cassel, Lillian. Computing Programs in Small Colleges. Communications of the ACM; 1985; 28(6).

4. Berztiss, Alfs. A Mathematically Focused Curriculum for Computer Science. Communications of the ACM; 1987; 30(5).

5. Bradley, James. The Role of Mathematics in the Computer Science Curriculum. SIGSCE Bulletin; 1988; 20(1).

6. Gibbs, Norman; Tucker, Allen. Model Curriculum For a Liberal Arts Degree in Computer Science. Communication of the ACM; 1986, 29(3).

7. IEEE Computer Society Education Activities Board. The Model Program in Computer Science and Engineering. IEEE Computer Society Press; December, 1983.

8. Knuth, Donald. Computer Science and Its Relation to Mathematics. American Mathematical Monthly; 1974; 81(4).

9. Mathematical Association of America. Discrete Mathematics in the First Two Years. Committee Report; 1986.

10. Mathematical Association of America. Calculus For a New Century: A Pump, Not a Filter. National Colloquium Report; 1988; MAA Notes No. 8.

11. Mathematical Association of America. Toward a Lean and Lively Calculus. Conference Report; 1986; MAA Notes No. 6.

12. Ralston, Anthony. Computer Science, Mathematics and the Undergraduate Curricula in Both. American Mathematical Monthly; 1981; 88(7).

13. Ralston, Anthony. The First Course in Computer Science Needs a Mathematical Corequisite. Communications of the ACM; 1984, 27(10).

14. Ralston, Anthony; Shaw, Mary. Curriculum '78 - Is Computer Science Really That Unmathematical? Communications of the ACM; 1980; 23(2)

15. Shaw, M. ed. The Carnegie-Mellon Curriculum for Undergraduate Computer Science. Springer-Verlag; 1984.

IMPLEMENTING A GKS-LIKE GRAPHICS PACKAGE ON A MICROCOMPUTER

Michael K. Mahoney

Computer Science and Engineering Department
California State University, Long Beach
Long Beach, CA 90840

Abstract

A variable-length project for an introductory upper-division computer graphics course for majors is described. The project consists of the implementation of a graphics package based on the Graphical Kernel System (GKS, an ISO and ANSI standard) and application programs which demonstrate features of GKS. Any microcomputer with graphics capabilities equipped with an appropriate compiler can be used for the project. It is assumed that the reader is familiar with the basic concepts of 2D computer graphics. A brief introduction to GKS is included.

Introduction

GKS is the first international graphics application programmer interface (**API**) standard. This paper describes how a computer graphics student can implement a major portion of GKS and write and run application programs to test his implementation. The project can be modified so that it takes a few weeks or a few months to complete. The student should have a background in linear algebra and structured programming with data structures.

Asking students to implement a working graphics system based on a published "standard" is not new. The authors of [Fole82], [Harr83] and [Maho86] have discussed Core-like implementations. (**Core** is the name of the functional specification for a graphics system published by the ACM SIGGRAPH Graphics Standards Planning Committee [Core79].) However Core, unlike GKS, doesn't provide language bindings and never went through the lengthy ANSI standardization process.

Advantages

There are two main reasons the computer graphics student should implement this GKS-like package. First, the standard terminology and concepts of GKS will give him (her) a base on which to understand the variety of graphics terms and systems currently in use. This base will help make him a "portable" graphics programmer which will help him succeed in the field. It will also introduce him to substantial portions of other graphics standards such as GKS-3D, PHIGS, CGI and CGM. Many of the terms and concepts in these standards are similar to those in GKS (see [Bono86] and [Chin88]). Second, the student can see how basic graphics concepts such as transformations, segmentation and device independence are merged to form a complete system. If he studies these concepts individually he is left wondering how all the parts fit together and fails to see the "big picture".

GKS Functions

GKS provides a device-independent functional specification for a graphics system which can address multiple workstations [GKS84]. It does not, however, specify how to implement such a system. The GKS functions are divided into the following groups:

Control Functions - to open GKS, activate and clear workstations, etc.

Output Primitives - to build objects which make up generated pictures

Output Attributes - to determine the visual appearance of output primitives

Workstation Attributes - to define bundles of attributes

Transformation Functions - to specify mappings between coordinate systems

Segment Functions - to create and manipulate segments

278

Utility Functions - to set up matrices for segment transformations
Input Functions - to handle input from workstations
Metafile Functions - for the long-term storage of pictures
Inquiry Functions - to inquire about workstations, operating states, colors, etc.
Error Handling Functions - to handle errors

Scope of the Implementation

An appropriate assignment is to implement a GKS-like package which addresses *one* workstation and includes most of the control, output primitive and attribute, workstation attribute, transformation, segment and utility functions. An application program which calls only these functions should (with minor modifications) run properly were it linked with a "legal" GKS implementation. The appendix lists one possible subset of GKS functions for the assignment.

This GKS-like package allows an application programmer to control the workstation and structure pictures into pieces (**segments**) that can be manipulated (displayed, deleted, transformed) separately. It provides him with the tools to model simple objects in 2D world coordinates (**WC**) and specify normalization transformations which map from WC to normalized device coordinates (**NDC**) and workstation transformations which map from NDC to physical device coordinates (**PDC**). Thus the project contains all the major components which make up the 2D viewing pipeline.

Modules (Files) of the Implementation

It makes sense to divide the project into three main files. The application program resides in one file, the GKS functions, segment storage and segment interpreter reside in a second (GKS) file, while the device driver routines reside in a third. The files are divided roughly among the three coordinate systems WC, NDC and PDC. Graphics output data passes from the application program file to the GKS file to the device driver file.

Only the *calls* of GKS functions appear in the application program file while the implementations of those functions appear in the GKS file. The division between these two

files is very clear and shouldn't be altered. It illustrates the API that is defined by GKS.

The division between the GKS and device driver files is determined by the device-independent/device-dependent interface. The device driver file contains the device-dependent part of the implementation which supports the graphics hardware in the workstation. It generates device-dependent output and (if implemented) handles device-dependent interaction. See [MGKS83] for further discussion of this interface.

Hardware and Compilers

The focus here is on microcomputers because they can be inexpensively equipped with good graphics capabilities, are easier to use than most alternatives and function well as workstations in the GKS sense. Availability is also a key reason. Most colleges now have microcomputer labs and many students have their own micros which allow them to work at home.

Students in my courses have chosen to implement the GKS-like package on both IBM PC/XT/AT (or compatible) and Macintosh II computers. The preferred PC-type system is equipped with EGA graphics hardware or better. The preferred Mac II system is equipped with color. The package is a delight to implement on a "loaded" Mac II due to the Mac's speed, resolution, range of colors and QuickDraw graphics interface. A monochrome Mac can be used but the lack of color leads to much less satisfactory pictures and color table manipulations.

On PC-type computers my graphics students have used Turbo Pascal 4.0 (**TP4**), Turbo C 1.5 and QuickC 1.0 - all with outstanding results. (Later versions of these compilers work even better.) The TP4 and Turbo C environments are similar and their graphics interface routines are nearly identical. This makes it easy to allow students in the same class to use either compiler. Any good Pascal or C compiler with access to the QuickDraw routines is a great choice on the Mac.

I suspect that the most common microcomputer installation at colleges is TP4 on PC-type computers. Therefore details of the project will be described in that setting.

The Project in Turbo Pascal

Separate compilation, essential to the implementation, is accomplished in TP4 through the use of program-like **units**. The **interface section** of a TP4 unit contains declarations which are available ("public") to any program or unit that "uses" this unit. The **implementation section** of a TP4 unit contains implementations of the routines declared in the interface section and any other "private" declarations and routines.

Returning to the three project modules, suppose we call the application program file APPROG.PAS, the GKS unit file GKS.PAS and the device driver unit file DDRIVER.PAS (see Figure 1). Declarations of all GKS constants, data types and functions (procedures) are placed in the interface section of GKS.PAS so they can be referenced by the application program. Implementations of the GKS procedures and other supporting routines are placed in the implementation section of GKS.PAS. The interface section of DDRIVER.PAS contains the declarations which are referenced in GKS.PAS.

Figure 1 shows how graphics output data passes through the system. It indicates that APPROG.PAS "uses" GKS.PAS which in turn "uses" DDRIVER.PAS which in turn "uses" GRAPH.TPU. GRAPH.TPU is the compiled TP4 standard unit file that contains implementations of the TP4 built-in graphics routines such as LineTo, FloodFill, etc.. These TP4 routines call on the hardware-specific code in EGAVGA.BGI to drive the EGA or VGA hardware. Thus the device driver is actually contained in 3 files. However, students only need code DDRIVER.PAS.

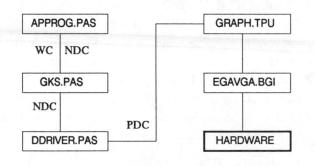

Figure 1

Calls of GKS procedures in APPROG.PAS pass most points to GKS.PAS in WC (some points such as viewport corners are passed in NDC). Calls of device driver routines in GKS.PAS pass NDC points to DDRIVER.PAS which in turn passes PDC points to GRAPH.TPU. DDRIVER.PAS contains *all* calls of TP4 graphics routines. (If a Mac is used then all calls of QuickDraw routines are in the device driver file.) One can easily "make" this system in the TP4 environment.

Presenting the Project

Lectures on hardware, simple algorithms and a few other basics of computer graphics (e.g. the material in Chapters 1-4 of [Hear86]) should be given before the project is assigned. Then the pertinent parts of a language binding, the state lists and what is stored in a segment should be distributed and discussed. This information (Pascal binding) and much more on GKS can be found in [Ende86]. An application program (call it DEMO1) which demonstrates control functions, a few output primitives and attributes, segments and segment visibility is an excellent way to begin discussing the GKS functionality and API. The different project modules can be illustrated with a diagram similar to Figure 1.

Various segment data structures could also be discussed (see [Hear86] and [Fole82]). One which is relatively easy to implement stores each segment as a simple linked list. In Pascal each segment entry could be a record which contains the following fields: an operand, an NDC point, a pointer to the next segment entry and pointers to other data structures containing text, fill area vertices etc..

Students have found diagrams like Figure 2 very helpful. It indicates how graphics output data is passed from an application program all the way through a TP4 package to the hardware. WC points are passed from the GKS output primitive routine GPolyline to the normalization transformation routine which converts them to NDC. The Put_Seg_Entry and Get_Seg_Entry routines place data in and retrieve data from segment storage. In Figure 2 this data consists of the converted points together with move or line operands.

Interpret_Seg, the segment interpreter routine, calls the segment transformation routine to multiply (transform)

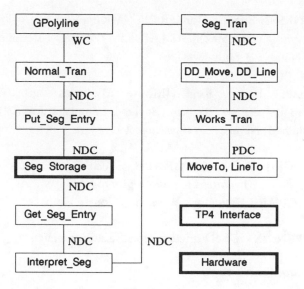

Figure 2

NDC points by matrices specified in the application program. Then it uses the segment entry operands to determine which device driver routines (e.g. DD_Move, DD_Line) should receive these transformed NDC points. These DD routines call the workstation transformation routine to convert points to PDC and then pass the converted points to TP4 routines such as MoveTo and LineTo. The division between GKS.PAS and DDRIVER.PAS falls between the segment transformation and DD routines.

The project assignment can be given in parts. Part 1 could consist of the implementation of that part of the package which properly runs the application program DEMO1. This gives students a reachable goal within a 4-6 week time period and the instructor an easy way to test their work.

Part 1 could also include an application program that the student has to *write*. Any set of pictures which can be displayed as combinations of visible and invisible fixed segments is a good choice. For example, consider the digits 0 through 9 as seen on a digital watch. Students could display them in order by flipping the visibilities of three horizontal and four vertical bar-shaped segments.

Part 2 of the project could consist of the implementation of more output primitives and attributes, bundles and segment transformations. As with Part 1, an appropriate

application program (DEMO2) would be helpful for presenting and testing Part 2. DEMO2 could demonstrate simple animation techniques and how a segment can be transformed and then inserted into another segment. Students could write their own application programs which build on these techniques. For example, one of the bar-shaped segments in the digits example above could be rotated and/or translated and then inserted to create the others.

It's a good idea for the instructor to implement each part of the project before assigning it. Then he can distribute executable files which visually demonstrate how the GKS functions in the DEMO application programs work.

Variations of the Assignment

There are a number of approaches to take with this assignment. One approach is to have students implement the package from scratch according to the guidelines above. This covers a large part of the "Computer Graphics Systems" course described by Cunningham in [SIGG87] and takes 2-3 months.

Another approach is to give students an implementation of the GKS API part of the package and then have them implement device driver algorithms. For example, students could be allowed to use only a few basic TP4 graphics routines (e.g. PutPixel) and be required to implement line, ellipse, fill, clipping and/or spline curve algorithms themselves. This approach takes less time.

A third approach is to extend the project described above and build an entire course around it. More algorithms, GKS functions and a sophisticated segment storage data structure could be added. For example, many of the GKS input functions could be implemented using a mouse. This would be relatively easy to do on a Mac since it's already equipped with a mouse and software interface (QuickDraw). Details on how it can be done in TP4 are in [Port88].

See [MGKS83] for a discussion of the implementation of a different GKS subset, "Minimal GKS", which addresses multiple workstations but doesn't contain segments.

Conclusion

I have introduced GKS and described a major microcomputer project based on it. I've provided some ideas for presenting the project in the classroom and attempted to convince you of its value and flexibility. I can honestly say that I've never enjoyed implementing or presenting a project as much as this one and have never seen students so enthusiastic about programming. Give it a try! I think you'll find the same result.

References

[Bono86] Bono, Peter et. al., Feature Articles, IEEE *Computer Graphics and Applications*, Volume 6, Number 8 (Aug. 1986).

[Chin88] Chin, Janet, "Education and Graphics Standards", IEEE *Computer Graphics and Applications*, Volume 8, Number 1 (Jan. 1988).

[Core79] "Status Report of the Graphics Standards Planning Committee," ACM *Computer Graphics*, Volume 13, Number 3 (Aug. 1979).

[Ende86] Enderle, G., Kansy, K., and Pfaff, G., *Computer Graphics Programming, GKS - The Graphics Standard*, Second Edition, Springer-Verlag, New York, 1986.

[Fole82] Foley, J.D., and van Dam, A., *Fundamentals of Interactive Computer Graphics*, Addison-Wesley Publishing Company, Reading, Mass., 1982.

[GKS84] "Special GKS Issue", ACM *Computer Graphics*, Feb. 1984.

[Harr83] Harrington, Steven, *Computer Graphics, A Programming Approach*, McGraw-Hill Book Company, New York, 1983.

[Hear86] Hearn, D., and Baker, M.P., *Computer Graphics*, Prentice- Hall, 1986.

[Maho86] Mahoney, Michael, K., "Hardware Independent Programming for a Computer Graphics Course", ACM *SIGCSE Bulletin*, Volume 18, Number 4 (Dec. 1986).

[MGKS83] Simons, Randall, W., "Minimal GKS", ACM *Computer Graphics* (SIGGRAPH Proceedings), Volume 17, Number 3 (July 1983).

[Port88] Porter, Kent, "Mouse Mysteries Part II: Graphics", *Turbo Technix* (Borland Language Journal) Volume 1, Number 5 (July/August 1988).

[SIGG87] ACM SIGGRAPH, *Teaching Computer Graphics: An Interdisciplinary Approach*, 1987 ACM SIGGRAPH Educator's Workshop Course Notes.

APPENDIX - GKS Functions for the Assignment

Control Functions

OPEN GKS, CLOSE GKS, OPEN WORKSTATION
CLOSE WORKSTATION, ACTIVATE WORKSTATION, DEACTIVATE WORKSTATION, CLEAR WORKSTATION
REDRAW ALL SEGMENTS ON WORKSTATION

Output Primitive (and Output Attribute) Functions

POLYLINE, FILL AREA, TEXT
GENERALIZED DRAWING PRIMITIVE
(and most of the associated attribute functions)

Workstation Attribute Functions

SET POLYLINE REPRESENTATION,
SET FILL AREA REPRESENTATION,
SET TEXT REPRESENTATION,
SET COLOR REPRESENTATION

Transformation Functions

SET WINDOW, SET VIEWPORT,
SELECT NORMALIZATION TRANSFORMATION,
SET CLIPPING INDICATOR, SET WORKSTATION WINDOW,
SET WORKSTATION VIEWPORT

Segment Functions

CREATE SEGMENT, CLOSE SEGMENT, RENAME SEGMENT,
DELETE SEGMENT, INSERT SEGMENT, SET VISIBILITY,
SET SEGMENT TRANSFORMATION, SET SEGMENT PRIORITY

Utility Functions

EVALUATE TRANSFORMATION MATRIX,
ACCUMULATE TRANSFORMATION MATRIX

Teaching Introductory and Advanced Computer Graphics Using Micro-Computers

G. Scott Owen
Department of Mathematics and Computer Science
Georgia State University
Atlanta, Georgia 30303

ABSTRACT

In the past few years there have been significant advances in both the computational and graphics capabilities of micro-computers. In graphics the standard (for the IBM compatible world) has advanced from the Computer Graphics Adapter (CGA) through the Enhanced Graphics Adapter (EGA) to the present Video Graphics Array (VGA). With the multiple color capability of the VGA, images can be constructed which use graphics shading algorithms. This allows us to teach more advanced concepts in introductory courses and even to teach some topics in advanced courses using these machines. In this paper I will discuss how these hardware improvements have allowed for changes in our introductory graphics course and also our experience in teaching an advanced course using these machines.

INTRODUCTION

A difficulty in teaching computer graphics has always been the hardware requirements. Before the advent of micro-computers with graphics capabilities, even introductory graphics courses needed expensive (at least $3,000) graphics terminals connected to central mainframes. Teaching advanced concepts, such as shading techniques or ray tracing, required very expensive color displays and access to powerful machines for computation. As a result, few colleges and universities offered computer graphics courses and many of those that did used text oriented displays to simulate graphics.

With the introduction of micro-computers with graphics capabilities and reasonable languages, more schools started offering introductory courses. As long as nothing sophisticated was attempted these machines worked quite well. For example, the first computer graphics course which I taught was in 1982, using Apple II computers running UCSD-Pascal. In 1985 we switched to IBM PC's and compatibles but the course remained relatively unchanged, until recently.

In graphics hardware the standard (for the IBM compatible world) has advanced from the Computer Graphics Adapter (CGA) with 640 x 200 pixel resolution with 2 colors, through the Enhanced Graphics Adapter (EGA) with 640 x 350 pixel resolution with 16 colors out of a palette of 64 colors, to the present Video Graphics Array (VGA). The VGA has 640 x 480 pixel resolution and 16 colors out of a palette of 256 K colors or 320 x 200 pixels with 256 colors from a palette of 256K colors (6 bits per gun). With the VGA, images can be constructed with multiple shades of one color, e.g., as used in graphics shading algorithms.

The computer center at Georgia State University (GSU) had IBM compatible micro-computers, with CGA capabilities only, until early 1988. They then purchased approximately 100 IBM PS/2 Model 50's, which use the VGA. Fortunately, they also purchased color monitors which supported the VGA. I say fortunately since, as in many institutions, the computer science department at GSU has little or no input into the purchases of the Computer Center. Unfortunately, none of the Model 50's were purchased with a math coprocessor (80287).

In the sections below I will describe our Computer Graphics course before the acquisition of the IBM PS/2 systems, how the course was modified, and how we were able to offer an advanced course using these machines.

BACKGROUND OF STUDENTS

At GSU the computer science curriculum contains a substantial amount of mathematics. We require 20 hours of calculus (4 courses of 5 hours each, all of our courses are 5 hours per quarter), 10 hours of statistics, 5 hours of discrete mathematics, and 5 hours of linear algebra. The students usually have not completed all these courses when they take the introductory graphics course but they generally have finished the calculus sequence, the discrete mathematics, and the linear algebra course. Thus, they have a sound mathematical background and are familiar with vectors and matrices.

Since the introductory course, Computer Graphics Algorithms, is a senior level (or introductory graduate level) course, the students have had at least the first three programming courses, Programming Principles I and II (which includes Pascal and a brief introduction to FORTRAN), and the Data Structures course, which uses Ada [OWEN87]. Many of them also have had the Programming Languages course which introduces them to C, among other languages. Many of our students have their own machines, ranging from older IBM PC compatibles to IBM PS/2 Model 60's.

INTRODUCTORY COURSE

The introductory graphics course, **Computer Graphics Algorithms**, is taught twice a year, in winter and summer quarters, with an average enrollment of 15-30 students per class. The text used in the introductory course is [HEAR86], which is an excellent text for an algorithms oriented course. When this book was first used I covered the entire book except for chapter 14, which is on advanced concepts. The students had four programming projects for the quarter. Each program was graded on meeting the project specifications, on the user interface, and on programming style. The projects could be done using Pascal (Turbo Pascal), Ada, or C.

To facilitate the teaching of the course I have developed a complete set of overhead foils which includes all of the course material. The students make their own copies of these foils and use them in class. This allows the material to be covered more quickly since I don't have to redraw all the figures and the students can concentrate on understanding rather than note taking.

When the course was first taught the emphasis was more on the fundamental algorithms. For example, the first project was to derive the complete Bresenham line drawing algorithm, from the first octant example given in the text, and then to write a program using the complete algorithm to draw lines. The second project involved plotting the cosine function in both the top and bottom half of the screen. This illustrated the concepts of the Window and Viewport and the mapping from world coordinates to physical device coordinates. The students had to construct their own small GKS graphics package for this project.

The third project was to write a program which defined a two dimensional polygon and performed transformations on it such as scaling, rotation, translation, x-shearing, and y-shearing. The program was menu driven with the graphics display area on the left part of the screen and a menu section on the right. The polygon could be redrawn after each transformation or the transformations could be concatenated before redrawing. Along with the above transformations, the menu included options to clear the graphics area, change the Window, and change the Viewport (always restricted to the left graphics display area).

The students had to implement full line clipping (either Liang-Barsky [LIAN84] or Sutherland-Cohen [HEAR86]). For bonus points the students could implement polygon scan conversion, to fill the polygon, and polygon clipping. Several of these algorithms are partially given as code examples in [HEAR86], but it still took time to fully implement them.

The fourth project was to extend the third project into three dimensions and to include backface removal on a polyhedron represented by a polygon mesh. All of the transformations were in 3D and included rotations about the X, Y, Z axes and about any arbitrary axis specified by two points, input by the user. As in the third project, there was an on-screen menu listing the available graphics commands. The viewing transformation included options for perspective or orthographic views, and some students included oblique viewing. The problem specified only 2D clipping but some students performed full 3D clipping.

In assigning the above set of projects there was a threefold objective. The first, obvious, objective was for the students to gain a mastery of the graphics techniques involved. A second objective was for them to gain a qualitative understanding of the effect of different types of 2 and 3 dimensional transformations and the concatenation of these transformations.

The third objective was for the students to gain a better understanding of some principles from software engineering, particularly software maintenance and reusable code. Rather than four unrelated projects, the above sequence allowed the students to build each project from the results of the previous one. The total code size of the four projects was about 4,000 lines with the fourth project about 1200-1500 lines of source code, much of it from the previous projects. All of the above projects could be easily done on an IBM PC with a CGA board using the 640 x 200 pixel resolution mode.

As stated above, in the winter of 1988, GSU purchased systems with VGA capability. In the spring of 1988 we offered the first advanced computer graphics course, described in the next section. Partially as a result of teaching this course I decided to change the emphasis of the introductory course and to take greater advantage of the VGA systems.

The new version of the introductory graphics course was taught in the summer of 1988. The major change was to shift the projects by one, i.e. the previous second project became the first, etc. The new fourth project was to be the student's choice and had to use more advanced graphics techniques. The students were supplied with a small GKS based graphics package, written by myself in Turbo Pascal. This package performs line drawing (using **polyline** it performs the complete 2D viewing transform), clipping, setting a window and viewport, activating the workstation in any graphics mode, plus a few other miscellaneous functions.

The package does not use any Turbo Pascal graphics but instead uses the IBM rom bios interrupt 10h routines. It allows for the detecting of the display type (CGA, EGA, or VGA) and the setting of the palette for the EGA or VGA. It can be used either with Turbo Pascal versions 3.01, 4.0, or 5.0. The students who programmed in C or Ada did their own conversions of this package. If anyone wants this GKS package please send me a 5.25" floppy disk or 3.5" micro-floppy disk, and I will send you the package.

Even though the students did not have to implement their own line drawing, clipping, or viewing transformation procedures, these topics still received as much class and test emphasis as before. I did **not** de-emphasize any of this fundamental material, I just covered more additional advanced material by slightly increasing my presentation pace.

In the new version of the course I was able to cover much of the advanced material in chapter 14 of Hearn and Baker.

This included color models (RGB, CMY, and HSV), lighting models with simple terms for the ambient, diffuse, and Phong approximation to specular reflections, and three shading models (constant or faceted, Gouraud, and Phong). There was also a lecture giving an overview of Ray Tracing, using the ACM SIGGRAPH notes [GLASS87].

For their fourth programming project, over half of the students chose to build on their third project (3D transformations of a polyhedron) and to implement faceted shading with ambient and diffuse lighting terms. They all used the 640 x 480 16/256K color mode of the VGA, setting the palette registers to 16 shades of one color e.g. green or red. Some students used a simple polyhedron such as a cube while others generated more complex ones such as a sphere or an arbitrary shape. The PS/2 Model 50's, even without math co-processors, were quite adequate for this project.

Some of the other interesting student projects included a fractal mountain which had some shading, a program to use the cursor keys to change the HSV coordinate values with concurrent display of the generated color (using the 256/256K color mode of the VGA), real time animation using the double frame buffer of the EGA modes, and an implementation of the floating horizon hidden line algorithm [ROGE85].

Even though I have some qualms about not having the students implement their own graphics primitives and develop their own GKS package, I was satisfied with the course change. The students became quite excited about learning more advanced techniques, producing more complex, as well as more colorful, images, and they enjoyed the course more. As the frontier of computer graphics research continues to advance, more advanced techniques will migrate into the introductory course.

ADVANCED COMPUTER GRAPHICS

The first offering of the Advanced Computer Graphics course was in Spring, 1988. This was an advanced graduate level (M. S.) course with the introductory graphics course as the prerequisite. The graphics hardware available for the course was the previously mentioned Model 50 VGA systems and two departmental IBM PS/2 Model 80's (both with 80387 chips, one at 16 Mhz and one at 20 Mhz).

The primary text was [ROGE85] with [HEAR86] used as a review text. The proposed course outline was as follows: Review of Color lookup tables, Brief introduction to VGA hardware, Programming the VGA (at the ROM Bios level), GKS Package for the VGA, Antialiasing

Algorithms, Hidden Line & Surface Algorithms (Backface removal, Painter's algorithm, Floating Horizon, Z-Buffer, Ray Tracing), Rendering Algorithms (Simple Illumination Models, Shading Models: Faceted, Gouraud, Phong, Advanced Illumination Model (Cook - Torrance), Transparency, Shadows, Texture, Global Illumination Model using Ray Tracing), Fractals, Scientific Visualization, and Image Processing.

While [ROGE85] covers most of the above topics, it was necessary to read the original papers, primarily from ACM SIGGRAPH proceedings, to fully understand the material. The course reading list is given in Appendix I.

There were four student projects for the course. The first project was to implement faceted shading and the Z-buffer hidden surface algorithm for an image composed of several polyhedrons. I gave the students the procedures for solid polygon clipping and scan conversion. The second project was to modify the first project to include Gouraud shading. The third project was to add Phong shading and specular highlights. For these projects the students used Turbo Pascal 4.0 and the 320 x 200 pixel 256/256K mode of the VGA. The fourth project was to investigate different rendering effects using ray tracing.

One of the students had obtained a freeware ray tracing program by David B. Wecker. This program, in C, had originally been written for the Commodore Amiga and modified for the IBM using Microsoft C 4.0. The program did not directly create a graphics image but instead generated an image file of RGB values (5 bits per gun). Thus, it was necessary to write a program to display the image files on a VGA system. Since the program could produce an image file with up to 32,768 colors, this involved determining the 256 most used colors and using these to set the VGA palette. Any remaining colors were mapped to the closest of the 256 displayable colors in RGB space.

Using this program, the students investigated such effects as transparency, creating different types of fractal islands, photographic depth-of-field effects, etc. This involved running the ray tracing program with many different inputs. Whereas the Model 50's were adequate for the first three projects (although slow on the Phong shading), we did not even try to use them for the ray tracing program but used the Model 80 systems.

Most of the runs took between 20-60 minutes on the Model 80 (20 mhz) and we found this machine to be about 8 times faster than an 8 Mhz Zenith AT (with an 80287). The students prepared batch files of several data sets which were run overnight. One problem with the ray tracing program was that it would occasionally crash and lock up the machine. This could be catastrophic if it occurred at the beginning of a large batch file for several students. We overcame this problem by using DeskView, a multitasking system for MS-DOS. Each student's batch file used a separate copy of the ray tracing program so that if one student's program crashed it only locked up that Deskview task and did not affect the other student's jobs.

Since this was the first time the course was taught, not all of the target material was covered, which was mainly my fault as some of the material was new to me and this slowed me down. Fractals were only briefly mentioned, and ray tracing was not covered as extensively as I would have liked. I used the ACM SIGGRAPH course notes on ray tracing and for the next course the entire set of notes will be covered.

The advanced course will be next offered in spring, 1989, and will contain about 30% more material than the first course. Since the introductory course now contains some of what was the advanced course material, more advanced topics can be covered. As mentioned above, ray tracing will be covered more extensively as will fractals. Other topics to be covered may include radiosity and more material on splines and CAD related topics.

This course had only a few students and so it was possible to demonstrate the programs on one of the Model 80 computers without a projection system. In the low resolution VGA mode, a Model 80 can construct an image of a Phong shaded polyhedron in a few seconds. Thus, we could vary the light source intensity and position, the coefficients of reflection, etc. and quickly see the results.

CONCLUSION

As the research frontier in computer graphics progresses, more advanced material will be moved into introductory courses, allowing the advanced graphics courses to stay close to the frontier. Fortunately, advances in computer hardware make this feasible for most institutions. 80286 based VGA systems work quite well in teaching simple shading algorithms. With a math coprocessor (80287) they can also be used for Phong shading and specular highlights. For more heavily computational programs, such as ray tracing, a faster machine, such as an 80386/80387 is needed. Another advantage of using micro-computers is that the students can do much of the development work on their own home systems and then use the school's systems only when needed.

There are no completely adequate texts for advanced courses in computer graphics. Using [ROGE85] as a base was satisfactory but it had to be heavily supplemented. The best resource for advanced graphics is the annual set of ACM SIGGRAPH course notes. These can be obtained at a special price of about $350 for the complete set. The best secondary resources are the literature i.e., ACM SIGGRAPH, ACM Transactions on Graphics, and IEEE Computer Graphics and Applications. A new IEEE tutorial text on Image Synthesis [JOY88] has just been published and will be used for the next advanced course. This text contains many of the papers which I used in the first course.

References

[GLAS87] Glassner, A., "An Overview of Ray Tracing", Course Notes Introduction to Ray Tracing Siggraph '87, 1987.

[HEAR86] Hearn, D. and Baker, M. P., Computer Graphics, Prentice-Hall, 1986.

[JOY88] Joy, K., Grant, C., Max, Nelson, and Hatfield, L., Computer Graphics: Image Synthesis, IEEE Computer Society Press, 1988.

[LIAN84] Liang, Y. D., and Barsky, B. A., "A New Concept and Method for Line Clipping", ACM Transactions on Graphics, 3(1), 1-22, January, 1984.

[OWEN87] Owen, G. S., "Using Ada on Microcomputers in the Undergraduate Curriculum", Papers of the Eighteenth SIGCSE Technical Symposium on Computer Science Education, Vol. 19.1, p. 374, February, 1987.

[ROGE85] Rogers, D. F., Procedural Elements for Computer Graphics, McGraw-Hill, 1985.

Appendix I Reading List for Advanced Computer Graphics

Blinn, J. F. "Models of Light Reflection for Computer-Synthesized Pictures", ACM SIGGRAPH '77 proceedings, Computer Graphics, 11(2), 192-198, 1977.

Blinn, J. F. "Simulation of Wrinkled Surfaces", ACM SIGGRAPH '78 proceedings, Computer Graphics, 12(3), 286-292, 1978.

Blinn, J. F. and M. E. Newell, "Texture and Reflection in Computer Generated Images", CACM 19, pp. 542-547, 1976.

Cook, R. L., and K. E. Torrance, "A Reflectance Model for Computer Graphics", ACM SIGGRAPH '81 proceedings, Computer Graphics, 15(3), 307-316, 1981. This article was later reprinted in ACM Transactions on Graphics 1(1), 7-24, 1982.

Kay, D. S., and, D. Greenburg, "Transparency, Refraction and Ray Tracing for Computer Synthesized Images", ACM SIGGRAPH '79 proceedings, Computer Graphics, 13(2), 158-164, 1979.

Phong, B. T., "Illumination for Computer Grenerated Images", Communications of the ACM, 18(6), 311-317, 1975.

THE RELATION OF THE ADVANCED PLACEMENT EXAMINATION
TO COMPUTER SCIENCE PROGRAMS

Over eight thousand high school seniors are taking the advanced placement examination in Computer Science. Over fifteen hundred colleges and universities use Advanced Placement Examination grades in determination of advanced placement and/or credit in Computer Science. As such, the topics covered on the examination will have wide influence on the preparation of incoming Freshmen.

This panel will focus on how the examination and the institutions are interacting. This discussion will be from the perspectives of how students are prepared for the examination, test question development, how the tests are graded, and how the results are used.

Panel Chair: Charles M. Shub
                Computer Science Department
                University of Colorado at Colorado Springs

Panelists: Nell Dale
                Computer Science Department
                University of Texas at Austin

                Michael Clancy
                University of California at Berkeley

                Stuart Reges
                Computer Science Department
                Stanford University

                Margaret Brenneman
                High School Teacher
                Knoxville, Tennessee

PANEL

WHERE DO "DISCRETE STRUCTURES" TOPICS BELONG IN A COMPUTER SCIENCE CURRICULUM?

Computer science departments have not come to a consensus on the presentation and teaching of those topics which commonly go under the heading of "discrete structures". Some of the questions that need to be resolved are:

1) What is the purpose of teaching "discrete structures" to computer science majors?

2) When should it be taught to them?

3) Should such a course be different than a discrete mathematics course taught to math majors' that is, should a separate course be taught in the computer science department?

4) If taught in the CS department, what topics should be included?

5) Should the title of such a course be "Discrete Structures", or would another name be more suitable? Or should these topics just merely be included within other computer science courses?

With a new ACM curriculum effort under way, it is essential that the above questions be addressed.

Panel Chair: Donald J. Bagert, Jr.
                Texas Tech University

Panelists: Judith L. Gersting
                Purdue University at Indianapolis

                Richard Johnsonbaugh
                De Paul University

                William B. Robinson
                Data General Corporation

                Angela Shiflet
                Wofford College

                Allen Tucker
                Bowdoin College

A PROGRESS REPORT FROM A JOINT ACM/IEEE-CS TASK FORCE
NEW RECOMMENDATIONS FOR THE UNDERGRADUATE CURRICULUM

In the spring of 1988, ACM and the Computer Society of the IEEE formed a joint task force to develop a new model for undergraduate programs in the discipline of computing. The report from this task force is intended to provide guidelines and recommendations for undergraduate programs names "computer science", "computer science engineering" , and other similar designations, in various academic settings.

The task force has initially concentrated on the core requirements for undergraduate programs, with the objective of defining a common core to support all programs in the discipline. The content of the core has been motivated by considering the minimal body of knowledge and capabilities that every graduate of a computing program should have. The core content includes not only technical subject matter, but also such topics as ethics and professionalism.

Thus far the task force has used the work of the Task Force on the Core of Computer Science (Denning, et al, C. ACM. January 1989) as the basis for defining the core material in the discipline. The nine areas of computer science, as defined in the Core Task Force Report, have also been used for the model curriculum. The core content has further been subdivided into topic modules, currently called "knowledge units", that can be combined in various ways for teaching purposes. A collection of principles, concepts, and objectives that occur throughout the curriculum have also been determined, and these are called "recurring themes".

Panel Chair: A.J. Turner
Clemson University

Panelists: Allen B. Tucker (Task Force Co-Chair)
Bowdoin College

Bruce H. Barnes (Task Force Co-Chair)
National Science Foundation

Kim B. Bruce
Williams College

Doris K. Lidtke
Towson State University

PANEL

COMPUTER SCIENCE ACCREDITATION: A CONTINUING PROCESS

The computer science accreditation process is into the fourth year of visits and is continuing to review programs and standards.   This fourth year also starts a series of revisits to those programs which were granted the three year accreditation designation.   Results from the initial and continuing process will be addressed by a panel of visitors and institutions. Future directions and expectations will be examined for input in the process to better serve the institutions and computer science programs.

<u>Panel Chair:</u>   Gerald L. Engel
                University of Connecticut at Stamford

<u>Panelists:</u>   Raymond Miller
              University of Maryland

              A. Joe Turner
              Clemson University

              Stewart Zweben
              Ohio State University

PANEL

PERSPECTIVES OF ARTIFICIAL INTELLIGENCE AND EXPERT SYSTEMS: FROM THE CLASSROOM TO INDUSTRY

Artificial Intelligence and Expert Systems are very popular topics in both education and in business. There are various issues regarding the way in which AI and ES are taught in the college and university setting. The question is are these courses preparing our students for a career in industry? The focus of this panel discussion is to explore this issue. There will be discussion about the use of AI and ES in the classroom. Then there will be discussion about the uses and implementations of AI and ES in industry.

Panel Chair: Larry Travis
                University of Wisconsin-Madison

Panelists: Morris Firebaugh
                University of Wisconsin

                Joseph Giarratano
                University of Houston

                Ed Mahler
                Du Pont Company

                Paul Harmon
                Harmon and Associates

PANEL

ACCREDITATION AND TWO-YEAR COLLEGE COMPUTER SCIENCE PROGRAMS

Accreditation of computer science programs at four-year colleges in the United States and Canada is a reality. Criteria have already been established for computer related programs at two-year colleges in Canada. Members of the panel will discuss the merits and feasibility of an accreditation process for computer science programs at two-year colleges in the United States.

Panel Chair: John Impagliazzo
                Chair, Department of Computer Science
                Hoffstra University
                ACM Accreditation Committee

Panelists: Karl Klee
                Coordinator, Computer Science and Mathematics
                Jamestown Community College
                Two-Year College Representative

                Ronald M. Davis
                Chair, Division of Mathematics, Computers and
                      Engineering
                DeKalb College
                Two-Year College Representative

                Gerald Engel
                Department of Computer Science and Engineering
                University of Connecticut
                Computing Sciences Accreditation Board

                A. Joe Turner
                Chair, Department of Computer Science
                Clemson University
                Chair, Computer Science Accreditation Commission

PANEL

CIS ACCREDITATION: AN UPDATE WITH AACSB INPUT

After input from several professional meetings, the working group is finalizing the initial guidelines for accreditation of computer information systems programs. The professional societies have provided further input to the process along with meetings of various regional institutions and agencies. The panel will report on the results from the various meetings held within the last year and provide their recommendation for the CIS accreditation process.

Panel Chair: Robert Cannon
               University of South Carolina

Panelists: John T. Gorgone
               Bentley College

               Thomas I.M. Ho
               Purdue University

               John D. McGregor
               Murray State University

FINAL REPORT OF THE ACM/IEEE COMPUTER SOCIETY / MAA TASK FORCE ON TEACHING COMPUTER SCIENCE WITHIN MATHEMATICS DEPARTMENTS

The Task Force on Teaching Computer Science within Mathematics Departments was established jointly by the ACM, the IEEE Computer Society, and the Mathematical Association of America in the Spring of 1986, with Zaven Karian of Denison University as chair. The charge to the Task Force reads in part:

> To examine issues of professional standards and professional development for faculty members of college mathematics departments who now teach partly or wholly courses in computer science. The purpose of the Task Force is twofold: to recommend means of professional development for faculty that will insure productive, fulfilling careers, and to recommend steps that departments must take to insure quality instruction in computer science ...

Hearings were held at the ACM Computer Science Conference and at the Joint Mathematics meeting in early 1987, and the final report was submitted to the sponsoring associations in August 1988.

During this session, members of the panel will describe the most significant aspects of the task force recommendations in the general areas of
  (1) Faculty qualifications and development,
  (2) Faculty workloads,
  (3) Retention, tenure and promotion,
  (4) Equipment and laboratory support,
  (5) Professional issues, and
  (6) Combined versus separate departments of mathematics and computer science.

We note that while this report was originally intended to address problems in departments of mathematics which provide instruction in computer science, much of it is relevant to any relatively small or new department (whether combined or separate) which includes computer science.

Panel Chair: Kim Bruce
               Williams College

Panelists: Bruce Klein
               Grand Valley State College

               Stan Seltzer
               Ithaca College

PANEL

THE NSF PEER REVIEW PROCESS

Purpose: Describe the application of the NSF proposal review
criterion and the review process. Four reviewers will
discuss the application of the review criterion and
their observations of the peer review process. The
NSF representative will describe how the peer review
process is combined with other criterion to award
grants.

Panel Chair: John Beidler
Department of Computer Science
University of Scranton

Panelists: Margaret Reek
Rochester Institute of Technology

PANEL

COMPUTER SCIENCE TEACHING CERTIFICATE FOR SECONDARY EDUCATION

Since the invention of microcomputers, Senior High Schools and now Junior High School and some Elementary Schools have gradually introduced courses dealing with computer science. In the mid-eighties, in many states, Department of Educations started thinking of creating a high school graduation requirement in the area of Computer Literacy. there are several sides to this issue: 1) defining the requirement, 2) staffing and 3) certification. Some States have started from the back door by first having the computer literacy as a high school graduation requirement and now are facing other problems: what to teach and who should teach the courses. The panelists in this proposal represent the view of a number of States, with respect to computer education, including: California, Minnesota, Indiana, Maryland, Vermont and North Dakota.

The major topics for discussion in the panel will include the following:

1. What is the position of the Department of Education in different states?

2. What kind of certification is being required for the teachers, if any? A sample of certification requirements for several States that have adopted some form of requirement will be discussed.

3. What kind of courses are currently being taught at the secondary level? All of the panelists are in direct contact with teachers teaching such courses or have been involved in training teachers to teach such courses or both.

4. The role of the Computer Science Departments and the Computer Science societies such as ACM, DPMA, and IEEE/CS in helping Computer Science Education at the Secondary level.

Panel Chair: Ali Behforooz
               Towson State University

Panelists: Curtis R. Bring, Moorhead State University

               John F. Dalphin, Towson State University

               Joyce C. Little, Towson State University

               William A. Stannerd, Cal State, Bakersfield

PANEL

HIGH SCHOOL PREPARATION FOR COMPUTER SCIENCE

At the 1988 SIGCSE Conference in Atlanta, a report was presented by an ACM Task Force on the Core of Computer Science. They recommend a three-course introductory sequence for beginning undergraduate CS majors, including three processes basic to the computing discipline -- theory, abstraction and design. The sequence assumes that entering freshmen, "who aspire to becoming computing majors already have a background of programming in some language." (p. 11, Draft 3). At the same conference, one speaker recommended that topics from discrete mathematics be taught within the context of Computer Science courses and not as a separate subject in Mathematics. Another claimed that even good students find concepts such as relations, especially inverses, extremely difficult to understand, and need to focus on these ideas separately. At one of the regional conferences, a speaker from a leading Computer Science university suggested that CS students "were born knowing physics and calculus."

Just how well prepared are our current high school graduates? This panel, composed of teachers and one other involved regularly with high school students, will address this question. Kenneth Appel is a high school physics teacher responsible for the Computer Science program at Yorktown High School, and a grader for the AP Computer Science Examination. Timothy Corica serves on the governing committee for this same exam, and is chair of the Mathematics Department at the Peddie School, which prepares students for the Ivy League, particularly Princeton. Julie Gross teaches mathematics and computing at "one of the ten best high schools in New York state," which enrolls 40% minority students. Our panelist from the Bronx High School of Science, can speak on the preparedness and interests of students selected by examination as the most scientifically talented in New York City. Maryam Hastings represents Women and Mathematics (WAM), a committee of the Mathematical Association of America (MAA) devoted to the encouragement of women and minorities in the high schools, to consider mathematical sciences.

Panelists have been asked to read the Denning Report and respond to the following questions:

Given graduating high school students who might do well in Computer Science,

1. How successful were they when studying Calculus? Can they construct good proofs? Is Calculus the best choice for most with mathematical aptitude?

2. How much probability, statistics and logic do they understand?

3. How are their algebra skills? Can they use them easily to solve fairly complex ("word") problems?

4. Do they program with ease in at least one high level language such as Pascal or C? Assembly language? About how many hours per week were they able to spend programming?

5. Can they translate fairly complex problems into algorithms and then into working code?

6. Will they be able to understand the level of abstraction suggested by the Task Force for the introductory sequence?

7. Are your answers to the questions above any different for minority students? Women students?

8. How has your school staffed its Calculus courses? Programming courses? Other senior-level mathematics courses?

The last half hour will be devoted to a dialogue between the panelists and members of the audience.

Panel Chair: Doris C. Appleby
              Mathematics/CS
              Marymount College

Panelists: Kenneth Appel
              Yorktown High School

              Julie Gross
              Ossining High School

              Timothy Corica
              Department of Mathematics
              The Peddie School

              Maryam Hastings
              Mathematics/CS
              Marymount College

CASE DEVELOPMENT PROCESS

Donald R. Chand
Bentley College
Waltham, MA 02154

The CASE method is an accepted and successful approach for teaching business disciplines but it has not been used widely in teaching computer science and information systems. One reason for this is the lack of cases available to support the teaching needs in a computer related discipline. The objective of this session is to discuss the process of generating case material needed for developing cases.

The first presentation in this session will focus on the issues of case development for supporting the teaching needs in computer science and information systems. The other two presentations will discuss the development of case material in two different organizational settings.

The following issues will be addressed in this first presentation.

- The role of the case method in teaching computer related disciplines.

- The problems of developing cases in a new field.

- The institutional environment needed for effective case development and implementation.

- The process for generating case leads and case materials.

- The guidelines for case writing.

AN ANATOMY OF AN END-USER STRATEGY: A CASE STUDY

Stuart A. Varden
Pace University
Information Systems Department
Pleasantville, N. Y. 10570

This case describes a project that was conducted during the summer of 1987 as part of the Pace University Information Systems Faculty-in-Residence Program. The corporation, people and events described in the case are real, but the identities have been changed.

The purpose of the project was to conduct an assessment of the effectiveness of Olympic Corporation's Headquarters Information Systems (I/S) department in providing I/S services to its headquarters departments. I/S management was particularly interested in an independent study and recommendations regarding its end-user computing strategy. Two years earlier, I/S had reorganized. It created a new unit, called Customer Services, which is the primary point of contact between the user community and I/S. I/S introduced new policies and practices that were designed to promote user self-reliance by encouraging users to learn fourth generation query languages and tools.

An early test of its new approach was Olympic's Equipment Acquisition Planning Department (EAPD) project. This department has the task of forecasting and developing an acquisition plan for computer and communications equipment. EAPD needed to replace its out-of-date planning system, and approached I/S for help. I/S saw the EAPD project as ideal to introduction its new service philosophy. EAPD, however, was expecting I/S to develop a turnkey system, and was reluctant to devote time and effort to develop I/S skills within the department.

After several half-hearted attempts and many heated meetings, an impasse developed. EAPD refused to comply with the new I/S end-user strategy and I/S refused to develop a turnkey system. Finally, EAPD retained help from a third party to develop the new planning system. The system is now in operation, but it is I/S that must maintain the system it did not create.

After studying the two-year of the project, the investigator offered the followed recommendations. They deal mainly with strategies for end-user computing.

- The I/S end-user strategy should emphasize technology transfer.

- When introducing a new technology to a user, user education becomes an important part of the marketing effort.

- The customer services function within I/S should establish a procedure for assessing the user's technical skill level and general readiness to adopt and adapt to new technologies.

- The technical skills of Customer Services Representatives should be maintained at a high level.

- All functions within the I/S department should strive to show the user a unified I/S department.

- Establish a career path for individuals who perform I/S functions within a user setting who are not "traditional" I/S professionals.

End-User Computing in a Public Accounting Firm: A Case Study

Joseph O'Connor
Donald Chand
Dennis Anderson
Computer Information Systems
Bentley College
Waltham, MA 02154-6270

End-User Computing is a term used for describing a growing phenomenon in organizations where non data processing persons have direct personal control of information technology involving the use of computers as part of their job, the selection of hardware and software, the development of applications, the customization of programs, and management of data. This has resulted in a host of information systems management issues associated with the successful implementation of end-user computing in organizations.

A teaching case in this area is an ideal tool for increasing the "vocabulary of experience" of the student by drawing upon the learning experiences of specific organizations and for providing concrete situations for enhancing and practicing decision making in this area.

Since the eventual goal is to use the details of the case study for developing a teaching case, the approach we used for generating the case materials is critical. Therefore the focus of this presentation is on the approach we used for performing this case study.

The first step in our approach involved a comprehensive review of the MIS research literature on end-user computing. The purpose of this review was to develop a framework and sensitivity for performing the case study. The research literature on end-user computing provided a classification vocabulary, instruments for recording and measuring facts, a taxonomy of issues affecting end-user computing, and a rich source of management strategies available for addressing these issues. It also made us aware of the nuances of end-user computing that made us more sensitive to subtle details.

The second step involved tracing the evolution of end-user computing in a specific public accounting firm to identify the end-user computing issues that relate to public accounting firms and what strategies were used to address them.

In this presentation we will focus on the process for generating case materials, and the end-user computing issues relevant to a large public accounting firm and ways for dealing with them will be covered indirectly.

TUTORIAL

HUMAN FACTORS AND SOFTWARE PRODUCTIVITY

Raghava Gowda
Computer Science Department
University of Dayton
Dayton, Ohio 45469

The objective of this tutorial is to provide a framework for teaching the role and impact of human factors on software productivity. The material for this tutorial is based on the author's Ph. D. dissertation entitled "Influence of Individual Characteristics and Group Cohesiveness on Programmer Productivity". It will introduce the participant to valid instruments for measuring individual programmer characteristics and group dynamics, metrics for measuring software productivity, and guidelines for implementing time reporting procedures.

Major Topics:

Software Productivity Issues
Programmer Productivity Model
Human Factors:
. Individual Characteristics
. Group Cohesiveness
Software Productivity Measures
Influence of Human Factors on Software Productivity
Measuring Software Productivity in an Organization
Integration of Software Productivity topics in Computer Science Curriculum

Target Audience:

Educators teaching software engineering and systems design courses
Anyone interested in learning the impact of human factors on software productivity

TUTORIAL

NEURAL NETWORKS: ISSUES AND IDEAS

Norman E. Sondak
Information and Decision Systems
San Diego State university
&
Vernon K. Sondak
Medical Center
University of Michigan

Neural networks offer the potential for solving complex, non-deterministic problems at high speeds. This tutorial will introduce the fundamental concepts of neural networks, discuss the simulation of neural networks on digital computers, survey the current applications of neurocomputing, compare and contrast expert systems and neurocomputing, and review the future of this technology.

Major Topics:

Artificial Intelligence and the Brain
Biological Information Processing
What are Neural Network Computers ?
History of Neural Network Computers
Artificial Neural Systems
Paradigms
  . Perceptron, Adaline, and Madaline
  . The Learning Machine
  . BAM (Bidirectional Associate Memory)
  . BSB (Brain-state-in-a-box)
  . Hopfield
  . Boltzman Machine
  . Back Propagation
  . Sigma Pi Units
  . Master-Slave Systems
  . Research Issues
The Commercialization of Neural Networks
Neural Networks in Defence
Neural Networks and Expert Systems
The Future of Neurocomputing

Target Audience:

Anyone interested in learning about neural networks

WORKSHOP

USING EXCELERATOR IN SYSTEMS DEVELOPMENT COURSES

Iraj Hirmanpour
Computer Science Department
Embry-Riddle University
Daytona Beach, FL 32014

This workshop will provide a framework, tools and strategies for using CASE technology in systems development courses. It will provide an introduction to CASE technology, demonstrate the teaching of structured techniques using Excelerator, and illustrate the development of a systems in Excelerator. The instructor will provide the illustrations, assignments, and sample cases which he uses in his system design courses and seminars.

Major Topics:

Rationale for teaching systems courses using CASE technology
Introduction to CASE technology
Teaching features of Excelerator
. Data dictionary facility
. Graphic facility
. Screen and report generator
. Documentation facility
. Analyzer
. Interfacing
. Housekeeping
Data Flow Modeling
Entity Relationship Modeling
Structured Software Design
Prototyping

Duration:
Two 90 minutes sessions

Intended Audience:

Educators teaching or preparing to teach system design courses
Anyone interested in learning Excelerator

WORKSHOP

USING PROLOG IN EXPERT SYSTEMS COURSES

Sridhar A. Raghavan
Bentley College
Waltham, MA 02154-6270

This workshop will provide a framework, tools and strategies for teaching expert system concepts in Prolog. It will demonstrate that Prolog is the most appropriate tool for teaching expert system concepts, provide a systematic approach for developing student's basic problem-solving skill in Prolog, teach the principles and techniques underlying diagnostic and planning expert systems, and illustrate the development of expert systems shells. The instructor will provide the illustrations, assignments, and sample Prolog programs which he uses in his expert system courses and seminars.

Major Topics:

Rationale for teaching expert systems using Prolog
Introducing students to Prolog syntax and semantics
Teaching Prolog inferencing process
A Library of Prolog Programming idioms
Exercising Prolog on a database problem
Teaching recursive formulation of problems
Teaching diagnostic expert systems techniques:
. problem formulation
. questioning techniques
. explanation facilities
. uncertainty handling
Teaching planning expert systems techniques:
. problem formulation
. simple planning alogorithm
. hierarchical planning
Knowledge representation schemes in Prolog
Techniques for developing expert system shells

Duration:
Two 90 minutes sessions

Intended Audience:

Educators teaching or preparing to teach courses on expert system
Anyone interested in learning of prolog and expert systems

COMPUTER TRIVIA
Carolyn McCreary
The American University, Washington, D.C.

When I was teaching the beginning computing course for non-computer science majors, *Introduction to Computing*, I realized that I was presenting many computer literacy facts not presented to our majors throughout their entire curriculum. In particular, *Introduction to Computing* included a chapter on the evolution of computers that I felt would be of great interest to our majors, especially the advanced students who had enough experience and knowledge to appreciate the developmental steps involved in devising today's computers. Hoping to increase student awareness of computer evolution and to spark an interest in the subject, I have developed a set of trivia questions. They can be used as an entertaining way of presenting facts, encouraging discussions and building community among the students. The questions are appropriate for any student/faculty function or in the classroom and as my colleagues remark, many questions are not really trivia but important facts. The questions are divided into six categories and are appropriate for used with the Horn Abbot game *Trivial Pursuit* or with a tic-tac-toe game such as Hollywood Squares, or like the television quiz game Jeopardy.

The categories are:

H: History and Future of Computing
P: Famous People in Computing
A: Computer Architecture and Hardware
C: Computer Science Theory & Applications
L: Programing Languages and Compilers
I: Information Systems

SAMPLE QUESTIONS

C. When several processors can access common data, it is necessary that writing the data be an indivisible operation. The segment of the code that must be indivisible is called_____

C. Critical Section

H. Babbage's invention that was the forerunner of the computer is called the _____

H. Analytical Engine or difference machine

P. Who is the countess of Lovelace, daughter of Lord Byron, who is regarded as the first computer programmer?

P. Ada

A. Name three special registers found in most CPUs.

A. accumulator
program counter
instruction register

I. Trapdoor, time bomb, and salami slice are all methods for _____

I. committing computer crime

L. What computer language is based on horn clauses and first order predicate calculus?

L. Prolog

The complete set contains 300 questions, 50 from each category. To obtain the complete set, send $5.00 to:
ACM chapter
CSIS
American University
4400 Massachusetts Ave., N.W.
Washington, D.C. 20016

LIST OF AUTHORS (REFEREED PAPERS)

From Generation to Generation:
The 21st SIGCSE Technical Symposium

February 23-24, 1990
Washington, DC

Post-Symposium Workshops February 25

Come Celebrate the 21st Symposium and the 21st Birthday of SIGCSE

The twenty-first SIGCSE Symposium will include paper and panel sessions, tutorials, birds-of-a-feather sessions, a keynote address by the winner of the SIGCSE award for outstanding contributions to Computer Science Education, Thursday exhibits, some new resource displays and a new SIGCSE luncheon on Friday, plus ample opportunity to exchange ideas with colleagues. Send a paper (4 copies, not more than 12 pages double spaced), panel proposal (including an abstract and list of participants, not exceeding one page), ideas for tutorial subjects, special sessions, and other activities to the appropriate member of the Symposium committee listed below. Submission deadline is September 1, 1989.

SIGCSE Symposium Cochairmen

Richard H. Austing
Department of Computer Science
Unversity of Maryland
College Park, MD 20742
(301) 454 2002

Lillian N. Cassel
Department of Mathematical Sciences
Villanova University
Villanova, PA 19085
(215) 645 7341

Papers

Gayle Yaverbaum
Felty and Company
4211 Elmerton Ave.
Harrisburg, PA 17109

(215) 787 8810

Panels, Tutorials, Case Studies

Harriet Taylor
Dept. of Computer Science
Louisiana State University
Baton Rouge, LA 70803

(504) 388 1495

Special Events

Joyce Currie Little
Dept. of Computer and
Information Sciences
Towson State University
Towson, MD 21204
(301) 321 3701